CRIMINAL JUSTICE

Twenty-First Edition

Editor
John J. Sullivan
Mercy College, Dobbs Ferry

John J. Sullivan, professor and former chairman of the Department of Law, Criminal Justice, and Safety Administration at Mercy College, received his B.S. in 1949 from Manhattan College and his J.D. in 1956 from St. John's Law School. He was formerly captain and director of the Legal Division of the New York City Police Department.

Editor
Joseph L. Victor
Mercy College, Dobbs Ferry

Joseph L. Victor is professor and chairman of the Department of Law, Criminal Justice, and Safety Administration at Mercy College. Professor Victor has extensive field experience in criminal justice agencies, counseling, and administering human service programs. He earned his B.A. and M.A. at Seton Hall University, and his Doctorate of Education at Fairleigh Dickinson University.

A Library of Information from the Public Press
Dushkin/McGraw·Hill
Sluice Dock, Guilford, Connecticut 06437

Visit us on the Internet—http://www.dushkin.com

The Annual Editions Series

ANNUAL EDITIONS is a series of over 65 volumes designed to provide the reader with convenient, low-cost access to a wide range of current, carefully selected articles from some of the most important magazines, newspapers, and journals published today. ANNUAL EDITIONS are updated on an annual basis through a continuous monitoring of over 300 periodical sources. All ANNUAL EDITIONS have a number of features that are designed to make them particularly useful, including topic guides, annotated tables of contents, unit overviews, and indexes. For the teacher using ANNUAL EDITIONS in the classroom, an Instructor's Resource Guide with test questions is available for each volume.

VOLUMES AVAILABLE

Abnormal Psychology
Adolescent Psychology
Africa
Aging
American Foreign Policy
American Government
American History, Pre-Civil War
American History, Post-Civil War
American Public Policy
Anthropology
Archaeology
Biopsychology
Business Ethics
Child Growth and Development
China
Comparative Politics
Computers in Education
Computers in Society
Criminal Justice
Criminology
Developing World
Deviant Behavior
Drugs, Society, and Behavior
Dying, Death, and Bereavement

Early Childhood Education
Economics
Educating Exceptional Children
Education
Educational Psychology
Environment
Geography
Global Issues
Health
Human Development
Human Resources
Human Sexuality
India and South Asia
International Business
Japan and the Pacific Rim
Latin America
Life Management
Macroeconomics
Management
Marketing
Marriage and Family
Mass Media
Microeconomics

Middle East and the Islamic World
Multicultural Education
Nutrition
Personal Growth and Behavior
Physical Anthropology
Psychology
Public Administration
Race and Ethnic Relations
Russia, the Eurasian Republics, and Central/Eastern Europe
Social Problems
Social Psychology
Sociology
State and Local Government
Urban Society
Western Civilization, Pre-Reformation
Western Civilization, Post-Reformation
Western Europe
World History, Pre-Modern
World History, Modern
World Politics

Cataloging in Publication Data
Main entry under title: Annual Editions: Criminal Justice. 1997/98.
    1. Criminal Justice, Administration of—United States—Periodicals. I. Sullivan, John J., comp. II. Victor, Joseph L., comp. III. Title: Criminal justice.
HV 8138.A67   364.973.05   77–640116
ISBN 0–697–37231–6

© 1997 by Dushkin/McGraw-Hill, Guilford, CT 06437, A Division of The McGraw-Hill Companies.

Copyright law prohibits the reproduction, storage, or transmission in any form by any means of any portion of this publication without the express written permission of Dushkin/McGraw-Hill, and of the copyright holder (if different) of the part of the publication to be reproduced. The Guidelines for Classroom Copying endorsed by Congress explicitly state that unauthorized copying may not be used to create, to replace, or to substitute for anthologies, compilations, or collective works.

Annual Editions® is a Registered Trademark of Dushkin/McGraw-Hill,
A Division of The McGraw-Hill Companies.

Twenty-First Edition

Cover image © 1996 PhotoDisc, Inc.

Printed in the United States of America

Printed on Recycled Paper

Editors/Advisory Board

Members of the Advisory Board are instrumental in the final selection of articles for each edition of ANNUAL EDITIONS. Their review of articles for content, level, currentness, and appropriateness provides critical direction to the editor and staff. We think that you will find their careful consideration well reflected in this volume.

EDITOR

John J. Sullivan
Mercy College, Dobbs Ferry

Joseph L. Victor
Mercy College, Dobbs Ferry

ADVISORY BOARD

Harry N. Babb
SUNY at Farmingdale

Peter D. Chimbos
Brescia College–University of Western Ontario

Joseph A. DeSanto
Iona College

Helen E. Taylor Greene
Old Dominion University

Kenneth Haas
University of Delaware

Raymond A. Helgemoe
University of New Hampshire

Paul Lang Jr.
Radford University

Michael A. Langer
Loyola University Water Tower Campus

Moses A. Leon
Pima Community College

Matthew C. Leone
University of Nevada

Robert J. McCormack
College of New Jersey

John J. McGrath
Mercy College, Bronx

Stephen G. O'Brien
Macomb Community College

Barbara Raffel Price
CUNY John Jay College of Criminal Justice

Dinah A. Robinson
Auburn University–Main

George E. Rush
California State University, Long Beach

Leslie Samuelson
University of Saskatchewan

Linda Stabile
Prince Georges Community College

David R. Struckhoff
Loyola University Water Tower Campus

Kenneth Venters
University of Tennessee

Staff

Ian A. Nielsen, Publisher

EDITORIAL STAFF

Roberta Monaco, Developmental Editor
Addie Raucci, Administrative Editor
Cheryl Greenleaf, Permissions Editor
Deanna Herrschaft, Permissions Assistant
Diane Barker, Proofreader
Lisa Holmes-Doebrick, Program Coordinator
Joseph Offredi, Photo Coordinator

PRODUCTION STAFF

Brenda S. Filley, Production Manager
Charles Vitelli, Designer
Shawn Callahan, Graphics
Lara M. Johnson, Graphics
Laura Levine, Graphics
Mike Campbell, Graphics
Juliana Arbo, Typesetting Supervisor
Jane Jaegersen, Typesetter
Marie Lazauskas, Word Processor
Kathleen D'Amico, Word Processor
Larry Killian, Copier Coordinator

To the Reader

In publishing ANNUAL EDITIONS we recognize the enormous role played by the magazines, newspapers, and journals of the *public press* in providing current, first-rate educational information in a broad spectrum of interest areas. Many of these articles are appropriate for students, researchers, and professionals seeking accurate, current material to help bridge the gap between principles and theories and the real world. These articles, however, become more useful for study when those of lasting value are carefully *collected, organized, indexed,* and *reproduced* in a *low-cost format,* which provides easy and permanent access when the material is needed. That is the role played by ANNUAL EDITIONS. Under the direction of each volume's *academic editor,* who is an expert in the subject area, and with the guidance of an *Advisory Board,* each year we seek to provide in each ANNUAL EDITION a current, well-balanced, carefully selected collection of the best of the public press for your study and enjoyment. We think that you will find this volume useful, and we hope that you will take a moment to let us know what you think.

During the 1970s, criminal justice emerged as an appealing, vital, and unique academic discipline. It emphasizes the professional development of students who plan careers in the field and attracts those who want to know more about a complex social problem and how this country deals with it. Criminal justice incorporates a vast range of knowledge from a number of specialties, including law, history, and the behavioral and social sciences. Each specialty contributes to our fuller understanding of criminal behavior and of society's attitudes toward deviance.

In view of the fact that the criminal justice system is in a constant state of flux, and because the study of criminal justice covers such a broad spectrum, today's students must be aware of a variety of subjects and topics. Standard textbooks and traditional anthologies cannot keep pace with the changes as quickly as they occur. In fact, many such sources are already out of date the day they are published. *Annual Editions: Criminal Justice 97/98* strives to maintain currency in matters of concern by providing up-to-date commentaries, articles, reports, and statistics from the most recent literature in the criminal justice field.

This volume contains units concerning crime and justice in America, victimology, the police, the judicial system, juvenile justice, and punishment and corrections. The articles in these units were selected because they are informative as well as provocative. The selections are timely and useful in their treatment of ethics, punishment, juveniles, courts, and other related topics.

Included in this volume are a number of features designed to be useful to students, researchers, and professionals in the criminal justice field. These include a *topic guide* for locating articles on specific subjects; the *table of contents abstracts,* which summarize each article and feature key concepts in bold italics; and a comprehensive *bibliography, glossary,* and *index.* In addition, each unit is preceded by an *overview* that provides a background for informed reading of the articles, emphasizes critical issues, and presents challenge questions.

We would like to know what you think of the selections contained in this edition. Please fill out the postage-paid *article rating form* on the last page and let us know your opinions. We change or retain many of the articles based on the comments we receive from you, the reader. Help us to improve this anthology—annually.

John J. Sullivan

Joseph L. Victor
Editors

Contents

UNIT 1

Crime and Justice in America

Seven selections focus on the overall structure of the criminal justice system in the United States. The current scope of crime in America is reviewed, and topics such as criminal behavior, drugs, and organized crime are discussed.

To the Reader	iv
Charts and Graphs	1
Topic Guide	2
Overview	4

1. **An Overview of the Criminal Justice System,** *Report to the Nation on Crime and Justice,* Bureau of Justice Statistics, U.S. Department of Justice, March 1988. — 6
   What is the sequence of events in the *criminal justice system*? This report reveals that the response to crime is a complex process, involving citizens as well as many agencies, levels, and branches of government.

2. **The Real Problems in American Justice,** *U.S. News & World Report,* October 9, 1995. — 11
   "Each year, 4.3 million violent crimes are committed, but barely more than 200,000 people are convicted of felonies and a little over half end up going to prison," this report reveals. The 10 major *"flaws" in the criminal justice system,* such as plea bargaining, police failures, the jury system, and repeaters of violent crime, are discussed.

3. **What to Do about Crime,** James Q. Wilson, *Commentary,* September 1994. — 14
   James Q. Wilson discusses crime in America and those who commit it. He proposes some innovative approaches to dealing with *crime,* such as *problem-oriented policing,* expanding the right of police to *stop and frisk* suspects, developing technologies that will permit the police to detect from a distance persons who are carrying weapons, and enforcing *truancy* laws.

4. **Who Is the Mob Today?** Peter Maas, *Parade,* February 25, 1996. — 25
   Potent new criminal elements, mostly from *Russia* and *China,* loom ominously on the law enforcement horizon. Is *"Cosa Nostra"* being replaced with new *ethnic* crime groups?

5. **Disintegration of the Family Is the Real Root Cause of Violent Crime,** Patrick F. Fagan, *USA Today Magazine (Society for the Advancement of Education),* May 1996. — 28
   Patrick Fagan argues that "the popular assumption that there is an association between *race* and crime is false." He cites *illegitimacy* as the key factor. The absence of marriage and the failure to maintain intact families impact on the incidence of crime among whites as well as blacks.

The concepts in bold italics are developed in the article. For further expansion please refer to the Topic Guide, the Glossary, and the Index.

UNIT 2

Victimology

Six articles discuss the impact of crime on the victim. Topics include the rights of crime victims and the consequences of family violence and rape.

6. **The Evolution of Street Gangs: A Shift toward Organized Crime,** Michael C. McCort, *The Police Chief,* June 1996. — 31
   Police lieutenant Michael McCort presents a brief history of the development of ***ethnic street gangs*** in the United States. He states that today's street gangs present a diverse and complex problem that must be dealt with in a diverse and comprehensive manner by law enforcement.

7. **Experts Are at Odds on How Best to Tackle Rise in Teen-Agers' Drug Use,** Gina Kolata, *New York Times,* September 18, 1996. — 35
   As ***drug*** use among people in their teens begins to rise sharply, experts in ***drug abuse*** say there is an opportunity to halt this incipient epidemic in its tracks. However, there is a disagreement as to the right remedy.

Overview — 38

8. **Criminal Victimization 1994,** Craig Perkins and Patsy Klaus, *Bureau of Justice Statistics Bulletin, U.S. Department of Justice,* April 1996. — 40
   This report presents information on ***criminal victimization*** in the United States during 1994. Of the 42.4 million crimes U.S. residents age 12 or older experienced, 31 million were ***property crimes***, 10.9 million were ***crimes of violence***, and one-half million were ***personal thefts***.

9. **True Crime,** Cheryl Russell, *American Demographics,* August 1995. — 48
   Safety-conscious baby boomers and the media fuel an overwhelming ***public fear of crime***. An examination of the data reveals that much fear is misplaced. Yet the worst crimes are increasing, and life can be dangerous, especially in the South.

10. **Protecting Our Seniors,** Ronald J. Getz, *Police,* September 1995. — 57
    Elder abuse and neglect are coming out of the closet as police interact with social agencies to improve the quality of life for ***senior citizens***.

11. **Nobody's Victim,** Stephanie B. Goldberg, *ABA Journal,* July 1996. — 61
    Stephanie Goldberg reviews the background of prosecutor Sarah Buel. Buel left an ***abusive partner*** to save her life, and since then, she's been saving others.

12. **Helping to Prevent Child Abuse—and Future Criminal Consequences: Hawai'i Healthy Start,** Ralph B. Earle, *National Institute of Justice Program Focus,* October 1995. — 67
    As the ***criminal justice system*** increasingly focuses its attention on the reduction of crime and violence, the ***prevention of child abuse*** and ***neglect*** has become a critical priority.

13. **Is Street Crime More Harmful than White-Collar Crime?** Kurt Finsterbusch and George McKenna, *Dushkin Publishing Group/McGraw-Hill,* 1996. — 76
    The authors present this pro/con essay in which professor John DiIulio contends that street criminals should be the focus of crime study. Jeffrey Reiman, professor of philosophy, argues that uncorrected pollution, medical malpractice, and dangerous working conditions are far more serious than street crimes.

The concepts in bold italics are developed in the article. For further expansion please refer to the Topic Guide, the Glossary, and the Index.

UNIT 3

The Police

Six selections examine the role of the police officer. Some of the topics discussed include the stress of police work, utilization of policewomen, and ethical policing.

Overview 86

14. **Police and the Quest for Professionalism,** Barbara Raffel Price, *Law Enforcement News,* June 15, 1995. 88
    Professionalism has long been a goal of the American *police* community. Barbara Price explores some of the reasons for this and explains factors that might impede reaching this goal. Some see *community policing* as the key to solving the problems.

15. **Police Work from a Woman's Perspective,** James M. Daum and Cindy M. Johns, *The Police Chief,* September 1994. 90
    A survey of *female police officers* indicates that there are still some problems of acceptance, some *sexual harassment,* and unequal treatment. The survey also considers the impact of the job on individual *women.*

16. **The Community's Role in Community Policing,** Wesley G. Skogan, *National Institute of Justice Journal,* August 1996. 93
    One of the key elements in a successful *community policing* program is the community itself. Wesley Skogan discusses challenges in sustaining community involvement and offers some suggestions as to how to keep the public involved.

17. **Incorporating Diversity: Police Response to Multicultural Changes in Their Communities,** Brad R. Bennett, *FBI Law Enforcement Bulletin,* December 1995. 96
    Brad Bennett discusses the findings of a study undertaken to determine how four California law enforcement agencies responded to *demographic* changes in their communities. Bennett argues that the country is being called on to open its arms to people from many different *ethnic* backgrounds. He says police departments must do their parts to respond to *multicultural* changes.

18. **LEN Interview: Police Chief Robert E. Ford of Port Orange, Fla.,** Marie Simonetti Rosen, *Law Enforcement News,* September 15, 1996. 101
    An experienced *police* administrator discusses far-ranging issues such as *quality of life* crimes, *community policing,* and, for police officers, report-*writing skills* and *college education* requirements.

19. **Police Cynicism: Causes and Cures,** Wallace Graves, *FBI Law Enforcement Bulletin,* June 1996. 108
    Cynicism is an attitude of "contemptuous distrust of human nature and motives." Cynical, distrustful *police officers* can hinder a department's efforts to forge collaborative relationships with the *community.* Wallace Graves discusses problems that can arise when cynicism creeps into a police department and suggests some remedies.

UNIT 4

The Judicial System

Five selections discuss the process by which the accused are moved through the judicial system. Prosecutors, courts, the jury process, and judicial ethics are reviewed.

Overview 112

20. **Abuse of Power in the Prosecutor's Office,** Bennett L. Gershman, *The World & I,* June 1991. 114
    Bennett Gershman, a distinguished law professor, discusses the power that a *prosecutor* possesses in determining whom to bring to trial, whom to charge with a capital crime, and what evidence will be introduced or withheld. He also cites examples of the abuse of these powers.

21. **The Rehnquist Reins,** David J. Garrow, *New York Times Magazine,* October 6, 1996. 121
    David Garrow explores the role of William H. Rehnquist as *chief justice of the United States* and his relationships with other members of the *Supreme Court.* This is an interesting insight into the personalities and the inner workings of the Court.

The concepts in bold italics are developed in the article. For further expansion please refer to the Topic Guide, the Glossary, and the Index.

UNIT 5

Juvenile Justice

Seven selections review the juvenile justice system. The topics include effective ways to respond to violent juvenile crime, juvenile detention, and children in gangs.

22. **'We're in the Fight of Our Lives,'** Bernard Gavzer, *Parade*, July 28, 1996. — 131

    "*Criminal justice* in America is in a state of collapse," says Judge Harold J. Rothwax, who has presided over criminal cases in New York City for over 25 years. He argues for eliminating both the *exclusionary rule* and the requirement for a *unanimous jury* verdict, and he calls for restrictions on *peremptory challenges* to prospective jurors.

23. **Unlocking the Jury Box,** Akhil Reed Amar and Vikram David Amar, *Policy Review*, May/June 1996. — 134

    "*Jury* service offers Americans an unequaled opportunity to participate democratically in the administration of *justice*. But on its present course, this vital egalitarian institution may shrivel up, avoided by citizens, manipulated by lawyers and litigants, and ridiculed by the general public," say Akhil and Vikram Amar. Their critical review of the jury system today makes suggestions for reform.

24. **Do You Swear That You Will Well and Truly Try . . . ?** Barbara Holland, *Smithsonian*, March 1995. — 141

    Trial by *jury* has had its ups and downs, but it beats what led up to it—trial by combat and ordeal by fire, water, or poison. This article presents an interesting history of the concept of trial by jury.

Overview — 146

25. **Rethinking the Sanctioning Function in Juvenile Court: Retributive or Restorative Responses to Youth Crime,** Gordon Bazemore and Mark Umbreit, *Crime & Delinquency*, July 1995. — 148

    Gordon Bazemore and Mark Umbreit assert that a restorative sanctioning model could provide a clear alternative to the punishment-centered sanctioning approaches now dominant in juvenile justice. *Restorative justice* responds to crime by addressing the harm that results when an offense is committed, gives first priority to victim reparation, and addresses the need to build safer communities.

26. **Juvenile Probation: The Workhorse of the Juvenile Justice System,** Patricia McFall Torbet, *Juvenile Justice Bulletin, U.S. Department of Justice,* March 1996. — 159

    In 1993 nearly 1.5 million *delinquency* cases were handled by *juvenile courts*. Virtually every one of those cases had contact with a *probation officer* at some point. This report presents a comprehensive picture of *juvenile probation* activity in the nation.

27. **Crime Time Bomb,** *U.S. News & World Report*, March 25, 1996. — 164

    Rising *juvenile crime,* and worries that it will get worse, lead cities, states, and Congress to seek a balance between *tougher laws* and *preventive measures.*

28. **Controlling Crime before It Happens: Risk-Focused Prevention,** J. David Hawkins, *National Institute of Justice Journal*, August 1995. — 167

    J. David Hawkins advocates using the *public health model to reduce violence in America's communities.* The model calls for (1) identifying factors that put young people at risk for violence, in order to reduce or eliminate these factors, and (2) strengthening the protective factors that buffer the effects of exposure to risk.

The concepts in bold italics are developed in the article. For further expansion please refer to the Topic Guide, the Glossary, and the Index.

UNIT 6

Punishment and Corrections

Nine selections focus on the current state of America's penal system and the effects of sentencing, probation, overcrowding, and capital punishment on criminals.

29. **Street Gangs—Future Paramilitary Groups?** Robert J. Bunker, *The Police Chief,* June 1996.   173
"Of all the concerns related to *street gangs,* probably the one that should be most closely watched is the interrelationship of these gangs to the *U.S. military,*" says Robert Bunker. "Street gang members with military training would bring a whole new dimension to *law enforcement's* struggle with these criminal groups."

30. **States Revamping Laws on Juveniles as Felonies Soar,** Fox Butterfield, *New York Times,* May 12, 1996.   176
"Almost all 50 states have overhauled their laws in the past two years, allowing more *youths* to be tried as adults and scrapping longtime protections like the confidentiality of *juvenile court* proceedings," Fox Butterfield reports.

31. **The Search for a Proper Punishment,** Randall Edwards, *APA Monitor,* December 1995.   179
"Many *psychologists* say that incarcerating *children,* in juvenile facilities or adult prisons, fails to reduce *juvenile crime.* They warn that warehousing delinquent youth bleeds money from *rehabilitation* and treatment programs that could more effectively prevent crime," writes Randall Edwards.

Overview   182

32. **Correctional Populations in the United States, 1994,** *Bureau of Justice Statistics Executive Summary, U.S. Department of Justice,* July 1996.   184
An estimated 5.1 million adults were under some form of *correctional supervision* in 1994. Nearly three-quarters of these people were on *probation* or *parole.* About 2.7 percent of the U.S. adult resident population were under correctional care or supervision in 1994, up from 1.1 percent in 1980.

33. **Doing Soft Time,** Jon Jefferson, *ABA Journal,* April 1994.   187
Faced with rising crime and falling revenues, governments are looking for alternative ways to sentence and rehabilitate *offenders.*

34. **Going to Meet the Man,** Mansfield B. Frazier, *Prison Life,* October 1996.   191
Mansfield Frazier offers practical advice to fellow former inmates about field *parole officers* and *parole supervision.* After debunking some common myths, he asserts that "the new-breed parole officer would rather keep you out of the joint than send you back."

35. **Eddie Ellis at Large,** Pam Widener, *Prison Life,* October 1996.   193
Former Black Panther *Eddie Ellis* spent 23 years in New York State's toughest *prisons* for a crime he did not commit. Released a few years ago, he has worked tirelessly to make needed changes in his own community and in the *justice system.*

36. **Probation's First 100 Years: Growth through Failure,** Charles J. Lindner, *Journal of Probation and Parole,* Spring 1993.   202
During the 100-year existence of *probation,* inadequate resources frequently have been identified as an underlying factor contributing to the ineffectiveness of offender supervision.

The concepts in bold italics are developed in the article. For further expansion please refer to the Topic Guide, the Glossary, and the Index.

37. A Woman behind Bars Is Not a Dangerous Man, Adrian Nicole LeBlanc, *New York Times Magazine,* June 2, 1996.
Adrian LeBlanc points out that *"prison administrators, corrections officers* and *inmates* consistently express an awareness of the differences between incarcerated women and men." Yet, despite these differences, she reports, "the treatment of *imprisoned women* is based on a correctional model that is based on muddy assumptions about violent men." — 210

38. The Color of Justice, John H. Trumbo, *Death Row,* 1995.
There are more nonwhite men on *death row* than their Caucasian counterparts, a fact supported by the numbers. The real question is this: Is the disparity due to *racial discrimination* or some other not-so-black-and-white issues? — 217

39. Anger and Ambivalence, David A. Kaplan, *Newsweek,* August 7, 1995.
Most Americans support *capital punishment,* yet few inmates are actually executed. This essay explores the reasons why the country has mixed feelings about putting people to death. — 223

40. Death Row, U.S.A., *NAACP Legal Defense and Educational Fund,* Summer 1996.
As of July 31, 1996, there had been a total of 335 *executions* since the 1976 reinstatement of *capital punishment.* This report also identifies 40 jurisdictions with *capital punishment statutes,* and indicates that there were 3,153 inmates on death row. — 226

Crime Statistics	**228**
Glossary	**237**
Index	**241**
Article Review Form	**244**
Article Rating Form	**245**

The concepts in bold italics are developed in the article. For further expansion please refer to the Topic Guide, the Glossary, and the Index.

Charts and Graphs

Sequence of Events in the Criminal Justice System	6–7
Criminal Justice Employment by Level of Government	9
Outcome of Arrests for Serious Cases	10
A Portrait of Justice?: Violent Crimes	12
Anti-Drug Programs	36
Criminal Victimizations—Highlights	40
Criminal Victimizations and Victimization Rates	41
Murder in the United States, 1994	42
Victimizations Reported to the Police, 1993–94	42
Victimization Rates for Persons Age 12 or Older	43
Property Victimization Rates	44
Victimization Rates for Violent and Property Crime	44
Number of Victimizations Experienced	45
Rates of Violent Victimizations by Age of Victim	45
Victim-Offender Relationship	46
What Police Reports Say	49
What Crime Victims Say	49
Most Violent Metros	50
Young and Wild	51
Safe Havens	52
Crime Central	54
Most Murderous Metros	56
How Americans Are Murdered	84
How Americans Are (Really) Murdered	85
Police Officers' Behavior Changes	91
Ethnic Changes in Total Population	100
Current and Restorative Assumptions	152
"Messages" of Sanctions	153
Probation Supervision	160
Probation Caseloads	161
Number of Probation Officers	161
Probation Caseloads Are Growing	162
Offences against Other Persons	162
Youth Violence Outpaces Adult Crime	164
Explosion of Juvenile Crimes	165
Profile of Young Killers	166
Teenagers and Guns	166
Risk Factors and Their Association with Behavior Problems	169
Development of Protective Factors	171
Changing Face of Homicide	177
Changing Juvenile Laws	178
Correctional Populations	184
Incarceration Rates	185
U.S. Military Confinement Summary	186
Global Prisoners	188
Crimes of the Times	188
Crime and Punishment	189
Race of Death Row Inmates	219
Race of Defendants Executed	219
Race of Victims	219
Executions by Race—by State	221
Death Row, U.S.A.	226
Crime Clock, 1995	228
Crime in the United States, 1986–1995 Index	229
Index of Offenses Reported:	
Murder	230
Forcible Rape	231
Robbery	232
Aggravated Assault	233
Burglary	233
Larceny-Theft	234
Motor Vehicle Theft	235

The concepts in bold italics are developed in the article. For further expansion please refer to the Topic Guide, the Glossary, and the Index.

Topic Guide

This topic guide suggests how the selections in this book relate to topics of traditional concern to students and professionals involved with the study of criminal justice. It is useful for locating articles that relate to each other for reading and research. The guide is arranged alphabetically according to topic. Articles may, of course, treat topics that do not appear in the topic guide. In turn, entries in the topic guide do not necessarily constitute a comprehensive listing of all the contents of each selection.

TOPIC AREA	TREATED IN	TOPIC AREA	TREATED IN
Attorneys	20. Abuse of Power in the Prosecutor's Office 21. Rehnquist Reins 22. 'We're in the Fight of Our Lives' 23. Unlocking the Jury Box	Crime	1. Overview of the Criminal Justice System 3. What to Do about Crime 4. Who Is the Mob Today? 5. Disintegration of the Family Is the Real Root Cause of Violent Crime 9. True Crime 13. Is Street Crime More Harmful than White Collar Crime?
Battered Families	10. Protecting Our Seniors 11. Nobody's Victim 12. Helping to Prevent Child Abuse		
Bias	15. Police Work from a Woman's Perspective 17. Incorporating Diversity 38. Color of Justice	Crime Victims	See Victimology
		Criminal Justice	1. Overview of the Criminal Justice System 2. Real Problems in American Justice 20. Abuse of Power in the Prosecutor's Office 22. 'We're in the Fight of Our Lives' 23. Unlocking the Jury Box
Children	See Juveniles		
Community Policing	3. What to Do about Crime 14. Police and the Quest for Professionalism 16. Community's Role in Community Policing 17. Incorporating Diversity 18. LEN Interview with Police Chief Robert E. Ford 19. Police Cynicism		
		Cynicism	19. Police Cynicism
		Death Penalty	38. Color of Justice 39. Anger and Ambivalence 40. Death Row, U.S.A.
Constitutional Rights	21. Rehnquist Reins 22. 'We're in the Fight of Our Lives' 23. Unlocking the Jury Box	Defense Counsel	22. 'We're in the Fight of Our Lives'
		Delinquency	See Juveniles
Corrections	32. Correctional Populations in the United States, 1994 33. Doing Soft Time 34. Going to Meet the Man 35. Eddie Ellis at Large 36. Probation's First 100 Years 37. Woman behind Bars Is Not a Dangerous Man	Drugs	4. Who Is the Mob Today? 7. Experts Are at Odds on How Best to Tackle Rise in Teen-Agers' Drug Use
		Elder Abuse	10. Protecting Our Seniors
Courts	20. Abuse of Power in the Prosecutor's Office 21. Rehnquist Reins 22. 'We're in the Fight of Our Lives' 23. Unlocking the Jury Box 25. Rethinking the Sanctioning Function in Juvenile Court	Ethics	20. Abuse of Power in the Prosecutor's Office
		Exclusionary Rule	22. 'We're in the Fight of Our Lives'
		Family Violence	10. Protecting Our Seniors 11. Nobody's Victim 12. Helping to Prevent Child Abuse
		Fear of Crime	9. True Crime

TOPIC AREA	TREATED IN	TOPIC AREA	TREATED IN
Gangs	6. Evolution of Street Gangs 29. Street Gangs—Future Paramilitary Groups?	Probation	36. Probation's First 100 Years
Gender	15. Police Work from a Woman's Perspective 37. Woman behind Bars Is Not a Dangerous Man	Prosecution	20. Abuse of Power in the Prosecutor's Office 22. 'We're in the Fight of Our Lives'
Judges	21. Rehnquist Reins 22. 'We're in the Fight of Our Lives'	Punishment	See Corrections
Jury	22. 'We're in the Fight of Our Lives' 23. Unlocking The Jury Box 24. Do You Swear That You Will Well and Truly Try . . . ?	Race	4. Who Is the Mob Today? 6. Evolution of Street Gangs 17. Incorporating Diversity 38. Color of Justice
Juveniles	7. Experts Are at Odds on How Best to Tackle Rise in Teen-Agers' Drug Use 25. Rethinking the Sanctioning Function in Juvenile Court 26. Juvenile Probation 27. Crime Time Bomb 28. Controlling Crime before It Happens 29. Street Gangs—Future Paramilitary Groups? 30. States Revamping Laws on Juveniles as Felonies Soar	Sentencing	25. Rethinking the Sanctioning Function in Juvenile Court 33. Doing Soft Time
		Sexual Harassment	15. Police Work from a Woman's Perspective
		Stop and Frisk	3. What to Do about Crime
		Stress	15. Police Work from a Woman's Perspective 19. Police Cynicism
		Supreme Court	21. Rehnquist Reins
		Truancy	3. What to Do about Crime
Organized Crime	4. Who Is the Mob Today? 6. Evolution of Street Gangs	Victimology	8. Criminal Victimization 1994 9. True Crime 10. Protecting Our Seniors 11. Nobody's Victim 12. Helping to Prevent Child Abuse 13. Is Street Crime More Harmful than White Collar Crime?
Parole	32. Correctional Populations in the United States, 1994 34. Going to Meet the Man 35. Eddie Ellis at Large		
Police	14. Police and the Quest for Professionalism 15. Police Work from a Woman's Perspective 16. Community's Role in Community Policing 17. Incorporating Diversity 18. LEN Interview with Police Chief Robert E. Ford 19. Police Cynicism	Violence	5. Disintegration of the Family Is the Real Root Cause of Violent Crime 8. Criminal Victimization 1994 10. Protecting Our Seniors 11. Nobody's Victim 12. Helping to Prevent Child Abuse 27. Crime Time Bomb
		White Collar Crime	13. Is Street Crime More Harmful than White Collar Crime?
Prevention	28. Controlling Crime before It Happens	Women	11. Nobody's Victim 15. Police Work from a Woman's Perspective 37. Woman behind Bars Is Not a Dangerous Man
Prisons	37. Woman behind Bars Is Not a Dangerous Man		

Crime and Justice in America

Opening this unit, the essay "An Overview of the Criminal Justice System" charts the flow of events in the administration of justice. The report "The Real Problems in American Justice" declares that the criminal justice system is in crisis from "cops to prison." Calls for action to help stem the flow of crime are discussed in "What to Do about Crime." James Q. Wilson offers some controversial suggestions, such as expanding police powers to stop and frisk.

Organized crime is no longer the exclusive province of the Mafia as new ethnic groups become involved. "Who Is The Mob Today?" by Peter Maas focuses on the rise of Chinese and Russian crime groups. "The Evolution of Street Gangs: A Shift toward Organized Crime" presents a brief history of the development of ethnic street gangs.

The rise of drug use by youngsters is of national concern. However, in "Experts Are at Odds on How Best to Tackle Rise in Teen-Agers' Drug Use," Gina Kolata shows that there are diverse views on treatment. And in the last reading, "Disintegration of the Family Is the Real Root Cause of Violent Crime,", Patrick Fagan calls illegitimacy that root cause.

Looking Ahead: Challenge Questions

What indications are there of ethnic street gangs in your community?

Should the police be given more power to stop and search people on the street or should they not? Defend your answer.

To what degree are drugs a problem with teen-agers in your community? How adequate are the treatment programs available?

UNIT 1

Article 1

An Overview of the Criminal Justice System

The response to crime is a complex process that involves citizens as well as many agencies, levels, and branches of government

The private sector initiates the response to crime

This first response may come from any part of the private sector: individuals, families, neighborhood associations, business, industry, agriculture, educational institutions, the news media, or any other private service to the public.

It involves crime prevention as well as participation in the criminal justice process once a crime has been committed. Private crime prevention is more than providing private security or burglar alarms or participating in neighborhood watch. It also includes a commitment to stop criminal behavior by not engaging in it or condoning it when it is committed by others.

Citizens take part directly in the criminal justice process by reporting crime to the police, by being a reliable participant (for example, witness, juror) in a criminal proceeding, and by accepting the disposition of the system as just or reasonable. As voters and taxpayers, citizens also participate in criminal justice through the policymaking process that affects how the criminal justice process operates, the resources available to it, and its goals and objectives. At every stage of the process, from the original formulation of objectives to the decision about where to locate jails and prisons and to the reintegration of inmates into society, the private sector has a role to play. Without such involvement, the criminal justice process cannot serve the citizens it is intended to protect.

The government responds to crime through the criminal justice system

We apprehend, try, and punish offenders by means of a loose confederation of agencies at all levels of government. Our American system of justice has evolved from the English common law into a complex series of procedures and decisions. There is no single criminal justice system in this country. We have many systems that are similar, but individually unique.

Criminal cases may be handled differently in different jurisdictions, but court decisions based on the due process guarantees of the U.S. Constitution require that specific steps be taken in the administration of criminal justice.

The description of the criminal and juvenile justice systems that follows portrays the most common sequence of events

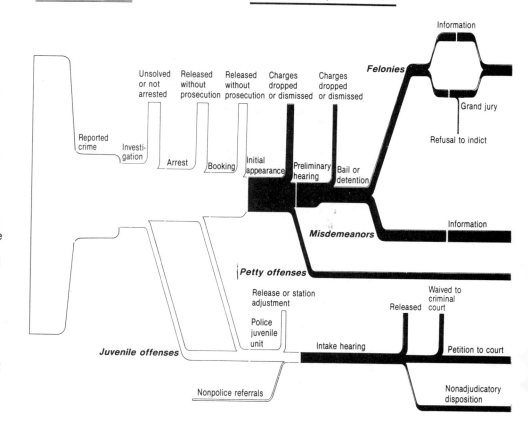

What is the sequence of events in the criminal justice system?

Note: This chart gives a simplified view of caseflow through the criminal justice system. Procedures vary among jurisdictions. The weights of the lines are not intended to show the actual size of caseloads.

From the *Report to the Nation on Crime and Justice,* March 1988, pp. 56-60. Reprinted by permission of the U.S. Department of Justice, Bureau of Justice Statistics.

1. Overview of the Criminal Justice System

in the response to serious criminal behavior.

Entry into the system

The justice system does not respond to most crime because so much crime is not discovered or reported to the police. Law enforcement agencies learn about crime from the reports of citizens, from discovery by a police officer in the field, or from investigative and intelligence work.

Once a law enforcement agency has established that a crime has been committed, a suspect must be identified and apprehended for the case to proceed through the system. Sometimes, a suspect is apprehended at the scene; however, identification of a suspect sometimes requires an extensive investigation. Often, no one is identified or apprehended.

Prosecution and pretrial services

After an arrest, law enforcement agencies present information about the case and about the accused to the prosecutor, who will decide if formal charges will be filed with the court. If no charges are filed, the accused must be released. The prosecutor can also drop charges after making efforts to prosecute (*nolle prosequi*).

A suspect charged with a crime must be taken before a judge or magistrate without unnecessary delay. At the initial appearance, the judge or magistrate informs the accused of the charges and decides whether there is probable cause to detain the accused person. Often, the defense counsel is also assigned at the initial appearance. If the offense is not very serious, the determination of guilt and assessment of a penalty may also occur at this stage.

In some jurisdictions, a pretrial-release decision is made at the initial appearance, but this decision may occur at other hearings or may be changed at another time during the process. Pretrial release and bail were traditionally intended to ensure appearance at trial. However, many jurisdictions permit pretrial detention of defendants accused of serious offenses and deemed to be dangerous to prevent them from committing crimes in the pretrial period. The court may decide to release the accused on his/her own recognizance, into the custody of a third party, on the promise of satisfying certain conditions, or after the posting of a financial bond.

In many jurisdictions, the initial appearance may be followed by a preliminary hearing. The main function of this hearing is to discover if there is probable cause to believe that the accused committed a known crime within the jurisdiction of the court. If the judge does not find probable cause, the case is dismissed; however, if the judge or magistrate finds probable cause for such a belief, or the accused waives his or her right to a preliminary hearing, the case may be bound over to a grand jury.

A *grand jury* hears evidence against the accused presented by the prosecutor and decides if there is sufficient evidence to cause the accused to be brought to trial. If the grand jury finds sufficient evidence, it submits to the court an indictment (a written statement of the essential facts of the offense charged against the accused). Where the grand jury system is used, the grand jury may also investigate criminal activity generally and issue indictments called grand jury originals that initiate criminal cases.

Misdemeanor cases and some felony cases proceed by the issuance of an *information* (a formal, written accusation submitted to the court by a prosecutor). *In some jurisdictions*, indictments *may be* required in felony cases. However, the accused may choose to waive a grand jury indictment and, instead, accept service of an information for the crime.

Adjudication

Once an indictment or information has been filed with the trial court, the accused is scheduled for arraignment. At the arraignment, the accused is informed of the charges, advised of the

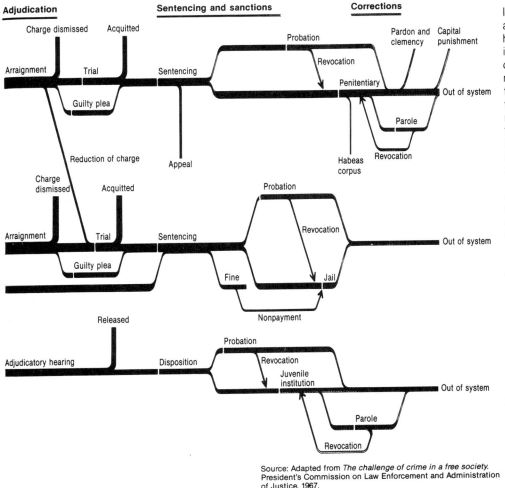

Source: Adapted from *The challenge of crime in a free society.* President's Commission on Law Enforcement and Administration of Justice, 1967.

1. CRIME AND JUSTICE IN AMERICA

rights of criminal defendants, and asked to enter a plea to the charges. Sometimes, a plea of guilty is the result of negotiations between the prosecutor and the defendant, with the defendant entering a guilty plea in expectation of reduced charges or a lenient sentence.

If the accused pleads guilty or pleads *nolo contendere* (accepts penalty without admitting guilt), the judge may accept or reject the plea. If the plea is accepted, no trial is held and the offender is sentenced at this proceeding or at a later date. The plea may be rejected if, for example, the judge believes that the accused may have been coerced. If this occurs, the case may proceed to trial.

If the accused pleads not guilty or not guilty by reason of insanity, a date is set for the trial. A person accused of a serious crime is guaranteed a trial by jury. However, the accused may ask for a bench trial where the judge, rather than a jury, serves as the finder of fact. In both instances the prosecution and defense present evidence by questioning witnesses while the judge decides on issues of law. The trial results in acquittal or conviction on the original charges or on lesser included offenses.

After the trial a defendant may request appellate review of the conviction or sentence. In many criminal cases, appeals of a conviction are a matter of right; all States with the death penalty provide for automatic appeal of cases involving a death sentence. However, under some circumstances and in some jurisdictions, appeals may be subject to the discretion of the appellate court and may be granted only on acceptance of a defendant's petition for a *writ of certiorari*. Prisoners may also appeal their sentences through civil rights petitions and writs of habeas corpus where they claim unlawful detention.

Sentencing and sanctions

After a guilty verdict or guilty plea, sentence is imposed. In most cases the judge decides on the sentence, but in some States, the sentence is decided by the jury, particularly for capital offenses such as murder.

In arriving at an appropriate sentence, a sentencing hearing may be held at which evidence of aggravating or mitigating circumstances will be considered. In assessing the circumstances surrounding a convicted person's criminal behavior, courts often rely on presentence investigations by probation

agencies or other designated authorities. Courts may also consider victim impact statements.

The sentencing choices that may be available to judges and juries include one or more of the following:
• the death penalty
• incarceration in a prison, jail, or other confinement facility
• probation—allowing the convicted person to remain at liberty but subject to certain conditions and restrictions
• fines—primarily applied as penalties in minor offenses
• restitution—which requires the offender to provide financial compensation to the victim.

In many States, State law mandates that persons convicted of certain types of offenses serve a prison term.

Most States permit the judge to set the sentence length within certain limits, but some States have determinate sentencing laws that stipulate a specific sentence length, which must be served and cannot be altered by a parole board.

Corrections

Offenders sentenced to incarceration usually serve time in a local jail or a State prison. Offenders sentenced to less than 1 year generally go to jail; those sentenced to more than 1 year go to prison. Persons admitted to a State prison system may be held in prisons with varying levels of custody or in a community correctional facility.

A prisoner may become eligible for parole after serving a specific part of his or her sentence. Parole is the conditional release of a prisoner before the prisoner's full sentence has been served. The decision to grant parole is made by an authority such as a parole board, which has power to grant or revoke parole or to discharge a parolee altogether. The way parole decisions are made varies widely among jurisdictions.

Offenders may also be required to serve out their full sentences prior to release (expiration of term). Those sentenced under determinate sentencing laws can be released only after they have served their full sentence (mandatory release) less any "goodtime" received while in prison. Inmates get such credits against their sentences automatically or by earning it through participation in programs.

If an offender has an outstanding charge or sentence in another State, a

detainer is used to ensure that when released from prison he or she will be transferred to the other State.

If released by a parole board decision or by mandatory release, the releasee will be under the supervision of a parole officer in the community for the balance of his or her unexpired sentence. This supervision is governed by specific conditions of release, and the releasee may be returned to prison for violations of such conditions.

The juvenile justice system

The processing of juvenile offenders is not entirely dissimilar to adult criminal processing, but there are crucial differences in the procedures. Many juveniles are referred to juvenile courts by law enforcement officers, but many others are referred by school officials, social services agencies, neighbors, and even parents, for behavior or conditions that are determined to require intervention by the formal system for social control.

When juveniles are referred to the juvenile courts, their *intake* departments, or prosecuting attorneys, determine whether sufficient grounds exist to warrant filing a petition that requests an *adjudicatory hearing* or a request to transfer jurisdiction to criminal court. In some States and at the Federal level prosecutors under certain circumstances may file criminal charges against juveniles directly in criminal courts.

The court with jurisdiction over juvenile matters may reject the petition or the juveniles may be diverted to other agencies or programs in lieu of further court processing. Examples of diversion programs include individual or group counseling or referral to educational and recreational programs.

If a petition for an adjudicatory hearing is accepted, the juvenile may be brought before a court quite unlike the court with jurisdiction over adult offenders. In disposing of cases juvenile courts usually have far more discretion than adult courts. In addition to such options as probation, commitment to correctional institutions, restitution, or fines, State laws grant juvenile courts the power to order removal of children from their homes to foster homes or treatment facilities. Juvenile courts also may order participation in special programs aimed at shoplifting prevention, drug counseling, or driver education. They also may order referral to criminal court for trial as adults.

1. Overview of the Criminal Justice System

Despite the considerable discretion associated with juvenile court proceedings, juveniles are afforded many of the due-process safeguards associated with adult criminal trials. Sixteen States permit the use of juries in juvenile courts; however, in light of the U.S. Supreme Court's holding that juries are not essential to juvenile hearings, most States do not make provisions for juries in juvenile courts.

The response to crime is founded in the intergovernmental structure of the United States

Under our form of government, each State and the Federal Government has its own criminal justice system. All systems must respect the rights of individuals set forth in court interpretation of the U.S. Constitution and defined in case law.

State constitutions and laws define the criminal justice system within each State and delegate the authority and responsibility for criminal justice to various jurisdictions, officials, and institutions. State laws also define criminal behavior and groups of children or acts under jurisdiction of the juvenile courts.

Municipalities and counties further define their criminal justice systems through local ordinances that proscribe additional illegal behavior and establish the local agencies responsible for criminal justice processing that were not established by the State.

Congress also has established a criminal justice system at the Federal level to respond to Federal crimes such as bank robbery, kidnaping, and transporting stolen goods across State lines.

The response to crime is mainly a State and local function

Very few crimes are under exclusive Federal jurisdiction. The responsibility to respond to most crime rests with the State and local governments. Police protection is primarily a function of cities and towns. Corrections is primarily a function of State governments. More than three-fifths of all justice personnel are employed at the local level.

	Percent of criminal justice employment by level of government		
	Local	State	Federal
Police	77%	15%	8%
Judicial (courts only)	60	32	8
Prosecution and legal services	58	26	17
Public defense	47	50	3
Corrections	35	61	4
Total	62%	31%	8%

Source: *Justice expenditure and employment, 1985*, BJS Bulletin, March 1987.

Discretion is exercised throughout the criminal justice system

Discretion is "an authority conferred by law to act in certain conditions or situations in accordance with an official's or an official agency's own considered judgment and conscience." Discretion is exercised throughout the government. It is a part of decisionmaking in all government systems from mental health to education, as well as criminal justice.

Concerning crime and justice, legislative bodies have recognized that they cannot anticipate the range of circumstances surrounding each crime, anticipate local mores, and enact laws that clearly encompass all conduct that is criminal and all that is not. Therefore, persons charged with the day-to-day response to crime are expected to exercise their own judgment within *limits* set by law. Basically, they must decide—
• whether to take action

• where the situation fits in the scheme of law, rules, and precedent
• which official response is appropriate.

To ensure that discretion is exercised responsibly, government authority is often delegated to professionals. Professionalism requires a minimum level of training and orientation, which guides officials in making decisions. The professionalism of policing discussed later in this chapter is due largely to the desire to ensure the proper exercise of police discretion.

The limits of discretion vary from State to State and locality to locality. For example, some State judges have wide discretion in the type of sentence they may impose. In recent years other States have sought to limit the judges' discretion in sentencing by passing mandatory sentencing laws that require prison sentences for certain offenses.

Who exercises discretion?

These criminal justice officials...	...must often decide whether or not or how to—
Police	Enforce specific laws Investigate specific crimes Search people, vicinities, buildings Arrest or detain people
Prosecutors	File charges or petitions for adjudication Seek indictments Drop cases Reduce charges
Judges or magistrates	Set bail or conditions for release Accept pleas Determine delinquency Dismiss charges Impose sentence Revoke probation
Correctional officials	Assign to type of correctional facility Award privileges Punish for disciplinary infractions
Paroling authority	Determine date and conditions of parole Revoke parole

1. CRIME AND JUSTICE IN AMERICA

More than one agency has jurisdiction over some criminal events

The response to most criminal actions is usually begun by local police who react to violation of State law. If a suspect is apprehended, he or she is prosecuted locally and may be confined in a local jail or State prison. In such cases, only one agency has jurisdiction at each stage in the process.

However, some criminal events because of their characteristics and location may come under the jurisdiction of more than one agency. For example, such overlapping occurs within States when local police, county sheriffs, and State police are all empowered to enforce State laws on State highways.

Congress has provided for Federal jurisdiction over crimes that—
• materially affect interstate commerce
• occur on Federal land
• involve large and probably interstate criminal organizations or conspiracies
• are offenses of national importance, such as the assassination of the President.

Bank robbery and many drug offenses are examples of crimes for which the States and the Federal Government both have jurisdiction. In cases of dual jurisdiction, an investigation and a prosecution may be undertaken by all authorized agencies, but only one level of government usually pursues a case. For example, a study of FBI bank robbery investigations during 1978 and 1979 found that of those cases cleared—

• 36% were solved by the FBI alone
• 25% were solved by a joint effort of the FBI and State and local police
• 40% were solved by the State and local police acting alone.

In response to dual jurisdiction and to promote more effective coordination, Law Enforcement Coordinating Committees have been established throughout the country and include all relevant Federal and local agencies.

Within States the response to crime also varies from one locality to another

The response differs because of statutory and structural differences and differences in how discretion is exercised. Local criminal justice policies and programs change in response to local attitudes and needs. For example, the prosecutor in one locality may concentrate on particular types of offenses that plague the local community while the prosecutor in another locality may concentrate on career criminals.

The response to crime also varies on a case-by-case basis

No two cases are exactly alike. At each stage of the criminal justice process officials must make decisions that take into account the varying factors of each case. Two similar cases may have very different results because of various factors, including differences in witness cooperation and physical evidence, the availability of resources to investigate

and prosecute the case, the quality of the lawyers involved, and the age and prior criminal history of the suspects.

Differences in local laws, agencies, resources, standards, and procedures result in varying responses in each jurisdiction

The outcomes of arrests for serious cases vary among the States as shown by Offender-based Transaction Statistics from nine States:

	% of arrests for serious crimes that result in . . .		
	Prose-cution	Convic-tion	Incarcer-ation
Virginia	100%	61%	55%
Nebraska	99	68	39
New York	97	67	31
Utah	97	79	9
Virgin Islands	95	55	35
Minnesota	89	69	48
Pennsylvania	85	56	24
California	78	61	45
Ohio	77	50	21

Source: Disaggregated data used in *Tracking offenders: White-collar crime*, BJS Special Report, November 1986.

Some of this variation can be explained by differences among States. For example, the degree of discretion in deciding whether to prosecute differs from State to State; some States do not allow any police or prosecutor discretion; others allow police discretion but not prosecutor discretion and vice versa.

Article 2

The real problems in American justice

A system in crisis from cops to courts to prisons

The criminal justice system was low on Americans' list of esteemed institutions long before the O. J. Simpson case became a national obsession. A recent survey by *U.S. News* found only 8 percent with a "great deal" of confidence in the courts, and the public routinely complains of excessive costs and delays, as well as laxity in sentencing.

Clearly, the system is broken in fundamental ways: Each year, 4.3 million violent crimes are committed, but barely more than 200,000 people are convicted of felonies, and a little over half end up going to prison for more than a year. Here's a rundown of the major flaws:

1. Police solve too few crimes. Law enforcers never have had it easy, but their modern success rate is staggeringly low. Only 24 percent of robberies and 13 percent of burglaries are cleared by an arrest. Homicide clearance rates are down from 86 percent in 1970 to 66 percent in 1993. Fewer witnesses are willing to testify against today's armed teens. A larger witness-protection program would help.

But the biggest problem is manpower. Some help is on the way as up to 100,000 community-patrol officers are hired under last year's federal anticrime law. And shootings already are falling in some New York City precincts, where more police are returning to the beat to deal with both serious crimes and low-level offenses. But critics warn that local patrols take away from investigative units.

2. Sleuths lose vital evidence. Harried police officers inadvertently contaminate key items. Crime laboratories, which do everything from alcohol testing to DNA analysis, can compound the problem. Historically, they have been a low priority for public funds. Technicians often receive scant training, and, until recently, few of the nation's 358 labs worked under any quality control. But quality is improving, and new technologies are spreading. An Automated Fingerprint Identification System helps police at more than 80 agencies match fingerprints found at crime scenes to those in a national database. The system registers "hits" in more than 10 percent of cases. One area where quality remains suspect: the system of coroners and medical examiners. One reason is that only a few areas employ doctors trained to investigate unnatural deaths.

3. Dangerous suspects commit crimes while awaiting trials on other charges. Defendants have a legal right to be considered for release before trial, and nearly two thirds of those charged with serious crimes—including one fourth of accused murderers—are allowed out on the street while awaiting trial. While most of them stay out of trouble, a disturbingly high 1 out of 3 either is rearrested, fails to appear in court on time or commits some infraction that results in a bail revocation.

This year, Republicans in the House approved a "jail, not bail" bill that would allow states to spend new federal prison money to build local jails for pretrial inmates. Experts like D. Alan Henry of the Pretrial Services Resource Center complain that such "solutions" will only worsen the system's unfairness: Many of those who can afford to post bail will do so—regardless of how serious their crimes—while poor suspects will remain stuck behind bars.

4. Prosecutors make bargains with too many criminals. In 9 cases out of 10, no trial ever is held. The defendants accept plea bargains that let them plead guilty, usually to just a few of the charges. Critics argue that to move cases along, prosecutors too readily abandon charges that could bring tougher penalties. Although that does happen, just as common is overcharging—filing counts of dubious provability to pressure defendants.

A few places have moved to curb abuses. The most prominent example is Alaska, which banned plea bargaining in 1975. A study by the federal State Justice Institute found that the policy has improved the screening of cases and contributed to longer prison terms. However, researchers found that in some areas, bargaining over pleas has been replaced by bargaining over the charges filed.

5. Criminal cases take too long. The interval between arrest and sentencing averages 274 days nationwide for murders and 172 days for violent crimes generally. The length of the few cases that go to trial is less of a problem. The National Center for State Courts reports that trials average about 11 hours, much shorter than the time it took for single witnesses to testify in the Simpson extravaganza. Murder trials typically last one to two weeks, depending on the circumstances. California trials tend to take longer.

Still, "we can do a lot better" at expediting cases once they reach court, says Barry Mahoney of the Denver-based Justice Management Institute. Mahoney's group and others offer trial-management training to judges, but probably fewer than 10 percent nationwide have taken it. A bigger problem: There aren't enough judges to juggle all witnesses, defendants and lawyers that come to court.

6. The jury system is flawed. It took 11 weeks to choose 12 jurors and 12 alternates in the Simpson trial. Then, the jury was forced to live in a hotel for nine months under guard, which frayed nerves and cost taxpayers more than $2.5 million. The jury process is so cumbersome, says Joseph DiGenova, former federal prosecutor in Washington, D.C., that "procedures instituted a century or two ago . . . are not adequate today."

Ideas abound to simplify jury service. Some reformers urge curtailing the elaborate process of allowing prosecution and defense to eliminate potential jurors, often on the advice of expensive consultants who analyze candidates for expected biases. Once the trial is underway, a few states, including Arizona, are experimenting with permitting jurors to ask

From *U.S. News & World Report*, October 9, 1995, pp. 52, 54-55. © 1995 by U.S. News & World Report. Reprinted by permission.

1. CRIME AND JUSTICE IN AMERICA

questions of witnesses. California prosecutors, noting that 14 percent of Los Angeles County trials end with a hung jury, are pressing the state legislature to allow less-than-unanimous jury verdicts—which Oregon and Louisiana already do.

7. Trials are consumed more with tactics than truth. Many believe that defense lawyers search not for truth but for "preventing evidence of a defendant's guilt from reaching the jury," says James Wootton of the Safe Streets Alliance, an anticrime group based in Washington, D.C. Conservatives in Congress are trying to blunt the "exclusionary rule," which prevents illegally obtained evidence from being used in trials. They would allow such evidence if it was provably gathered in good faith. Others would go further. Law Prof. Joseph Grano of Wayne State University advocates that defense lawyers be required to ask their clients whether they committed the crime and to encourage the guilty to accept responsibility.

But defense lawyers will resist basic changes. "It's been a long time since I went to court looking for the truth," concedes Raymond Brown, a prominent Newark defense attorney. He says a proper role of the defense is forcing prosecutors to prove guilt.

8. Suspects get inadequate legal aid. Simpson is spending millions on a "dream team" defense. The reality for most criminal suspects is that they are fortunate to get much attention at all from overworked public defenders or court-appointed attorneys. Most such advocates are competent: They achieve roughly the same results as high-priced attorneys The problem is that there are too many cases and too little time. Experts say full-time defense lawyers should handle at most 150 felony cases each year. The actual number in many areas is much higher: Defenders in southwest Florida are assigned some 300 cases and up to 50 appeals a year.

Although a system of public defenders is in place, its resources are limited and declining. Congress, for example, is on the verge of eliminating federal funding for a network of centers that help defenders prepare cases of candidates for the death penalty. Critics say the centers help give attorneys ammunition to prolong cases unnecessarily; supporters respond that better sorting of the evidence can actually expedite trials and prevent needless appeals—not to mention helping ensure that innocent persons are not executed or put in prison for life.

9. Some criminals strike over and over. A few criminals commit a disproportionate amount of violence, but identifying and incapacitating them has proved impossible. Limits on prison space and an inability to predict recidivists mean that nearly 6 of every 10 serious offenders are not sentenced to prison. More than 4 in 10 are arrested within three years for another serious crime. Of those who serve time, most are paroled before serving 40 percent of their time.

Several states are moving to abolish parole, and others are clamping down on early releases. Pennsylvania has slowed releases of violent offenders to a trickle. In South Carolina, retired naval officer Jim Grego founded Citizens Against Violent Crime 11 years ago when his daughter was seriously wounded in an assault by a twice-paroled felon. Now that the group has lobbied for tougher standards, the state paroles 25 to 30 percent of applicants compared with 75 percent a decade ago. Meanwhile, many states are beefing up habit-

A PORTRAIT OF JUSTICE?

An estimated 4.37 million violent crimes are committed each year (including murder, rape, robbery and aggravated assault), but only a tiny fraction of criminals are put behind bars.

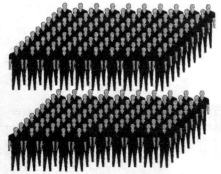

Note: These data are the latest available. Annual violent crimes and violent crimes reported to police include multiple crimes per defendant.

USN&WR–Basic data: U.S. Dept. of Justice

2. Real Problems

ual-offender laws, often by requiring life sentences for those who commit two or three violent offenses.

But get-tough measures can backfire. Some states that have eliminated parole have seen costs soar as prison populations explode. And in California, the "three strikes and you're out" law requiring life terms for third-time offenders is causing more defendants to demand trials, thus clogging the courts. "The real crisis in L.A. County is the impact of three strikes," says presiding trial Judge James Bascue.

10. The justice system is insensitive to the public, particularly crime victims. Except for their court testimony, victims traditionally have been shut out when penalties are assessed. This view is changing, albeit slowly. A growing crime-victims movement has succeeded in recognizing victim rights in most states, at least on paper. The challenge is giving those rights real meaning. Victims are campaigning for "restorative justice," a program to involve them more in the sentencing process. In many cases, that means requiring convicts to provide victims restitution for losses or encouraging assailants to face their victims.

Some courts, traditionally remote institutions, are acting to improve public relations. Connecticut indoctrinates its court employees in "total quality management," partly to help citizens seeking information about cases.

Many justice reforms require an infusion of tax money. "The public gets the justice system it pays for," says Donald Rebovich of the National District Attorneys Association. Other changes would necessitate fundamental rewriting of criminal law—something that has proved remarkably resistant to reform. Defense lawyers argue that the system generally works well, even if it results at times in a criminal's going free. So it's reasonable to expect that long after the Simpson case is over, the justice system will lurch along—and so will the public's frustration and outrage.

TED GEST WITH DORIAN FRIEDMAN
AND TIMOTHY M. ITO

Article 3

What To Do About Crime

James Q. Wilson

Few of the major problems facing American society today are entirely new, but in recent years most of them have either taken new forms or reached new levels of urgency. To make matters more difficult, in many cases the solutions formerly relied upon have proved to be ineffective, leaving us so frustrated that we seize desperately on proposals which promise much but deliver little.

In the hope of bringing greater clarity to the understanding of these problems, and of framing workable solutions and policies, we are inaugurating this new series of articles. Like James Q. Wilson's below, each subsequent piece in the series will begin with a reexamination of a particular issue by a writer who has lived with and studied it for a long time and who will then proceed to suggest "What To Do About" it. Among those already scheduled for publication in the coming months are Charles Murray and Richard J. Herrnstein on welfare; Gertrude Himmelfarb on the universities; William J. Bennett on our children; Robert H. Bork on the First Amendment; and Richard Pipes on Russia.

JAMES Q. WILSON, *professor of management and public policy at UCLA, is the author of many books and articles on crime, including* Thinking about Crime; Varieties of Police Behavior; *and* Crime and Human Nature *(written with Richard J. Herrnstein). He is also the editor of* Crime and Public Policy *and co-editor, with Joan Petersilia, of* Crime *(from ICS Press).*

WHEN the United States experienced the great increase in crime that began in the early 1960's and continued through the 1970's, most Americans were inclined to attribute it to conditions unique to this country. Many conservatives blamed it on judicial restraints on the police, the abandonment of capital punishment, and the mollycoddling of offenders; many liberals blamed it on poverty, racism, and the rise of violent television programs. Europeans, to the extent they noticed at all, referred to it, sadly or patronizingly, as the "American" problem, a product of our disorderly society, weak state, corrupt police, or imperfect welfare system.

Now, 30 years later, any serious discussion of crime must begin with the fact that, except for homicide, most industrialized nations have crime rates that resemble those in the United States. All the world is coming to look like America. In 1981, the burglary rate in Great Britain was much less than that in the United States; within six years the two rates were the same; today, British homes are more likely to be burgled than American ones. In 1980, the rate at which automobiles were stolen was lower in France than in the United States; today, the reverse is true. By 1984, the burglary rate in the Netherlands was nearly twice that in the United States. In Australia and Sweden certain forms of theft are more common than they are here. While property-crime rates were declining during most of the 1980's in the United States, they were rising elsewhere.[1]

America, it is true, continues to lead the industrialized world in murders. There can be little doubt that part of this lead is to be explained by the greater availability of handguns here. Arguments that once might have been settled with insults or punches are today more likely to be settled by shootings. But guns are not the whole story. Big American cities have had more homicides than comparable European ones for almost as long as anyone can find records. New York and Philadelphia have been more murderous than London since the early part of the 19th century. This country has had a violent history; with respect to murder, that seems likely to remain the case.

But except for homicide, things have been getting better in the United States for over a decade. Since 1980, robbery rates (as reported in victim surveys) have declined by 15 percent. And even with regard to homicide, there is relatively good news: in 1990, the rate at which adults killed one another was no higher than it was in 1980, and in many cities it was considerably lower.

This is as it was supposed to be. Starting

---

[1] These comparisons depend on official police statistics. There are of course errors in such data. But essentially the same pattern emerges from comparing nations on the basis of victimization surveys.

From *Commentary*, September 1994, pp. 25-34. © 1994 by James Q. Wilson. Reprinted by permission.

3. What to Do about Crime

around 1980, two things happened that ought to have reduced most forms of crime. The first was the passing into middle age of the postwar baby boom. By 1990, there were 1.5 million fewer boys between the ages of fifteen and nineteen than there had been in 1980, a drop that meant that this youthful fraction of the population fell from 9.3 percent to 7.2 percent of the total.

In addition, the great increase in the size of the prison population, caused in part by the growing willingness of judges to send offenders to jail, meant that the dramatic reductions in the costs of crime to the criminal that occurred in the 1960's and 1970's were slowly (and very partially) being reversed. Until around 1985, this reversal involved almost exclusively real criminals and parole violators; it was not until after 1985 that more than a small part of the growth in prison populations was made up of drug offenders.

Because of the combined effect of fewer young people on the street and more offenders in prison, many scholars, myself included, predicted a continuing drop in crime rates throughout the 1980's and into the early 1990's. We were almost right: crime rates did decline. But suddenly, starting around 1985, even as adult homicide rates were remaining stable or dropping, *youthful* homicide rates shot up.

Alfred Blumstein of Carnegie-Mellon University has estimated that the rate at which young males, ages fourteen to seventeen, kill people has gone up significantly for whites and incredibly for blacks. Between 1985 and 1992, the homicide rate for young white males went up by about 50 percent but for young black males it *tripled.*

The public perception that today's crime problem is different from and more serious than that of earlier decades is thus quite correct. Youngsters are shooting at people at a far higher rate than at any time in recent history. Since young people are more likely than adults to kill strangers (as opposed to lovers or spouses), the risk to innocent bystanders has gone up. There may be some comfort to be had in the fact that youthful homicides are only a small fraction of all killings, but given their randomness, it is not much solace.

THE United States, then, does not have *a* crime problem, it has at least two. Our high (though now slightly declining) rates of property crime reflect a profound, worldwide cultural change: prosperity, freedom, and mobility have emancipated people almost everywhere from those ancient bonds of custom, family, and village that once held in check both some of our better and many of our worst impulses. The power of the state has been weakened, the status of children elevated, and the opportunity for adventure expanded; as a consequence, we have experienced an explosion of artistic creativity, entrepreneurial zeal, political experimentation—

and criminal activity. A global economy has integrated the markets for clothes, music, automobiles—and drugs.

There are only two restraints on behavior—morality, enforced by individual conscience or social rebuke, and law, enforced by the police and the courts. If society is to maintain a behavioral equilibrium, any decline in the former must be matched by a rise in the latter (or vice versa). If familial and traditional restraints on wrongful behavior are eroded, it becomes necessary to increase the legal restraints. But the enlarged spirit of freedom and the heightened suspicion of the state have made it difficult or impossible to use the criminal-justice system to achieve what custom and morality once produced.

This is the modern dilemma, and it may be an insoluble one, at least for the West. The Islamic cultures of the Middle East and the Confucian cultures of the Far East believe that they have a solution. It involves allowing enough liberty for economic progress (albeit under general state direction) while reserving to the state, and its allied religion, nearly unfettered power over personal conduct. It is too soon to tell whether this formula—best exemplified by the prosperous but puritanical city-state of Singapore—will, in the long run, be able to achieve both reproducible affluence and intense social control.

Our other crime problem has to do with the kind of felonies we have: high levels of violence, especially youthful violence, often occurring as part of urban gang life, produced disproportionately by a large, alienated, and self-destructive underclass. This part of the crime problem, though not uniquely American, is more important here than in any other industrialized nation. Britons, Germans, and Swedes are upset about the insecurity of their property and uncertain about what response to make to its theft, but if Americans only had to worry about their homes being burgled and their autos stolen, I doubt that crime would be the national obsession it has now become.

Crime, we should recall, was not a major issue in the 1984 presidential election and had only begun to be one in the 1988 contest; by 1992, it was challenging the economy as a popular concern and today it dominates all other matters. The reason, I think, is that Americans believe something fundamental has changed in our patterns of crime. They are right. Though we were unhappy about having our property put at risk, we adapted with the aid of locks, alarms, and security guards. But we are terrified by the prospect of innocent people being gunned down at random, without warning and almost without motive, by youngsters who afterward show us the blank, unremorseful faces of seemingly feral, presocial beings.

1. CRIME AND JUSTICE IN AMERICA

CRIMINOLOGY has learned a great deal about who these people are. In studies both here and abroad it has been established that about 6 percent of the boys of a given age will commit half or more of all the serious crime produced by all boys of that age. Allowing for measurement errors, it is remarkable how consistent this formula is—6 percent causes 50 percent. It is roughly true in places as different as Philadelphia, London, Copenhagen, and Orange County, California.

We also have learned a lot about the characteristics of the 6 percent. They tend to have criminal parents, to live in cold or discordant families (or pseudo-families), to have a low verbal-intelligence quotient and to do poorly in school, to be emotionally cold and temperamentally impulsive, to abuse alcohol and drugs at the earliest opportunity, and to reside in poor, disorderly communities. They begin their misconduct at an early age, often by the time they are in the third grade.

These characteristics tend to be found not only among the criminals who get caught (and who might, owing to bad luck, be an unrepresentative sample of all high-rate offenders), but among those who do not get caught but reveal their behavior on questionnaires. And the same traits can be identified in advance among groups of randomly selected youngsters, long before they commit any serious crimes—not with enough precision to predict which individuals will commit crimes, but with enough accuracy to be a fair depiction of the group as a whole.[2]

Here a puzzle arises: if 6 percent of the males causes so large a fraction of our collective misery, and if young males are less numerous than once was the case, why are crime rates high and rising? The answer, I conjecture, is that the traits of the 6 percent put them at high risk for whatever criminogenic forces operate in society. As the costs of crime decline or the benefits increase; as drugs and guns become more available; as the glorification of violence becomes more commonplace; as families and neighborhoods lose some of their restraining power—as all these things happen, almost all of us will change our ways to some degree. For the most law-abiding among us, the change will be quite modest: a few more tools stolen from our employer, a few more traffic lights run when no police officer is watching, a few more experiments with fashionable drugs, and a few more business deals on which we cheat. But for the least law-abiding among us, the change will be dramatic: they will get drunk daily instead of just on Saturday night, try PCP or crack instead of marijuana, join gangs instead of marauding in pairs, and buy automatic weapons instead of making zip guns.

A metaphor: when children play the schoolyard game of crack-the-whip, the child at the head of the line scarcely moves but the child at the far end, racing to keep his footing, often stumbles and falls, hurled to the ground by the cumulative force of many smaller movements back along the line. When a changing culture escalates criminality, the at-risk boys are at the end of the line, and the conditions of American urban life—guns, drugs, automobiles, disorganized neighborhoods—make the line very long and the ground underfoot rough and treacherous.

MUCH is said these days about preventing or deterring crime, but it is important to understand exactly what we are up against when we try. Prevention, if it can be made to work at all, must start very early in life, perhaps as early as the first two or three years, and given the odds it faces—childhood impulsivity, low verbal facility, incompetent parenting, disorderly neighborhoods—it must also be massive in scope. Deterrence, if it can be made to work better (for surely it already works to some degree), must be applied close to the moment of the wrongful act or else the present-orientedness of the youthful would-be offender will discount the threat so much that the promise of even a small gain will outweigh its large but deferred costs.

In this country, however, and in most Western nations, we have profound misgivings about doing anything that would give prevention or deterrence a chance to make a large difference. The family is sacrosanct; the family-preservation movement is strong; the state is a clumsy alternative. "Crime-prevention" programs, therefore, usually take the form of creating summer jobs for adolescents, worrying about the unemployment rate, or (as in the proposed 1994 crime bill) funding midnight basketball leagues. There may be something to be said for all these efforts, but crime prevention is not one of them. The typical high-rate offender is well launched on his career before he becomes a teenager or has ever encountered the labor market; he may like basketball, but who pays for the lights and the ball is a matter of supreme indifference to him.

Prompt deterrence has much to recommend it: the folk wisdom that swift and certain punishment is more effective than severe penalties is almost surely correct. But the greater the swiftness and certainty, the less attention paid to the procedural safeguards essential to establishing guilt. As a result, despite their good instincts for the right answers, most Americans, frustrated by the restraints (many wise, some foolish) on swiftness and certainty, vote for proposals to increase severity: if the penalty is 10 years, let us make it 20 or 30; if the penalty is life imprisonment, let us make it death; if the penalty is jail, let us make it caning.

---

[2] Female high-rate offenders are *much* less common than male ones. But to the extent they exist, they display most of these traits.

3. What to Do about Crime

Yet the more draconian the sentence, the less (on the average) the chance of its being imposed; plea bargains see to that. And the most draconian sentences will, of necessity, tend to fall on adult offenders nearing the end of their criminal careers and not on the young ones who are in their criminally most productive years. (The peak ages of criminality are between sixteen and eighteen; the average age of prison inmates is ten years older.) I say "of necessity" because almost every judge will give first-, second-, or even third-time offenders a break, reserving the heaviest sentences for those men who have finally exhausted judicial patience or optimism.

Laws that say "three strikes and you're out" are an effort to change this, but they suffer from an inherent contradiction. If they are carefully drawn so as to target only the most serious offenders, they will probably have a minimal impact on the crime rate; but if they are broadly drawn so as to make a big impact on the crime rate, they will catch many petty repeat offenders who few of us think really deserve life imprisonment.

Prevention and deterrence, albeit hard to augment, at least are plausible strategies. Not so with many of the other favorite nostrums, like reducing the amount of violence on television. Televised violence may have some impact on criminality, but I know of few scholars who think the effect is very large. And to achieve even a small difference we might have to turn the clock back to the kind of programming we had around 1945, because the few studies that correlate programming with the rise in violent crime find the biggest changes occurred between that year and 1974. Another favorite, boot camp, makes good copy, but so far no one has shown that it reduces the rate at which the former inmates commit crimes.

Then, of course, there is gun control. Guns are almost certainly contributors to the lethality of American violence, but there is no politically or legally feasible way to reduce the stock of guns now in private possession to the point where their availability to criminals would be much affected. And even if there were, law-abiding people would lose a means of protecting themselves long before criminals lost a means of attacking them.

As for rehabilitating juvenile offenders, it has some merit, but there are rather few success stories. Individually, the best (and best-evaluated) programs have minimal, if any, effects; collectively, the best estimate of the crime-reduction value of these programs is quite modest, something on the order of 5 or 10 percent.[3]

W<small>HAT</small>, then, is to be done? Let us begin with policing, since law-enforcement officers are that part of the criminal-justice system which is closest to the situations where criminal activity is likely to occur.

It is now widely accepted that, however important it is for officers to drive around waiting for 911 calls summoning their help, doing that is not enough. As a supplement to such a reactive strategy—comprised of random preventive patrol and the investigation of crimes that have already occurred—many leaders and students of law enforcement now urge the police to be "proactive": to identify, with the aid of citizen groups, problems that can be solved so as to prevent criminality, and not only to respond to it. This is often called community-based policing; it seems to entail something more than feel-good meetings with honest citizens, but something less than allowing neighborhoods to assume control of the police function.

The new strategy might better be called problem-oriented policing. It requires the police to engage in *directed*, not random, patrol. The goal of that direction should be to reduce, in a manner consistent with fundamental liberties, the opportunity for high-risk persons to do those things that increase the likelihood of their victimizing others.

For example, the police might stop and pat down persons whom they reasonably suspect may be carrying illegal guns.[4] The Supreme Court has upheld such frisks when an officer observes "unusual conduct" leading him to conclude that "criminal activity may be afoot" on the part of a person who may be "armed and dangerous." This is all rather vague, but it can be clarified in two ways.

First, statutes can be enacted that make certain persons, on the basis of their past conduct and present legal status, subject to pat-downs for weapons. The statutes can, as is now the case in several states, make all probationers and parolees subject to nonconsensual searches for weapons as a condition of their remaining on probation or parole. Since three-fourths of all convicted offenders (and a large fraction of all felons) are in the community rather than in prison, there are on any given day over three million criminals on the streets under correctional supervision. Many are likely to become recidivists. Keeping them from carrying weapons will materially reduce the chances that they will rob or kill. The courts might also declare certain dangerous street gangs to be continuing criminal enterprises, membership in which constitutes grounds for police frisks.

---

[3] Many individual programs involve so few subjects that a good evaluation will reveal no positive effect even if one occurs. By a technique called meta-analysis, scores of individual studies can be pooled into one mega-evaluation; because there are now hundreds or thousands of subjects, even small gains can be identified. The best of these meta-analyses, such as the one by Mark Lipsey, suggest modest positive effects.

[4] I made a fuller argument along these lines in "Just Take Away Their Guns," in the *New York Times Magazine*, March 20, 1994.

1. CRIME AND JUSTICE IN AMERICA

Second, since I first proposed such a strategy, I have learned that there are efforts under way in public and private research laboratories to develop technologies that will permit the police to detect from a distance persons who are carrying concealed weapons on the streets. Should these efforts bear fruit, they will provide the police with the grounds for stopping, questioning, and patting down even persons not on probation or parole or obviously in gangs.

Whether or not the technology works, the police can also offer immediate cash rewards to people who provide information about individuals illegally carrying weapons. Spending $100 on each good tip will have a bigger impact on dangerous gun use than will the same amount spent on another popular nostrum—buying back guns from law-abiding people.[5]

Getting illegal firearms off the streets will require that the police be motivated to do all of these things. But if the legal, technological, and motivational issues can be resolved, our streets can be made safer even without sending many more people to prison.

THE same directed-patrol strategy might help keep known offenders drug-free. Most persons jailed in big cities are found to have been using illegal drugs within the day or two preceding their arrest. When convicted, some are given probation on condition that they enter drug-treatment programs; others are sent to prisons where (if they are lucky) drug-treatment programs operate. But in many cities the enforcement of such probation conditions is casual or nonexistent; in many states, parolees are released back into drug-infested communities with little effort to ensure that they participate in whatever treatment programs are to be found there.

Almost everyone agrees that more treatment programs should exist. But what many advocates overlook is that the key to success is steadfast participation and many, probably most, offenders have no incentive to be steadfast. To cope with this, patrol officers could enforce random drug tests on probationers and parolees on their beats; failing to take a test when ordered, or failing the test when taken, should be grounds for immediate revocation of probation or parole, at least for a brief period of confinement.

The goal of this tactic is not simply to keep offenders drug-free (and thereby lessen their incentive to steal the money needed to buy drugs and reduce their likelihood of committing crimes because they are on a drug high); it is also to diminish the demand for drugs generally and thus the size of the drug market.

Lest the reader embrace this idea too quickly, let me add that as yet we have no good reason to think that it will reduce the crime rate by very much. Something akin to this strategy, albeit one using probation instead of police officers, has been tried under the name of "intensive-supervision programs" (ISP), involving a panoply of drug tests, house arrests, frequent surveillance, and careful records. By means of a set of randomized experiments carried out in fourteen cities, Joan Petersilia and Susan Turner, both then at RAND, compared the rearrest rates of offenders assigned to ISP with those of offenders in ordinary probation. There was no difference.

Still, this study does not settle the matter. For one thing, since the ISP participants were under much closer surveillance than the regular probationers, the former were bound to be caught breaking the law more frequently than the latter. It is thus possible that a higher fraction of the crimes committed by the ISP than of the control group were detected and resulted in a return to prison, which would mean, if true, a net gain in public safety. For another thing, "intensive" supervision was in many cases not all that intensive—in five cities, contacts with the probationers only took place about once a week, and for all cities drug tests occurred, on average, about once a month. Finally, there is some indication that participation in treatment programs was associated with lower recidivism rates.

Both anti-gun and anti-drug police patrols will, if performed systematically, require big changes in police and court procedures and a significant increase in the resources devoted to both, at least in the short run. (ISP is not cheap, and it will become even more expensive if it is done in a truly intensive fashion.) Most officers have at present no incentive to search for guns or enforce drug tests; many jurisdictions, owing to crowded dockets or overcrowded jails, are lax about enforcing the conditions of probation or parole. The result is that the one group of high-risk people over which society already has the legal right to exercise substantial control is often out of control, "supervised," if at all, by means of brief monthly interviews with overworked probation or parole officers.

Another promising tactic is to enforce truancy and curfew laws. This arises from the fact that much crime is opportunistic: idle boys, usually in small groups, sometimes find irresistible the opportunity to steal or the challenge to fight. Deterring present-oriented youngsters who want to appear fearless in the eyes of their comrades while indulging their thrill-seeking natures is a tall order. While it is possible to deter the crimes they commit by a credible threat of prompt sanctions, it is easier to reduce the chances for risky group idleness in the first place.

---

[5] In Charleston, South Carolina, the police pay a reward to anyone identifying a student carrying a weapon to school or to some school event. Because many boys carry guns to school in order to display or brag about them, the motive to carry disappears once any display alerts a potential informer.

3. What to Do about Crime

In Charleston, South Carolina, for example, Chief Reuben Greenberg instructed his officers to return all school-age children to the schools from which they were truant and to return all youngsters violating an evening-curfew agreement to their parents. As a result, groups of school-age children were no longer to be found hanging out in the shopping malls or wandering the streets late at night.

There has been no careful evaluation of these efforts in Charleston (or, so far as I am aware, in any other big city), but the rough figures are impressive—the Charleston crime rate in 1991 was about 25 percent lower than the rate in South Carolina's other principal cities and, for most offenses (including burglaries and larcenies), lower than what that city reported twenty years earlier.

All these tactics have in common putting the police, as the criminologist Lawrence Sherman of the University of Maryland phrases it, where the "hot spots" are. Most people need no police attention except for a response to their calls for help. A small fraction of people (and places) need constant attention. Thus, in Minneapolis, *all* of the robberies during one year occurred at just 2 percent of the city's addresses. To capitalize on this fact, the Minneapolis police began devoting extra patrol attention, in brief but frequent bursts of activity, to those locations known to be trouble spots. Robbery rates evidently fell by as much as 20 percent and public disturbances by even more.

Some of the worst hot spots are outdoor drug markets. Because of either limited resources, a fear of potential corruption, or a desire to catch only the drug kingpins, the police in some cities (including, from time to time, New York) neglect street-corner dealing. By doing so, they get the worst of all worlds.

The public, seeing the police ignore drug dealing that is in plain view, assumes that they are corrupt whether or not they are. The drug kingpins, who are hard to catch and are easily replaced by rival smugglers, find that their essential retail distribution system remains intact. Casual or first-time drug users, who might not use at all if access to supplies were difficult, find access to be effortless and so increase their consumption. People who might remain in treatment programs if drugs were hard to get drop out upon learning that they are easy to get. Interdicting without merely displacing drug markets is difficult but not impossible, though it requires motivation which some departments lack and resources which many do not have.

The sheer number of police on the streets of a city probably has only a weak, if any, relationship with the crime rate; what the police do is more important than how many there are, at least above some minimum level. Nevertheless, patrols directed at hot spots, loitering truants, late-night wanderers, probationers, parolees, and possible gun carriers, all in addition to routine investigative activities, will require more officers in many cities. Between 1977 and 1987, the number of police officers declined in a third of the 50 largest cities and fell relative to population in many more. Just how far behind police resources have lagged can be gauged from this fact: in 1950 there was one violent crime reported for every police officer; in 1980 there were three violent crimes reported for every officer.

I HAVE said little so far about penal policy, in part because I wish to focus attention on those things that are likely to have the largest and most immediate impact on the quality of urban life. But given the vast gulf between what the public believes and what many experts argue should be our penal policy, a few comments are essential.

The public wants more people sent away for longer sentences; many (probably most) criminologists think we use prison too much and at too great a cost and that this excessive use has had little beneficial effect on the crime rate. My views are much closer to those of the public, though I think the average person exaggerates the faults of the present system and the gains of some alternative (such as "three strikes and you're out").

The expert view, as it is expressed in countless op-ed essays, often goes like this: "We have been arresting more and more people and giving them longer and longer sentences, producing no decrease in crime but huge increases in prison populations. As a result, we have become the most punitive nation on earth."

Scarcely a phrase in those sentences is accurate. The probability of being arrested for a given crime is lower today than it was in 1974. The amount of time served in state prison has been declining more or less steadily since the 1940's. Taking all crimes together, time served fell from 25 months in 1945 to 13 months in 1984. Only for rape are prisoners serving as much time today as they did in the 40's.

The net effect of lower arrest rates and shorter effective sentences is that the cost to the adult perpetrator of the average burglary fell from 50 days in 1960 to 15 days in 1980. That is to say, the chances of being caught and convicted, multiplied by the median time served if imprisoned, was in 1980 less than a third of what it had been in 1960.[6]

---

[6] I take these cost calculations from Mark Kleiman, *et al.*, "Imprisonment-to-Offense Ratios," Working Paper 89-06-02 of the Program in Criminal Justice Policy and Management at the Kennedy School of Government, Harvard University (August 5, 1988).

1. CRIME AND JUSTICE IN AMERICA

Beginning around 1980, the costs of crime to the criminal began to inch up again—the result, chiefly, of an increase in the proportion of convicted persons who were given prison terms. By 1986, the "price" of a given burglary had risen to 21 days. Also beginning around 1980, as I noted at the outset, the crime rate began to decline.

It would be foolhardy to explain this drop in crime by the rise in imprisonment rates; many other factors, such as the aging of the population and the self-protective measures of potential victims, were also at work. Only a controlled experiment (for example, randomly allocating prison terms for a given crime among the states) could hope to untangle the causal patterns, and happily the Constitution makes such experiments unlikely.

Yet it is worth noting that nations with different penal policies have experienced different crime rates. According to David Farrington of Cambridge University, property-crime rates rose in England and Sweden at a time when both the imprisonment rate and time served fell substantially, while property-crime rates declined in the United States at a time when the imprisonment rate (but not time served) was increasing.

Though one cannot measure the effect of prison on crime with any accuracy, it certainly has some effects. By 1986, there were 55,000 more robbers in prison than there had been in 1974. Assume that each imprisoned robber would commit five such offenses per year if free on the street. This means that in 1986 there were 275,000 fewer robberies in America than there would have been had these 55,000 men been left on the street.

Nor, finally, does America use prison to a degree that vastly exceeds what is found in any other civilized nation. Compare the chance of going to prison in England and the United States if one is convicted of a given crime. According to Farrington, your chances were higher in England if you were found guilty of a rape, higher in America if you were convicted of an assault or a burglary, and about the same if you were convicted of a homicide or a robbery. Once in prison, you would serve a longer time in this country than in England for almost all offenses save murder.

James Lynch of American University has reached similar conclusions from his comparative study of criminal-justice policies. His data show that the chances of going to prison and the time served for homicide and robbery are roughly the same in the United States, Canada, and England.

OF LATE, drugs have changed American penal practice. In 1982, only about 8 percent of state-prison inmates were serving time on drug convictions. In 1987, that started to increase sharply; by 1994, over 60 percent of all federal and about 25 percent of all state prisoners were there on drug charges. In some states, such as New York, the percentage was even higher.

This change can be attributed largely to the advent of crack cocaine. Whereas snorted cocaine powder was expensive, crack was cheap; whereas the former was distributed through networks catering to elite tastes, the latter was mass-marketed on street corners. People were rightly fearful of what crack was doing to their children and demanded action; as a result, crack dealers started going to prison in record numbers.

Unfortunately, these penalties do not have the same incapacitative effect as sentences for robbery. A robber taken off the street is not replaced by a new robber who has suddenly found a market niche, but a drug dealer sent away is replaced by a new one because an opportunity has opened up.

We are left, then, with the problem of reducing the demand for drugs, and that in turn requires either prevention programs on a scale heretofore unimagined or treatment programs with a level of effectiveness heretofore unachieved. Any big gains in prevention and treatment will probably have to await further basic research into the biochemistry of addiction and the development of effective and attractive drug antagonists that reduce the appeal of cocaine and similar substances.[7]

In the meantime, it is necessary either to build much more prison space, find some other way of disciplining drug offenders, or both. There is very little to be gained, I think, from shortening the terms of existing non-drug inmates in order to free up more prison space. Except for a few elderly, nonviolent offenders serving very long terms, there are real risks associated with shortening the terms of the typical inmate.

Scholars disagree about the magnitude of those risks, but the best studies, such as the one of Wisconsin inmates done by John DiIulio of Princeton, suggest that the annual costs to society in crime committed by an offender on the street are probably twice the costs of putting him in a cell. That ratio will vary from state to state because states differ in what proportion of convicted persons is imprisoned—some states dip deeper down into the pool of convictees, thereby imprisoning some with minor criminal habits.

But I caution the reader to understand that there are no easy prison solutions to crime, even if we build the additional space. The state-prison population more than doubled between 1980 and 1990, yet the victimization rate for robbery fell by only 23 percent. Even if we assign all of that gain

---

[7] I anticipate that at this point some readers will call for legalizing or decriminalizing drugs as the "solution" to the problem. Before telling me this, I hope they will read what I wrote on that subject in the February 1990 issue of COMMENTARY. I have not changed my mind.

3. What to Do about Crime

to the increased deterrent and incapacitative effect of prison, which is implausible, the improvement is not vast. Of course, it is possible that the victimization rate would have risen, perhaps by a large amount, instead of falling if we had not increased the number of inmates. But we shall never know.

Recall my discussion of the decline in the costs of crime to the criminal, measured by the number of days in prison that result, on average, from the commission of a given crime. That cost is vastly lower today than in the 1950's. But much of the decline (and since 1974, nearly all of it) is the result of a drop in the probability of being arrested for a crime, not in the probability of being imprisoned once arrested.

Anyone who has followed my writings on crime knows that I have defended the use of prison both to deter crime and incapacitate criminals. I continue to defend it. But we must recognize two facts. First, even modest additional reductions in crime, comparable to the ones achieved in the early 1980's, will require vast increases in correctional costs and encounter bitter judicial resistance to mandatory sentencing laws. Second, America's most troubling crime problem—the increasingly violent behavior of disaffected and impulsive youth—may be especially hard to control by means of marginal and delayed increases in the probability of punishment.

Possibly one can make larger gains by turning our attention to the unexplored area of juvenile justice. Juvenile (or family) courts deal with young people just starting their criminal careers and with chronic offenders when they are often at their peak years of offending. We know rather little about how these courts work or with what effect. There are few, if any, careful studies of what happens, a result in part of scholarly neglect and in part of the practice in some states of shrouding juvenile records and proceedings in secrecy. Some studies, such as one by the *Los Angeles Times* of juvenile justice in California, suggest that young people found guilty of a serious crime are given sentences tougher than those meted out to adults.[8] This finding is so counter to popular beliefs and the testimony of many big-city juvenile-court judges that some caution is required in interpreting it.

There are two problems. The first lies in defining the universe of people to whom sanctions are applied. In some states, such as California, it may well be the case that a juvenile *found guilty of a serious offense* is punished with greater rigor than an adult, but many juveniles whose behavior ought to be taken seriously (because they show signs of being part of the 6 percent) are released by the police or probation officers before ever seeing a judge. And in some states, such as New York, juveniles charged with having committed certain crimes, including serious ones like illegally carrying a loaded gun or committing an as-

sault, may not be fingerprinted. Since persons with a prior record are usually given longer sentences than those without one, the failure to fingerprint can mean that the court has no way of knowing whether the John Smith standing before it is the same John Smith who was arrested four times for assault and so ought to be sent away, or a different John Smith whose clean record entitles him to probation.

The second problem arises from the definition of a "severe" penalty. In California, a juvenile found guilty of murder does indeed serve a longer sentence than an adult convicted of the same offense—60 months for the former, 41 months for the latter. Many people will be puzzled by a newspaper account that defines five years in prison for murder as a "severe" sentence, and angered to learn that an adult serves less than four years for such a crime.

The key, unanswered question is whether prompt and more effective early intervention would stop high-rate delinquents from becoming high-rate criminals at a time when their offenses were not yet too serious. Perhaps early and swift, though not necessarily severe, sanctions could deter some budding hoodlums, but we have no evidence of that as yet.

For as long as I can remember, the debate over crime has been between those who wished to rely on the criminal-justice system and those who wished to attack the root causes of crime. I have always been in the former group because what its opponents depicted as "root causes"—unemployment, racism, poor housing, too little schooling, a lack of self-esteem—turned out, on close examination, not to be major causes of crime at all.

Of late, however, there has been a shift in the debate. Increasingly those who want to attack root causes have begun to point to real ones—temperament, early family experiences, and neighborhood effects. The sketch I gave earlier of the typical high-rate young offender suggests that these factors are indeed at the root of crime. The problem now is to decide whether any can be changed by plan and at an acceptable price in money and personal freedom.

If we are to do this, we must confront the fact that the critical years of a child's life are ages one to ten, with perhaps the most important being the earliest years. During those years, some children are put gravely at risk by some combination of heritable traits, prenatal insults (maternal drug and alcohol abuse or poor diet), weak parent-child attachment, poor supervision, and disorderly family environment.

---

[8] "A Nation's Children in Lock-up," *Los Angeles Times*, August 22, 1993.

1. CRIME AND JUSTICE IN AMERICA

If we knew with reasonable confidence which children were most seriously at risk, we might intervene with some precision to supply either medical therapy or parent training or (in extreme cases) to remove the child to a better home. But given our present knowledge, precision is impossible, and so we must proceed carefully, relying, except in the most extreme cases, on persuasion and incentives.

We do, however, know enough about the early causes of conduct disorder and later delinquency to know that the more risk factors exist (such as parental criminality and poor supervision), the greater the peril to the child. It follows that programs aimed at just one or a few factors are not likely to be successful; the children most at risk are those who require the most wide-ranging and fundamental changes in their life circumstances. The goal of these changes is, as Travis Hirschi of the University of Arizona has put it, to teach self-control.

Hirokazu Yoshikawa of New York University has recently summarized what we have learned about programs that attempt to make large and lasting changes in a child's prospects for improved conduct, better school behavior, and lessened delinquency. Four such programs in particular seemed valuable—the Perry Preschool Project in Ypsilanti, Michigan; the Parent-Child Development Center in Houston, Texas; the Family Development Research Project in Syracuse, New York; and the Yale Child Welfare Project in New Haven, Connecticut.

All these programs had certain features in common. They dealt with low-income, often minority, families; they intervened during the first five years of a child's life and continued for between two and five years; they combined parent training with preschool education for the child; and they involved extensive home visits. All were evaluated fairly carefully, with the follow-ups lasting for at least five years, in two cases for at least ten, and in one case for fourteen. The programs produced (depending on the project) less fighting, impulsivity, disobedience, restlessness, cheating, and delinquency. In short, they improved self-control.

They were experimental programs, which means that it is hard to be confident that trying the same thing on a bigger scale in many places will produce the same effects. A large number of well-trained and highly motivated caseworkers dealt with a relatively small number of families, with the workers knowing that their efforts were being evaluated. Moreover, the programs operated in the late 1970's or early 1980's before the advent of crack cocaine or the rise of the more lethal neighborhood gangs. A national program mounted under current conditions might or might not have the same result as the experimental efforts.

Try telling that to lawmakers. What happens when politicians encounter experimental successes is amply revealed by the history of Head Start: they expanded the program quickly without assuring quality, and stripped it down to the part that was the most popular, least expensive, and easiest to run, namely, preschool education. Absent from much of Head Start are the high teacher-to-child case loads, the extensive home visits, and the elaborate parent training—the very things that probably account for much of the success of the four experimental programs.

IN THIS country we tend to separate programs designed to help children from those that benefit their parents. The former are called "child development," the latter "welfare reform." This is a great mistake. Everything we know about long-term welfare recipients indicates that their children are at risk for the very problems that child-helping programs later try to correct.

The evidence from a variety of studies is quite clear: even if we hold income and ethnicity constant, children (and especially boys) raised by a single mother are more likely than those raised by two parents to have difficulty in school, get in trouble with the law, and experience emotional and physical problems.[9] Producing illegitimate children is not an "alternative life-style" or simply an imprudent action; it is a curse. Making mothers work will not end the curse; under current proposals, it will not even save money.

The absurdity of divorcing the welfare problem from the child-development problem becomes evident as soon as we think seriously about what we want to achieve. Smaller welfare expenditures? Well, yes, but not if it hurts children. More young mothers working? Probably not; young mothers ought to raise their young children, and work interferes with that unless *two* parents can solve some difficult and expensive problems.

What we really want is *fewer illegitimate children*, because such children, by being born out of wedlock are, except in unusual cases, being given early admission to the underclass. And failing that, we want the children born to single (and typically young and poor) mothers to have a chance at a decent life.

Letting teenage girls set up their own households at public expense neither discourages illegitimacy nor serves the child's best interests. If they do set up their own homes, then to reach those with the fewest parenting skills and the most difficult children will require the kind of expensive and intensive home visits and family-support programs characteristic of the four successful experiments mentioned earlier.

---

[9] I summarize this evidence in "The Family-Values Debate," COMMENTARY, April 1993.

One alternative is to tell a girl who applies for welfare that she can only receive it on condition that she live either in the home of *two* competent parents (her own if she comes from an intact family) or in a group home where competent supervision and parent training will be provided by adults unrelated to her. Such homes would be privately managed but publicly funded by pooling welfare checks, food stamps, and housing allowances.

A model for such a group home (albeit one run without public funds) is the St. Martin de Porres House of Hope on the south side of Chicago, founded by two nuns for homeless young women, especially those with drug-abuse problems. The goals of the home are clear: accept personal responsibility for your lives and learn to care for your children. And these goals, in turn, require the girls to follow rules, stay in school, obey a curfew, and avoid alcohol and drugs. Those are the rules that ought to govern a group home for young welfare mothers.

Group homes funded by pooled welfare benefits would make the task of parent training much easier and provide the kind of structured, consistent, and nurturant environment that children need. A few cases might be too difficult for these homes, and for such children, boarding schools—once common in American cities for disadvantaged children, but now almost extinct—might be revived.

Group homes also make it easier to supply quality medical care to young mothers and their children. Such care has taken on added importance in recent years with discovery of the lasting damage that can be done to a child's prospects from being born prematurely and with a very low birth weight, having a mother who has abused drugs or alcohol, or being exposed to certain dangerous metals. Lead poisoning is now widely acknowledged to be a source of cognitive and behavioral impairment; of late, elevated levels of manganese have been linked to high levels of violence.[10] These are all treatable conditions; in the case of a manganese imbalance, easily treatable.

My FOCUS on changing behavior will annoy some readers. For them the problem is poverty and the worst feature of single-parent families is that they are inordinately poor. Even to refer to a behavioral or cultural problem is to "stigmatize" people.

Indeed it is. Wrong behavior—neglectful, immature, or incompetent parenting; the production of out-of-wedlock babies—*ought* to be stigmatized. There are many poor men of all races who do not abandon the women they have impregnated, and many poor women of all races who avoid drugs and do a good job of raising their children. If we fail to stigmatize those who give way to temptation, we withdraw the rewards from those who resist them. This becomes all the

more important when entire communities, and not just isolated households, are dominated by a culture of fatherless boys preying on innocent persons and exploiting immature girls.

We need not merely stigmatize, however. We can try harder to move children out of those communities, either by drawing them into safe group homes or facilitating (through rent supplements and housing vouchers) the relocation of them and their parents to neighborhoods with intact social structures and an ethos of family values.

Much of our uniquely American crime problem (as opposed to the worldwide problem of general thievery) arises, not from the failings of individuals but from the concentration in disorderly neighborhoods of people at risk of failing. That concentration is partly the result of prosperity and freedom (functioning families long ago seized the opportunity to move out to the periphery), partly the result of racism (it is harder for some groups to move than for others), and partly the result of politics (elected officials do not wish to see settled constituencies broken up).

I SERIOUSLY doubt that this country has the will to address either of its two crime problems, save by acts of individual self-protection. We could in theory make justice swifter and more certain, but we will not accept the restrictions on liberty and the weakening of procedural safeguards that this would entail. We could vastly improve the way in which our streets are policed, but some of us will not pay for it and the rest of us will not tolerate it. We could alter the way in which at-risk children experience the first few years of life, but the opponents of this—welfare-rights activists, family preservationists, budget cutters, and assorted ideologues—are numerous and the bureaucratic problems enormous.

Unable or unwilling to do such things, we take refuge in substitutes: we debate the death penalty, we wring our hands over television, we lobby to keep prisons from being built in our neighborhoods, and we fall briefly in love with trendy nostrums that seem to cost little and promise much.

Much of our ambivalence is on display in the 1994 federal crime bill. To satisfy the tough-minded, the list of federal offenses for which the death penalty can be imposed has been greatly enlarged, but there is little reason to think that executions, as they work in this country (which is to say, after much delay and only on a few offenders), have any effect on the crime rate and no reason to think that executing more federal prisoners (who account, at best, for a tiny fraction of all homicides) will reduce the murder rate. To

---

[10] It is not clear why manganese has this effect, but we know that it diminishes the availability of a precursor of serotonin, a neurotransmitter, and low levels of serotonin are now strongly linked to violent and impulsive behavior.

1. CRIME AND JUSTICE IN AMERICA

satisfy the tender-minded, several billion dollars are earmarked for prevention programs, but there is as yet very little hard evidence that any of these will actually prevent crime.

In adding more police officers, the bill may make some difference—but only if the additional personnel are imaginatively deployed. And Washington will pay only part of the cost initially and none of it after six years, which means that any city getting new officers will either have to raise its own taxes to keep them on the force or accept the political heat that will arise from turning down "free" cops. Many states also desperately need additional prison space; the federal funds allocated by the bill for their construction will be welcomed, provided that states are willing to meet the conditions set for access to such funds.

Meanwhile, just beyond the horizon, there lurks a cloud that the winds will soon bring over us. The population will start getting younger again. By the end of this decade there will be a million more people between the ages of fourteen and seventeen than there are now. Half of this extra million will be male. Six percent of them will become high-rate, repeat offenders—30,000 more muggers, killers, and thieves than we have now.

Get ready.

The FBI is tracking other big crime organizations besides Cosa Nostra

WHO IS THE MOB TODAY?

PETER MAAS

THE FACE OF organized crime is changing in America. For 65 years, Cosa Nostra, the American version of Italy's Mafia, had held undisputed sway over criminal enterprises across the U.S. While Cosa Nostra ("Our Thing") remains a dangerous force to be reckoned with, it no longer enjoys the unique dominance it once had. Just as Cosa Nostra asserted its supremacy over Jewish and Irish crime groups in the late 1920s and early '30s, today potent new criminal elements settling here—principally Russian and Chinese—loom ominously on the law-enforcement horizon.

> **Potent new criminal elements, mostly mobsters from Russia and China, loom ominously on the law-enforcement horizon.**

In recognition of this threat, the FBI has formed special Russian and Chinese organized-crime squads similar to the ones it has successfully employed in recent years against Cosa Nostra. The Russians and Chinese have yet to achieve full flower in the underworld, and FBI director Louis J. Freeh means to nip them in the bud.

For decades under the late J. Edgar Hoover, the FBI's official position was that the existence of Cosa Nostra was

Reuters/Corbis-Bettmann

The Present Hundreds from across the U.S. witness the 1994 gangland-style funeral of Benny Ong, head of the most powerful *tong* in New York's Chinatown.

a myth. "We cannot allow the same kinds of mistakes to be made today," Freeh told Congress. "The failure of American law enforcement, including the FBI . . . permitted the development of a powerful, well-entrenched organized crime syndicate [that required] 35 years of concerted law-enforcement effort and the expenditure of incredible resources to address."

The downward turning point for Cosa Nostra began in the 1960s with the dramatic revelations of Joseph Valachi, a "soldier" in the secret brotherhood, who first described its oath of fealty—complete with the drawing of blood and burning the image of a saint—and how it was structured in paramilitary fashion into 25 crime "families" throughout the U.S. It came full cycle with the defection of the highest-ranking Cosa Nostra member ever to testify: Salvatore (Sammy the Bull) Gravano, the No. 2 man in the Gambino crime family. His 1992 testimony put the family boss, John Gotti—known as "The Teflon Don" because of

1. CRIME AND JUSTICE IN AMERICA

his ability to avoid prison—behind bars for the rest of his life.

As a result—according to James Moody, a deputy assistant director who formerly was chief of the FBI's organized-crime section—the Gambino family, at the time the most powerful in the nation, has been reduced from 35 active "crews," or family units, to 10.

Of the remaining four families in the greater New York area, only the Genovese family has escaped relatively unscathed. Its reputed boss, Vincent (The Chin) Gigante, has thus far evaded prosecution on the grounds that he is mentally unfit to stand trial. He is often seen padding around the streets of Greenwich Village in a bathrobe and pajamas, muttering incoherently to himself. Federal authorities, convinced it's all a hoax, will attempt to try him again this year on multiple charges, including conspiracy to murder. "We've just got to get the courts to realize that he's crazy all right—like a fox," Moody told me.

Moody ticked off the current status of Cosa Nostra families elsewhere, beset by broad-based federal statutes—both criminal and civil—under the innovative Racketeer Influenced and Corrupt Organizations (RICO) Act that followed the Valachi revelations in 1963. "In the Boston region now, all we have active is one crew in Rhode Island," said Moody. In Philadelphia: "Almost everybody is in jail." In Cleveland: "Technically, there is no real family." In Detroit: "The family's still there, but I think good things may occur in the future."

In Milwaukee, St. Louis and Kansas City, he went on, the local families "have almost ceased to exist." In Chicago— once a Cosa Nostra crown jewel, with such famous past bosses as Al Capone and Sam Giancana—a new FBI approach of targeting one family crew at a time has proved effective. In Los Angeles and San Francisco, what's left of the families is small potatoes. In "open" Las Vegas, where all the families can operate, the casino business has gotten too big even for Cosa Nostra, although it still hovers on the fringe of things. In Buffalo, however, the family remains "pretty strong," especially with its alleged stranglehold over a local construction union.

While Cosa Nostra families generally are hanging on the ropes, the idea is to keep hammering them. Otherwise, "they'll come back fast," Moody noted. "Until we get to the point where a young man decides he doesn't want to be a member because it'll put him in jail for the rest of his life, we haven't won yet."

Still, the situation is well enough in hand to enable an undermanned FBI to divert agents from its Cosa Nostra squad and others from counterintelli-gence squads—now that the Cold War is over—to meet a new domestic menace: Russian organized crime.

Its rise has been startlingly swift. The initial influx of Russians—about 300,000—occurred in the late 1970s and early 1980s, when immigration barriers were temporarily lifted to allow persecuted Jews to leave the Soviet Union. A large number of these immigrants, however, turned out not to be Jewish at all and included "second-echelon" criminal elements. They settled primarily in the Brighton Beach section of Brooklyn, which quickly was dubbed "Little Odessa." As with past ethnic waves of new arrivals, these hoodlums began by victimizing their own people. And at first, according to Moody, the FBI considered it a local police problem.

But that would not long be the case. In 1989, the number of visitors' visas to the U.S. from Russia was 3000. By 1994, just two years after the collapse of the Communist regime, 129,500 such visas had been issued in Moscow, St. Petersburg and Kiev alone. Now came a flood of high-ranking, hardened, organized criminals—"the first team," as Moody put it.

After the Cold War, a flood of high-ranking criminals came here from Russia—"very tough, very smart, very educated, very violent."

Moody got an inkling of what lay ahead when he attended a 1991 international crime conference. Its host was the Russian Ministry of Internal Affairs (MVD), which was trying to cope with a sudden onslaught of savage gang warfare in Moscow (one of the bitter fruits of democracy) that made the bloodletting of Chicago in the 1920s look like play school. "You don't understand what these people are like," Moody recalled being told. "They're very tough, very smart, very educated and very violent. They attack police officers. They don't care."

And soon the U.S. was awash with Russian-instigated gangland murders, complex tax and health-care fraud schemes, vicious extortions, money laundering, major drug trafficking and huge auto-theft rings with the cars being shipped back for sale in Russia (Jeep Cherokees are especially favored).

The FBI's Russian squad in New York, led by the supervisory agent Ray Kerr, was formed in May 1994. Due to the cooperation between the FBI and the MVD, Kerr's squad got an immediate break—the kind that FBI Director Freeh was hoping for. The MVD warned the FBI that a man named Vyacheslav Ivankov, whom they believed to be a Russian version of a Cosa Nostra "godfather," had left Moscow for America, where he was to manage and control Russian gangland activities in the U.S. He was placed under immediate surveillance. Along with his residence in Brighton Beach, he took another one in Denver and was spotted meeting Russian organized-crime figures not only there but also in Miami, Los Angeles, Boston, suburban New Jersey and Toronto.

Then, the Justice Department says, Ivankov made a mistake while masterminding an extortion plot against two Russian emigrés who owned a Wall Street investment advisory firm. Ivankov allegedly demanded separate payments of $5 million and $3.5 million, accompanied by threats of mayhem. Last April 26—presumably, the government says, to get the message across—the father of one of the extortion targets was beaten to death in a Moscow train station.

Russian organized crime counts on fear to keep its victims silent, but the two targets had gone to the FBI. A tap was put on Ivankov's phone, and he was overheard discussing the plot, FBI officials say. In June he was awakened and arrested at the apartment of a girlfriend. At a press conference, the head of the FBI's New York office, Jim Kallstrom, dryly observed: "He muttered something to the agents in Russian. It didn't sound too nice." Then, after being fingerprinted and photographed, the handcuffed Ivankov spat and kicked at reporters and photographers.

As Ray Kerr pointed out, however, "We aren't there yet with the Russians the way we are with Cosa Nostra. We have to learn more about how they are structured, who answers to whom, how many different groups there are here. That's what we're looking at right now."

Then there are the Chinese mobsters. The Chinese population is exploding in the U.S., and with it comes China's own brand of organized crime. It arrives in three layers: First are the Hong Kong-based *triads*, secret criminal societies that predate even the Sicilian Mafia. Second are the Chinese-American *tongs*, ostensibly business and fraternal associations in America's various Chinatowns, which have been known to ape

4. Who Is the Mob Today?

the criminal enterprises of the *triads*. Third are the violent Chinese street gangs—with names like Ghost Shadows and White Tigers—which, the FBI believes, both the *triads* and *tongs* use to enforce their rackets.

At the moment, the main trade of the *triads* in the U.S. is the importation of China White, the purest form of heroin yet developed, which has become the fastest-growing drug of choice throughout much of the country. The *triads* and *tongs* also organize the smuggling of tens of thousands of illegal Chinese immigrants into the U.S., who then receive slave wages in garment sweatshops, restaurants and brothels until they pay off fees ranging from $30,000 to $50,000.

In New York, for instance, three *tong* chieftains were accused by the Justice Department of carving up Chinatown into designated zones, using street gangs to oversee gambling, extortion and murder operations. They demand as much as $100,000 to open a restaurant and $20,000 a week to let gambling dens function. To make matters worse, two Chinese-American police detectives in New York pleaded guilty to feeding Chinese gangsters advance information about raids on gambling and prostitution houses.

A bright spot in the fight against organized crime is San Francisco. Long sensitive to Chinese crime, the FBI has two Chinese-American agents who gained Chinatown's confidence and quickly thwarted a Hong Kong *triad*'s incursion into the Bay Area. According to Tom Fuentes, head of the FBI's organized-crime unit in San Francisco, a major investigation also is under way involving shipments of goods hijacked in Russia and sold legitimately in the U.S., the laundered cash then returned to Russia's gangland coffers.

Meanwhile, the Colombian cocaine cartels present a special problem. Unlike the Russians and Chinese, the drug overlords have no intention of settling here, preferring to remain in their native havens, where they reap many millions from the manufacture and delivery of their deadly product. Under intense U.S. pressure, the Colombian government recently arrested six cartel kingpins. Whether this was only window dressing remains to be seen.

The bottom line is that organized crime still represents an enormous peril to the well-being of this nation. The only difference is that today it has become multicultural.

And the expense of fighting it is significant. But, as Louis Freeh said, "Let us learn from the past and pay the price now, before it becomes too costly later on."

Disintegration of the Family

VIOLENT

"... The popular assumption that there is an association between race and crime is false. Illegitimacy, not race, is the key factor. It is the absence of marriage and the failure to maintain intact families that explain the incidence of crime among whites as well as blacks."

Patrick F. Fagan

SOCIAL SCIENTISTS, criminologists, and many other observers at long last are coming to recognize the connection between the breakdown of families and various social problems that have plagued American society. In the debate over welfare reform, for instance, it now is a widely accepted premise that children born into single-parent families are much more likely than those in intact families to fall into poverty and welfare dependency.

While the link between the family and chronic welfare dependency is understood much better these days, there is another link—between the family and crime—that deserves more attention. Entire communities, particularly in urban areas, are being torn apart by crime. We desperately need to uncover the real root cause of criminal behavior and learn how criminals are formed in order to be able to fight this situation.

There is a wealth of evidence in the professional literature of criminology and sociology to suggest that the breakdown of family is the real root cause of crime in the U.S. Yet, the orthodox thinking in official Washington assumes that it is caused by material conditions, such as poor employment opportunities and a shortage of adequately funded state and Federal social programs.

The Violent Crime Control and Law Enforcement Act of 1994, supported by the Clinton Administration, perfectly embodies Washington's view of crime. It provides for

Mr. Fagan is William H.G. Fitzgerald Fellow for Family and Cultural Studies, Heritage Foundation, Washington, D.C. This article is based on a Hillsdale (Mich.) College Center for Constructive Alternatives seminar on "Crime in America: Fighting Back with Moral and Market Virtues."

5. Disintegration of the Family Is the Real Root Cause of CRIME

billions of dollars in new spending, adding 15 social programs on top of a welfare system that has cost taxpayers five trillion dollars since the War on Poverty was declared in 1965. There is no reason to suppose that increased spending and new programs will have any significant positive impact. Since 1965, welfare spending has grown 800% in real terms, while the number of major felonies per capita today is roughly three times the rate prior to 1960. As Sen. Phil Gramm (R.-Tex.) rightly observes, "If social spending stopped crime, America would be the safest country in the world."

Still, Federal bureaucrats and lawmakers persist in arguing that poverty is the primary cause of crime. In its simplest form, this contention is absurd; if it were true, there would have been more crime in the past, when more people were poorer. Moreover, in less-developed nations, the crime rates would be higher than in the U.S. History defies the assumption that deteriorating economic circumstances breed crime and improving conditions reduce it. America's crime rate actually rose during the long period of economic growth in the early 20th century. As the Great Depression set in and incomes dropped, the crime rate also fell. It went up again between 1965 and 1974, when incomes rose. Most recently, during the recession of 1982, there was a slight dip in crime, not an increase.

Washington also believes that race is the second most important cause of crime. The large disparity in crime rates between whites and blacks often is cited as proof. However, a closer look at the data shows that the real variable is not race, but family structure and all that it implies in terms of commitment and love between adults and children.

A 1988 study of 11,000 individuals found

29

1. CRIME AND JUSTICE IN AMERICA

that "the percentage of single-parent households with children between the ages of 12 and 20 is significantly associated with rates of violent crime and burglary." The same study makes it clear that the popular assumption that there is an association between race and crime is false. Illegitimacy, not race, is the key factor. It is the absence of marriage and the failure to form and maintain intact families that explains the incidence of crime among whites as well as blacks.

There is a strong, well-documented pattern of circumstances and social evolution in the life of a future violent criminal. The pattern may be summarized in five basic stages:

Stage one: Parental neglect and abandonment of the child in early home life. When the future violent criminal is born, his father already has abandoned the mother. If his parents are married, they are likely to divorce by the third year of his life. He is raised in a neighborhood with a high concentration of single-parent families. He does not become securely attached to his mother during the critical early years. His child care frequently changes.

The adults in his life often quarrel and vent their frustrations physically. He, or a member of his family, may suffer one or more forms of abuse, including sexual. There is much harshness in his home, and he is deprived of affection.

He becomes hostile, anxious, and hyperactive. He is difficult to manage at age three and is labeled a "behavior problem." Lacking his father's presence and attention, he becomes increasingly aggressive.

Stage two: The embryonic gang becomes a place for him to belong. His behavior continues to deteriorate at a rapid rate. He satisfies his needs by exploiting others. At age five or six, he hits his mother. In first grade, his aggressive behavior causes problems for other children. He is difficult for school officials to handle.

He is rejected socially at school by "normal" children. He searches for and finds acceptance among similarly aggressive and hostile youngsters. He and his friends are slower at school. They fail at verbal tasks that demand abstract thinking and at learning social and moral concepts. His reading scores trail behind the rest of his class. He has lessening interest in school, teachers, and learning.

By now, he and his friends have low educational and life expectations for themselves. These are reinforced by teachers and family members. Poor supervision at home continues. His father, or father substitute, still is absent. His life primarily is characterized by aggressive behavior by himself and his peers and a hostile home life.

Stage three: He joins a delinquent gang. At age 11, his bad habits and attitudes are well-established. By age 15, he engages in criminal behavior. The earlier he commits his first delinquent act, the longer he will be likely to lead a life of crime.

His companions are the main source of his personal identity and his sense of belonging. Life with his delinquent friends is hidden from adults. The number of delinquent acts increases in the year before he and his friends drop out of school.

His delinquent girlfriends have poor relationships with their mothers, as well as with "normal" girls in school. A number of his peers use drugs. Many, especially the girls, run away from home or just drift away.

Stage four: He commits violent crime and the full-fledged criminal gang emerges. High violence grows in his community with the increase in the number of single-parent families. He purchases a gun, at first mainly for self-defense. He and his peers begin to use violence for exploitation. The violent young men in his delinquent peer group are arrested more than the nonviolent criminals, but most of them do not get caught at all.

Gradually, different friends specialize in different types of crime—violence or theft. Some are more versatile than others. The girls are involved in prostitution, while he and the other boys are members of criminal gangs.

Stage five: A new child—and a new generation of criminals—is born. His 16-year-old girlfriend is pregnant. He has no thought of marrying her; among his peers this simply isn't done. They stay together for awhile until the shouting and hitting start. He leaves her and does not see the baby anymore.

One or two of his criminal friends are experts in their field. Only a few members of the group to which he now belongs—career criminals—are caught. They commit hundreds of crimes per year. Most of those he and his friends commit are in their own neighborhood.

For the future violent criminal, each of these five stages is characterized by the absence of the love, affection, and dedication of his parents. The ordinary tasks of growing up are a series of perverse exercises, frustrating his needs, stunting his capacity for empathy as well as his ability to belong, and increasing the risk of his becoming a twisted young adult. This experience is in stark contrast to the investment of love and dedication by two parents normally needed to make compassionate, competent adults out of their offspring.

The impact of violent crime

When one considers some of the alarming statistics that make headlines today, the future of our society appears bleak. In the mid 1980s, the chancellor of the New York City school system warned: "We are in a situation now where 12,000 of our 60,000 kindergartners have mothers who are still in their teenage years and where 40% of our students come from single-parent households."

Today, this crisis is not confined to New York; it afflicts even small, rural communities. Worse yet, the national illegitimacy rate is predicted to reach 50% within the next 12-20 years. As a result, violence in school is becoming worse. The Centers for Disease Control recently reported that more than four percent of high school students surveyed had brought a firearm at least once to school. Many of them, in fact, were regular gun carriers.

The old injunction clearly is true—violence begets violence. Violent families are producing violent youths, and violent youths are producing violent communities. The future violent criminal is likely to have witnessed numerous conflicts between his parents. He may have been physically or sexually abused. His parents, brothers, and sisters also may be criminals, and thus his family may have a disproportionate negative impact on the community. Moreover, British and American studies show that fewer than five percent of all criminals account for 50% of all criminal convictions. Over all, there has been an extraordinary increase in community violence in most major American cities.

Government agencies are powerless to make men and women marry or stay wed. They are powerless to guarantee that parents will love and care for their children. They are powerless to persuade anyone to make and keep promises. In fact, government agencies often do more harm than good by enforcing policies that undermine stable families and by misdiagnosing the real root cause of such social problems as violent crime.

Nevertheless, ordinary American are not powerless. They know full well how to fight crime effectively. They do not need to survey the current social science literature to know that a family life of affection, cohesion, and parental involvement prevents delinquency. They instinctively realize that paternal and maternal affection and the father's presence in the home are among the critical elements in raising well-balanced children. They acknowledge that parents should encourage the moral development of their offspring—an act that best is accomplished within the context of religious belief and practice.

None of this is to say that fighting crime or rebuilding stable families and communities will be easy. What *is* easy is deciding what we must do at the outset. Begin by affirming four simple principles: First, marriage is vital. Second, parents must love and nurture their children in spiritual as well as physical ways. Third, children must be taught how to relate to and empathize with others. Finally, the backbone of strong neighborhoods and communities is friendship and cooperation among families.

These principles constitute the real root solution to the problem of violent crime. We should do everything in our power to apply them in our own lives and the life of the nation, not just for our sake, but for that of our children.

Article 6

The Evolution of Street Gangs
A Shift Toward Organized Crime

Lieutenant Michael C. McCort, Phoenix Police Department, Arizona

Over the past 15 years, street gangs have undergone a swift and dramatic change that has had a significant impact upon America. The problem that was once restricted to large cities is now shared by small suburban and rural communities as well. These gangs have become a driving influence on violent crime, drug trafficking and community stability. All segments of American society are affected in terms of crime, safety, community image and quality of life.

The criminal justice system has been largely unprepared for the swift growth of the problem. Despite increased efforts at the local, state and federal levels, the problem continues to grow. While street gangs continue to influence crime on a local level, parallel events may signal the development of a more sophisticated form of gang-related criminal activity on a national scale.

An examination of recent developments in street gang activity in comparison to historical patterns, social/cultural processes and gang migration trends reveals an evolutionary process that has been characteristic of ethnic gangs throughout American history. Today's gangs are just as susceptible to this process.

Where that evolution will lead today's gangs is not completely understood. It is certain, however, that law enforcement must consider the potential emergence of a new organized crime system. Street gangs are undergoing continuous change, and police cannot afford to rely on understandings forged in the past. It is a function of leadership to look toward the future and anticipate changes that will affect crime and public safety—to develop intervention strategies that meet changing events as they occur, rather than after they become a crisis. In this context, effort must be directed at the growing structure of organized gang activity, as well as the street-level crime problem.

This article does not suggest the wholesale transition of the entire street gang subculture. For the most part, street gangs will likely remain loose-knit social entities, involved primarily in street-level crime. However, individuals or elements of the subculture are evolving into a more sophisticated level of organized crime. Furthermore, it is suggested that this event can be predicted by simple analysis of social history and current events.

General Development

Ethnic gangs have been in existence since the early days of America. Historically, they have been a product of social/cultural issues that have remained somewhat consistent across ethnic lines. Social scientists studying gangs have consistently reported common factors in their formation and development. Despite ethnic origins, gangs form out of a need for association, protection and defense against economic and social isolation. For this reason, they undergo classic changes in response to their environment as a means of survival.

The impact gangs have on a community has been a concern of criminal justice professionals and social scientists for some time. Frederick Thrasher published an early study of Chicago's urban gangs in 1927, describing the gangs of that period as "lawless, godless, and wild." Their propensity for violence was considered to be "beyond the control of police and social service agencies."[1] Gangs of that era pale in comparison to today's street gangs.

Historically, different ethnic gangs began their existence as small territorial groups involved in petty crime within their own urban underclass neighborhoods. Individual members formed associations and engaged in crime for personal success. Over time, some successful groups developed structure as their enterprises grew and extended beyond their confined areas.

Various organized crime groups (past and present) were offshoots of neighborhood gangs. Irish, Jewish and other immigrant communities experienced gangs as a means to deal with economic, social and cultural isolation. The present-day Italian-American La Costra Nostra (LCN) had its roots in early 20th-century gangs from Chicago and New York. Many ethnic gangs with similar origins have become quite large and have migrated from their original stomping grounds. Some exhibit levels of organization and sophistication.

Today, the most notable street gangs include groups like the Crips, Bloods, Black Gangster Disciple Nation and Vice Lords. Currently, Crips and Bloods have the highest recognition and exposure on a national level. They are known coast to coast, and law enforcement across the country has frequent contact with their members. Many adolescents emulate aspects of these gangs, probably due in part to the level of exposure they get in the entertainment industry (movies and gangster rap).

Ethnic Succession

Ethnic succession of gangs and organized crime is a traceable phenomenon in

---

Reprinted from the *Police Chief* magazine, June 1996, pp. 33-38, 51-52. © 1996 by The International Association of Chiefs of Police, Inc., 515 N. Washington St., Alexandria, VA 22314, U.S.A. Further reproduction without express written permission from IACP is strictly prohibited.

1. CRIME AND JUSTICE IN AMERICA

America. In a 1973 study, sociologist Francis Ianni examined organized crime as a social system and identified circumstances motivating the evolution of organized crime groups through history. The origins of many criminal enterprises have been linked to early neighborhood gangs.

Rather than viewing criminal organizations as formal units, conceived specifically to achieve criminal goals, Ianni viewed them as "social groupings contrived by culture and responsive to sociocultural change." Organized crime was described as "a feature of the social, economic and political structure of American society."[2] The study described an evolutionary progression of ethnic groups, making comparisons among Irish, Jewish and Italian gangs. The progression came about as behaviors and patterns in relationships changed, influenced by social and economic events.

Taking the sociological perspective, ethnic underclasses use crime as a means to escape poverty, enhance ego, express aggression and achieve upward mobility.[3] As wealth is gained, power and influence are achieved. Over time, successful criminal groups acquire sophistication, structure and organization as mechanisms for survival.

In 1973, Ianni believed Blacks and Hispanics were possibly beginning a transition to displace the Italian-Americans in organized crime. Taking a broader view of current gang activity makes this possibility seem plausible.

History of Ethnic Organized Crime

The evolution of Caucasian ethnic gangs lends perspective to current gang development. In the late 1800s, Irish immigrants formed gangs and engaged in criminal activity as a means to climb the social ladder. They emerged in large cities and claimed specific neighborhoods as their territory.

Initially, they preyed upon their own communities, using theft, extortion, gambling and prostitution as sources of income. As wealth grew, power, status and political influence were obtained. Structure evolved as their network expanded, and over time they developed organized criminal enterprises. In some instances, political influence was significant, and local elections were controlled in their respective territories. In recent times, some cities have experienced attempts at political influence. In 1994, several Black Gangster Disciple members ran for local office in Chicago.

During the early 1900s, large-scale Italian immigration took place. As their populations settled in large urban centers, groups formed for cultural protection. Like other gangs, they engaged in criminal activity—preying on their own, slowly developing sophistication and extending their network. In New York's Lower East side, the Five Points Gang emerged, and individuals such as Johnny Torrio and Al Capone established themselves as leaders in the Italian gang scene.

Prior to Prohibition, the gangs of the day were fragmented, independent and territorial. Prohibition, however, served as a catalyst for major gang evolution. Illicit alcohol was a lucrative business that propelled gang expansion, organization and consolidation.

As the markets each gang controlled began to tighten, they struggled for market share. Territorial disputes spurred violence and created competition, which affected profit. Increased violence brought public attention, and law enforcement applied added pressure. Individuals sought new markets and migrated outside traditional territories to establish new trade. Networks formed and expanded. Coordination to maintain the networks brought organization.

Individuals like Lucky Luciano emerged as leaders and forged more formalized structures to maximize profits. Although Irish and Jewish gangs dominated in the early stages, the Italian gangs eventually displaced them to become the dominant organized crime system of the era.

As Prohibition ended, a replacement for the lucrative alcohol trade was sought. Narcotics trafficking became a profitable business for gangs of the era—as it has for today's gangs—stimulating the development of international associations. By the 1960s, the LCN had become an international organized crime network and the United States' premier criminal organization. In today's environment, certain gang drug dealers have international associations with Latin American drug cartels that supply cocaine.

The LCN was involved in drugs, gambling, loansharking, pornography, prostitution and labor racketeering. Assault, murder, extortion and public corruption became recognized trademarks. Its influence also reached into legitimate business and politics.

It is interesting to note that until a leadership meeting in Appalachia was discovered by a New York state trooper in 1957, law enforcement didn't realize a national organization or union of gangs existed. Prior to that discovery, fragmented law enforcement efforts had little impact on organized crime.

The Importance of Crack

The discovery of "crack" or "rock" cocaine in the early 1980s had a significant impact on the evolution of street gangs and their influence upon society. Crack did for street gangs what Prohibition did for Irish and Italian ethnic gangs of the 1920s.

In comparison to other illegal drugs, crack is a dealer's dream. It is relatively cheap and easy to obtain, easy to produce and easy to conceal for transportation and sale; it also has a short but intense high that produces a strong user craving. In business terms, crack is a cost-effective product to buy, produce and sell.

Although prices vary from market to market, cocaine can generally be bought cheaply in Southern California and sold at a large profit in other locations. For example, an ounce of powder cocaine might be purchased in Los Angeles for $300 and sold as crack on the street in Wichita for $1,500—a 400 percent profit. Throughout history, profit has been a driving force in bringing about change and propelling gang evolution.

Gang Migration

The scale of gang migration over the past 10 years has been significant, bringing the problem to communities that had never before experienced gangs.

In little more than a decade, for example, Los Angeles Crips and Bloods have gone from a Southern Californian phenomenon to a nationwide problem. In 1993, the National Drug Intelligence Center published a survey of Crip and Blood activity, reporting their presence in 155 cities throughout the country. Of course, L.A. gangs are not the only ones spreading from traditional territories. To a lesser extent, Black Gangster Disciples and Vice Lords have shown up in many eastern, southeastern and midwestern cities.

Drs. Maxson and Klein of the University of Southern California noted in their *Interim Survey Report on Gang Migration* that over 700 surveyed cities reported experience with some type of gang migration, compared to only 200 cities that had street gangs a decade earlier. The spread of street gangs is occurring at a level never before experienced.

Law enforcement is operating under the assumption that migrating gangs lack sophistication. Even so, gang culture facilitates at least an informal ability to link, communicate and provide support. What

6. Evolution of Street Gangs

exists across the country is a network of gang associations that establish a basic infrastructure for criminal activity. It also establishes a basic structure for advanced organization if manipulated in that direction.

Factors Motivating Migration

Gang migration is often motivated by the desire to make money through sales of illegal drugs, mostly crack cocaine. Although there are other factors, such as imitation of gangs with popular reputations and migration for housing or employment opportunities, a large portion is the result of drug trafficking by gang entrepreneurs.

The typical gang drug dealer probably does not make a decision to travel to a new city after a formal meeting or strategic planning session.[4] The decision is more likely motivated by personal ambition and the expectation of acquiring income. However, police intelligence has not been able to accurately determine the level of strategic support and organization related to gang drug dealing across the country.

> *Living in an environment of poverty and gang culture promotes values very different from societal norms. Crime is seen as a logical means to escape poverty, enhance status and obtain power.*

Street gang culture supports individual ambition to gain status through illegal ventures. Young gang members establish themselves by demonstrating tough, recklessly violent attitudes. They go through an informal apprenticeship, earning their reputations by committing thefts, robberies and shootings. Referred to as "coming up," this process prepares youth to fulfill roles that support drug dealing in today's competitive markets.

Drug dealers—seen as "high rollers"—are usually older members with established reputations. They have money, power and status in their environments.

Drug dealing provides the means to demonstrate success by flaunting clothes, gold jewelry and nice cars. They are respected role models for younger gang members.

Living in an environment of poverty and gang culture promotes values very different from societal norms. Crime is seen as a logical means to escape poverty, enhance status and obtain power. It permits upward mobility within their environment. This is particularly true when socially approved routes are considered out of reach. Because drug dealing is seen as a prestigious way to gain wealth, there is no shortage of motivated and ambitious persons willing to enter the business.

Changes in gang drug markets support migration. As crack markets become saturated with dealers, competition for profit increases. Laws of supply and demand force dealers to reduce prices to maintain their customer base. Competition spurs violence to protect one's market share and defend against rivals. In turn, the increase in violence attracts public concern, which brings law enforcement pressure. The combination of these factors often induces ambitious dealers to seek more attractive markets to ply their trade in a less-competitive environment.

Los Angeles experienced this phenomenon during the 1980s, with widespread migration to new markets in California and, eventually, to other states. As the same conditions are replicated in the new markets, new locations are sought. As urban markets become saturated, suburban and rural areas become targets. Because there is no shortage of either cocaine or dealers, migration continues.

Gang members have a supportive resource network they can rely on to develop their business ventures. In new locations, they exploit the gang's reputation, particularly where violence is concerned. They have access to experienced and willing manpower, a supply of modern weapons and a unique transportation system. They also have access to large quantities of inexpensive, quality product, which is obtained easily across southwestern borders. In addition, having experienced police tactics in their home territories, they are skilled in resisting police interdiction in communities where law enforcement is generally unprepared for their invasion.

Migrant gang members are a powerful force against local dealers who are less sophisticated and lack the supportive infrastructure of the gang. When a gang dealer moves to a new location, he brings the supportive resources of the gang—particularly its reputation. He will intimidate with violence, cut prices, recruit locals and make alliances in order to swiftly

establish himself in the local market. With little time to adapt, law enforcement is hampered in its efforts to develop intelligence and organize an effective response.

As elements of specific gangs spread and create new relationships, a loose network develops. The associations solidify, and structure grows. As gangs adapt to market changes and police tactics, a greater level of sophistication is needed to maintain the networks. Over time, organization evolves through the natural course of events. The initial values of street gang members undergo a dynamic shift, becoming more pronounced over time. The old identity is replaced by new values that support success of the business.

Today's Gangs

The developmental history of today's street gangs is strikingly similar to gangs of the past. Like the ethnic gangs that evolved into organized crime groups, street gangs exist because they fill a need for economic, social and cultural protection. Currently, there is no collective understanding of the extent of this evolution, or the likelihood of its leading to organized crime. However, there are drug-dealing gangs that appear to be evolving as gangs of the past did.

For example, L.A.'s original street gangs followed the same general patterns as most gangs. They were small, fragmented, territorial groups, with individual and separate identities. Their activities had little impact on the community at large.

During the late 1960s and early '70s, black gangs in L.A. began to shift from traditional roles. Crips came into existence and quickly earned a reputation for violence—extorting money and committing assaults and robberies. Bloods emerged to protect themselves from the large and violent Crip gangs. In short order, L.A.'s black gangs came under the umbrella identity of Crip or Blood. The original gang culture changed, but gangs remained indigenous to the L.A. area until the discovery of crack cocaine.

These two factions now consist of many different neighborhood groups or "sets" that share a common identity but remain somewhat autonomous within their particular geographical areas. The grouping is more of a union of gang sets than a consolidated empire. Drug-dealing elements of these gangs have linked across the United States, with some connections to Latin America.

Similarly, a number of small street gangs in Chicago have joined coalitions such as the Black Gangster Disciple Na-

1. CRIME AND JUSTICE IN AMERICA

tion (BGDN) and the Vice Lords. Both groups are heavily involved in narcotics trafficking. These particular gangs typically possess a more defined structure and organization than the gangs of the Southwest. The BGDN and Vice Lords have established drug-trafficking links across the United States. In some cases, their network includes links to the L.A.-based Crips and Bloods.

Successful gang drug enterprises generate large sums of money that require methods of laundering the money back into the economy. In addition, financial wealth provides a means to procure influence and power. Factions of the BGDN and Vice Lords have been very successful at acquiring businesses to launder money. They have also been successful at political action. These activities take a certain amount of coordination and organization to create an aura of legitimacy and insulate the gang business from police interference.

A comparison of current and historical gang activity demonstrates the evolutionary nature of certain street gangs.

Among the types of businesses purchased by BGDN and Vice Lord members and uncovered by law enforcement are laundries, bars, restaurants, auto repair shops and similar ventures. In certain investigations, it was demonstrated that the businesses were purchased with gang drug money and operated to launder drug money for the gang.

The BGDN's political action group, known as the "21st Century Vote," has become influential in Chicago politics. The group seeks to elect candidates that are sensitive to the gang. They organize members as a political force, run public rallies, sponsor public information campaigns and attempt to influence their followers to vote as instructed. While they use community improvement as a platform, the bottom line is an active, coordinated attempt to legitimize the gang's ac-

tivity and insulate its lucrative illegal activities.

In 1994, Larry Hoover, the recognized founder of the BGDN and a convicted, imprisoned murderer, sought to change the gang's image. From prison, he attempted to change the BGDN charter and rename the gang "Better Growth and Development." Confiscated excerpts from BGDN bylaws have proposed to advance the "GD Nation" through political, social and economic means. In these documents, members have been urged to use drug monies to purchase new businesses as a means to launder illegal profits.

Although Hoover was in prison for the execution-style murders of three individuals, there were attempts to portray him as a reformed community leader and social visionary. In 1993, the Chicago mayor, three city aldermen (one of them an ex-police officer) and a state representative actively supported Hoover's early release from prison. In 1994, two BGDN gang members ran for local office and came close to being elected. This activity is reminiscent of 1920s Chicago, when Al Capone sought an image of legitimacy by helping followers work their way into the political process through corruption of local politicians and judges.

A comparison of current and historical gang activity demonstrates the evolutionary nature of certain street gangs. While the subculture remains unsophisticated and oriented to street-level criminal activity, there are elements that are advancing their sophistication and level of organization. In addition, a nationwide network of gang-related drug contacts exists. Currently, the networks are thought to be very informal. However, the potential for their developing into a more formal system does exist.

Conclusion

The evolution of organized crime is a product of combining influences that work together over time, causing a social unit to respond to its environment and opportunities. In a broad sense, this process has been characteristic of ethnic criminal groups throughout American history.

At present, some mainstream professionals consider it unlikely that street gangs will become a national organized crime enterprise with the sophistication of the LCN. Yet, they are susceptible to the

same economic, social and cultural processes as ethnic gangs of the past.

Their evolution may not take the exact path of the LCN's, but some form is likely to occur—in fact, it may already exist.

Today's street gangs are more violent than any gangs of the past. Their violence is motivated by more obscure reasons, such as status, reputation and pride. Their membership includes a larger portion of the population, and the street gang subculture enjoys a greater acceptance from youth.

Add leadership and an organized criminal element, and American society faces a serious national crime problem on a scale unmatched in this country's history. Law enforcement must be prepared to respond to the new dynamics of gang crime with different prevention, intervention and suppression tactics.

Street gangs are a diverse and complex problem that must be addressed in a diverse and comprehensive manner. Law enforcement can take a leadership role in a collective effort to solve the problem. The effort requires partnerships between local, state and federal criminal justice agencies. This is necessary to combine unique talents to share intelligence, investigate and dismantle organized groups. It requires partnerships with social services, education, private business and other groups that have a stake in the issue.

Because the underlying causes are rooted in complex social issues, the community must be involved. Society has the ultimate power to control crime. This power can be nurtured into a common acceptance of shared human values that will permit peace and harmony.

Citizens have a right to live in peace, free from fear and the negative effects gangs have on our quality of life. If we are to be successful in this endeavor, we must recognize the changing nature of gangs, engage in long-term planning and develop complementary strategies to address the problems posed by street gangs.

[1] J.H. Skolnick, *Gang Organization and Migration and Drugs, Gangs and Law Enforcement?* (California Department of Justice, 1993), p. 1.

[2] Francis A.J. Ianni, *Ethnic Succession in Organized Crime, Summary Report*, U.S. Department of Justice, Dec. 1973, p. 3 and p. 12.

[3] *Ibid*, p. 14.

[4] Skolnick, p. 18.

Article 7

Experts Are at Odds on How Best to Tackle Rise in Teen-Agers' Drug Use

GINA KOLATA

As drug use among teen-agers begins to rise sharply after years of decline, experts in drug abuse say there is an opportunity to halt the incipient epidemic in its tracks. But they disagree on the right remedy.

The most popular anti-drug program is DARE, for Drug Abuse Resistance Education, which is used in nearly 75 percent of the nation's school systems. But several leading academic experts, supported by the National Institute on Drug Abuse, say that the program does not work and that other programs that have been effective are not being used. Its supporters, on the other hand, note the widespread acceptance of their program. And few if any schools have adopted the programs favored by the academic experts.

There is little question that drug abuse among adolescents is dramatically increasing, according to national surveys. For example, Dr. Lloyd D. Johnston of the University of Michigan found that the number of eighth graders trying any illicit drug, nearly doubled, to 21 percent in 1995 from 11 percent in 1991.

Conflicting claims on what works and what does not in curbing drug use.

With the release of the latest survey data by Dr. Johnston and others, drug abuse has become an issue in the Presidential campaigns. Bob Dole is blaming President Clinton for the increases, and Mr. Clinton is saying the trend began in the Bush Administration. But both political parties and experts in drug abuse say something must be done.

Of course, levels of drug use are still far below what they were at the peak of the last epidemic, and not everyone agrees that the present upturn in drug use signals a new epidemic. Dr. David Musto, a historian of medicine at Yale University, notes that it is possible that drug use has blipped up and then gone down in the past, without turning into an epidemic. But, Dr. Musto said, since drug use has never before been so carefully watched, there is no way of knowing how significant the current pattern is. But drug use today certainly falls far short of what it was at the peak of the last epidemic, he pointed out. In 1979, for example, more than half of the high school seniors in Dr. Johnston's survey, which began in 1975, said they had used an illicit drug in the last 12 months.

But Dr. Herbert Kleber, who directs the Center on Addiction and Substance Abuse at Columbia University, said, "What's scary is not simply that the curve is rising but that it's rising exponentially. It's a steeply rising curve."

Dr. Richard R. Clayton, director of the Center for Prevention Research at the University of Kentucky in Lexington, also worries that an epidemic is nigh. And, Dr. Clayton said, the increasing drug use coincides with a "demographic explosion."

"By 2010," he said, "we will have more teenagers than at any time in history. We are at the front end of what could be a disaster for the whole society."

In past epidemics, researchers say, drug use peaked, then dropped of its own accord as people who once thought drugs glamorous saw first hand their dark side.

So when a new, naïve group of adolescents starts experimenting with drugs, there are two courses of action, Dr. Johnston said.

"You can let nature run its course," he said, and let the teenagers learn through experience or by watching their friends experiment that drug abuse is abhorrent. Or, through

From *The New York Times*, September 18, 1996, p. B7. © 1996 by The New York Times Company. Reprinted by permission.

1. CRIME AND JUSTICE IN AMERICA

CASE STUDIES

Anti-Drug Programs: a Comparison

In a guide to school drug programs called "Making the Grade," Drug Strategies, a nonprofit research institution, evaluated many different studies of several anti-drug programs.

Here is how the most widely used program, Drug Abuse Resistance Education, or DARE, compared with Life Skills Training, a program that several studies have found to be effective.

	DARE	LIFE SKILLS TRAINING
WHERE USED	In nearly three-quarters of the nation's schools	In very few school systems
GRADE LEVELS	K-12	6-8 or 7-9
CHANGE IN DRUG USE	Numerous studies have yielded inconsistent findings.	Smoking, alcohol and marijuana use by 7th-graders reduced between 50-75 percent after the test. By the end of high school, results eroded only slightly.
COMMENTS	No consistent results. Some studies showed impact on knowledge and attitudes about tobacco, alcohol and drugs, and more favorable attitudes toward police.	Significant impact on knowledge and attitudes about tobacco, alcohol and drugs after 3 years (6-year data on knowledge and attitudes has not yet been analyzed).

education programs and other efforts, perhaps an epidemic can be stopped.

Most school systems are taking the second route, trying to stop drug use through education. But a vigorous dispute has developed over what anti-drug programs are effective. Several academic experts say that DARE has no lasting effect, a view that its supporters deny.

The program is taught by specially trained police officers who come into the schools and teach children how to resist drugs. DARE was developed in Los Angeles in 1983, under Daryl Gates, who was then the city's chief of police, along with the Los Angeles Unified School District. Aggressively marketed, the program was there "at the right place at the right time," Dr. Clayton said, and quickly filled an educational void. It was attractive to school systems because the money for DARE programs came out of a city's administrative funds, to pay for the police officers, and not out of the school budget. There was no need for teacher training—the police officers did it all.

And parents, school systems and police departments loved it. Dr. Joseph F. Donnemeyer of Ohio State University in Columbus, who recently surveyed parents and teachers in Ohio, said he was struck by their enthusiastic support for the program.

Glenn Levant, the president of DARE America, a private, nonprofit corporation in Los Angeles, said New York City had just signed on to the program and this month sent 100 police officers for training.

Academic researchers are more critical. They say the program has failed the acid test of science. "DARE has been evaluated in a reasonably rigorous way by 5 to 10 different researchers in different parts of the country," said Dr. Clayton, the author of one of these studies.

Researchers asked whether children who had been through the program were less likely to smoke, drink, or use drugs than those who had not had the program but "failed to find lasting effects," Dr. Clayton said.

Mathea Falco, whose Drug Strategies group scrutinized all the published studies on prevention programs, said the program was "remarkably effective about marketing." But, she said, "the DARE evaluations did not show behavioral change."

Although no one knows why the program has not caused lasting behavioral changes, Dr. Clayton said it made some assumptions that were not backed by research. For example, one lesson is devoted to self-esteem, and yet, he said, researchers have found "very little correlation between drug use and self-esteem."

Another possible problem, said Dr. Gilbert J. Botvin, who directs the Institute for Prevention Research at Cornell University Medical College, is that police officers—authority figures—might not be the right people to teach adolescents that drug use is not cool.

But Mr. Levant said the program did work. Although he could not point to a large prospective study of DARE with a control group, the kind of test favored by the academic experts, he said that he knew of about 70 evaluations of the program and that "all of the evaluations talk about the positive benefits of the program."

Dr. Kleber, who is the head of the program's scientific advisory board, said that it had evolved and improved over time, but that the available assessments looked only at the old DARE model. For example, he said, the program was originally offered in fifth and sixth grades. Now it is a program that goes from kindergarten through 12th grade.

"If there's anything we know," Dr. Kleber said, "it's that one shot doesn't work" in preventing drug abuse.

But the revised program is too new to have been evaluated in longterm studies. Yet, academic scientists say, there are alternatives, programs that have been proved to work, but that are virtually unknown, not marketed, and ignored.

For example, Dr. Botvin developed and tested a program called Life Skills Training. It has undergone 10 rigorous evaluations, the largest involving 4,466 seventh graders who were followed until the end of high school. Behavioral changes initiated by the program lasted the entire six years of the study. The use of cigarettes, alcohol and marijuana among teen-agers who had had the program was half that of similar teen-agers who had not had the program.

But Dr. Botvin said that he was unaware of any widespread use of his program, and that he himself was not marketing it.

"Researchers are not good at disseminating findings," he said. "A lot of it is published in scientific journals, that's the

7. Experts Are at Odds

currency of our careers. There isn't any incentive to publish in places that practitioners are likely to read."

Dr. Kleber said that alternatives to DARE might look good when they were tested by their proponents, but that they had not undergone the sort of real-world use that its programs were put through. So, he said, these programs may not be quite as effective as they at first appear.

But Dr. Zili Sloboda, director of the division of epidemiology and prevention research at the National Institute on Drug Abuse, said that incredible as it might seem, the real reason that competing programs were rarely used was that school systems did not know about them, and the social scientists who designed them had failed to market them.

"You know how researchers are," Dr. Sloboda said. "I hate to say it, but it's true. We tend to be in our own worlds."

She said the drug-abuse institute, which paid for this work, was now trying to promote the programs itself.

The director of the National Institute on Drug Abuse, Dr. Alan I. Leshner, is "going out on the road, traveling all over the country" to tell communities about other drug education programs, Dr. Sloboda said. The institute has also made videos about the new programs, is teaching drug abuse prevention coordinators for the states about the programs, and is holding a conference in Washington on Sept. 19 and 20 to bring together researchers and people who make decisions about prevention programs.

At this point, said Dr. Linda Dusenbury, a drug abuse researcher at Cornell University Medical College, experts might do well to look to DARE as a model. Although Dr. Dusenbury said she doubted its merits in preventing drug abuse, it does have one stellar quality—it managed to get itself in widespread use.

"It is absolutely the model we should look to to get a program disseminated," Dr. Dusenbury said. "None of the other programs have had that kind of success."

Victimology

For many years, crime victims were not considered an important topic for criminological study. Now, however, criminologists consider focusing on victims and victimization essential to understanding the phenomenon of crime. The popularity of this area of study can be attributed to the early work of Hans von Hentig and the later work of Stephen Schafer. These writers were the first to assert that crime victims play an integral role in the criminal event, that their actions may actually precipitate crime, and that unless the victim's role is considered, the study of crime is not complete.

In recent years a growing number of criminologists have devoted increasing attention to the victim's role in the criminal justice process. Generally, areas of particular interest include calculating costs of crime to victims, taking surveys of victims to measure the nature and extent of criminal behavior, establishing probabilities of victimization risks, studying victim precipitation of crime and culpability, and designing services expressly for victims of crime. As more criminologists focus their attention on the victim's role in the criminal process, victimology will take on even greater importance.

This unit provides sharp focus on key issues. From the lead report, "Criminal Victimization 1994," we learn that of the 42.4 million crimes U.S. residents age 12 or older experienced in 1994, 31 million were property crimes, 10.9 million were crimes of violence, and one-half million were personal thefts. In spite of that frightening picture, the next reading, "True Crime," asserts that careful examination of the data reveals that much fear among citizens is misplaced. It is true, however, that the worst crimes are increasing and that it is particularly dangerous to live in certain regions of the country.

In the essay that follows, "Protecting Our Seniors," Ronald Getz focuses on victimization of the elderly, mani-fested in abuse and neglect. The police are networking with social agencies in order to improve the quality of life for seniors. The issue of domestic violence is examined in "Nobody's Victim," which tells the story of Sarah Buel, once a battered woman herself, who escaped her abusive partner and now works to save other abused women.

Preventing child abuse and neglect has become a critical priority, as the criminal justice system focuses its attention on crime and violence reduction. "Helping to Prevent Child Abuse—and Future Criminal Consequences: Hawai'i Healthy Start" offers a strategy to curb this menace. The last unit article is entitled "Is Street Crime More Harmful than White Collar Crime?" In their pro-and-con answers to this question, one professor contends that street criminals should be the focus of crime study. The other professor argues that medical malpractice and dangerous working conditions are far more serious than street crime.

Looking Ahead: Challenge Questions

What lifestyle changes might you consider to avoid becoming victimized?

How successful are crime victims when they fight their assailants?

According to "Criminal Victimization 1994," how many crime victims were there in the United States? What are the trend and patterns in victimization?

What can be done to help solve abuse and neglect of the elderly?

Does marital status influence victimization risk? Defend your answer.

Is street crime more harmful that white-collar crime? If you were the victim of a mugging, how would this influence your answer?

UNIT 2

Article 8

National Crime Victimization Survey

Criminal Victimization 1994

Craig Perkins
Patsy Klaus
BJS Statisticians

In 1994 U.S. residents age 12 or older experienced approximately 42.4 million crimes. Thirty-one million (73%) were property crimes, 10.9 million (26%) were crimes of violence, and approximately a half million (1%) were personal thefts.

The National Crime Victimization Survey (NCVS) indicates there were 51 violent victimizations per 1,000 persons age 12 or older and 308 property crimes per 1,000 households.

The National Crime Victimization Survey measures personal and household offenses, including crimes not reported to police, by interviewing all occupants age 12 or older in a nationally representative sample of U.S. households.

Violent crimes include rape/sexual assault, robbery, and both aggravated and simple assault, as measured by the NCVS, and murders from FBI data on homicides reported to the police (see box "Murder in the United States, 1994").

Pocket picking, purse snatching, and attempted purse snatching comprise personal theft. Property crimes consist of household burglary, motor vehicle theft, and thefts of other property.

10.9 million violent crimes in 1994

The 10.9 million violent victimizations included: 430 thousand rapes/sexual assaults, 1.3 million robberies, over 2.5 million aggravated assaults, and 6.6 million simple assaults (table 1).

Highlights

Criminal victimization experienced in the U.S. in 1994

	Number in millions	Rate per 1,000[a]	Percent of measured crime	Percent of this crime reported to police
All crimes	42.4	–	100%	36%
Violent crime	10.9	51	26%	42%
Simple assault	6.6	31	16	36
Aggravated assault	2.5	12	6	52
Robbery	1.3	6	3	55
Rape/Sexual assault	.4	2	*	32
Personal theft[b]	.5	2	1%	33%
Property crime	31.0	308	73%	34%
Property thefts	23.8	236	56	27
Household burglary	5.5	54	13	50
Motor vehicle theft	1.8	18	4	78

–Not applicable.
*Less than .1%.
[a]Per 1,000 persons age 12 or older, or per 1,000 households
[b]Includes pocket picking and purse snatching.

- In 1994 for every 1,000 persons age 12 or older, there occurred:
  — 2 rapes or attempted rapes
  — 3 assaults with serious injury
  — 4 robberies with property taken.

- The violent crime rate has been essentially unchanged since 1992, following a slight increase between 1985 and 1991. Property crime continued a 15-year decline.

- The young, blacks, and males were most vulnerable to violent crime:
  — 1 in 9 persons age 12 to 15, compared to 1 in 196 age 65 or more
  — 1 in 16 blacks, compared to 1 in 20 whites
  — 1 in 17 males, compared to 1 in 24 females

- Compared to those households with annual incomes of $15,000 or more, persons in households with incomes of less than $15,000 were:
  — 3 times more likely to be raped or sexually assaulted
  — 2 times more likely to be robbed
  — 1½ times more likely to be a victim of an aggravated assault.

- Almost two-thirds of victims of completed rapes did not report the crime to the police.

- Two-thirds of victims of rape or sexual assault knew their assailants.

- A third of robbery victims were injured as a result of the incident.

From *Bureau of Justice Statistics Bulletin*, NCJ-158022, April 1996, pp. 1-8. Reprinted by permission of the U.S. Department of Justice, Bureau of Justice Statistics.

8. Criminal Victimization 1994

Table 1. Criminal victimizations and victimization rates, 1993-94: Estimates from the redesigned National Crime Victimization Survey

Type of crime	Number of victimizations (1,000's) 1993	Number of victimizations (1,000's) 1994	Victimization rates (per 1,000 persons age 12 or older or per 1,000 households) 1993	Victimization rates (per 1,000 persons age 12 or older or per 1,000 households) 1994
All crimes	43,547	42,359	...	...
Personal crimes[1]	11,365	11,349	53.7	53.1
Crimes of violence	10,848	10,860	51.3	50.8
Completed violence	3,213	3,205	15.2	15.0
Attempted/threatened violence	7,635	7,654	36.1	35.8
Rape/Sexual assault	485	433	2.3	2.0
Rape/attempted rape	313	316	1.5	1.5
Rape	160	168	.8	.8
Attempted rape	152	149	.7	.7
Sexual assault	173	117[b]	.8	.5[a]
Robbery	1,291	1,299	6.1	6.1
Completed/property taken	815	795	3.9	3.7
With injury	274	288	1.3	1.3
Without injury	541	507	2.6	2.4
Attempted to take property	476	504	2.3	2.4
With injury	96	122	.5	.6
Without injury	381	382	1.8	1.8
Assault	9,072	9,128	42.9	42.7
Aggravated	2,563	2,478	12.1	11.6
With injury	713	679	3.4	3.2
Threatened with weapon	1,850	1,799	8.7	8.4
Simple	6,509	6,650	30.8	31.1
With minor injury	1,356	1,466	6.4	6.9
Without injury	5,153	5,184	24.4	24.3
Personal theft[2]	517	489	2.4	2.3
Property crimes	32,182	31,011[a]	322.1	307.6[a]
Household burglary	5,984	5,482[a]	59.9	54.4[a]
Completed	4,824	4,573	48.3	45.4
Forcible entry	1,856	1,725	18.6	17.1
Unlawful entry without force	2,968	2,847	29.7	28.2
Attempted forcible entry	1,160	910[a]	11.6	9.0[a]
Motor vehicle theft	1,961	1,764	19.6	17.5[b]
Completed	1,291	1,172	12.9	11.6
Attempted	670	591	6.7	5.9
Theft	24,238	23,765	242.6	235.7[b]
Completed[3]	23,020	22,743	230.4	225.6
Less than $50	9,653	9,377	96.6	93.0
$50-$249	7,682	7,874	76.9	78.1
$250 or more	4,253	4,251	42.6	42.2
Attempted	1,218	1,022[a]	14.3	10.1[a]

Note: Completed violent crimes include completed rape, sexual assault, completed robbery with and without injury, aggravated assault with injury, and simple assault with minor injury. The total population age 12 or older was 211,524,770 in 1993; in 1994 it was 213,747,400. The total number of households in 1993 was 99,926,400; in 1994 it was 100,808,030.
...Not applicable.
[a]The difference is significant at the 95% confidence level.
[b]The difference is significant at the 90% confidence level.
[1]The victimization survey cannot measure murder because of the inability to question the victim.
[2]Includes pocket picking, purse snatching, and attempted purse snatching.
[3]Includes thefts in which the amount taken was not ascertained. In 1993 this category accounted for 1,433,000 victimizations and in 1994, 1,241,000 .

FBI data indicated 23,305 homicides and nonnegligent manslaughters were reported to police during 1994 (see box "Murder in the United States, 1994").

In terms of crime rates, for every 1,000 persons age 12 or older, there were 51 victims of violence, including:

— 1 sexual assault,
— 2 rapes or attempted rapes per 1,000,
— 6 completed or attempted robberies,
— 12 aggravated assaults, and
— 31 simple assaults.

Murders were the least frequent violent victimization — about 9 murder victims per 100,000 persons.

Attempted violent crimes accounted for 71% (7.7 million) of the 10.9 million crimes of violence. Attempted violent crimes included attempted rapes, attempted robberies, and attempted or threatened violence — including threats with weapons.

Almost a quarter (2.7 million) of all violent victimizations resulted in an injury to the victim. Minor injuries include bruises, black eyes, or broken teeth. Rape, gun shot or knife wounds, or other injuries requiring hospitalization constitute serious harm.

In 1994 a third of all robberies resulted in an injury to the victim. In 36% of completed and 24% of attempted robberies the victim sustained an injury.

There was little or no change between 1993 and 1994 in most NCVS measured crimes. Comparisons between these years are discussed in more detail on pages 44 and 45.

31 million burglaries, motor vehicle thefts, and household thefts

In 1994 the NCVS measured 31 million household burglaries, motor vehicle thefts, and thefts of other property, accounting for 73% of the more than 42 million victimizations. During the year, households experienced 1.8 million motor vehicle thefts, 5.5 million household burglaries, and 23.8 million thefts of other property.

Of the almost 5.5 million household burglaries, 4.6 million, or 83%, were completed burglaries. In the remaining 0.9 million (17%), the offender attempted forcible entry. In a third of the completed burglaries, the burglar forced entry into the home; in two-thirds, the burglar gained entry through an unlocked door or open window.

Of the 22.7 million completed thefts of property, there were 9.4 million (41%) property thefts of less than $50, 7.9 million (35%) between $50 and $249, 4.3 million (19%) of $250 or more, and 1.2 million (5%) in which the property value was not known.

2. VICTIMOLOGY

Murder in the United States, 1994

In its annual compilation of local police agency statistics for 1994, the FBI reported 23,305 murders and nonnegligent manslaughters — a 5% decrease from the previous year.

The national murder rate was 9 per 100,000 inhabitants.

In its annual report *Crime in the United States*, the FBI defines murder as the willful (nonnegligent) killing of one human being by another. The incidence of murder varies by U.S. region, and characteristics of murder victims vary according to sex, race, and age.

The South and the West, with 56% of the population, accounted for almost 66% of all homicides

	Percent	
Region	Homicides	U.S. population
Total	**100%**	**100%**
South	42	35
West	23	21
Midwest	20	24
Northeast	16	20

Supplemental demographic information was available for 22,076 murder victims. About 51% of these victims were black, 46% were white, and the remainder were Asians, Pacific Islanders, and Native Americans.

Victims were likely to be male and relatively young: 78% were male and 65% were under age 35. About 11% were under age 18.

Forty-seven percent of murder victims were related to or acquainted with their assailants; 13% of victims were murdered by strangers, while 40% of victims had an unknown relationship to their murderer.

Husbands or boyfriends killed 28% of female murder victims; wives or girlfriends, 3% of male victims.

Expressed as rates per 1,000 households, there were 54 burglaries, 18 motor vehicle thefts, and 236 property thefts.

Victimizations reported to law enforcement authorities

Overall, 42% of the violent crimes committed in 1994 were reported to police (table 2). Thirty-six percent of rapes, 20% of attempted rapes, and 41% of sexual assaults were brought to the attention of law enforcement

authorities. Fifty-five percent of robberies, 52% of aggravated assaults, and 36% of simple assaults were reported to police.

Victims reported approximately a third of all property crimes. Motor vehicle theft was the most frequently reported property crime (78%), and theft of

Table 2. Victimizations reported to the police, 1993-94: Estimates from the redesigned National Crime Victimization Survey

Type of crime	Number of victimizations reported (1,000's)		Percent of victimizations reported to the police	
	1993	1994	1993	1994
All crimes	15,299	15,187	35.1%	35.9%
Personal crimes[a]	4,654	4,673	40.9%	41.2%
Crimes of violence	4,514	4,513	41.6	41.6
Completed violence	1,723	1,752	53.6	54.7
Attempted/threatened violence	2,791	2,761	36.5	36.1
Rape/Sexual assault	140	137	28.8	31.7
Rape/attempted rape	106	90	34.0	28.3
Rape	56	61	34.7	36.1
Attempted rape	51	29	33.4	19.6
Sexual assault	33	47	19.4	40.7
Robbery	724	719	56.1	55.4
Completed/property taken	551	512	67.6	64.4
With injury	189	192	69.0	66.7
Without injury	362	320	66.9	63.1
Attempted to take property	173	207	36.3	41.1
With injury	46	65	48.3	53.4
Without injury	127	142	33.3	37.2
Assault	3,650	3,657	40.2	40.1
Aggravated	1,362	1,278	53.2	51.6
With injury	414	411	58.1	60.6
Threatened with weapon	948	867	51.3	48.2
Simple	2,288	2,379	35.2	35.8
With minor injury	671	727	49.5	49.6
Without injury	1,617	1,652	31.4	31.9
Personal theft[b]	140	160	27.0%	32.6%
Property crimes	10,646	10,514	33.1%	33.9%
Household burglary	2,924	2,770	48.9	50.5
Completed	2,492	2,425	51.7	53.0
Forcible entry	1,391	1,308	75.0	75.8
Unlawful entry without force	1,101	1,117	37.1	39.2
Attempted forcible entry	432	345	37.3	37.9
Motor vehicle theft	1,523	1,379	77.7	78.2
Completed	1,206	1,083	93.4	92.4
Attempted	317	296	47.4	50.0
Theft	6,198	6,365	25.6	26.8
Completed[c]	5,850	6,061	25.4	26.6
Less than $50	1,147	1,218	11.9	13.0
$50-$249	1,987	2,097	25.9	26.6
$250 or more	2,424	2,462	57.0	57.9
Attempted	348	304	28.6	29.8

Note: Completed violent crimes include completed rape, sexual assault, completed robbery with and without injury, aggravated assault with injury, and simple assault with minor injury.
[a]The victimization survey cannot measure murder because of the inability to question the victim. Personal crimes include purse snatching and pocket picking, not shown separately under personal theft.
[b]Includes pocket picking, purse snatching, and attempted purse snatching.
[c]Includes thefts in which the amount taken was not ascertained.

8. Criminal Victimization 1994

other property the least reported crime (27%).

The 1994 data indicated patterns in reporting to police. For example, victims were more likely to report incidents to police where:

— violent crimes were completed
— an injury resulted
— items valued at $250 or more were stolen
— forcible entry occurred.

Victims cite many reasons for deciding whether or not to report particular crimes to law enforcement authorities.*

Victims of violent incidents most often cite as a reason for reporting the crime to the police the desire to prevent future acts of violence. Victims also reported incidents because they thought it was the right thing to do.

Among victims who chose not to report a violent crime to the police, many indicated that they felt the matter was private or personal in nature.

Victims of personal and property thefts frequently reported the incidents to enable recovery of their stolen property and to collect insurance, or chose not to report because they had been able to recover their property or because the theft attempt had been unsuccessful.

Characteristics of victims of violence

Males, blacks, Hispanics, the young, the poor, and inner city dwellers were the most vulnerable to violence (table 3).

Except for rape/sexual assault, every violent crime victimization rate for males was higher than for females.

Males were about twice as likely as females to experience robbery and aggravated assault. However, there were 4 rapes or sexual assaults per 1,000 females age 12 or older compared to 0.2 rapes per 1,000 males.

Blacks were more likely than whites or persons of other races — Asians or Native Americans — to be victims of robbery or aggravated assault.

*For analysis of reasons why victims reported or did not report crimes, see *Criminal Victimization in the United States, 1993,* BJS, NCJ-15157.

In 1994 there were 16.6 aggravated assaults per 1,000 black persons, 10.9 per 1,000 whites, and 11.9 per 1,000 persons in other racial categories. The victimization rates for rape/sexual assault were not significantly different among the three racial groups.

Persons under age 25 had higher violent victimization rates than those 65 or older. Persons age 16 to 19 were about 30 times more likely than persons age 65 or older to be victimized by assault.

Hispanics had higher violent crime rates than Non-Hispanics.

Persons from households with lower incomes were more vulnerable to violent crime than those from higher income households. Persons with household incomes of less than $15,000 per year had significantly higher violent crime rates for all categories of violent crime when compared with those who had household incomes of $15,000 or more per year.

	Rates per 1,000 persons age 12 or older	
Type of crime	Annual household income of less than $15,000	Annual household income of $15,000 or more
Violent crime	68.6	46.9
Rape/sexual assault	4.7	1.3
Robbery	8.7	4.9
Aggravated assault	16.5	10.6
Simple assault	38.8	30.2

Table 3. Victimization rates for persons age 12 or older, by type of crime, sex, age, race, ethnicity, income, and locality of residence of victims, 1994

	Victimizations per 1,000 persons age 12 or older							
		Crimes of violence						
					Assault			
Characteristics	All crime	All crimes of violence	Rape/ Sexual assault	Robbery	Total	Aggra-vated	Simple	Personal theft
Sex								
Male	61.7	59.6	.2	8.1	51.3	15.3	35.9	2.0
Female	45.1	42.5	3.7	4.1	34.7	8.1	26.6	2.5
Age								
12-15	117.4	114.8	3.1	12.0	99.7	22.2	77.6	2.6
16-19	125.9	121.7	5.1	11.8	104.8	33.7	71.1	4.2
20-24	102.5	99.2	5.0	11.3	82.9	26.6	56.4	3.3
25-34	63.2	60.9	2.9	7.5	50.6	13.7	36.9	2.3
35-49	41.4	39.5	1.6	5.2	32.8	7.6	25.2	1.9
50-64	16.8	15.1	.2*	2.3	12.6	3.3	9.3	1.7
65 or older	7.2	5.1	.1*	1.4	3.6	1.2	2.4	2.1
Race								
White	51.5	49.4	1.9	4.8	42.7	10.9	31.8	2.1
Black	65.4	61.8	2.7	14.0	45.0	16.6	28.4	3.6
Other	49.1	47.6	2.5*	9.0	36.1	11.9	24.2	1.6*
Ethnicity								
Hispanic	63.3	59.8	2.6	9.8	47.4	16.2	31.2	3.5
Non-Hispanic	51.9	49.8	2.0	5.6	42.1	11.1	31.0	2.1
Household income								
Less than $7,500	88.3	83.6	6.7	11.1	65.8	20.5	45.3	4.7
$7,500-$14,999	60.8	58.6	3.3	7.1	48.1	13.8	34.3	2.2
$15,000-$24,999	51.7	49.9	2.3	5.9	41.7	13.2	28.5	1.8
$25,000-$34,999	51.3	49.3	1.2	4.6	43.5	11.3	32.3	2.0
$35,000-$49,999	49.3	46.8	.9	4.8	41.1	10.1	31.0	2.6
$50,000-$74,999	47.6	46.1	.8	4.2	41.1	9.5	31.6	1.5
$75,000 or more	42.7	40.0	.9*	4.5	34.6	8.0	26.5	2.7
Residence								
Urban	67.6	63.6	2.7	10.9	50.1	14.8	35.2	4.0
Suburban	51.8	49.6	1.8	5.1	42.7	11.0	31.7	2.2
Rural	39.8	39.2	1.7	2.6	34.9	9.2	25.8	.6

Note: The victimization survey cannot measure murder because of the inability to question the victim.

*Estimate is based on about 10 or fewer sample cases.

43

2. VICTIMOLOGY

Higher property crime victimization rates: households of blacks, Hispanics, the poor, urban dwellers, and renters

Minorities, urban dwellers, and those who rent their homes experienced the highest rates of property crime. The impact of income varied, depending on the type of property crime.

Black households suffered higher rates of property victimization for all property crime than did white households (341 versus 302 per 1,000 households, respectively).

dents (296) or rural area dwellers (246).

Renters had significantly higher property crime rates than home owners.

Recent trends

Between 1993 and 1994 there were no changes in violent crimes measured by NCVS, except for a decline in sexual assault. While sexual assault decreased, the overall rape/sexual assault category showed no change.

Motor vehicle theft and property theft rates showed statistically significant declines between 1993 and 1994. There was some evidence of declines in the rates and levels of overall property crimes, household burglary, attempted forcible entry, and attempted theft.

Since its inception in 1973, the survey has identified fluctuations in crime levels and rates over extended periods. Because of the survey design, the data presented in this bulletin are not directly comparable with data collected prior to 1993. While some crimes exhibit short-term changes that differ from previous longer-term trends, many patterns discernible for 1992-94 continue general trends in crime rates that existed during previous years.

Violent crime rates generally declined from 1981 to 1986 (a drop of 20%), and then rose from 1986 to 1991 (up 15%). Since 1992, violent crime victimization rates have remained generally stable. Both victimization levels and rates show little change in 1992, 1993, and 1994 (table 5).

Robbery rates increased slightly during the late 1980's, but never reached the peak rates experienced earlier in the decade. Since 1992 the robbery rate has remained unchanged.

Aggravated assault levels have shown yearly fluctuations but the overall trend was slightly downward from 1974 to 1991. Neither the increase in

Table 4. Property victimization rates, by type of crime, race, ethnicity, income, residence, and form of tenure of head of household, 1994

	Victimizations per 1,000 households			
Characteristics	Total	Burglary	Motor vehicle theft	Theft
Race				
White	301.9	51.7	15.6	234.6
Black	341.3	70.8	26.6	243.8
Other	334.9	64.3	34.1	236.5
Ethnicity				
Hispanic	425.5	71.0	39.9	314.5
Non-Hispanic	298.0	53.1	15.6	229.3
Household Income				
Less than $7,500	295.8	78.6	13.9	203.2
$7,500-$14,999	296.6	65.4	15.2	216.0
$15,000-$24,999	307.0	60.5	16.3	230.2
$25,000-$34,999	307.1	50.9	20.0	236.3
$35,000-$49,999	325.8	51.6	17.0	257.2
$50,000-$74,999	356.3	39.6	20.7	296.0
$75,000 or more	356.6	40.9	17.7	297.9
Residence				
Urban	376.4	69.4	29.3	277.7
Suburban	296.5	46.5	15.6	234.3
Rural	246.4	49.6	6.9	189.8
Form of tenure				
Home owned	272.2	45.5	14.5	212.2
Home rented	371.2	70.3	22.8	278.1

Hispanic households had a significantly higher rate of property crime victimization than non-Hispanics (426 incidents per 1,000 households versus 298, respectively) (table 4).

Households earning $50,000 or more annually had a theft rate 50% higher than those households earning less than $7,500 annually. Households earning under $7,500 a year suffered almost twice the rate of household burglary compared to those with the highest annual earnings.

City residents experienced higher rates of property crime (376 per 1,000 households) than either suburban resi-

Table 5. Victimization rates and comparison of changes in victimization rates for violent and property crimes, 1992-94

	Victimization rates per 1,000			Percent change of victimizations per 1,000	
Type of crime	1992	1993	1994	1992-94	1993-94
Crimes of violence	49.3	51.3	50.8	3.0%	-1.0%
Rape/Sexual assault	2.9	2.3	2.0	-31.0	-13.0
Robbery	6.2	6.1	6.1	-1.6	0
Assault	40.2	42.9	42.7	6.2	-.5
Aggravated assault	11.1	12.1	11.6	4.5	-4.1
Simple assault	29.1	30.8	31.1	6.9	1.0
Personal theft*	2.3	2.4	2.3	0	-4.2%
Property crimes	325.3	322.1	307.6	-5.4%	-4.5%
Household burglary	58.7	59.9	54.4	-7.3	-9.2
Motor vehicle theft	18.6	19.6	17.5	-5.9	-10.7
Theft	248.0	242.6	235.7	-5.0	-2.8

*Includes pocket picking, purse snatching, and attempted purse snatching.

aggravated assault from 1992 to 1993 nor the decrease from 1993 to 1994 is statistically significant.

Theft rates declined slightly in 1994 from the previous year, continuing a steady decrease that has persisted since 1979.

Burglary rates continued a downward trend that has existed since the survey began in 1973.

Motor vehicle theft rates steadily increased for several years beginning in the mid-1980's. There is some

8. Criminal Victimization 1994

evidence of a decline in the motor vehicle theft rate from 1993 to 1994.

Except for an increase in reporting of sexual assault and theft, there were no statistically significant changes in reporting of crimes to police between 1993 and 1994 (table 6).

Juvenile victims

Teenagers and young adults were more likely to become victims of violent crime than older persons. In 1994, about a third of all victims of violent crime were ages 12 to 19. Almost half of all victims of violence were under age 25.

In the same year, there were 111 rapes/sexual assaults, robberies, or aggravated or simple assaults for every 1,000 persons under age 25.

This rate was more than twice as high as that for persons between ages 25 and 49 and about 11 times as high as that for persons age 50 or older (table 7).

Table 6. Number of victimizations experienced and percent reported to the police, 1993-94

| | Victimizations | | | | | |
| | Number (1,000's) | | | Percent reported to the police | | |
Type of crime	1993	1994	Percent change, 1993-94	1993	1994	Difference between percents, 1994-93
All crimes	43,547	42,359	-2.7%	35.1%	35.9%	.8
Personal crimes	11,365	11,349	-.1	40.9	41.2	.3
Crimes of violence	10,848	10,860	.1	41.6	41.6	0
Rape/Sexual assault	485	433	-10.7	28.8	31.7	2.9
Rape/sexual attempted	313	316	1.0	34.0	28.3	-5.7
Sexual assault	173	117	-32.4	19.4	40.7	21.3
Robbery	1,291	1,299	.6	56.1	55.4	-.7
Assault	9,072	9,128	.6	40.2	40.1	-.1
Aggravated	2,563	2,478	-3.3	53.2	51.6	-1.6
Simple	6,509	6,650	2.2	35.2	35.8	.6
Personal theft*	517	489	5.4%	27.0%	32.6%	5.6
Property crimes	32,182	31,011	-3.6%	33.1%	33.9%	.8
Household burglary	5,984	5,482	-8.4	48.9	50.5	1.6
Motor vehicle theft	1,961	1,764	-10.0	77.7	78.2	.5
Completed	1,291	1,171	-9.3	93.4	92.4	-1.0
Attempted	670	591	-11.8	47.4	50.0	2.6
Theft	24,238	23,765	-2.0	25.6	26.8	1.2

*Includes pocketpicking, purse snatching, and attempted purse snatching.

While making up 23% of the population age 12 or older, persons from 12 to 24 were victims of almost half of all violent crime

Victim's age	Percent of population 12 or older	Percent of violent victimizations
Total	100%	100%
12 to 15	7	16
16 to 19	7	16
20 to 24	8	17
25 to 34	20	23
35 to 49	28	21
50 to 64	16	5
65 or older	14	1

These large differences in victimization rates by age occurred for each of the violent crimes measured by the survey. For example, there were 4 rape/sexual assaults per 1,000 for persons under age 25, 2 per 1,000 for those ages 25 to 49, and 0.1 per 1,000 for those age 50 or more.

Rates for robbery were twice as high for those under 25 as for those ages 25 to 49. For persons under age 25, the robbery rates were 12 per 1,000 compared with 2 per 1,000 for those persons age 50 or more.

Table 7. Rates of violent victimizations by age of victim, 1992-94

Type of crime by age of victim	Victimization rates per 1,000			Percent distribution		
	1992	1993	1994	1992	1993	1,994
All violent crime	49	51	51	100%	100%	100%
12 to 15	114	121	115	16	17	16
16 to 19	107	117	122	15	15	16
20 to 24	98	94	99	18	16	17
25 to 34	58	59	61	24	23	23
35 to 49	39	43	40	21	23	22
50 to 64	13	17	15	4	5	5
65 or older	5	6	5	2	2	1
Robbery	6	6	6	100%	100%	100%
12 to 15	13	14	12	15	16	14
16 to 19	11	12	12	12	12	13
20 to 24	14	11	11	21	15	16
25 to 34	8	7	8	27	24	24
35 to 49	4	5	5	16	22	23
50 to 64	2	3	2	6	8	6
65 or older	2	1	1	5	3	3
Aggravated assault	11	12	12	100%	100%	100%
12 to 15	20	23	22	13	14	14
16 to 19	27	30	34	16	16	19
20 to 24	23	27	27	19	20	20
25 to 34	13	15	14	23	24	23
35 to 49	10	9	8	23	20	18
50 to 64	3	4	3	4	5	5
65 or older	1	1	1	2	1	1

2. VICTIMOLOGY

The rates of aggravated assault were almost 3 times as high for victims under 25 as for those ages 25 to 49.

	Rates per 1,000 persons age 12 or older		
Type of crime	12-24	25-49	50 or older
Violent crime	110.9	48.4	10.3
Rape/sexual assault	4.4	2.1	.1
Robbery	11.7	6.1	1.9
Aggravated assault	27.3	10.1	2.3
Simple assault	67.5	30.0	6.0

Examining violent incidents

Excluding those crimes in which the victim/offender relationship was not known, 53% of persons victimized by violence did not know their assailant. Almost 8 out of 10 robberies were committed by strangers compared to 3 out of 10 of all rapes/sexual assaults. Just over half of all rapes/sexual assaults were committed by people either well-known or casually known to the victim (table 8).

While overall violent crimes were about as likely to occur during the day as during the night, some crimes exhibited different patterns.

Fifty-three percent of incidents of violent crime occurred between 6 a.m. and 6 p.m. About two-thirds of simple assaults, compared to a third of aggravated assaults, took place during these hours. Approximately two-thirds of rapes/sexual assaults occurred at night — 6 p.m. to 6 a.m.

In 1994 about a quarter of incidents of violent crime occurred at or near the victim's home. Among common locales for violent crimes were on the street other than those near the victim's home (20%), at school (13%), or at a commercial establishment (13%).

Twenty-three percent of victims of violent crime reported being involved in some form of leisure activity away from home at the time of their victimization. Twenty-two percent said they were at home, and another 22% mentioned they were at work or traveling to or from work when the crime occurred.

One in five violent crimes occurred in or near the victim's home. Including these, almost half occurred within a mile from home and about 70% within five miles. Only 5% of victims of violent crime reported that the crime took place more than fifty miles from their home.

In 3 out of 10 incidents of violent crimes, offenders used or threatened to use a weapon. NCVS defines assaults involving weapons as aggravated; thus almost all aggravated assaults (95%) involved a weapon. (Assaults without weapons are classified as aggravated if the victim suffers a serious injury.) Offenders had or used a weapon in slightly more than half of all robberies, compared with 16% of all rapes/sexual assaults.

Summary of crime characteristics

Rapes/sexual assaults

• Two-thirds were committed by someone acquainted with, known to, or related to the victim.

• Two-thirds occurred in the evening or at night.

Table 8. Victim-offender relationship, victim's activity, weapons, and characteristics of the criminal incident, by crimes of violence, 1994

	Crimes of violence					
	Total violent crime	Rape/ Sexual assault	Robbery	Assault		
Characteristics of incident				Total	Aggravated	Simple
Total	100%	100%	100%	100%	100%	100%
Victim/offender relationship*						
Relatives	9%	11%	6%	9%	7%	10%
Well-known	23	35	13	24	21	25
Casual acquaintance	15	21	3	16	12	18
Stranger	53	33	77	51	60	48
Time of day						
6 a.m. to 6 p.m.	53%	31%	42%	62%	36%	62%
6 p.m. to midnight	35	37	43	37	33	33
Midnight to 6 a.m.	12	32	15	1	32	5
Location of crime						
At or near victim's home or lodging	26%	37%	24%	26%	25%	26%
Friend's/relative's/neighbor's home	7	21	4	7	9	7
Commercial places	13	7	8	14	11	15
Parking lots/garages	8	6	12	7	9	7
School	13	3	4	15	7	18
Streets other than near victim's home	20	8	37	18	26	15
Other*	13	17	10	13	12	13
Victim's activity						
At work or traveling to or from work	22%	8%	16%	23%	21%	24%
School	13	5	7	14	8	16
Activities at home	22	38	17	22	19	23
Shopping/errands	4	2	11	3	4	3
Leisure activities away from home	23	32	21	23	28	21
Traveling	10	6	20	9	12	7
Other	7	8	8	7	9	6
Distance from victim's home						
Inside home or lodging	5%	34%	14%	14%	12%	14%
Near victim's home	16	10	13	15	16	15
1 mile or less	24	12	29	21	22	21
5 miles or less	26	14	22	24	25	24
50 miles or less	24	23	19	22	20	22
More than 50 miles	5	6	4	4	5	4
Weapons [b]						
No weapons present	71%	84%	45%	73%	5%	100%
Weapons present	29	16	55	27	95	0
Firearm	12	6	31	10	35	0
Other type of weapon [c]	17	10	25	17	60	0

*Excludes "don't know" relationships.
[a]Includes areas on street other than near victim's home, on public transportation or inside station, in apartment yard, park, field, playground, and other areas.
[b]An aggravated assault is any assault in which an offender possesses or uses a weapon or inflicts serious injury.
[c]Includes knives, other sharp objects, blunt objects, and other types of weapons.

46

8. Criminal Victimization 1994

- About 6 in 10 occurred in the victim's or someone else's home.

- More than a third occurred as the victim engaged in activities in the home; another third occurred during leisure activities away from the home.

- Offenders had a weapon in 16% of all rape/sexual assault victimizations.

Robberies

- Almost 8 in 10 were committed by strangers.

- About 4 in 10 occurred in the daytime; another 4 in 10 occurred in the evening before midnight.

- Robberies occurred in a variety of situations:

— 1 in 5 during leisure activities
— 1 in 5 during travel and almost 1 in 5 at home
— 1 in 6 while at work or commuting to/from work
— 1 in 10 while shopping
— 1 in 14 at school.

- Weapons were present in 55% of robberies.

- More than half occurred at or within a mile of the victim's home.

Assaults

- Strangers committed 1 in 2 simple assaults and 6 in 10 aggravated assaults.

- Simple assaults were almost twice as likely as aggravated assaults to be committed during the daytime.

- For both aggravated and simple assaults, about 1 in 4 occurred at or near the victim's home.

- 25% of aggravated assaults and 15% of simple assaults occurred on streets other than near the victim's home.

- In aggravated assaults, offenders had a firearm in more than 1 in 3 incidents and another type of weapon in 6 of 10. Simple assaults do not involve the use of weapons.

Survey methodology

The National Crime Victimization Survey measures personal and household offenses, including crimes not reported to police, by interviewing all the occupants age 12 or older of housing units that have been selected to comprise a representative sample. The sample also includes persons living in group quarters, such as dormitories, rooming houses, and religious group dwellings. Excluded are crew members of merchant vessels, Armed Forces personnel living in military barracks or temporary housing, and institutionalized persons, such as correctional facility inmates and hospital or hospice patients.

A Bureau of the Census representative interviews each housing unit at 6-month intervals, spreading out the complete sample of household interviews over the entire year. In 1994, Bureau of the Census interviewed approximately 120,000 residents in 56,000 housing units about the crimes they had experienced in the previous 6 months. Response rates were 96% of eligible housing units and 92% of individuals in interviewed households.

Since sample survey data provide the estimates in the Bulletin, these estimates are subject to sampling variation. Comparisons presented in this report are statistically significant at the 95% confidence level, meaning that the estimated difference is greater than twice the standard error. Statements of comparison qualified by language such as "slightly," "somewhat," or "marginal" indicate statistical significance at the 90% level (1.6 standard error).

The NCVS redesign

Data based on the redesign are not comparable to data before 1993. *Criminal Victimization 1993* was the first yearly Bulletin that presented data from the redesigned survey. A number of fundamental changes were introduced when the survey was redesigned. These changes were phased into the sample over several years. For information about these changes refer to *Criminal Victimization in the United States, 1993*, NCJ-151657.

The Bureau of Justice Statistics is the statistical agency of the U.S. Department of Justice. Jan M. Chaiken, Ph.D., is director.

BJS Bulletins are a publication series that presents the first release of findings from permanent data collection programs.

Craig Perkins and Patsy Klaus of the Bureau of Justice Statistics wrote this report. Bruce Taylor provided statistical review. Tom Hester and Tina Dorsey edited the report. Marilyn Marbrook, assisted by Jayne Robinson and Yvonne Boston, administered production.

April 1996, NCJ-158022

Article 9

TRUE CRIME

> **SUMMARY**
>
> **The media and safety-conscious baby boomers fuel an overwhelming public fear of crime. A close look at the data shows that much of the fear is misplaced. Yet the worst crimes are increasing, and life can be especially dangerous in southern and smaller metros. In the next decade, more criminals and a less tolerant public will transform Americans' lives.**

Cheryl Russell

Cheryl Russell is author of The Official Guide to the American Marketplace *(New Strategist, 1995) and editor-in-chief of New Strategist Publications in Ithaca, New York.*

The hour is late. The city street lies dark and empty. Solitary footsteps echo on the pavement. Ahead, an ominous shape lurks in a storefront. Suddenly you're face to face with a gun-wielding, homicidal maniac. You panic. Is it time to run, or time to turn off the TV?

Crime in America has come home. Ask anyone; they can tick off the names, dates, and grisly details from the Oklahoma bombing, the O.J. Simpson double-murder trial, the kidnapping and murder of Polly Klaas, the drowning of Susan Smith's children, the roadside slaying of Michael Jordan's father, the Long Island Railroad massacre, the never-ending string of post office shootings, and on and on. Crime was the number-one issue of concern to the public in 1994, according to the Conference Board. Ninety percent of Americans say that crime is a "serious" problem.

No one escapes the repercussions of Americans' obsession with crime. Some segments of the economy even profit from it. Forty-three percent of Americans have had special locks installed on their doors, and 18 percent have burglar alarms, according to a 1993 Gallup Poll. Half of American households own guns, and sales of personal-security devices such as mace and pepper spray have been brisk in recent years.

More businesses are hurt than helped by the fear of crime. Downtown areas lose shoppers to suburban shopping malls, while tourists and homebuyers shy away from areas where the media have publicized particularly heinous offenses.

Not only do Americans think crime is a terrible problem; they believe it's getting worse. Nearly nine in ten say there was more crime in 1993 in the U.S. than there was a year before, according to a Gallup poll. This perspective accounts for the popularity of a get-tough attitude toward criminals, from stiffer penalties for juvenile offenders to three-strikes-you're-out life terms for repeat felony criminals. Support for the death penalty has grown from just under 50 percent in the early 1960s to 80 percent in 1994.

But is crime really overwhelming America? The public says yes, but crime statistics are contradictory—and so are the experts. Separating the myths from the facts is the best way to understand the current mood of the public. And when you take a close look, one thing becomes clear. Every organization should position itself for a future in which fear of crime is likely to play a major role.

FUEL FOR FEAR

Crime has become a hot issue for a number of reasons, beginning with the

From *American Demographics* magazine, August 1995, pp. 22-31. © 1995 by American Demographics, Inc. Reprinted by permission.

9. True Crime

The Books on Crime

The two sets of government crime statistics are contradictory, but both agree that violent crime is increasing.

WHAT POLICE REPORTS SAY

(crimes reported to police per 100,000 population in 1992, 1984, and 1974, by type of crime, and percent change in crime rate, 1984-92 and 1974-92)

	1992	1984	1974	percent change 1984-92	percent change 1974-92
violent crime, total	757.5	539.2	461.1	40.5%	64.3%
rape	42.8	35.7	26.2	19.9	63.4
robbery	263.6	205.4	209.3	28.3	25.9
aggravated assault	441.8	290.2	215.8	52.2	104.7
property crime, total	4,902.7	4,492.1	4,389.3	9.1	11.7
burglary	1,168.2	1,263.7	1,437.7	–7.6	–18.7
larceny	3,103.0	2,791.3	2,489.5	11.2	24.6
motor-vehicle theft	631.5	437.1	462.2	44.5	36.6

WHAT CRIME VICTIMS SAY

(victimizations per 100,000 people aged 12 or older or per 100,000 households, in 1992, 1984, and 1974, and percent change in victimization rate, 1984-92 and 1974-92)

	1992	1984	1974	percent change 1984-92	percent change 1974-92
violent crime, total	3,210	3,140	3,300	2.2%	–2.7%
rape	70	90	100	–27.3	–30.0
robbery	590	570	720	4.0	–17.3
aggravated assault	900	900	1,040	–0.5	–13.8
property crime, total	15,220	17,870	23,570	–14.8	–35.4
burglary	4,890	6,410	9,310	–23.7	–47.5
larceny	8,320	9,940	12,380	–16.3	–32.8
motor-vehicle theft	2,010	1,520	1,880	32.2	6.9

Source: Federal Bureau of Investigation, Uniform Crime Reports 1993; and Bureau of Justice Statistics Bulletin, Criminal Victimization 1992, October 1993

media. The public's concern with crime rises and falls in lockstep with media reporting about the issue. High-profile crimes create sensational news coverage. And the greater the news coverage, the larger the proportion of Americans who cite crime as the most important problem facing the country, according to a 1994 analysis in *The Public Perspective* by Jeffrey D. Alderman, director of polling for ABC News. Public concern with crime follows news coverage of crimes with an exactness that proves the importance of the media in shaping public opinion.

In 1994, a *Los Angeles Times* poll asked Americans whether their feelings about crime were based on what they read or saw in the media, or on what they had personally experienced. While 65 percent named the media, only 21 percent named personal experience, and 13 percent said both.

Another reason for the public's heightened concern about crime is the expansion of the middle-aged population. People in the huge baby-boom generation, now aged 31 to 49, are more concerned than young adults about crime. Baby boomers are also more active in protecting themselves from crime. People aged 30 to 49 are more likely than those younger or older to have installed special locks, to have a dog for protection, to have bought a gun, to carry a weapon, or to have a burglar alarm.

In 1995, 38 percent of all American adults are in the 35-to-54 age group, a larger proportion than at any time since the 1950s. The share in this age group will rise to 40 percent by 2000. The middle-aged population is struggling to protect its homes, careers, financial assets, and especially its children. No wonder crime is one of its top concerns.

There is some evidence that the public's fear of crime is driven by a burgeoning population of parents and the crime-crazy media, but not by the facts. Overall crime rates are lower today than they were in the early 1980s. At that time, baby boomers were crime-prone young adults who drove the rates up. And while

> **Sixty-one percent of Americans say they feel "very safe" at home.**

most Americans believe the crime problem is severe, they think it is much worse elsewhere than it is in their community. Seventy-nine percent of Americans think crime is one of the nation's biggest problems, but only 14 percent name crime as one of the biggest problems in their neighborhood. Sixty-one percent of Americans say they feel "very safe" at home. And most Americans say they are not afraid to walk alone at night near their home.

The average American's fear of crime may be a fear for the future. Forty-three percent say that crime in their local area is increasing. While most Americans feel safe in their home and neighborhood, many do not feel secure in their community or when traveling elsewhere. These feelings will intensify in the years ahead, because those most afraid of crime are a growing segment of the population. Moreover, the worst crime does appear to be on the rise.

A LOOK AT THE DATA

How bad is the crime scene? The answer isn't easy to find, because the United

2. VICTIMOLOGY

The Most Violent Metros

Many smaller metropolitan areas have higher rates of violent crime than the bigger metros Americans fear the most.

(50 metropolitan areas with the largest number of violent crimes* per 100,000 population, 1993)

rank	metropolitan area	violent crime rate	rank	metropolitan area	violent crime rate
1	Miami, FL	2,136.2	26	Orlando, FL	1,118.2
2	New York, NY	1,865.5	27	Memphis,TN-AR-MS	1,109.3
3	Alexandria, LA	1,833.0	28	Nashville, TN	1,098.7
4	Los Angeles-Long Beach, CA	1,682.4	29	Stockton-Lodi, CA	1,091.6
5	Tallahassee, FL	1,546.0	30	Riverside-San Bernardino, CA	1,089.8
6	Baton Rouge, LA	1,510.7	31	San Francisco, CA	1,088.1
7	Little Rock-North Little Rock, AR	1,453.1	32	Fresno, CA	1,084.6
8	Jacksonville, FL	1,419.9	33	Greenville-Spartanburg-Anderson, SC	1,080.0
9	Pueblo, CO	1,403.9	34	Fayetteville, NC	1,076.5
10	Baltimore, MD	1,356.1	35	Pine Bluff, AR	1,058.8
11	Gainesville, FL	1,328.6	36	Waco, TX	1,052.6
12	New Orleans, LA	1,312.6	37	Florence, SC	1,045.8
13	Jackson, TN	1,294.7	38	El Paso, TX	1,031.0
14	Albuquerque, NM	1,273.6	39	Newark, NJ	1,030.9
15	Tampa-St. Petersburg-Clearwater, FL	1,223.4	40	Tuscaloosa, AL	1,009.3
16	Charlotte-Gastonia-Rock Hill, NC-SC	1,204.4	41	Fort Lauderdale, FL	1,005.4
17	Anniston, AL	1,183.6	42	Modesto, CA	992.1
18	Sumter, SC	1,179.1	43	Albany, GA	990.0
19	Gadsden, AL	1,177.5	44	Shreveport-Bossier City, LA	987.9
20	Birmingham, AL	1,146.8	45	Lakeland-Winter Haven, FL	984.3
21	Jersey City, NJ	1,144.1	46	Lake Charles, LA	977.7
22	Ocala, FL	1,141.7	47	Greenville, NC	975.5
23	Oakland, CA	1,137.5	48	Monroe, LA	973.5
24	Sioux City, IA-NE	1,133.8	49	Las Vegas, NV-AZ	959.5
25	Columbia, SC	1,129.1	50	Vineland-Millville-Bridgeton, NJ	953.2

* *Murder, rape, robbery, aggravated assault*

Source: Crime in the United States, *1993, Federal Bureau of Investigation, 1994*

States keeps two sets of books on crime. One, the FBI's Uniform Crime Reports (UCR), is an annual collection of reported crime in over 16,000 communities across the country. The figures are voluntarily submitted to the FBI by police agencies in those communities. Overall, 95 percent

> **The public's willingness to report crime varies by type of crime.**

of the population is covered by the police agencies that submit their crime data to the FBI, including 97 percent of the metropolitan population and 86 percent of nonmetro residents.

The second data set on crime is the Justice Department's national survey of households, called the National Crime Victimization Survey. In this survey, interviewers ask respondents whether anyone in the household has been a crime victim in the past year. Because many crimes are never reported to police, the National Crime Victimization Survey uncovers much more crime than the police report to the FBI.* By comparing these two data sets, analysts can estimate the amount of crime reported to police.

In 1992, only 39 percent of what the Justice Department refers to as "victimizations" were reported to police. Yet the public's willingness to report crime varies by type of crime. In 1992, the public re-

* *The FBI collects statistics on murder and non-negligent manslaughter, forcible rape, robbery, aggravated assault, burglary, larceny, motor-vehicle theft, and arson. The National Crime Victimization Survey covers all but murder/nonnegligent manslaughter and arson.*

ported 53 percent of rapes, 51 percent of robberies, 49 percent of assaults, 41 percent of household theft, and 30 percent of personal theft. Motor-vehicle theft is most likely to be reported to the police—75 percent in 1992—because such thefts must be reported to make claims on auto insurance.

Over time, the gap between actual and reported crime has narrowed as Americans have become increasingly willing to complain of misdeeds. The 39 percent reporting level of 1992 was up from 32 percent in 1973. The proportion of aggravated assaults reported to the police increased from 52 percent to 62 percent during those years. The proportion of personal theft reported to police rose from 22 to 30 percent. Today's older, better-educated public is more comfortable interacting with authorities than was the

9. True Crime

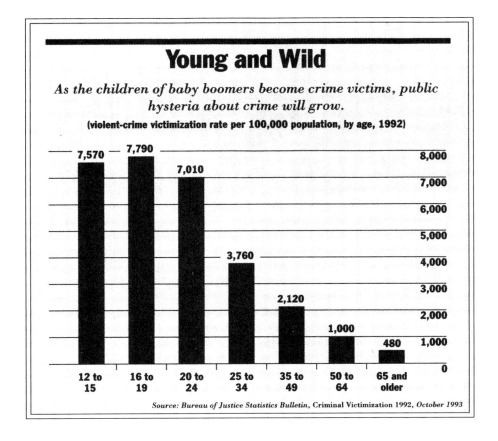

Young and Wild

As the children of baby boomers become crime victims, public hysteria about crime will grow.

(violent-crime victimization rate per 100,000 population, by age, 1992)

- 12 to 15: 7,570
- 16 to 19: 7,790
- 20 to 24: 7,010
- 25 to 34: 3,760
- 35 to 49: 2,120
- 50 to 64: 1,000
- 65 and older: 480

Source: *Bureau of Justice Statistics Bulletin*, Criminal Victimization 1992, October 1993

public of two decades ago. This increases the likelihood of reporting crime. In addition, the introduction of 911 emergency phone services makes it easier for people to report crime.

The two databases on crime seem to contradict each other in many cases. The Uniform Crime Reports show crime rising over the past 20 years, while the National Crime Victimization Survey shows crime falling. The total crime rate rose from 4,850 offenses per 100,000 population in 1974 to 5,660 per 100,000 in 1992, a 17 percent increase, then dropping slightly to 5,483 per 100,000 in 1993, according to the UCR. In contrast, the household survey shows the percentage of households "touched" by crime falling from 32 to 23 percent from 1975 to 1992. The exclusion of murder and arson from the household survey cannot explain this contradiction, because the two datasets show crime rates moving in opposite directions even for specific types of crime. For example, the UCR statistics show the rate of aggravated assault rising from 2.16 to 4.42 assaults per 1,000 people between 1974 and 1992, a 105 percent increase. In contrast, the victimization survey shows the aggravated assault rate falling from 10.4 to 9.0 assaults per 1,000 people aged 12 or older during those years.

The trends revealed by the two datasets agree in only two areas. Both show

> **The introduction of 911 emergency phone services makes it easier for people to report crime.**

burglary declining and motor-vehicle theft rising. But while the FBI finds that the burglary rate fell 19 percent between 1974 and 1992, the household survey says it fell 48 percent. And while the FBI reports that motor-vehicle theft is up 37 percent, the household survey says just 7 percent.

Which dataset is right? The public finds the FBI's rising crime rates most believable, because it is closer to the carnage they see on TV. But most experts believe that the trends revealed in the victimization survey are more accurate because of changes in Americans' propensity to report crime. As people report a larger proportion of crime to police, then the UCR statistics will show an increase even if crime rates remain the same. For example, the fact that a larger proportion of aggravated assaults was reported to police in 1993 than in 1974 could account for much of the increase in aggravated assault reported in the UCR.

The trends in the UCR statistics are questionable because of reporting problems. Yet the trends revealed by the victimization survey may not be completely accurate because they are affected by changes in household size, household location, and the age structure of the population. Single-person households are less likely to be victimized by crime than are larger households. Households in central cities are more likely to be victimized than those in suburban areas. If household size declines and an increasing share of households are located in the suburbs, as in the past 20 years, the proportion of households victimized by crime will decline while crime rates remain unchanged.

The Justice Department reports that if households in 1992 were the same size as those in 1975, the proportion "touched" by crime would have been 23.7 percent in 1992 rather than 22.6 percent. But it would still fall far below the 32 percent of 1975. Adjusting for changes in household location would raise it even further, because it turns out that most of the decline in the proportion of households touched by crime is due to the drop in property crime rather than violent crime. The victimization survey shows the burglary rate dropping by 47 percent between 1973 and 1992, household larceny falling by 22 percent, and personal theft down 35 percent. Violent crime rates, on the other hand, have barely budged.

The changing age structure of the population also affects the crime trends revealed by the victimization survey.

2. VICTIMOLOGY

SAFETY ZONES

City-dwellers on both coasts tend to think that nothing happens in the Midwest. Although Wisconsinites and Minnesotans may resent having their homes portrayed as boring, they can also have the last laugh. One of the things that isn't happening in the Midwest is crime.

Of the ten metropolitan areas with the lowest assault rates, eight are in Wisconsin and Minnesota, according to the 1993 Federal Bureau of Investigation's Uniform Crime Reports. Bangor, Maine, and Provo-Orem, Utah, are the other two. Four Wisconsin metros rank at the bottom of the list for violent crimes in general.

Wausau, Wisconsin, may be the safest metropolitan area in the country. It has the lowest assault and rape rates, second-lowest burglary rate, third-lowest car-theft rate, fourth-lowest murder rate, and ninth-lowest property-crime rate. Its combined violent crime rate in 1993 was 67 per 100,000 people, versus 2,136 in top-ranked Miami. Other Wisconsin metros also rank tops for lack of crime. Appleton-Oshkosh-Neenah, Sheboygan, and La Crosse each appear on three bottom-ten lists, and Eau Claire appears on two.

Wausau's Deputy Police Chief Paul Luoma modestly declines the credit for his town's low crime rates. "We try to be pro-active, and you have to be visible, but I don't think law enforcement can take credit,"Luoma says. "We have a high employment rate—people don't have a lot of time on their hands. The general values of the community and strong education system keep the crime rate low, too."

But even Wausau has an increasing problem with small-gang activity. "It depends on what you call a gang," says Luoma. "Gangs in a small community could be five to ten individuals causing vandalism." The minority population in Wausau has increased tenfold within the last decade, and it con-

sists largely of Hmong and Laotian immigrants who sometimes don't get along. He says the kids band together to create self-assurance. "They put tattoos on their arms, wear their hats a different way, and it's all because they want to be recognized. They're saying 'Hey, I'm a person.'" Luoma acknowledges that there's no short-term solution to these problems.

Sergeant John Roach of Bangor says it's difficult to say why the Maine metro places second-lowest in assault rates, but he attributes some of it to an aggressive pursuit of abusers in domestic assault cases. "We count domestic assaults the same as assaults," Roach says. "If there is any sort of evidence of abuse, the abuser is automatically arrested." He says this is true for the entire state of Maine, not just Bangor.

Outside of the Midwest, metros with older residents and low mobility rates have lower-than-average crime rates. Johnstown, Pennsylvania, has the country's largest share of householders who have not moved since 1959—24 percent—and it also has the nation's lowest property-crime and larceny rates, third-lowest burglary rate, and ninth-lowest car-theft rate. One in five householders in Steubenville-Weirton, Ohio-West Virginia, has stayed put for more than 30 years. The metro has the nation's second-lowest property-crime and larceny rates, fifth-lowest rape and burglary rates, and sixth-lowest car-theft rate.

One expects smaller and more out-of-the-way metros such as Lewiston-Auburn, Maine, and Florence, Alabama, to see less crime than New York and Los Angeles. But one of the country's biggest cities also has relatively low crime rates. Pittsburgh ranks no higher than 81st place out of 245 (see "The Most Violent Metros") metro areas for any of the seven types of crimes studied, and it ranks seventh from the bottom for larceny.

—Jennifer Fulkerson

SAFE HAVENS

Cooler climates seem to put violence on ice.

(metros with the lowest violent crime rate per 100,000 people, 1993)

rank	metropolitan area	violent crime rate
1	Wausau, WI	66.5
2	Eau Claire, WI	91.4
3	Appleton-Oshkosh-Neenah, WI	106.4
4	Sheboygan, WI	116.1
5	Bangor, ME	125.7
6	Provo-Orem, UT	141.9
7	Bismarck, ND	175.2
8	Williamsport, PA	176.9
9	Lewiston-Auburn, ME	183.5
10	Fayetteville-Springdale-Rogers, AR	196.0

Source: Crime in the United States, 1993, *Federal Bureau of Investigation, 1994*

Adults are much more likely to be victimized by crime than are older people. Even if crime rates remain unchanged, the overall crime rate should have dropped over the past two decades due to the aging of the population. The fact that the victimization survey shows no significant decline despite the aging of the population suggests that the age-adjusted rate of violent crime is actually on the rise.

Both datasets show violent crime increasing as a proportion of all crime. In the UCR, violent crime grew from 10 to 14 percent of all reported crime from 1974 to 1993. The victimization survey shows the same trend, with violent crime growing from 15 to 20 percent of all crime during those years. This trend alone is enough to alarm the public, since a larger share of the crime around them is of the most-feared type—the random act of violence committed by a stranger.

The UCR shows the rate of violent crime rising fairly steadily since the mid-1970s, peaking in 1992, and standing just below that peak in 1993. The household survey shows the rate of violent crime rising through the early 1980s, falling slightly, then rising again in the early 1990s. The latest statistics from both surveys show violent crime rates today to be close to their all-time high. No wonder people are alarmed.

The trend in violent crime is especially ominous, because the young-adult population—the segment most likely to commit acts of violence—is currently at a low point, due to the small baby-bust generation. As the young-adult population expands with the children of the baby boom in the next decade or so, we can expect a significant increase in violent crime simply because of demographic change.

SMALL, SOUTHERN, AND DANGEROUS

Crime may be pervasive, but each crime is local. This adds another layer of confusion to the crime story. The media's obsessive reporting of every gory detail has increased the public's fear of crime in areas where well-publicized crimes occur. Because the largest number of crimes occur in the most populous metropolitan areas, many people have an exaggerated sense of danger in these places. At the same time, they feel safe in smaller metropolitan areas that may be more dangerous than some big cities. This public confusion is documented in a 1993 Gallup poll that asked Americans to rank cities according to their danger of crime. Out of a list of 15 cities, Americans correctly ranked Miami and New York as first and second in crime danger. UCR statistics show that the metropolitan area with the highest violent crime rate is Miami, with 2,136 per 100,000 people.* Second is New York, with 1,866. The public ranked Washington, D.C., as the 4th most dangerous city, with two-thirds saying Washington, D.C. is

---

Demogram

Peter Tyler

Age: 26
Occupation: Police officer in a small city
Why he's a police officer: "It's just go, go, go. I like the variety of calls. You see rich and poor, young and old. You'll go from breaking up a fight to untangling an automobile accident to rescuing an animal. It's never boring."
How to avoid being mugged: "Use common sense. Don't go in dark unlit areas. Don't walk through bad areas alone. Don't display your money, like counting it at an ATM. Assume that people are always watching you. If it happens, do what you're told and don't try to be a hero. Try to get a good description. When it's over, get to the phone."
How to avoid a burglary: "If the bad guys really want to get in, they will. So if there's something you really value, take it with you or put it in storage. And this is so obvious, but do lock your windows and doors. When I do saturation detail in areas where a lot of young people live, I can't believe how many places we can get into."
The root of all evil: In his experience, drugs and alcohol are directly involved in the vast majority of robberies and assaults by strangers. "I see zombies walking around strung out at 4 a.m., needing a rock of crack, and I know they'll do anything to get the money."
Crime and the young black officer: "When I'm in plain clothes, I do get the feeling, often, that people are wary of me. Race is sort of the baseline. But a lot depends on how you act and what you wear, so I'm careful not to provoke people. It used to bother me, but at this point it's more amusing than anything else. I'll walk into a store and the clerk will run over to me-'can I help you?'-and then keep an eye on me until I leave. All the time I'm thinking, 'You don't know who I am, and you'd sure be embarrassed if you did.'"

> **We can expect a significant increase in violent crime simply because of demographic change.**

---

* *The National Crime Victimization Survey is not large enough to supply data for metropolitan areas, so the Uniform Crime Reports are the only source of local data on crime.*

2. VICTIMOLOGY

Crime Central

The violent crime rate is dropping in the most violent metros' central cities

(violent crime rate per 100,000 in central cities of the 10 most violent metropolitan areas, 1993, 1994, and percent change 1993-94)

central city	1993	1994	percent change 1993-94
Miami, FL	3,900	3,400	−12.3%
New York, NY	2,100	1,900	−11.0
Alexandria, LA	**	**	**
Los Angeles, CA	2,400	2,100	−13.3
Tallahassee, FL	2,000	1,700	−14.8
Baton Rouge, LA	3,000	2,400	−19.0
Little Rock, AR	3,300	3,000	−10.2
Jacksonville, FL	1,700	1,500	−10.5
Pueblo, CO	1,700	1,400	−17.3
Baltimore, MD	3,000	2,800	−5.3

*See table, p. 25
**Data not available.*

Source: Federal Bureau of Investigation

---

a dangerous place to live or visit. But its violent crime rate (771 per 100,000 people) places it 88th among the 245 metro areas reporting violent crimes to the FBI in 1993. This rate is far below that of San Francisco or Dallas. Yet only 42 percent of the public think San Francisco is dangerous, and just 24 percent think Dallas is dangerous.

The metropolitan area with the third-highest rate of violent crime is one most Americans have never heard of: Alexandria, Louisiana. The fourth is no sur-

> **The rate of violent crime peaks in July and August, when hot weather shortens tempers.**

prise—Los Angeles-Long Beach. Fifth is Tallahassee, Florida. Other lesser-known cities on the top-ten list are Baton Rouge,

Louisiana; Little Rock, Arkansas; Jacksonville, Florida; and Pueblo, Colorado.

The UCR statistics show that the South is a region plagued by crime. Of the ten metros with the highest rates of violent crime, seven are in the South. Of the top 20, 16 are in the South. Of the top 50, 35 are in the South. Several factors account for the South's high rate of crime. One is the warm climate, which allows people to get out and into trouble year-round. The rate of violent crime peaks in July and August, when hot weather shortens tempers, according to the FBI.

Another reason for the South's high rate of violent crime may be the rapid growth of many of the region's metropolitan areas. The list of the nation's fastest-growing metros looks very similar to the list of the most dangerous. Florida alone is home to 9 of the 50 metropolitan areas with the highest rates of violent crime: Miami (1), Tallahassee (5), Jacksonville (8), Gainesville (11), Tampa (15), Ocala (22), Orlando (26), Fort Lauderdale (41), and Lakeland (45). Other fast-growing metros are also on

the list, such as Charlotte-Gastonia, North Carolina (16) and Las Vegas (49). These popular metropolitan areas—many touted as wonderful retirement and recreation areas—have much higher crime rates than the cities Americans fear, such as Atlanta (54th in its rate of violent crime), Boston (85), Washington, D.C. (88), and Philadelphia (114).

The FBI's local crime rates are often criticized by civic leaders in crime-prone cities. And in fact, many variables can skew these data. If fewer robberies are reported in New York City than in Tallahassee, for example, New York's rate will look too low, while Tallahassee's will look too high. When Tallahassee launched an aggressive campaign against sex crimes in the mid-1980s, the number of reported rapes increased three times faster than the overall crime rate. Wherever police are aggressive against criminals but approachable to the public, a high proportion of total crimes will be reported.

Still, the FBI data are the only source of information on local crime rates. And the same regional patterns show up in the crime most difficult to hide: murder. New York ranks 5th and Washington, D.C. ranks 28th among the 255 metropolitan areas that supplied their 1993 murder statistics to the FBI. But the nation's highest murder rate is in New Orleans, followed by Shreveport-Bossier City, Louisiana; Jackson, Mississippi; and Jackson, Tennessee. Of the ten metropolitan areas with the highest murder rates,

> **Of the ten metropolitan areas with the highest murder rates, seven are in the South.**

seven are in the South. Among the top 20, 17 are in the South. Among the top 50, 38 are in the South.

Murder is not included in the Justice Department's victimization survey. But

9. True Crime

the UCR statistics show that 24,530 Americans were murdered in 1993, or 9.5 murders per 100,000 people. This rate is up 20 percent from a low of 7.9 in 1984 and 1985. This is cause for concern, because the increase occurred despite the shrinking size of the crime-prone young-adult population.

THE NEXT DECADE OF CRIME

The experts agree that violent crime will increase in the years ahead, for demographic reasons alone. The number of Americans aged 15 to 24 is projected to rise 14 percent between 1995 and 2005. Those most likely to commit crime or to be victimized by crime are teenagers and young adults. What's more, crime-prone age groups are getting wilder in the 1990s. The violent crime victimization rate for 16-to-19-year-olds rose from 73.8 to 77.9 per 1,000 between 1989 and 1992, according to the Justice Department's

survey. The rate for 12-to-15-year-olds rose from 62.9 to 75.7, and the rate among 20-to-24-year-olds rose from 57.8 to 70.1. Young black men are now so vulnerable to crime that homicide is the leading cause of death for black men aged 15 to 24.

Violent crime may also increase as people's sense of community dwindles. The emergence of highly individualistic generations in the U.S. and other countries has weakened community standards and eroded public trust. The percentage of Americans who think most people can be trusted fell from 55 percent in 1960 to 36 percent in 1993. The emergence of a highly individualistic population that is indifferent toward public judgment has disturbing consequences that ripple through society. One of the consequences is an increase in violence at society's margins.

As violent crime increases in the next decade, the powerful baby-boom generation will have children entering the age

group most likely to be victimized by crime. These converging trends will probably increase public hysteria over crime in years to come. Specifically:

• Expect middle-aged Americans to demand more protection for their children, whether they are toddlers in day care or young adults in college. Institutions of higher education are likely to discover that the old-fashioned policy of *in loco parentis* has powerful advantages as a marketing tool. Strict on-campus discipline will appeal to fearful parents who are unwilling to grant their children inde-

> **When the baby-boom generation retires, it may retreat behind the walls of a gated community.**

T A K I N G   I T   F U R T H E R

ONLINE

Many of the data analyses used to create this article are available online and free to *American Demographics* subscribers. These data are posted as spreadsheets in DBF and WKS formats and are available through our site on the World Wide Web; point your Web browser to http://www.marketingtools.com. If you don't have internet access, dial our electronic bulletin board, modem access number (607) 273-5579.

Our Web site and electronic bulletin board allow you to download rankings of crime rates per 100,000 population based on the FBI's Uniform Crime Reports for 1993. We offer nine tables that cover all metropolitan areas that reported crimes to the FBI. The tables describe the following crimes: overall violent crimes, murder, aggravated assault, rape, robbery, overall property crimes, car theft, burglary, and larceny.

In addition, 1993 and 1994 data are available for these crimes as reported in 194 cities with more than 100,000 population. Please note that 46 metros did not report crime data to the FBI, and an additional 23 are missing some information. These data will be updated on our online services when the 1994 metro data are published in October 1995.

HARDCOPY

To obtain a printed copy of the FBI's Uniform Crime Reports, *Crime in the United States 1993*, call the Superintendent of Documents, U.S. Government Printing Office; telephone (202) 783-3238. A variety of reports analyzing data from the National Crime Victimization Survey are available from the Bureau of Justice Statistics. These include *Crime and the Nation's Households, 1992; Criminal Victimization 1993*; and *Highlights from 20 years of Surveying Crime Victims: The National Crime Victimization Survey, 1973-92*. In addition, the *Sourcebook of Criminal Justice Statistics*, published annually, includes data from both the UCR and the victimization survey. To order these reports, call the Justice Department at (800) 732-3277. Single copies of reports are free.

For more information about international crime statistics, see *Understanding Crime: Experiences of Crime and Crime Control*, edited by Anna Alvazzi del Frate, Ugljesa Zvekic, and Jan J.M. van Dijk, United Nations Interregional Crime and Justice Research Institute, United Nations Publication No. 49, Rome, August 1993, available for $45 from United Nations Publications, telephone (800) 253-9646.

2. VICTIMOLOGY

Most Murderous Metros

Most of the metropolitan areas with the highest murder rates are located in the South.

(50 metropolitan areas with the largest number of murders per 100,000 population, 1993)

rank	metropolitan area	murder rate	rank	metropolitan area	murder rate
1	New Orleans, LA	37.7	26	Monroe, LA	15.8
2	Shreveport-Bossier City, LA	25.8	27	Rocky Mount, NC	15.8
3	Jackson, MS	25.2	28	Washington, DC-MD-VA-WV	15.8
4	Jackson, TN	23.3	29	Galveston-Texas City, TX	15.5
5	New York, NY	23.2	30	Danville, VA	15.3
6	Memphis,TN-AR-MS	21.9	31	Jacksonville, FL	15.1
7	Fayetteville, NC	21.7	32	Vineland-Millville-Bridgeton, NJ	15.0
8	Los Angeles-Long Beach, CA	21.3	33	Montgomery, AL	14.9
9	Gary-Hammond, IN	20.2	34	Dallas,TX	14.6
10	Little Rock-North Little Rock, AR	20.1	35	Riverside-San Bernardino, CA	14.6
11	Alexandria, LA	19.8	36	Savannah, GA	14.6
12	Pine Bluff, AR	19.7	37	Anniston, AL	14.4
13	Birmingham, AL	19.3	38	Oakland, CA	14.4
14	Baton Rouge, LA	19.1	39	Florence, SC	14.2
15	Albany, GA	18.7	40	Laredo, TX	13.9
16	San Antonio, TX	18.6	41	Columbus, GA-AL	13.7
17	Miami, FL	18.1	42	Las Vegas, NV-AZ	13.1
18	Richmond-Petersburg, VA	17.4	43	Mobile, AL	13.0
19	Baltimore, MD	17.2	44	Gadsden, AL	12.9
20	Texarkana, TX-AR	17.1	45	Augusta-Aiken, GA-SC	12.8
21	Fresno, CA	16.9	46	Stockton-Lodi, CA	12.8
22	Charlotte-Gastonia-Rock Hill, NC-SC	16.6	47	Bakersfield, CA	12.5
23	Waco, TX	16.4	48	Flint, MI	12.4
24	Houston, TX	15.9	49	Atlanta, GA	12.2
25	Detroit, MI	15.8	50	Norfolk-Virginia Beach-Newport News, VA-NC	12.1

Source: Crime in the United States, 1993, *Federal Bureau of Investigation, 1994*

pendence at the vulnerable age of 18.

• The public's fear of crime will ensure an ongoing fascination with true crime stories. In this respect, the O.J. Simpson trial is just a harbinger of things to come. Expect at least one major crime story to be at the top of the news at all times from now on.

• The public will shy away from gratuitous fictional violence, because they are so afraid of the real thing. Audiences will demand happy endings from their fiction because there are so many tragedies in real life.

• The personal-security industry will offer increasingly creative high-tech ways to protect oneself, from alarms and security cards to hidden cameras. A growing number of crimes will be captured on videotape and fed to the suppliers of 24-hour news.

• The gun lobby will lose power as an older, educated public demands reasonable compromise in the gun control de-bate. A growing number of politicians will advocate gun control as their constituents tire of random violence.

• Retailers, restaurateurs, shopping malls, office buildings, train stations, and other public places will offer more visible security. Expect growing demand for guards, metal detectors, and escorts. Even neighborhoods will become more security-conscious. When the baby-boom generation retires, it may retreat behind the walls of a gated community.

Article 10

Protecting Our Seniors

Elder abuse and neglect [are] coming out of the closet as police network with social agencies to improve the quality of life for senior citizens.

Ronald J. Getz

Ronald J. Getz is a free-lance writer based in Largo, Fla.

Unlike spouses or children, they're often voiceless and abandoned by their families. These victims of elder abuse and neglect are usually terribly vulnerable, isolated and dependent on others. It's a national tragedy; yet it's considered a low priority among many segments of society—including some law enforcement agencies.

"Society treats dogs and animals —and protects them—better than we do some of our own elderly parents and grandparents," said Lt. Rick Duran of the Tampa (Fla.) Police Department, who instructs cops on how to recognize indicators of abuse and neglect of the elderly.

"Elder abuse and neglect is the nation's hidden problem," he said. "It's like child or spousal abuse was 20 years ago."

Abuse is an all-inclusive term encompassing physical, emotional and psychological abuse, financial victimization, neglect by another person and self-neglect. The violence ranges from rape and homicide to a case where a son withheld insulin from his diabetic mother "because it cost too much."

In fact, most elderly victims are abused or neglected in their own homes by family members or paid caregivers—not necessarily by strangers in long-term care facilities.

The following are some typical examples of the more than one million cases of elder abuse and neglect that occur in this country each year:

■ A deputy found an elderly man abandoned by his children with no heat or hot water in his home. The bed was saturated with urine, and the man was covered with his own excrement. His body was a mass of lesions and sores that were infested with maggots. A foot had to be amputated.

■ A home health aide—previously convicted of dealing in stolen property and grand theft—was assigned by a hospital in Sun City, Fla., to care for an 86-year-old man after open heart surgery. The woman and her husband systematically drained his assets to buy cars and gamble, took out a $22,000 mortgage on his home, and attempted to divert his direct deposit checks to their use before they were finally caught. The bank threatened foreclosure, but—after public pressure—announced that "no further actions will be taken for 30 days."

■ Officials closed down the Riverside Nursing Home in Tampa and removed 19 residents on stretchers after the administrators ignored repeated citations and scores of deficiencies. One resident restricted to soft foods died from choking on a hot dog. Another was treated for dehydration and malnutrition after not being fed for five days.

As the population gets older and social services are reduced, cases like these are expected to escalate.

"Police administrators should plan now for the changing demographics of tomorrow," said Dr. Wilbur L. Rykert, director of the National Crime Prevention Institute at the University of Louisville in Kentucky.

Rykert calls law enforcement officers "the first line of defense" for victims of neglect and abuse. "In the past, law enforcement addressed youth crimes by creating specialized juvenile units," he said. "Now, law enforcement administrators must make similar contributions to the overall good of America by specifically addressing the crime problems of our aging society." (See "The Graying of America".)

An Alliance for Change

Take, for example, Hillsborough County, Fla., which encompasses the city of Tampa and has a larger senior population (350,000) than 16 individuals states. The Tampa Bay P.D. receives about 3,000 calls each year reporting cases of elder abuse and neglect, and there are 20,000 cases statewide.

Nonetheless, not one law enforcement agency had a formal program or systematic training in place to deal with this lethal and rapidly growing problem—until now.

In Tampa Bay, an alliance of law enforcement, social service agencies and members of the aging network launched a unique program focusing on "first responders"—usually cops on the streets—who have first contact with the elderly. Initiated in Hillsborough Coun-

2. VICTIMOLOGY

ty in 1992, the First Responder's Program has received recognition for excellence by the National Center on Elder Abuse.

At the time, Joe Breen, who helped launch the program, was serving as a supervisor of Adult Protective Services for Florida's Department of Health and Rehabilitative Services.

"What I found was that my investigators were explaining the laws dealing with elder abuse and neglect to law enforcement," said Breen, who is now a program manager of Mental Health-Care Inc. "The officers just weren't that knowledgeable of the Florida statutes. Moreover, they were inappropriately 'Baker Acting' everybody."

In other words, they were using Florida's Baker Act to get court orders to commit an elderly person to a ward for mental health treatment against the person's wishes when the person was mentally competent.

Breen realized that there had to be a better way to educate police about elder laws. That was the catalyst for earning a federal grant to underwrite "A First Responder's Guide to Abuse, Neglect, and Exploitation of the Elderly and Disabled Adult" with the support of the West Central Florida Area Agency on Aging (AAA).

An advisory team was then formed, consisting of law enforcement —including Lt. Duran and Dpty. Georgia Veitch of the Hillsborough County Sheriff's Office (HCSO)—social service agencies, and emergency medical services to advise West Central Florida AAA on what first responders needed to know when dealing with the elderly and disabled.

"First we created the training manual," said Leslee Boykin of AAA. "Then we distilled the manual into a handy pamphlet, because the officers on the street told us they wanted something easy to understand that they could throw in the glove compartment of the squad car or carry that would give them information in a hurry."

Linking the Pieces

What the team ended up with was actually a package consisting of three modules: the First Responder's Guide

with basic information and vital resources, the training manual and a videotape. The latter, hosted by news anchor Kelly Ring of the Fox Network, was intended to stimulate discussion during training sessions by showing actual cases of at-risk seniors in abusive relationships.

The package is now being updated for release in 1996 to incorporate feedback from law enforcement and to make it even more user-friendly.

The guide also provides a concise overview of the elderly population, types of abuse, neglect and exploitation, a primer on the law and a list of resources. It includes a directory of agencies describing their services and phone numbers.

"We needed something unique for the elderly, because many of the problems law enforcement deals with are not criminal in nature," Duran said. "For instance, many are simply self-neglect.

"Then there are family situations that are legally defined as elder abuse, and we arrest the perpetrator. But just locking people up wasn't the solution either," Duran continued. "Our idea was to link up law enforcement with the social services network so that we can direct the elderly to the part of the system where they belong."

If the elderly person was being abused, for instance, then law enforcement could step in. But with the First Responder's program, the officer has a full array of options.

"Maybe the older person needs Meals on Wheels," Duran said, "or counseling for the family to defuse a violent situation.

"It could be someone in the early stages of Alzheimer's who we connect with the Alzheimer's Wanderer's Identification Program."

According to Duran, police officers want systems in place that *work,* so officers can direct a person to the appropriate services—as long as it's not a criminal justice matter—and then "get them out of there." That's the reason First Responder's has been so invaluable to cops on the streets.

"You get an officer on the street at three in the morning and there's no social services support," said Duran. "That officer's got to make life-and-

death decisions pretty much on his own. Besides that, the social services network is so confusing and hard to navigate (that) an officer just doesn't have the time to figure it all out."

The training component of the First Responder's package has been equally useful.

"We were the first in Florida to develop a curriculum for law enforcement dealing with elder abuse and neglect," Boykin said. "It really took off. As a result of this program, other Area Agencies on Aging have developed similar courses, and personnel in five counties have been trained."

A Three-Way Street

One organization that has been instrumental in improving the quality of life for seniors is TRIAD, which represents the combined forces of the sheriff, the chiefs of police within the county and senior citizens. The group's mission is to reduce the criminal victimization of the elderly and improve law enforcement services to older persons.

The group gets input from an advisory group known as Seniors and Law Enforcement Together (SALT), which evaluates its activities, supports training for law enforcement and community awareness programs, and is an advocacy group that supports law enforcement and legislation affecting senior citizens.

In 1993, the first law enforcement agencies in Florida to organize a TRIAD included the Hillsborough Sheriff's Office, as well as the Tampa, Temple Terrace and Plant City Police Departments. That same year, HCSO was the first law enforcement agency in the Tampa Bay area to establish a Crimes Against the Elderly Unit (CATE).

"Law enforcement has to make a commitment to the elderly and back that up with resources," said Hillsborough County Sheriff Cal Henderson.

"Law enforcement agencies throughout the nation are now recognizing the importance of community policing. What we're doing with our crimes against seniors program is a natural extension of that philosophy," he added. "It makes sense to take advantage of the willingness of

10. Protecting Our Seniors

seniors and social agencies that want to work with us to improve the quality of life for our elderly."

Working Out the Details

According to Veitch, who heads the CATE unit for the Hillsborough Sheriff's Office, there has to be at least one officer who is designated as the lead person in dealing with crimes against the elderly.

"When there isn't someone responsible for a particular law enforcement responsibility, then nobody is. And normally nothing gets done. Right now most departments don't have even one deputy or officer responsible for crimes against seniors, and that has to change," Veitch said.

One of the first steps the sheriff's office undertook was to initiate in-service training so that all certified personnel would have two hours of instruction on the First Responder's Guide. HCSO conducted a three-day specialized school to familiarize every one of its 900 deputies with the Florida statutes covering crimes against the elderly.

In conjunction with the training, Veitch developed a slide presentation—with support of the Florida Health and Rehabilitative Services Department—to graphically show officers what the at-risk population must endure.

"Cops can get jaded because they've just about seen it all," said Veitch. "Unless you get their attention, they're just going to blow it off because it doesn't mean anything to them. Believe me, I got their attention by showing (cops) elderly victims with burns, battered seniors, bed sores infested with larvae, malnutrition and roaches in food."

Veitch has trained seven deputies who are certified as elder abuse investigators and can assume training responsibilities throughout the agency.

"Ultimately, every squad will have a designated person to handle elder abuse cases," Veitch said. "Each of these elder abuse investigators will have specialized training in dealing with abuse and know how to prepare and handle reports."

Lobbying for Support

Later this year, Veitch will lead a two-day school for HCSO investigators. The training will cover such subjects as financial exploitation, the protocol for emergency removal of an at-risk senior and an update on Florida statutes.

Meanwhile, the Hillsborough County TRIAD is lobbying the Florida Department of Law Enforcement to have a mandated statewide curriculum on crimes against the elderly. HCSO is also joining forces with the Fort Myers P.D. and other agencies to develop a statewide curriculum on elder abuse, which will be completed in 1996 under another federal grant.

In addition, the TRIAD is collaborating with senior groups and social service agencies to change the Florida statutes, so the laws dealing with elder abuse and neglect are consistent, provide for appropriate punishment, are enforceable and result in convictions. Too often, law enforcement representatives nationwide find that cases are thrown out—or not even prosecuted—because the statutes are vague or are ruled unconstitutional.

Early this year, HCSO sponsored a conference on aging sanctioned by the White House entitled "Seniors Impacted By Violence."

The conference, which featured experts from law enforcement, government, universities and the private sector, served as a forum to raise the visibility of crimes against the elderly and encourage greater support of senior abuse and neglect initiatives.

Findings and information from the conference formed the basis for proposals presented by Veitch, who was selected as one of a handful of law enforcement delegates to participate in a recent White House Conference on Aging.

The Graying of America

Take one look at the demographics of America and it's evident why concern about violence and the elderly is very real. America is getting older—and fast. The total population of the United States has tripled in this century, but now there are 10 times as many people 65 years and over; that group has increased from about three million in 1900 to more than 31 million in 1990. And it could reach 70 million by the middle of the next century.

Another way of illustrating the rapidly aging face of America is to note that one in eight Americans were elderly in 1900. Today, the number is one in five. This is the fastest growing demographic group in America.

The sheer mass of the elderly population is one aspect of the challenge facing law enforcement. But there's also the unsettling scale of the violence and hurt inflicted on the elderly. Crime statistics are notoriously unreliable when it comes to determining the incidence of abuse. But most experts now believe that at least one million elderly are abused every year. And the number may be much higher.

Given the prevalence of elder abuse, it would seem that this is an issue that would scream out for attention, headlines and tabloid television. Hardly.

Early this year, "Parade Magazine"—which is distributed as an insert in newspapers to 33 million homes—ran a Special Intelligence Report entitled "Let's Try a Week Without Violence." The magazine registered its dismay and shock over the 2.5 million women who are victims of violent crime and the 2.7 million cases of suspected child abuse. Conspicuously absent was any mention of elders.

—*Ronald J. Getz*

2. VICTIMOLOGY

Assessing At-Risk Elders

Another priority for law enforcement here was to develop a simple information system deputies could use to report and assess calls involving elders at risk.

"For example we found that we have multiple 9-1-1 calls involving the same person," Veitch said, "so officers on three shifts would be responding and filling out paperwork on the same call. That meant a lot of duplication and wasted effort."

Veitch created an Elder Referral Card System (ERCS)—a simple three-by-five card—that deputies complete when they find a senior at risk or in need of services. To reinforce the card referral system, Veitch went to every roll call to explain how the cards worked.

"We told the deputies that if they found a senior that was endangered or was just lonesome and calling 9-1-1, we needed a referral card," she said. "We didn't care if it was a barking dog call or a homicide, or whether or not they filed a report. In addition, we gave them an incentive, because we told them they could get credit for community-oriented policing by turning in a referral card."

The CATE unit now receives about 60 referral cards each month. Once referrals are made to the appropriate agencies, the card is copied and sent to the deputies, so they can see the results and find out what happened to the person in question.

Information from ERCS is then inputted into a computer as part of a database that investigators can draw on for statistical information and data on crimes against the elderly. The information can also be used to assess successes and serve as a guide for program changes.

Connecting with Senior Citizens

Duran emphasizes that the elder program is a way for law enforcement to build bridges with important constituencies in the community. He asserts that it's not only the right thing to do, but it's also politically smart. As a group, seniors volunteer more often than any other single segment of the population, and they have the highest turnout during elections.

"Not only does this system serve our senior citizens, but it's practical," Duran said. "So it's something police departments should initiate in their own self-interest."

Moreover, he said, the First Responder program cuts down on wasted time and unnecessary emergency calls.

"We get people off the 9-1-1 line by plugging them into the telephone reassurance center at the Suicide Prevention Center, where they have volunteers that can call the seniors once a day and talk to them ... Then there's the cases we discover (where there's a) dire need."

A case in point is the experience of Hillsborough County Dpty. Kevin Sowers, who responded when neighbors called to voice their concern about an elderly woman they'd not seen for some time.

When Sowers arrived at her home, he found the woman living in filth, malnourished, dehydrated, with no hot water and too weak to even operate the dial on her rotary telephone.

"Inside—and outside—the place was a mess," Sowers recalls.

The house was entangled in overgrown trees and shrubs, debris was strewn inside and out, there were piles of unwashed clothes and filth throughout the living areas. Sowers called an ambulance, and the woman was dispatched to a hospital's emergency room.

"Some people may think this isn't a law enforcement function, but it is," Sowers said. "Left vacant, that woman's home would have become an easy target for vandals or burglars," Sowers said. "Its deterioration would have led to neighborhood decay, which kills property values and breeds crime."

And, most importantly, the woman might have died or been permanently impaired.

Sowers could have left the matter in the hands of health care professionals. But when he called Florida's Health and Rehabilitative Services Department, he discovered the woman would be forced to go to a nursing home unless her home could be made habitable.

"I said if all we need to do is a massive clean up, I could get it done," Sowers said.

Sowers organized a task force, including himself and five other deputies, who volunteered to clean up the residence. When the deputies were finished with their rehab project, they hauled away two dump-truck loads and an industrial trash bin loaded with garbage and waste.

"Being in law enforcement, we tend to see the worst of people every day," Sowers said. "It's easy to get negative. But this has really charged us up."

Taking a Proactive Approach

Veitch believes that law enforcement needs to be out front in combatting crimes against the elderly with this kind of proactive attitude. And the TRIAD and SALT groups are an effective way to energize society and raise awareness.

But generally, society still doesn't understand the range of violence the elderly face. For example, Florida has an elder abuse hotline, and it's a felony not to report physical abuse, neglect or exploitation of the elderly. But, Veitch admits, not many people know about the hotline.

That's one reason the First Responder's Program is so important.

"Crimes against the elderly in Hillsborough County are taken seriously by our officers, and now we follow up on complaints," Veitch added.

"We know that some of these abuse charges can't be substantiated, and many cases aren't prosecuted because of ambiguities in the law or other circumstances," she continued, "but it's worth investigating every single case—regardless of whether a crime is prosecuted or not—to protect the thousands of seniors in our community who are being victimized, neglected and abused. In many cases, we're the first—and only—line of defense for these older Americans."

Article 11

Nobody's Victim

**Sarah Buel left an abusive partner to save her life.
Since then, she's been saving others.**

STEPHANIE B. GOLDBERG

Stephanie B. Goldberg, a lawyer, is a senior editor at the ABA Journal.

A great believer in guided imagery, Sarah Buel walks audiences nationwide through exercises in imagining the future. She declares with evangelical fervor: "Everything I need is streaming toward me, and I can feel it."

Then she urges those present to conjure up images of money, power and influence—not to better themselves but in service of a single principle: putting an end to domestic violence.

In the wake of Buel's speeches, coalitions form and organizations are energized to try new strategies that ultimately will save women's lives. This is not hyperbole but fact—in Quincy, Mass., where Buel is a prosecutor, there has been only one domestic homicide in the past decade, while neighboring boroughs rack up 15 or so every year.

Buel, 42, a petite, blond-haired woman who looks like a grown-up version of the storybook heroine Heidi, has come to occupy a unique position as what might be described as the spiritual center of the domestic violence-prevention movement. Although she works as a prosecutor, Buel's real job seems to be touching people's hearts so they can no longer see domestic violence as somebody else's problem.

"She is the driving force, the passion, the source of energy in this office," says her boss, District Attorney William Delahunt.

"She inspires people to take action," says Sandra Dempsey of the Philadelphia chapter of Physicians for Social Responsibility. "She gets them to bear witness." After Buel spoke to that group, it mobilized other local organizations to produce a coordinated response to domestic violence.

"She [was] the most extraordinary student I have ever had," says her former law professor, Harvard's Charles Ogletree, who watched with pride as Buel, with other students, found time to create two pro bono student-advocacy projects on behalf of battered women and women in prison.

There is also a deep vein of generosity in this woman who, a friend says, once used a Christmas bonus to buy blankets for the homeless and, on another occasion, cashed in her retirement account to give a fresh start to two women newly released from prison.

Buel has spoken on domestic violence in every state in the country and has trained thousands of people—physicians, lawyers, court personnel and social workers—about detecting and preventing domestic violence. It's not simply the intensity with which she speaks—for hours, without any notes—but the story she has to tell.

Once upon a time, Buel was a battered woman herself. She has also been a paralegal, a day-care worker, a customer representative for an electric company and a welfare mother on the long, improbable journey that ultimately led to Harvard Law School, from which she graduated with honors in 1990.

Actually, says longtime friend Sherry St. Germain, a Vermont silversmith, Buel is a graduate of the school of hard knocks. "She must have told you," says St. Germain, "about how she used to drive past Harvard and say, 'One day you're going to let me in.'"

"I've been very lucky," says Buel with characteristic understatement. "I see myself as very blessed."

After leaving Quincy's domestic violence unit in 1991 to head up another city's unit and then take a fel-

Get-tough efforts by police and prosecutors, plus increasing public awareness, are paying off in the fight against domestic violence

Reprinted with permission from *ABA Journal*, July 1996, pp. 48-53. Reprinted by permission of the American Bar Association.

2. VICTIMOLOGY

lowship at Radcliffe, Buel came back in 1994 to work in the juvenile offender division. Despite her official posture, she is less interested in convictions than in rescuing kids before they are irretrievably damaged. ("A very healthy attitude in a prosecutor," notes Ogletree.) That these children more often than not come out of violent homes doesn't surprise her. Buel, like many others working against domestic violence, sees this crime as the progenitor, the incubator of crime in society.

The child who grows up with violence accepts it as the norm, she says. "It's absolutely essential for a child to have some adult to love and believe in him," declares Buel from the driver's seat of her battered 1987 Honda. Without love, "Children disengage and get that dead look in their eyes. When they stop caring about themselves and other people, they start acting out in violence."

Buel learned about violence firsthand when she was pregnant with her son almost 22 years ago. Her then-partner, whom she takes care not to identify, struck her in the face. "I remember being incredibly shocked," Buel recalls. The abuse, both physical and verbal, continued for the next two years—Buel is not comfortable going into the specifics. She left and came back twice, finally leaving for good in 1977. She remembers mornings when she would lie in bed, trying to gauge whether this was going to be a bad day from the way her partner breathed in his sleep.

"It was like walking on eggshells," Buel says, using a figure of speech that takes on special meaning to victims of domestic violence.

Beyond Expectations

Over lunch, Buel reflects on the amazing turns her life has taken. In high school, her grades were nothing special, and a guidance counselor told her to forget higher education—she wasn't college material. Little did he know that Buel would labor seven years for her undergraduate degree, taking night courses at a number of colleges before receiving her diploma from Harvard's Extension School in Cambridge, Mass.

Born in Chicago into a family of five children, Buel would move 10 times while growing up. Her father left the family when she was 9, though he has maintained contact. She always assumed she would become a teacher or nursery school instructor, though deep down she knew she wanted to be a lawyer. Nope, her grandmother said, girls can't be lawyers. "But you can work for a lawyer like Della on *Perry Mason.*"

Buel idolized her mother, an Austrian Jewish refugee. The refugee experience shaped her mother's life, Buel says, both in her willingness to extend aid to anyone in the family or neighborhood who needed it and in her refusal to make waves politically. Buel inherited her mother's compassion, but not her timidity.

Her infatuation with the law began at age 12, when she was able to extract a refund from an auto mechanic who had cheated her mother. She realized that law was a sword she could brandish to right wrongs. "It bothered me that in the richest country in the world there were people going hungry," Buel says.

At 20, she found herself in the Bronx working in a day-care center while her companion, her high school sweetheart, attended a training program. Noticing empty apartment buildings in her neighborhood, she started working with a community organization to reclaim them for indigent families. "I had read about it

Organizing an Anti-Violence Offensive

In the early 1980s, battered women's advocates in search of a test site for their new ideas found what they were looking for in Duluth, Minn. With its modest size (roughly 85,000), Duluth lent itself well to the then-radical notion of coordinating the work of all the key players in the justice system to combat domestic violence.

That effort evolved into the Domestic Abuse Intervention Project, which independently tracks and monitors sectors of the justice system.

An important step was the Duluth police chief's agreement to impose a mandatory arrest policy for batterers on an experimental basis, according to Michael Paymar, the St. Paul-based training and technical assistance coordinator for an educational resource group called the National Training Project of Duluth.

Simply getting police to arrest alleged batterers "was an enormous change initially," says Joan Zorza, a New York City lawyer who provides consultation and training on domestic violence issues.

Meanwhile, other players in the system—from prosecutors to judges—got together to change the way domestic violence cases were handled. All agreed to new policies and protocols, though Paymar says the judges were initially reluctant due to fear of crowded dockets and diminished discretion. Mental health professionals responded to the call by developing treatment programs that gave courts an alternative to imprisonment.

Cooperation instead of turf protection defined the Duluth model. "In some ways they were willing to give up discretion, which is very dear to professionals, . . . to achieve a larger common goal that they bought into," says Denise Gamache, the Minneapolis-based associate director of the Battered Women's Justice Project.

Duluth's initial gains masked a problem that plagues efforts to bring batterers to justice: lack of cooperation from victims. Mandatory arrests and a "no-drop" prosecution policy (under which a case would go forward even if the victim would not) forced the issue out in the open. The city's yearly misdemeanor caseload, which numbered little more than a handful before 1980, soared to 300–350, says Mary Asmus, chief prosecutor with the Duluth City Attorney's Office. A whopping 80 percent of misdemeanor cases resulted in convictions during the early years of the program, she says.

But many of these convictions represented guilty pleas entered by stunned defendants reeling from the shock of having been arrested in the first place, Asmus says. When the novelty of mandatory arrest subsided, so did the hefty percentage of easy wins.

Out of concern that vigorous prosecution traumatized victims, the city attorney's office relaxed its no-drop policy in the mid-1980s, with a corresponding nosedive in conviction rates. Misdemeanor convictions dropped to roughly 20 percent between 1985 and 1988, Asmus estimates.

The no-drop policy has since been revived. "Now every case is like guerrilla warfare," Asmus says. The conviction rate is back to 80 percent, which "really means something to me now," she adds.

11. Nobody's Victim

Prosecuting Without the Witness

Change began to ferment in San Diego in the mid-'80s. The prime movers were Casey Gwinn, then a greenhorn prosecutor, now the city attorney-elect; Norm Stamper, then a high-ranking member of the San Diego Police Department, now the chief of police in Seattle; and San Diego police officer Anne O'Dell. O'Dell is a former battered wife who concealed the fact, even when she became the department's first domestic violence coordinator in 1990.

An early test case came in 1986, a high-profile one involving San Diego Municipal Court Judge Joseph Davis. Davis was accused of beating his girlfriend, who was five months' pregnant. A judge dismissed the charges against Davis after a jury deadlock. The prosecution later attributed the loss to lack of admissibility of evidence. According to Gwinn and O'Dell, the trial judge kept out 911 tapes, testimony from the victim's doctors, testimony from some neighbors, and evidence concerning a restraining order issued against Davis.

In the wake of this defeat, efforts were focused on perfecting the technique of so-called "victimless" prosecution. This approach stresses evidence gathering and trial techniques that do not rely on a victim's participation or assent to proceed.

"That is, without a doubt, what revolutionized our handling of domestic abuse cases in San Diego," Gwinn says. "If you require a victim to press charges or prosecute, you've just drawn a target on her chest."

During 1995, 33 percent of misdemeanor cases against batterers went to trial without the presence of the witness at all. In 19 percent of cases, the victim testified for the defense, while recantation occurred in another 15 percent of cases where the victim initially gave information favorable to the prosecution.

The painstaking effort appears to be worth it. San Diego credits a downturn in domestic homicides to both victimless prosecutions and to its aggressive approach to misdemeanors, which is viewed as a means to forestall more serious cases down the line.

Proof that the system works is the explosion of the docket load—from 20 cases in 1986 to 1,500 today, with a corresponding reduction in homicides of nearly 70 percent since 1985. "It's the early intervention," Gwinn says.

For More Information

The ABA Commission on Domestic Violence will release a manual, *Impact of Domestic Violence on Your Legal Practice,* which explains how lawyers can get involved with this issue. Contact the commission at (202) 662–1737.

---

being done in other cities," Buel says. "She was an activist from way back," adds her friend St. Germain.

Buel has said that all she needed to do to trigger a beating in those days was talk about going to law school. She was allowed to read the *New York Daily News* but not the *New York Times.* Her partner became more and more controlling, escorting her everywhere she went, demanding to know how she spent her time. "At first the attention is flattering," Buel says. "But after a while it becomes suffocating."

Was he afraid he would lose her if she went to college? "Definitely," she says, noting the irony of how abusive spouses engineer the very thing they fear most.

At that time, there was no one Buel could turn to. The battered women's movement—which evolved as an offshoot of rape prevention—was just gathering steam. In the coming years, much effort would go into educating the public that domestic violence is a crime. That it touches every strata of society. That it is about power and control much more than anger. That many battered women do not flee their assailants but stay with them because a spark in them has gone dead. Somehow, Buel was able to keep that flame alive.

Too ashamed to tell her friends and family, she confided only in her parish priest. No one seemed to notice her gradual withdrawal, and calling the police was not an option. Besides her own son, she was caring for the two young children of relatives who were in transition.

Eventually she fled to Lebanon, N.H., near her mother's home. Her partner pursued her, surprising her at a laundry.

"Won't someone call the police? This man has attacked me," cried Buel to the crowd of onlookers. There were bruises on her face. Not one person came to her aid.

"It's a family matter. I'm taking her home," Buel's abuser announced. They left together but stopped at the home where she was staying. Miraculously, Buel persuaded him to go back to New York alone. Before leaving she had made arrangements for the two children in her care, but she still had a 2-year-old son to rear. She went to work at a shoe factory before finding a job at the local Legal Services office as a paralegal—her first position as an advocate.

"In all the time she worked for us," recalls her former boss, lawyer Mark Larsen, now in private practice in New Hampshire, "we never knew she had had a problem with domestic violence."

On the Road

Buel's job was to travel throughout the state explaining the law to indigent people, preventing their electricity from being cut off, giving advice on how to get Social Security, welfare and medical benefits.

At the same time, she and three other women worked to create a network of safe houses in the area so that battered women could seek refuge.

Another project was starting a three-county Women, Infants and Children program with vouchers for food that enabled pregnant women on welfare and poor families to get adequate nutrition. "I still see women with their vouchers at the grocery store," comments Larsen, "and I always think of Sarah."

The question remains: Some women are shattered by violence, so how was Buel able to regroup so quickly?

She credits her mother with making her feel that she didn't deserve to be abused, that she could pursue

2. VICTIMOLOGY

her dreams. She also was sustained by religious faith—and still is, she adds, noting she was reared in her father's Catholicism. And little things made a difference, including the public assistance funds that tided her over at one point.

Up for the Challenge

"One thing led to another" is how Buel explains her gradual ascent to public prominence as an advocate. Much to her surprise, she found herself sitting on the boards of local groups (today she is a member of the ABA Commission on Domestic Violence). It was never anything she sought, she maintains. She remembers how her voice quavered and her knees knocked the first time she gave a speech.

"She grew by leaps and bounds," says Larsen, who has stayed in touch with Buel over the years.

Her voice became louder and more authoritative. Between 1980 and 1985 she lived in Massachusetts, Denver and Seattle. All the while she was taking courses toward her undergraduate degree. Buel returned to Massachusetts in 1985 and became director of the state committee on domestic violence policy.

That same year, Buel also did something quite unwise for an aspiring law student: She publicly called for accountability from a Massachusetts sitting judge, charging that the judge botched the case of a battered wife who was then murdered when five months' pregnant. The resentment she created lingers to this day, Buel says. "I'm asked to do judicial training programs everywhere in the country—except Massachusetts."

Buel got her undergraduate degree and was accepted to Harvard Law School in 1987, though a faculty member later told her that some questioned the wisdom of her admission. It was an unlikely place for someone who wanted to practice poverty law.

Buel says it was a great time in her life. "I loved every minute of law school," she says. Her friend Suzanne Groisser, a Manhattan district attorney, remembers her first impression of Buel: "I met her when I was a first-year and she was a second-year. She was speaking at a public interest conference and had this incredible passion." The two would go on to found a project that trained law students to act as advocates for battered women.

But later, Buel lets on, there were disappointments. She got the feeling that many faculty members didn't find battered women's problems intellectually challenging. A family law course gave advice on how to draft prenuptial agreements, not protective orders. Another professor was distant when she met to talk about tort remedies for domestic violence. There was a faculty feminist reading group that was closed to students, even though, Buel notes, she was a contemporary in age and certainly in life experience.

Did it make a difference to students to know that one of their own had been an activist and a battered woman?

"Her life experience was invaluable. She brought an awareness of how the system worked," says Ogletree, who praises Buel's conviction and commitment.

What's unique about Buel, he says, is her nonadversarial posture. In trial advocacy class, she fought to retain her own style and spoke softly, even in court. "I never pace," says Buel, who eschews theatrics.

Once a defense lawyer who opposed her told her point-blank that she was not a real litigator. Never-

---

Tipping the Scales in Favor of Victims

Influenced by the interagency cooperation in Duluth and San Diego's emphasis on victimless prosecution, the Seattle and King County area of Washington state has launched programs geared toward greater victim involvement in the justice system.

Although Seattle had a history of activism on the issue, an informal group of city workers founded the Domestic Violence Task Force in 1990 to find ways to update Seattle's approach to domestic violence. The city has since established a municipal domestic-violence office to coordinate the efforts of different law enforcement agencies.

Seattle moved its program into high gear by hiring Norm Stamper away from the San Diego Police Department and making him chief of police. Stamper arrived in early 1994 and implemented reforms right off the bat.

In November 1994, Stamper brought on a special police unit for domestic abuse cases. An innovation was devoting significant resources to misdemeanor crimes, a tactic also favored in San Diego.

Lt. Debbie Allen, who heads the unit, says an average of 500 misdemeanor cases come through her office each month. The unit has a computerized program for performing triage—giving priority to cases that require immediate attention because they present a risk of serious violence or homicide.

Stamper points out that one of his favorite measures is a California law that Washington has adopted. The law makes it a crime to interfere with reporting domestic violence or with a victim's seeking medical attention. Under the new law, which went into effect in June, tactics used by batterers to foil calls for help, such as yanking the phone out of the wall, are illegal. "It was leverage that could be used to jail somebody," he says.

So far, Seattle has seen an apparently stunning payoff from Stamper's presence. Compared with the 16 domestic homicides from January through September 1995, there were zero from October through this April, according to Judith Shoshana, director of the Seattle City Attorney's Domestic Violence Unit, which handles misdemeanors rather than felonies.

At the county level, specialized advocacy groups target specific populations, says Lynn Gordon, domestic violence program manager for King County, which includes Seattle along with other municipalities. The county is now implementing the second of two five-year comprehensive plans.

A product of that plan, King County's fledgling felony domestic-violence unit, was flooded with cases in short order. Established in 1994 within the county prosecutor's office, officials originally anticipated only 650 case filings its first year. Yet it handled 470 files during its first six months, which county officials interpret as proof the program is working.

Corporate America Taking Up the Cause

It was a worker's blowout with a supervisor over lagging performance that brought domestic abuse into focus in the mid-'80s for Polaroid Corp. in Cambridge, Mass. Jim Hardeman, the corporate employee-assistance program manager and a child-abuse survivor, says the employee and her male supervisor looked to him for help. The worker admitted to beatings at home, especially if she deviated from the rigid schedule for leaving work.

Hardeman took action by organizing a battered-women's program at the Norwood, Mass., production facility, dubbing it a "self-image" group to shield participants. News spread by word of mouth. The company produced a video documenting victims' accounts that was aired at mandatory business meetings, and that sparked company wide activism.

The Polaroid Foundation made grants to shelters and provided funds to aid women turned away from shelters.

And Polaroid marketed an instant camera that uses grid film to portray the relative size of a wound. Law enforcement agencies and other buyers get free training in photographic documentation of evidence, Hardeman adds.

Other coporations have joined the movement:

• State Farm Life Insurance Co., based in Bloomington, Ill., did a turnaround after being taken to task by the media for denying health and life insurance to a battered woman. In May 1995, the company founded the Corporate Alliance to End Partner Violence, which focuses on prevention programs.

• The National Workplace Resource Center is the brainchild of the Family Violence Prevention Fund, a San Francisco-based nonprofit. Esta Soler, the fund's executive director, says companies that sign on with the center agree to provide financial support, professional talent for the center's advisory committee, and help in developing corporate domestic-violence programs.

• The Body Shop has built its effort around the power of visual imagery. "People rally around icons," says Lorilei Beer, spokeswoman for the Wake Forest, N.C.-based company. The Body Shop made a whistle its icon when it launched a campaign in 1995 urging people to "blow the whistle" on violence against women. Besides donating profits from whistle sales to relevant organizations, the company sponsors public events to boost awareness of violence against women.

• Liz Claiborne Inc. teamed up with New York public relations firm Patrice Tanaka & Co. Inc. to create the "Women's Work" campaign. The campaign commissions high-profile artistic interpretations of domestic abuse themes: One features a blowup of a man's crooked arm and fist with the message "Lethal Weapon" emblazoned above. The campaign has also donated money to advocacy groups.

• Finally, the Walt Disney Co. and the ABA Commission on Domestic Violence have co-produced the *It's Not OK* video for children affected by domestic abuse.
—*Lisa Stansky*

Making Men Part of the Solution

Jackson Katz in Boston is uniquely poised to tackle the perception that domestic violence is a women's issue.

A former high-school football star with a university minor in women's studies, Katz helped found the Mentors in Violence Prevention Project. The project, based in Boston at Northeastern University's Center for the Study of Sport in Society, contracts with groups such as high schools and universities to present a traveling informational program.

Katz says his primary targets are male student athletes, whom he encourages to act and speak out against violence to women.

He emphasizes that the phrase "men's violence against women" is more apt than the ubiquitous "violence against women." Katz explains: "Our silence is a form of consent and complicity in other men's violence."

Katz uses a playbook to guide program participants through various scenarios, ranging from a guy who slaps his girlfriend at a party to gang rape. The program also aims to reach students in other group-culture contexts, such as fraternities.

On the other coast, in California, rehabilitation of batterers has become a growing trend. "I got looked at askance for working with men and putting my energy into these guys," says Alyce LaViolette, the founder of Alternatives to Violence, a private battering-treatment program that began in 1979 and that now operates in Long Beach and West Los Angeles.

Getting batterers to take responsibility for their actions is slow going, LaViolette says. "It takes about six months to cut through the bull," she notes, adding that she usually sees a change in attitude after a year of group sessions. Significant shifts take hold after two to three years.

Susan Cayouette, clinical director of Emerge, a Boston-based treatment program for batterers that was established in 1977, points out that the courts are increasing their demand for such programs. "Ninety-five percent of the people we see are court-ordered, probably."

Cayouette sees the expansion of treatment programs, however, as potentially problematic, especially if the result is treating domestic abuse as a sickness rather than a crime.

As with many of the women activists in the movement, some men join the effort for personal reasons. Mark Wynn of the Domestic Violence Division of the Nashville Metropolitan Police says his family lived under a reign of terror imposed by his violent stepfather.

For 12 of his 18 years as a police officer, Wynn has focused on domestic violence issues. He does not define the struggle against violence in the home along gender lines. "It's not about a women's movement, it's not about a feminist agenda, it's about people's civil rights," Wynn says.

2. VICTIMOLOGY

theless, Buel won the case. "She is a really great trial lawyer," Delahunt says.

Her first job out of school was as a prosecutor in Middlesex County, Mass., but she left six months later to work in a jurisdiction that she thought moved more quickly against domestic violence. That was Quincy, the city where she now lives and volunteers two nights a week at the Germantown Youth Center.

Further to Go

"I don't think I'd be a good judge," Buel says as she trudges from the parking lot to the courthouse. "People have suggested it, but I always say, 'I'm an advocate.' If a lawyer messed up a case in my courtroom, I'd find it very upsetting.

"I find politics interfere too much with doing the right thing," she adds.

And, in truth, Buel—who is often commended for her exceeding delicacy—has been known not to do the politic thing.

At a press conference in Tampa in 1994, she chastised Hillsborough County state attorney Harry Lee Coe for saying that he saw his goal as keeping families together.

Buel said bluntly that was a "dangerous, misguided notion." The press had a field day, but Buel says she doesn't regret speaking out. "I'd have hated to be a battered woman living in Tampa." She reports that since then, they have done a lot to get up to speed.

She also had a run-in with a former boss who, she charges, was irked by her high profile, which eclipsed his own. According to Buel, he was so miffed at her invitation to testify on domestic violence at hearings chaired by Sen. Joseph Biden that she had to take a vacation day to do it.

"I don't understand," Buel says, "why anyone would not be able to see how something like that makes us all look good."

"Sarah does what she does because she believes in it," says St. Germain. "She's a zealot all right, but flexible and willing to compromise. She is not at all self-aggrandizing."

Her situation is much more accommodating in Quincy, where Delahunt allows her to work four-day weeks so she can keep speaking around the country. "When you have a special employee," he says, "you do what you can to keep her."

But not for long. Buel was set to move to Austin, Texas, at the end of June with her fiancé. "He's taught me that it's OK to have fun, to be less workaholic." Among Buel's plans for her life in Austin is starting a national domestic violence training institute.

Her work always continues no matter where she is. There will be cases to try, people to train and counsel, speeches to give, her story to tell. The moral is always the same: Will it, and it will happen.

"I really believe we can wipe out domestic violence in our lifetime," Buel says. "We know what to do. We just have to do it." Her voice is soft, but her face is incandescent as she looks off into the distance.

Article 12

Helping To Prevent Child Abuse— and Future Criminal Consequences: Hawai'i Healthy Start

Ralph B. Earle, Ph.D.

Traditionally, the prevention of child abuse and neglect has fallen under the purview of health and social service agencies. Increasingly, however, violence against children is a critical priority for criminal justice officials as well. Not only are child abuse and neglect crimes against society's most vulnerable members, they also may lead to crime perpetrated later in life by the victims themselves. Reducing the twofold effect of child abuse and neglect on the safety and well-being of American communities presents a formidable challenge for all segments of society.

Highlights

The violence committed by youths too often is traced to the abuse and neglect they suffered in their early years. The link between child maltreatment and later criminal behavior by its victims has made the criminal justice, health, and social service systems partners in prevention. As part of its research initiative on family violence, the National Institute of Justice (NIJ) is investigating interdisciplinary approaches involving children, their families, and their communities. This Program Focus describes the Hawai'i Healthy Start program, which uses home visitors from the community to provide services to at-risk families. Its goals are to reduce family stress and improve family functioning, improve parenting skills, enhance child health and development, and prevent abuse and neglect.

Of Special Interest:

■ Unlike other similar programs, Hawai'i Healthy Start follows the child from birth (or before) to age 5 with a range of services, and it assists and supports other family members.

■ To ensure systematic enrollment, Healthy Start signs up most families right after delivery of the child, although approximately 10 percent of families are enrolled prenatally.

■ Healthy Start has formal agreements with all hospitals in Hawai'i to enable it to perform postpartum screening through a review of the mother's medical record or a brief inperson interview. Fewer than 1 percent of mothers refuse to be interviewed, 4 to 8 percent later refuse offers of services, and about 7 percent cannot be located after release from the hospital.

■ Paraprofessional home visitors call on families weekly for the first 6 to 12 months. Early in the relationship, the home visitor helps parents develop an Individual Support Plan, specifying the kinds of services they want and need and the means by which to receive them.

■ As part of its oversight, the Maternal Child Health Branch requires completion of a series of Infant/Child Monitoring Questionnaires to identify problems in child development at 4, 12, 20, and 30 months. If these show developmental delays, further assessments are performed and appropriate services are offered.

■ In 1994 a confirmed child care abuse and neglect case cost the Hawai'i family welfare system $25,000 for investigation, related services, and foster care. In contrast, Hawai'i Healthy Start officials estimate an annual average cost of $2,800 per home visitor case.

■ Preliminary evaluation findings indicate that Healthy Start families have lower abuse/neglect rates and their children are developing appropriately for their ages.

From *National Institute of Justice, Program Focus*, NCJ-156216, October 1995, pp. 2-12. Reprinted by permission of the U.S. Department of Justice, National Institute of Justice.

2. VICTIMOLOGY

A growing amount of data appears to support the concept of a "cycle of violence" that begins with child abuse and neglect. One recent national study showed that being the victim of abuse and neglect as a child increases the chances of later juvenile delinquency and adult criminality by 40 percent. Even among children who are neglected but not abused, one in eight will later be arrested for a violent offense.[1] Children who experience severe violence in the home are approximately three times as likely as other children to use drugs and alcohol, get into fights, and deliberately damage property. Abused and neglected children are four times as likely to steal and to be arrested.[2]

Long before some victims of child abuse and neglect inflict pain and loss on others, they are caught up in a child welfare system that is costly and overburdened. For example, from 1994 to 1995 in Hawai'i, each confirmed case of child abuse or neglect cost nearly $15,000 per year for investigation and services. Foster care added another $10,000 per year. Home care for a drug-exposed child cost $18,000 per year, and foster care for that child, $46,000.[3] For both social and financial reasons, the criminal justice and family welfare systems have a strong incentive to reduce child abuse and neglect.

Although both intuition and existing scientific data indicate a predisposition to crime and violence among many abused and neglected children, more research is needed to determine the exact nature of the link, as well as the relationship of associated factors, such as socioeconomic status.[4] Nonetheless, preliminary findings underscore the need for the criminal justice system to support and work in partnership with child abuse and neglect prevention efforts and the communities they serve as a means of reducing crime in both the short term and the long run.

The Hawai'i Healthy Start Model

As part of its research initiative on family violence, the National Institute of Justice (NIJ) is interested in interdisciplinary approaches involving children, their families, and their communities.[5] The U.S.

Advisory Board on Child Abuse and Neglect identified home visiting in 1991 as the most promising means for preventing the maltreatment of children. One example of this approach is Hawai'i Healthy Start, a statewide, multisite home visitation program designed to screen, identify, and work with at-risk families of newborns to prevent abuse and promote child development.

Home visitation programs have become increasingly popular in recent years as a means to address a number of social problems and individual needs. Programs designed primarily for families with newborns have diverse goals and services. The goals of Hawai'i Healthy Start are to:

- Reduce family stress and improve family functioning.

- Improve parenting skills.

- Enhance child health and development.

- Prevent abuse and neglect.

Although it shares the same name as 15 infant mortality prevention programs on the mainland, Healthy Start's services are not limited to the months before and after a child's birth. Instead, Hawai'i Healthy Start serves the child until age 5. The program includes early identification of families at risk for child abuse and neglect, community-based home visiting support and intervention services, linkage to a "medical home" and other health care services, and coordination of a wide range of community services, primarily for the parents and their newborn, but also for other

family members.[6] To avoid confusion with similarly named and focused programs (see "Federal 'Healthy Start' Program" and "Healthy Families America"), the program featured in this Program Focus is referred to throughout as Hawai'i Healthy Start.

Program History

The development of Hawai'i Healthy Start was strongly influenced by the late Dr. Henry Kempe, a researcher at the University of Colorado Health Sciences Center and Director of the National Center for Prevention and Treatment of Child Abuse and Neglect in Denver. Kempe operated residential treatment and prevention programs and developed a checklist to identify families at risk of abusing or neglecting their children.

In the early 1970's Kempe screened 500 families in the Denver area and identified 100 as being at risk for child abuse and neglect. He randomly assigned these 100 families to two groups. One group received home visiting services; the other received only the usual medical services. In each group of 50, he followed 25 families for 3 years. Among the families provided services, there were no hospitalizations for abuse, although three families gave a child up for adoption. Among the 25 nonserviced families, however, five children were hospitalized variously for head injuries, scaldings, and fractures.

In 1973 Dr. Calvin Sia, a prominent pediatrician in Hawai'i, and members of

Federal "Healthy Start" Program To Reduce Infant Mortality

In 1991 the U.S. Department of Health and Human Services began a 5-year program, also called "Healthy Start," to reduce infant mortality by 50 percent in 15 mainland communities. The Federal program was designed to strengthen the maternal and infant care system in these communities through six recommended activities: perinatal care, family planning and infant care, psychosocial services, facilitating services, individual development, and community development and public education.

The Federal Healthy Start program is trying to reduce deaths during the first year of life. It does not provide the child development and stress management services offered by Hawai'i Healthy Start or by the Healthy Families America programs. The Chicago Healthy Start program, however, recently adopted Hawai'i's model at four sites as part of its strategy to prevent domestic violence.

12. Helping to Prevent Child Abuse

Healthy Families America:

Home Visitation To Prevent Child Abuse and Neglect on the Mainland

In January 1992 the National Committee to Prevent Child Abuse (NCPCA), in partnership with Ronald McDonald Children's Charities (RMCC) and in collaboration with the Hawai'i Family Stress Center, launched the Healthy Families America (HFA) initiative. Building on two decades of research and the experiences of Hawai'i Healthy Start in putting that research into practice, HFA was designed to help establish home visitation programs, service networks, and funding opportunities in each State so that all new parents can receive necessary education and support. As of spring 1995, HFA programs had been implemented at 101 pilot sites in 20 States on the mainland.[7]

NCPCA, in collaboration with the Hawai'i Family Stress Center, provides training and technical assistance to HFA home visitation programs, using Hawai'i Healthy Start as one example of an effective program. NCPCA also has prepared a number of other individuals across the country to serve as trainers for State and local HFA efforts. Although each HFA site has aimed to meet the needs and build on the strengths of its community, all have embraced the 12 HFA criteria for effective programs as defined by research and the experience of Hawai'i Healthy Start.

HFA programs have been funded by a mix of private foundations, Federal funds, block grants, and State appropriations. Arizona, Indiana, and Oregon have passed multimillion dollar appropriations for statewide services.

The HFA goal is to offer **all** new parents in each service area at least one or two home visits. Thus far in practice, however, most programs have provided services primarily to families with the greatest needs. The programs serve a range of populations, from inner-city African Americans in Atlanta to Central American immigrants in Fairfax, Virginia.

NCPCA is coordinating efforts to help each program develop an evaluation component, including a national network of evaluators to collaborate on common outcome measures. All sites track child abuse and neglect cases and monitor child development and immunization; many sites use Nursing Child Assessment Satellite Training (NCAST) assessments.

The first HFA program to provide outcome data from an outside evaluation was in Arizona. Out of the 111 families enrolled in 1992, two families had validated reports of abuse, and one family had a validated report of neglect following the entrance of the target child in the project. The combined abuse and neglect rate (CAN) was 2.7 percent, compared with 2.1 percent for the Hawai'i families. However, the Arizona families were at higher risk than their Hawai'ian counterparts: 50 percent had a previous history of abuse (versus 38 percent in Hawai'i), and they had a higher percentage of severe risk items on the Kempe Family Stress Checklist. At age 6 months, only four of 57 children screened showed delay in one area of development; none showed delay in more than one area.[8]

Sia's developmental work continued with a community service grant from 1978 to 1981 to extend services to five additional sites on neighboring islands.

Healthy Start was an outgrowth of these early programs. It was designed at the request of the Hawai'i Senate Ways and Means Chairman, Mamoru Yamasaki, who was concerned with the State's increasing costs of corrections and social services. Originally intending to fund a delinquency prevention project in a high school, Yamasaki recognized the relationship between early abuse and delinquency and decided instead to begin with infants of families at risk for child abuse and neglect.

Healthy Start began in Hawai'i in July 1985 as a State-funded demonstration child abuse and neglect prevention program at a single site on O'ahu, the most populous island, with an annual budget of $200,000. The original prevention program concept was expanded to include broader implementation and more comprehensive objectives. Hawai'i Healthy Start was designed to serve all families of newborns at risk within the catchment area, follow the children to age 5, link all infants to a medical home that would serve them through childhood, and intensify the focus on parent-child attachment and interaction, child health, and child development.

After 3 years, Healthy Start had served 241 high-risk families, 176 of which were served for at least 1 year. No cases of child abuse and only four cases of child neglect were reported among the 241 families. Based on these results, between 1988 and 1990 the program was expanded through general funds appropriated by the State legislature to 13 sites across the State, with an annual budget of over $8 million for fiscal year 1995.

Hawai'i's Child Protective Service (CPS) Advisory Committee invited Kempe to help them put together a plan for the prevention and treatment of child abuse and neglect among families in Hawai'i. One year later, Gail Breakey, current Director of the Hawai'i Family Stress Center, and Sia obtained a 3-year grant from the National Center for Prevention and Treatment of Child Abuse and Neglect to implement the home visiting program developed by Kempe and the CPS Advisory Committee. They began a small prevention program on O'ahu, which yielded results similar to Kempe's work. Three home visitors provided emotional support and taught child development to 70 families for 12 to 18 months. Breakey's and

Administration, Budget, and Management

The Maternal Child Health Branch of the Hawai'i Department of Health administers the State appropriations, monitors the program, and evaluates the seven not-for-profit private agencies that deliver

2. VICTIMOLOGY

Healthy Start services. The programs conducted by the seven agencies vary in terms of budget and caseload. The smallest has an annual budget of $290,000 and serves 150 families; the largest spends over $1 million to serve 350 to 400 families each year. In 1990 actual screening, assessment, and case management services cost $2,500 per case. Where available, respite care services cost $476 per child per year.

To establish a new program, Hawai'i Healthy Start officials recommend a yearly budget of $349,000 to handle 140 cases per year, allocating about $283,000 to personnel costs, $34,000 to operating expenses, and $32,000 to overhead. This budget does not include funds for evaluation, but it would fund a program manager at $35,000, a supervisor at $30,000, one family assessment worker and six family support workers (who serve as the home visitors) from $19,000 to $21,000, and a secretary at $21,000. At this level, the supervisor would direct five home visitors and/or family assessment workers. The program manager would supervise up to three additional home visitors. Hawai'i Healthy Start maintains about a 1:5 ratio of supervisors to staff and recommends that other programs try to do the same— regardless of the level of staff training— to ensure adequate supervision critical to program success and avoid overburdening supervisors.

Clientele

In 1994 Healthy Start made initial contact with 65 percent of the more than 16,000 newborns of civilian families in the State. From these 10,485 contacts, 2,800 families (27 percent) enrolled in home visitation services. Enrolled families tend to be young (parents under 24 years old); of Hawai'ian (32 percent), Caucasian (23 percent), Filipino (18 percent), or Japanese (10 percent) ancestry; and low-income (50 percent receive welfare), with the father unemployed and the mother undereducated. Thirty-eight percent of the families have a history of substance abuse; 43 percent have a history of domestic violence; and 22 percent are homeless or living in temporary, overcrowded

conditions with other families. About 65 percent of enrolled women are single.

Service Flow

Enrollment. Hawai'i Healthy Start enlists most families immediately after delivery of the child, as this is the best way of ensuring systematic enrollment. About 10 percent of families are enrolled prenatally through contacts with clinics, obstetricians, and public health nurses. Private physicians are encouraged to refer pregnant women who may need services to the program. For those who enter the program before a child's birth, Hawai'i Healthy Start has developed a curriculum for home visitors to use with women and those of their husbands or partners who are involved with the family. Home visitors help them understand the physiological and emotional effects of pregnancy and prepare them for taking care of the baby. Hawai'i Healthy Start also stresses regular prenatal care and assists enrolled women in identifying and using a primary care physician for both preventive care and later infant treatment.

Screening at birth. Throughout Hawai'i, postpartum screening begins in the hospital with either a review of the mother's medical records or a brief inperson interview. The program has formal agreements with each hospital. Using the Healthy Start screening questionnaire, the family assessment worker checks 15 items as true, false, or unknown. ("See Healthy Start Screening Instrument.")

Three situations prompt an assessment interview:

- The mother is single, separated, or divorced; had poor prenatal care; or sought an abortion.

- Responses for two or more items are "true."[9]

- Responses for seven or more items are "unknown."

This first screening determines who requires an indepth assessment interview. One family assessment worker can perform 550 screenings and 225 assessments per year.

Assessment. If the screening suggests the need for assessment, the family assessment worker visits the mother and introduces her to the Healthy Start program. If the father is present, he is also interviewed. All interviews are voluntary. According to the family assessment worker supervisor at Kapiolani Medical Center for Women and Children (where about half of all children on O'ahu are born), mothers of newborns are usually quite willing to talk about any concerns having to do with their home situations. Less than 1 percent refuse to be interviewed.

During a casual conversation, which takes from 45 minutes to an hour, the family assessment worker covers the ten topics on the Kempe Family Stress Checklist. Immediately after leaving the room, the family assessment worker scores the ten items as normal (0), mild (5), or severe (10). This screening assessment identifies the

Healthy Start Screening Instrument

1. Marital Status: Single, Separated, Divorced	9. Late or No Prenatal Care
2. Partner Unemployed	10. History of Abortions
3. Inadequate Income or Unknown	11. History of Psychiatric Care
4. Unstable Housing	12. Unsuccessful Abortion
5. No Phone	13. Relinquishment for Adoption
6. Education Under 12 Years	14. Marital or Family Problems
7. Inadequate Emergency Contacts	15. History of Current Depression
8. History of Substance Abuse	

12. Helping to Prevent Child Abuse

factors that place the family at high risk for abuse and neglect. Families scoring above 25 are invited and encouraged to become enrolled in services. Depending on the community served, about 85 to 95 percent accept, 4 to 8 percent refuse, and about 7 percent cannot be found after they leave the hospital, usually because they move and cannot be contacted. (Some families who score in the 10–20 point range are assessed as "clinically positive" if the family assessment worker senses that the mother or father is not forthcoming. These families are offered services.) If a family scores above 40 and does not accept services, the supervisor will consider referring the family to the Child Protective Services.

The first home visit. Paraprofessional home visitors call on families weekly (or more frequently, if needed) for the first 6 to 12 months. The first 1 1/2 hour visit is spent describing the program and the role of the home visitor. The home visitor usually starts the conversation with something like the following:

> I work with the Healthy Start program. I have new information about babies that I didn't know about when I was raising my kids. It can make being a mother easier, but not easy! Also, you can look at me as your information center about this community. I live here, too, and I didn't know about WIC [Special Supplemental Food Program for Women, Infants, and Children] or the well baby clinic before I started this job.

> I hope you will learn to think of me as your "special" friend, someone here completely for you and the baby. I am here to talk when you need to share something that concerns you. I know that it is hard to start with a new baby and to have so much on your mind.

If the mother—or, if present, the father—is reluctant, the home visitor will ask if it is all right to come back the following week or offer a ride to the doctor, if needed.[10]

During the first 3 months of weekly visits, the primary focus is on helping the par-

ents with basic family support, such as learning how to mix formula and wash the baby and understanding the baby's early stages of development and sleep patterns, as well as on answering the most common question, "Why does my baby cry so much?"

Family support plan. A great deal of the home visitor's time is spent listening to parents and providing emotional support; helping them obtain food, formula, and baby supplies; assisting them with housing and job applications; getting them to appointments; and providing informal counseling on a wide range of issues, including domestic violence and drug abuse. As one home visitor put it, "It's hard to teach the mother about child development when her eyes are only on her own crises." Therefore, early in their relationship, the home visitor and the family develop an Individual Family Support Plan, which lists the services that Healthy Start provides, plus assistance available from other social service agencies. The family checks the services they want to receive during the next 6 months. The plan spells out "What we want," "Ways to get it," "Who can help," "Target date," and "What happened." The parent(s), the home visitor, and the supervisor complete and sign the plan, which also records the other service providers involved with the family.

Assessing development. During the first few weeks, the home visitor watches for signs that the mother is bonding to the infant. If she is not, the visitor models the attachment behavior (e.g., showing the mother how to hold and talk to the baby while making eye contact).

Healthy Start mothers complete a series of Infant/Child Monitoring Questionnaires, designed to identify problems in child development at 4, 8, 12, 16, 20, 24, 30, 36, and 48 months. If necessary, the home visitor reads the questions to the mother. Separate forms are used for girls and boys. Each form has five sections, covering communication, gross motor skills, fine motor skills, adaptive skills, and personal-social skills. Some questions asked at 4 months are:

- "Does your baby chuckle softly?"
- "While on her back, does your baby move her head from side to side?"
- "Does your baby generally hold her hands open or partly open?"
- "When you put a toy in her hand, does your baby look at it?"
- "When in front of a large mirror, does your baby smile or coo at herself?"

As part of its oversight, the Maternal Child Health Branch requires assessments at 4, 12, 20, and 30 months. If these reveal any developmental delays in the infant, assessments at 8, 16, and 24 months are performed. Periodic assessments are also used to determine when the family is stable enough for biweekly visits. The assessment is then repeated every 6 months to determine if visits can be safely reduced to every month, and then to every 3 months. Each family stays in the program until the child is 5 years old.

Meeting multiple needs. In addition to using the family support plan and the Infant/Child Monitoring Questionnaire, the program attempts to meet the families' multiple needs through the following:

- Parent skill building, individually and in groups, to provide parents with information about the needs of their children (primarily the newborn, but also older children) at each stage of development and what activities may be used to cope with these needs.

- Nursing Child Assessment Satellite Training (NCAST) assessment of feeding, the home, and teaching, in order to plan interventions.

- Interagency coordination and referrals.

- A toy-lending library.

- Parent support groups to increase self-esteem and reduce social isolation.

Some Healthy Start agencies in Hawai'i also provide these services:

- Respite care, to enable parents to participate in socialization groups, recreational activities, or parenting classes, or to attend to personal needs.

71

2. VICTIMOLOGY

• A male home visitor who works with the father to reduce high-risk behavior.

• Parent-child play mornings to increase bonding and interaction.

• A child development specialist who monitors and tracks the child's development and coordinates referrals for developmental testing and services, as needed.

Focusing on child development. A major clinical challenge to Hawai'i Healthy Start has been how to strengthen the focus on child development. Most of the families served are described as "chaotic"; they are poor, live in substandard housing, are unemployed, and have emotional and frequently substance abuse problems. Home visitors are often caught up in the multiple and recurring crises of the parents and in helping the family deal with these immediate problems. This makes it difficult for the home visitor to turn the parents' attention to the child's emotional and social needs and to engage them in active intervention with the child.

Hawai'i Healthy Start has responded to this challenge in some of its agencies by adding child development specialists to the team. If the home visitor cannot fully address a child's developmental needs, a specialist goes to the home to teach the parents how to interact more constructively with their child. The crux of healthy development, in the view of Hawai'i Healthy Start, is to encourage parents to see their children as enjoyable and to play with them spontaneously.

Staff Qualifications, Training, and Supervision

Both home visitors and family assessment workers are required, at minimum, to have a high school degree or General Equivalency Degree. Several staff have completed some college work, while others have a bachelor's or associate's degree. Recruited through newspaper advertisements, they are interviewed first in groups of three or four and then individually. Each structured interview includes at least one sample vignette that asks the applicant to react to a specific

situation. Ideally, applicants have been well-nurtured themselves, have strong social support systems, and have effective parenting skills. The presence of these attributes is established through extensive interviews about their childhood and the discipline they experienced.

All home visitors, family assessment workers, and supervisors attend a 6-week orientation, covering topics such as team building, child abuse and neglect, cultural sensitivity, child development, stress management, early identification of risk factors, supporting family growth, and promoting parent-child interaction and child development. Ten to 14 weeks later, staff receive an additional 2 weeks of training. Home visitors and family assessment workers receive at least 1 day of inservice training per quarter, plus informal training during case management sessions and weekly team meetings.

Family assessment workers. In addition to the training described above, family assessment workers receive intensive training in interview techniques, the entire assessment process, and community referral sources. Every day, the supervisor reviews all screenings and assessment interviews for completeness and appropriate disposition. Because the family assessment workers work only 6 days a week and maternity stays are shrinking to 24 hours, some families are missed at the hospital and instead reached at home by telephone. A monthly log compares the number of births with the number of families screened and documents action taken for those not seen at birth. Also monthly, each supervisor shadows two family assessment workers and documents observations as they conduct an assessment. And, once a month, the supervisor calls two families who refused an interview or services to discuss the reasons why. Finally, once a year, 20 intake files are chosen at random for quality assurance review by management.

Home visitors. In addition to training received with other staff, home visitors are taught how to enter the home, work nonjudgmentally, and empower families. They also are trained in cultural competence regarding parenting and ways to promote mother/child bonding and child development.

Home visitors are sometimes matched ethnically to the family, but overall compatibility is the most important criterion in assignment. Some of the Hawai'i Healthy Start programs use male home visitors to work with families in which the father is involved with the child. Supervisors review the caseloads with each home visitor for 2 hours each week; the supervisory ratio is one to five or six. Home visitors' caseloads vary from 15 to 25 families, depending on the families' level of risk and the home visitor's experience. All home visitors work 40 hours per week, with a daily average of three $1\frac{1}{2}$ hour visits; the remaining time is spent on case management.

Links to the Criminal Justice System

While Healthy Start does not have formal working agreements with the criminal justice system in Hawai'i, it does collaborate with Family Court and related agencies, particularly in cases of domestic violence. A home visitor may accompany the mother or father to Family Court for support. The Court also may ask the home visitor for a report on the family to help decide a case's disposition. When warranted, the home visitor encourages the mother to develop a safety plan, including having telephone numbers for and transportation to the spouse abuse shelter and a bag packed with necessities for herself and her child(ren). The home visitor also encourages the batterer to attend anger management classes staffed and run by other community agencies. Where corresponding classes are available for partners, mothers are encouraged also to attend.

In addition, Healthy Start staff work closely with Hawai'i's victim assistance program. Healthy Start staff make presentations to victim advocates on the program's services and its clients' needs. In turn, victim advocates train program staff on court procedures and accept referrals, usually battered women who need assistance through the court system. On occasion, judges have referred pregnant women or new mothers involved in the criminal justice system to the program,

12. Helping to Prevent Child Abuse

but their participation is on a voluntary basis. When a mother is incarcerated at the time of birth, program staff try to work with her both before and after she is released. If the father is incarcerated, staff encourage family visits, if appropriate. Also, if the family has a probation or parole officer, staff try to coordinate services.

Hawai'i Healthy Start is linked directly to the criminal justice system through its aims to prevent child abuse and neglect. Another significant but more indirect link lies in Hawai'i Healthy Start's long-term potential to reduce later criminal behavior documented as characteristic of many child abuse and neglect victims. At the very least, a decreased rate of child mistreatment would represent a strong and positive step toward long-term crime prevention.

Evaluation

Internal outcome evaluation of Hawai'i Healthy Start has been conducted primarily in terms of confirmed cases of abuse and neglect. Between July 1987 and June 1991, 13,477 families were screened and/or assessed, 9,870 of which were determined to be at low risk. Of the 3,607 families at high risk, 1,353 were enrolled in Healthy Start, 901 were enrolled in less intensive home-visiting programs, and another 1,353 went unserved, due to limited program capacity.

Among the 1,353 Healthy Start families, the confirmed rates for abuse and neglect were 0.7 percent and 1.2 percent, respectively. The combined abuse/neglect (CAN) rate was 1.9 percent. The CAN rate for at-risk families not served was 5.0 percent, quite low, compared with results from studies using control groups denied services.[11] However, the percentage may actually be higher because the at-risk families not served in Hawai'i were not monitored for abuse and neglect, nor were their medical records reviewed. The 3.1 percent difference in CAN rates between Healthy Start and unserved at-risk families is a conservative estimate and represents about 42 cases prevented during the 4-year period. (The CAN rate for the 9,870 low-risk families was 0.3 percent.)[12]

At $15,000/case/year, the 42 fewer abuse and neglect cases attributable to Healthy

Start between 1987 and 1991 represent a savings of over $1.26 million in child protection services (CPS) costs alone. (The average CPS case lasts 2 years.)

Although there are many other signs of the program's success (see "Indicators of Success for Hawai'i Healthy Start"), formal evaluation results are pending. Currently, two randomized control evaluations are being conducted, one by Deborah Daro and Karen McCurdy of the National Committee to Prevent Child Abuse (NCPCA), the other by Ann Duggan and Sharon Buchbinder of the Johns Hopkins University School of Medicine, Loretta Fuddy of Hawai'i Maternal and Child Care, and Calvin Sia.

In its second year, the NCPCA study is observing newborn to 18-month-old children served by the Hawai'i Family Stress Center at two locations on O'ahu. The study is looking at multiple outcomes— potential for child abuse, parenting skills, the mother's social support, the child's mental development, and the physical en-

---

Indicators of Success for the Hawai'i Healthy Start Program

Between July 1987 and June 1991, 2,254 families were served by Healthy Start. Indicators of the program's success over this 3-year period include:

■ Ninety percent of 2-year-olds in families receiving services were fully immunized.

■ Eighty-five percent of the children in served families had developed appropriately for their ages.[13]

■ Of the 90 families (4 percent) known to CPS at or prior to intake with a confirmed combined abuse/neglect report for siblings or imminent danger status, no further reports occurred during these families' program enrollment. Three cases were reported after the families left the program.

■ No instances of domestic homicide have been recorded since the program's inception.

---

vironment in the home. Results are expected in 1996.

The Johns Hopkins study is just starting. A prospective study, it will follow children throughout the State for 5 years. This study will cover child abuse and neglect, service delivery, adequacy of medical care, use of community resources, home environment, child health, child development, and school readiness. It will also include a cost/benefit analysis. Some data will be available in 3 years, but the entire study will not be completed until 1999.

Current Issues in Home Visitation

Heading into the late 1990's, home visitation programs like Hawai'i Healthy Start face significant questions regarding program structure and service delivery. Although much research remains to be conducted, several indepth studies provide evidence of the effectiveness of some home visiting programs and indicate what factors may lead to their success.

Breadth of services. Among the many program issues being discussed and researched are the breadth of services offered and the qualifications of staff who deliver the services. Although there appears to be a general consensus among researchers that home visitation programs should attempt to address a wide range of clients' needs, this view is tempered by the opinion that programs should have realistic expectations of what they can accomplish.[14] One review of randomized trials of home visitation programs designed to prevent child abuse and neglect found that programs with the most positive effects used comprehensive approaches to address a number of family needs.[15] Moreover, the successful programs provided both prenatal and postnatal services. (Recognizing the shortcoming of delaying outreach until birth, Hawai'i Healthy Start is currently planning a statewide program to provide prenatal care to all who need it.) Home visitation programs that, for instance, concentrate primarily on teaching mothers how to stimulate their infants' educational development or on providing only basic

73

2. VICTIMOLOGY

emotional support have shown little success.[16] It has been suggested that home visitation programs collaborate extensively with other community resources and service providers to address families' needs.[17]

Staff qualifications. Perhaps one of the more widely discussed questions regarding home visitation programs is whether professionals (particularly nurses) or paraprofessionals (usually individuals from the community with little advanced education) should be the primary service deliverers. Researchers and practitioners point to a number of advantages and disadvantages to using either professionals or paraprofessionals. It should be noted, however, that no systematic study comparing the two types of home visitors has been completed yet.

In general, professionals' expertise—and the confidence this inspires among clients and in themselves—seems to promote effective service delivery and more easily forestall job stress. One review indicated that programs with the most positive effects employed nurses as home visitors. However, it remains unclear whether the greater success stemmed from nurses' qualifications and training, clients' perceptions of nurses' qualifications, the comprehensiveness of services that programs with nurses tend to provide, or some other factor or combination of these.[18] The main disadvantages of nurses and other professionals are that they are expensive and scarce.

The majority of new home visiting programs, including Hawai'i Healthy Start, employ primarily paraprofessionals as service providers. Disadvantages of using paraprofessionals as home visitors include their relative lack of expertise and credibility, increased staff turnover due to job burnout, and need for extensive training and supervision. Also, although paraprofessionals may command smaller salaries than professionals, the level of training and supervision required may cancel out any potential financial savings to a program.[19] However, paraprofessionals from within the community being served may be better able to recruit families and communicate with them—because of shared beliefs, language or dialect, and experi-

ences—than professionals outside that community. Paraprofessionals also may better serve as role models for clients.[20]

For example, Hawai'i Healthy Start staff say that the program's paraprofessionals establish rapport with families easily and are not threatening (as, staff say, professionals can be). Staff recruitment interviews specifically screen for people who are warm, caring, and nonjudgmental. Paraprofessionals are taught to accept the family "as it is" and to be patient with slow progress. In general, service deliverers from the community are considered necessary to obtain participants' trust.

Summary

As the criminal justice system increasingly focuses its attention on crime and violence reduction, the prevention of child abuse and neglect has become a critical priority. This approach takes on added urgency in light of research documenting the cycle of violence that begins with child mistreatment and can lead to later delinquency and criminal behavior. By providing comprehensive home visitation services to families at risk for child abuse and neglect, Hawai'i Healthy Start is taking an important step toward reducing both child abuse and later crime by many of its victims. As such, Hawai'i Healthy Start and similar home visitation programs may warrant the support of the criminal justice system and society.

Notes

[1] Cathy Spatz Widom, *The Cycle of Violence*, National Institute of Justice Research in Brief, Washington, DC: U.S. Department of Justice, 1992, 3; Widom, *Victims of Childhood Sexual Abuse—Later Criminal Consequences*, National Institute of Justice Research in Brief, Washington, DC: U.S. Department of Justice, 1995, 4.

[2] Richard J. Gelles and John W. Harrop, "The Nature and Consequences of the Psychological Abuse of Children: Evidence from the Second National Family Violence Survey." Paper presented at the Eighth National Conference

on Child Abuse and Neglect, Salt Lake City, Utah, October 24, 1989.

[3] Source: John Walters, Hawai'i Department of Human Services.

[4] National Committee for Prevention of Child Abuse, *Child Abuse: Prelude to Delinquency?* Research Conference Findings, April 7–10, 1984, Washington, DC: Office of Juvenile Justice and Delinquency Prevention, U.S. Department of Justice, September 1986.

[5] See William DeJong, *Building the Peace: The Resolving Conflict Creatively Program (RCCP)*, National Institute of Justice Program Focus, Washington, DC: U.S. Department of Justice, 1994; DeJong, *Preventing Interpersonal Violence Among Youth: An Introduction to School, Community, and Mass Media Strategies*, National Institute of Justice Issues and Practices in Criminal Justice, Washington, DC: U.S. Department of Justice, 1994.

[6] *Healthy Start: Hawai'i's System of Family Support Services,* Honolulu: Hawai'i Department of Health, 1992, i.

[7] "Healthy Families America Third Year Progress Report," National Committee to Prevent Child Abuse, Chicago, IL, March 1995.

[8] Craig W. LeCroy and José B. Ashford, *Arizona Healthy Families First Year Outcome Evaluation Report*, Tucson, AZ: LeCroy, Ashford & Milligan, 1994, 13–14.

[9] The program hired an epidemiologist to determine this score. Using the results of the Kempe Family Stress Checklist as the measure of high and low risk, a score of two or more negative factors produces interviews of the largest percentage of high-risk families while avoiding interviews of the largest percentage of low-risk families (i.e., it maximizes the sum of specificity and sensitivity). About 4 to 5 percent of true high-risk families are missed by this criterion and are later reported to Child Protective Services. Even with these cases included, however, the Confirmed Abuse and Neglect rate of the noninterviewed families is less than 0.5 percent, which indicates that the criterion is very efficient.

[10] Vicki A. Wallach and Larry Lister, "Stages in the Delivery of Home-Based Services to Parents at Risk of Child Abuse: A Healthy Start Experience." Reprinted with permission of the *Journal of Scholarly Inquiry for Nursing Practice*, 9, no. 2, 1995 (in press). Published by Springer Publishing.

[11] Kempe found five confirmed cases in 25 control group families in Denver, and Olds found a 19 percent rate of confirmed abuse and neglect among a control group of poor, unmarried teenagers in Elmira, New York. See David Olds and Harriet Kitzman, "Can

12. Helping to Prevent Child Abuse

Home Visitation Improve the Health of Women and Children at Environmental Risk?" *Pediatrics*, 86, no. 1, 1990: 112.

[12] Loretta Fuddy, "Outcomes for the Hawai'i Healthy Start Program, 1992 (revised 1/94)," Honolulu: Hawai'i Department of Health, 1994. See also Gail Breakey and Betsy Pratt, "Healthy Growth for Hawai'i's Healthy Start: Toward a Systematic Statewide Approach to the Prevention of Child Abuse and Neglect," *Zero to Three,* April 1991.

[13] Loretta Fuddy, "Outcomes for the Hawai'i Healthy Start Program, 1992 (revised 1/94)."

[14] Deanna S. Gomby, Carol S. Larson, Eugene M. Lewit, and Richard E. Behrman, "Home Visiting: Analysis and Recommendations," *The Future of Children*, Center for the Future of Children, Los Altos, CA, 3, no. 3, Winter 1993: 18; Heather B. Weiss, "Home Visits: Necessary but Not Sufficient," *The Future of Children*, Center for the Future of Children, Los Altos, CA, 3, no. 3, Winter 1993: 120.

[15] David L. Olds and Harriet Kitzman,

"Review of Research on Home Visiting for Pregnant Women and Parents of Young Children," *The Future of Children*, Center for the Future of Children, Los Altos, CA, 3, no. 3, Winter 1993: 88.

[16] Olds, "Can Home Visitation Improve the Health of Women and Children at Environmental Risk?" 113–114; Weiss, "Home Visits: Necessary but Not Sufficient," 120, 122.

[17] Weiss, "Home Visits: Necessary but Not Sufficient," 122–123.

[18] Olds, "Can Home Visitation Improve the Health of Women and Children at Environmental Risk?" 115.

[19] Douglas R. Powell, "Inside Home Visiting Programs," *The Future of Children*, Center for the Future of Children, Los Altos, CA, 3, no. 3, Winter 1993: 35–36.

[20] Barbara Hanna Wasik, "Staffing Issues for Home Visiting Programs," *The Future of*

Children, Center for the Future of Children, Los Altos, CA, 3, no. 3, Winter 1993: 144–45.

About This Study

Ralph B. Earle, Ph.D., is an independent evaluator living in Hawai'i. The author reviewed the training materials, assessment instruments, and developmental materials for Hawai'i Healthy Start; interviewed Gail Breakey, Director of the Hawai'i Family Stress Center; and met with Healthy Start supervisors and staff. Julie Esselman, a research analyst at Abt Associates Inc., in Massachusetts, assisted the author. For further information, contact Gladys Wong, Program Head for Healthy Start, at (808) 946-4771.

Article 13

Is Street Crime More Harmful Than White-Collar Crime?

ISSUE SUMMARY

The word *crime* entered the English language (from the Old French) around A.D. 1250, when it was identified with "sinfulness." Later, the meaning of the word was modified: crime became the kind of sinfulness that was rightly punishable by law. Even medieval writers, who did not distinguish very sharply between church and state, recognized that there were some sins for which punishment was best left to God; the laws should punish only those that cause harm to the community. Of course, their concept of harm was a very broad one, embracing such offenses as witchcraft and blasphemy. Modern jurists, even those who deplore such practices, would say that the state has no business punishing the perpetrators of these types of offenses.

What, then, should the laws punish? The answer depends in part on our notion of harm. We usually limit the term to the kind of harm that is tangible and obvious: taking a life, causing bodily injury or psychological trauma, and destroying property. For most Americans today, particularly those who live in cities, the word *crime* is practically synonymous with street crime. Anyone who has ever been robbed or beaten by street criminals will never forget the experience. The harm that these criminals cause is tangible, and the connection between the harm and the perpetrator is very direct.

But suppose the connection is not so direct. Suppose, for example, that A hires B to shoot C. Is that any less a crime? B is the actual shooter, but is A any less guilty? Of course not, we say; he may even be more guilty, since he is the ultimate mover behind the crime. A would be guilty even if the chain of command were much longer, involving A's orders to B, and B's to C, then on to D, E, and F to kill G. Organized crime kingpins go to jail even when they are far removed from the people who carry out their orders. High officials of the Nixon administration, even though they were not directly involved in the burglary attempt at

the Democratic National Committee headquarters at the Watergate Hotel complex in 1972, were imprisoned.

This brings us to the topic of white-collar crime. The burglars at the Watergate Hotel were acting on orders that trickled down from the highest reaches of political power in the United States. Other white-collar criminals are as varied as the occupations from which they come. They include stockbrokers who make millions through insider trading, as Ivan Boesky did; members of Congress who take payoffs; and people who cheat on their income taxes, like hotel owner and billionaire Leona Helmsley. Some, like Helmsley, get stiff prison sentences when convicted, though many others (like most of the officials in the Watergate scandal) do little or no time in prison. Do they deserve stiffer punishment, or are their crimes less harmful than the crimes of street criminals?

Although white-collar criminals do not directly cause physical harm or relieve people of their wallets, they can still end up doing considerable harm. The harm done by Nixon's aides threatened the integrity of the U.S. electoral system. Every embezzler, corrupt politician, and tax cheat exacts a toll on our society. Individuals can be hurt in more tangible ways by decisions made in corporate boardrooms: Auto executives, for example, have approved design features that have caused fatalities. Managers of chemical companies have allowed practices that have polluted the environment with cancer-causing agents. And heads of corporations have presided over industries wherein workers have been needlessly killed or maimed.

Whether or not these decisions should be considered crimes is debatable. A crime must always involve "malicious intent," or what the legal system calls *mens rea*. This certainly applies to street crime—the mugger obviously has sinister designs—but does it apply to every decision made in a boardroom that ends up causing harm? And does that

Reprinted with permission from *Taking Sides: Clashing Views on Controversial Social Issues, 9/e*, edited by Kurt Finsterbusch and George McKenna, Dushkin Publishing Group/Brown & Benchmark Publishers, 1996, pp. 282-289.

harm match or exceed the harm caused by street criminals? In the following selections, John J. DiIulio, Jr., focuses on the enormous harm done—especially to the poor—by street criminals. Not only does street crime cause loss, injury, terror, and death for individuals, he argues, but it also causes neighborhood decline, community disintegration, loss of pride, business decline and failure, hampered schools, and middle-class flight to the suburbs. According to Jeffrey Reiman, white-collar crime also does more harm than is commonly recognized. By his count, white-collar crime causes far more deaths, injuries, illnesses, and financial loss than street crime. In light of this, he argues, we must redefine our ideas about what crime is and who the criminals are.

—Kurt Finsterbusch and George McKenna

YES John J. DiIulio, Jr

John J. DiIulio, Jr., is an associate professor of politics and public affairs at Princeton University in Princeton, New Jersey. His publications include *No Escape: The Future of American Corrections* (Basic Books, 1991).

THE IMPACT OF INNER-CITY CRIME

My grandmother, an Italian immigrant, lived in the same Philadelphia row house from 1921 till her death in 1986. When she moved there, and for the four decades thereafter, most of her neighbors were Irish and Italian. When she died, virtually all of her neighbors were black. Like the whites who fled, the first blacks who moved in were mostly working-class people living just above the poverty level.

Until around 1970, the neighborhood changed little. The houses were well-maintained. The children played in the streets and were polite. The teenagers hung out on the street corners in the evenings, sometimes doing mischief, but rarely—if ever—doing anything worse. The local grocers and other small businesspeople (both blacks and the few remaining whites) stayed open well past dark. Day or night, my grandmother journeyed the streets just as she had during the days of the Great Depression, taking the bus to visit her friends and relatives, going shopping, attending church, and so on.

She was a conspicuous and popular figure in this black community. She was conspicuous for her race, accent, and advanced age; she was popular for the homespun advice (and home-baked goods) she dispensed freely to the teenagers hanging out on the corners, to the youngsters playing ball in the street in front of her house, and to their parents (many of them mothers living without a husband).

Like the generations of ethnics who had lived there before them, these people were near the bottom of the socioeconomic ladder. I often heard my grandmother say that her new neighbors were "just like us," by which she meant that they were honest, decent, law-abiding people working hard to advance themselves and to make a better life for their children.

But in the early 1970s, the neighborhood began to change. Some, though by no means all, of the black families my grandmother had come to know moved out of the neighborhood. The new neighbors kept to themselves. The exteriors of the houses started to look ratty. The streets grew dirty. The grocery and variety stores closed or did business only during daylight hours. The children played in the schoolyard but not in front of their homes. The teenagers on the corners were replaced by adult drug dealers and their "runners." Vandalism and graffiti became commonplace. My grandmother was mugged twice, both times by black teenagers; once she was severely beaten in broad daylight.

In the few years before she died at age eighty-four, and after years of pleading by her children and dozens of grandchildren, she stopped going out and kept her doors and windows locked at all times. On drives to visit her, when I got within four blocks of her home, I instinctively checked to make sure that my car doors were locked. Her house, where I myself had been raised, was in a "bad neighborhood," and it did not make sense to take any chances. I have not returned to the area since the day of her funeral.

My old ethnic and ghetto neighborhood had become an underclass neighborhood. Why is it that most readers of this article avoid, and advise their friends and relatives to avoid, walking or driving through such neighborhoods? Obviously we are not worried about being infected somehow by the extremely high levels of poverty, joblessness, illiteracy, welfare dependency, or drug abuse that characterize these places. Instead we shun these places because we suppose them to contain exceedingly high numbers of predatory street criminals, who hit, rape, rob, deal drugs, burglarize, and murder.

This supposition is absolutely correct. The underclass problem, contrary to the leading academic and journalistic understandings, is mainly a crime problem. It is a crime problem, moreover, that can be reduced dramatically (although not eliminated) with the human and financial resources already at hand.

Only two things are required: common sense and compassion. Once we understand the underclass problem as a crime problem, neither of those two qualities should be scarce. Until we understand the underclass problem as a crime problem, policymakers and others will continue to fiddle while the underclass ghettos of Philadelphia, Newark, Chicago, Los Angeles, Miami, Washington, D.C., and other cities burn. . . .

2. VICTIMOLOGY

The Truly Deviant

Liberals . . . have understood the worsening of ghetto conditions mainly as the by-product of a complex process of economic and social change. One of the latest and most influential statements of this view is William Julius Wilson's *The Truly Disadvantaged: The Inner City, the Underclass, and Public Policy* (1987).

Wilson argues that over the last two decades a new and socially destructive class structure has emerged in the ghetto. As he sees it, the main culprit is deindustrialization. As plants have closed, urban areas, especially black urban areas, have lost entry-level jobs. To survive economically, or to enjoy their material success, ghetto residents in a position to do so have moved out, leaving behind them an immobilized "underclass." . . .

Wilson has focused our attention on the socioeconomic straits of the truly disadvantaged with an elegance and rhetorical force that is truly admirable.[1] But despite its many strengths, his often subtle analysis of the underclass problem wrongly deemphasizes one obvious possibility: "The truly disadvantaged" exist mainly because of the activities of "the truly deviant"—the large numbers of chronic and predatory street criminals—in their midst. One in every nine adult black males in this country is under some form of correctional supervision (prison, jail, probation, or parole).[2] Criminals come disproportionately from underclass neighborhoods. They victimize their neighbors directly through crime, and indirectly by creating or worsening the multiple social and economic ills that define the sad lot of today's ghetto dwellers.

Predatory Ghetto Criminals

I propose [another] way of thinking about the underclass problem. The members of the underclass are, overwhelmingly, decent and law-abiding residents of America's most distressed inner cities. Fundamentally, what makes them different from the rest of us is not only their higher than normal levels of welfare dependency and the like, but their far higher than normal levels of victimization by predatory criminals.

This victimization by criminals takes several forms. There is *direct victimization*—being mugged, raped, or murdered; being threatened and extorted; living in fear about whether you can send your children to school or let them go out and play without their being bothered by dope dealers, pressured by gang members, or even struck by a stray bullet. And there is *indirect victimization*—dampened neighborhood economic development, loss of a sizable fraction of the neighborhood's male population to prison or jail, the undue influence on young people exercised by criminal "role models" like the cash-rich drug lords who rule the streets, and so on.

Boldly stated, my hypothesis is that this victimization causes and perpetuates the other ills of our underclass neighborhoods. Schools in these neighborhoods are unable to function effectively because of their disorderly atmosphere and because of the violent behavior of the criminals (especially gang members) who hang around their classrooms. The truly deviant are responsible for a high percentage of teen pregnancies, rapes, and sexual assaults. Similarly, many of the chronically welfare-dependent, female-headed households in these neighborhoods owe their plights to the fact that the men involved are either unable (because they are under some form of correctional supervision) or unwilling (because it does not jibe well with their criminal lifestyles) to seek and secure gainful employment and live with their families. And much of the poverty and joblessness in these neighborhoods can be laid at the door of criminals whose presence deters local business activity, including the development of residential real estate.

Blacks are victims of violent crimes at much higher rates than whites. Most lone-offender crime against blacks is committed by blacks, while most such crimes against whites are committed by whites; in 1986, for instance, 83.5 percent of violent crimes against blacks were committed by blacks, while 80.3 percent of violent crimes against whites were committed by whites. This monochrome picture of victim-offender relationships also holds for multiple-offender crimes. In 1986, for example, 79.6 percent of multiple-offender violent crimes against blacks were committed by blacks; the "white-on-white" figure was 59.4 percent.

Criminals are most likely to commit crimes against people of their own race. The main reason is presumably their physical proximity to potential victims. If so, then it is not hard to understand why underclass neighborhoods, which have more than their share of would-be criminals, have more than their share of crime.

Prison is the most costly form of correctional supervision, and it is normally reserved for the most dangerous felons—violent or repeat offenders. Most of my readers do not personally know anyone in prison; most ghetto dwellers of a decade or two ago probably would not have known anyone in prison either. But most of today's underclass citizens do; the convicted felons were their relatives and neighbors—and often their victimizers.

For example, in 1980 Newark was the street-crime capital of New Jersey. In the Newark area, there were more than 920 violent crimes (murders, non-negligent manslaughters, forcible rapes, robberies, and aggravated assaults) per 100,000 residents; in the rest of the state the figure was under 500, and in affluent towns like Princeton it was virtually nil. In the same year, New Jersey prisons held 5,866 criminals, 2,697 of them from the Newark area.[3] In virtually all of the most distressed parts of this distressed city, at least one of every two hundred residents was an imprisoned felon.[4] The same basic picture holds for other big cities.[5]

13. Street Crime

Correlation, however, is not causation, and we could extend and refine this sort of crude, exploratory analysis of the relationship between crime rates, concentrations of correctional supervisees, and the underclass neighborhoods from which they disproportionately come. But except to satisfy curiosity, I see no commanding need for such studies. For much the same picture emerges from the anecdotal accounts of people who have actually spent years wrestling with—as opposed to merely researching—the problem.

For example, in 1988 the nation's capital became its murder capital. Washington, D.C., had 372 killings, 82 percent of them committed on the streets by young black males against other young black males. The city vied with Detroit for the highest juvenile homicide rate in America. Here is part of the eloquent testimony on this development given by Isaac Fulwood, a native Washingtonian and the city's police-chief designate:

> The murder statistics don't capture what these people are doing. We've had in excess of 1,260 drug-related shootings. . . . People are scared of these kids. Someone can get shot in broad daylight, and nobody saw anything. . . . Nobody talks. And that's so different from the way it was in my childhood.

The same thing can be said about the underclass neighborhoods of other major cities. In Detroit, for instance, most of the hundreds of ghetto residents murdered over the last six years were killed within blocks of their homes by their truly deviant neighbors.

To devise meaningful law-enforcement and correctional responses to the underclass problem, we need to understand why concentrations of crime and criminals are so high in these neighborhoods, and to change our government's criminal-justice policies and practices accordingly.

Understanding the Problem

We begin with a chicken-and-egg question: Does urban decay cause crime, or does crime cause urban decay?

In conventional criminology, which derives mainly from sociology, ghettos are portrayed as "breeding grounds" for predatory street crime. Poverty, joblessness, broken homes, single-parent families, and similar factors are identified as the "underlying causes" of crime.[6] These conditions cause crime, the argument goes; as they worsen—as the ghetto community becomes the underclass neighborhood—crime worsens. This remains the dominant academic perspective on the subject, one that is shared implicitly by most public officials who are close to the problem.

Beginning in the mid-1970s, however, a number of influential studies appeared that challenged this conventional criminological wisdom.[7] Almost without exception, these studies have cast grave doubts on the classic socio-logical explanation of crime, suggesting that the actual relationships between such variables as poverty, illiteracy, and unemployment, on the one hand, and criminality, on the other, are far more ambiguous than most analysts freely assumed only a decade or so ago. . . .

Locks, Cops, and Studies

Camden, New Jersey, is directly across the bridge from Philadelphia. Once-decent areas have become just like my grandmother's old neighborhood: isolated, crime-torn urban war zones. In February 1989 a priest doing social work in Camden was ordered off the streets by drug dealers and threatened with death if he did not obey. The police chief of Camden sent some extra men into the area, but the violent drug dealers remained the real rulers of the city's streets.

The month before the incident in Camden, the Rockefeller Foundation announced that it was going to devote some of its annual budget (which exceeds $100 million) to researching the underclass problem. Other foundations, big and small, have already spent (or misspent) much money on the problem. But Rockefeller's president was quoted as follows: "Nobody knows who they are, what they do. . . . The underclass is not a topic to pursue from the library. You get out and look for them."

His statement was heartening, but it revealed a deep misunderstanding of the problem. Rather than intimating that the underclass was somehow hard to locate, he would have done better to declare that his charity would purchase deadbolt locks for the homes of ghetto dwellers in New York City who lacked them, and subsidize policing and private-security services in the easily identifiable neighborhoods where these poor people are concentrated.

More street-level research would be nice, especially for the networks of policy intellectuals (liberal and conservative) who benefit directly from such endeavors. But more locks, cops, and corrections officers would make a more positive, tangible, and lasting difference in the lives of today's ghetto dwellers.

Notes

1. In addition, he has canvassed competing academic perspectives on the underclass; see William Julius Wilson, ed., "The Ghetto Underclass: Social Science Perspectives," *Annals of the American Academy of Political and Social Science* (January 1989). It should also be noted that he is directing a $2.7 million research project on poverty in Chicago that promises to be the most comprehensive study of its kind yet undertaken.

2. According to the Bureau of Justice Statistics, in 1986 there were 234,430 adult black males in prison, 101,000 in jail, an estimated 512,000 on probation, and 133,300 on parole. There were 8,985,000 adult black males in the national residential population. I am grateful to Larry Greenfeld for his assistance in compiling these figures.

2. VICTIMOLOGY

3. I am grateful to Hank Pierre, Stan Repko, and Commissioner William H. Fauver of the New Jersey Department of Corrections for granting me access to these figures and to related data on density of prisoner residence; to Andy Ripps for his heroic efforts in organizing them; and to my Princeton colleague Mark Alan Hughes for his expert help in analyzing the data.

4. Ten of the thirteen most distressed Newark census tracts were places where the density of prisoner residence was that high. In other words, 76.9 percent of the worst underclass areas of Newark had such extremely high concentrations of hardcore offenders. In most of the rest of Newark, and throughout the rest of the state, such concentrations were virtually nonexistent.

5. In 1980 in the Chicago area, for example, in 182 of the 1,521 census tracts at least one of every two hundred residents was an imprisoned felon. Fully twenty of the thirty-five worst underclass tracts had such extraordinary concentrations of serious criminals; in several of them, more than one of every hundred residents was behind prison bars. I am grateful to Wayne Carroll and Commissioner Michael Lane of the Illinois Department of Corrections for helping me with these data.

6. For example, see the classic statement by Edwin H. Sutherland and Donald R. Cressey, *Principles of Criminology*, 7th rev. ed. (Philadelphia: J. P. Lippincott, 1966).

7. See, for example, James Q. Wilson, *Thinking About Crime* (New York: Basic Books, 1975), especially the third chapter.

Excerpted from John J. DiIulio, Jr., "The Impact of Inner-City Crime," *The Public Interest*, no. 96 (Summer 1989), pp. 28–46. Copyright © 1989 by National Affairs, Inc. Reprinted by permission of *The Public Interest* and the author.

NO   Jeffrey Reiman

Jeffrey Reiman is the William Fraser McDowell Professor of Philosophy at American University in Washington, D.C. He is the author of over 40 articles and numerous books on moral, political, and legal philosophy, including *Justice and Modern Moral Philosophy* (Yale University Press, 1992).

A CRIME BY ANY OTHER NAME

If one individual inflicts a bodily injury upon another which leads to the death of the person attacked we call it manslaughter; on the other hand, if the attacker knows beforehand that the blow will be fatal we call it murder. Murder has also been committed if society places hundreds of workers in such a position that they inevitably come to premature and unnatural ends. Their death is as violent as if they had been stabbed or shot. . . . Murder has been committed if society knows perfectly well that thousands of workers cannot avoid being sacrificed so long as these conditions are allowed to continue. Murder of this sort is just as culpable as the murder committed by an individual.

—Frederick Engels
The Condition of the Working Class in England

What's in a Name?

If it takes you an hour to read this chapter, by the time you reach the last page, two of your fellow citizens will have been murdered. *During that same time, at least four Americans will die as a result of unhealthy or unsafe conditions in the workplace!* Although these work-related deaths could have been prevented, they are not called murders. Why not? Doesn't a crime by any other name still cause misery and suffering? What's in a name?

The fact is that the label "crime" is not used in America to name all or the worst of the actions that cause misery and suffering to Americans. It is primarily reserved for the dangerous actions of the poor.

In the March 14, 1976 edition of the *Washington Star*, a front-page article appeared with the headline: "Mine Is Closed 26 Deaths Late." The article read in part:

Why, the relatives [of the twenty-six dead miners] ask, did the mine ventilation fail and allow pockets of volatile methane gas to build up in a shaft 2,300 feet below the surface?

Why wasn't the mine cleared as soon as supervisors spotted evidence of methane gas near where miners were driving huge machines into the 61-foot-high coal seam? . . .

[I]nvestigators of the Senate Labor and Welfare Committee . . . found that there have been 1,250 safety violations at the 13-year-old mine since 1970. Fifty-seven of those violations were serious enough for federal inspectors to order the mine closed and 21 of those were in cases where federal inspectors felt there was imminent danger to the lives of the miners working there. . . .

Federal inspectors said the most recent violations found at the mine were three found in the ventilation system on Monday—the day before 15 miners were killed.

Next to the continuation of this story was another, headlined: "Mass Murder Claims Six in Pennsylvania." It described the shooting death of a husband and wife, their three children, and a friend in a Philadelphia suburb. This was murder, maybe even mass murder. My only question is, "Why wasn't the death of the miners also murder?"

Why do twenty-six dead miners amount to a "disaster" and six dead suburbanites a "mass murder"? "Murder" suggests a murderer, whereas "disaster" suggests the work of impersonal forces. If more than 1,000 safety violations had been found in the mine—three the day before the first explosion—was no one responsible for failing to eliminate the hazards? Was no one responsible for *preventing* the hazards? If someone could have prevented the hazards and did not, does that person not bear responsibility for the deaths of twenty-six men? Is he less evil because he did not want them to die although he chose to leave them in jeopardy? Is he not a murderer, perhaps even a *mass* murderer?

These questions are at this point rhetorical. My aim is not to discuss this case but rather to point to the blinders we wear when we look at such a "disaster." Perhaps there will be an investigation. Perhaps someone will be held responsible. Perhaps he will be fined. But will he be tried for *murder?* Will anyone think of him as a murderer? *And if not, why not?* Would the miners not be safer if such people were treated as murderers? Might they not still be alive? ... Didn't those miners have a right to protection from the violence that took their lives? *And if not, why not?*

Once we are ready to ask this question seriously, we are in a position to see that the reality of crime—that is, the acts we label crime, the acts we think of as crime, the actors and actions we treat as criminal—is *created:* It is an image shaped by decisions as to *what* will be called crime and *who* will be treated as a criminal.

The Carnival Mirror

... The American criminal justice system is a mirror that shows a distorted image of the dangers that threaten us—an image created more by the shape of the mirror than by the reality reflected. What do we see when we look in the criminal justice mirror?

On the morning of September 16, 1975, the *Washington Post* carried an article in its local news section headlined "Arrest Data Reveal Profile of a Suspect." The article reported the results of a study of crime in Prince George's County, a suburb of Washington, D.C. It read in part that

The typical suspect in serious crime in Prince George's County is a black male, aged 14 to 19. . . .

This is the Typical Criminal feared by most law-abiding Americans. His crime, according to former Attorney General John Mitchell (who was by no means a typical criminal), is forcing us "to change the fabric of our society, . . . forcing us, a free people, to alter our pattern of life, . . . to withdraw from our neighbors, to fear all strangers and to limit our activities to 'safe' areas." These poor, young, urban (disproportionately) black males comprise the core of the enemy forces in the war against crime. They are the heart of a vicious, unorganized guerrilla army, threatening the lives, limbs, and possessions of the law-abiding members of society—necessitating recourse to the ultimate weapons of force and detention in our common defense. They are the "career criminals" President Reagan had in mind when he told the International Association of Chiefs of Police, assuring them of the tough stance that the federal government would take in the fight against crime, that "a small number of criminals are responsible for an enormous amount of the crime in American society."

... The acts of the Typical Criminal are not the only acts that endanger us, nor are they the acts that endanger us the most. We have a greater chance . . . of being killed or disabled, for example, by an occupational injury or disease, by unnecessary surgery, or by shoddy emergency medical services than by aggravated assault or even homicide! Yet even though these threats to our well-being are graver than that posed by our poor, young, urban, black males, they do not show up in the FBI's Index of serious crimes. The individuals who are responsible for them do not turn up in arrest records or prison statistics. *They never become part of the reality reflected in the criminal justice mirror, although the danger they pose is at least as great and often greater than those who do!*

Similarly, the general public loses more money *by far* . . . from price-fixing and monopolistic practices and from consumer deception and embezzlement than from all the property crimes in the FBI's Index combined. Yet these far more costly acts are either not criminal, or if technically criminal, not prosecuted, or if prosecuted, not punished, or if punished, only mildly. In any event, although the individuals responsible for these acts take more money out of the ordinary citizen's pocket than our Typical Criminal, they rarely show up in arrest statistics and almost never in prison populations. *Their faces rarely appear in the criminal justice mirror, although the danger they pose is at least as great and often greater than those who do.*

The inescapable conclusion is that the criminal justice system does not simply *reflect* the reality of crime; it has a hand in *creating* the reality we see.

The criminal justice system is like a mirror in which society can see the face of the evil in its midst. Because the system deals with some evil and not with others, because it treats some evils as the gravest and treats some of the gravest evils as minor, the image it throws back is distorted like the image in a carnival mirror. Thus, the image cast back is false, not because it is invented out of thin air, but because the proportions of the real are distorted: Large becomes small and small large; grave becomes minor and minor grave. Like a carnival mirror, although nothing is reflected that does not exist in the world, the image is more a creation of the mirror than a picture of the world. . . .

This is my point. Because we accept the belief . . . that the model for crime is one person specifically intending to harm another, we accept a legal system that leaves us unprotected against much greater dangers to our lives and well-being than those threatened by the Typical Criminal. . . .

Work May Be Dangerous to Your Health

Since the publication of *The President's Report on Occupational Safety and Health* in 1972, numerous studies have documented both the astounding incidence of disease, injury, and death due to hazards in the workplace *and* the fact that much or most of this carnage is the consequence of the refusal of management to pay for safety measures and of government to enforce safety standards.

In that 1972 report, the government estimated the number of job-related illnesses at 390,000 per year and the number of annual deaths from industrial disease at 100,000. For 1986, the Bureau of Labor Statistics [BLS] of the U.S. Department of Labor estimates 136,800 job-related illnesses and 3,610 work-related deaths. Note that the latter figure

2. VICTIMOLOGY

applies only to private-sector work environments with eleven or more employees. It is not limited to death from occupational disease but includes all work-related deaths, including those resulting from accidents on the job.

Before considering the significance of these figures, it should be pointed out that there is wide agreement that occupational diseases are seriously underreported. *The Report of the President to the Congress on Occupational Safety and Health* for 1980 stated that

> recording and reporting of illnesses continue to present measurement problems, since employers (and doctors) are often unable to recognize some illnesses as work-related. The annual survey includes data only on the visible illnesses of workers. To the extent that occupational illnesses are unrecognized and, therefore, not recorded or reported, the illness survey estimates may understate their occurrence.

. . . For these reasons, plus the fact that BLS's figures on work-related deaths are only for private workplaces with eleven or more employees, we must supplement the BLS figures with other estimates. In 1982, then U.S. Secretary of Health and Human Services Richard Schweiker stated that "current estimates for overall workplace-associated cancer mortality vary within a range of five to fifteen percent." With annual cancer deaths currently running more than 460,000, that translates into between 23,000 and 69,000 job-related cancer deaths per year. In testimony before the Senate Committee on Labor and Human Resources, Dr. Philip Landrigan, director of the Division of Environmental and Occupational Medicine at the Mount Sinai School of Medicine in New York City, stated that

> Recent data indicate that occupationally related exposures are responsible each year in New York State for 5,000 to 7,000 deaths and for 35,000 new cases of illness (not including work-related injuries). These deaths due to occupational disease include 3,700 deaths from cancer. . . .
>
> Crude national estimates of the burden of occupational disease in the United States may be developed by multiplying the New York State data by a factor of 10. New York State contains slightly less than 10 percent of the nation's workforce, and it includes a broad mix of employment in the manufacturing, service and agricultural sectors. Thus, it may be calculated that occupational disease is responsible each year in the United States for 50,000 to 70,000 deaths, and for approximately 350,000 new cases of illness.

It is some confirmation of Dr. Landrigan's estimates that they imply work-related cancer deaths of approximately 37,000 a year—a figure that is squarely in the middle of the range implied in Secretary Schweiker's statement on this issue. Thus, even if we discount OSHA's [Occupational Safety and Health Administration's] 1972 estimate of 100,000 deaths a year due to occupational disease or Dr. Landrigan's estimate of between 50,000 to 70,000, we would surely be erring in the other direction to accept the BLS figure of 3,610. We can hardly be overestimating the actual toll if we set it at 25,000 deaths a year resulting from occupational disease.

As for the BLS estimate of 136,800 job-related illnesses, here, too, there is reason to assume that the figure considerably understates the real situation. Dr. Landrigan's estimates suggest that the BLS figure represents less than half of the actual number. However, the BLS figure is less accurate than its figure for job-related deaths for at least two reasons: It is not limited to firms with eleven or more employees and symptoms of illness generally can be expected to appear sooner after contracting an illness than does death. To stay on the conservative side, then, I shall assume that there are annually in the United States approximately 150,000 job-related illnesses and 25,000 deaths from occupational diseases. How does this compare to the threat posed by crime? Before jumping to any conclusions, note that the risk of occupational disease and death falls only on members of the labor force, whereas the risk of crime falls on the whole population, from infants to the elderly. Because the labor force is less than half the total population (110,000,000 in 1986, out of a total population of 241,000,000), to get a true picture of the *relative* threat posed by occupational diseases compared to that posed by crime we should *halve* the crime statistics when comparing them to the figures for industrial disease and death. Using the 1986 statistics, this means that the *comparable* figures would be:

	Occupational Disease	Crime (halved)
Death	25,000	10,000
Other physical harm	150,000	400,000

. . . It should be noted further that the statistics given so far are *only* for occupational *diseases* and deaths from those diseases. They do not include death and disability from work-related injuries. Here, too, the statistics are gruesome. The National Safety Council reported that in 1986, work-related accidents caused 10,700 deaths and 1.8 million disabling work injuries, at a total cost to the economy of $34.8 billion. This brings the number of occupation-related deaths to 36,700 a year. If, on the basis of these additional figures, we recalculated our chart comparing occupational to criminal dangers, it would look like this:

	Occupational Hazard	Crime (halved)
Death	36,700	10,000
Other physical harm	1,950,000	400,000

Can there be any doubt that workers are more likely to stay alive and healthy in the face of the danger from the

13. Street Crime

underworld than in the face of what their employers have in store for them on the job? . . .

[T]he vast majority of occupational deaths result from disease, not accident, and disease is generally a function of conditions outside a worker's control. Examples of such conditions are the level of coal dust in the air (about 10 percent of all active coal miners have black lung disease) or textile dust (some 85,000 American cotton textile workers presently suffer breathing impairments caused by acute byssinosis or brown lung, and another 35,000 former mill workers are totally disabled with chronic brown lung) or asbestos fibers (a study of 632 asbestos-insulation workers between 1943 and 1971 indicates that 11 percent have died of asbestosis and 38 percent of cancer; two doctors who have studied asbestos workers conclude "we can anticipate three thousand excess respiratory, cardiopulmonary deaths and cancers of the lung—three thousand excess deaths *annually* for the next twenty or thirty years"), or coal tars ("workers who had been employed five or more years in the coke ovens died of lung cancer at a rate three and a half times that for all steelworkers"; coke oven workers also develop cancer of the scrotum at a rate five times that of the general population). Also, some 800,000 people suffer from occupationally related skin disease each year (according to a 1968 estimate by the U.S. surgeon general), and "the number of American workers experiencing noise conditions that may damage their hearing is estimated [in a 1969 Public Health Service publication of the Department of Health, Education and Welfare] to be in excess of 6 million, and may even reach 16 million."

To blame the workers for occupational disease and deaths is simply to ignore the history of governmental attempts to compel industrial firms to meet safety standards that would keep dangers (such as chemicals or fibers or dust particles in the air) that are outside of the worker's control down to a safe level. This has been a continual struggle, with firms using everything from their own "independent" research institutes to more direct and often questionable forms of political pressure to influence government in the direction of loose standards and lax enforcement. So far, industry has been winning because OSHA has been given neither the personnel nor the mandate to fulfill its purpose. . . .

When inspectors do find violations, the penalties they can assess are severely limited by the OSHA law that Congress has not updated since it established the agency. The maximum penalty for a serious OSHA violation is $1,000; an employer who acts willfully can be fined up to $10,000 for each incident. . . .

Even when the agency hits employers hard, however, the sting does not often last very long. The big proposed fines that grab headlines are seldom paid in full. The two record-breaking citations of last year, against Union Carbide Corporation for $1.37 million and Chrysler for $910,000, were each settled this year for less than a third of the original amounts.

According to *Occupational Hazards,*

. . . NIOSH's [National Institute for Occupational Safety and Health's] budget, rather than being increased, had continued to be cut—by as much as 47 percent since 1980, when adjusted for inflation. And that while nations such as Finland spend approximately $2 per worker each year on occupational disease surveillance, the United States spends about 2¢ per worker.

. . . Is a person who kills another in a bar brawl a greater threat to society than a business executive who refuses to cut into his profits in order to make his plant a safe place to work? By any measure of death and suffering the latter is by far a greater danger than the former. Because he wishes his workers no harm, because he is only indirectly responsible for death and disability, while pursuing legitimate economic goals, his acts are not called "crimes." Once we free our imagination from the irrational shackle of the one-on-one model of crime, can there be any doubt that the criminal justice system does *not* protect us from the gravest threats to life and limb? It seeks to protect us when danger comes from a young, lower-class male in the inner city. When a threat comes from an upper-class business executive in an office, the criminal justice system looks the other way. This is in the face of growing evidence that for every American citizen murdered by some thug, two American workers are killed by their bosses.

Health Care May Be Dangerous to Your Health

. . . On July 15, 1975, Dr. Sidney Wolfe of Ralph Nader's Public Interest Health Research Group testified before the House Commerce Oversight and Investigations Subcommittee that there "were 3.2 million cases of unnecessary surgery performed each year in the United States." These unneeded operations, Dr. Wolfe added, "cost close to $5 billion a year and kill as many as 16,000 Americans." Wolfe's estimates of unnecessary surgery were based on studies comparing the operations performed and surgery recommended by doctors who are paid for the operations they do with those performed and recommended by salaried doctors who receive no extra income from surgery.

. . . In an article on an experimental program by Blue Cross and Blue Shield aimed at curbing unnecessary surgery, *Newsweek* reports that

a Congressional committee earlier this year [1976] estimated that more than 2 million of the elective operations performed in 1974 were not only unnecessary—but also killed about 12,000 patients and cost nearly $4 billion.

. . . In fact, if someone had the temerity to publish a *Uniform Crime Reports* that really portrayed the way Americans are murdered, the FBI's statistics on the *type of weapon used*

2. VICTIMOLOGY

Table 1

How Americans Are Murdered

Total	Firearms	Knife or Other Cutting Instrument	Other Weapon: Club, Arson, Poison, Strangulation, etc.	Personal Weapon: Hands, Fists, etc.
19,257[a]	11,381	3,957	2,609	1,310

[a] Note that this figure diverges somewhat from the figure of 20,613 murders and nonnegligent manslaughters used elsewhere in the FBI *Uniform Crime Reports,* 1987; see for example, p. 7.
Source: FBI *Uniform Crime Reports,* 1987: "Murder Victims: Weapons Used, 1986."

in murder would have to be changed for 1986, from those shown in Table 1 to something like those shown in Table 2.

The figures shown in Table 2 would give American citizens a much more honest picture of what threatens them. We are not likely to see it broadcast by the criminal justice system, however, because it would also give American citizens a more honest picture of *who* threatens them.

We should not leave this topic without noting that, aside from the other losses it imposes, unnecessary surgery was estimated to have cost between $4 and $5 billion in 1974. The price of medical care has nearly tripled between 1974 and 1986. Thus, assuming that the same number of unneeded operations were performed in 1986, the cost of unnecessary surgery would be between $12 and $15 billion. To this we should add the unnecessary 22 percent of the 6 billion administered doses of medication. Even at the extremely conservative estimate of $3 a dose, this adds about $4 billion. In short, assuming that earlier trends have continued, there is reason to believe that unnecessary surgery and medication cost the public between $16 and $19 billion annually—far outstripping the $11.6 billion taken by thieves that concern the FBI. This give us yet another way in which we are robbed of more money by practices that are not treated as criminal than by practices that are.

Waging Chemical Warfare Against America

. . . "A 1978 report issued by the President's Council on Environmental Quality (CEQ) unequivocally states that 'most researchers agree that 70 to 90 percent of cancers are caused by environmental influences and are hence theoretically preventable.' " This means that a concerted national effort could result in saving 300,000 or more lives a year and reducing each individual's chances of getting cancer in his or her lifetime from one in four to one in twelve or less. . . .

The simple truth is that the government that strove so mightily to protect us against a guerrilla war 10,000 miles from home [the Vietnam War, in which the United States spent around $165 billion] is doing next to nothing to protect us against the chemical war in our midst. This war is being waged against us on three fronts:

- Air pollution
- Cigarette smoking
- Food additives

Not only are we losing on all three fronts, but it looks like we do not even have the will to fight. . . .

In 1970, Lester B. Lave and Eugene P. Seskin reviewed more than fifty scientific studies of the relationship between air pollution and morbidity and mortality rates for lung cancer, nonrespiratory tract cancers, cardiovascular disease, bronchitis, and other respiratory diseases. They found in every instance a *positive quantifiable relationship.* Using sophisticated statistical techniques, they concluded that a 50 percent reduction in air pollution in major urban areas would result in:

- A 25 percent reduction in mortality from lung cancer (using 1974 mortality rates, this represents a potential saving of 19,500 lives per year)
- A 25 percent reduction in morbidity and mortality due to respiratory disease (a potential saving of 27,000 lives per year)
- A 20 percent reduction in morbidity and mortality due to cardiovascular disease (a potential saving of 52,000 lives per year). . . .

A more recent study, done in 1978 by Robert Mendelsohn of the University of Washington and Guy Orcutt of Yale University, estimates that air pollution causes a total of 142,000 deaths a year. . . .

Based on the knowledge we have, there can be no doubt that air pollution, tobacco, and food additives amount to a chemical war that makes the crime wave look like a football scrimmage. Quite conservatively, I think we can estimate the death toll in this war as at least a quarter of a million lives a year—*more than ten times the number killed by criminal homicide! . . .*

Summary

Once again, our investigations lead to the same result. The criminal justice system does not protect us against the gravest threats to life, limb, or possessions. Its definitions of crime are not simply a reflection of the objective dangers

13. Street Crime

Table 2
How Americans Are (Really) Murdered

Total	Occupational Hazard & Disease	Inadequate Emergency Medical Care	Knife or Other Cutting Instrument Including Scalpel	Firearms	Other Weapon: Club, Poison, Hypodermic, Prescription Drug	Personal Weapon: Hands, Fists, etc.
114,957	61,700	20,000	15,957[a]	11,381	4,609[a]	1,310

[a] these figures represent the relevant figures in Table 1 plus the most conservative figures for the relevant categories discussed in the text.

that threaten us. The workplace, the medical profession, [and] the air we breathe . . . lead to far more human suffering, far more death and disability, and take far more dollars from our pockets than the murders, aggravated assaults, and thefts reported annually by the FBI. What is more, this human suffering is preventable. A government really intent on protecting our well-being could enforce work safety regulations, police the medical profession, [and] require that clean air standards be met, . . . but it does not. Instead we hear a lot of cant about law and order and a lot of rant about crime in the streets. It is as if our leaders were not only refusing to protect us from the major threats to our well-being but trying to cover up this refusal by diverting our attention to crime—as if this were the only real threat. As we have seen, the criminal justice system is a carnival mirror that presents a distorted image of what threatens us. . . . All the mechanisms by which the criminal justice system comes down more frequently and more harshly on the poor criminal than on the well-off criminal take place *after* most of the dangerous acts of the well-to-do have been excluded from the definition of crime itself.

From Jeffrey Reiman, *The Rich Get Richer and the Poor Get Prison: Ideology, Class, and Criminal Justice,* 3rd ed. (Macmillan, 1990). Copyright © 1990 by Jeffrey Reiman. Reprinted by permission of Macmillan College Publishing Company. Notes omitted.

POSTSCRIPT

Is Street Crime More Harmful Than White-Collar Crime?

DiIulio implies that much of the social misery of America, including the persistence of poverty, can be traced

to the "truly depraved" street criminals in our central cities. Is this focus too narrow? Surely there are many other sources of the social crisis that afflicts our central cities. Reiman's focus, on the other hand, may be overly broad. He claims that more people are killed and injured by "occupational injury or disease, by unnecessary surgery, and by shoddy emergency medical services than by aggravated assault or even homicide!" Can shoddy medical services be categorized as a crime? And could the residents of city ghettos, where most of the violent crime occurs, ever be convinced that they face a greater risk from occupational injury or disease than from street criminals? In the end, the questions remain: What is a crime? Who are the criminals?

A set of readings that support Reiman's viewpoint is *Corporate Violence: Injury and Death for Profit* edited by Stuart L. Hills (Rowman & Littlefield, 1987). Further support is provided by Marshall B. Clinard, *Corporate Corruption: The Abuse of Power* (Praeger, 1990). *White-Collar Crime* edited by Gilbert Geis and Robert F. Meier (Free Press, 1977) is a useful compilation of essays on corporate and political crime, as is Gary Green's *Occupational Crime* (Nelson-Hall, 1990). Four other books that focus on crime in high places are J. Douglas and J. M. Johnson, *Official Deviance* (J. B. Lippincott, 1977); J. Anthony Lukas, *Nightmare: The Underside of the Nixon Years* (Viking Press, 1976); Marshall B. Clinard, *Corporate Elites and Crime* (Sage Publications, 1983); and David R. Simon and Stanley Eitzen, *Elite Deviance* (Allyn & Bacon, 1982). A work that deals with the prevalence and fear of street crime is Elliott Currie, *Confronting Crime: An American Challenge* (Pantheon Books, 1985). Two works on gangs, which are often connected with violent street crime, are Martin Sanchez Jankowski, *Islands in the Street: Gangs and American Urban Society* (University of California Press, 1991) and Felix M. Padilla, *The Gang as an American Enterprise* (Rutgers University Press, 1992). One interesting aspect of many corporate, or white-collar, crimes is that they involve crimes of obedience, as discussed in Herman C. Kelman and V. Lee Hamilton, *Crimes of Obedience: Toward a Social Psychology of Authority and Responsibility* (Yale University Press, 1989).

The Police

The role of the police in America is a difficult one, and as the police deal with a growing, diverse population, their job becomes more difficult. The need for a more professional, well-trained police officer is obvious. In the first unit article, "Police and the Quest for Professionalism," Barbara Raffel Price presents a short overview of the problems that police face as they strive for professionalism. Public confidence, respect, and higher education are essential. Price supports community policing as one step toward reaching the goal of professionalism. In "Police Work from a Woman's Perspective," James Daum and Cindy Johns explore the problems that are still present as women assume a greater role in policing. Many female police officers still face unacceptance, sexual harassment, and unequal treatment.

In "The Community's Role in Community Policing," and again in an interview with a Florida police chief (see "LEN Interview: Police Chief Robert E. Ford of Port Orange, Fla."), there are discussions of problems with officers who cannot properly prepare reports and the advantages of officers' having a college education.

"Incorporating Diversity: Police Response to Multicultural Changes in Their Communities," by Brad Bennett, reports on a study done in California concerning how four police agencies responded to demographic changes in their communities. In "Police Cynicism: Causes and Cures," Wallace Graves discusses the negative impact of cynicism within a police agency. According to Graves, cynical, distrustful police officers can hinder a department's ability to form collaborative relationships within the community.

Looking Ahead: Challenge Questions

Is there "community policing" in your community? If not, why not? If so, is it working?

How important do you consider a college education as a requirement for entry into police work?

Do the police in your community reflect accurately the racial mix of the community?

UNIT 3

Article 14

Police & the Quest for Professionalism

Barbara Raffel Price

Barbara Raffel Price is the Dean of Graduate Studies and a professor of criminal justice at John Jay College of Criminal Justice.

Since the early 1900's, under the leadership of August Vollmer, the father of American policing, law enforcement has been fascinated by the possibilities of professionalism. For the police in those early years, professionalism meant control of their work world with an end to interference from corrupt politicians who appointed unqualified patrolmen and interfered with or controlled hiring, firing and assignment. For Vollmer, professionalism also held a loftier meaning—something he called "scientific policing," which emphasized a style of policing that was detached, objective and, especially, adopted techniques that took advantage of the latest scientific advances in detecting and solving crimes and in approaches to patrolling a community.

Soon after Vollmer appeared on the scene, the police incorporated the term "professionalism" into their public rhetoric. However, policing remained an occupation that had far to go before it would be considered a profession. The principal barrier to professionalism, then as now, is the fact that policing is in one fundamental way unlike any other field striving to professionalize: It has the duty and the right to use coercion, an act that fosters a work culture antithetical to professionalism (which is usually understood to mean service to the client).

Professionalism normally entails:

- A transmittable body of knowledge which is constantly growing and being refined;
- A code of ethics defining relations between members of the profession and the public, including an obligation to render services exclusive of any other considerations;
- High standards for membership, often including higher education and formal training;
- Accountability through peer review and, therefore, continuous evaluation and improvement through research of professional practices;
- At some point in the evolution of the occupation, acknowledgement from outsiders that the occupation is a profession.

Although these demanding criteria arguably present significant obstacles to efficient policing, many continue to believe in and work toward the professionalization of law enforcement. Central to that effort over the years—dating back at least to the Wickersham Commission in 1931—has been an insistence that educational levels of police be raised. More recently, in 1973, the National Commission on Criminal Justice Standards and Goals urged that by 1982, every police department in the United States require four years of college education. In 1995, however, only a relative handful of departments require recruits to have a college degree. It bears mentioning, too, that most police unions have vehemently opposed education for recruits, as they have other components of professionalization, including peer review and accountability.

"If there is a future to the professionalization of policing, many believe it rests in pursuing community policing. Others insist that it is an impossible dream."

Why is professionalism a goal of law enforcement? The most basic answer is that public confidence in the police is essential for order maintenance and stability in the community. When the police are distrusted, government itself is undermined. Professionalism instills confidence and respect because it means to the public that the practitioners have internalized values of service, even altruism, self-control and commitment to high ideals of behavior. Further, professionalism implies higher education. Many have argued that higher education will help police gain an understanding of their role in a democratic society and a fuller comprehension of the responsibilities that come with

Reprinted with permission from *Law Enforcement News,* June 15, 1995, p.8. © 1995 by LEN, Inc., and John Jay College of Criminal Justice, New York, NY.

14. Police and the Quest for Professionalism

police power. The President's Crime Commission in 1967 observed that the complexities of policing "dictate that officers possess a high degree of intelligence, education, tact and judgment" and said it was "essential . . . that the requirements to serve in law enforcement reflect the awesome responsibility" facing the personnel selected.

Since the 1960s, when the Federal Government began to assume a major role in upgrading the quality of law enforcement, significant progress has been made, notwithstanding that policing remains fraught with problems. Police are better educated today. Departments are more representative of the communities and populations they serve. Police are more restrained in the use of deadly force. Research on policing, virtually nonexistent in the 1950s, has expanded to a considerable volume generated by universities, private research institutes, nonprofit foundations and Federal agencies. Much more of it is needed.

With the introduction of the patrol car and the two-way radio, the hallmarks of police professionalism were efficiency, as measured by clearance rates, and speed in response to calls. Following the widespread urban unrest of the mid- to late 1960s, law enforcement developed a strategy of community relations that stressed police sensitivity to diverse needs and cultures within the community.

For the past few years, the focus within policing has been directed toward a new, comprehensive strategy called, variously, community policing or problem-oriented policing. In order to work, community policing requires professional police who have acquired nontraditional police skills so that they can involve the community as a co-participant in the control of crime and maintenance of order. Community policing also requires that communities develop consensus as to what steps should be taken to prevent or reduce crime and it requires cooperation and follow-through by the police and the community.

The question arises as to whether a level of trust sufficient to work with the police exists in those communities that are most crime-ridden. Community policing also raises questions as to whether police have the requisite community organization skills, problem-solving skills, and the ability to mobilize scarce community resources to solve problems.

If there is a future to the professionalization of policing, many in law enforcement believe it rests in pursuing community policing. But others insist that it is an impossible dream—from the community's standpoint there is too little cohesion or ability to respond to police initiatives; from the police standpoint, the requisite skills are difficult to obtain and require mid-management support and facilitation that has, to date, been notably lacking. And then there is the question of availability of resources in the community and their efficacy for solving problems.

About the same time that community policing was taking root around the country, the beating of Rodney King by Los Angeles police was recorded on home video and broadcast worldwide. Other similar incidents of police violence have been noted as well. Public support and trust of the police eroded substantially in the wake of such episodes. Moreover, some have noted the irony of this happening even as advancing professionalism on a variety of fronts (education, organizational structure, accountability and technology) has altered some agencies dramatically within the past decade.

The loss of confidence in the police is due, in part, to the steady increase in the high visibility of crime, including drug abuse, youth gangs, organized crime, and terrorism, and the sense—almost certainly false—that we now have a more disorderly and violent society than at any time in our history. Certainly with the abandonment of President Lyndon Johnson's "war on poverty," socioeconomic divisions have widened, and racism continues to be a major source of tension. In this context, the prognosis for community policing, which has been hailed by the police themselves as "smarter policing" and as the best hope yet for the professionalization of policing, is guarded at best.

With police brutality still a significant factor in 1995, it is difficult to claim that professionalism has taken hold in law enforcement. Eradicating the excessive use of force and the scourge of police corruption are the most critical internal issues police face if they are to continue on the long and arduous course toward professionalism. There have been many successes of late for law enforcement, especially in communications technology, forensics, information systems, interagency cooperation, and the development of a commitment to their peers, if not to professional conduct. But until attitudes of the police toward those they serve can be changed, they will continue to make their own jobs more difficult and more dangerous—and professionalism for the police will not come to pass.

Article 15

Police Work From a Woman's Perspective

James M. Daum, Ph.D., Police Psychologist, Lippert, Daum and Associates; and Lieutenant Cindy M. Johns, Cincinnati Police Division

Since women have joined the ranks, much attention has been paid to their impact on the police organization and the community. However, comparatively little research has been conducted to determine how the police organization and the community have affected the female police officer. Common wisdom might lead one to believe that becoming a police officer would bring about a more radical change in a woman's life than in a man's. Police work remains a predominantly male occupation, and there is still a remnant of the traditional belief that assertiveness, aggressiveness, physical capability and emotional toughness are "male" characteristics necessary to perform competently as a police officer. When a woman displays these very same characteristics, she is often perceived as "cold," "pushy" or somehow in violation of the role socially prescribed for her gender.

For a man, a career in law enforcement is an option he can select without question. To become an officer, he must demonstrate that he possesses the knowledge, skills and abilities to do the job. In contrast, a woman aspiring to become a police officer is often viewed as unusual. This makes her "different" from other women. In order to become an officer, she must not only prove that she has the "KSAs", but also deal with the obstacles posed by being a true minority. Rather than proving that she can be as good as any other officer, she has to prove that she is as good as any *male* officer. In other words, there is pressure for her to be what she is not—which is male.

She also faces the problem of not being taken seriously as an officer. Although this lack of respect occurs most frequently among her fellow (male) officers, she sometimes encounters this same problem in the community, from citizens who request a male officer after she responds to the call. Although legal and formal organizational barriers no longer exist, a woman is still subjected to the stereotype of being one of "the weaker sex" and therefore not as capable as a man. As such, she must fight a steep uphill battle to gain acceptance as an officer.

What type of impact might such barriers and pressures have upon the female police officer? One might expect a high stress level, along with such side effects as undesirable changes in personality, health, job performance and home life. However, it could also be argued that working to combat stereotypes and gain acceptance has reward value, and that job success might provide a greater feeling of accomplishment. All that can be stated with certainty is that for women, being socialized into a police organization presents a considerable challenge.

Procedure

Eighty-one of the 122 female police officers of a metropolitan police department completed surveys while attending a one-day workshop that addressed issues of women in policing. Participation in this workshop was voluntary, so 41 of these police women did not attend. Thus, the survey results do not represent all of the female members of the department. However, it can be asserted that those who filled out the surveys have an interest in women's issues in policing, and are therefore probably aware of gender-related problems facing female officers.

Of the 12 supervisors and 69 officers who responded, 51 worked in patrol, with the remaining 30 serving in a non-patrol capacity. Eighteen respondents had been with the department for two or fewer years, 23 had been police officers for three to five years, 12 had been officers for six to 10 years and the remaining 27 had been with the division for more than 10 years. Fifty-two respondents were white, 28 were African-American and one was Hispanic.

Results

It is important to note that these findings represent the perceptions of the women who completed the surveys. Their opinions were not verified by consulting outside sources of information, such as performance evaluations, disciplinary records or other documentation. The focus of this study is not on the police department itself, but rather the perceptions, attitudes and behaviors developed among female officers through their exposure to police work.

Acceptance

Asked whether they felt accepted by other officers, supervisors, civilian city employees and the public, very few reported having difficulty being accepted by civilian employees (7 percent) or the public (10 percent). Likewise, there was general agreement that they were accepted by other female officers, as well as by female supervisors. However, 42 percent did not feel accepted by male officers, and 55 percent expressed the opinion that male supervisors did not accept them.

To assess the female officers' confidence on the job, they were asked to compare their job performance with that of male officers. The vast majority (76 percent) felt that they perform the job as well as male officers. It is significant to note, however, that almost one-fourth (24 percent) expressed the opinion that they do a better job than do male officers.

More than two-thirds (68 percent) of the female officers surveyed felt that they had to do a lot more work to receive the same credit as their male counterparts; only 30 percent believed that they were given just as much credit for their work as their male counterparts.

Asked to compare the code of conduct for male and female officers, only 4 percent felt that male officers had a stricter code of conduct, whereas 58 percent believed

15. Police Work

female officers faced tougher standards; 38 percent saw no difference. Some respondents expressed the opinion that grooming standards were stricter for females, and that their behavior was more closely scrutinized than that of males.

Another issue related to acceptance is the attitude of the recruit's field training officer (FTO). Respondents were split fairly evenly on this question, with slightly over half (52 percent) reporting that they experienced no reluctance on the part of the FTO and the remaining 48 percent reporting having sensed some displeasure about having a female as a partner.

Although the majority (57 percent) saw no difference in morale between male and female officers, a substantial percentage (35 percent) felt that morale was lower among female officers. Several respondents noted that, since the majority of officers are men and they prefer to work and socialize with each other, women tend to be left out and feel disenfranchised from the organization; others observed that there are more "men-only" outings among male officers.

Many respondents expressed the need for the department to realize that female officers have different needs and to adjust its thinking accordingly; others stressed the need for official recognition that women do the job just as well, albeit differently. There were also comments about not wanting to be pampered or given the "quiet beats."

A number of respondents expressed the desire to be treated as equals and receive more support, as well as appreciation for doing a good job. "Just let me feel good about being a female cop," noted one respondent, perhaps summarizing what most female officers felt.

Changes in Attitude and Behavior

Ninety-seven percent of the female officers surveyed firmly agreed that becoming a police officer has changed them in significant ways. Although most of the group were generally pleased with these changes, there were a substantial number who were displeased. Some like feeling more self-confident and less naive. Others mentioned having more distrust of others. Being able to relate more easily to people was listed as a desirable change, whereas being colder, more skeptical and less tolerant were mentioned as undesirable changes. Common themes were that the job produces a negative outlook, less patience, more forcefulness and greater irritability. Overall, there seemed to be a general awareness that exposure to life's harsher realities has significantly changed perceptions and attitudes.

Asked if being a police officer has affected relationships outside the police department, many of these officers reported feeling set apart from others and subjected to stereotypes put forth by the media. Others mentioned that the shifts they work afford little time for relationships, or that it is more difficult to start a relationship because a potential date is uncomfortable with a "cop."

It might be expected that a stressful job would have an impact on the officer's tendency to curse, smoke or use alcohol. Respondents reported the following changes in these behaviors:

	Never Have	More	Less	Same	Quit
Smoking	57%	6%	5%	13%	19%
Drinking	16%	13%	29%	35%	7%
Cursing	3%	63%	8%	24%	2%

It could be said that becoming a police officer appears to have had some positive impact in the areas of smoking and drinking, in that 24 percent have either quit smoking or smoke less than previously, and a total of 36 percent have either decreased their alcohol intake or quit altogether. It is obvious that most of these women find that they curse more now than they did before.

These officers also noted unpleasant changes in sleeping and eating habits, as well as attitude. Changes in sleeping or eating habits were usually attributed to shift work and the corresponding need to alter one's daily schedule. A negative eating habit mentioned by several officers is having to eat more "fast food" instead of home-cooked meals.

Sixty-five percent of respondents reported regularly engaging in one or more stress-reducing activities, including playing team and individual sports, walking, reading, spending time with family, bike riding and doing aerobics. Also mentioned were tending to animals (household pets, horses), exercising, talking out problems and enjoying outdoor activities.

Sexual Harassment

Respondents considered several behaviors to be part and parcel of sexual harassment, including jokes, inappropriate touching, requests for sex, sexually degrading comments or gestures and other threatening behaviors. Some respondents also mentioned being treated differently because of their sex.

Sixty-two percent of the survey respondents had experienced some form of sexual harassment (as defined above)

from a co-worker or supervisor. Of these, one-third confronted the offender, and 6 percent talked to their supervisors about it. A few contacted a representative of the EEOC, but 21 percent took no action at all. Very few took strong measures to address the problem.

Job Goals

Given the difficulties facing female police officers, one might expect discouragement and disenchantment. However, 80 percent stated that they plan to work for the department until retirement. There were very few with definite plans to leave within the foreseeable future, although some mentioned getting another position after finishing college. Only one respondent stated that she sees better opportunities for advancement and promotion outside of a police career. Fifty-six percent of the patrol officers planned on working toward promotion, and 31 percent were seeking a specialized assignment. Only 13 percent preferred to stay on as patrol officers.

There was substantial confidence among female officers that they will be able to succeed in garnering a promotion or preferred assignment—implying either that no major organizational obstacles are perceived or that female officers have confidence in their ability to surmount whatever obstacles there might be. Such confidence may also result from the department's policy of encouraging placement of minorities in preferred assignments.

Seventy-one percent reported that if they had to start over again, they would still become police officers. Therefore, most felt that they had made the right choice and were receiving enough reward and satisfaction from their careers. The 29 percent who would have pursued another career stated that they have remained on the job primarily due to the salary, benefits and job security. A few said they have continued as police officers because they were taught to "tough it out," or that they enjoyed the status that comes with the profession.

Summary

The results of this survey suggest that female police officers continue to struggle to gain acceptance from their male counterparts. The prevailing opinion among respondents to this survey is that they do not receive equal credit for their job performance, even though they believe that they are as capable as male officers. They also sense some degree of ostracism from the male social network, which has a negative impact on their

91

3. THE POLICE

morale. They feel a need to be accepted as female officers, rather than being evaluated according to "male" criteria. Many have experienced some form of sexual harassment from co-workers and supervisors, but did not assertively address the problem.

Exposure to police work produces a change in social attitudes for female officers. Some become more confident, more socially comfortable and less naive, but others become colder, less trusting and less tolerant of others. Most of the officers who responded to the survey regularly engage in healthy activities to relieve stress. Many have decreased their smoking and use of alcohol. Their sleeping and eating habits are adversely affected because of lifestyle adjustments to shift work.

Despite these problems, most do not regret the decision to become a police officer. They plan to continue with the job and are optimistic about career advancement. For these officers, the career is worth the struggle, and although they have yet to gain full acceptance, they see themselves as making valuable contributions to their departments and communities.

Article 16

The Community's Role in Community Policing

Wesley G. Skogan

Discussions about community policing often involve a number of assumptions about the role that the community will play. These assumptions often appear on reflection to have been arrived at too casually. It is usually anticipated that citizens will be eager to step forward to work with police. Discussions of problem solving frequently assume that police and residents will engage in joint as well as coordinated efforts to tackle neighborhood problems. There even is talk about the role that police can play in fostering the development of community organizations and mobilizing the organizations in problem solving and community-building activities.

It is also widely assumed that crime *prevention* is probably more dependent on the community than on the police side of the community policing equation and that in the final analysis, the police play an ancillary role in maintaining social control. In this view, the police can keep their part of the bargain by being more "customer oriented." They will be more effective when citizens' priorities help shape their agenda, and the subsequent buildup of trust will rebound in the form of greater police-citizen cooperation and mutual support.

Challenges in sustaining community involvement

Although the community side of community policing is as critical as any, many cities have experienced difficulty getting neighborhood residents involved. The Vera Institute of Justice found in its NIJ-sponsored study of community policing in eight cities that "all eight...sites experienced extreme difficulty in establishing a solid community infrastructure on which to build their community policing programs."[1] The researchers concluded that, of all the implementation problems these programs faced, "the most perplexing...was the inability of the police departments to organize and maintain active community involvement in their projects."[2] They found that the list of problems in sustaining community involvement in policing was long.

Police-citizen cooperation. Above all, police and citizens may have a history of not getting along with each other. Especially in disadvantaged neighborhoods, there too often is a record of antagonistic relationships between residents and the police, who may be perceived as arrogant, brutal, and uncaring—not as potential partners. Residents may fear that more intensive policing could generate new conflicts between them, including harassment and indiscriminate searches.

This concern about police behavior was documented in a recent study of community policing in Chicago. It revealed that Hispanics and African Americans were almost three times as likely as whites to think that police serving their neighborhoods were impolite and more than twice as likely to think they treated people unfairly. Among Hispanics, about 35 percent felt police were not concerned about the problems facing people in their neighborhoods; 25 percent of African Americans but only 15 percent of whites also felt this way.

Organizational involvement. Organizations representing the interests of community members also may not have a track record of cooperating with police. Low-income and high-crime areas often lack the organizational infrastructure needed to get people involved. Since their constituents often fear the police, groups representing low-income and minority areas may be more interested in monitoring police misconduct and pressing for greater police accountability to civilians, not in getting involved with them.

Research that has examined participation in crime prevention programs has revealed that in disadvantaged neighborhoods it is not easily initiated or sustained. Crime and fear stimulate withdrawal from, not involvement in, community life. In crime-ridden neighborhoods, mutual distrust and hostility often are rampant; residents may view each other with suspicion rather than neighborliness, and this undermines their capacity to forge collective responses to local problems. Because they fear retaliation by drug dealers and neighborhood toughs, programs requiring public meetings or organized cooperation may be less successful in areas with high levels of fear.

Understanding community policing. It is also difficult to get out the community policing message. Nothing in the past has really prepared many Americans for this new police mission. Residents are unlikely to understand community policing's goals and tactics. Vera Institute researchers found in their eight-city study that none of the cities had recognized the need to train residents in their appropriate roles. They con-

From *National Institute of Justice Journal,* August 1996, pp. 31-34. Reprinted by permission of the U.S. Department of Justice, National Institute of Justice.

3. THE POLICE

cluded, "[A]ny potential for the success of community policing will be limited if major commitments to community education and training are not forthcoming."[3]

There also may be no reason for residents of crime-ridden neighborhoods to think anything about community policing except, "here today, gone tomorrow." Too often their past is strewn with broken promises and programs that flowered but then wilted when funding dried up or newspapers looked the other way. They are rightly skeptical that it will be any different this time, especially when they discern that the police officers they deal with are not fully committed to the program.

Victims' experiences. Research indicates that people with direct, personal experience with crime are much more dissatisfied with police service (when other factors are held equal). The experience that crime victims often have with the criminal justice system has been referred to as "the second wound." During the 1970s there was a great deal of interest in providing better police service to victims, and in many places victims of domestic violence and sexual assault continue to receive specialized treatment. Few community policing programs, however, seem to feature services for victims.

Community diversity. Some of these problems multiply when program boundaries imposed by police departments bundle together diverse communities. Suspicion and fear may divide the area along race, class, and lifestyle lines, leaving residents and the organizations that represent them at odds with one another. They will probably point fingers at each other over who causes what problems, and the police are likely to be pressured to choose sides. Groups contending over access to housing, municipal services, infrastructure maintenance, and public-sector jobs and contracts also may find themselves battling one

another over policing priorities and for the ear of the district commander.

Community policing then threatens to become politicized. In an evaluation of community policing in Houston, researchers found that the program favored the interests of racially dominant groups and the established interests in the community. This was reflected in turn in the impact of the program, whose positive effects were confined to whites and homeowners.[4]

The Houston experience illustrates that policing by consent is difficult in places where the community is fragmented by race, class, and lifestyle. If, instead of trying to find common interests in diverse areas, the police deal mainly with elements of their own choosing, they will appear to be taking sides. It is easy for them to focus community policing on supporting those with whom they get along best and share a similar outlook. As a result, the "local priorities" they represent will be those of some in the community but not all. Critics of community policing are concerned that it can extend the familiarity of police with citizens past the point where police professionalism and commitment to the rule of law control their behavior. To act fairly and constitutionally and to protect minority rights, the police must sometimes act contrary to majority opinion. As one criminologist notes, community policing must develop a process by which officers can be given sufficient autonomy to do good without increasing the likelihood of their doing evil.[5]

Can it work?

Can community policing live up to the expectations of its supporters? Can the public get involved and see clear benefits from the program? The answers to these questions are not clear, for few systematic evaluations of community policing have

examined the role of citizen participation in any detail. Most of my observations are drawn from an ongoing evaluation of a community policing program in Chicago.

The support of the public must be won, not assumed. Police need to be responsive to citizens' concerns, and they have to be able to deliver on community policing's commitment to neighborhood problem solving. Responsiveness requires organizational design: There have to be regular and widely recognized channels by which the public can articulate its concerns and priorities, and there has to be assurance that someone who is responsible for responding at the police end is listening carefully. In Chicago the mechanism is beat meetings. These small gatherings are held all over the city on a regular schedule; they bring together residents and the officers who work in their area to discuss community problems.

The capacity of the police to deliver on commitments they make to deal with those problems has been greatly enhanced by the city's effective integration of community policing with the efforts of other city service agencies. Beat teams are able to command quick attention to problems they identify as priorities. People will come back to meet with police again if they see that concrete things happen as a result of their attendance.

Train citizens, not just police. The public needs to know what they can expect from the police and what they themselves can contribute to coordinated neighborhood problem-solving efforts. They have been trained in the past to call 911 quickly when a crime occurs, but now the range of issues the police may get involved in and the repertoire of responses they can bring to bear has greatly increased. These are sophisticated concepts, and community policing may require some aggressive marketing so that citizens

16. Community's Role in Community Policing

will understand their new powers as consumers of the wide range of products now being offered by customer-oriented agencies. The public also has to understand that theirs is not just a passive role and that "police-community partnerships" are a two-way street. When they discuss possible solutions to neighborhood problems, police are going to ask what resources and personal commitments residents can bring to the table.

Once they are trained, residents are in a much better position to make informed judgments about their priorities, be they programs for victims or more aggressive action against abandoned cars. Untrained citizens are likely to define their expectations of police in traditional terms and expect more patrols and arrests to solve their problems for them. Trained residents are more likely to understand how they can confront the parents of troublemaking youths, picket irresponsible landlords, boycott merchants who refuse to clean up their alleys, and use their clout to extract resources from the city for neighborhood problem-solving efforts—all things that the police *cannot* do.

Get organizations involved. One of the conclusions of the Chicago evaluation is that it is difficult to sustain autonomous citizen action, even with the support of the police. Community policing needs community organizations. Organizations

develop agendas that keep their energies focused even when key leaders tire or turn to other affairs. They provide a locus for identification and commitment, and they provide important social benefits for participants. This commitment and solidarity can in turn sustain the membership during tough moments or in the face of extraordinary demands on their time. Organizations are needed to turn people out for meetings even when the weather is bad. They also lend supporters of community policing the political capacity they may need if the program flounders, threatens to get off track, or needs protection from its opponents.

Public forums and organizations are also good places to confront diversity issues. We have observed organizations working in support of community policing struggle to build their political base in parts of their district that they previously had ignored. We have seen citizens rise in beat meetings to ask where minority residents of their beat were and how more could be encouraged to attend the gatherings. District-level advisory committees that represent all major factions have brought together leaders of warring groups in a forum that encouraged them to identify concrete problems and solutions acceptable to all. Sometimes this took a year because the political interests they represented were real and truly conflicting ones. Community policing programs, however, are not immune

from the forces that often impede the development of effective collective responses to community problems.

Notes

1. Grinc, Randolph M., "'Angels in Marble': Problems in Stimulating Community Involvement in Community Policing," *Crime and Delinquency*, 40, 3 (July 1994):442. See also Sadd, Susan, and Randolph Grinc, *Implementation Challenges in Community Policing: Innovative Neighborhood-Oriented Policing in Eight Cities*, Research in Brief, Washington, D.C.: U.S. Department of Justice, National Institute of Justice, December 1995.

2. Grinc, "'Angels in Marble'": 437.

3. Ibid.:455.

4. Skogan, Wesley G., *Disorder and Decline: Crime and the Spiral of Decay in American Cities*, New York: The Free Press, 1990.

5. Mastrofski, Steven, "Community Policing as Reform: a Cautionary Tale," in *Community Policing: Rhetoric or Reality?*, eds. Jack Greene and Steven Mastrofski, New York: Praeger, 1988:47–67.

Wesley G. Skogan, Ph.D., is a professor of political science and urban affairs at Northwestern University. He currently is conducting an evaluation of Chicago's community policing program, with support from NIJ grant 94–IJ–CX–0046.

Article 17

Incorporating Diversity
Police Response to Multicultural Changes in Their Communities

BRAD R. BENNETT, D.P.A.

A great demographic change is taking place in the United States, making the population much more multicultural and diverse than it used to be. As with other kinds of social changes, law enforcement agencies must adapt to the population shifts in their communities.

This article discusses the findings of a study undertaken to determine how law enforcement agencies in four California cities responded to demographic changes that took place in their communities between 1980 and 1994. The departments in San Jose, Long Beach, Stockton, and Garden Grove[1] now police cities where African Americans, Asians, and Hispanics represent almost 50 percent of the population, an average of a 17-percent increase in the ethnic population since 1980. The departments have employed a number of strategies to best serve their changing communities.

REPRESENTATION AND INCORPORATION

All four police departments have made concerted efforts to incorporate into their organizations the varied and diverse members of their communities. Through recruiting and hiring strategies, citizen participation, training programs both for employees and community members, community outreach initiatives, and community policing, each department has embraced its diverse community groups.

Recruiting and Hiring

San Jose developed a philosophy that recognizes and espouses the value of a diversified work force. This philosophy provided the fundamental ingredient that fostered the attitude necessary to lay the foundation for a successful recruiting and hiring strategy. Many of San Jose's recruiting efforts involve officers as culturally diverse as the applicants they seek. The recruiters seek out potential applicants by attending events, such as festivals and job fairs, frequented by people from a variety of ethnic backgrounds, by advertising in bilingual publications, and by offering incentives to applicants who speak more than one language.

In addition to these fairly traditional approaches, San Jose also developed some unique ways to recruit and promote ethnically diverse employees. The department's program rewards officers with up to 40 hours of paid leave if the individuals they recruit become police officers. The department also helps all officer candidates to overcome obstacles, cultural or otherwise, in preparing for the department's written tests. Mentors from ethnically diverse police officer associations within the department help newly hired officers acclimate to the department.

San Jose's efforts to incorporate representatives of diverse groups do not stop at the entry level. The department continually monitors the composition of special units, such as the detective, gang, training, and personnel units, to ensure that they represent the department and the community. Officers can serve in special units for only 3 years so that all members of the department have an opportunity to do so.

The department also incorporates diversity into its promotional procedures. Recruiting efforts and community relations are enhanced when community members from diverse backgrounds see people similar to themselves in a variety of positions and ranks throughout the department.

Similar to San Jose, the Long Beach, Garden Grove, and Stockton Police Departments have taken steps to recruit and hire personnel who reflect the cultural composition of their communities. Special emphasis has been placed on recruiting Asian applicants because of the large increase in Asian populations

From FBI Law Enforcement Bulletin, December 1995, pp. 1-6. Reprinted by permission of the Federal Bureau of Investigation, U.S. Department of Justice.

17. Incorporating Diversity

in these communities over the past decade.

All three departments hired individuals specifically to work with the Asian community and to attract more Asian applicants. Community leaders in Long Beach also help by training people within their cultural groups so they can qualify as potential candidates for positions within the police department and in city government in general. In addition, Long Beach established an Asian Affairs Advisory Committee, while Garden Grove works with the City Cultural Cohesiveness Committee to improve its recruiting efforts.

Citizen Participation

All four departments have undertaken successful efforts that bring diverse individuals into their organizations at different levels. These include civilian community service officer, reserve officer, police cadet, Law Enforcement Explorer, and Police Athletic League programs. Such initiatives provide excellent opportunities for police departments to familiarize citizens with agency operations.

These police departments also use a variety of methods for determining the concerns of community members. Forming advisory groups representative of the entire community has proven to be one effective way to establish collaborative relationships with diverse groups. Advisory groups give residents a voice and help them ensure that the department understands their unique needs and serves them in a professional manner. Such groups also prompt police agencies to be more open and responsive to the community.

In addition to forming advisory boards, departments developed neighborhood groups and solicited information through focus groups and citizen surveys. As many agencies move toward a more service-oriented, community-involved approach to policing, it will become increasingly important for the police to try to represent the wide variety of community groups in the ranks of employees and to incorporate the voices of the full range of citizens.

TRAINING

All four police departments conduct training programs to teach employees about the many cultures within their communities. The length of the programs varies tremendously, from a few-hour presentation to a week-long course.

In the two larger departments, San Jose and Long Beach, the programs are components of advanced officer training and are offered only to sworn personnel. The two smaller agencies, Stockton and Garden Grove, provide training to all employees. Most of the programs call on community members to facilitate the training, and the departments have developed rather uncommon approaches to their cultural diversity training.

In San Jose, the police chief sought input from members of the advisory board to design the cultural diversity training program for the department. Based on their suggestions, the training starts with a segment on change. It addresses a wide range of concerns relevant to individual and organizational change, including understanding the process of change and overcoming resistance. The initial instruction and the discussions that arose from it helped to eliminate many of the barriers that often occur when dealing with new issues, ideas, and approaches.

> **"...to be responsive to all citizens, police departments must find out what their communities need."**

The Long Beach Police Department collaborated with the National Conference of Christians and Jews to develop its 40-hour cultural awareness training course for all department employees. In addition to general topics related to cultural diversity, the program addresses some nontraditional subjects of interest, such as Anglo cultures, the police culture, the homeless, and various religions.

Long Beach also emphasizes cultural diversity awareness in its basic recruit training academy. Recruits receive 8 hours of classroom instruction devoted to diversity awareness, and then they spend 16 training hours with citizens from the various ethnic groups within the city. Recruits and citizens thus have an opportunity to interact in a nonconfrontational, positive way.

In addition to cultural awareness training, all four departments encourage or provide training in the various languages spoken within their communities. Bilingual or multilingual officers can be very helpful to their departments and their communities. Unfortunately, as communities become more and more diverse, the number of languages spoken increases as well, and it becomes difficult for agencies to cope. Still, by encouraging all officers to learn other languages, departments can facilitate communication with the full spectrum of community members.

COMMUNITY OUTREACH

To respond to the needs of their diverse communities, the police agencies in the study tried a variety of approaches, including police substations, citizen police academies, and youth programs. Many of these initiatives did not target ethnic neighborhoods in particular; instead, they impacted the police department's responsiveness to all community members.

Police Substations

The San Jose and Garden Grove departments have placed substations in areas where very distinct populations live. Police employees, repre-

3. THE POLICE

sentatives from other government agencies, and citizen volunteers who speak the residents' languages staff the substations.

Staff members work closely with merchants, apartment complex owners, and residents to ensure police responsiveness to the needs of each community. Especially in large cities, substations provide citizens the opportunity to access needed government services. They also enable government employees to establish personal relationships with community members.

Citizen Police Academies

A number of police departments across the United States have adopted citizen police academies. Through these academies, police agencies seek to educate community members about the roles and responsibilities of police officers and to familiarize the public with the departments and how they work within the community.

San Jose and Garden Grove both have citizen police academies. San Jose includes a wide variety of community members in its classes. Garden Grove requires members of its community policing advisory board to attend the academy to acquaint them with the functions, policies, and operations of the police department.

As noted, to be responsive to all citizens, police departments must find out what their communities need. Similarly, departments also should educate their communities about the functions of the police department, as well as any changes that occur within the department. An open exchange of information between each community and its police department promotes understanding and greater cooperation.

Youth Programs

All four departments have developed youth-centered programs to enhance their relationships with young people in their communities. These programs generally focus on at-risk youth, who often come from culturally diverse backgrounds.

Initiatives include assigning beat officers to schools, conducting educational programs, and sponsoring Police Athletic Leagues. Officers teach Drug and Alcohol Resistance Education (D.A.R.E.), participate in after-school activities, and become involved in the schools as role models, mentors, and counselors.

Involving diverse youth in Law Enforcement Explorer and police cadet programs also has proven advantageous. Youngsters learn self-discipline and often develop improved self-esteem. For students interested in law enforcement careers, these programs expose them to the department and provide them opportunities to learn about policing.

Through these programs, the departments have focused on getting the police and young people together in positive circumstances. Relationships between police and children have improved tremendously in the schools where officers have been assigned. Young people and officers get involved with each other in positive settings that benefit both groups. Positive contacts made

> **A common theme became apparent during the study of these four California police departments: Leadership makes a difference.**

through these programs often translate into improved relationships between officers and the children's families as they interact outside the school environment.

COMMUNITY POLICING

Many members of the law enforcement profession believe that community policing provides the best method for being responsive to and involved in the community. As an organizational philosophy, it promotes a set of values and corresponding procedures that form the basis for police-community interaction to solve problems. Community policing reverses the notion that the police have sole responsibility for maintaining public order, recognizing instead that the community at large is responsible for the conditions that generate crime.

Empowering the community to solve its own problems is the key to making community policing work. This means that the police and members of the community—neighbors, families, individuals, schools, organizations, churches, and businesses—must accept the challenge to assume joint responsibility for the community's safety and well-being.

The four departments studied, similar to many police agencies across the country, have taken steps to implement community policing. Many of the initiatives already described are components of those efforts. Most of the agency personnel interviewed for this study believe that this approach offers the best opportunity for responding effectively to changing and diverse communities. Only by listening to and working with community members can the police determine what needs to be done and how best to do it.

Officers in San Jose, Stockton, and Garden Grove were reassigned from normal patrol duties to specific neighborhoods. These officers formed partnerships with community groups to identify and solve neighborhood problems. The police arranged their priorities based on the problems identified by residents. Some of the strategies employed by these departments for solving community problems included community surveys, meetings, education, and involvement; neighborhood cleanups; citizen patrols; school and youth programs; government and social service involve-

17. Incorporating Diversity

ment; and community empowerment initiatives.

The San Jose, Stockton, Long Beach, and Garden Grove departments are all moving toward implementing community policing departmentwide. These departments believe that to be successful they must involve all stakeholders in tailoring their philosophies and processes to meet the specific needs of their communities. Department employees, as well as community members, must participate in the development of community policing as a law enforcement approach in order for it to be effective. Such participation raises two important sets of expectations—those between individual employees and the police organization and those between the community members and the organization. Police leaders must work to balance these expectations in order to move effectively toward community policing.

To begin this process, the agencies formed internal committees composed of a cross-section of department members to determine the particular approach most suit-able for each department. After establishing a general internal philosophy and approach, representatives from the agencies then met with community members to design specific strategies for the various communities within their cities.

Everyone involved in implementing community policing should recognize that it is not a fixed or standardized program. It is not a structured model of policing that can be replicated and transferred from agency to agency with ease. Rather, departments must adopt philosophies and approaches that meet the unique needs of their communities. Only in this way will community policing provide the promised benefits for police departments who want to serve their diverse communities effectively.

LEADERSHIP

A common theme became apparent during the study of these four California police departments: Leadership makes a difference. New leaders in each organization led all four departments in making significant strides toward enhanced re-sponsiveness to their communities. Interviews with department members revealed that what distinguished the new leaders from their predecessors was the ability to translate intentions into realities. Because they could deal effectively with their constituencies both inside and outside the organization, these leaders could turn their visions for their departments into action and reality.[2]

The current leaders recognized the influence of relationships among the agency, the individual employees, and the community members on organizational responsiveness. The leaders first addressed internal issues, because it is important to attend to employees' needs before addressing the needs of the community. Next, they developed strategies for dealing with police-community relationships.

These strategies reflect both a concern for community problems and a social responsibility that goes beyond law enforcement. They include service dimensions that recognize that crime prevention is a community matter and suggest that the

---

Increased Population Diversity

During the 1980s, 6 million people legally immigrated to the United States. In the previous two decades combined, only 7.4 million immigrants legally entered the country. Census information shows that between 1980 and 1990 the country's population of Asians doubled, from 1.5 percent to 3 percent of the U.S. population. The Hispanic population grew by half, from 6.4 percent to 9 percent of the population by 1990. Despite the rapid growth among immigrant groups, African Americans continue to be the largest minority group in the United States, representing 12.1 percent of the population in 1990.

The diversity of the United States is expected to expand even more. Projections by the U.S. Census Bureau suggest that Asians will continue to be the fastest-growing race in America, reaching 11 percent of the population by the year 2050. Hispanics are expected to eclipse African Americans as the largest minority group by the year 2010 and to increase to 21 percent of the population by 2050. By that year, the number of African Americans probably will rise to 16 percent of the total population, while the number of whites will fall from 75 percent to 53 percent of the population. By 2050, the U.S. population will be divided almost evenly between minorities and non-Hispanic whites.[4]

Source: Chris Swingle, "U.S. Minorities Expected to Grow by 2050," *Democrat and Chronicle*, Rochester, New York, December 1992, 1.

3. THE POLICE

police broaden their approach beyond merely responding to crime. The approaches adopted by the leaders of all four agencies recognize that the police must become more problem-oriented; they must scrutinize problems, obtain as much information as possible from everyone involved or affected, and only then develop solutions.[3]

CONCLUSION

All four agencies set the goal of being responsive to their changing communities. As shown by the various strategies and programs employed by each agency, there are many ways to achieve that goal. Developing positive relationships with young people from diverse backgrounds, actively seeking input on departmental operations from the full spectrum of community members, conducting imaginative police training in the areas of cultural sensitivity and improved communication, and adopting the community policing philosophy moved these agencies toward their goals.

There is no guarantee that every effort to improve police service to a changing and diverse society will be successful. Yet, these four agencies show that imaginative and resourceful moves toward responding to

Ethnic Changes in Total Population

	1980 Ethnic Population	1990 Ethnic Population	Increase
San Jose	36%	50.4%	14.4%
Long Beach	33%	50.5%	17.5%
Stockton	43%	56.0%	13.0%
Garden Grove	22%	45.3%	23.3%

changes in their communities can be made.

The United States historically has been noted for incorporating people from all over the world into a common society. Once again, the country is being called upon to open its arms to people from many backgrounds, and police departments must do their part. By embracing all segments of their communities, agencies can tap into the vast resources of their many members. By drawing on those strengths, the police and the public can work together to make communities safer for everyone.

Endnotes

[1] The 1990 census showed the populations of these cities as: San Jose, 782,248; Long Beach, 429,423; Stockton, 226,255; and Garden Grove, 149,700.

[2] Warren Bennis, "The Artform of Leadership," in *Public Administration in Action*, ed. Robert B. Denhardt and Barry Hammond (Pacific Grove, CA: Brooks/Cole Publishing, 1992), 311-315.

[3] Roy Roberg and Jack Kuykendall, *Police Organization and Management, Behavior, Theory, and Processes* (Pacific Grove, CA: Brooks/Cole Publishing, 1990), 48-52.

Article 18

Law Enforcement News interview

Police Chief Robert E. Ford of Port Orange, Fla.

"I don't believe we've even begun to scratch the surface in most departments. Right now a lot of community policing around the country is lip service, and a lot of it is small specialized units."

Marie Simonetti Rosen

After 10 years in office, one might think the job of police chief would become somewhat routine, as a kind of "been there, done that" attitude creeps in. Not so for Chief Robert E. Ford of the Port Orange, Fla., Police Department, who is clearly not the type to be satisfied with force of habit. He is a driven executive who is constantly "paying attention to details," a critical component of his overall philosophy and management style. He wants to know how best to provide "service, service, service" to his community and, as important, he wants his officers to do the best job possible with the least amount of stress—even though he would be the first to admit that reconciling the two can sometimes be stressful in itself.

Ford initiated his version of community policing about three years ago, first training the officers and then launching the new approach department-wide. As others have found, the process wasn't easy. The "hardest stage," he says, was monitoring and follow-up. "It took about three years of constant mumbling and grumbling. . . . I'm sure [the officers] would call it supervisory harassment." However one describes it, patrol officers in Port Orange now have the responsibility to investigate nearly all crime on their beats, with only a few cases being turned over to detectives.

Officers in Port Orange, which lies adjacent to Daytona Beach, may complain about the "Chinese water torture" of being "talked to death" about strategies, but Ford is not without his own frustrations. He is frustrated by recruits who lack good writing skills, by a Federal im-

migration agency that is so shorthanded it can't respond to his community's needs, by criminologists who give the field of policing little in the way of relevant, useful research, by a "distant" relationship with prosecutors. A strong believer in problem-oriented approaches throughout the department, he appears to deal with on-the-job frustrations by incorporating his own problem-solving methods.

Take, for example, officer morale. It's no secret that low morale is often taken for granted as part of the job. But Ford's interest in improving morale led him to conduct his own investigation by way of management-labor "encounter" groups. What he found was that much of the stress his officers were experiencing was caused by report writing—a skill that many police officials find lacking these days. After isolating the problem, Ford came up with a solution that included development of computer software that provides model reports officers can "click into on their laptops."

Ford is one of a handful of police administrators with a doctoral degree— in his case, in criminology, from the University of Illinois—and the Chief, who never minces words, is especially critical of his chosen field of study. There's a sense among criminologists that "enforcement is wrong," a kind of necessary evil, he opines. "I read all those books, I did all that research and every day I make decisions that the data will not give me any answers on," says Ford, who wants the fields of criminology and criminal justice to pay more attention to the practitioner.

A former Commissioner of Central Police for Erie County, N.Y., Ford may be "flying by the seat of my pants," as he puts it, but it's clear that the Port Orange Police Department is doing something—a lot of things—right. The police have managed to dramatically reduce crime and calls for service, as well as forging new, productive relations with residents. After 10 years as chief, the professional challenges are still there, but so is the excitement and the satisfaction.

LAW ENFORCEMENT NEWS: Port Orange, like many communities around the country, has experienced a reduction in crime in the past few years. Could you describe the nature and scope of the decrease, and what you think is responsible for it?

FORD: For a 10-year period we've had a very significant drop in crime, along with a continued drop in crime calls, so that our rates are now one-third of other communities right in our own area. We attribute that to a serious of strategies, some of which could be labeled community policing. We do a different type of community policing than some jurisdictions because, I guess community policing today is whatever you want to call it. Basically what we've done is give a great deal of attention to detail and a great deal of attention to follow-up, and we have a program that's really been successful where the patrol officer is given responsibility for his beat and needs to investigate all crimes on his beat. He does a full investigation; they're not turned over to detectives. Some are, but only a few. They're responsible for

Reprinted with permission from *Law Enforcement News*, September 15, 1996, pp. 8-9, 11. © 1996 by John Jay College of Criminal Justice/CUNY, New York City.

3. THE POLICE

> *"We had periods of very negative morale, and I'm telling anyone that's getting into major changes like this to expect three or four years of a great deal of dynamic tension within the department. Then it eases out. We're now getting relatively mellow about it."*

follow-ups, for contacting the victim and the offender, and for dealing with outcome. This has had a dramatic impact in that we are solving crimes we never solved before on minor offenses, and like the old saying, a stitch in time saves nine. What we're finding is very much like what they found on the New York subway system. If you pay attention to the graffiti, if you pay attention to the minor offenses, the panhandling and all that, the big ones never come. Now the officers did not like it at first. But once they got into actually taking responsibility, they began to have some dramatic impact. We also make wide use of crime analysis, constantly looking at patterns, and we do a lot of directed actions. We use a series of different strategies, and plainclothes details if necessary. We really pay attention to identifying problem areas and then addressing them in a variety of ways. That has been quite successful in reducing crime.

LEN: It sounds as if you're describing a kind of focus on quality of life. Do you think that's contributing to the decrease as well?

FORD: Let me give you an example. If we can catch juveniles doing car breaks, we're finding that they don't graduate to burglaries. If we can catch people earlier, like catch a burglar after his first five burglaries, as opposed to waiting and finally catching him after his 55th burglary, we have avoided having 40 burglaries that we would have had if we hadn't paid attention earlier. So a couple of things are happening. One, we're cutting the sense of offenders that they can get away with it, so a group of them are simply abandoning their criminal careers. For those who are more career-minded criminals, we're catching them earlier in the process, thus avoiding a whole series of crimes. Our strategies have been very successful for us. There is, however, some evidence that we have driven of-

fenders out of our community into neighboring communities. So while we have seen almost a 50-percent reduction of crime within our community, we've seen some rise around us.

LEN: What does this do to your relationship with your neighboring police chiefs?

FORD: They haven't figured it out yet—although one or two have already made comments about how I'm sending them my best miscreants [*laughs*].

LEN: You noted a moment ago that community policing looks different in every department. Could you describe the process that Port Orange went through in implementing community policing?

FORD: What we did was a very different process from most agencies, in that I decided very early on that we weren't going to do specialized squads. We were either going to make the whole department a community police department, or none of it. We weren't going to make little units that we'd call community policing. As I travel around the country, I see terrible feuds going on between community police units and, say, patrol—just constant tensions. So we decided not to do that. We first sat down as a staff and planned what is community policing for us, identified little increments of it, trained the officers in those increments, issued orders as to what they needed to be doing, gave them the training they needed to do it. Then, basically, we continued to monitor and follow up. That was the hardest stage. It took us literally about three years of constant mumbling and grumbling, I guess—I'm sure they'd call it supervisory harassment—to gradually move their thinking in the direction of community policing. For example: they don't go back to the same call, the same house, day after day; they need to develop strategies. So we had to monitor that they were, in fact, doing

what they were supposed to be doing. Whenever there were disputes between neighbors, instead of just writing it up, they needed to take action to either resolve the dispute or to get them into arbitration. We make heavy use of alternative strategies other than arrest for a lot of the public disturbance or public order problems. So they had to get involved in that, and what it means was that our crime analysts spend an awful lot of time just monitoring different reports, and bringing constant sustained pressure to bear on them to move in a new direction. It's sort of like everything in learning theory; it takes a long time to break old habits. And it's just pressure.

Beyond lip service

LEN: Do you believe community policing has been fully institutionalized now?

FORD: I don't believe we've even begun to scratch the surface in most departments. Right now a lot of community policing around the country is lip service, and a lot of it is small specialized units. I think its full impact will not be felt until you see them actually making it a true department-wide activity.

LEN: You mentioned alternative strategies, such as the use of arbitrators. Are there other examples of this? What kinds of connections or links have you made with other agencies to help you with alternatives?

FORD: This has probably been the most difficult part of our strategy at this point, linkages. Because if you think police can be resistant to change, you should meet public works. To make for options, we've been trying to make linkages with the garbage department, code enforcement, all sorts of other people and groups. We've been fairly successful with a few, like arbitration. They've been very help-

> *"We do quite a bit of training here, talk them to death about strategies. They call it Chinese water torture, a little dripping on their heads. But it does have an effect."*

18. LEN Interview

ful. We have a county arbitration unit here that is delighted to work with us. We've been empowered in the State of Florida to issue juvenile civic citations—boy, I feel like I'm back in Chicago. The police officer in Florida, can, if the officer so chooses, can set the penalty, can be the judge and jury. The parents of the child have to agree so it never goes to court. It's all handled internal to the Police Department. Every Saturday we have community service, where all the youth get together with young officers that I assign, and they do projects around the community. This is called Payback. So when they get caught in a minor offense like shoplifting, possession of minor amounts of marijuana, alcohol, vandalism, et cetera, et cetera, now we do not send them into the system, for the new offenders at least. We treat them through this civil process. Interestingly, with the graffiti people, what we've found is that if you make youth clean graffiti, they'll never do it again.

LEN: But that's a major responsibility you've given to your officers. The wrong kind of intervention, or an officer who perhaps doesn't interact well with, say, the juvenile's parents or guardians, might lead to a worse situation being created for the Department. . . .

FORD: Well, this is something you have to monitor. Yes, this has not been done without tremendous problems and energy. We think it's worth it. It has turned out to be very popular in the community, but it has had its cost internally to the Department. A lot of the officers did not like it, and have responded somewhat negatively, and it just has been constant feedback. We do quite a bit of training here, talk them to death about the strategies. They call it Chinese water torture, a little dripping on their heads. But it does have an effect. Now the officers, interestingly, have reached stage two, where they all admit the programs work. They say they're very effective.

LEN: That must [have] given them some satisfaction.

FORD: Yes, but you haven't hear[d] Part B of that. We did this analysis, sitting down with the officers and trying in a more psychological type of interview to find out why they don't like this. The answers that came back were quite surprising. One, I feel responsible. I can't go home and just kick off my shoes and never think about it again; it comes back to haunt me, and I have to worry about what I'm going to do tomorrow. Two, I can't come to work and just get into the

patrol car and just ride around and wait for calls. I have to make my day. I have to plan my day, I have a certain number of things I have to accomplish each day, and this is very frustrating and very threatening. So we're talking about a whole different way of looking at work. They have to plan, they have to think, they have to time-manage. It's a very different way of looking at the world.

Not like the movies

LEN: What is the average age of your officers?

FORD: Our officers are very young. We're in an expanding, growing area of Florida, and the average age for the whole Department is probably under 30. In a way, they feel betrayed because this isn't what they saw on television and the movies; this is not what policing is supposed to be about. The older officers' problem was that they didn't like the proactive side of it, because we're saying that for every negative action in the community, you must take an action to address that. And this isn't soft artsy-craftsy stuff. So the older officers are more active in avoiding work; the younger ones are more frustrated with . . .

LEN: The social-work side of the job?

FORD: Yes, and pre-planning and time management. I wouldn't say they're angry about it; they're frustrated.

LEN: Do you think that frustration will ebb in time?

FORD: We are seeing, by the month, a decline in the anger about it as they get used to it. It's very much like changing report forms. They have a nervous breakdown; they hate the new report, and then five years later when you're changing that report, they love that report and they hate the new one. So as they get used to it, we're seeing them get much more relaxed. We have periods of very negative morale, and I'm telling anyone that's getting into major changes like this to expect three or four years of a great deal of dynamic tension within the department. Then it eases out. We're now getting relatively mellow about it; we're getting used to it.

LEN: Have you taken advantage of the Clinton Administration's COPS program?

FORD: We have, in two ways. We're getting some technology—laptop comput-

ers—and we've gotten some additional personnel.

LEN: How do you plan to employ the personnel?

FORD: We're putting them right out in the field as zone officers. We justify that because the type of community policing we're doing demands more time of the individual officers, so to free up more time for some of the problem-solving they're doing, some of the addressing of community concerns and the like, we're adding some additional officers to free up the whole patrol division.

LEN: How many officers are you getting?

FORD: We didn't get many; we got four.

Fear of commitment

LEN: Was your community happy with the commitment that you had to make to keep them?

FORD: No. One of the big problems with COPS is that the community has to make a commitment to keep them for the long run, and I live in a very conservative community that doesn't like to make commitments. We could have gotten far more, but they were not going to make the financial commitment.

LEN: Some politicians want to change the COPS program into block grants to the states. How do you feel about that?

FORD: I don't have any strong feeling either way. You'd have to tell me how the block grants were to be administered and what for and the like. Normally, I'd say it's better the way it is right now unless I could see what the option was. There are block grants that have been very favorable, there are block grants that have not. For a lot of communities it would help if they could have some sustained, long-term funding, because you have to pick the officers up in three or four years. So some of the communities that most need the officers won't make the commitment.

LEN: We often ask police officials what you might call the "blank-check" question. That is, if you were given a blank check, and you could fill out the amount to do anything you wanted in your department, how would you spend the money?

FORD: I would like to hire some additional trained professionals in a couple

103

3. THE POLICE

> *Would I like to make the whole department college-trained? Absolutely. But I don't fool myself that we could compete and have sufficient numbers to fill our positions by just hiring college-trained. We can't do it.*

of areas. For example, I'd like to have a full-time attorney for the Department. I'd like to have a couple of psychologists/police officers that I could send out. One-third of what we deal with is really mental-health problems, and I've given up on expecting the mental-health system to do anything. I think there's a lot of intervention we could do on the street that would be very helpful if we had people who were trained. A lot of these people could be training the actual guys who are going to do it; they could be serving as trainers. So I would like to see some funds set aside for us to hire quality professionals with special skills to assist us in making our decisions more sophisticated and more on target for what we're trying to accomplish.

I before E . . .

LEN: An analysis that you did found that one of the biggest morale problems had to do with report-writing skills. . . .

FORD: We were undergoing a lot of changes, and it was very frustrating for the officers. We started looking at what exactly were the sources of some of the problems. We have these group encounters—we call them management-labor, but they're more like encounter groups. We meet with each shift and we sit and talk about what's frustrating them. I went out and spent several days on patrol myself, wrote all the reports, and found out that I couldn't understand all their complaints because it took me less than an hour to write all my reports. In every encounter group we had, the No. 1 complaint among the officers was paperwork. So we did all sorts of things to adjust the paperwork. The No. 1 complaint from the administration about the officers was also paperwork. We had fascinating little things like, "He read him his Amanda rights." Finally I watched them do the reports, and one of the things I found out was they couldn't write them. We started doing some one-on-one discussions with young officers as to what was the most frustrating thing on the job, and it kept coming out writing skills. We tried addressing that and they got dreadfully insulted and threatened by it, and they got angrier and angrier. As we tracked this down, we were finding

out that basically a large proportion of our officers' writing skills were so bad that every time they came to a report, they actually winced and felt terrible stress. And over the last year, we have found the No. 1 cause of stress for our officers was writing reports, not facing guns or responding to calls. They won't admit it outright, but increasingly we're hearing the undertow that they *know* they're not good writers. When they write they're embarrassed, they're frustrated, they're threatened and they get angry. A lot of the supervisors were seeing this as disciplinary in nature when it really isn't. Either we address the underlying cause, which is the writing skills, or we're never going to accomplish anything. We're finding out that an awful lot of our problems were related to this kind of reaction-formation to writing.

LEN: You had mentioned the development of a software program or template that allows the officers to pick and choose statements that are applicable to a particular incident, a kind of fill-in-the-blanks approach . . .

FORD: We're developing it here. We had found out that spelling was atrocious, but the major problem was that there was no order or rhyme or reason. Writing is far more than just putting the words on paper; writing is mental organization, so you put out a clear message to the topic you're addressing. That was what was most killing them. They were writing far longer reports than they needed to, and no one could understand what they were saying because they were so disorganized. So the first thing we said was "Why can't *we* organize them. We started with model reports for them to look at. Then we went one step further; we said, well, we've got these point-and-click PCs, these little laptops. For all of our crimes, we find that 98 percent of them are pretty much the same as the other ones. So why don't we take the five elements of burglary and give them a model burglary report, which they can click into on their laptop, pick the sentence that fits their thing, or just have them insert words at certain key points? So on a burglary, you would start first with the date: On or about the date, fill in the date, this person did enter, and then we would have a few options, and they can

click on the options. For now, it looks like that for about 90 percent of our routine reports, we can give them canned narratives that they can just point and click and put phrases or words in and solve most of the problems they're having.

LEN: In the context of the system you described earlier, where the beat officer has to follow through on every case, would an instant report form be missing the kind of little details that a beat cop could provide to help solve the incident?

FORD: They can, and that is the down side of any model report form in that they never fully address the uniqueness of the event. We try to deal with that by putting a kind of little bottom piece where they just have to write phrases of other significant things that are important for the case. There are no easy solutions. There's a good reason why they should learn to write well. It's just that I am finding out it takes three to five years to significantly improve writing skills. There are certain reports that we cannot mock up for them; they're still going to have to do that. What I'm trying to do is reduce the stress level so they can learn.

College material

LEN: The writing problem raises at least tangentially the issue of recruitment and how police agencies in Florida conduct that process. Like a handful of states, Florida hires police through the community college system. Could you describe how that works?

FORD: Basically, the community colleges have a curriculum that is administered like other technical skills curriculums, where students can choose to go into this career pattern and receive the necessary training. Once they receive the training, which is about a semester in length, they then go out and look for jobs among the various police departments that are hiring. So they already come to the police department with the certification. When they finish the basic class, they have to take a test, a proficiency test that the state administers. Once they take that, they are potentially accredited as a police officer that one hires.

104

18. LEN Interview

LEN: You've worked in other places. What do you see as the advantages or disadvantages of Florida's system?

FORD: The advantage is that it saves us a fortune. Basically it saves us six months of full pay, and all the other resources that are necessary to run a police academy. For agencies like ours it would be very difficult to do that. The negative side is that while we have some influence over the curriculum, we don't have what I consider to be enough, and it's not tailored to our own agency's needs. Take writing, for example, I would like them to write a report every day during school on every topic they cover. They don't push that. So they're not as attuned to the way we would like things done. And the course work they teach is not always relevant to the jobs the officers are going to be assuming in the local departments.

LEN: If that's the case, do you then have to do some training once the new recruit has come on board?

FORD: Once the new recruit comes on board we have to do extensive training because, first of all, they've been filling out different forms than ours, and while that doesn't sound like a big thing, it is. They don't have any of the procedures down. If you run your own academy, when you teach them burglary, you're going to use your own burglary report. You're going to use your own procedures for that or this. We get a generic, and they're going to have to learn the idiosyncrasies of our systems.

LEN: How much influence does a police department, or all the chiefs in Florida, have on a curriculum that you feel may be not up to date or truly relevant? Is there a way to change it?

FORD: They can have an influence, especially if they stand united. But you'll find there's a great deal of diversity among police officials, so it's very hard to get the police chiefs themselves to stand united on any one type of curriculum. What I would like to see is something I'm working on right now. I am willing to cover the cost of giving them the technical skills if they can give me a more versatile, more deeply trained, more vision-oriented police cadet. What we're talking about now is expanding the current program to make the police academy training part of a bachelor's of criminal justice, with a specialization in police. You get your bachelor's degree, and as part of your training some of your course work will be police-oriented.

LEN: Are you saying that the associate's degree isn't enough at this point?

FORD: It's clearly not enough. Every day, I am sometimes just shocked at what I have to ask them to do. You know, they need medical training; they're the first respondents to an injury or accident. I had to laugh the other day. It was at a domestic, listening to a 24-year-old, never married young male officer giving marital advice to a couple. The advice, by the way, was not bad! But it was entertaining that he'd be doing it. The problem is that they don't even get an associate's degree when they come out of community college; it's just one semester—15 credits. So what I'm saying is, I need someone that's learned good thought processes, problem-solving skills, a little general overview of Constitutional law, a little general overview of psychology and sociology, diversity, and who comes to us with that type of thing, which is probably bachelor's level.

LEN: Higher education has been a tough nut to crack in this field. Of those departments that have educational requirements, there still are not that many requiring a bachelor's. Do you think the approach you're describing would cause a fuss in Florida, or in policing generally?

FORD: One of the problems is that I don't think we could at this time. We could not fill our vacancies if we demanded college degrees. Would I like to make the whole department college-trained? Absolutely. But I don't fool myself that we could compete and have sufficient numbers to fill our positions by just hiring college-trained. We can't do it. What we do here is the other option, which is once they're here, we work with them to help them get their college degree. The city pays all tuition. We have about a third to half of our people now pursuing degrees. We also have cutoffs for promotion. Above a certain rank you have to have a bachelor's degree. So we're back-dooring it, but it's a long process.

LEN: Is the salary scale in your department competitive to attract a college educated person?

FORD: Not in my department, and not in this area. I was just at a department in Anchorage, Alaska, which does have a college degree as a requirement, but their salaries are competitive, and they have no trouble finding college-educated people.

A doctor in the house

LEN: You have a doctorate in criminology. Is there a conflict between your role as a police chief and your training as a criminologist?

FORD: I would say the biggest conflict, and I get very frustrated, is because I read all those books. I did all that research, and every day I make decisions that the data will not give me any answers on; I have to fly by the seat of my pants. What you'll find is our field simply does not have clear directives. Our theories are so poorly developed at this point that there are more paradigms that give us a little sense of the area, but not any real direction on the day-by-day decisions. Also, there has been a tremendous fragmentation between the university and the applied people in the field. A lot of what's going on in the field has no relevance to what the university people think is important. And in turn, what the university people think is important has very little relevance often to the people in the field.

LEN: What advice, then, would you offer to the disciplines of criminology or criminal justice in the university setting? What kind of menu would you like to see them work up that would better help you as police chief?

FORD: I would like to see them spend more time on the practical problems of criminal justice as applied in the field. With any of the ones we talked about, from police morale to the social psychology of police violence, a lot of what I hear in academic circles does not ring true for what I'm experiencing. For example, one of the things I'm finding out is that if you organize a police department well, if you pay attention to detail, if you really do follow-up, and you really try to manage your crime problem, you probably can reduce crime in your area by 50 to 70 percent. I had always been trained that the police have *no* impact upon crime.

Is enforcement wrong?

LEN: You've second-guessed a follow-up question. Criminologists are reluctant to attribute recent crime reductions around the country to improved police work. Why do you think that is?

FORD: There's a sort of a sense among criminologists that enforcement is wrong. It's a university thing; it's part of their culture. I was always trained that there is no positive outcome for enforcement;

3. THE POLICE

> *"The major problem with police is not brutality; it's laziness. This is a profession where you can successfully get by by doing nothing. There's this one famous quote: Many arrests, many problems; few arrests, few problems; no arrests, no problems."*

about the best thing we can say about enforcement is that it's a necessary evil, and probably only necessary because of people's backward thinking, and you'd tick the public off too much if you removed it. My sense is enforcement can be a very positive and a very successful thing. Particularly if you're dealing with juveniles, you can make a significant impact in their lives and the decisions they're making now can be changed by their brushes with the system, that there is learning going on through negative consequences. I've found that an awful lot of public order and peace can be maintained by early and reasonable intervention. It does mean we're going to have to be a little more sophisticated than we were in the past. It does mean we're going to have to pay more attention to things we tended to ignore in the past. But I came to my current department with the general belief that all I could do was make marginal differences, and now it's clear—and now I think we're seeing it in several areas of the country—that major differences have occurred due to intelligent decision-making and decent intervention.

LEN: If criminologists aren't giving police what they need, should the police as a profession approach them somehow?

FORD: Absolutely. I saw a little of that occur at a crime summit or something conducted by NIJ recently. For the first time I saw college professors being confronted by police chiefs who were saying, "You guys are irrelevant. You college professors are out there doing your own thing, you're not of help to anyone other than yourself, and you need to be more on target." I would love to have some cookbooks in policing: like if you have a burglary pattern, this is what you should be doing. There's a whole series of research that I think we need—you know, what is the best way to address juveniles? Should we be strict or easy with the first offense? What type of intervention? There's so many decisions that I have to make every day, and I just don't have data or information to base them on.

LEN: Let's look at a specific example—the Minneapolis study on domestic violence and the follow-up replications.

When those replication studies were conducted, they brought a mixed bag of answers: You should arrest if the abuser is employed, but maybe arresting someone who's unemployed might contribute to recidivism. At the time, the research seemed to be a major attempt on the part of the field of criminology. . . .

FORD: It was an exciting attempt. Whether it was successful or not, it showed two things to me. One, if they do research that tells an answer, the field will listen. It had dramatic impact throughout this country. And the other thing is that research is real hard. We have a multiplicity of variables out there. I don't know why they're shocked that the results are going to be complex, because it's a complex world. What they need to be doing now is getting down to defining the other variables we need to take into account in our decision-making. Just like when you come in with a sore leg, it isn't always broken. And doctors are beyond leeching any sore leg, so they look at the different options. So I would love to see more research like that. The Kansas City Patrol experiments were *great.*

What I would love to see has to do with my misgivings about community policing, because I don't see the research out there that would give a stronger feeling of how it's working. You never trust your own experiences, because we all tend to vote for our own successes. But I'd love to see some real hard-core research on what happened in the New York City subways when they confronted them the way they did. I'd also love to see some research on what's happening now in several major cities. Why suddenly the slump?

No problems

LEN: Police chiefs we've spoken to have attributed their successes to improved police work, a concentrated effort to deal with quality-of-life issues, and simply paying attention to crime and doing whatever they can to solve it. . . .

FORD: You know, one of the things that I always tell the public is that the major problem with police is not brutality; it's

laziness. This is a profession where you can successfully get by by doing nothing. There's this one famous quote: Many arrests, many problems; few arrests; few problems; no arrests, no problems.

LEN: Perhaps because the police have so much discretion in how they fill their workday, there's an irony here in light of what you said earlier about how some officers are frustrated because they have to now plan their days in a certain way. That leads me to believe that there must be some kind of feedback or monitoring procedures in place.

FORD: We have what's called case management—that's the first phase of it—where a crime analyst looks at every report that comes in, looks at what the officer did, and suggests additional steps for the officer to take. These go on a computerized file which the patrol commander reviews daily to see that the officer is keeping up with his investigatory workload. For instance, if you had a case in domestic violence, the officer now must go back and check with the wife that she's all right and that things are all right. With any type of family violence, they have to call back. It remains on their caseload. So we do monitor the caseloads. We also have a new thing that I had to change because I got into some political problems with it. We called it the point system. We gave them points for each activity each day and just monitored their activities. People called it a quota, but I didn't think it was one. They got activity points for stopping and talking to people, for getting out of the car and doing a business check—in other words, we took a full range of everything we wanted a police officer to do during the day and simply counted the number of times they did it, and assigned them a weight according to their importance to us. Then we changed that weight depending on what was going on at a given time of year.

LEN: This didn't go over very well?

FORD: Well, they didn't like the concept of points, so I changed it to hours of productive labor. Now we count the amount of time you spent on a shift, and we define how long things should take. So each month I get a report on every officer

18. LEN Interview

on how many hours of his patrol day was spent in gainful activity. And then I can break it down by type of activity.

LEN: One can see how this would help you, but is this helping the officers, perhaps by allowing them to get a good look at how they really spend their time?

FORD: Interestingly, they like it. They hated it at first. And you know why they like it? They've already set quotas for themselves: "You can't yell at me, I'm a good officer. I've done this much work." So it gives them certainty in a very uncertain field. "I am doing a decent job, I don't have to fear anything. You can't yell at me as a manager. You've got to treat me with respect. I'm a hard worker; look at what I did." It gives them feedback. One of the things an officer says is, "I don't have any guidelines for what I'm supposed to do all day, so how do I know if I'm doing a good job or not? Well, this gives them that. It wasn't meant to, but it does. So I now get, "My evaluation should be higher because look at the amount of work I do." It's a prime thing on their evaluations because I'm trying desperately to make evaluations somewhat objective.

Shades of difference

LEN: You've been a police official in the Buffalo, N.Y., area as well as in Chicago. Could you speak from experience about the differences in policing in these very different parts of the country, and any comparisons that might apply?

FORD: There's a great deal of difference; in fact, we find that here constantly. One of the things that's interesting is the different cultures of policing. One of the shocking things coming from the Northeast to Florida, for instance, is the decline of the blue curtain. If an officer in my department took a bribe, his partner would be here in three minutes to tell on him. They will not tolerate that. I see it as a positive thing in that they have a better standard, an understanding of professional ethics, and they do enforce it among each other. So that's one thing that's a real difference here, particularly among the suburban and more progressive agencies, the sheer shock that anything wrong is being done. The second difference is workload. They make far more arrests, and are far more active.

LEN: You think the workload in the Northeast isn't as heavy?

FORD: Well, whether it's heavy or not, they're only going to respond at a certain

pace. You'll see that. So the blue curtain's different, the ethics are different, the whole approach is different.

LEN: You have a fairly large volunteer force, the Volunteers in Policing. Are they well trained?

FORD: We give them fairly decent training. It's amazing the number of jobs police officers do that do not necessarily demand any police skills. For example, traffic control. They do that. We do vacation house checks. People who move here from New York City are always shocked at the level of service. If you go out of town for vacation, we will check your house twice a day.

LEN: That's impressive.

FORD: This is service, service, service. There's nothing our residents won't call us for.

I'll give you my funny New York City story. We had a series of burglaries going on in the vicinity of our local high school. After about the third or fourth one, we said it must be the high school kids, and it's about the time of their break. So we send a police car to the high school at the same time we're answering an alarm, and sure enough, three or four of them come running across the lawn carrying videos and with gold jewelry hanging out of their pockets. We placed them under arrest and, being new offenders, they immediately talked to us and they gave everything up. Well, all the burglaries were reported except one. Now I, being a naturally cynical police administrator, immediately thought that Records lost the report, so we went to the house and asked the woman had she been burgled. I could tell by the accent—she said "Whaddaya want!?"— that she was from New York and had just come down here. She wouldn't open the door. We said, "Police. Did you have a burglary here?" "Whaddaya wanna know?" "Well, ma'am we've recovered your property"—it was about $8,000 worth of property—"that the burglar said he took from your house, and we want to verify that the burglary in fact occurred here and that it is yours." She opened the door and said, "You got my property back? Yes, I was burgled." "Ma'am, did you report it?" "No, are you allowed to here?" " What do you mean?" "Well, I'm just moved down here from Queens, where I got burgled last year, and the New York Police Department people said, 'Don't call us if it's under $10,000; we don't respond.'"

Of course, the officers were standing with me, and they were looking cross-eyed; they couldn't understand it at all.

You wouldn't report it? They report everything here!

LEN: Florida is one of the country's hubs for immigration, both legal and illegal, and is one of the states asking the Federal Government for help when it comes to paying the tab for criminality by illegal aliens. What kind of relationship do you have with the Immigration and Naturalization Service?

FORD: We talk with INS frequently, and we receive no satisfaction. I had illegal aliens, a whole bunch of them, and I was upset because this group had been involved in a murder two years ago. So I called INS. "I'm sorry," he told me, "we don't have anybody to send. How many do you have? Only 15? No, we don't send anyone for less than 50." There is no hope. We've got illegals all over the place and we treat them like regular citizens. And there's nothing you can do to them because they're illegals.

I had another terrible case with an illegal alien who was running a child-care center, and I caught him selling cocaine. I complained to our social services department that he shouldn't be running a child-care center, and they told me, "What does cocaine have to do with child care?" So he went to jail for the cocaine, and stayed in the country, and then we caught him on 29 counts of child sexual assault. I called Immigration, and we told them that we were going to hold a press conference and make a big public story about how he was still in the country. Finally, after a series of threats like that, he was deported. On their behalf, they say they're overwhelmed and just can't cope. But we just assume they're not there, and we're going to have to cope with whatever we can cope with. The illegals all know it too.

LEN: How would you characterize your philosophy of policing?

FORD: My philosophy is that policing is like everything else—hard work and attention to detail will win. The one thing that is really delightful about working here, as opposed to a big city, is that you know your residents and they know you. The police and the residents like each other and they get along well. It's so neat to see that type of system working, where the officers are actually beginning to like their community, and their community is liking them, and there's some sort of coherence. Now when we go on a crime call, the residents are there helping. It wasn't always that way. Once the police make the move to relax the barriers between themselves and the residents, marvelous things happen.

107

Article 19

Police Cynicism
Causes and Cures
WALLACE GRAVES

What makes a junkyard dog so mean and a cop so cynical? In the case of the dog, it is a matter of conditioning. The police officer undergoes a similar, but much more complex, process. Unfortunately, the public sometimes perceives the results to be the same.

Cynicism often adversely affects officers' productivity, impacts the morale of their colleagues, and chills community relations. It also tends to breed a poor quality of life for officers and their families. In some cases, cynicism can be a precursor to emotional problems, misconduct, brutality, and even corruption.

Cynical, distrustful officers hinder a department's efforts to forge collaborative relationships with members of the community. Therefore, police leaders must build a culture of policing that prevents cynicism and promotes a healthy, positive environment. This article examines police cynicism—what it is, what causes it, and how to prevent it.

WHAT IS CYNICISM?

Cynicism is an attitude of "contemptuous distrust of human nature and motives."[1] A cynic expects nothing but the worst in human behavior. In short, cynicism is the antithesis of idealism, truth, and justice—the very virtues that law enforcement officers swear to uphold.

Most research on police cynicism took place in the late 1960s and mid-1970s. Using test groups, researchers conducted studies that revealed cynicism to be more prevalent in large urban police departments and in the lower ranks, especially among college-educated officers. The degree of cynicism among officers studied generally increased during their first 10 years of service, then declined slightly, and finally leveled off. Notably, officers in the studies who received meritorious awards experienced lower levels of cynicism.[2]

Recent research has focused on burnout and stress, two emotional conditions related to cynicism and caused largely by the excessive demands of the police profession. As with cynicism, burnout and stress can result in reduced performance, alienation, and the use of defense mechanisms. Burnout, stress, and cynicism produce two main unhealthy responses from police officers: Withdrawal from society and antipathy to idealism.

Withdrawal from Society

The sordid reality of the streets, particularly in large cities that have higher crime rates and more anonymity, often shocks officers fresh from the academy. As a result, many of the situations they experience cause them to lose faith in others and develop an us-versus-them view in the process. They soon begin to trust only other police officers, the only people who they believe understand how the world really is. Unfortunately, senior partners oftentimes reinforce such views.

As a consequence, officers socialize with fewer and fewer people outside of the law enforcement circle and might even gradually withdraw from their families and friends. If carried too far, this phenomenon courts domestic disaster. It can even lead to suicide.

As officers withdraw further and further from society, they lose their social safety net—the norms and values that help them make sense of the world—and fall deeper into a state of confusion, alienation, apathy, and frustration. This social estrangement is compounded as officers eventually lose respect for the law. Almost simultaneously, they learn to manipulate the law in their everyday dealings with what they

From *FBI Law Enforcement Bulletin*, June 1996, 16-20. Reprinted by permission of the Federal Bureau of Investigation, U.S. Department of Justice.

believe to be a dysfunctional judicial system.[3]

Antipathy to Idealism

One of the main reasons young people go into law enforcement is to serve society.[4] When confronted with an unexpectedly hostile or indifferent public, or with a justice system that allows criminals to go free, idealistic officers feel betrayed and victimized by such injustice. They soon learn that the idealism of the academy and of the Law Enforcement Code of Ethics does not reflect reality.

As they lose respect for law and society, these officers might lose their self-respect as well. Embittered, they cannot attack the public they have sworn to protect; so, they nurse their hatreds and become victims of cynicism.

Cynical officers no longer show concern for the values that led them to police service in the first place. Instead, they often view those values with contempt. Unlike employees in other occupations, police officers usually will not leave for another job because they are disillusioned with more than just the job. Like many combat veterans returning from war, they believe that their world has changed forever, no matter what job they hold.

WHAT CAUSES CYNICISM?

In addition to the conditions on the streets and the officers' ensuing loss of respect for the law, occupational stagnation also contributes to police cynicism.[5] This specialization often restricts patrol officers' opportunities for new and enriching experiences. For those officers who cannot be promoted, which happens to be the majority, the job provides few incentives and little built-in satisfaction. Instead, it may become tedious, especially for officers with a college education and high expectations. In a society that defines success in materialistic terms, the lack of promotability causes further frustration, disap-

pointment, and a decrease in self-esteem.

Two concepts introduced here merit further exploration—the need for work to be rewarding and the effects of an excessively materialistic society on police officers. Some researchers postulate that work itself must yield feelings of achievement, responsibility, personal growth, and recognition to satisfy the worker's ego and self-actualization needs.[6] According to police cynicism studies, present methods of policing necessarily do not meet this need for the patrol officer.[7]

The second issue involves the effects of the high value placed on material success in American society. Many researchers over the years have identified the American dream of material success as a significant factor contributing to the soaring crime rate.[8] Such ambition promotes deviant behavior as individuals trade ethical values for personal gain, thus creating a culture of crime. Police officers not only see this phenomenon in the streets, where everyone is out for themselves, but they also might see it demonstrated by their own political and law enforcement leaders.

Some believe that cynicism has become an ingrained part of everyday life in this country. People adopt a cynical attitude as a reaction to and a defense against dashed hopes—hopes that have been culturally induced and socially reinforced.[9] As members of society, police officers fall victim to the same types of social forces that befall everyone else.

HOW CAN CYNICISM BE PREVENTED?

Just as some of the causes of police cynicism correspond to the causes of burnout and stress among other types of employees, some methods of prevention and cure that help them also work for law enforcement. Leadership plays a significant part.

Competent, principle-centered, people-oriented leadership, as espoused by some current writers[10] on the topic, is required if the law enforcement profession is to develop an ethos based on universally acknowledged ethics, principles, and values. This ethos must accommodate and encourage personal ambition, but not exclude other values and goals.

Leadership

Police leaders must demonstrate their commitment to the ideals of honesty, fairness, justice, courage, integrity, loyalty, and compassion. Leaders who fail to prove themselves trustworthy help spread the seeds of cynicism.

Police leaders must exhibit appropriate conduct by example, not just by words. They also must nurture their employees by working to expose officers to the many good people and good deeds in their communities so they see more than just the bad.

By explaining the intent of rules of evidence and providing comprehensive and continuous training on the subject, leaders can help officers feel confident and empowered in the legal arena. Such confidence can help officers respect the judicial system rather than feel manipulated by it. Most important, leaders need to build a culture of integrity within their agencies, so that officers have something to believe in when all else seems to fail.

Research on cynicism suggests that principle-centered, compassionate leadership inspires employees and therefore decreases cynicism. To be effective, however, such leadership must be consistent over a long period of time. Role models and mentors also have a positive effect. Employee-oriented leadership and team building provide essential elements of a positive, "upbeat company."[11]

The research further recommends other ways to help prevent employees from becoming cynical, including job enrichment programs,

3. THE POLICE

participatory management styles where employees share responsibility and have a say in workplace policies and practices, and reward systems in which employees have a voice.[12] In policing, as in society in general, an increased emphasis must be placed on sharing power and rewards with employees at all levels.

Every element of effective leadership, from setting an example to listening actively to employees, affects cynicism. As leaders promote esprit de corps, they directly help build esteem and self-worth among employees. Establishing standards, providing the training to reach those standards, and continuously offering refresher training builds officers' competence, which in turn builds their confidence. Following up with positive recognition or guidance when necessary creates and maintains good morale.

Those who write about motivation nearly always discuss the power of positive recognition. In *A Passion for Excellence*, Tom Peters recommends using any excuse to celebrate employee success.[13] Police managers have an obligation to their employees and their agencies to use this and all leadership tools to combat the debilitating disease of cynicism.

Recruiting

Experts routinely recommend that employees become involved in something larger than themselves to combat burnout and cynicism. An organizational culture committed to a quality product, the community, and/or the environment can accomplish this. Caution must be exercised here, however, because thwarted idealism might have made the public servant cynical in the first place. Their idealistic visions of public service did not match the realities, which caused them to lose faith and become cynical.

To prevent a repeat of this scenario, some researchers recommend providing a realistic job preview to potential applicants.[14] Recruits should know the exact realities of

policing from the outset. At present, some departments offer limited orientation for the families of officers, but few, if any, offer a realistic preview to officers. College police science courses also could address such issues.

> " *Cynicism often adversely affects officers' productivity, impacts the morale of their colleagues, and chills community relations.* "

Training

In addition to a realistic job preview, recruit and ongoing roll call training should be provided on the subjects of cynicism, burnout, and stress management. While many departments offer psychological services to employees once symptoms develop, few offer preventative training.

Police officers must be taught the early warning signs of stress and burnout, as well as the difference between healthy suspicion and insidious cynicism. Once they know how to identify these problems, officers should be taught productive coping techniques and stress management methods. Left to their own devices, too many officers choose counterproductive methods, such as alcohol abuse and withdrawal. In addition, officers' families should receive similar training so that they can provide first-line detection and long-term support to their loved ones.[15]

Mentors and Peer Counselors

Because distraught officers often feel most comfortable talking to their colleagues, peer counseling provides another method for treating cynicism once symptoms appear. A

more proactive measure, however, would be to recruit peer counselors as mentors for new officers.

Mentors provide instruction and help officers manage their expectations early in their assimilation into the police culture. By establishing realistic expectations, officers are less likely to become disillusioned by actual police work.

Community Policing

Community policing offers police departments a unique opportunity to combat cynicism. Involving the police and the public in collaborative problem solving has the positive side effect of reducing officers' alienation and withdrawal.

In community policing, management empowers employees, and trust is given and ultimately received. When officers feel that they can trust management and that management trusts them, cynicism declines. In such a relationship, two-way accountability ensures that tasks get completed.

The empowerment aspect of community policing enables leaders to help employees develop their potential through creative and innovative problem solving. This leads to a better quality of service to the community achieved with greater efficiency and effectiveness. Particularly at the patrol level where studies have shown the levels of cynicism to be the highest, community policing can provide an outlet for accomplishment that builds employees' self-esteem and fulfills their needs for growth.

CONCLUSION

Police leaders must take a moment to reflect on cynicism, acknowledge its harmful effects, and use the tools available to prevent it. These tools—employee- and principle-centered leadership, realistic job previews, training, positive recognition, and empowerment—will serve to develop an organizational culture where personal ambition becomes second to the good of the

19. Police Cynicism

organization and the good of the community.

Police cynicism is insidious and costly. It can attack officers of all ranks in departments of all sizes. Its cumulative effects sneak up on its victims, crushing their idealism and enthusiasm before they even realize what has happened.

Cynicism robs the profession of the very values needed to accomplish its goals. Each time it creates a negative contact with a citizen or impinges on professionalism and productivity among the ranks, cynicism impacts on police officers everywhere.

The demands of policing in the next century require that police leaders examine this disease and take action against it. Cynicism does not have to be a natural part of policing. With realistic expectations, strong and compassionate leadership, and continuous training, officers can avoid the conditions that lead to the pitfalls of cynicism and maintain their ideals and values.

Endnotes

[1] Kenneth R. Behrend, "Police Cynicism: A Cancer in Law Enforcement?" *FBI Law Enforcement Bulletin*, August 1980, 1.

[2] Arthur Neiderhoffer, *Behind the Shield: The Police in Urban Society* (Garden City, NY: Doubleday Anchor, 1969); and Robert Regoli, *Police in America* (Washington, DC: R.F. Publishing, Inc., 1977).

[3] Ibid.

[4] John Stratton, *Police Passages* (Manhattan Beach, CA: Glennon, 1984), 32.

[5] Supra note 2.

[6] Bert Scanlon and J. Bernard Keys, *Management and Organizational Behavior* (New York: John Wiley & Sons, 1979), 223 and 229. Herzberg discussed the need for achievement, which complements Maslow's work on the fulfillment of needs. Maslow theorized that all motivation was based on satisfying a hierarchy of needs, progressing from basic physiological and safety needs to social and ego needs, and ultimately to self-actualization, a sense of reaching one's fullest potential.

[7] Supra note 2.

[8] See, for example, Steven Messner and Richard Rosenfeld, *Crime and the American Dream* (Belmont, CA: International Thompson, 1993).

[9] Donald L. Kanter and Philip H. Mirvis, *The Cynical Americans* (San Francisco: Jossey-Bass, 1989).

[10] See, for example, Stephen Covey, *Principle Centered Leadership* (NY: Simon & Schuster, 1991).

[11] Supra note 9.

[12] Ibid.

[13] Tom Peters and N. Austin, *A Passion for Excellence* (New York: Time Warner, 1986).

[14] Supra note 9.

[15] James T. Reese, *Behavioral Science in Law Enforcement* (Quantico, VA: FBI National Center for the Analysis of Violent Crime, 1987).

The Judicial System

The fallout from the O. J. Simpson criminal case is still being felt. All aspects of the criminal justice system have been scrutinized, especially the jury system. In "Abuse of Power in the Prosecutor's Office," law professor Bennett Gershman presents a critical analysis of the prosecutor, "the most dominant figure in the American criminal justice system." Because of the awesome power that prosecutors exercise, abuse is possible. Abuses that most frequently occur could happen in connection with the prosecutor's power to bring charges, to control information used to convict those on trial, and to influence juries. This essay is not an indictment of all prosecutors, but it is meant to stimulate discussion.

The views of Judge Harold Rothwax, as expressed in "We're in the Fight of Our Lives," should also provoke vigorous reaction. Rothwax advocates for the elimination of the exclusionary rule and the unanimous jury verdict requirement. Additionally, peremptory challenges should be restricted, according to Rothwax. Also included is an article reviewing the Rehnquist era of the Supreme Court. The inner workings of the Court and an interesting insight into the Court's personalities are revealed.

The last two readings in this unit deal with various aspects of the jury process. In "Do You Swear That You Will Well and Truly Try . . . ?" Barbara Holland presents a brief history of the development of the jury. While trial by jury has had its ups and downs, it is certainly a lot better than what led up to it—trial by combat and ordeal by fire, water, or poison. In "Unlocking The Jury Box," Akhil and Vikram Amar offer a critical review of today's jury system. "If the jury system is to remain a central institution of democracy and citizenship, it must be refined."

Looking Ahead: Challenge Questions

What are some of the moral and ethical issues involved in prosecutorial misconduct?

Should the "exclusionary rule" be abandoned? Defend your answer.

Is the American jury system in trouble? Explain your answer.

UNIT 4

Article 20

ABUSE OF POWER IN THE PROSECUTOR'S OFFICE

Bennett L. Gershman

Bennett L. Gershman is professor of law at Pace University. He is the author of Prosecutorial Misconduct *and several articles on law dealing with such topics as entrapment and police and prosecutorial ethics. For ten years, he was a prosecutor in New York.*

The prosecutor is the most dominant figure in the American criminal justice system. As the Supreme Court recently observed, "Between the private life of the citizen and the public glare of criminal accusation stands the prosecutor. [The prosecutor has] the power to employ the full machinery of the State in scrutinizing any given individual." Thus, the prosecutor decides whether or not to bring criminal charges; whom to charge; what charges to bring; whether a defendant will stand trial, plead guilty, or enter a correctional program in lieu of criminal charges; and whether to confer immunity from prosecution. In jurisdictions that authorize capital punishment, the prosecutor literally decides who shall live and who shall die. Moreover, in carrying out these broad functions, the prosecutor enjoys considerable independence from the courts, administrative superiors, and the public. A prosecutor cannot be forced to bring criminal charges, or be prevented from bringing them. Needless to say, the awesome power that prosecutors exercise is susceptible to

abuse. Such abuses most frequently occur in connection with the prosecutor's power to bring charges; to control the information used to convict those on trial; and to influence juries.

The prosecutor's charging power includes the virtually unfettered discretion to invoke or deny punishment, and therefore the power to control and destroy people's lives. Such prosecutorial discretion has been called "tyrannical," "lawless," and "most dangerous." Prosecutors may not unfairly select which persons to prosecute. But this rule is difficult to enforce, and the courts almost always defer to the prosecutor's discretion. In one recent case, for example, a prosecutor targeted for prosecution a vocal opponent of the Selective Service system who refused to register, rather than any of nearly a million nonvocal persons who did not register. The proof showed that the defendant clearly was selected for prosecution not because he failed to register but because he exercised his First Amendment rights. This was a legally impermissible basis for prosecution. Nevertheless, the courts refused to disturb the prosecutor's decision, because there was no clear proof of prosecutorial bad faith. Many other disturbing examples exist of improper selection based on race, sex, religion, and the exercise of constitutional rights. These

The article originally appeared in *The World & I*, June 1991, pp. 477-487. Reprinted by permission of *The World & I*, a publication of The Washington Times Corporation. © 1991.

20. Abuse of Power

cases invariably are decided in the prosecutor's favor. The reasoning is circular. The courts presume that prosecutors act in good faith, and that the prosecutor's expertise, law enforcement plans, and priorities are ill suited to judicial review.

Unfair selectivity is one of the principal areas of discretionary abuse. Another is prosecutorial retaliation in the form of increased charges after defendants raise statutory or constitutional claims. Prosecutors are not allowed to be vindictive in response to a defendant's exercise of rights. Nevertheless, proving vindictiveness, as with selectiveness, is virtually impossible. Courts simply do not probe the prosecutor's state of mind. For example, prosecutors often respond to a defendant's unwillingness to plead guilty to a crime by bringing higher charges. In one recent case, a defendant charged with a petty offense refused to plead guilty despite prosecutorial threats to bring much higher charges. The prosecutor carried out his threat and brought new charges carrying a sentence of life imprisonment. The court found the prosecutor's conduct allowable. Although the prosecutor behaved in a clearly retaliatory fashion, the court nevertheless believed that the prosecutor needed this leverage to make the system work. If the prosecutor could not threaten defendants by "upping the ante," so the court reasoned, there would be fewer guilty pleas and the system would collapse.

Finally, some prosecutions are instituted for illegitimate personal objectives as opposed to ostensibly valid law enforcement objectives. Such prosecutions can be labeled demagogic and usually reveal actual prosecutorial malice or evil intent. Telltale signs of demagoguery often include the appearance of personal vendettas, political crusades, and witch hunts. Examples of this base practice abound. They have involved prosecutions based on racial or political hostility; prosecutions motivated by personal and political gain; and prosecutions to discourage or coerce the exercise of constitutional rights. One notorious example was New Orleans District Attorney James Garrison's prosecution of Clay Shaw for the Kennedy assassination. Other examples have included the prosecutions of labor leader James Hoffa, New York attorney Roy Cohn, and civil rights leader Dr. Martin Luther King.

HIDING EVIDENCE

A prosecutor's misuse of power also occurs in connection with legal proof. In the course of an investigation, in pretrial preparation, or even during a trial, prosecutors often become aware of information that might exonerate a defendant. It is not unusual for the prosecutor to have such proof, in view of the acknowledged superiority of law enforcement's investigative resources and its early access to crucial evidence. The adversary system relies on a fair balance of opposing forces. But one of the greatest threats to rational and fair fact-finding in criminal cases comes from the prosecutor's hiding evidence that might prove a defendant's innocence. Examples of prosecutorial suppression of exculpatory evidence are numerous. Such conduct is pernicious for several reasons: It skews the ability of the adversary system to function properly by denying to the defense crucial proof; it undermines the public's respect for and confidence in the public prosecutor's office; and it has resulted in many defendants being unjustly convicted, with the consequent loss of their liberty or even their lives.

Consider the following recent examples. Murder convictions of Randall Dale Adams in Texas, James Richardson and Joseph Brown in Florida, and Eric Jackson in New York all were vacated because the prosecutors hid crucial evidence that would have proved these defendants' innocence. The Adams case—popularized by the film *The Thin Blue Line*—depicts Texas "justice" at its worst. Adams was convicted in 1977 of murdering a policeman and sentenced to die largely on the testimony of a juvenile with a long criminal record who made a secret deal with the prosecutor to implicate Adams, and the testimony of two eyewitnesses to the killing. The juvenile actually murdered the policeman, as he later acknowledged. At Adams' trial, however, the prosecutor suppressed information about the deal and successfully kept from the jury the juvenile's lengthy record.

4. THE JUDICIAL SYSTEM

The prosecutor also withheld evidence that the two purported eyewitnesses had failed to identify Adams in a line-up, and permitted these witnesses to testify that they had made a positive identification of Adams. A Texas court recently freed Adams, finding that the prosecutor suborned perjury and knowingly suppressed evidence.

Richardson—whose case was memorialized in the book *Arcadia* was condemned to die for poisoning to death his

tor misrepresented to the jury that ballistics evidence proved the defendant's guilt, when in fact the prosecutor knew that the ballistics report showed that the bullet that killed the deceased could not have been fired from the defendant's weapon.

Eric Jackson was convicted of murder in 1980 for starting a fire at Waldbaum's supermarket in Brooklyn in which a roof collapsed and six firefighters died. Years later, the attorney who repre-

---

Abuses most frequently occur in connection with the prosecutor's power to bring charges, to control the information used to convict those on trial, and to influence juries.

---

seven children in 1967. The prosecutor claimed that Richardson, a penniless farm worker, killed his children to collect insurance. A state judge last year overturned the murder conviction, finding that the prosecutor had suppressed evidence that would have shown Richardson's innocence. The undisclosed evidence included a sworn statement from the children's babysitter that she had killed the youngsters; a sworn statement from a cellmate of Richardson's that the cellmate had been beaten by a sheriff's deputy into fabricating his story implicating Richardson; statements from other inmates contradicting their claims that Richardson confessed to them; and proof that Richardson had never purchased any insurance.

Brown's murder conviction recently was reversed by the Eleventh Circuit. Brown was only hours away from being electrocuted when his execution was stayed. That court found that the prosecutor "knowingly allowed material false testimony to be introduced at trial, failed to step forward and make the falsity known, and knowingly exploited the false testimony in its closing argument to the jury." The subornation of perjury related to the testimony of a key prosecution witness who falsely denied that a deal had been made with the prosecutor, and the prosecutor's misrepresentation of that fact to the court. In addition, the prosecu-

sented the families of the deceased firemen in a tort action discovered that one of the prosecutor's expert witnesses at the trial had informed the prosecutor that the fire was not arson related, but was caused by an electrical malfunction. At a hearing in the fall of 1988, the prosecutor consistently maintained that nothing had been suppressed and offered to disclose pertinent documents. The judge rejected the offer and personally inspected the prosecutor's file. The judge found in that file two internal memoranda from two different assistant district attorneys to an executive in the prosecutor's office. Each memorandum stated that the expert witness had concluded that the fire had resulted from an electrical malfunction and had not been deliberately set— and that the expert's conclusion presented a major problem for the prosecution. None of this information was ever revealed to the defense. On the basis of the above, the court vacated the conviction and ordered the defendant's immediate release.

To be sure, disclosure is the one area above all else that relies on the prosecutor's good faith and integrity. If the prosecutor hides evidence, it is likely that nobody will ever know. The information will lay buried forever in the prosecutor's files. Moreover, most prosecutors, if they are candid, will concede that their inclination in this area is not to reveal information that might damage his or her case. Ironically, in this important area in which the prosecutor's fairness, integrity, and good faith are so dramatically put to the test, the courts have defaulted. According to the courts, the prosecutor's good or bad faith in secreting evidence is irrelevant. It is the character of the evidence that counts, not the character of the prosecutor. Thus, even if a violation is deliberate, and with an intent to harm the defendant, the courts will not order relief unless the evidence is so crucial that it would have changed the verdict. Thus, there is no real incentive for prosecutors to disclose such evidence.

Hopefully, in light of the recent disclosures of prosecutorial misconduct, courts, bar associations, and even legislatures will wake up to the quagmire in criminal justice. These bodies should act vigorously and aggressively to deter and punish the kinds of violations that recur all too frequently. Thus, reversals should be required automatically for deliberate suppression of evidence, and the standards for reversal for nondeliberate suppression relaxed; disciplinary action against prosecutors should be the rule rather than the exception; and legislation should be enacted making it a crime for prosecutors to willfully suppress evidence resulting in a defendant's conviction.

MISBEHAVING IN THE COURTROOM TO SWAY THE JURY

Finally, the prosecutor's trial obligations often are violated. The duties of the prosecuting attorney during a trial were well stated in a classic opinion fifty years ago. The interest of the prosecutor, the court wrote, "is not that it shall win a case, but that justice shall be done. As such, he is in a peculiar and very definite sense the servant of the law, the twofold aim of which is that guilt shall not escape or innocence suffer. He may prosecute with earnestness and vigor—indeed, he should do so. But, while he may strike hard blows, he is not at liberty to strike a foul one."

Despite this admonition, prosecutors continually strike "foul blows." In one leading case of outrageous conduct, a prosecutor concealed from the jury in a murder case the fact that a pair of undershorts

with red stains on it, a crucial piece of evidence, was stained not by blood but by paint. In another recent case, a prosecutor, in his summation, characterized the defendant as an "animal," told the jury that "the only guarantee against his future crimes would be to execute him," and that he should have "his face blown away by a shotgun." In another case, the prosecutor argued that the defendant's attorney knew the defendant was guilty; otherwise he would have put the defendant on the witness stand.

The above examples are illustrative of common practices today, and the main reason such misconduct occurs is quite simple: It works. Indeed, several studies have shown the importance of oral advocacy in the courtroom, as well as the effect produced by such conduct. For example, a student of trial advocacy often is told of the importance of the opening statement. Prosecutors would undoubtedly agree that the opening statement is indeed crucial. In a University of Kansas study, the importance of the opening statement was confirmed. From this study, the authors concluded that in the course of any given trial, the jurors were affected most by the first strong presentation that they saw. This finding leads to the conclusion that if a prosecutor were to present a particularly strong opening argument, the jury would favor the prosecution throughout the trial. Alternatively, if the prosecutor were to provide a weak opening statement, followed by a strong opening statement by the defense, then, according to the authors, the jury would favor the defense during the trial. It thus becomes evident that the prosecutor will be best served by making the strongest opening argument possible, thereby assisting the jury in gaining a better insight into what they are about to hear and see. The opportunity for the prosecutor to influence the jury at this point in the trial is considerable, and many prosecutors use this opportunity to their advantage, even if the circumstances do not call for lengthy or dramatic opening remarks.

An additional aspect of the prosecutor's power over the jury is suggested in a University of North Carolina study, which found that the more arguments counsel raises to support the different substantive arguments offered, the more the

4. THE JUDICIAL SYSTEM

jury will believe in that party's case. Moreover, this study found that there is not necessarily a correlation between the amount of objective information in the argument and the persuasiveness of the presentation.

For the trial attorney, then, this study clearly points to the advantage of raising as many issues as possible at trial. For the prosecutor, the two studies taken together would dictate an "action-packed" opening statement, containing as many arguments as can be mustered, even those that might be irrelevant or unnecessary to convince the jury of the defendant's guilt. The second study would also dictate the same strategy for the closing argument. Consequently, a prosecutor who through use of these techniques attempts to assure that the jury knows his case may, despite violating ethical standards to seek justice, be "rewarded" with a guilty verdict. Thus, one begins to perceive the incentive that leads the prosecutor to misbehave in the courtroom.

Similar incentives can be seen with respect to the complex problem of controlling evidence to which the jury may have access. It is common knowledge that in the course of any trial, statements fre-

dence on the decisions of jurors. The authors of the test designed a variety of scenarios whereby some jurors heard about an incriminating piece of evidence while other jurors did not. The study found that the effect of the inadmissible evidence was directly correlated to the strength of the prosecutor's case. The authors of the study reported that when the prosecutor presented a weak case, the inadmissible evidence did in fact prejudice the jurors. Furthermore, the judge's admonition to the jurors to disregard certain evidence did not have the same effect as when the evidence had not been mentioned at all. It had a prejudicial impact anyway.

However, the study also indicated that when there was a strong prosecution case, the inadmissible evidence had little, if any, effect. Nonetheless, the most significant conclusion from the study is that inadmissible evidence had its most prejudicial impact when there was little other evidence upon which the jury could base a decision. In this situation, "the controversial evidence becomes quite salient in the jurors' minds."

Finally, with respect to inadmissible evidence and stricken testimony, even if

---

In one leading case of outrageous conduct, a prosecutor concealed from the jury in a murder case the fact that a pair of undershorts with red stains on it, a crucial piece of evidence, was stained not by blood but by paint.

---

quently are made by the attorneys or witnesses despite the fact that these statements may not be admissible as evidence. Following such a statement, the trial judge may, at the request of opposing counsel, instruct the jury to disregard what they have heard. Most trial lawyers, if they are candid, will agree that it is virtually impossible for jurors realistically to disregard these inadmissible statements. Studies here again demonstrate that our intuition is correct and that this evidence often is considered by jurors in reaching a verdict.

For example, an interesting study conducted at the University of Washington tested the effects of inadmissible evi-

one were to reject all of the studies discussed, it is still clear that although "stricken testimony may tend to be rejected in open discussion, it does have an impact, perhaps even an unconscious one, on the individual juror's judgment." As with previously discussed points, this factor—the unconscious effect of stricken testimony or evidence—will generally not be lost on the prosecutor who is in tune with the psychology of the jury.

The applicability of these studies to the issue of prosecutorial misconduct, then, is quite clear. Faced with a difficult case in which there may be a problem of proof, a prosecutor might be tempted to try to sway the jury by adverting to a matter that might be highly prejudicial. In this connection, another study has suggested that the jury will more likely consider inadmissible evidence that favors conviction.

Despite this factor of "defense favoritism," it is again evident that a prosecutor may find it rewarding to misconduct himself or herself in the courtroom. Of course, a prosecutor who adopts the unethical norm and improperly allows jurors to hear inadmissible proof runs the risk of jeopardizing any resulting conviction. In a situation where the prosecutor feels that he has a weak case, however, a subsequent reversal is not a particularly effective sanction when a conviction might have been difficult to achieve in the first place. Consequently, an unethical courtroom "trick" can be a very attractive idea to the prosecutor who feels he must win. Additionally, there is always the possibility of another conviction even after an appellate reversal. Indeed, while a large number of cases are dismissed following remand by an appellate court, nearly one-half of reversals still result in some type of conviction. Therefore, a pros-

moral standards, the problem of courtroom misconduct will inevitably be tolerated by the public.

Moreover, when considering the problems facing the prosecutor, one also must consider the tremendous stress under which the prosecutor labors on a daily basis. Besides the stressful conditions faced by the ordinary courtroom litigator, prosecuting attorneys, particularly those in large metropolitan areas, are faced with huge and very demanding caseloads. As a result of case volume and time demands, prosecutors may not be able to take advantage of opportunities to relax and recover from the constant onslaught their emotions face every day in the courtroom.

Under these highly stressful conditions, it is understandable that a prosecutor occasionally may find it difficult to face these everyday pressures and to resist temptations to behave unethically. It is not unreasonable to suggest that the conditions under which the prosecutor works can have a profound effect on his attempt to maintain high moral and ethical standards. Having established this hy-

---

An unethical courtroom ''trick'' can be a very attractive idea to the prosecutor who feels he must win.

---

ecutor can still succeed in obtaining a conviction even after his misconduct led to a reversal.

An additional problem in the area of prosecutor-jury interaction is the prosecutor's prestige; since the prosecutor represents the "government," jurors are more likely to believe him. Put simply, prosecutors are the "good guys" of the legal system, and because they have such glamor, they often may be tempted to use this advantage in an unethical manner. This presents a problem in that the average citizen may often forgive prosecutors for ethical indiscretions, because conviction of criminals certainly justifies in the public eye any means necessary. Consequently, unless the prosecutor is a person of high integrity and able to uphold the highest

pothesis, we see yet another reason why courtroom misconduct may occur.

WHY PROSECUTORIAL MISCONDUCT PERSISTS

Although courtroom misconduct may in many instances be highly effective, why do such practices continue in our judicial system? A number of reasons may account for this phenomenon, perhaps the most significant of which is the harmless error doctrine. Under this doctrine, an appellate court can affirm a conviction despite the presence of serious misconduct during the trial. As one judge stated, the "practical objective of tests of harmless er-

4. THE JUDICIAL SYSTEM

ror is to conserve judicial resources by enabling appellate courts to cleanse the judicial process of prejudicial error without becoming mired in harmless error."

Although this definition portrays harmless error as having a most desirable consequence, this desirability is undermined when the prosecutor is able to misconduct himself without fear of sanction. Additionally, since every case is different, what constitutes harmless error in one case may be reversible error in another case. Consequently, harmless error determinations do not offer any significant precedents by which prosecutors can judge the status of their behavior. Moreover, harmless error determinations are essentially absurd. In order to apply the harmless error rule, appellate judges attempt to evaluate how various evidentiary items or instances of prosecutorial misconduct may have affected the jury's verdict. Although it may be relatively simple in some cases to determine whether improper conduct during a trial was harmless, there are many instances when such an analysis cannot be properly made but nevertheless is made. There are numerous instances in which appellate courts are deeply divided over whether or not a given error was harmless. The implications of these contradictory decisions are significant, for they demonstrate the utter failure of appellate courts to provide incentives for the prosecutor to control his behavior. If misconduct can be excused even when reasonable judges differ as to the extent of harm caused by such misbehavior, then very little guidance is given to a prosecutor to assist him in determining the propriety of his actions. Clearly, without such guidance, the potential for misconduct significantly increases.

A final point when analyzing why prosecutorial misconduct persists is the unavailability or inadequacy of penalties visited upon the prosecutor personally in the event of misconduct. Punishment in our legal system comes in varying degrees. An appellate court can punish a prosecutor by simply cautioning him not to act in the same manner again, reversing his case, or, in some cases, identifying by name the prosecutor who misconducted himself. Even these punishments, however, may not be sufficient to dissuade prosecutors from acting improperly. One noteworthy case describes a prosecutor who appeared before the appellate court on a misconduct issue for the third time, each instance in a different case.

Perhaps the ultimate reason for the ineffectiveness of the judicial system in curbing prosecutorial misconduct is that prosecutors are not personally liable for their misconduct. During the course of a trial, the prosecutor is absolutely shielded from any civil liability that might arise due to his or her misconduct, even if that misconduct was performed with malice. To be sure, there is clearly a necessary level of immunity accorded all government officials. Without such immunity, much of what is normally done by officials in authority might not be performed, out of fear that their practices would later be deemed harmful or improper. Granting prosecutors a certain level of immunity is reasonable. Allowing prosecutors to be completely shielded from civil liability in the event of misconduct, however, provides no deterrent to courtroom misconduct.

For the prosecutor, the temptation to cross over the allowable ethical limit must often be tremendous, because of the distinct advantages that such misconduct creates with respect to assisting the prosecutor to win his case by effectively influencing the jury. Most prosecutors must inevitably be subject to this temptation. It takes a constant effort on the part of every prosecutor to maintain the high moral standards necessary to avoid such temptations. Despite the frequent occurrences of courtroom misconduct, appellate courts have not provided significant incentives to deter it. Inroads will not be made in the effort to end prosecutorial misconduct until the courts decide to take a stricter, more consistent approach to this problem.

Article 21

THE REHNQUIST REINS

The Chief Justice has brought order to the Court and won striking support for judicial restraint. But Anthony Kennedy turns out to be the decisive voice.

David J. Garrow

David J. Garrow is the author of "Liberty and Sexuality" and "Bearing the Cross," which won the Pulitzer Prize in 1987. He wrote about Justice David H. Souter for the Magazine in 1994.

WHEN THE SUPREME COURT RECONVENES TOMORROW morning, William H. Rehnquist will mark his 10th anniversary as the 16th Chief Justice of the United States. The Rehnquist Court's first decade may best be remembered for such surprisingly "liberal" decisions as the 1992 reaffirmation of Roe v. Wade and this year's vindication of gay rights in a case from Colorado. In both exceptional cases, Rehnquist was in dissent on the losing sides, but those outcomes are unrepresentative of his winning record in crucial, if less publicized, areas of the law.

Rehnquist's most far-reaching triumphs have come in cases raising fundamental questions of federalism, involving the distribution of power between the Federal Government and the states. One year ago, in United States v. Lopez, for the first time in 58 years a court majority restricted Congress's ability to expand Federal authority after it enacted an anti-gun-possession law. This June, in the otherwise unsung death penalty case of Felker v. Turpin, Rehnquist ratified a significant victory in a longstanding war over the power of Federal courts to review and potentially reverse state inmates' criminal convictions. This seemingly abstruse battle over greatly truncating Federal courts' habeas corpus jurisdiction demonstrates how successfully Rehnquist has extended his own staunchly conservative, lifelong beliefs into a judicial agenda that has significantly remade major portions of American law.

But as decisions like Romer v. Evans, the Colorado gay rights case, and 1992's reaffirmation of Roe in Planned Parenthood of Southeastern Pennsylvania v. Casey exemplify, the "Rehnquist Court" is only sometimes the Rehnquist Court. That's true only when the Chief Justice is able to win the determinative fifth vote of the one crucial Justice who most oftentimes is the deciding voice whenever the Court is split 5 to 4—Anthony Kennedy. When he chooses to side with the High Court's four moderates, the "Rehnquist Court" is turned into the "Kennedy Court." In the meantime, Rehnquist will no doubt continue his drive to shrink the influence of Federal courts in American life.

MONDAY MORNING, JUNE 3, 1996, MARKED A POTENTIALLY culminating moment for the 72-year-old Chief Justice.

Just as it will be tomorrow, the court's magisterial courtroom is packed to capacity. United States Senators and members of the House sit toward the front. Former clerks to several Justices have come from as far away as California just to watch; senior members of the Court's press corps squeeze into two tightly packed wooden benches on the left. Members of the marshal's staff shush tourists in the rear of the intimate chamber.

At precisely 10 A.M., a marshal brings the courtroom to its feet as the nine Justices emerge from behind the velvet curtain to take their seats on the elevated bench. Chief Justice Rehnquist declares that several decisions are ready for announcement, and in quick succession the authors of the majority opinions offer brief summaries of the new holdings.

Only at 10:28 A.M. does Rehnquist reach the event the capacity crowd has come to see. "We'll hear argument now in No. 95-8836, Ellis Wayne

From *The New York Times Magazine,* October 6, 1996, pp. 65-71, 82, 85. © 1996 by David J. Garrow. Reprinted by permission.

4. THE JUDICIAL SYSTEM

Felker v. Tony Turpin." The Chief Justice, too, has been waiting for this opportunity for a long time.

The Court's regular argument calendar ended more than five weeks earlier, on April 24; for all of May and June, the Justices normally would have devoted themselves simply to finishing up their opinions in cases that had been argued during the standard October-through-April schedule. However, on that very same April 24, President Clinton signed into law a new statute awkwardly titled the Antiterrorism and Effective Death Penalty Act of 1996.

Long under consideration by Congress, the new law includes a host of provisions intended to reduce and hasten Federal court review of criminal offenders' challenges to the finality of their state court convictions—including challenges by convicted murderers sentenced to death. Prisoners have an initial right to appellate court review; those who fail can pursue subsequent challenges by filing petitions for writs of habeas corpus—literally "you have the body" but in essence a Federal court order overturning a state court conviction. The new law imposes stringent limits on *any* Federal court consideration of a *second* or additional habeas petition from a convict. Death-row prisoners often file petition after petition, thereby delaying their executions even if their sentences are never overturned; some noncapital felons file such papers year after year.

Opponents of the new law argued that, if allowed to stand, it would eventually open the floodgates to speedier executions of the 3,153 prisoners now on death row nationwide. For Rehnquist, however, the limiting of Federal habeas corpus reflects not some sort of personal blood lust for the death penalty. It instead bespeaks his commitment to a federalism-centered view of American politics and government, which encompasses many other issues in addition to Federal court respect for the finality of state court criminal convictions. "The core" of Rehnquist's theory, one scholar has written, "is the idea of state sovereignty," above and beyond Federal Government control.

Testifying at his 1986 confirmation hearings for promotion to Chief Justice, Rehnquist acknowledged that "my personal preference has always been for the feeling that if it can be done at the local level, do it there. If it cannot be done at the local level, try it at the state level, and if it cannot be done at the state level, then you go to the national level."

Rehnquist strongly opposed an expansive habeas role for the Federal courts even long before President Richard M. Nixon nominated him to the Supreme Court in the fall of 1971. Then a 47-year-old Assistant Attorney General, Rehnquist had joined the Justice Department in 1969 at the behest of his fellow Arizonan, Deputy Attorney General Richard G. Kleindienst, whom he had come to know during

15 years of law practice in Phoenix. But 1969 hadn't marked Rehnquist's first job in Washington, for way back in 1952 and 1953—just after he had graduated first in his class from Stanford Law School—young Rehnquist had served for 18 months as one of two law clerks to the highly regarded Supreme Court Justice Robert H. Jackson. Rehnquist had enjoyed his clerkship immensely, but when he himself was nominated to the High Court in 1971, his work for Jackson generated a major controversy when a Rehnquist memorandum arguing *against* any Supreme Court voiding of segregated schools and *for* a continued endorsement of the old doctrine of "separate but equal" was discovered in Jackson's file on Brown v. Board of Education. Rehnquist unpersuasively insisted—as he would again during his 1986 confirmation hearings for Chief Justice—that the memo represented an articulation of *Jackson's* views rather than his own. The Senate nonetheless confirmed him on a vote of 68 to 26.

Jackson's papers also contain a Rehnquist memo with a minority view on *another* Brown case, Brown v. Allen, a 1953 ruling little known to the general public but justly famous among criminal law practitioners as the modern fount of an expansive approach to Federal courts' habeas jurisdiction. In that memo, Rehnquist argued that Federal courts should not grant habeas petitions involving any issue that had been considered by a state court unless the defendant had been denied the right to counsel. In 1953, that recommendation had no more impact than did Rehnquist's advice in the other Brown case, but three decades later, once he sat on the High Court in his own right, habeas excesses reappeared as a subject of his special concern. In a 1981 opinion involving a death-row petitioner, Coleman v. Balkcom, Rehnquist complained that in light of habeas's "increasing tendency to postpone or delay" death-penalty enforcement, "stronger measures are called for" beyond the Court's simple denial of repeated death-row appeals.

Reminded of his Jackson clerkship memos in a 1985 interview with this Magazine—the last such interview Rehnquist has granted—he frankly acknowledged that "I don't know that my views have changed much from that time." Four years later, Chief Justice Rehnquist vented his continuing anger at repetitive filings in a 5-4 majority opinion rebuffing an application from an ostensibly penniless petitioner named Jessie McDonald. "Since 1971," Rehnquist observed, McDonald "has made 73 separate filings with the Court, not including this petition, which is his eighth so far this term." Rejecting the solicitude of four dissenters who objected to the majority's order instructing the clerk's office to reject any further unpaid filings from

122

21. Rehnquist Reins

McDonald, Rehnquist emphasized that "every paper filed with the clerk of this Court, no matter how repetitious or frivolous, requires some portion of the institution's limited resources."

A few months later, Rehnquist took up his capital habeas cudgel in his role as head of the Judicial Conference, the administrative arm of the Federal judiciary. Failing in an effort to obtain majority support for a recommendation calling upon Congress to limit Federal habeas jurisdiction, Rehnquist nonetheless forwarded a report to the Senate Judiciary Committee. In an unprecedented public letter, 14 of the conference's 26 other members objected to the Chief Justice's action. Rehnquist refused to back down.

Congress did not act, but in April 1991 Rehnquist achieved much of his legislative goal *judicially* in a 6-3 court ruling that starkly limited successive habeas petitions and vindicated his 1981 call for action in Coleman. Decrying "the abusive petitions that in recent years have threatened to undermine the integrity of the habeas corpus process," the majority stressed that "perpetual disrespect for the finality of convictions disparages the entire criminal justice system."

But even that ruling in McCleskey v. Zant did not set as high a hurdle to successive petitions as Rehnquist sought. Warning that America cannot afford "the luxury of state and Federal courts that work at cross purposes or irrationally duplicate" each others' efforts, the Chief Justice continued to emphasize that "capital habeas corpus still cries out for reform." Come April 1996, after 24 years on the court and 10 years as Chief Justice, it seemed with the Felker case that Rehnquist's wish had finally come true.

WHEN REHNQUIST WAS NOMINATED TO SUCCEED THE retiring Warren E. Burger as Chief Justice by President Ronald Reagan in 1986, his colleagues were unanimously pleased and supportive. Fourteen years of working together had built good personal relations even between Rehnquist and his ideological opposites, William J. Brennan and Thurgood Marshall. Brennan startled one acquaintance by informing him that "Bill Rehnquist is my best friend up here," and a Washington attorney, John D. Lane, who privately interviewed all seven other Justices on behalf of the American Bar Association's Committee on the Federal Judiciary, informed the Senate Judiciary Committee that Rehnquist's nomination was met with "genuine enthusiasm on the part of not only his colleagues on the Court but others who served the Court in a staff capacity and some of the relatively lowly paid individuals at the Court. There was almost a unanimous feeling of joy."

Rehnquist's colleagues looked forward to his installation as "Chief" in part because they welcomed the departure of his overbearing, manipulative and less-than-brilliant predecessor, Burger, who had succeeded the legendary Earl Warren 17 years earlier. Reporters always stressed that Burger *looked* the part of Chief Justice of the United States, but among his fellow Justices there was virtually unanimous agreement that his skills at leading the Conference—the Justices' own name for their group of nine—had been woefully lacking. John Lane told the Judiciary Committee that one Justice said that "he looks for a tremendous improvement in the functioning of this Court" under Rehnquist. Based upon all the Justices' comments, Lane reported, "I came away with a very strong opinion that Justice Rehnquist will make an excellent Chief Justice."

Much of the 1986 debate over Rehnquist's promotion focused upon newly augmented allegations that 20-odd years earlier he had taken part in Republican Party efforts to intimidate black voters at Phoenix polling places. The charges were not provable, but the final Senate confirmation vote of 65 to 33 was closer than Rehnquist's backers had expected and in its wake the new Chief Justice privately told friends that he felt the Judiciary Committee hearings had treated him very badly. "He took it somewhat personally," one acquaintance remembered, but within the Court there was immediate agreement that Rehnquist was far superior to Burger in leading the Conference's discussion of cases.

Ten years before, in a 1976 law review essay on "Chief Justices I Never Knew," Rehnquist had stressed the importance of firmly run sessions in which each Justice, speaking in order of seniority, stated his views succinctly and without interruption: "A give and take discussion between nine normal human beings, in which each participates equally, is not feasible." He also acknowledged how a "Chief Justice has a notable advantage over his brethren: he states the case first and analyzes the law governing it first. If he cannot, with this advantage, maximize the impact of his views, subsequent interruptions of colleagues or digressions on his part or by others will not succeed either." Citing Harlan Fiske Stone and Felix Frankfurter as brilliant Justices of the past whose efforts to influence their colleagues had generally failed, Rehnquist added that "the power of persuasion is a subtle skill, dependent on quality rather than quantity."

In his 1987 book, "The Supreme Court," Rehnquist gently noted that "I have tried to make my opening presentation of a case somewhat shorter than Chief Justice Burger made his." Jus-

4. THE JUDICIAL SYSTEM

tice Harry A. Blackmun often disagreed substantively with Rehnquist, but he was quick to praise Rehnquist's management skills. "The Chief in conference is a splendid administrator," he told one semiprivate gathering. Unlike the Burger years, "we get through in a hurry. If there's anything to be criticized about it, he gets through it in too much of a hurry at times."

Warren Burger was seen by his colleagues as a Chief who often abused his power to assign the writing of majority opinions whenever he was not in dissent. One Rehnquist clerk from the mid-1970's still recalls how Burger, unhappy with the political humor of a Rehnquist-produced skit at the Court's 1975 Christmas party, the next month assigned Rehnquist only one opinion, in an Indian tax case. Most Justices expected Rehnquist to eschew such gamesmanship, and the record of the past decade generally bears that out. Some former clerks contend in private that in recent years Anthony Kennedy has fared far better in receiving important assignments from Rehnquist than other Justices, but Rehnquist as Chief is far more concerned with maximizing the speed and efficiency of the Court's opinion-writing than with playing favorites.

In a 1989 memo to his colleagues, Rehnquist divulged that "the principal rule I have followed in assigning opinions is to give everyone approximately the same number of assignments of opinions for the Court during any one term." But, he warned, any Justice who failed to circulate a first draft of a majority opinion within four weeks or who failed to circulate the first draft of an anticipated dissent within four weeks of the majority opinion or who had not voted in any case in which both majority and dissenting opinions had circulated would now be looked upon less favorably. "It only makes sense," he asserted, "to give some preference to those who are 'current' with respect to past work."

Rehnquist's announcement provoked an immediate objection from John Paul Stevens, now the second-most-senior Justice to the Chief himself. An iconoclastic and generally liberal thinker, Stevens in recent years has outpaced all of his colleagues in his number of individual dissents and concurrences. Reminding Rehnquist that "too much emphasis on speed can have an adverse effect on quality," Stevens warned that it "may be unwise to rely too heavily" on rigid deadlines, especially when a Justice's investment in a major dissent, or a handful of dissents, might create a lag. "I do not think a Justice's share of majority opinions should be reduced because he is temporarily preoccupied with such an opinion, or because he is out of step with the majority in a large number of cases." Rehnquist remained largely unmoved, chiding his colleagues just a few weeks later about several de-

cisions that were running behind schedule. "I suggest that we make a genuine effort to get these cases down 'with all deliberate speed.' "

EIGHT DAYS AFTER PRESIDENT CLINTON SIGNED THE NEW HABEAS legislation into law, a three-judge panel of the Court of Appeals for the 11th Circuit applied the statute in denying a request from a Georgia death-row inmate, Ellis Wayne Felker, to file a successive petition. Convicted 13 years earlier of murdering a 19-year-old woman soon after being released from prison on a prior felony conviction, Felker now was finally facing actual execution; three times before, the Supreme Court had turned aside appeals. Later that very same day, May 2, Felker's attorneys asked the High Court to review how the new law prohibited Felker from appealing the circuit court's refusal.

Less than 24 hours later, the Supreme Court granted Felker's request for a hearing and set oral argument on his challenge to the new law for exactly one month later. The Court's swift action—the first such accelerated hearing in six years and the fastest grant of review since the famous Pentagon Papers case, New York Times Co. v. United States, a quarter-century earlier—brought a cry of protest from the four least conservative Justices, John Paul Stevens, David H. Souter, Ruth Bader Ginsburg and Stephen G. Breyer. Formally dissenting, they called the majority's action "both unnecessary and profoundly unwise" and declared that review of the new law "surely should be undertaken with the utmost deliberation, rather than unseemly haste."

One question posed by Felker was whether the new limits on appeals involving second or successive habeas petitions represented a Congressional diminution of the Supreme Court's own appellate jurisdiction. That would be a constitutional issue of the highest order; not since the Civil War era had the Court directly confronted it. Felker's lawyers, focusing on an avenue Congress had failed to address, noted in their brief that the new law did not expressly affect the Court's authority to consider "original" habeas petitions filed directly with it. Conceding that the High Court's use of "original habeas" would be "exceptional and discretionary," Felker's attorneys nonetheless acknowledged that "no unconstitutional interference with this Court's appellate jurisdiction exists if Congress merely eliminates one procedure for review but leaves in place an equally efficacious alternative."

Henry P. Monaghan, a Columbia University law professor and an experienced Supreme Court advocate, spoke for Felker when oral argument got under way on June 3. The present-day Rehnquist Court is as vocal and energetic a nine-member bench as any attorney could imagine confronting (only Justice Clarence Thomas is usually silent, but the liberal icons William Brennan and Thurgood Marshall were likewise generally quiet), and Rehnquist himself—along with Justices Souter, Breyer, Ginsburg and Antonin Scalia—is an outspoken questioner, as both Monaghan and his opponent, Senior Assistant Attorney General Susan V. Boleyn of Georgia, soon found. "Why shouldn't we just try to apply the statute as written?" asked Rehnquist with some exasperation. "I mean, rather than trying to torture some meaning out of it that's not there?" Monaghan tried to demur, but drolly conceded that "this statute passed by Congress with respect to second petitions is not the work of Attila the Hun."

Susan Boleyn, however, faced a far tougher grilling. "That's not a very specific position, Ms. Boleyn," the Chief Justice interjected before she had uttered her fourth sentence. Peppering her with questions, Rehnquist asked how she would distinguish a 19th-century decision, Ex Parte Yer-

---

ONE ANGRY MAN

Antonin Scalia's Decade

William Rehnquist's 10th anniversary as Chief Justice is also Antonin (Nino) Scalia's 10th anniversary as an Associate Justice. Nominated to Rehnquist's seat when Rehnquist was promoted to replace Warren Burger, Scalia—a four-year veteran of the United States Court of Appeals for the District of Columbia Circuit—faced no opposition. He was confirmed, 98-0, after less than five minutes of Senate floor discussion.

During Scalia's first few years on the Court, commentators wondered whether his combination of intelligence and gregariousness would make him into the Rehnquist Court's real intellectual leader. As Laurence H. Tribe, a Harvard law professor, told The Boston Globe in 1990: "There is no question Scalia is brilliant. What remains to be seen is if he is wise."

Six years later, the verdict is all but unanimous: Scalia is rash, impulsive and imprudent, a Justice who in case after case would rather insult his colleagues' intelligence than appeal to them. Judge Alex Kozinski, a conservative member of the United States Court of Appeals for the Ninth Circuit, pronounced his judgment as early as 1992: "Commentators said, 'This is the guy who, through his charm and intellect, will forge a conservative consensus.' He hasn't done it." The New Republic's Jeffrey Rosen, contending that Scalia "has intellectual contempt for most of his colleagues," suggests that the relatively young Justice—Scalia is now 60—calls to mind the sad career of another brilliant judicial failure, Felix Frankfurter.

One former Scalia clerk insists that the Justice is "100 percent impervious" to public criticism. But Scalia is hardly ignorant of his bad-boy reputation; three years ago, he insisted to one Washington audience that "I am not a nut." In comments to the Supreme Court Historical Society, Scalia observed that dissenting opinions "do not, or at least need not, produce animosity and bitterness among the members of the Court." But even more revealing was a statement Justice Sandra Day O'Connor made to a Ninth Circuit judicial conference. Reminding her audience of the old saying that "sticks and stones will break my bones but words will never hurt me," O'Connor added, "That probably isn't true."

A colleague confirms that O'Connor has been "deeply wounded" by the insults Scalia has sent her way, starting in 1989 in the abortion case Webster v. Reproductive Health Services. O'Connor analysis, Scalia wrote there, "cannot be taken seriously."

A former Scalia clerk acknowledges that Scalia "completely alienated" O'Connor and "lost her forever," and a former Rehnquist clerk notes how O'Connor's "personality is in many ways just the opposite of Justice Scalia's. She's very willing to build consensus on opinions." But Scalia, says another ex-clerk, is not only "in love with his own language," he also believes that "what he's doing is a matter of principle. He knows how right he is."

On the next-to-last day of the 1995–96 term, Scalia turned his rhetorical guns on Rehnquist, who had committed the grievous sin of concurring with the Court's 7-1 majority in striking down the Virginia Military Institute's exclusion of women from a state institution. In his lonely, splenetic dissent, Scalia called the majority's equal protection analysis "irresponsible" and mocked Rehnquist's separate views as "more moderate than the Court's but only at the expense of being even more implausible." Saying Rehnquist erroneously suggested that Virginia "should have known . . . what this Court expected of it" because of an earlier Court ruling, Scalia truculently asserted that "any lawyer who gave that advice to the Commonwealth ought to have been either disbarred or committed."

Scalia's characterization of the Chief Justice's views represented the first time in memory that one member of the Court had suggested that another might be better situated in a nonjudicial institution, but virtually nothing that Scalia might say could worsen the reputation he has made for himself among students of the Court. Harvard's Laurence Tribe decries Scalia's "extreme stridency and disrespect for opposing views." Another well-known law professor, far less liberal than Tribe and a social colleague of several Justices, ruefully looks back on the Senate's 1987 rejection of Supreme Court nominee Robert H. Bork and concludes that Bork would have been "more civil and more broad-minded than Scalia by a long shot." Indeed, Scalia, he contends, "has become precisely what the Bork opponents thought Bork would be."

—D.J.G.

4. THE JUDICIAL SYSTEM

ger. Boleyn struggled. "Well, I think that this Court has recognized exceptions to its jurisdiction both in the constitutional venue under Article III—." An unhappy Rehnquist cut her off. "Are you familiar with the Yerger case?" "Yes, Your Honor, but I'm not familiar with what exactly you're asking me to respond to."

It only got worse. Breyer, telling her, "I'm sorry, I don't understand," asked Boleyn a fast-paced hypothetical and demanded an answer. "Do we have jurisdiction to hear it? Yes or no." Boleyn said no, but Breyer objected: "I thought from your brief the answer was yes."

Asked in 1992 by C-span's Brian Lamb whether he could tell if attorneys are nervous during oral argument, Rehnquist jocularly replied that "I assume they're all nervous—they should be." Occasionally—most often in the months before his wife's slow death from cancer in October 1991—Rehnquist has rebuked or snapped at lawyers who have been unprepared or who have committed the tiny but grievous sin of calling him Judge rather than Chief Justice.

The day after the Felker argument, the Justices met in private conference to discuss the case. The substance of that meeting isn't likely to be known for a long time; accounts of conference discussions generally become available only years after the event, with release of the handwritten notes of one or more Justices. Even then, some Justices' papers—Thurgood Marshall's are the most recent example—shed next to no light on conference discussions, for not all Justices take notes. Those of William O. Douglas and Brennan offer reliable guides to the 1960's, 70's and 80's, but every modern Court scholar knows full well that the ultimate treasure trove for the years 1970 through 1994 will, in time, be the conference notes of now-retired Justice Blackmun.

In his own chambers, Rehnquist instructs each of his three clerks to have their first drafts of his opinions ready for his review within 10 to 14 days. Some wags insist that Rehnquist has three clerks—seven other Justices now have four, Stevens has three—primarily to ease the arrangements for his weekly tennis-match doubles, but Rehnquist treats his young aides in a warm, low-key manner. He revises their drafts by orally dictating amended wording into a recorder, and he volunteered in his 1987 book that "I go through the draft with a view to shortening it, simplifying it and clarifying it."

In Rehnquist's first 15 years on the Court, commentators praised his writing as "clear, lucid, brief and mercifully free of bureaucratese." One commended "the somewhat peculiar references to history, the classics and gamesmanship with which Rehnquist likes to sprinkle his opinions"—this June a Rehnquist concurrence included a passing reference to "Grover Cleveland's second inaugural address"—but since 1986 such acclaim has gradually diminished, with critics noting "the characteristic terseness of a Rehnquist opinion" and journalists labeling his prose "dry and to the point."

Rehnquist's June 28 opinion announcing the Court's *unanimous*—including the four Justices who had protested the accelerated hearing—resolution of Felker v. Turpin manifested all these traits. Back in 1987, Rehnquist acknowledged how "the Chief Justice is expected to retain for himself some opinions that he regards as of great significance," but Rehnquist traditionally has written a disproportionate number of criminal law rulings. The 12½-page Felker decision had been written, edited and circulated for other Justices' comments and agreement in little more than three weeks' time, and the substance of Rehnquist's—and the Court's—holding followed closely from the implications of the questions Rehnquist had put to Monaghan and Boleyn back on June 3.

Not long after Ellis Wayne Felker finally goes to the electric chair, the pace of death-row executions across America will pick up substantial speed. Rehnquist's victory may not yet be 100 percent complete; his triumph nonetheless is impressive, and still growing.

The new statute "makes no mention of our authority to hear habeas petitions filed as original matters in this Court" and thus, fully in keeping with Ex Parte Yerger, it "has not repealed our authority to entertain" such petitions. Therefore, Rehnquist held, "there can be no plausible argument that the Act has deprived this Court of appellate jurisdiction in violation of Article III." No constitutional collision thereby occurred, and the new statutory restrictions on Federal court consideration of successive habeas petitions could remain fully in place. Convicts and death-row prisoners *could* send "original" petitions directly to the High Court, but—just as Felker's lawyers had conceded in their brief—only in a rare instance of "exceptional circumstances" would such an appeal be granted.

Felker's own habeas request was denied; Georgia has not yet set a new date for Felker's execution.

Some habeas specialists, pointing back to Rehnquist's earlier 1991 judicial breakthrough in McCleskey, dismiss Felker's actual holding as "relatively insignificant." They emphasize that several pending challenges to other particular provisions of the new law, including Lindh v. Murphy, a case that was decided by the Court of Appeals for the Seventh Circuit in Chicago in late September, are likely to force Rehnquist and his colleagues to revisit the habeas battlefield sometime in 1997.

But such characterizations unintentionally minimize the extent and scale of Rehnquist's long-term agenda and long-term victory. Federal habeas jurisdiction is now only a shadow of what it was when Rehnquist first joined the Supreme Court, and what in 1981 in Coleman was a lonely individual call for action has now won decisive support from a solid Court majority and from bipartisan majorities in both houses of Congress as well as an ostensibly liberal Democratic President. Not long after Ellis Wayne Felker finally goes to the electric chair, the entire pace of death-row executions all across America will pick up substantial speed as one habeas petition after another is quickly cast aside by the courts. Rehnquist's victory may not yet be 100 percent complete; his triumph nonetheless is remarkably impressive and still growing.

FELKER IS THE LATEST IN A LINE OF FEDERALISM CASES that for Rehnquist began with a 1975 solo dissent in Fry v. United States, an opinion that directly foreshadowed the landmark 5-4 majority victory he would win exactly 20 years later in United States v. Lopez. In 1975, writing only for himself, Rehnquist had advocated "a concept of constitutional federalism which should . . . limit federal power under the Commerce Clause." In Lopez, writing on behalf of a 5-vote majority, Rehnquist dismissed the Justice Department's defense of the Federal anti-gun-possession law and declared that "if we were to accept the Government's arguments, we are hard-pressed to posit any activity by an individual that Congress is without power to regulate."

As early as 1982, a Yale Law Journal analysis of Rehnquist's jurisprudence by H. Jefferson Powell (now a high-ranking Clinton Justice Department appointee) cogently identified "federalism's role as the organizing principle in Rehnquist's work" and persuasively concluded that "Rehnquist's federalism does form a consistent constitutional theory."

In 1986, Rehnquist had volunteered that a one-third decline in the Court's annual caseload from 150 to 100 would be 'unseemly,' but by the 10th anniversary of his statement, the Court had reduced its annual workload by more than half—from 151 to 75.

More than 10 years later, in one of the three most important decisions of the 1995–96 term, Seminole Tribe of Florida v. Florida, another 5-vote Rehnquist majority forthrightly declared that "each State is a sovereign entity in our Federal system." Dissenting vigorously, Justice Souter protested how Rehnquist was deciding "for the first time since the founding of the Republic that Congress has no authority to subject a State to the jurisdiction of a Federal court at the behest of an individual asserting a Federal right." Souter's objection brought him a harsh rebuke from the Chief: the dissent's "undocumented and highly speculative extralegal explanation . . . is a disservice to the Court's traditional method of adjudication."

One core principle of Rehnquist's federalism, as the habeas battle has reflected, is a firm belief in a modest—some would say *excessively* modest—political and supervisory role for the Federal courts. Back in the early 1980's, the annual docket of the Supreme Court itself—the number of cases it chooses to hear, not the thousands upon thousands it turns aside—had grown to a peak of 151. Many voices, including both Burger and Rehnquist's, called unsuccessfully for the creation of a new, nationwide court of appeals to ease the pressure on the High Court's docket, but the idea died aborning and in recent years has completely vanished from both public—and private—discussion.

At his 1986 confirmation hearings, Rehnquist told the Senate Judiciary Committee that "I think the 150 cases that we have turned out quite regularly over a period of 10 or 15 years is just about where we should be at." Addressing whether that load might be too great and noting how the caseloads of Federal district and appellate courts were increasing rapidly, Rehnquist said that "my own feeling is that all the courts are so much bus-

4. THE JUDICIAL SYSTEM

ier today than they have been in the past, that there would be something almost unseemly about the Supreme Court saying, you know, everybody else is deciding twice as many cases as they ever have before, but we are going to go back to two-thirds as many as we did before."

A year later, in his 1987 book, Rehnquist cited the 150 figure and observed that "we are stretched quite thin trying to do what we ought to do." Privately, inside the Court, Rehnquist brooded about the annual "June crunch" of backlogged decisions awaiting finished opinions and suggested to his colleagues the "desirability of cutting down the number of cases set for argument in April," toward the end of the Court's year. But year by year the Court's annual caseload has shrunk further and further: from 132 cases in 1988–89 to 129 in 1989–90, to 112 in 1990–91, to 108 in 1991–92, to 107 in 1992–93, markedly to 84 in 1993–94, then to 82 in 1994–95 and finally to 75 in the just-completed term of 1995–96.

In 1986, Rehnquist had volunteered that a one-third decline in the Court's annual caseload from 150 to 100 would be "unseemly," but on the 10th anniversary of his statement, the Court had reduced its annual workload by *more than half*—from 151 to 75. Granted, a 1988 statute had virtually eliminated some mandatory appeals that the Court previously had been obligated to hear, whether or not a minimum of four Justices voted to accept the case, but the issue of the "incredible shrinking docket"— what Court watchers call it—has been one of the most striking developments of the Rehnquist years.

The Court, of course, issues no explanations for even so momentous a trend, but in April 1995, at the Third Circuit's annual dicial conference in White Sulphur Springs, W.Va., Justice Souter spoke extemporaneously about the docket shrinkage in remarks that were virtually unprecedented in their public frankness. Referring back to the early 1980's, when he was still an obscure New Hampshire state judge, Souter recalled that in reading Supreme Court opinions at the time, it "seemed to me . . . some of those opinions had the indicia of rush and hurriedness about them." Now he realized, given the caseloads of those years, that those shortcomings "could not have been otherwise and the remarkable thing is that the number of really fine things that came down in that period was as high as it was."

Souter said he was "amazed" that the docket annually had continued to shrink throughout the 1990's, but he stressed that "nobody sets a quota; nobody sits at the conference table and says: 'We've taken too much. We must pull back.' . . . It simply has happened." Identifying a host of contributing factors, Souter noted the "diminishing supply" of

new Federal statutes in the late 1980's and early 1990's, and how "not much antitrust work" and "not much civil rights" work, beyond voting cases, had been generated by the Reagan and Bush Administrations' Justice Department. In the criminal area, "drug prosecution does not make for Supreme Court cases these days" because of how Fourth Amendment search-and-seizure standards have "been pretty much raked over. . . . The basic law, the basic standards which have been governing and do govern most of the appeals that people want to bring to us are products of the 60's and the 70's and the 80's. There hasn't been an awful lot for us to take."

In addition, Souter added, according to a comprehensive account of his remarks in the Pennsylvania Law Weekly, 12 years of Reagan-Bush judicial nominations had produced "a relative homogeneity" and "a diminished level of philosophical division within the Federal courts." But, he emphasized, "I know of no one on my court who thinks that we're turning away cases which by traditional standards . . . we should be taking. In fact, it's just the contrary."

Once, he confessed, when the numbers were declining, "I said out loud as well as to myself that if that continued, I was going to start voting to take interesting Federal questions whether there was a conflict [among lower Federal courts] or not." However, Souter went on, "those were rash words," for "as it turned out, I didn't have to make good on that" because more cases began attracting 4 or more affirmative votes. "About 100 a year is about right," Souter concluded, and the number for the upcoming 1996–97 term seems destined to rise from this past year's remarkable minimum of 75.

With a total caseload of 75 (34 of which were decided unanimously), there are not all that many opinions to spread out over nine months of work for nine Justices—and 34 law clerks. The image of clerks working seven-day-a-week, 12-hour-a-day jobs is a polite fiction of the past, and—though it is considered rude to mention it—many Court observers know that a typical at-the-office workday for the Chief Justice of the United States often stretches from about 9:10 A.M. to 2:30 P.M. Some Justices—Souter, Kennedy and Stevens among them—work decidedly longer hours, but Rehnquist's crusade to shrink the role and responsibilities of the Federal courts has definitely born fruit right at home.

Rehnquist has certainly registered historic doctrinal achievements—in habeas law, in United States v. Lopez, in Seminole Tribe and in the 1994 "takings clause" decision in Dolan v. City of Tigard, but there is no denying Rehnquist has been on the losing side in the two most important, highly visible constitutional holdings of the last five years: 1992's

128

vindication of abortion rights in Planned Parent-hood v. Casey and, just a few months ago, the remarkable voiding of a homophobic, antigay Colorado state constitutional amendment in Romer v. Evans. The 6-3 Romer ruling, in which two swing Justices, Anthony Kennedy and Sandra Day O'Connor, sided with the "liberal" foursome of Stevens, Souter, Ginsburg and Breyer rather than with Rehnquist, Scalia and Thomas, was without doubt the most important and symbolically momentous decision of the 1995–96 term.

Romer's majority opinion, written by Kennedy, featured a rhetorical verve rare for the High Court. The Colorado amendment "seems inexplicable by anything but animus toward the class that it affects," Kennedy explained, and "disqualification of a class of persons from the right to seek specific protection from the law is unprecedented in our jurisprudence." Declaring that "it is not within our constitutional tradition to enact laws of this sort," Kennedy pointed out that a statute "declaring that in general it shall be more difficult for one group of citizens than for all others to seek aid from the government is itself a denial of equal protection of the laws in the most literal sense." The state amendment "classifies homosexuals not to further a proper legislative end but to make them unequal to everyone else. This Colorado cannot do. A State cannot so deem a class of persons a stranger to its laws."

In a style and tone to which his colleagues have become all too well accustomed, Scalia angrily and vituperatively dissented. Joined by both Rehnquist and Thomas, Scalia protested that the majority's holding "places the prestige of this institution behind the proposition that opposition to homosexuality is as reprehensible as racial or religious bias." Avowing that his fellow Justices have "no business imposing upon all Americans the resolution favored by the elite class from which the Members of this institution are selected," Scalia alleged that "our constitutional jurisprudence has achieved terminal silliness" and complained of how Kennedy's opinion was "so long on emotive utterance and so short on relevant legal citation." Declaring that Colorado's action was "eminently reasonable" since citizens are "entitled to be hostile toward homosexual conduct," Scalia maintained that "the degree of hostility reflected by" the state enactment was "the smallest conceivable." His final blast was explicitly contemptuous: "Today's opinion has no foundation in American constitutional law, and barely pretends to."

BUT THE MOST IMPORTANT JUSTICE ON the 1996 Rehnquist court is not the angry Antonin Scalia; it's the man who ascended to the Court in the wake of Robert H. Bork's rejection:

Anthony Kennedy. A quiet and thoughtful Californian, Kennedy throughout his eight-year tenure has been both the crucial fifth vote for virtually all of Rehnquist's major victories *and* the decisive vote and voice when Rehnquist has suffered historic defeats in cases like Casey and Romer. Occasionally apologetic in tone ("sometimes we must make decisions we do not like," Kennedy volunteered in the 1989 flag-burning decision, Texas v. Johnson), Kennedy term after term has been the balance wheel of the Rehnquist Court. Early on, in 1988–89, when Rehnquist and the now-retired William Brennan disagreed in *every one* of that year's 31 5-4 outcomes, Kennedy was with Rehnquist 29 times. (Johnson was one of the two exceptions.) In 1991–92, when Kennedy dissented from only 8 of the term's 108 decisions, his crucial "liberal" votes in both Casey and an important school prayer decision, Lee v. Weisman, drew intense flack from conservative critics.

The following term, 1992–93, Kennedy dissented in only 5 of 107 cases, and the year after that, when he was in the majority in *every one* of the term's 14 5-4 decisions, he again dissented in only 5 cases out of 84. In 1994–95, Kennedy was in the majority in 13 of the term's 16 5-4 cases, including both Lopez and the highly publicized Congressional term limits decision, and in the just-completed 1995–96 term, Kennedy again was the Court's least frequent dissenter (in just 5 of 75 cases) and was in the majority in 9 of the 12 5-4 outcomes.

Now Kennedy is again under fire from extreme conservatives for his memorable majority opinion in Romer (National Review magazine labels him "the dimmest of the Court's intellectual lights"), but among serious Court watchers the impression is growing that Kennedy has more than found his footing. David O'Brien of the University of Virginia calls Kennedy "more principled, less of a pragmatist" than other Justices. Peter J. Rubin, a Washington attorney and a former two-year High Court clerk, points out that Kennedy "understands the moment of what he's doing" and stresses how there can be "no question after Romer about his integrity and courage."

Legal historians sometimes wonder whether the "Brennan Court" and the "Powell Court" might actually be more accurate monikers for the 1960's, 70's and early 80's than the "Warren Court" and the "Burger Court." And in that same spirit, Peter Rubin readily agrees that, yes, "it's the Kennedy Court." But, Romer and Casey notwithstanding, in most other particulars the court of 1996 is indeed the "Rehnquist Court," and it is likely to stay the Rehnquist Court for longer than most commentators now think.

Prior to the death of his wife, Nan, in October 1991, most people who knew Rehnquist expected

4. THE JUDICIAL SYSTEM

him to step down as Chief Justice sooner rather than later. In July 1991, Rehnquist apologetically turned down the newly retired Thurgood Marshall's request for home-to-office transportation in a court car, while adding that "in all probability I will be in the same boat you are within a couple of years." Eleven months later, Rehnquist told C-Span's Brian Lamb that while he enjoyed his job, "I wouldn't want to hold it forever." In September 1995, when he underwent major back surgery to remedy a long-festering problem that had suddenly mushroomed into crippling pain, what Tony Mauro of Legal Times called Rehnquist's "rumored plan for retiring from the Court after the next Presidential election" looked all the more certain.

But a wide sample of former Rehnquist clerks say "not so" and predict against any Rehnquist retirement in the summer of 1997, especially—as some of them hesitantly volunteer—if Bill Clinton is re-elected this November. The Wall Street Journal columnist Paul Gigot has slyly pronounced

Rehnquist's scheduled departure, but a former clerk says the Chief already has begun hiring the clerks who will join him next summer.

"I think he's too committed and too interested in winning the battles he's been fighting to retire during the Presidency of a Democrat," says one Court insider with a high personal opinion of Rehnquist. He adds, with emphasis, that the Chief is "extraordinarily politically savvy" and that Bill Rehnquist "plays for the long, long, long run," as his entire career consistently demonstrates.

"He's more inclined to stay," says another former Rehnquist clerk who keeps in regular touch and who feels that the Chief does not want to leave during a Democratic Presidency but "would never say it."

"He enjoys his work," this clerk states. "He never expected to be in the majority as much as he is now," and the ongoing victories—like Lopez and Seminole Tribe on federalism, and in the habeas arena with cases like Felker—all incline him to stay, not retire. "He's fully in stride right now."

Article 22

'We're In The Fight Of Our Lives'

Bernard Gavzer

At 2 a.m. on Nov. 20, 1990, Leonardo Turriago was pulled over for speeding by two state troopers. They asked if they could look into his van, and Turriago said they could. Inside, the troopers saw a trunk and asked Turriago about it. He sprang open its lock, then ran away. Opening the trunk, the troopers found the body of a man shot five times.

Turriago was quickly caught. In his apartment, police found 11 pounds of cocaine and guns. The suspect told them where to look for the murder weapon, and it was recovered. Turriago was convicted of a second-degree murder and sentenced to 45 years to life.

The defense appealed, saying the troopers had no right to search the van. On June 6, 1996, Turriago's conviction was overturned. A New York appellate court ruled that the police search was not justified and had been coerced.

that criminals are going free," he says. "There is no respect for the truth, and without truth, there can be no justice."

Judge Harold Rothwax *has spent 25 years presiding over criminal cases in New York City. What he has seen has convinced him that our courts must be changed if our justice system is to survive.*

While the search for truth should be the guiding principle of our courts, instead, the judge says, "Our system is a carefully crafted maze, constructed of elaborate and impenetrable barriers to the truth."

A lank and slightly bent man who looks in repose as though he's leaning into the wind, the 65-year-old jurist has detailed his views in a recently published book, *Guilty: The Collapse of Criminal Justice.* Nothing less than sweeping change, he insists, is required to save our system.

Practices we have taken for granted—such as the *Miranda* warning, the right to counsel, even unanimous jury verdicts—need to be reconsidered, says the judge. "You know," Rothwax confided, "more than 80 percent of the people who appear before me are probably guilty of some crime."

"riminal Justice in America is in a state of collapse," says Judge Harold J. Rothwax, who has spent 25 years presiding over criminal cases in New York City. "We have formalism and technicalities but little common sense. It's about time America wakes up to the fact that we're in the fight of our lives."

Rothwax believes cases such as Turriago's illustrate that the procedural dotting of every "i" and crossing of every "t" has become more important than the crime's substance. "The bottom line is

DEFENDANT		LOCATION	
SPECIFIC WARNING REGARDING INTERROGATIONS			
1. YOU HAVE THE RIGHT TO REMAIN SILENT.			
2. ANYTHING YOU SAY CAN AND WILL BE USED AGAINST YOU IN A COURT OF LAW.			
3. YOU HAVE THE RIGHT TO TALK TO A LAWYER AND HAVE HIM PRESENT WITH YOU WHILE YOU ARE BEING QUESTIONED.			
4. IF YOU CANNOT AFFORD TO HIRE A LAWYER ONE WILL BE APPOINTED TO REPRESENT YOU BEFORE ANY QUESTIONING, IF YOU WISH ONE.			
SIGNATURE OF DEFENDANT		DATE	
WITNESS		TIME	
☐REFUSED SIGNATURE	SAN FRANCISCO POLICE DEPARTMENT		PR. 9.1.4

UPI/Bettmann

From *Parade,* July 28, 1996, pp. 4-6. © 1996 by Parade Publications. Reprinted by permission.

4. THE JUDICIAL SYSTEM

Rothwax insists there is a fundamental difference between the investigative and the trial stages of a case. The investigative stage is marked by the notion of probable guilt, he asserts, not the presumption of innocence. "Until a defendant goes on trial, he is probably guilty," the judge says, noting that by the time a person reaches trial he has been deemed "probably guilty" several times. "When a person is arrested, indicted by a grand jury, held in detention or released on bail, it is all based on probable guilt," Rothwax adds. "Once *on trial*, he is presumed innocent."

A criminal trial *should be a search for the truth. Instead, Judge Rothwax says, "Our system is a maze constructed of elaborate and impenetrable barriers to the truth. . . . Without truth there can be no justice."*

Many of the judge's views have drawn criticism from others in the criminal justice arena. "I think there is a problem with a sitting judge who may think people are guilty before they've been judged guilty." says Norman Reimer, chair of the New York County Lawyers Association's criminal justice section. "In this country you are presumed innocent by everyone and anyone until you are convicted by a jury." Even at the time of arrest? "You absolutely are, beyond any doubt, presumed innocent," says Reimer.

The positions the judge has staked out in what he regards as his crusade to bring sense to the criminal justice system have shocked those who long associated him with strong liberal causes. A lifelong Democrat, Rothwax was a senior defense trial attorney for the Legal Aid Society in New York and a stalwart of the New York Civil Liberties Union early in his career.

"I represented Lenny Bruce and Abbie Hoffman, the Black Panthers and the Vietnam war protesters," he says. "I am today as much a civil libertarian as ever. But that does not mean I must close my eyes to the devastation that has occurred in criminal justice. We have the crime, but where is the justice? It is all tilted in favor of the criminal, and it is time to bring this into balance."

The interests of the victim weigh solidly in Rothwax's courtroom in the Criminal Court Building in Manhattan. However, he is troubled by some decisions of the U.S. Supreme Court, saying: "Its rulings over the last 35 years have made the criminal justice system incomprehensible and unworkable."

Although neither the Supreme Court nor the Courts of Appeals decide the guilt or innocence of a defendant, they do make rulings on the constitutionality of acts by the police and lower courts and thus have a significant impact on our justice system. Key practices of our current system—which have come about as a result of Supreme Court rulings in recent decades—need to be changed, Rothwax believes. Among them are:

• *The Miranda warning:* In New York, Alfio Ferro was arrested in 1975 in connection with a fur robbery that turned into a murder. In the lockup, a detective—without saying a word—dropped some of the stolen furs in front of Ferro's cell. Ferro then made incriminating statements that led to his conviction for second-degree murder.

In 1984, an appellate court overturned the conviction, saying that the detective's action amounted to interrogation and violated Ferro's *Miranda* rights. The *Miranda* warning requires that the suspect be told he has a right to remain silent, that any statement he makes might be used against him and that he has the right to have a lawyer present.

"*Miranda* came about because of abuses such as prolonged custodial interrogation, beatings and starving in order to get a confession," says Rothwax. "I think those abuses have been largely dealt with. Now the police officer is put in the position of telling a suspect in a murder or rape, 'Look, you don't have to tell us anything, and that may be the best thing for you.' And it produces a situation in which a proper confession is thrown out because of the way in which it was read or that it wasn't read at the right time."

Rothwax believes *Miranda* can be replaced by the recording of an arrest and interrogation through videotapes, tape recorders and other technology. This would probably show whether a confession or statement was coerced.

• *The exclusionary rule:* This winter, Federal Judge Harold Baer Jr. refused to admit as evidence 80 pounds of cocaine and heroin obtained in the arrest of a drug courier in the Washington Heights neighborhood of New York City. The evidence was excluded because, said Baer, the police had violated the Fourth Amendment protection against unreasonable search and seizure when they searched the car in which the drugs were found.

The police said their search was proper in view of the fact that they saw men hastily loading bags into an out-of-state car in a high drug area in the middle of the night, and the men ran away when the police approached. Judge Baer, however, said just because the men ran off was no reason to suspect them of a crime. In Washington Heights, the judge said, it was not unusual for even innocent people to flee, because police there were regarded as "corrupt, violent and abusive."

Under a growing chorus of criticism, Judge Baer first reversed himself and then asked that the case to assigned to another judge. It was. Rothwax says this is the sort of muddled episode which arises from the exclusionary rule, producing "truth and justice denied on a technicality."

"The Supreme Court has consistently ruled that evidence seized in violation of the Fourth Amendment *should* be excluded from a criminal trial. But if you read the Fourth Amendment, nowhere does it say that *illegally* obtained evidence *must* be excluded," says Rothwax. "In my view, when you exclude or suppress evidence, you suppress the truth."

22. 'We're in the Fight of Our Lives'

Judge Rothwax has a remedy: "Make the exclusionary rule *discretionary* instead of mandatory. If it was at the discretion of the judge, there could be a test of reasonableness. A judge could consider factors such as whether a police officer acted with objective reasonableness and subjective good faith. As it is now, the exclusionary rule is irrational, arbitrary and lacks proportion. No wonder that in 90 percent of exclusionary cases, the police don't know what the law is."

• *The right to counsel:* In 1982, Kenneth West of New York, an alleged drug dealer, was suspected of being involved in killing a man who had taken his parking place. His lawyer, at a police lineup, told the police not to question West in his absence. Nothing came of the case for three years. Then police arrested a former cohort of West who said West had been one of the shooters. The informer secretly taped West talking about the killing. West was convicted, but in 1993 the New York Court of Appeals reversed the conviction, saying the secret taping amounted to questioning him without the presence of counsel.

The right to counsel is provided by the Sixth Amendment. "It is essential there be a right to counsel,' Judge Rothwax says. "But the amendment doesn't say it has to be during police questioning and investigation. As a result of technicalities over this issue of counsel, I have seen murderers go free. Make it clear that the right to a lawyer shouldn't be a factor in the *investigative* stage but only in pre-trial and trial stages."

• *Instructions to the jury:* After closing arguments in the O. J. Simpson murder trial, Judge Ito took great care in telling jurors that Simpson's failure to take the stand in his own defense should in no way be taken to mean anything negative or to draw any other adverse conclusion.

This instruction to the jury occurs in all cases in which the defense asks for it, because a Supreme Court ruling in 1981 that said not to do so amounted to a violation of the Fifth Amendment. (The Fifth Amendment states that no person shall be forced to testify against himself.) "The Fifth Amendment does *not* say that one might not draw reasonable inferences from the silence of a defendant," Judge Rothwax says. "I think we must find a way to return to the standard that existed before, that the judge could tell the jury that the failure to explain could amount to an inability to explain."

The judge would like to see other changes made to the jury system. Among them:

1) *Unanimous jury verdicts should no longer be required.* Why? Rothwax cites a murder case he presided over. "It was an overwhelming case of clear guilt. Yet there was a hung jury. One juror was convinced the defendant was not guilty. How did she know? Well, as she explained it, 'Someone that good-looking could not commit such a crime.' We had to retry the case, and the man was quickly found guilty."

By allowing verdicts to be decided by a vote of 11–1 or 10–2, Rothwax says, there would be a reduced risk that a single juror could cause a retrial or force a compromise in the face of overwhelming evidence of guilt.

2) *Peremptory challenges to prospective jurors should be strictly limited or abolished.* Peremptory challenges allow lawyers to knock someone off the jury without giving any reason. "As we saw in the Simpson case," Rothwax says, "it makes it possible to stack a jury so that the most educated juror is excused, and you end up with a jury that can be manipulated to accept innuendo as evidence."

Judge Rothwax regards the entire conduct of the Simpson trial as an unspeakable insult to the American people, one that left them "feeling wounded and deeply distrustful of the system." He adds: "There was an opportunity to show a vast audience the potential vitality of justice at work. Instead we were assaulted by an obscene circus. We saw proof that the American courtroom is dangerously out of order."

Not everyone agrees with the judge's assessments. "All the arguments Rothwax makes have been addressed and answered in the legal literature," says Yale Kamisar, the Clarence Darrow Distinguished Professor at the University of Michigan and a constitutional scholar. "I think millions of Americans will agree with him, but he has presented a lopsided argument. I think he's wrong."

To sit with Rothwax in court, as this writer did, is to get a sense of his urgency for reform. In three hours, there was a procession of men and women charged with felonies from murder to drug dealing. Rothwax was all business, and he was tough with everyone. After 47 cases had been considered and dealt with, the judge turned to me and asked, with irony, about the defendants we had seen: "Did you notice the huge display of remorse?" There hadn't been any. "That's why," he said, "we are in the fight of our lives."

133

Article 23

The Founders of our nation understood that no idea was more central to our Bill of Rights—indeed, to government of the people, by the people, and for the people—than the citizen jury. It was cherished not only as a bulwark against tyranny but also as an essential means of educating Americans in the habits and duties of citizenship. By enacting the Fifth, Sixth, and Seventh Amendments to the Constitution, the Framers sought to install the right to trial by jury as a cornerstone of a free society.

Today that cornerstone is crumbling. In recent years, a parade of notorious criminal trials has called into question the value of citizen juries. The prosecutions of Oliver North, O.J. Simpson, William Kennedy Smith, the Menendez brothers, and the assailants of Rodney King and Reginald Denny have made armchair jurors of millions of Americans. Now the failings of the system seem obvious to anyone with a television:

• In search of "impartial" jurors, the selection process seems stacked against the educated, the perceptive, and the well informed in favor of those more easily manipulated by lawyers and judges. Attorneys exercising their rights to strike candidates from the pool cynically and slyly seek to exclude jurors on the basis of race, gender, and other supposed indicators of bias.

• Courts subject citizens to repeated summonses, intrusive personal questioning, and long and inefficient trials. Unsurprisingly, many citizens avoid jury duty.

• In court, jurors serve a passive role dictated by rules that presume jurors are incapable of impartial deliberation and that provide little help in understanding points of law or evaluating testimony.

• The public perceives that the scales of justice tip in favor of rich defendants with high-priced counsel.

More than a million Americans serve as jurors on state courts each year. Jury service offers these Americans an unequaled opportunity to participate democratically in the administration of justice. But on its present course, this vital egalitarian institution may shrivel up, avoided by citizens, manipulated by lawyers and litigants, and ridiculed by the general public. To be sure, the system has inherent limitations; "correct" verdicts cannot be guaranteed. But given the jury's present form, society is bearing the costs of a jury system's vices without enjoying a jury system's virtues. Our task is to demonstrate why the citizen jury is worth defending, and to propose a number of specific reforms designed to restore the jury to its rightful status in a democracy under law.

A Cornerstone of Democracy

The Framers of the Constitution felt that juries—because they were composed of ordinary citizens and because they owed no financial allegiance to the government—were indispensable

Unlocking
The Jury Box

Akhil Reed Amar
& Vikram David Amar

to thwarting the excesses of powerful and overzealous government officials. The jury trial was the only right explicitly included in each of the state constitutions penned between 1776 and 1789. And the criminal jury was one of few rights explicitly mentioned in the original federal constitution proposed by the Philadelphia Convention. Anti-federalists complained that the proposed constitution did not go far enough in protecting juries, and federalists eventually re-

134   From *POLICY REVIEW*, May/June 1996, pp. 38-44. © 1996 by The Heritage Foundation. Reprinted by permission.

23. Unlocking the Jury Box

sponded by enacting three constitutional amendments guaranteeing grand, petit, and civil juries.

The need for juries was especially acute in criminal cases: A grand jury could block any prosecution it deemed unfounded or malicious, and a petit jury could likewise interpose itself on behalf of a defendant charged unfairly. The famous Zenger case in the 1730s dramatized the libertarian advantages of juries. When New York's royal government sought to stifle its newspaper critics through criminal prosecution, New York grand juries refused to indict, and a petit jury famously refused to convict.

But the Founders' vision of the jury went far beyond merely protecting defendants. The jury's democratic role was intertwined with other ideas enshrined in the Bill of Rights, including free speech and citizen militias. The jury was an essential democratic institution because it was a means by which citizens could engage in self-government. Nowhere else—not even in the voting booth—must Americans come together in person to deliberate over fundamental matters of justice. Jurors face a solemn obligation to overlook personal differences and prejudices to fairly administer the law and do justice.

As the great historian of anti-federalist thought, Herbert Storing, put it, "The question was not fundamentally whether the lack of adequate provision for jury trial would weaken a traditional bulwark of individual rights (although that was also involved) but whether it would fatally weaken the role of the people in the administration of government."

Perhaps most important was the jury's educational mission. Through the jury, citizens would

No idea is more central to democratic government than a well-informed citizen jury.

learn self-government by doing it. In the words of Alexis de Tocqueville, "The jury is both the most effective way of establishing the people's rule and the most effective way of teaching them how to rule." This learning, of course, would carry over to other political activity. As Tocqueville explained:

"Juries, especially civil juries, instill some of the habits of the judicial mind into every citizen, and just those habits are the very best way of

4. THE JUDICIAL SYSTEM

preparing people to be free. . . . They make all men feel that they have duties toward society and that they take a share in its government. By making men pay more attention to things other than their own affairs, they combat that individual selfishness which is like rust in society. . . . [The jury] should be regarded as a free school which is always open and in which each juror learns his rights, . . . and is given practical lessons in the law. . . . I think that the main reason for the . . . political good sense of the Americans is their long experience with juries in civil cases."

Once we see how juries serve as major avenues for popular education and political participation, the connections early American observers drew between jury service and other means of political participation—especially voting—make more sense. Tocqueville keenly understood these linkages: "The jury system as understood in America seems to me to be as direct and extreme a consequence of the . . . sovereignty of the people as universal suffrage. They are both equally powerful means of making the majority prevail. . . . The jury is above all a political institution [and] should be made to harmonize with the other laws establishing the sovereignty. . . . For society to be governed in a settled and uniform manner, it is essential that the jury lists should expand or shrink with the lists of voters. . . .

"[In general] in America all citizens who are electors have the right to be jurors."

We have come to think of voting as the quintessential act of democratic participation. Historically, the role of the people in serving on juries was often likened to the role of voters

> **T**ocqueville explained, "Juries instill some of the habits of the judicial mind into every citizen . . . those habits are the very best way of preparing people to be free."

selecting legislative bodies, and even to the role of legislators themselves. Indeed, the jury's place in the judicial framework was closely related to the idea of bicameralism: Just as the legislature comprised two equal branches, an upper and a lower, juries and judges constituted the lower and upper branches, respectively, of the judicial department.

The Supreme Court has reinforced the linkage of jury service and voting as part of a "package" of political rights. For example, in a 1991 case challenging race-based exclusions in jury selection, Justice Anthony Kennedy observed in his majority opinion that "with the exception of

voting, for most citizens the honor and privilege of jury duty is their most significant opportunity to participate in the democratic process. . . . Whether jury service may be deemed a right, a privilege or a duty, the State may no more extend it to some of its citizens and deny it to others on racial grounds than it may invidiously discriminate in the offering and withholding of the elective franchise."

Later in the same term, Justice Kennedy again invoked the similarity between jury service and voting, observing that just as government cannot escape from constitutional constraints by farming out the tasks of administering elections and registering voters, neither can it evade constitutional norms by giving private parties the power to pick jurors.

The link between jury service and other rights of political participation such as voting was also recognized and embraced by the drafters of the Reconstruction amendments and implementing legislation, and still later by authors of various 20th-century voting amendments. For example, the framers of the Fifteenth Amendment, which prohibited race-based discrimination in voting, understood well that the voting they were protecting included voting on juries. That amendment, drafted and ratified in the 1860s, proved to be a template for later amendments protecting women, the poor, and the young from voting discrimination.

Justice's Weak Link?

The weaknesses of jury trials are sometimes ascribed to the mediocre capacity of ordinary citizens to adjudicate matters of law and fact in an increasingly complex society. It is true that jurors will not always decide "correctly," any more than voters will always choose the most qualified candidates for public office. But the real problem is not that we rely too much on men and women of ordinary intelligence and common sense to decide questions of fact and value in the courtroom. The problem is that we rely too little. The jury is crippled by constraints imposed by the court professionals.

In the era of the Founders, the jury was no more egalitarian than was suffrage, limited by race and sex and by tests of personal traits thought necessary for judging cases. Over two centuries, even as the right of jury service was gradually extended to all citizens of voting age, the freedom of jurors to participate in the finding of fact in the courtroom was constricted. Contrary to the spirit in which the jury trial was woven into our constitutional fabric, judges and lawyers have aggrandized their own roles in litigation at the expense of the jury.

The deepest constitutional function of the

jury is to serve not the parties but the people—by involving them in the administration of justice and the grand project of democratic self-government. Alas, over the years, the search for adversarial advantage by attorneys won out over the values of public education and participation.

Judges, charged with protecting these enduring constitutional values, have at times done just the opposite in order to maintain their control over trials. The jury was to check the judge—much as the legislature was to check the executive, the House of Representatives to check the Senate, and the states to check the national government.

It is not surprising that we—as jurors, as citizens—have not fought off these creeping assaults. The benefits of jury service are widely dispersed—they redound to fellow citizens as well as the individual jurors. But the individual juror bears all of the cost—the hassle, the inconvenience, the foregone wages—of jury service.

If the jury system is to remain a central institution of democracy and citizenship, it must be refined. Jury trials must attract engaged and thoughtful citizens; the rules of the courts must treat jurors as sovereign, self-governing citizens rather than as children. To this end, we suggest a number of reforms. In many instances, these changes would require no new laws, but merely a willingness on the part of the courts to unleash the common sense of the ordinary citizen.

I. Respect jurors

First, we must try to design the system to welcome jurors. All too often they are mistreated by the trial process, forced to wait in cramped and uncomfortable quarters while the judge and lawyers question jury candidates, who are often dismissed from selection without explanation. We should use juries to reconnect citizens with each other and with their government. After serving on a jury, a citizen should, in general, feel better—less cynical, more public-regarding—about our system.

II. Make juries more representative

Earlier in the nation's history, juries were impaneled under the elitist principle that only the propertied or the highly educated possessed the habits of citizenship needed to serve well. Now that we know better, it is perverse that professional and literate citizens often are exempted or struck from the jury pool. When juries produce stupid verdicts, it is often because we let interested parties pick stupid jurors in stupid ways. It is a scandal that only those who had never heard of Oliver North were permitted to judge him. Now that we have ceded so much control over trials to the court regulars, this shouldn't come as a surprise—it is akin to letting lobbyists hand-pick candidates for office.

A juror should have an open mind but not an empty mind. We must empower juries in ways that make them more representative and less vulnerable to encroachments of the judicial professionals, without turning them into professionals themselves.

Limit peremptory challenges. By and large, the first 12 persons picked by lottery should form the jury. The jury—and not just the jury pool summoned for each case—should be as representative of the entire community as possible. Peremptory challenges (a device that allows lawyers to remove a specified number of jurors from the panel without having to show "cause") should be eliminated; they allow prosecutors and defense attorneys to manipulate demographics and chisel an unrepresentative panel out of a representative pool. Juries should represent the people, not the parties.

Consider the analogies outlined earlier. Our society does not let an individual defendant hand-pick the legislature to fashion the norms governing his conduct; or the prosecutor who pursues him; or the grand jury that indicts him; or the judge who tries him; or the appellate court that reviews his case. We do not set out—and we'll resist the temptation to wisecrack—to pick the most stupid people imaginable to populate our legislatures or our judiciary. And we are especially uneasy about depriving citizens of the right to vote on the basis of discretionary criteria that may mask racial or sexual stereotyping.

Some major arguments have been advanced to support peremptories. First is the idea of legitimacy: The parties will respect a decision reached by a body they helped to select. But what about the legitimacy of verdicts for the rest of society—We, the people, whom the jury system is supposed to serve? After all, the parties regard the trial judge, the appellate court, the legislature, and the grand jury as legitimate, even though the defendant didn't personally select any of them or exercise any peremptory challenges. In the name of principle, the court professionals are merely disguising a power grab at the expense of the jury.

Second, some argue that peremptories allow counsel to probe jurors with incisive questions during the selection process to unearth "cause" to remove particular jurors. Lawyers need peremptories to vigorously exercise this right, the argument goes, lest they offend a juror for whom no provable grounds exist for a "for cause" dismissal. Our response to this is that "for cause" dismissals should be limited; jurors should not have to recuse themselves by different criteria than do judges. If "for cause" challenges are re-

4. THE JUDICIAL SYSTEM

stricted, the prophylactic argument for peremptories collapses.

The Supreme Court has made clear that no constitutional right to peremptories exists: They are a relic of an imperfectly democratic past. At the Founding, we suspect, peremptories were exercised mainly as a polite way of dismissing folks with personal knowledge of the parties. In a homogeneous jury pool, peremptory challenges would rarely skew the demographics of the eventual jury. But to vindicate the Fifteenth and Nineteenth Amendments, we must close off attempts by lawyers to exploit race and gender in jury selection in a way that deprives some citizens of their right to participate as democratic equals.

Jury pay. We should pay jurors for their time. Payment at a fair, flat rate will permit a broad cross section of society to serve. Our analogy to a bicameral legislature suggests that payment is appropriate, for judges and legislators are paid for their time. To decline to compensate citizens for their sacrifice—or to pay them a token $5 per day as is done in many California courts—is in effect to impose a functionally regressive poll tax that penalizes the working poor who want to serve on juries, but who cannot afford the loss of a week's pay. Payment should come from the government, not private employers. All jurors are equal as jurors, and should be paid equally: One person, one vote, one paycheck.

III. Restore the notion of duty

Jury service is not only a right, but also a duty. Few of us have militantly insisted that we perform this obligation, just as few of us insisted in the last 30 years that we pay our fair share of the intergenerational tax burden. The *Economist* reports that half of all Californians called for jury duty in the state's criminal courts ignore the summons. Citizens should not escape so easily.

Few exemptions. Exemptions from service should be extremely limited: If you are the brother-in-law of the plaintiff, you may be excused; but you may not be excused merely because you happen to read the newspaper or work in a profession. The idea of the jury is rooted in equality; just as all defendants are treated equally before the law, all jurors have equal claims as well as obligations to play a part in the administration of justice. This measure would expand the size of the jury pool, enforce the universality of required service, and raise the average education level of juries.

Yearly service. The Swiss defend their country with a citizen militia that regularly requires a citizen to serve a periodic stint of active service. Similarly, we should ask each citizen to devote, say, one week a year to jury service, depending on the needs of his or her jurisdiction. Each citizen could register in advance for the week that is most convenient, and except for genuine emergencies, citizens should then be obliged to serve when their turn comes. Courts should be willing to provide professional day care or day-care vouchers to enable homemakers to take their turns in this project in collective self-governance.

Enforcing the duty. And how should this obligation be enforced? Progressive fines are probably the best option. If you miss your week, you should pay two weeks' salary. (Flat fines, by contrast, would be functionally regressive and create incentives for highly paid citizens to dodge service.) If for some reason fines didn't work, perhaps we could consider a more radical recoupling of jury service with voting: If you want to opt out of the responsibilities of collective self-government, fine—but you may not then exercise any of its rights. You may choose to be a citizen, with democratic rights and duties, or a subject, ruled by others. On this view, you are not entitled to vote outside juries if you are unwilling to serve and vote inside juries. If you are not willing to engage in regular focused deliberation with a random cross section of fellow voters, you should not be governing the polity, just as you may not vote in the Iowa presidential caucuses unless you attend and hear the arguments of your peers.

Serial jurors. Each jury, once constituted, should be able to try several cases in a row. If you can hear four quick cases in your week a year, so much the better. The grand jury reviews more

Over the years, the professionals of the court have conspired to strip jurors of their ability to evaluate the facts.

that one indictment, the judge sits on more than one case, and the legislature may decide more than one issue in a session. The quality of deliberations is likely to improve with practice. The burden of jury service will be more evenly distributed—one week for everyone—and more trials can take place if we get rid of all the wasteful preliminaries like elaborate jury questioning and peremptories. Indeed, perhaps a jury should hear both civil and criminal cases in its week. One week a year will not turn citizens into government bureaucrats, though it will give them regular practice in the art of deliberation and self-government.

IV. Free jurors to do their jobs

Juries today are often criticized for reaching foolish decisions. But it's not all their fault.

Nothing is more important to fulfilling the democratic aims of jury service—including just outcomes—than active participation by the jurors. Over the years, the court professionals have conspired to strip jurors of their ability to evaluate the facts. Running the courtroom to maximize their own convenience, they have often slighted the jury's legitimate needs to understand its role, the law, and the facts. The bicameral analogy is instructive: Would we expect the House of Representatives to perform its duties competently if its access to information and ideas were entirely determined by the Senate?

Taking notes. Many judges do not allow jurors to take notes. This is idiocy. Judges take notes, grand jurors take notes, legislators take notes—what's going on here? This prohibition is based on the misguided beliefs that note-taking distracts jurors from the testimony and that deliberation would be unfairly dominated by jurors with extensive records. Neither fear outweighs the benefit of giving jurors the means to highlight key evidence and keep track of their impressions, particularly in long trials.

Plain-English instructions. Judges should give the panel, at the *outset* of a case, the basic elements of the charged offenses—in English, not legalese—so jurors can consider them and check them off in their notebooks as the trial unfolds.

Questioning of witnesses. Jurors should be allowed to question witnesses by passing queries to the judge. This allows jurors to pierce the selective presentation of facts offered by counsel, and it also keeps jurors more attentive to proceedings. Best of all, it would expose any lingering confusion about testimony in the minds of the jurors, giving prosecutors and defense counsel the chance to address these concerns. Consider, for example, the possibility that each of the jurors in the O.J. Simpson trial had a different pet theory of police conspiracy. If each juror could submit questions, prosecutors would have had an opportunity to understand, address, and debunk many of these mutually inconsistent and factually insupportable theories.

Discussion among jurors prior to deliberation. A ban on such discussion assumes that jurors are superhumanly capable of suspending all judgment for days or weeks and that conversation can only contaminate their faculties. Common sense suggests that it is human nature to form provisional judgments; at least by discussing a case prior to deliberation, jurors can test each other's impressions of the evidence and begin to hone their understandings of key points before these points are lost in the rush of the proceedings. Such a reform must, of course, be accompanied by reminders from the judge that jurors may not reach final conclusions about guilt or innocence until they have heard all the evidence.

Support staff. We should allow juries to hire support staff when it is necessary. In a world of increasing complexity and specialization of labor, few can do an important job well without such help. If legislators and judges can have staffs, why not grand juries? We trivialize jurors when we insist that they alone remain trapped in the 18th-century world of generalists. Perhaps every court should hire a permanent staff with undivided loyalty to the jury itself, and subject to "term limits" to prevent the staff from entrenching itself and using the jury to advance its own agenda.

V. Avoid hung juries

When hung juries occur, mistrials waste the time and resources of all concerned. They even harm defendants in cases where the jury was leaning toward acquittal, because a mistrial allows a vindictive prosecutor a second bite at the apple. All this brings us to another controversial—and we admit extremely tentative—suggestion. Perhaps, just perhaps, we should move, even in criminal cases, away from unanimity toward majority or supermajority rule on juries. Founding history is relatively clear—a criminal jury had to be unanimous. But this clear understanding was not explicitly inscribed into the Constitution, and the modern Supreme Court has upheld state rules permitting convictions on 10-2 votes. (England today also permits 10-2 verdicts in criminal cases.)

Three arguments support our suggestion that nonunanimous verdicts should be upheld. First, at the Founding unanimity may have drawn its strength from certain metaphysical and religious ideas about Truth that are no longer plausible: to wit, that all real truths would command universal assent. Second, most of our analogies tug toward majority rule—used by legislatures, appellate benches, voters, and grand juries—or supermajority rule: In impeachment proceedings, for example, a two-thirds vote in the Senate is required for conviction.

Last, and most important, all our other suggestions lead the modern American jury system away from its historical reliance on unanimity. At the founding of our nation, unanimity *within* a jury was nestled in a cluster of other rules that now must fall. In early days, blacks, women, the poor, and the young were excluded from voting and jury service. Peremptory challenges probably made juries even more homogenous. But now that all adult citizens may serve on juries, and we have eliminated all the old undemocratic barriers, preserving unanimity might also be undemocratic, for it would create an extreme minority veto unknown to the Founders.

4. THE JUDICIAL SYSTEM

Even at the Founding, unanimous jury verdicts may have existed in the shadow of a custom of majority or supermajority rule. Jurors would discuss the case and vote on guilt; and even if the minority were unconvinced about the verdict, they would in the end vote with the majority after they had been persuaded that the majority had listened to their arguments in good faith. This custom bears some resemblance to legislative "unanimous consent" rules. A single lawmaker may often slow down proceedings—force her colleagues to deliberate more carefully on something that matters to her—but in the end she may not prevent the majority from implementing its judgment. Perhaps the same should hold true for juries.

In allowing juries to depart from unanimity, we must try to preserve the ideal of jury deliberation and self-education. Jurors should communicate with each other seriously and with respect. Fans of unanimity argue that it promotes serious deliberation—everyone's vote is necessary, so everyone is seriously listened to. But unanimity cannot guarantee *mutual* tolerance: What about an eccentric holdout who refuses to listen to, or even try to persuade, others?

Nonunanimous schemes can be devised to promote serious discussion. Jurors should be told that their job is to communicate with others who have different ideas, views, and backgrounds. Judges could also advise jurors that their early deliberations should focus on the evidence and not jurors' tentative leanings or votes, and that they should take no straw polls until each juror has had a chance to talk about the evidence on both sides.

We suggest a scheme in which a jury must be unanimous to convict on the first day of deliberations, but on day two, 11-1 would suffice; on day three, 10-2; and so on, until we hit our bedrock limit of, say, two-thirds (for conviction) or simple majority (for acquittal).

VI. Educate the People

Once we start thinking about the jury from the perspective of democracy rather than adjudication—from the viewpoint of the citizenry rather than the litigants—other possibilities open up. Recall Tocqueville's description of the jury as a "free school . . . always open" to educate the people in citizenship. If this is the big idea, why not take advantage of new video technology to advance it? Think of how C-SPAN broadcasts of legislative debates and hearings have contributed to the education of the public. The courts could likewise tape jury deliberations for use as high-school teaching materials about democracy in action (perhaps delaying the release of sensitive cases). Of course, we would have to ensure that these records would not be used to impeach jury verdicts.

Let the Changes Begin

The vision we have sketched is a demanding one. Yet many states are already taking up the challenge, enacting reforms by statute or by court policy. The court system of New York state is mulling over reforms to make the experience of serving more efficient and convenient for citizens, and many states already have a one-day, one-trial policy. New Jersey and New York last year joined the 25 or so states that eliminate exemptions based on profession. Arizona is the leader in endorsing proposals, such as note-taking and questioning witnesses, to increase jurors' participation in the process. Oregon and Louisiana allow nonunanimous verdicts in some cases, and Arizona allows a jury to ask the lawyers to explain evidence again if it has reached an impasse in deliberations.

But much more needs to be done. Until America's state and federal judicial systems live up to the ideals embedded in their founding documents and learn to trust the capacity of ordinary citizens to dispense justice, a cornerstone of democracy will continue to crumble.

Akhil Reed Amar is Southmayd Professor of Law at Yale Law School. Vikram David Amar is Acting Professor of Law at the University of California at Davis and a visiting professor of law at the University of California at Berkeley. For citational support and further discussion of the themes addressed in this article, see Vikram David Amar, "Jury Service as Political Participation Akin to Voting," 80 Cornell L. Rev. 203 (1995) and Akhil Reed Amar, "Reinventing Juries: Ten Suggested Reforms," 28 U.C. Davis L. Rev. 1169 (1995).

Article 24

Do you swear that you will well and truly try...?

Trial by jury has had some ups and downs, but it beats what led up to it—trial by combat, and ordeal by fire, water or poison

Barbara Holland

Barbara Holland is the author of a book on the lives of U.S. Presidents. Justly or unjustly, she wrote for SMITHSONIAN about the illustrious Adams family.

When law and order began, the only court was the head of the family group, and father knew best. His word was law and there was no appeal. If Papa was a bully, maybe Mama could pack up the kids and move to a different family. Or spike his soup with the leaves and berries her mother had told her about. In any case, what happened in the family was nobody's business but the family's.

Presently people developed agriculture and settled down, clustering together in groups of families. We acquired garden plots and portable private property—and controversy as we know it was born. Old paterfamilias still decided family matters, but coping with interfamilial strife called for group arbitration to prevent a homicidal free-for-all (or try to prevent it; the human animal has a natural taste for homicidal free-for-alls). Controversy gave birth to law.

Law is an ever-deepening pile of decisions that, once made, become permanent. This is a great timesaver. If it's wrong for A to steal B's battle-ax on Tuesday, then it's automatically wrong for C to steal D's battle-ax Wednesday, whether the matter is written down or just preserved as remembered usage. We don't need to thrash it out over and over again.

We do need to find out whether C really stole the ax, or if D just lost the thing and blamed it on C. To establish this, we check with the neighbors. Is D a famous liar? Does he have a grudge against C? Has anyone seen C chopping up Saxons with the ax? These folk are witnesses. If we find the ax under C's bed, that's evidence.

The laws are established, facts discovered, witnesses heard and judgment made. These functions have been separated in our fancier world, but in the early tribunals they were all one. The group called in to consider the matter was made up of witnesses; if no law already applied to the case, they made one that would; they talked it over and decided.

The good thing about juries is that they're amateurs. The bad thing about juries is that they're amateurs.

They were all amateurs. Laws were so simple that ordinary folk could understand them. Now professionals have taken over the courts and, I hear, get well paid for it, but juries are still amateurs called in for the occasion,

From *Smithsonian*, March 1995, pp. 108, 110, 112, 114, 116-117. © 1995 by Barbara Holland. Reprinted by permission. Barbara Holland's most recent book is *Bingo Night at the Fire Hall.*

4. THE JUDICIAL SYSTEM

unattached to the system. The good thing about juries is that they're amateurs. The bad thing about juries is that they're amateurs.

Rome refined the system and separated the law from the facts. A magistrate defined the dispute, cited the law and referred the problem to a citizen judex—a fellow of some standing—who called in a few associates to help. They listened to the speeches, weighed the evidence and pronounced sentence. (Nobody was supervising them, so it helped if one of them was a lawyer, to explain.) This was more orderly than a tribunal. The Romans were passionately fond of order and wrote down all their laws in books.

They were also fond of a good public spectacle, and a convicted criminal could always opt for the arena and entertain the citizens by duking it out with other criminals or prisoners of war. A talented gladiator not only got to live, but he could wind up as a popular sports hero, surrounded by pretty ladies. The Romans loved a winner, regardless of his criminal record.

Meanwhile, the Scandinavians were gathering regularly in tribunals, called Things, dating back further than anyone remembered. Groups of delegates met to represent their districts, and committees of 12 or of multiples of 12 were picked to administer or invent the laws.

Twelve is the solemn number. When Morgan of Glamorgan, Prince of Wales, established trial by jury in A.D. 725, he wrote, "For as Christ and his Twelve Apostles were finally to judge the world, so human tribunals should be composed of the king and twelve wise men." Maybe, though apparently Christ was following an older tradition. The number 12 crops up all over. The zodiac has 12 signs, based on 12 constellations; we divide our days into twice-12 hours; 12 midnight rings in the witching hour. We buy our eggs by the dozen and undertake semimystical cures in 12 steps. Scandinavian folktales offer us 12 princesses, trolls with 12 heads, and 12 princes changed into 12 wild swans by a troll.

Maybe 12 has ancient powers. After all, the opinion of 11 jurors is merely an opinion, but the opinion of 12 is magic, transforming the presumed innocent into the guilty like a prince turned into a frog.

So the Scandinavians gathered and chose up groups of 12. (Then as now, the parties could object if they spotted their archenemy or their victim's glowering father among the 12.) They swore to vote justly and then decided the matter according to what seemed to them to be natural rightness.

It's pleasant to think of them meeting century after century for this civilized rite of community justice, a society taking responsibility for its common good conduct. Unfortunately, Northern Europe doesn't remember the Norsemen as calm, thoughtful, reasonable fellows; the Things may have been as uproarious in practice as they were virtuous in principle. Heads may have cracked.

After Rome fell apart, its former empire went all to sixes and sevens, and its orderly laws decayed into gib-

---

Under Saxon law, if you could carry several pounds of glowing red-hot iron in your bare hands for nine steps or walk barefoot over nine red-hot plowshares without getting any blisters, you were not guilty.

---

berish. In Britain, the possibly legendary King Arthur had to send his possibly legendary knights out to ride around righting wrongs and rescuing maidens from sexual harassment, a far from comprehensive judicial system. There were still trials, though, with an ordeal serving as jury.

Great faith has been placed in trial by ordeal, all the way from the Old Testament to the Australian outback. The idea is that something out there "knows" who's guilty and will point to him if given a chance. The chance usually involves fire or water or poison.

Poison was recommended in the Bible and was popular in Africa and Brahmanic India for trials by ordeal. Those who survived at all, though likely to be ill, were considered innocent. The Saxons developed a variation called "corsnaed," a morsel of something that would choke the guilty (perhaps their throats were dry with apprehension). Godwin, Earl of Kent, is said to have choked on his.

Under Saxon law, if you could carry several pounds of glowing red-hot iron in your bare hands for nine steps or walk barefoot over nine red-hot plowshares without getting any blisters, you were not guilty. Similar proof was accepted in Hindu and Scandinavian law. In Britain, Africa and parts of Asia, plunging your arm into boiling water, oil or lead without the usual results proved your innocence.

Water was also knowledgeable stuff. The innocent sank; the guilty floated and could be fished out and dealt with. This was the customary method of identifying witches, who were cross-tied thumb-to-toe before being thrown in. True witches refused to drown and were dried off and burned at the stake.

Alongside this undignified jurisprudence, the Saxons were actually working out a human jury system, but it was available only to the honest. If your neighbors knew you for a liar, or you'd perjured yourself in the past, or, presumably, if you were a stranger just passing through, you weren't "oath-worthy" and went directly to the red-hot iron or the drowning pond. But if you were a person of known honesty in your district and were accused of a crime, you swore, "By the Lord, I am guiltless both in deed and counsel of the charge of which X accuses me," and that was that. However, if you were accused by a

24. Do You Swear?

group, you had to parry with a group of your own, called "compurgators." You asked 11 thanes—freeholders—to join you and swear to your honesty in the matter. If you couldn't round up 11 who believed you, you took off your shoes for the hot plowshares.

In those days, honesty was the best policy. Honesty, and a loyal group of bribable drinking buddies. Ethelred, noticing this flaw, provided for a group of 12 senior thanes to investigate and act as an accusatory jury; 8 votes could convict.

Justice was still a neighborhood matter. Everyone was supposed to know everyone else and have some firsthand knowledge of what happened. Rather recently, we've turned this concept on its head, and juries are supposed to know nothing at all before they sit down in the box—to be but as empty vessels into which the liquor of admissible evidence is poured. In inflammatory cases, the trial even gets moved to another area to ensure the jurors' indifference.

Television's ubiquitousness makes it harder to find jurors sufficiently isolated to qualify: jurors too listless to turn TV on, too apathetic to have an opinion, and too morose even to lend an ear at the watercooler. (Nobody's actually proved that ignorance promises fairness. In fact, a study of English trials between 1550 and 1750 showed that juries overwhelmingly acquitted the people they knew and convicted passing strangers.)

A 17th-century prisoner complained that one of the jurors was a dear friend of the prosecutor's, and the judge snapped, "And do you challenge a juryman because he is supposed to know something of the matter? For that reason the juries are called from the neighborhood, because they should not be wholly strangers to the fact."

In Saxon times, a nosy curiosity about the neighbors was required by law. A regulation sometimes credited to King Alfred (not to be confused with the possibly legendary Arthur) in the ninth century divided everyone into groups, or "tythings," of ten families who were all held responsible for one another's behavior. Canute's law read, "And we will that every freeman be brought into a 'hundred,' and into a tything." Nonmembers were outlaws; members, called "hundredors," oversaw law and order and one another's personal lives. In murder cases, if they didn't produce a culprit within a month and a day, they all paid a fine. Every man was his brother's keeper. This made life simpler for the police, but it seems to be an idea whose time has gone.

The "hundreds" were democratic, mixing the washed and the unwashed and giving the latter a voice. The county court, presided over by the sheriff, met every six months, and 12-man juries chosen for their personal knowledge of a case decided matters concerning their hundred. Below the county court was the court of the hundred, which was convened every four weeks as a local police court, keeping order and protecting rights, its juries sworn to "accuse no innocent man, nor conceal any guilty one." Disgruntled parties could appeal to the king.

Folks back then were so primitive that they thought the victim, rather than the law, had been damaged, and bodily harm was redeemed at so much for a finger, so much for an ear, all the way up to murder, which, in Alfred's time, cost 200 shillings, payable to the deceased's family. (Among the Germans it was payable in sheep.) Thieves paid the value of the stolen object plus a fine; repeat offenders and those who stole from the church paid with a hand or a foot as well.

A prudent jury weighed factors other than the evidence. (It was also the custom for the winner to pay each juror several guineas and take them all out to dinner.)

This would mean that if someone broke your arm while stealing your car, he paid for your arm and your car, and you got to keep the fine and possibly his foot too. Now he just goes to jail, and you get to pay for his room and board with taxes. Progress has been made.

When right made might

When William the Conqueror took over England in 1066, he left the Saxon system in place and added some Norman flourishes, like trial by combat. Combat was a judicial entertainment similar to the gladiatorial, in which right was thought to make might—whoever was right would win. The accuser had to do battle with the accused, causing the small and frail to think twice before complaining, but if you were no good at fighting you could hire someone to fight for you. The man with the fiercest hired help won—rather like hiring the most expensive lawyer today.

(Ordeals fell into disuse in the 13th century, but the right to trial by combat stayed on the books until Ashford v. Thornton in 1819.)

By Norman times, laws were more complicated, so professionals, called justiciars, were sent around to keep an eye on the courts and the rules of evidence, rather like judges. They knew more about the law and less about what had happened than the jurors did.

We were told in school that jury trials sprang newborn from the Magna Carta, but juries were around before 1215. The Magna Carta just guaranteed them as a right not to be ignored by capricious powers like bad King

4. THE JUDICIAL SYSTEM

John, but some kings went right on being capricious anyway. In these enlightened times, we merely torch the neighborhood if we don't like a verdict, but back then, juries got punished if the authorities didn't like it. Since juries were still considered witnesses, a wrong vote was considered perjury. Acquitting unpopular or possibly treasonous people got jurors hauled into the star chamber, where a group of the king's dear friends dealt severely with them. They lost their goods and chattels and went to jail for at least a year; sometimes their wives and children were thrown out of their houses, the houses demolished, the meadows destroyed and even the trees chopped down. A prudent jury weighed factors other than the evidence. (It was also the custom for the winner to pay each juror several guineas and take them all out to dinner.)

Humans being cantankerous, jurors occasionally voted their consciences anyway. Sometimes they even voted against the law. Juries have always given justice a bit of purely human wiggle-room. If they don't buy into the law as written, they can pummel it into shape—and a law under which nobody gets convicted eventually starves to death.

In 1650, under Cromwell, a newly reinstated law called for hanging adulteresses—and scarcely an adulteress was found in the land. In 1670 William Penn was tried for preaching Quaker doctrine, and he couldn't have been guiltier, caught red-handed and far from a first offense. The jurors stubbornly found in his favor and were fined 40 marks apiece for wrongness. Four of

---

Whatever it may read or watch, the modern jury doesn't know what it was designed to know—its neighbors—and a clever lawyer can sometimes play on it as upon a harp.

---

them refused to pay and spent a year in prison, until one was brought before the court on habeas corpus, and lo, it was decided that the law couldn't jail jurors for their decisions. We can't put them in jail anymore, but we can select them half to death.

As we limp toward the 21st century, the rural community of nosy neighbors has faded into history, and the problem now is, Who are these jurors? Prince Morgan called them "wise men." Under Edward I, they were to be 12 of the "better men" of the bailiwick. Under George IV, "good and lawful men." (Except for adulteresses, witches and common scolds, legal history doesn't

mention women; perhaps they're a recent invention.) It seems to have been so simple then, naming our good, wise, lawful peers. But how do we choose among strangers not necessarily wise but merely registered to vote?

Once the blatantly prejudiced have been sent packing, both sides take up the peremptory challenge of turning down jurors for the way they look, dress or comb their hair. A new professional has sprung up among us, the jury-selection consultant. For the O. J. Simpson trial, consultants submitted an 80-page list of 294 questions for prospective jurors, including essay questions like "What do you think is the main cause of domestic violence?" The theory is that we ordinary citizens are such a bunch of sheep that we'll always vote according to our kind, regardless of the evidence. The more narrowly the consultants can identify our kind, the easier it is to predict the vote.

The differing agendas of the prosecution and the defense complicate matters. Prosecution lawyer Jeffrey Toobin says that when he first came to the bar, he was always told to avoid men with beards (too independent) and teachers and social workers (too sympathetic), and aim for "the little old Lutheran lady in pearls, quick to judge and slow to forgive."

For the defense, Clarence Darrow advised not to "take a German; they are bull-headed. Rarely take a Swede; they are stubborn. Always take an Irishman or a Jew; they are the easiest to move to emotional sympathy." He preferred old men for their tolerance, but Samuel Leibowitz liked them young for their still-fresh sense of brotherhood and avoided self-made men, businessmen with close-set eyes, writers, professors and former policemen.

In his recent book *We, the Jury*, Jeffrey Abramson recommends a patchwork, arguing that the soul of the jury rises out of its diversity, the alchemy of a "collection of wisdom," as people of various ages, classes and backgrounds rub their conflicting viewpoints together to shape a consensus that represents us, the people. (Whether we're levelheaded enough to deserve representation is another matter. Last year an English jury convicted in a murder case after receiving a message from the deceased on a smuggled Ouija board. But hey, we're all we've got.) Abramson, anyway, has faith. He even agrees with Chief Justice John Marshall who once said that it's all right for jurors to have read the newspapers.

Whatever it may read or watch, the modern jury doesn't know what it was designed to know—its neighbors—and a clever lawyer can sometimes play on it as upon a harp. Such was William Howe of Howe and Hummel, defender of the underworld in rowdy post-Civil War New York. Howe was an enormous, lion-headed man with a wardrobe of costumes for his courtroom performances and a talent for crying copiously over any case, however dull. Once he delivered an hourlong summation, kneeling before the jury. Another time he convinced a jury that his client's trigger finger had acciden-

24. Do You Swear?

tally slipped, not once but six times. So many of his clients were forgers that his office accepted only cash, so many were thieves that his office safe contained nothing but a coal scuttle—but murderers were his meat and drink. He personally appeared for more than 650 of them. He virtually invented "temporary insanity." He wept; the jury wept. According to a newspaper account, during his defense of Annie Walden, the "Man-Killing Race-Track Girl," the "sobs of juror nine could have been heard in the corridors, and there was moisture in the eyes of all but one or two of the other jurors."

Howe kept a stable of white-haired mothers, distraught wives and cherubic children available to represent the family of the accused. He once pointed out his own wife and child, who happened to be in the courtroom, as his client's prospective widow and orphan. How would a New York jury know? And how the hometown juries of old would have laughed.

Here and there a voice suggests returning at least

minor offenses to neighborhood judicial counsels, as in the old courts of the hundreds, taking the law into our own hands where it began. This may be utopian. We don't want to know our 99 nearest neighbors, let alone be accountable for their behavior. Some of us don't even want to read the papers. We gripe about the results, but we leave civil order to the professionals. It wasn't designed to work that way.

British lawyers tell the story of a jury in New South Wales that was considering the matter of some stolen cows, about which the jurors certainly knew more than the court would ever learn. After deliberating, they returned a verdict of "Not guilty, if he returns the cows." The judge was outraged at this insult to the law and threw them back out to think again. Pigheaded and mutinous, they returned with a new verdict, "Not guilty—and he doesn't have to return the cows."

Perhaps justice, if not law, was served.

Juvenile Justice

Although there were variations within specific offense categories, the overall arrest rate for juvenile violent crime remained relatively constant for several decades. Then, in the late 1980s, something changed, bringing more and more juveniles charged with a violent offense into the justice system. The juvenile justice system is a twentieth-century response to the problems of dealing with children in trouble with the law or children who need society's protection. Juvenile court procedure differs from the procedure in adult courts because juvenile courts were based on the philosophy that their function was to treat and to help, not to punish and to abandon, the offender.

Recently, operations of the juvenile court have received criticism, and a number of significant Supreme Court decisions have changed the way the courts must approach the rights of children. In spite of these changes, however, the major thrust of the juvenile justice system remains one of diversion and treatment rather than adjudication and incarceration, although there is a trend toward dealing more punitively with serious juvenile offenders.

This unit's opening essay, "Rethinking the Sanctioning Function in Juvenile Court: Retributive or Restorative Responses to Youth Crime," asserts that a restorative sanctioning model could provide a clear alternative to punishment-centered sanctioning approaches now dominant in juvenile justice and could ultimately redefine the sanctioning function.

The report that follows, "Juvenile Probation: The Workhorse of the Juvenile Justice System," tells how extensively probation officers are involved with juvenile delinquency cases. Of the 1.5 million delinquency cases handled by the juvenile courts in 1993, virtually all had contact with a probation officer at some point. According to "Crime Time Bomb," juvenile crime is rising and will get worse.

How is this menace to be curbed? Somehow cities, states, and Congress need to strike a balance between passing tougher laws and implementing preventive measures.

J. David Hawkins advocates using the public health model to curb violence in "Controlling Crime before It Happens: Risk-Focused Prevention." He maintains that it is essential to identify and then eliminate the factors that put youth at risk for violence. Regarding the interrelationship of street gangs to the U.S. military, Robert Bunker, in "Street Gangs—Future Paramilitary Groups?" expresses his concern that gang members with military training would bring a whole new dimension to law enforcement's struggle with these criminal groups.

"States Revamping Laws on Juveniles as Felonies Soar" makes the point that "almost all 50 states have overhauled their laws in the past two years, allowing more youths to be tried as adults and scrapping longtime protections like the confidentiality of juvenile court proceedings."

The unit closes with an essay from the American Psychological Association's *Monitor*, "The Search for a Proper Punishment," which asserts that incarcerating youths fails to reduce juvenile crime.

Looking Ahead: Challenge Questions

What reform efforts are currently underway in the juvenile justice system?

What are some recent trends in juvenile delinquency? In what ways will the juvenile justice system be affected by these trends?

Is the departure of the juvenile justice system from its original purpose warranted or not?

UNIT 5

Article 25

Rethinking the Sanctioning Function in Juvenile Court: Retributive or Restorative Responses to Youth Crime

**Gordon Bazemore and
Mark Umbreit**

Gordon Bazemore: Associate Professor, School of Public Administration, Florida Atlantic University.
Mark Umbreit: Associate Professor, School of Social Work, University of Minnesota.

Although juvenile courts have always administered punishment to youthful offenders, parens patriae *and the individual treatment mission have historically assigned an ambivalent role to sanctioning. In the absence of a coherent sanctioning framework, a punitive model has recently gained dominance over dispositional decision making in juvenile court. This article examines the limitations of sanctioning choices presented by both the individual treatment mission and what some have referred to as a "retributive justice" paradigm. We then consider the implications of an alternative model—restorative justice—as a framework for a new approach to sanctioning consistent with a revitalized juvenile justice mandate.*

INTRODUCTION

The juvenile court is under the most severe attack it has experienced in the 95 years since its birth in 1899. For example, recent legislative changes mandating fixed sentences in adult prisons for youths meeting minimum age requirements (or no age requirements) in Georgia, Florida, Tennessee, and Oregon (Lemov

1994) challenge the viability of a separate court and justice system for young persons. Such changes represent only the most recent and extreme round of legislative assault on the jurisdiction of the juvenile court in more than a decade of transformation in policy and procedure. Although policymakers in some states have been more cautious in moves to abolish or dismantle their juvenile justice systems, what remains today in most jurisdictions can best be described as a "criminalized" or "punitive juvenile court" (Feld 1990) that has moved further away from its original goal of providing treatment in the "best interests" of youth.

In response, some have argued that the best hope for preserving the juvenile justice system is by "reaffirming" or "revitalizing" the individual treatment mission (Krisberg 1988; McHardy 1990; McAllair 1993). Others have argued that even a revitalized treatment mission is insufficient to sustain, or regain, public support for a separate and distinct juvenile justice system (Feld 1993). Whereas much of this debate has focused on the relative effectiveness of treatment, the need to improve assessment and classification, and the need for greater attention to due process in the juvenile court, other public and policymaker concerns have been largely ignored. Prominent among these concerns has been the absence of a clear and coherent sanctioning framework for juvenile offenders.

As coercive measures taken to enforce societal standards, criminal justice *sanctions,* depending on intent, may be directed toward rehabilitative, educative, regulatory, and/or compensatory ends—as well as retribution or deterrence (Packer 1968; Garland 1990). In the absence of a framework that incorporates and gives priority to such nonpunitive objectives, however, juvenile justice policymakers have adopted a one-dimensional approach to sanctioning based on what some have referred to as a *retributive justice* paradigm (Zehr 1990;

The authors wish to thank Ted Rubin and Martha Schiff for comments on an earlier version of this article. Don Gibbons provided helpful suggestions and extensive assistance with revisions on the final draft.

From *Crime & Delinquency,* July 1995, pp. 296-316. © 1995 by Sage Publications, Inc. Reprinted by permission.

Umbreit 1994). In this article, retributive justice refers to a broad ideological framework that gives priority to punishment and lesser emphasis to rehabilitative goals, places central focus on "desert" as the primary rationale for decision making, and expands the role of formal, adversarial, adjudicatory, and dispositional processes (Feld 1990, 1993).[1] Although this perspective is incompatible with the rationale for a separate and distinct justice system for juveniles based on their special developmental status and a concern with rehabilitative objectives (Feld 1990), the retributive approach to sanctioning has gained popularity because, in the minds of policymakers and the public, punitive sanctions serve to affirm community disapproval of proscribed behavior, denounce crime, and provide consequences to the lawbreaker.

In contrast, the traditional individual treatment mission clearly fails to accomplish these functions. Rather, treatment appears to be unrelated to the offense, to be related solely to the needs of juvenile lawbreakers, and to require nothing of offenders beyond participation in counseling or remedial services. It is difficult to convince most citizens that treatment programs provide anything other than benefits to offenders (e.g., services, recreational activities), and there is little in the message of the treatment response that attempts to communicate to an offender that he or she has harmed someone and should take action to repair damages wreaked upon the victim(s).

Should we give up entirely on the juvenile court? We stand with those who believe that abolition or dismemberment of the juvenile court, as well as the continued expansion of retributive sanctioning policies, represent extreme response to the internal contradictions that have been the source of much criticism leveled at the juvenile justice system. However, the punitive model and the traditional treatment model are not the only options for the juvenile court. Because neither provides an appropriate means of meeting the needs of communities to sanction youth crime, it is important to broaden the debate to consider alternative frameworks.

This article outlines the principles of one such alternative framework that could expand the limited range of available options, prioritize new objectives for sanctioning, and ensure that the use of sanctions is also consistent with other goals of juvenile justice intervention (e.g., rehabilitation and public safety). Drawing on recent theoretical developments that emphasize the importance of sanctioning in the control of criminal behavior (Braithwaite 1989; Garland 1990), the *restorative justice* perspective offers a blueprint to policymakers and juvenile justice professionals for developing an alternative to the retributive model. A restorative model would expand less punitive, less costly, and less stigmatizing sanctioning methods by involving the community and victims in sanctioning processes, thereby elevating the role of victims and victimized communities and giving priority to reparation, direct offender accountability to victims, and conflict resolution (Zehr 1990; Van Ness 1993; Umbreit 1994).

THE SANCTIONING FUNCTION AND JUVENILE JUSTICE

Sanctioning has always been viewed with ambivalence in the juvenile justice system. Although historically juvenile justice decision makers eschewed sanctioning in favor of providing individualized treatment in the "best interests of the child" (e.g., Mack 1909; Melton 1989), juvenile courts have often disguised punishment as treatment (Rothman 1980; Miller 1991) and have not been reluctant to confine offenders for failure to participate in mandated treatment or to comply with other court requirements (Rothman 1980; Bazemore 1994a). Such responses have been viewed as aberrant departures from the court's central mission, however, and juvenile justice decision makers have typically failed to formally acknowledge the sanctioning function. Rather, viewing sanctioning as an *alternative* to treatment, judges and other juvenile justice professionals often have been inconsistent and extreme in the response to juvenile crime (Thompson and McAnany 1984), foregoing sanctions altogether for many "low-end" or "medium-level" offenders deemed worthy candidates for services or treatment programs. On the other hand, those who have taxed decision makers' patience by repeat offending or noncompliance have often received a clearly punitive response—a response now increasingly likely to be administered in the criminal justice system, where little or no consideration is given to treatment needs (Feld 1990; Butts 1994).

The Rise and Impact of "Retributive Juvenile Justice"

One attempt to bring rationality to the erratic decision making in juvenile court sanctioning was through the application of the "just deserts" philosophy (von Hirsch 1976; Schneider and Schram 1983). Though intended to reduce arbitrary and excessive punitive actions, the "just deserts" policies and practices actually implemented—including mandatory and determinate sentencing, expanded prosecutorial powers, and fewer restrictions on transfer to adult court—resulted instead in an expansion of punishment. Specifically, retributive reforms in various states led to increased incarceration and longer stays in residential and detention facilities (Castellano 1986; McAllair 1993).

In addition, by giving new legitimacy to punishment for its own sake, policymakers sent signals to prosecutors and other decision makers that this was an appropriate and just response to delinquent behavior.[2] Moreover, as some criminologists have suggested, equating sanc-

5. JUVENILE JUSTICE

tioning with punitive measures aimed solely at causing pain and discomfort to the offender may fuel demand for more severe punishments, especially when it becomes apparent that current levels are not achieving the desired effect (Christie 1982; Wilkins 1991). In the juvenile justice context, this demand appears to have accelerated the sorting process through which an expanding group of offenders judged to require a punitive, adult-like response are increasingly distinguished from those viewed as deserving of treatment. Perhaps the most damaging effect of the retributive paradigm on the juvenile justice system has been its tendency to make nonpunitive "alternative sanctions" appear weak and less adequate than incarceration, thereby closing off consideration of inexpensive and less harmful responses to youth crime (Garland 1990; Wilkins 1991).

The Limits of Sanctioning Choices: Beyond Punishment and Treatment

Although few question the inevitability of some punishment or deny that any sanction may be experienced by the *offender* as punitive, it is possible to consider and give priority to different sanctioning objectives in the response to crime. In recent years a number of scholars have challenged the effectiveness of retributive punishment and argued that sanctions may also serve important expressive, educative, and symbolic functions (Braithwaite 1989; Wilkins 1991; Garland 1990). Quoting Durkheim (1961, pp. 181–2), for example, Braithwaite (1989) highlights the role of sanctioning in moral education and underscored the limitations of punishment aimed only at threats and offender suffering:

> Since punishment is reproaching, the best punishment is that which puts the blame . . . in the most expressive but least expensive way possible. . . . It is not a matter of making him suffer . . . or as if the essential thing were to intimidate and terrorize. Rather it is a matter of reaffirming the obligation at the moment when it is violated, to strengthen the sense of duty, both for the guilty party and for those witnessing the offense—those whom the offense tends to demoralize. (p. 178)

From this perspective, expressive sanctioning aimed at communicating value-based messages to offenders and the community and affirming obligations and accountability should be more effective in regulating conduct and more likely to promote community solidarity and peaceful dispute resolution (Griffiths and Belleau 1993; Wilkins 1991). Retributive punishment, on the other hand, may have several counterdeterrent effects on offenders, including stigmatization, humiliation, and isolation, that may minimize prospects for regaining self-respect and the respect of the community (Braithwaite 1989; Makkai and Braithwaite 1994). Punishment may also undermine self-restraint, create adjustment problems by exacerbating risk factors linked to future delinquency (Paternoster and Iovanni 1989),

and weaken conventional community bonds by damaging job prospects and peer, family, and other adult relationships (Zhang and Messner 1994). Moreover, as Durkheim and others have argued, punishment may become less effective the more often it is used, by attenuating feelings of shame or moralistic tendencies of offenders (Durkheim 1961; Garland 1990). Ironically, punishment may encourage lawbreakers to focus on themselves rather than on their victims and the community as they learn to "take the punishment" without taking responsibility for their misbehavior (Wright 1991).

Unfortunately, because it fails to acknowledge the sanctioning function and may even appear to excuse or minimize offender responsibility for crime, the treatment model offers little guidance to policymakers wishing to develop more meaningful and appropriate sanctioning options. As Byrne (1989) has observed in assessing the weaknesses of control/surveillance and treatment models in community corrections, both punishment and treatment responses are practically and conceptually incomplete. Taking a one-dimensional view of the offender, each model operates from a "closed system" logic (see also, Reiss 1986) that targets only offenders for service, punishment, or both and fails to include other parties critical to the resolution of crime. Specifically, victims can rarely count on reparation, assistance, or acknowledgment and typically do not participate in any meaningful way in the juvenile justice process (Galaway and Hudson 1990), and community members are seldom asked for input or informed of their potentially vital role in meeting sanctioning, rehabilitation, and public safety objectives. Both punitive and therapeutic interventions place offenders in a passive role—as the object of treatment or services on the one hand, and punishment and surveillance on the other (Eglash 1975), and few opportunities are provided for lawbreakers to actively make amends for their crimes or to practice productive behavior that might facilitate habilitation and reintegration. As atomized responses to delinquent behavior, neither treatment nor punishment is capable of uniting offender, community, family, and victim (McElrea 1993; Walgrave 1993).

Ultimately, as Wilkins (1991, p. 312) asserts, "it is now generally accepted that the problem of crime cannot be simplified to the problem of the criminal." The emerging interest in restorative justice as an alternative sanctioning model for juvenile justice is based in part on an increasing recognition of the inadequacy of sanctioning choices offered by the individual treatment mission and the retributive paradigm and frustration with the detachment of these models from the real problems of victims, offenders, and communities (Christie 1982). This interest does not presume immediate, clearly articulated solutions to current sanctioning problems in juvenile justice.

25. Sanctioning Function in Juvenile Court

Rather, it is based on a perceived need for an alternative "lens" (Zehr 1990) for viewing the problem of crime and a new framework to guide rational movement toward new solutions.

EXPLORING RESTORATIVE JUSTICE

Although it draws on ancient concepts and practices abandoned late in the Middle Ages as formal justice systems emerged and began to define the obligation of offenders as a debt to the king or lord (and later to the state) rather than to victims (Schafer 1970; Davis 1992), modern interest in restorative justice has been influenced by several developments in the 1970s and 1980s. Notably, the reemergence of restorative philosophy and practice grew out of experience with reparative sanctions and processes (e.g., restitution, victim-offender mediation) (Schneider 1985; Galaway and Hudson 1990; Umbreit and Coates 1993), the victims' movement, the rise of informal neighborhood justice and dispute resolution processes (Messmer and Otto 1992), and new thinking on equity and human relationships influenced in part by the women's movement and the peace and social justice movements (Pepinsky and Quinney 1991; Harris 1993).

Whereas retributive justice is focused on determining guilt and delivering appropriate punishment ("just deserts") through an adversarial process, restorative justice is concerned with the broader relationship between offender, victim, and the community (Zehr 1990; Van Ness 1993). Restorative justice differs most clearly from retributive justice (see Table 1) in its view of crime as more than simply lawbreaking—or a violation of government authority. Rather, what is most significant about criminal behavior is the injury to victims, communities, and offenders that is its result.[3]

According to its proponents, restorative justice seeks to respond to crime at the *micro* level by addressing the harm that results when a specific offense is committed, giving first priority to victim reparation, and at the *macro* level by addressing the need to build safer communities. Government and community should play collaborative and complementary roles in this response, with government/criminal justice assigned the responsibility for *order,* and the community the responsibility for restoring and maintaining peace (Van Ness 1993; Zehr 1990). As Table 1 suggests, restorative justice emphasizes the need for active involvement of victims, the community, and offenders in a process focused on denunciation of the offense, offender acceptance of responsibility (accountability), and reparation, followed by resolution of conflict resulting from the criminal act and offender reintegration.

RESTORATIVE SANCTIONING FOR JUVENILE JUSTICE

A restorative sanctioning model could provide clear alternatives to punishment-centered sanctioning approaches now dominant in juvenile justice and could ultimately redefine the sanctioning function. Specifically, by shifting the focus of offender accountability or "debt" from the state to the victim (see Table 1), restorative justice sanctions could meet the need of communities to provide meaningful consequences for crime, confront offenders, denounce delinquent behavior, and relay the message that such behavior is unacceptable—without primary reliance on punishment and incarceration. For this to occur, jurisdictions would need to agree on new priorities for sanctioning based on restorative values. Implementation, expansion, or both of the new policies and practices would then be undertaken to achieve clearly articulated goals and objectives consistent with a justice process that challenges the adversarial emphasis of retributive justice.

Values and Assumptions

The emphasis on victim needs, victim involvement, and elevation of the victim's role in restorative justice (Zehr 1990; Marshall and Merry 1990; Davis 1992; Umbreit 1994) is based in part on a reaction to the current state of affairs in which the quality and quantity of victim involvement is low and is driven by other priorities. Although "victims' rights" has become the watchword of many prosecutors and politicians, victim *needs* are not a major concern (Elias 1993). Rather, in most offender-driven juvenile and criminal justice systems, the interests of prosecutors, judges, defense attorneys, and even treatment program directors (e.g., in winning cases, processing offenders, or securing clients) take precedence over the needs and concerns of victims (Wright 1991; Messmer and Otto 1992). Despite frequent complaints about the inability of offenders to pay victim restitution, for example, many jurisdictions that do a poor job at enforcing restitution orders have been highly successful in the collection of offender fines and fees (Hillsman and Greene 1992). Indeed, in many probation and parole agencies, victim compensation and restitution have taken a back seat to the collection of monies used to support criminal justice agency functions (Shapiro 1990). Moreover, whereas prosecutors appear to spare no expense and effort to gain victim input for efforts to increase the probability of conviction and length of sentence, time and resources for providing victim services, mediation, and reparative programs seem always in short supply (Elias 1993).

Restorative justice is *not,* however, a "victims' rights" approach. Motivated by retributive rather than resto-

151

5. JUVENILE JUSTICE

rative values, some of the more vocal groups advocating victims' rights have often defined these as an *absence of offender rights* in a zero-sum game and have promoted political efforts to "get tough" with offenders through mandatory and determinate sentencing and other retributive policies (McShane and Williams 1992; Elias 1993). In contrast to such policies, restorative justice proponents promote a "victim-centered" approach that does not require that decision makers "choose sides" between victim and offender (Lawrence 1991).[4] Thus, while it places central emphasis on victim needs and the requirement that offenders are held account-

able to victims, the restorative justice paradigm also responds to the "mutual powerlessness" of offenders *and* victims in the current system and assumes the need for communities to provide opportunities for offender repentance and forgiveness following appropriate sanctioning (Wright 1991; Zehr 1990). Therefore, a core value in restorative justice is to balance the needs of offenders, victims, and community as three "customers" of justice systems. A core assumption is that neither public safety, rehabilitative, nor sanctioning goals can be effectively achieved without involvement of each of these parties in the justice process.

TABLE 1: Current and Restorative Assumptions

Current System	Restorative Justice
Crime is an act against the state, a violation of the law, an abstract idea	Crime is an act against another person and the community
The criminal justice system controls crime	Crime control lies primarily in the community
Offender accountability defined as taking punishment	Accountability defined as assuming responsibility and taking action to repair harm
Crime is an individual act with individual responsibility	Crime has both individual and social dimensions of responsibility
Punishment is effective a. threat of punishment deters crime b. punishment changes behavior	Punishment alone is not effective in changing behavior and is disruptive to community harmony and good relationships
Victims are peripheral to the process	Victims are central to the process of resolving a crime
The offender is defined by deficits	The offender is defined by capacity to make reparation
Focus on establishing blame or guilt, on the past (did he/she do it?)	Focus on problem solving, on liabilities/obligations, on the future (what should be done?)
Emphasis on adversarial relationship	Emphasis on dialogue and negotiation
Imposition of pain to punish and deter/prevent	Restitution as a means of restoring both parties; goal of reconciliation/restoration
Community on sideline, represented abstractly by state	Community as facilitator in restorative process

SOURCE: Adapted from Zehr (1990).

25. Sanctioning Function in Juvenile Court

TABLE 2: The "Messages" of Sanctions

	Individual Treatment	Retributive Punishment	Restorative Accountability
Offender	You are "sick" or disturbed and your behavior is not your fault. We will provide treatment or services in your best interest.	You are a bad person who willfully chose to commit an offense. We will punish you with swiftness and severity proportionate to the seriousness of the crime.	Your actions have consequences; you have wronged someone or the community through your offense. You are responsible for your crime and capable of restoring the victim or repaying the damages.
Victim	Our fundamental concern is the needs of the offender.	The first concern of the juvenile system is to make offenders suffer the consequences of their crime. You will benefit because the offender will be punished.	The juvenile justice system believes you are important and will do its best to ensure that the offender repays the debt incurred to you from the crime.
Community	We will do our best to rehabilitate offenders through providing appropriate treatment and services. Highly trained professionals will solve the problem. Leave it to us.	We will do our best to punish offenders to teach them that crime will not be tolerated. Threats are the best way to control behavior.	Requiring offenders to repay victims and the public for their crimes receives highest priority in the juvenile justice system. We need the help of the community. The community is a key player in holding offenders accountable.

SOURCE: Adapted from Schneider (1985).

Sanctioning Goals and Objectives

As suggested earlier, a retributive justice model gives priority to punishment as a *determining goal* (Robinson 1987) in juvenile court sanctioning. In contrast, the determining goal of sanctioning in restorative justice is to hold offenders accountable for reparation of harm caused to victims by their crimes (Walgrave 1993). Neither punitive nor lenient in its focus, restorative justice gauges success in sanctioning not by how much punishment was inflicted or treatment provided but by how much reparation, resolution, and reintegration was achieved.

Primary objectives. Restorative sanctioning objectives thus include behavioral, material, emotional, and cognitive outcomes for victims, offenders, and community members. For victims, success in sanctioning is measured by the degree of reparation of damages, the extent of involvement in the justice process, and the level of satisfaction with the process and its outcomes. For offenders, cognitive objectives emphasize gaining an understanding of the consequences of crime for victims, feelings of remorse, recognition that they have been sanctioned, and (ideally) development of empathy with victims. Positive behavioral outcomes include prompt repayment of victims and completion of community service and other reparative requirements (e.g., facing the victim in mediation). For the community, the most important objectives are overall satisfaction that justice has been served, a sense that offenders have been denounced and held accountable to victims, and a sense of peace and community healing and well being (Pepinsky and Quinney 1991; Yazzie 1994).

Finally, a larger educative objective of restorative sanctioning would be to relay a distinctive "message" to victims, offenders, and the community. Compared to the current message of neglect that characterizes both the retributive and the treatment models (Schneider 1985) (see Table 2), the restorative justice message suggests to victims and the community that the system views them as important and values their involvement. It also is intended to assure the community that promoting restoration and community peace is a top

153

5. JUVENILE JUSTICE

priority of the system (Davis 1992). Similarly, as Table 2 suggests, the message to lawbreakers that they are capable of, and responsible for, making amends for the harm caused by their crimes stands in sharp contrast to the message of "sick" or "evil" offenders with nothing to offer but their liberty (Christie 1982).

Limiting goals. In a restorative justice model, systemic concerns with rehabilitation/reintegration and public safety would receive balanced emphasis with sanctioning goals. Moreover, restorative justice would view rehabilitative and sanctioning goals as mutually compatible in a process in which members of the community reinforce the offender's obligation to redress the harm to victims, but then encourage—and create conditions to facilitate—offender reintegration following the shaming and reparative process (Makkai and Braithwaite 1994; McElrea 1993).

In addition, pursuit of full accountability to victims in sanctioning would be constrained by the *limiting* goals of risk management, fairness, and uniformity. Although restorative justice advocates are concerned that excessive use of secure confinement may limit the ability of offenders to fully repair harm to victims and meet other restorative objectives, all acknowledge that some proportion of the youthful offender population will need to be removed from the community and confined in secure facilities for public safety reasons. The goals of fairness and equity would likewise limit the pursuit of victim restoration when excessive requirements on specific lawbreakers that result from differences in victim needs and demands result in unfair and inappropriate consequences disproportionate to offender culpability (Van Ness 1993).

Restorative Process and Due Process

According to Braithwaite (1989, p. 8), in "low crime" societies, tolerance of deviance has clear limits and community members prefer to be actively involved in the response to lawbreakers by "shaming offenders, and, having shamed them, through concerted participation in integrating the offender back into the community." But whereas Native Americans and other aboriginal peoples, as well as the Japanese, have developed numerous sanctioning rituals for carrying out this *reintegrative shaming* process (Braithwaite 1989; Griffiths and Belleau 1993; McElrea 1993; Yazzie 1994), some have argued that the lack of institutional supports for such informal processes and the power of the formal adversarial system and Western legal processes have limited application and use of informal sanctioning mechanisms (Haley 1989, p. 274).

In contrast to the rule-driven, impersonal procedures of retributive justice focused on defining "winners and losers" and fixing blame (Zehr 1990; Messmer and Otto 1992), the restorative justice process would, however, necessarily rely heavily on informal resolution of un-

derlying problems, conflict reduction through dialogue and mediation, and efforts to achieve mutually satisfactory agreements. Such increased reliance on informal processes seems difficult to envision in a system in which formal rules and procedures are in part intended to protect offenders from the abuses of unrestricted retribution and may be especially troubling to youth advocates concerned about further slippage in current due process protections in juvenile courts (e.g., Feld 1990). Proponents of restorative justice would counter that in most cases the current court process is itself often highly informal rather than truly adversarial (see Eisenstein and Jacob 1991; Hackler 1991), but is based on negotiation and bargaining in the service of the retributive ends of the state (and the professional interests of attorneys) rather than the interests of fairness and due process. Moreover, in contrast to the "individualized" justice of *parens patriae,* restorative justice acknowledges and builds on group and community responsibility for crime (Van Ness 1993; McElrea 1993) rather than simply directing blame—and thus sanctions or treatment—at individual offenders.

Due process protections are also important to restorative justice advocates (e.g., Van Ness 1993; Walgrave 1993), and none has argued that it is necessary or desirable to weaken procedural protections for offenders to ensure restoration of victims or to bring about more rapid implementation of restorative policies (Messmer and Otto 1992). What some restorative justice advocates regard as an "obsession with process" in U.S. criminal and juvenile justice, however, may be due in part to the "high stakes" of being found guilty in a system that punishes with a great deal of severity (Wright 1991; Zehr 1990).[5] Thus the opposition of restorative justice advocates to the adversarial process is in large part due to opposition to the predominant emphasis on retributive punishment.

Practice, Programs, and Implementation

Current juvenile court sanctioning based on retributive justice is built around use of incarceration in its various forms, as well as an emphasis on surveillance, punishment, and control in probation and community supervision programs (Armstrong 1991). Based on the goals, objectives, and alternative processes outlined above, restorative justice sanctioning practices and programs would deemphasize retributive punishment in favor of restitution (Schneider 1985), victim-offender mediation (Umbreit and Coates 1993), restorative community service (Bazemore and Maloney 1994), victim awareness education (English and Crawford 1989), and other victim-oriented services. In addition to these now-familiar approaches, the shaming and reintegrative aspects of restorative sanctioning could be more specifically addressed and directly operationalized. Such offender interventions as community service crews that work with public employees to build homeless shelters or repair windows, doors, and other damage to homes victimized by break-ins; involving juveniles in community organizations where they can learn from their elders; direct service to victims where appropriate following mediation; and arranging for supervised home visits to victims come to mind (McElrea 1993; Bazemore and Maloney 1994).

Despite the strong potential of these and similar interventions, as well as the positive public acceptance and promising evaluation findings from empirical studies of restitution and victim-offender mediation programs (Schneider 1985, 1986; Butts and Snyder 1991; Umbreit and Coates 1993), there are dangers in a primary reliance on innovative programs and practices as the sole basis for reform. In recent years juvenile justice systems have been vulnerable to panaceas and "quick fix" solutions to complex problems (Finckenauer 1982) (e.g., boot camps, "Scared Straight"). Like Goldstein's (1979) profile of police departments obsessed with *tactics* rather than *outcomes* and emphasizing means over ends, systems adopting this "program driven" approach to reform typically fail to consider the fit between new programs and existing values, policies, and bureaucratic constraints of criminal justice agencies (McShane and Williams 1992). Programmatic reform, even when based on coherent, theoretical principles, may therefore lead to a dilution of even the most innovative practices to fit existing management protocols. Alternatively, it may simply add a new layer of progressive practices (e.g., based on restorative justice principles) onto a retributive policy core. In a system based on retributive justice values, programs and practices such as restitution and community service may be used as punitive "add-ons" rather than as primary sanctions directed toward restorative ends (Bazemore and Maloney 1994; Shapiro 1990). Similarly, increased involvement in the justice process is of little benefit to victims if the system uses them only to aid in securing convictions or in increasing the length or severity of punishment.

Specific dangers in simply initiating new restorative programs in the absence of wider systemic changes include the possibility that such programs will simply expand and strengthen social control, either by net widening, or by adding to current requirements imposed on offenders under court supervision (Krisberg and Austin 1981); the possibility of staff resistance to change when casework routines built around individual treatment, surveillance protocols, or both are disrupted (Maupin 1993); and the possibility that these programs will be judged by the performance standards of retributive or bureaucratic justice (e.g., increasing the number of cases handled) rather than by restorative justice outcomes (e.g., peace making, meeting victim needs) (Van Ness 1993). Ultimately, competing priorities of retributive justice and individual treatment may limit resources that can be allocated to pursuit of restorative objectives (e.g., involving victims, enabling offenders to pay restitution), and this limitation may quickly set up restorative programs for failure (Shapiro 1990). Moreover, in the absence of values clarification, reparative sanctions may be used primarily for punitive purposes (Bazemore and Maloney 1994) or as an ancillary component of treatment plans. Likewise, purportedly "victim-oriented" practices such as victim impact statements can be easily directed toward retributive ends (Elias 1993; McShane and Williams 1992).

On the other hand, if motivated by restorative values and viewed as primary sanctions rather than add-ons to other punishments and requirements, reparative sanctions can be effective tools for holding offenders accountable to victims and the community. Similarly, victim impact statements and similar mechanisms could be used effectively to determine the nature and type of reparation, increase victim involvement, and provide a more accurate assessment of victim needs. A restorative value framework could also provide the impetus for integrating now marginal victim-focused and reparative programs into the mainstream juvenile justice process and could provide a conceptual and policy basis for coordinating services of these disparate programs to better serve the needs of victims and communities.

DISCUSSION

Punitive values, goals, and policies will not disappear overnight. Although the juvenile justice system has shown progress in implementing programs consistent with a restorative approach (e.g., Schneider 1985; Umbreit & Coates 1993; Umbreit 1994), only a few juvenile courts have adopted these as prototypes for restructuring the sanctioning process based on a restorative philosophy. For the most part, restorative practices remain on the fringes, and their objectives are viewed as secondary to the concerns of retributive justice, as well as to those of individual treatment. In addition, a dramatic change in policy and management agendas governing juvenile justice systems is implied if these systems are to meet the challenge of restorative justice—for example, to identify and then engage communities and victims in the justice process (Van Ness 1993).

"Seeds" of Restorative Juvenile Justice
Despite these cautions and obstacles, policymakers wishing to move in the direction of a restorative justice approach can build on several inherent strengths of the model and take advantage of several opportunities created by the current crisis in juvenile justice policy.

5. JUVENILE JUSTICE

Movement toward increased formalization notwithstanding, juvenile justice in most jurisdictions retains an informal ethic and is more receptive to restorative approaches (Schneider 1985; Umbreit 1994) than criminal justice. In its contextual emphasis on crime as conflict (e.g., Zehr 1990), restorative justice may be highly compatible with this less formal process and situational approach to dispute resolution.

To move forward with the restorative agenda for juvenile court sanctioning, policymakers could exploit the potential for restorative justice to engage and integrate the interests of nontraditional juvenile justice constituencies (e.g., victims, employers) (Bazemore and Maloney 1994), while also building on innovative programs such as comprehensive restitution, restorative community service, and victim-offender mediation that exemplify the restorative process. Such programs could be used specifically to "pilot" practices and policies as models for entire *systems* rather than as "add-ons" to probation and the formal court process. Promising examples of such restorative sanctioning systems now can be found in several European countries and in Australia and New Zealand (Messmer and Otto 1992; Walgrave 1993; McElrea 1993; Marshall and Merry 1990). In the Australian and New Zealand "family group conference" model, for example, the victim and his/her supporters are given the opportunity to speak about how they have been affected by the crime and to condemn the behavior of young offenders. The offender, his/her family or community surrogates, a trained facilitator/mediator, and the victim then participate in designing appropriate ways for the offender to repair the harm and make amends to the victim and the community. This begins a reintegrative process for the delinquent in which members of the family and community take responsibility for monitoring offender compliance and facilitating victim and community healing (Makkai and Braithwaite 1994; McElrea 1993). U.S. cities are not the same as cities in New Zealand or Europe, and juvenile justice systems are larger, more complex, and more crisis-driven. However, it is possible to implement reforms based on these principles, which similarly challenge the adversarial process as pilot efforts in smaller components of such large systems and, as is most consistent with the restorative model, to do so on a neighborhood basis.[6]

CONCLUSION

As an emerging new paradigm, restorative justice sanctioning does *not* offer complete solutions to all of the complex issues facing juvenile justice policymakers. A meaningful and effective sanctioning model is only one aspect of the comprehensive agenda for reform currently needed in juvenile justice. As a holistic framework focused on a balanced response to the needs of offenders and communities, however, restorative justice also has implications for enhancing and building support for a more empowering, holistic, and effective reintegrative approach to rehabilitation (Bazemore and Maloney 1994) and for defining a new role for juvenile justice professionals in enhancing the safety and security of communities.

In addition, we have suggested that rethinking the way juvenile courts carry out the sanctioning function may be a prerequisite for more comprehensive reform aimed at preserving the juvenile court and a rehabilitative focus for juvenile offenders. The blueprint presented here, based on the principles of restorative justice, prescribes a comprehensive redesign of sanctioning policy. Such redesign would begin with change in values; acknowledgment of new "customers" of the system (i.e., victims and the community); the development of new goals and objectives; change in the justice process; and change in the priority assigned to various practices and programs.

From the vantage point of a retributive system steeped in supportive legal traditions and institutional frameworks, the goals and values of restorative justice are idealistic and utopian. At the same time, however, in the current climate of chaos and reaction in juvenile justice, such idealistic goals may be critical to ensure that balanced reform proceeds in a positive direction:

> Giving priority to reparation rather than retribution calls for a change in social ethics and a different ideology of society. That means a society governed with the aims of individual and collective emancipation, in which autonomy and solidarity are not seen as diametrically opposed, but viewed as mutually reinforcing principles. A society doing its utmost to avoid exclusion of its members, because it is a society which draws its strength not from fear but from the high social ethics by which it is governed. . . . Is this Utopia? Yes, but we need a utopia to motivate us and provide guidance for our actions in society. There is nothing more *practical* than a good utopia. (Walgrave 1993, p. 9)

NOTES

1. The retributive/punitive paradigm that emerged in the juvenile justice system in the 1980s was in no way a pure "just deserts" approach (Thompson and McAnany 1984). Rather, retributive juvenile justice as implemented combines the emphasis on the primacy of punishment philosophy and certain policy trappings (e.g., determinate sentencing guidelines) of "just deserts" with a general concern with deterrence, incapacitation, and more traditional punitive objectives supported by Reagan administration policymakers as part of a more general attack on "leniency" in juvenile court sanctioning (e.g., Regnery 1985). The increased formality and adversarial emphasis has generally *not* meant an increase in due-process protections or better representation for juvenile offenders (Feld 1993).

2. Whereas the pursuit of multiple justice goals characterizes most historical eras, by the late 1980s retributive punishment was well on its way toward becoming a *determining goal* (Robinson 1987) in juvenile court dispositions. Determining goals, which set the overall priority for sanctioning, require that certain presumptive components are always included in a disposition. *Limiting goals* define what must be excluded and restrict the overall inten-

25. Sanctioning Function in Juvenile Court

sity of sanctioning; for example, goals such as deterrence have often limited the pursuit of rehabilitative ends in juvenile justice.

3. Van Ness (1993) suggested that the term *restorative justice* was first coined by Albert Eglash (1975) in a paper in which he distinguished between retributive justice based on punishment, distributive justice based on therapeutic treatment, and restorative justice based on restitution. Though still unfamiliar in the United States, the term is widely used in Europe, and restorative justice has been on the agenda of policymakers and researchers for approximately a decade (Davis 1992; Messmer and Otto 1992). Whereas retributive and restorative justice are compatible in their common focus on the *offense act* (Davis 1992) and may be contrasted with the utilitarian focus on the offender, they differ in the emphasis on punishment versus reparation, obligation to the victim versus the state, and the emphasis (in restorative justice) on the future rather than the past (Zehr 1990; Davis 1992).

4. Elias (1993) has distinguished between this "official" retributive victims' movement and a "hidden" victims' movement that has often opposed the status quo—and therefore frequently been marginalized (e.g., Zehr 1990; Pepinsky and Quinney 1991). As McShane and Williams (1992) noted, victims and victims' advocacy groups were to a large extent coopted in various "get tough" prison expansion and mandatory sentencing initiatives in the 1980s.

5. This overemphasis on due process may have a number of unintended consequences according to these observers. For example, juveniles may be detained for longer periods or cases adjourned more frequently for continuances to accommodate the needs of attorneys (Hackler 1991). Whereas the parameters of offender and victim process rights and uniformity in restorative justice have yet to be completely defined (Messmer and Otto 1992), the restorative process should not be judged against an ideal adversarial process that rarely occurs in retributive justice (Elias 1993). In countries where restorative processes are more widely used in juvenile justice, a variety of mechanisms have been devised to protect offender rights and maximize access to nonadversarial options (Messmer and Otto 1992; Davis 1992).

6. The Minnesota Department of Corrections has recently adopted restorative justice as its mission, and other states and local jurisdictions are including restorative principles in their codes, mission, and purpose statements. Several U.S. juvenile systems are experimenting with restorative justice policies and practices by initiating small pilot projects as part of an "action research" demonstration effort funded by the Office of Juvenile Justice and Delinquency Prevention (OJJDP) (Bazemore 1994b). Points of view or opinions expressed in this document are, of course, those of the authors and do not necessarily represent the official position of OJJDP or the U.S. Department of Justice.

REFERENCES

Armstrong, Troy, ed. 1991. *Intensive Interventions With High-Risk Youths: Promising Approaches in Juvenile Probation & Parole.* New York: Criminal Justice Press.

Bazemore, Gordon. 1994a. "Understanding the Response to Reforms Limiting Discretion: Judges' Views of Restrictions on Detention Intake." *Justice Quarterly* 11:429–53.

———. 1994b. *Balanced and Restorative Justice: Program Summary.* Washington, DC: U.S. Department of Justice, Office of Juvenile Justice and Delinquency Prevention.

Bazemore, Gordon and Dennis Maloney. 1994. "Rehabilitating Community Service: Toward Restorative Service in a Balanced Justice System." *Federal Probation* 58:24–35.

Braithwaite, John. 1989. *Crime, Shame and Reintegration.* New York: Cambridge University Press.

Butts, Jeffrey. 1994. *Offenders in Juvenile Court, 1992.* Washington, DC: U.S. Department of Justice, Office of Juvenile Justice and Delinquency Prevention.

Butts, Jeffrey and Howard Snyder. 1991. *Restitution and Juvenile Recidivism.* Pittsburgh: National Center for Juvenile Justice.

Byrne, James M. 1989. "Reintegrating the Concept of Community Into Community-based Corrections." *Crime & Delinquency* 35:471–99.

Castellano, Thomas. 1986. "The Justice Model in the Juvenile Justice System: Washington State's Experience." *Law and Policy* 8:479–506.

Christie, Nils. 1982. *Limits to Pain.* Oxford: Martin Robertson.

Davis, Gwynn. 1992. *Making Amends: Mediation and Reparation in Criminal Justice.* London: Routledge.

Durkheim, Emile. 1961. *Moral Education: A Study in the Theory and Application of the Sociology of Education,* translated by E. K. Wilson and H. Schnurer. New York: Free Press.

Eglash, Albert. 1975. "Beyond Restitution: Creative Restitution." Pp. 91–101 in *Restitution in Criminal Justice,* edited by J. Hudson and B. Galaway. Lexington, MA: Lexington Books.

Eisenstein, James and Herbert Jacob. 1991. *Felony Justice: An Organizational Analysis of Criminal Courts,* 2nd ed. Boston: Little Brown.

Elias, Robert. 1993. *Victims Still: The Political Manipulation of Crime Victims.* Newbury Park, CA: Sage.

English, Sharon and Michael Crawford. 1989. "Victim Awareness Education Is Basic to Offender Programming" (monograph). Sacramento: California Youth Authority.

Feld, Barry. 1990. "The Punitive Juvenile Court and the Quality of Procedural Justice: Disjunctions Between Rhetoric and Reality." *Crime & Delinquency* 36:443–64.

———. 1993. "The Criminal Court Alternative to Perpetuating Juvenile [In] Justice." Pp. 3–13 in *The Juvenile Court: Dynamic, Dysfunctional, or Dead?* Philadelphia: Center for the Study of Youth Policy, School of Social Work, University of Pennsylvania.

Finckenauer, James. 1982. *Scared Straight! and the Panacea Phenomena.* Englewood Cliffs, NJ: Prentice-Hall.

Galaway, Burt and Joel Hudson, eds. 1990. *Criminal Justice, Restitution and Reconciliation.* Monsey, NY: Willow Tree Press.

Garland, David. 1990. *Punishment and Modern Society: A Study in Social Theory.* Chicago: University of Chicago Press.

Goldstein, Herman. 1979. "Improving Policing: A Problem-Oriented Approach." *Crime & Delinquency* 25:236–58.

Griffiths, Curt T. and Charlene Belleau. 1993. "Restoration, Reconciliation and Healing—The Revitalization of Culture and Tradition in Addressing Crime and Victimization in Aboriginal Communities." Paper presented at the meeting of the 11th International Congress on Criminology, Budapest, Hungary.

Hackler, James. 1991. "The Possible Overuse of Not Guilty Pleas in Juvenile Justice" (monograph). Edmonton, Alberta: Centre for Criminological Research, University of Alberta.

Haley, John. 1989. "Confession, Repentance, and Absolution." Pp. 195–211 in *Mediation and Criminal Justice: Victims, Offenders and Community,* edited by M. Wright and B. Galaway. London: Sage.

Harris, Kay. 1993. "Moving Into the New Millennium: A Feminist Perspective on Justice Reform." Pp. 166–7 in *Criminology as Peacemaking,* edited by H. E. Pepinsky and R. Quinney. Bloomington: Indiana University Press.

Hillsman, Sally and Judith Greene. 1992. "The Use of Fines as an Intermediate Sanction." Pp. 123–41 in *Smart Sentencing,* edited by J. M. Byrne, A. Lorigio, and J. Petersilia. Newbury Park, CA: Sage.

Krisberg, Barry. 1988. *The Juvenile Court: Reclaiming the Vision.* San Francisco: National Council of Crime and Delinquency.

Krisberg, Barry and James F. Austin. 1981. "Wider, Stronger, and Different Nets: The Dialectics of Criminal Justice Reform." *Journal of Research in Crime and Delinquency* 18:165–96.

Lawrence, Richard. 1991. "Reexamining Community Corrections Models." *Crime & Delinquency* 37:449–64.

Lemov, Penelope. 1994. "The Assault on Juvenile Justice." *Governing* December:26–31.

Mack, Julian. 1909. "The Juvenile Court." *Harvard Law Review* 23:104–22.

Makkai, Tony and John Braithwaite. 1994. "Reintegrative Shaming and Compliance With Regulatory Standards." *Criminology* 32:361–85.

Marshall, Tony and Sally Merry. 1990. *Crime and Accountability.* London: Home Office.

Maupin, James. 1993. "Risk Classification Systems and the Provision of Juvenile Aftercare." *Crime & Delinquency* 39:90–105.

McAllair, Daniel. 1993. "Reaffirming Rehabilitation in Juvenile Justice." *Youth and Society* 25:104–25.

McElrea, Frances W. M. 1993. "A New Model of Justice." Pp. 1–14 in *The Youth Court in New Zealand: A New Model of Justice,* edited by B. J. Brown. Auckland, New Zealand: Legal Research Foundation, Pub. 34.

5. JUVENILE JUSTICE

McHardy, Louis. 1990. "Looking at the Delinquency Problem from the Juvenile Court Bench." *International Review of Criminal Policy* 39/40:113–8.

McShane, Marilyn and Frank Williams IV. 1992. "Radical Victimology: A Critique of the Concept of Victim in Traditional Victimology." *Crime & Delinquency* 38:258–71.

Melton, Gary B. 1989. "Taking Gault Seriously: Toward a New Juvenile Court." *Nebraska Law Review* 68:146–81.

Messmer, Heinz and Hans-Uwe Otto, eds. 1992. *Restorative Justice on Trial: Pitfalls and Potentials of Victim Offender Mediation: International Research Perspectives*. Norwell, MA: Kluwer Academic Publishers.

Miller, Jerome. 1991. *Last One Over the Wall*. Columbus: Ohio State University Press.

Packer, Herbert. 1968. *The Limits of the Criminal Sanction*. Palo Alto, CA: Stanford University Press.

Paternoster, Raymond and Lynn Iovanni. 1989. "The Labeling Perspective and Delinquency: An Elaboration of the Theory and an Assessment of the Evidence." *Justice Quarterly* 6:359–94.

Pepinsky, Harold E. and Richard Quinney, eds. 1991. *Criminology as Peacemaking*. Bloomington: Indiana University Press.

Regnery, Alfred. 1985. "Getting Away With Murder: Why the Juvenile Justice System Needs an Overhaul." *Policy Review* 34:65–8.

Reiss, Albert, Jr. 1986. "Why Are Communities Important in Understanding Crime?" Pp. 1–33 in *Communities and Crime*, edited by A. J. Reiss and M. Tonry. Chicago: University of Chicago Press.

Robinson, Paul. 1987. "Hybrid Principles for the Distribution of Criminal Sanctions." *Northern University Law Review* 19:34–6.

Rothman, David. 1980. *Conscience and Convenience: The Asylum and Its Alternatives in Progressive America*. New York: Harper Collins.

Schafer, Steven. 1970. *Compensation and Restitution to Victims of Crime*. Montclair, NJ: Smith Patterson.

Schneider, Anne, ed. 1985. *Guide to Juvenile Restitution*. Washington, DC: U.S. Department of Justice, Office of Juvenile Justice and Delinquency Prevention.

_____. 1986. "Restitution and Recidivism Rates of Juvenile Offenders: Results From Four Experimental Studies," *Criminology* 24:533–52.

Schneider, Anne and Donna Schram. 1983. A *Justice Philosophy for the Juvenile Court*. Seattle: Urban Policy Research.

Shapiro, Carol. 1990. "Is Restitution Legislation the Chameleon of the Victims' Movement?" Pp. 73–80 in *Criminal Justice, Restitution, and Reconciliation*, edited by B. Galaway and J. Hudson. Monsey, NY: Willow Tree Press.

Thompson, Douglas and Patrick McAnany. 1984. "Punishment and Responsibility in Juvenile Court: Desert-based Probation for Delinquents." Pp. 137–75 in *Probation and Justice: Reconsideration of Mission*, edited by P. D. McAnany, D. Thompson, and D. Fogel. Cambridge, MA: Oelgeschlager, Gunn & Hain.

Umbreit, Mark. 1994. *Victim Meets Offender: The Impact of Restorative Justice and Mediation*. Monsey, NY: Criminal Justice Press.

Umbreit, Mark and Robert Coates. 1993. "Cross-site Analysis of Victim-Offender Mediation in Four States." *Crime & Delinquency* 39:565–85.

Van Ness, Daniel. 1993. "New Wine and Old Wineskins: Four Challenges of Restorative Justice." *Criminal Law Forum* 4:251–76.

von Hirsch, Andrew. 1976. *Doing Justice*. New York: Hill & Wang.

Walgrave, Lode. 1993. "Beyond Retribution and Rehabilitation: Restoration as the Dominant Paradigm in Judicial Intervention Against Juvenile Crime." Paper presented at the International Congress on Criminology, Budapest, Hungary.

Wilkins, Leslie T. 1991. *Punishment, Crime and Market Forces*. Brookfield, VT: Dartmouth Publishing Co.

Wright, Martin. 1991. *Justice for Victims and Offenders*. Buckingham, England: Open University.

Yazzie, Robert. 1994. "'Life Comes From It': Navajo Justice Concepts." *New Mexico Law Review* 24:175–90.

Zehr, Howard. 1990. *Changing Lenses: A New Focus for Crime and Justice*. Scottsdale, PA: Herald Press.

Zhang, Lening and Steven E. Messner. 1994. "The Severity of Official Punishment for Delinquency and Change in Interpersonal Relations in Chinese Society." *Journal of Research in Crime and Delinquency* 31:416–33.

Article 26

Juvenile Probation: The Workhorse of the Juvenile Justice System

Patricia McFall Torbet

In 1993 nearly 1.5 million delinquency cases were handled by juvenile courts. Virtually every one of those cases had contact with a probation officer at some point. Probation departments screened most of those cases to determine how they should be processed, made detention decisions on some of them, prepared investigation reports on most of them, provided supervision to over a half million of them, and delivered aftercare services to many of the juveniles released from institutions. Since 1929, when the first *Juvenile Court Statistics* report was published using 1927 data, probation has been the overwhelming dispositional choice of juvenile and family court judges. In 1993, 56 percent of all cases adjudicated for a delinquency offense received probation as the most severe disposition, compared with 28 percent that were placed in some type of residential facility, 12 percent that were given some other disposition (e.g., fines, restitution, or community service), and 4 percent that were dismissed with no further sanctions.

Over the past several years, the National Center for Juvenile Justice (NCJJ) has produced reports, parts of which describe the profession of probation or the youth on probation (see References). This information is compiled here to present the most comprehensive picture of juvenile probation activity in the Nation.

Generally, juvenile probation officers are college-educated white males, 30–49 years old, with 5–10 years of experience in the field. Typically the officers earn $20,000–$39,000 per year and receive standard benefits packages, but not necessarily annual salary increases. The average caseload is 41 juveniles. Although probation officers have some arrest powers, they do not normally carry weapons.

Some of the typical problems juvenile probation officers face are a lack of resources, not enough staff, and too many cases. Although they chose this line of work "to help kids," their greatest sources of frustration are an inability to impact the lives of youth, the attitudes of probationers and their families, and difficulties in identifying successes.

The Profession

What Is Juvenile Probation?

Juvenile probation is the oldest and most widely used vehicle through which a range of court-ordered services is rendered. Probation may be used at the "front end" of the juvenile justice system for first-time, low-risk offenders or at the "back end" as an alternative to institutional confinement for more serious offenders. In some cases probation may be voluntary, in which the youth agrees to comply with a period of informal proba-

tion in lieu of formal adjudication. More often, once adjudicated and formally ordered to a term of probation, the juvenile must submit to the probation conditions established by the court.

The official duties of juvenile probation professionals vary from State to State and can even differ between jurisdictions within a single State. Nonetheless, a basic set of juvenile probation functions includes: intake screening of cases referred to juvenile and family courts, predisposition or presentence investigation of juveniles, and court-ordered supervision of juvenile offenders.

Not all probation departments execute all three of these functions independently. For example, in some jurisdictions the prosecutor shares the intake responsibility with the probation officer, and in other jurisdictions the prosecutor has sole responsibility for the intake process. Similarly, probation responsibilities are not always limited to intake, investigation, and supervision. Some departments also provide aftercare for youth released from institutions; others may administer detention or manage local residential facilities or special programs.

How Are Probation Departments Organized?

Probation services are administered by the local juvenile court or by the State ad-

From *OJJDP Juvenile Justice Bulletin,* March 1996, pp. 1-5. Reprinted by permission of U.S. Department of Justice, Juvenile Justice and Delinquency Prevention.

5. JUVENILE JUSTICE

Table 1:
Probation Supervision Tends To Be Administered by Local Juvenile Courts or by a State Executive Branch Agency

State Administration		Local Administration	
Judicial Branch	**Executive Branch**	**Judicial Branch**	**Executive Branch**
Connecticut	Alaska	Alabama	**California**
Hawaii	**Arkansas**	Arizona	**Idaho**
Iowa	Delaware	**Arkansas**	**Minnesota**
Kentucky	Florida	**California**	**Mississippi**
Nebraska	**Georgia**	Colorado	New York
North Carolina	**Idaho**	District of	Oregon
North Dakota	**Kentucky**	Columbia	**Washington**
South Dakota	**Louisiana**	**Georgia**	**Wisconsin**
Utah	Maine	Illinois	
West Virginia	Maryland	Indiana	
	Minnesota	Kansas	
	Mississippi	**Kentucky**	
	New Hampshire	**Louisiana**	
	New Mexico	Massachusetts	
	North Dakota	Michigan	
	Oklahoma	**Minnesota**	
	Rhode Island	Missouri	
	South Carolina	Montana	
	Tennessee	Nevada	
	Vermont	New Jersey	
	Virginia	Ohio	
	West Virginia	**Oklahoma**	
	Wyoming	Pennsylvania	
		Tennessee	
		Texas	
		Virginia	
		Washington	
		Wisconsin	
		Wyoming	

Note: Bolded States indicate that probation is provided by a combination of agencies. Often larger, urban counties operate local probation departments, while the State administers probation in smaller counties.

Source: Hurst, H., IV, and Torbet, P. (1993). *Organization and Administration of Juvenile Services: Probation, Aftercare, and State Institutions for Delinquent Youth.* In Snyder, H. and Sickmund, M. (1995). *Juvenile Offenders and Victims: A National Report.* NCJ 153569.

ministrative office of courts in 23 States and the District of Columbia. In another 14 States, probation administration is a combination of structures, usually with services administered by the juvenile court in urban counties and by a State executive system of probation in smaller counties. In 10 States probation is administered statewide through an executive branch department. In three States, the county executive administers probation (Table 1).

While juvenile probation services continue to be predominantly organized under the judiciary, recent legislative activity has primarily transferred these services from the local juvenile court to a State court judicial department. The transfer of juvenile probation services to State judicial administration is consistent with the emerging pattern of State funding of courts.

How Many Juvenile Probation Officers Are There in the Country?

There are an estimated 18,000 juvenile probation professionals impacting the lives of juveniles in the United States. Eighty-five percent of these professionals are involved in the delivery of basic intake, investigation, and supervision services at the line officer level; the remaining 15 percent are involved in the administration of probation offices or the management of probation staff.

How Large Are Probation Officers' Caseloads?

Survey results of those officers who reported an active field supervision caseload indicate that the size of caseloads within departments ranged between 2 and more than 200 cases, with a typical (median) active caseload of 41. The optimal caseload suggested by respondents was 30 cases (Table 2).

A comparison of caseloads across geographic areas (urban, suburban, and rural) revealed substantial differences. The median caseload for urban officers was greater than the median caseload for suburban officers, which, in turn, was greater than the median caseload for rural officers. Similarly, urban and suburban juvenile probation officers reported a higher optimal caseload than rural officers. Rural officers are more likely than their urban or suburban counterparts to carry a mixed caseload of both adult and juvenile cases.

How Do Urban Counties Compare in Terms of Department Size?

Table 3 presents manpower rates for several urban jurisdictions. All have specialized juvenile probation departments; therefore, mixed caseloads of adults and juveniles are not an issue.

At first glance it appears that New York is understaffed relative to Chicago. However, the upper age of juvenile court jurisdiction in New York is 15; it is 16 in Illinois. Even though rate calculations control for upper age differences, older juveniles generate more delinquency referrals than younger juveniles. While 16-year-olds constitute about 14 percent of the population aged 10–16 nationwide, they account for more than 25 percent of delinquency referrals to courts in jurisdictions with an upper age of 16. The exclusion of 16-year-olds from juvenile jurisdiction has a dra-

26. Juvenile Probation

Table 2:
Probation Officers Report Differences in Their Actual and Optimal Caseloads

Caseload	Urban	Suburban	Rural	Overall
Current	47	40	30	41
Optimal	35	35	25	30

Source: Thomas, D. (1993). *The State of Juvenile Probation 1992: Results of a Nationwide Survey.* NCJ 159536.

matic effect on the need for juvenile probation staff.

In addition to mixed caseloads and upper age differences, other variables that impact department or caseload size include the range of functions performed by juvenile probation, the range of juvenile behaviors prohibited by law, and the number of crimes excluded from juvenile court jurisdiction. Moreover, the extent to which laws are enforced and crimes are cleared with an arrest varies between jurisdictions, as does the involvement of prosecutors and the use of diversion or informal handling.

How Much Do Juvenile Probation Officers Earn?

Over three-quarters of all survey respondents earned less than $40,000 per year. More than half (53 percent) of line staff earned less than $30,000 per year, but 13 percent earned $40,000 per year or more. Nearly 30 percent of the administrators earned more than $49,999 per year. Very few line staff reported earning salaries higher than that.

Only 28 percent of the respondents indicated that they routinely received annual salary increases; 30 percent replied that they received none; and 42 percent indicated that it varied whether they received increases. Of those that did receive annual salary increases, 50 percent received increases of less than 4 percent annually, 47 percent received increases of 4–6 percent, and fewer than 3 percent received increases in excess of 6 percent.

Table 3:
There Are Major Differences in the Number of Probation Officers in Urban Jurisdictions

City	1990 Census Population 10–Upper Age	Upper Age	Officers Reported 1993–1994	Duties I = Intake V = Investigation S = Supervision A = Aftercare D = Detention				Officers/ 10,000 Youth 10–Upper Age
New York, NY	536,300	15	175	I	V	S		3
Chicago, IL	469,000	16	318	I	V	S		7
Houston, TX	288,300	16	208	I	V	S		7
Detroit, MI	212,100	16	100	I	V	S		5
Los Angeles, CA	943,500	17	404	I	V	S		4
Orange, CA	242,000	17	148	I	V	S		6
Phoenix, AZ	225,400	17	275	I	V	S	D	12
Miami, FL	201,900	17	191	I	V	S	A	10
Philadelphia, PA	158,800	17	190	I	V	S	A	12
Cleveland, OH	142,500	17	105	I	V	S		7
Seattle, WA	137,100	17	95	I	V	S		7
Oakland, CA	120,500	17	120	I	V	S		10
Memphis, TN	95,600	17	65	I	V	S	A	7
Cincinnati, OH	92,200	17	34		V	S		4
Minneapolis, MN	91,700	17	82	I	V	S	A	9
Fairfax, VA	88,100	17	95	I	V	S	A	11
Newark, NJ	83,000	17	38			S		5
Baltimore, MD	70,500	17	142	I	V	S	A	20
Oklahoma City, OK	64,600	17	25	I	V	S		4

Note: "Officers Reported 1993–1994" count includes local juvenile probation administrators, supervisors, line staff, and special program staff (e.g., community service and drug and alcohol program officers).

Source: Hurst, H., IV, and Vereb, P. (1995). Special Analysis of the Juvenile Probation Officer Initiative Database.

5. JUVENILE JUSTICE

Youth on Probation

What Is the Volume of Cases Placed on Probation?

In 1993, 35 percent (520,600) of all formally and informally handled delinquency cases disposed by juvenile courts resulted in probation. Probation was the most severe disposition in over half (56 percent) of *adjudicated* delinquency cases, with annual proportions remaining constant for the 5-year period 1989–1993.

The 1.5 million delinquency cases handled by juvenile courts in 1993 represented a 23-percent increase from 1989. Similarly, the number of juvenile cases placed on probation (either formally or informally) increased 21 percent, from 428,500 in 1989 to 520,600 in 1993. The growth in probation caseloads was directly related to the general growth in referrals to juvenile courts. The likelihood of a probation disposition did not change, because judges did not increase the rate at which they used probation as a disposition. During this same period, the number of *adjudicated* cases placed on *formal* probation increased 17 percent, from 216,900 to 254,800, and the number of cases involving a person offense (homicide, rape, robbery, assault, kidnaping, etc.) resulting in formal probation increased 45 percent (Table 4).

What Is the Profile of Cases Placed on Probation?

Most cases (54 percent) placed on formal probation in 1993 involved youth adjudicated for property offenses; 21 percent involved person offenses; 18 percent involved public order offenses; and 7 percent involved drug law violations (Table 5). Even though most of the cases placed on probation are for property offenses (because most cases seen by juvenile courts are property cases), the offense profile of cases placed on formal probation changed slightly between 1989 and 1993, with an increase in the proportion of cases involving person offenses. Probation caseload changes reflected overall delinquency caseload changes in terms of growth and offense profile—the majority of cases processed by juvenile courts remained property offenses, but the court also experienced an increase in cases involving person offenses. To the extent that probation is a mirror of what juvenile courts are facing, it is not surprising that probation officers are finding more violent youth in their caseloads. Moreover, while there has not been a change in judicial use of probation as a disposition, the increase in

violent youth on probation may very well be a result of a lack of secure beds for these offenders. Probation is the only alternative.

Challenges to Probation

The field of probation is staffed by dedicated individuals who believe that young persons who break the law can change their behavior in favor of law-abiding activities. Probation departments cannot, however, limit their intake of probationers like private providers or State training schools, which routinely operate over capacity and often have caps on admissions. In that sense, probation is the "catch basin" of the juvenile justice system and is being confronted with increasing and, as indicated below, more dangerous caseloads.

In fact, one of the biggest issues facing the field of juvenile probation is on-the-job safety. There is a growing perception that the work of juvenile probation is increasingly dangerous. Almost one-third of the survey respondents reported that they had been assaulted on the job at some point in their careers. When asked whether, during the course of their duties, they were ever concerned about personal safety, 42 percent of the respondents reported that they were usually or always concerned.

Balancing juvenile probation officers' safety and the safety of the public with probationers' needs is a major challenge. Many departments have developed creative and successful intensive supervision and school-based programs that target special populations of probationers; however, there is increased pressure to do much more community-based programming.

Indeed, in the face of rising caseloads, fixed resources, public demand for more accountability, and serious safety concerns, the mission of probation will need to evolve even further to respond not only to juvenile offenders but also to the community.

An emerging issue for probation departments seeking some reasoned relief from

---

Table 4:
Probation Caseloads Are Growing

Offense	Number of Adjudicated Cases Placed on Formal Probation		
	1989	1993	Percent Change
Delinquency	216,900	254,800	17%
Person	37,200	53,900	45
Property	126,300	136,600	8
Drugs	17,600	17,500	0
Public Order	35,900	46,800	30

Note: Detail may not add to totals because of rounding. "Percent Change" calculations are based on unrounded numbers.

Source: Butts, J., et al. (1995). *Juvenile Court Statistics 1993.* NCJ 159535.

Table 5:
Offenses Against Other Persons Make Up a Growing Proportion of Probation Officers' Caseloads

Offense	1989	1993
Person	17%	21%
Property	58	54
Drugs	8	7
Public Order	17	18
Total	100%	100%
Cases Resulting in Formal Probation:	216,900	254,800

Note: Detail may not total 100 percent because of rounding.

Source: Butts, J., et al. (1995). *Juvenile Court Statistics 1993.* NCJ 159535.

26. Juvenile Probation

juvenile justice policies that shift between just deserts and treatment philosophies is whether to embrace a paradigm that encompasses yet another philosophy. The "balanced approach" and "restorative justice" concepts evoke new ways of looking not only at the delivery of probation services, but also the continuum of services available to respond to juvenile offenders in the community. The balanced approach (see Maloney, Romig, and Armstrong, 1988) espouses the potential value in any case of applying, to some degree, an entire set of principles—community protection, accountability, competency development, and/or treatment—along with individualized assessment. Restorative justice (see Umbreit, 1989) promotes maximum involvement of the victim, offender, and community in the justice process. These two concepts have been combined into the "balanced and restorative justice" model, which suggests that justice is best served when the community, victim, and youth receive balanced attention, and all gain tangible benefits from their interactions with the juvenile justice system. Future bulletins will address these issues in an attempt to support juvenile justice professionals on the front lines in finding new solutions to emerging problems. An upcoming OJJDP Program Summary will highlight the American Probation and Parole Association's program for early identification of and appropriate intervention for drug-involved youth.

For further information about the Juvenile Probation Officer Initiative, contact:

Doug Thomas, JPOI Coordinator
National Center for Juvenile Justice
710 Fifth Avenue
Pittsburgh, PA 15219
412–227–6950

References

Maloney, D., Romig, D., and Armstrong, T. (1988). "Juvenile Probation: The Balanced Approach." *Juvenile and Family Court Journal*, 39 (3).

Umbreit, M. (1989). "Victims Seeking Fairness, Not Revenge: Toward Restorative Justice." *Federal Probation*, September.

This bulletin was prepared using the following reports produced by the National Center for Juvenile Justice:

Butts, J., et al. (1995). *Juvenile Court Statistics 1993*. NCJ 159535.*

Hurst, H., IV. and Torbet, P. (1993). *Organization and Administration of Juvenile Services: Probation, Aftercare, and State Institutions for Delinquent Youth.*

Hurst, H., IV. and Vereb, P. (1995). Special Analysis of the Juvenile Probation Officer Initiative Database.

Snyder, H. and Sickmund, M. (1995). *Juvenile Offenders and Victims: A National Report.* NCJ 153569.*

Thomas, D. (1993). *The State of Juvenile Probation 1992: Results of a Nationwide Survey.* NCJ 159536.*

Torbet, P. (Editor). (1993). *Desktop Guide to Good Juvenile Probation Practice.* NCJ 128218.*

* Documents available from the Juvenile Justice Clearinghouse, 800–638–8736; all others available from NCJJ.

This bulletin was prepared under grant number 95–JN–FX–K003 from the Office of Juvenile Justice and Delinquency Prevention (OJJDP), U.S. Department of Justice.

Points of view or opinions expressed in this document are those of the author and do not necessarily represent the official position or policies of OJJDP or the U.S. Department of Justice.

CRIME TIME BOMB

Rising juvenile crime, and predictions that it is going to get worse, are prodding cities, states and Congress to seek a balance between tougher laws and preventive measures

When police officers in Tallahassee, Fla., got a report on a teenager breaking into an auto, they had an immediate suspect. Working at a nearby restaurant was a 16-year-old parolee who had racked up an astounding 147 points—representing 32 charges—on a scale tracking juvenile arrests. The boy was collared after he barricaded himself in an apartment building, and his extensive record prompted prosecutors to send him for trial in adult criminal court. The case is pending.

Other officials in Tallahassee are trying a kinder, gentler approach to curbing juvenile crime. One early beneficiary has been a single mother's fifth grader, who entered Project Fresh Start last summer after repeatedly getting into trouble. In six weeks of summer classes and counseling, followed by daily after-school sessions once school reopened, he went from "class problem to developing leader" and was named January's "student of the month," says the project's Dorothy Inman-Crews.

Tallahassee's divergent approaches typify the bitter struggle over how to combat the nation's fastest-growing crime problem: juvenile offenders. More-aggressive law enforcement has helped cut violent crime in many big cities, but homicide by youths under 17 tripled between 1984 and 1994 and a coming surge in the teen population could boost the juvenile murder total 25 percent by 2005. Youth violence with guns has been increasing at roughly the same pace, and teen drug use is rising after years of decline.

A series of tragedies—many involving young victims—put a human face on the statistics. A pregnant 15-year-old was shot to death on a St. Louis school bus. Two 16-year-old boys were charged in the murder of a Dutch woman tourist who mistakenly ended up in a rough Miami neighborhood. A young mother fell to her death under a New York subway car when a 15-year-old boy allegedly tried to steal her $60 earrings.

Growing anger. Victims of underage felons are demanding changes in the juvenile justice system and challenging the long-standing belief that youngsters who kill, rob and rape should be treated in a different way from adult criminals. Nancy Slaven Peters, whose 2½-year-old daughter was killed by two boys 6 and 10 years old in rural Ohio, says "anger set in big time" when authorities refused to give her information about the suspects. Peters and others are crusading to open the traditionally secret juvenile-court process.

States, cities and the U.S. Congress are responding to the grim statistics and depressing stories with a variety of new attacks on youth crime. In Congress, which is considering a rewrite of the 22-year-old law providing antidelinquency aid to states, Republican Sen. Fred Thompson of Tennessee declared last week that the statute has "failed miserably" to prevent youth violence. The Massachusetts House of Representatives has voted to require that accused murderers as young as 14 be tried as adults. Tennessee has eliminated any minimum age for trying some youths as adults, Oregon last year lowered its minimum age from 14 to 12 and Wisconsin put its at 10. Seeking middle ground, Virginia legislators last week agreed on a new policy that combines get-tough and preventive approaches.

The most vexing problem is the small minority of teens who kill or maim with little moral compunction. Citing a wave of "undisciplined, untutored, unnurtured young people," Judge David Grossmann of Cincinnati, president of a national juvenile judges' group, says that "gangs have become the alternative to a nurturing family." Many young murderers "are incapable of empathy," says Kathleen Heide, a Florida psychotherapist and criminologist. She mentions a teen who gunned down and paralyzed a jogger who refused to hand over a gold neck chain. Asked what a preferable outcome might have been, the gunman said: "He could have given me his rope [chain]. I asked him twice." Police officers are encountering more "kids with no hope, no fear, no rules and no life expectancy," says John Firman of the International Association of Chiefs of Police, which plans a "summit" on youth crime next month.

To conservatives, the answer is tougher prison terms and law enforcement tactics like Tallahassee's SHOCAP (Serious Habitual Offender Comprehen-

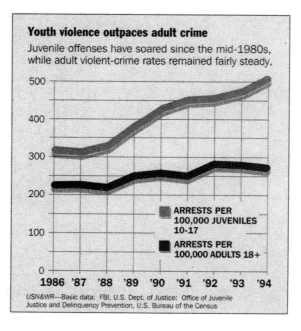

Youth violence outpaces adult crime
Juvenile offenses have soared since the mid-1980s, while adult violent-crime rates remained fairly steady.

ARRESTS PER 100,000 JUVENILES 10-17
ARRESTS PER 100,000 ADULTS 18+

USN&WR—Basic data: FBI, U.S. Dept. of Justice: Office of Juvenile Justice and Delinquency Prevention, U.S. Bureau of the Census

sive Action Program), which helped nab the auto break-in suspect. To liberals, the remedy is massive new spending on prevention plans like the one that may turn the fifth grader away from crime. As the two sides squabble, little gets done. Federal aid for SHOCAP ended quietly a few years ago, although more than 100 places use some form of the concept. And funding for prevention is limited amid conservative denunciations of crime-prevention programs.

Congressional conservatives, who argue that the federal antidelinquency statute is out of date, want to aid only states that try their most violent youths in adult courts. The White House signaled its own get-tough stance in January by sending Congress a plan for federal prosecutors to try some juveniles as adults without seeking judicial permission. (The bill is mainly symbolic because only a few dozen youths, mainly on military bases or Indian reservations, would be affected.) State lawmakers and judges "are responding to the public perception that juveniles ought to be held accountable," says James Wootton of the Safe Streets Alliance and former deputy chief of the federal antidelinquency office.

At the heart of the battle are juvenile courts, which were created beginning in 1899 to protect delinquents. The idea was to give young lawbreakers a combination of punishment, treatment and counseling to straighten out their lives. The modern-day reality, critics charge, is that too many are arrested, held and released time after time in a revolving-door process that ends only if a heinous crime is committed.

Absurd law? Now, a campaign against juvenile courts is spreading fast. Arizona Gov. Fife Symington is leading a petition drive for a state constitutional amendment that critics say could lead to the abolition of juvenile courts. Proponents say the aim is to send the most violent young suspects to adult trials, even if judges object. The current law making everyone under 18 a juvenile "is an absurdity," argues Symington aide Jay Heiler, a former prosecutor. "We've had kids arrested 10 or 15 times—that has to stop." People "are standing in line" to sign petitions, he says.

Critics charge that advocates of tougher measures are overreacting. "One heinous case has everyone jumping up and down saying all kids are doing it," complains Edward Loughran, a former head of Massachusetts's juvenile corrections agency. "Bad cases make bad law." Indeed, the move to lower the age at which juveniles can be tried as adults in Massachusetts began when a judge ruled that a 16-year-old should be tried as a juvenile for killing a woman who lived next door.

But statistics buttress the mounting concerns. Starting with the mid-1980s cocaine epidemic, competition among drug-sales rings led to a rash of gun purchases that made the streets more dangerous. The number of black males 14 through 17 is due to rise 26 percent by 2005—6 percent above the overall increase for that age group. Such youths are disproportionately affected by problems linked to crime, including poverty, family breakdowns and poor education. Not surprisingly, they also are disproportionately involved in crime: Sixty-one percent of juveniles arrested for homicide in 1994 were African-American, as were 52 percent of their victims. "Given our wholesale disinvestment in youth, we will likely have many more than 5,000 teen killers per year" after the new century dawns, says criminologist James Alan Fox of Northeastern University in Boston. (While the number of youths 14 or under arrested for murder has jumped 43 percent in two decades, the 1994 total of 379 is less than 2 percent of all homicides. And arrest figures can be misleading because juveniles tend to be rounded up in groups.)

Still, the nation has failed to make much headway with the "violent few." Layers of government, says Shay Bilchik of the Justice Department's antidelinquency agency, have long been "pointing fingers and blaming the other—a kind of hide-and-seek, grown-up style."

Consider the federal war on delinquency. After a commission named by President Lyndon Johnson touted a juvenile-justice overhaul in 1967 as "America's best hope for reducing crime," Congress responded in 1974 with the law now up for renewal, which aimed to help states separate teen and adult lawbreakers in prison. It largely worked, but it did not address the problem symbolized by Willie Bosket, who, after committing hundreds of street crimes, was charged in 1977 with killing two men in a New York subway. When the *Daily News* headlined the story, "He's

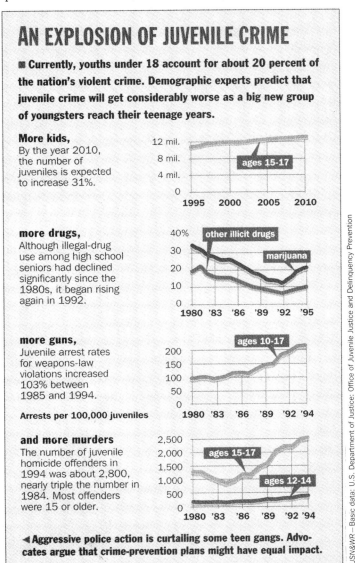

AN EXPLOSION OF JUVENILE CRIME

■ Currently, youths under 18 account for about 20 percent of the nation's violent crime. Demographic experts predict that juvenile crime will get considerably worse as a big new group of youngsters reach their teenage years.

More kids, By the year 2010, the number of juveniles is expected to increase 31%.

more drugs, Although illegal-drug use among high school seniors had declined significantly since the 1980s, it began rising again in 1992.

more guns, Juvenile arrest rates for weapons-law violations increased 103% between 1985 and 1994. Arrests per 100,000 juveniles

and more murders The number of juvenile homicide offenders in 1994 was about 2,800, nearly triple the number in 1984. Most offenders were 15 or older.

USN&WR – Basic data: U.S. Department of Justice: Office of Juvenile Justice and Delinquency Prevention

◄ Aggressive police action is curtailing some teen gangs. Advocates argue that crime-prevention plans might have equal impact.

5. JUVENILE JUSTICE

15 and He Likes to Kill—Because It's Fun," outraged state officials began the trend of allowing young teens to be tried as adults.

Hitting the hard core. Conflicting attitudes toward juvenile justice intensified during the presidency of Ronald Reagan, who tried to end the federal antidelinquency aid. When he failed, his advisers went after the hard core, launching experiments to develop treatment for chronic violators and inventing SHOCAP to track offenders' records, which long had been difficult for even public agencies to obtain.

Then the spotlight turned to fighting gangs and imposing mandatory prison terms for drug dealing. By 1992, President George Bush touted a program called "weed and seed," to weed out the worst young criminals and seed rehabilitation projects. Aid for SHOCAP was ended because the program operated only in medium-sized cities. In 1993, new Attorney General Janet Reno changed the focus again, to heading off delinquency from early ages. But prevention became a harder sell after Republicans, who ridiculed "midnight basketball," won control of Congress.

Hard-liners favor trying teen suspects as adults. Their aim is to give young criminals longer sentences than they could get in juvenile courts, which lose control when convicts reach either 18 or 21.

But the technique may be counterproductive. Because judges often view defendants transferred from juvenile courts as less dangerous than older convicts with longer crime records, youths tend to get shorter prison terms. In Florida, which has sent thousands of teens to trial as adults in recent years, criminologists conclude in a new study that youths tried as adults commit even more crimes after release than do those who remain in the juvenile system. Sending a youth for an adult trial may "stigmatize him as a lost cause and convince him he is no good," resulting in a return to crime, says Charles Frazier of the University of Florida. "We think we are hitting them hard but have the opposite effect."

Hybrid arrangements. Varying penalties between the adult and juvenile justice systems result in what law Prof. Barry Feld of the University of Minnesota calls a "punishment gap." Officials are experimenting with hybrid arrangements that might produce better results. In Jacksonville, Fla., for example, prosecutor Harry Shorstein has tried more than 1,100 young toughs as adults but then arranged to have them incarcerated in local jails that offer a variety of education and treatment programs. Youth crime in the area has dropped, bucking the general trend.

Many reformers argue that juvenile crime will ebb only when localities effectively combine get-tough and preventive approaches. The violence-prone youths of the future "are now 3 to 5 years old," says Barry Krisberg of the National Council on Crime and Delinquency. "We could change the crime projections if we wanted."

But only now are many communities launching broad attacks. Florida has set up 67 local panels to push programs like the one helping Tallahassee students. The U.S. Justice Department recently funded "Safe Futures" plans in six cities to establish a series of escalating penalties on young violators. If the kids do not stop committing crimes after modest sanctions, tougher punishment kicks in.

Crime fighters also are beginning to clamp down on teen firearm use. With federal aid, Boston police are going after gun-toting gangsters in high-crime neighborhoods. The federal community-policing drive is aiding antigun programs in 10 cities, including one in which Cleveland is opening a patrol station in a former crack house.

Other places are trying ideas like earlier curfews, holding parents responsible for their children's offenses, requiring school uniforms and helping institutions such as churches open their doors to teens after school, when violence rates are highest. That last idea wins praise from experts like Princeton University political scientist John Di-Iulio, who says inner-city neighborhoods boast too many "chaotic, dysfunctional, fatherless, Godless and jobless settings where . . . self-respecting young men literally aspire to get away with murder."

Get ready. The most pressing need may be dealing with young criminals after prison. The tendency now is for officials to say just before release, " 'Here's Johnny Jones. Get ready. He's coming out,' " says Troy Armstrong, a California State University criminologist who is designing "after care" plans to ease the transition from prison to jobs or school. That idea is praised by Johnny Rawls, 17 of Memphis, who told Senator Thompson that after he lived "a lousy life" of crime, a tough-minded treatment unit is turning him around: "I have done a lot of things that have hurt people, but I never really looked at it till I was forced to."

But it will be years before that gap is plugged. In the meantime, juvenile-detention centers are overcrowded and the odds that suspects will get competent attorneys are worsening, says a new American Bar Association report. Even if more youths are put behind bars, the projected violator totals are so high that "we can't build enough prisons to keep all of them locked up," says crime consultant Donna Hamparian of Columbus, Ohio.

There is scant hope that the pessimistic trends will stop anytime soon. And tough speeches may be "good for politicians' re-elections but don't make much sense," says Jesse Williams, a Philadelphia youth-corrections official. The tragic fact is that it may take an even greater bloodbath to force effective crime solutions to the top of the nation's agenda.

BY TED GEST WITH VICTORIA POPE

A PROFILE OF YOUNG KILLERS

■ The number of youths under 18 arrested for murder tripled between 1984 and 1994. Some 55 percent had juvenile accomplices and 30 percent had adult accomplices.

■ Juveniles kill strangers more than a third of the time; adults more often kill family members.

JUVENILES

8%
37%
55%

25 AND OVER

15%
25%
60%

■ FAMILY
■ STRANGERS
■ KNOWN

USN&WR—Data cover years 1988 to 1994. Basic data: James Alan Fox, Northeastern University, for U.S. Bureau of Justice Statistics. GRAPHIC BY TARA M. BLESSINGER—USN&WR

◄ Victor Brancaccio, 16, killed a woman who criticized his rap music. He got life.

TEENAGERS AND GUNS

■ Juvenile killings with firearms quadrupled between 1984 and 1994.

■ Handguns were used in two thirds of the youth homicides involving guns over a recent 15-year span.

Homicides by juveniles using guns
In 1994, 82 percent of juvenile murderers used guns.

Number of offenders

2,500
2,000
1,500
1,000
500
0

1980   '85   '90   '94

■ USED GUNS
■ DID NOT USE GUNS

USN&WR—Basic data: U.S. Department of Justice: Office of Juvenile Justice and Delinquency Prevention

◄ Police in many cities are bearing down on juvenile violators of firearms laws.

Article 28

Controlling Crime Before It Happens: Risk-Focused Prevention

J. David Hawkins

Traditionally, the juvenile justice system has employed sanctions, treatment, and rehabilitation to change problem behaviors after they have occurred. Advocates of a prevention-based approach to crime control invite the scorn of critics who believe prevention amounts to little more than "feel-good" activities. Yet the practitioner—the probation officer confronted daily with young people in trouble—is often aware of the need for effective prevention. As a probation officer in the early 1970's working with delinquent teenagers, I found myself asking, "Couldn't we have prevented these youngsters from getting to this point? Couldn't we have interceded before they were criminally referred to the courts?"

Once they have experienced the reinforcing properties of drugs and are convinced of crime's profitability, young people are difficult to turn around. Once invested in the culture of crime, they reject the virtues attributed to school and family, for reasons that are all too clear. For them, school is not a place of attachment and learning, but of alienation and failure; family is not a source of love and support, but of unremitting conflict.

Dealing with these youths as a probation officer, I saw my job as something akin to operating an expensive ambulance service at the bottom of a cliff. The probation

staff were the emergency team patching up those who fell over the edge. Many of us who have worked in juvenile corrections have come to realize that to keep young people from falling in the first place, a barrier is needed at the top of the cliff. In short, we believe that prevention is more effective and less costly than treatment after the fact. David Mitchell, chief judge of the juvenile court for Baltimore County, once observed, "It is of no value for the court to work miracles in rehabilitation if there are no opportunities for the child in the community. Until we deal with the environment in which they live, whatever we do in the courts is irrelevant."

Effective prevention based on the public health model

In prevention, where action precedes the commission of crime, it is wise to heed the admonition that guides physicians: "Above all, do no harm." Hard work and good intentions, by themselves, are not enough to ensure that a program to prevent violence or substance abuse will succeed, let alone that it will not make things worse.

Early prevention efforts in the "War on Drugs" serve to illustrate this point. Well-meaning people were concerned about substance abuse and decided to do something about it by introducing prevention programs

in the schools. They collected information, pictures, and even samples of illicit drugs, took these materials to the schools, and showed them to students; they talked about the behavioral and health effects of drugs and warned of the risks associated with their use. Contrary to intention and expectation, these drug information programs failed to reduce or eliminate drug use and, in some instances, actually led to its increase.[1] The real lesson learned in the schools was that information, which is neutral, can be employed to the wrong end, producing more harm than good. These early prevention workers had not envisioned drug information in the context of a comprehensive prevention strategy.

Increasingly, the preventive approach used in public health is being recognized as appropriate for use as part of a criminal justice strategy.[2] It is instructive to review an example of how the model has been applied to disease control. Seeking to prevent cardiovascular disease, researchers in the field of public health first identified risk factors; that is, the factors whose presence increased a person's chances of contracting the disease: tobacco use, high-fat diet, sedentary lifestyle, high levels of stress, and family history of heart disease. Equally important, they determined that certain protective factors (e.g., aerobic exercise or relaxation techniques) helped prevent the development of heart problems.

From the *National Institute of Justice Journal*, August 1995, pp. 10-18. Reprinted by permission of the U.S. Department of Justice, Office of Justice Programs.

167

5. JUVENILE JUSTICE

These public health researchers were concerned with halting the onset of heart disease in order to avoid risky, invasive, and costly interventions, such as angioplasty or bypass surgery, after the disease had taken hold. Their goal was to reduce or counter the identified risk factors for heart disease in the population at large; their strategy was to launch a massive public advocacy campaign, conducted in multiple venues (e.g., the media, government, corporations, schools), aimed at elimination of "at risk" behaviors (and the attitudes supporting them). If risk could not be avoided altogether, the campaign could at least promote those behaviors and attitudes that reduce risk of heart disease. Proof that this two-pronged strategy has been effective is in the numbers: a 45-percent decrease in the incidence of cardiovascular disease, due in large measure to risk-focused prevention.[3] Application of the same prevention principles to reduce the risks associated with problem behaviors in teenagers, including violence, can work as well.

Identifying risk factors for violence

Using the public health model to reduce violence in America's communities calls for first identifying the factors that put young people at risk for violence in order to reduce or eliminate these factors and strengthen the protective factors that buffer the effects of exposure to risk. Over the past few years, longitudinal research (that is, studies that follow youngsters from the early years of their lives into adulthood) has identified factors associated with neighborhoods and communities, the family, the schools, and peer groups, as well as factors residing in the individual that increase the probability of violence during adolescence and young adulthood. These factors, presented in exhibit 1, also have been shown to increase the probability of other health and behavior problems, including substance abuse, delinquency, teen pregnancy, and dropping out of school. It is important to note that only factors identified in *two or more* of these longitudinal studies to increase the probability of the checked health or behavior problem have been included in the exhibit. Although future research may reveal, for example, that alienation and rebelliousness place an individual at risk of violent behavior, consistent evidence does not yet exist to support this hypothesis.

In neighborhoods. Five risk factors arising from the community environment are known to increase the probability that a young person will engage in violence:

✦ *Availability of guns*. The United States has one of the highest rates of criminal violence in the world, and firearms are implicated in a great number of these crimes. In recent years, reports of gun-toting youths in inner-city schools and of violent incidents involving handguns in school environs have created mounting concern. Given the lethality of firearms, the increased likelihood of conflict escalating into homicide when guns are present, and the strong association between availability of firearms and homicide rates, a teenager having ready access to firearms through family, friends, or a source on the street is at increased risk of violence.

✦ *Community laws/norms favorable to crime*. Community norms are communicated through laws, written policies, informal social practices, and adult expectations of young people. Sometimes social practices send conflicting messages: for example, schools and parents may promote "just say no" themes while alcohol and substance abuse are acceptable practices in the community. Community attitudes also influence law enforcement. An example is the enforcement of laws that regulate firearms sales. These laws have reduced violent crime, but the effect is small and diminishes as time passes. A number of studies suggest that the reasons are community norms that include lack of proactive monitoring or enforcement, as well as the availability of firearms from jurisdictions having no legal prohibitions on sales or illegal access. Other laws related to reductions in violent crime, especially crime involving firearms, include laws governing penalties for licensing violations and for using a firearm in the commission of a crime.

✦ *Media portrayals of violence*. The highly charged public debate over whether portrayals of violence in the media adversely affect children continues. Yet research over the past 3 decades demonstrates a clear correlation between depictions of violence and the development of aggressive and violent behavior. Exposure to media violence also teaches violent problem-solving strategies and appears to alter children's attitudes and sensitivity to violence.

✦ *Low neighborhood attachment/community disorganization*. Indifference to cleanliness and orderliness, high rates of vandalism, little surveillance of public places by neighborhood residents, absence of parental involvement in schools, and low rates of voter participation are indicative of low neighborhood attachment. The less homogeneous a community in terms of race, class, religion, or mix of industrial to residential areas, the less connected its residents may feel to the overall community and the more difficult it is to establish clear community goals and identity. Higher rates of drug problems, juvenile delinquency, and violence occur in such places.

✦ *Extreme economic deprivation*. Children who live in deteriorating neighborhoods characterized by extreme poverty are more likely to develop problems

28. Controlling Crime

with delinquency, teen pregnancy, dropping out of school, and violence. If such children also have behavior and adjustment problems early in life, they are also more likely to have problems with drugs as they mature. The rate of poverty is disproportionately higher for African American, Native American, or Hispanic children than for white children; thus, children are differentially exposed to risk depending on their racial or cultural backgrounds.

In families. Obviously, the home environment, family dynamics, and parental stability play a major role in shaping children. Three risk factors for violence are associated with the family constellation: poor family management practices, including the absence of clear expectations and standards for children's behavior, excessively severe or inconsistent punishment, and parental failure to monitor their children's activities, whereabouts, or friends; family conflict, either between parents or between parents and children, which enhances the risk for all of the problem behaviors; and favorable parental attitudes and involvement in violent behavior, which increases the risk that children witnessing such displays will themselves become violent.

At school. Two indicators of risk for violence are associated with a child's experiences at school. Antisocial behavior of early onset (that is, aggressiveness in grades K–3, sometimes combined with isolation or withdrawal or sometimes combined with hyperactivity or attention-deficit disorder) is more frequently found in boys than girls and places the child at increased risk for problems, including violence, during adolescence. The risk factor also includes persistent antisocial behavior first exhibited in adolescence, such as skipping school, getting into fights, and misbehaving in class. Young people of both genders who engage in these behaviors during early adolescence are at increased risk for drug abuse, juvenile delinquency, violence, dropping out of school, and teen pregnancy. Academic failure, if it occurs in the late elementary grades and beyond, is a second school-related risk factor that is likely to result in violence and other problem behaviors. Specifically, it is the *experience* of failure that appears to escalate the risk, rather than ability per se.

Exhibit 1. Risk Factors and Their Association With Behavior Problems in Adolescents

Risk Factors	Adolescent Problem Behaviors				
	Substance Abuse	Delinquency	Teen Pregnancy	School Drop-Out	Violence
Community					
Availability of Drugs	✓				
Availability of Firearms		✓			✓
Community Laws and Norms Favorable Toward Drug Use, Firearms, and Crime	✓	✓			✓
Media Portrayals of Violence					✓
Transitions and Mobility	✓	✓		✓	
Low Neighborhood Attachment and Community Disorganization	✓	✓			✓
Extreme Economic Deprivation	✓	✓	✓	✓	✓
Family					
Family History of the Problem Behavior	✓	✓	✓	✓	
Family Management Problems	✓	✓	✓	✓	✓
Family Conflict	✓	✓	✓	✓	✓
Favorable Parental Attitudes and Involvement in the Problem Behavior	✓	✓			✓
School					
Early and Persistent Antisocial Behavior	✓	✓	✓	✓	✓
Academic Failure Beginning in Elementary School	✓	✓	✓	✓	✓
Lack of Commitment to School	✓	✓	✓	✓	
Individual/Peer					
Alienation and Rebelliousness	✓	✓		✓	
Friends Who Engage in a Problem Behavior	✓	✓	✓	✓	✓
Favorable Attitudes Toward the Problem Behavior	✓	✓	✓	✓	
Early Initiation of the Problem Behavior	✓	✓	✓	✓	✓
Constitutional Factors	✓	✓			✓

© 1993 Developmental Research and Programs, Inc.

169

5. JUVENILE JUSTICE

In peer groups and within the individual. If youngsters associate with peers who engage in problem behaviors (for example, drug abuse, delinquency, violence, sexual activity, or dropping out of school), they are much more likely to do the same. Further, the earlier in their lives that young people become involved in these kinds of experiences—or take their first drink of alcohol or smoke their first marijuana cigarette—the greater is the likelihood of prolonged, serious, and chronic involvement in health and behavior problems. Even when a young person comes from a well-managed family and is not burdened with other risk factors, associating with friends who engage in problem behaviors greatly increases the child's risk. In addition, certain constitutional factors—those that may have a biological or physiological basis—appear to increase a young person's risk. Examples of constitutional factors include lack of impulse control, sensation seeking, and low harm avoidance.

Protective factors

It is well known that some youngsters, even though they are exposed to multiple risk factors, do not succumb to violent, antisocial behavior. Research indicates that protective factors reduce the impact of negative risk factors by providing positive ways for an individual to respond to these risks. Three categories of protective factors have been identified:[4]

◆ Individual characteristics: A resilient temperament and positive social orientation.

◆ Bonding: Positive relationships with family members, teachers, or other adults.

◆ Healthy beliefs and clear standards: Beliefs in children's competence to succeed in school and avoid drugs and crime coupled with establishing clear expectations and rules governing their behavior.

Individual characteristics. Youths who seem able to cope more successfully than others with risk factors appear resilient: they are able to bounce back in the face of change or adversity; they experience less frustration in the face of obstacles and do not give up easily. They are also good-natured, enjoy social interaction, and elicit positive attention from others. Gender is another factor. Given equal exposure to risks, girls are less likely than boys to develop violent behavioral problems in adolescence. Finally, intelligence protects against certain problem behaviors, such as delinquency and dropping out of school, although it does not protect against substance abuse. Such individual characteristics enhance the likelihood that children will identify opportunities to make a personal contribution, develop the skills necessary to follow through successfully, and receive recognition for their efforts. However, these individual protective factors—resilient temperament, positive social orientation, gender, and intelligence—are innate and are extremely difficult to change.

Bonding. Several studies have revealed that children raised in environments in which they are exposed to multiple risk factors have nevertheless become productive, contributing members of the community. In interviews with these young people, they invariably note that someone took an interest in them. Some adult in the community—whether a parent, an aunt, a grandmother, a teacher, a youth worker, a minister, a businessperson—established a bond of affection and cared enough to reach out. Research has shown that the protective factor of bonding with positive, prosocial family members, teachers, or other significant adults or peers can be strengthened by preventive intervention.

Healthy beliefs and clear standards. When the adults with whom young people bond have healthy beliefs and well-defined standards of behavior, these serve as protection against the onset of health and behavior problems in those youngsters. Examples of healthy beliefs include believing it is best for children to be free of drugs and crime and to do well in school. Examples of well-defined standards include clear, consistent family prohibitions against drug and alcohol use, demands for good performance in school, and disapproval of problem behaviors. When a young person bonds to those who hold healthy beliefs and set clear standards, the two protective factors are reinforcing; they work in tandem by providing a model on which to base behavior and the motivation to practice approved behavior so that the bond is not jeopardized. Both bonding and healthy beliefs/clear standards mediate the relationship between a young person and the social environment, including community, family, schools, and peer groups; these protective factors can be encouraged and strengthened.

The preconditions of bonding. Bonding may take place with a caregiver, a family member or other significant adult, or it may represent an attachment to a social group. For bonding to occur, however, three conditions must be met. The first is the *opportunity for active involvement*. People become bonded to a family, a school class, or a community because they are given the chance to participate in the life of the group. In a classroom where the teacher calls on only the students in the front who raise their hands, the others are denied an opportunity for active involvement; as a result they may lose their commitment to education. The situation is similar in a family where the 13- or 14-year-old uses the home as a hotel—essentially a place to sleep—but has no responsibilities in the family. Youngsters need to be given the chance to contribute, in ways commensurate with their level of development, to life in the family,

170

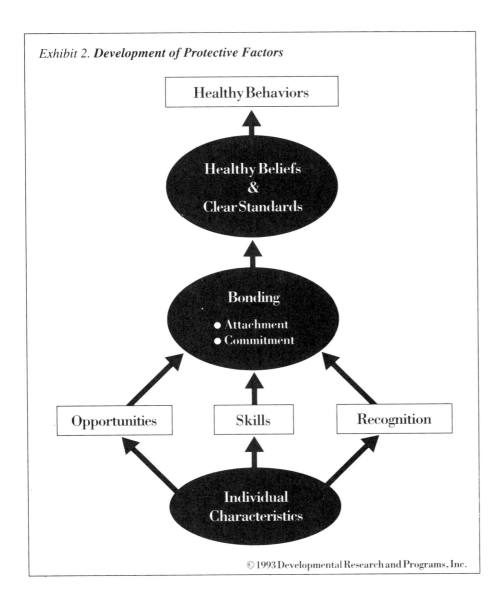

Exhibit 2. Development of Protective Factors

© 1993 Developmental Research and Programs, Inc.

28. Controlling Crime

developed and how they influence one another.

Community guidelines for preventive intervention

In designing preventive interventions for the 1990's and beyond, community leaders should keep in mind some key principles. The first is that prevention strategies should focus on *known* risk factors. Once communities identify the risk factors they need to address, the prevention program developed in response should be targeted to reducing those factors and to enhancing protective factors. Another guideline is that intervention should be planned to coincide with the point in a child's development that is optimal for achieving the desired outcome. Thus, prevention interventions need to be geared to the *appropriate developmental stages* of the child. If behavior problems at age 4, 5, and 6 are known to be associated with substance abuse and delinquency later in life, this means all youngsters should be taught in the early elementary grades the skills they need to manage and control their impulses in order to get along with others.

Allied to the principle of intervention at the appropriate stage is *early intervention*, necessary to prevent behavior problems from stabilizing and becoming entrenched. Ideally, prevention begins before the child is born to ensure that low-income mothers and other adult caregivers have the skills they need to nurture children. These skills will equip them to understand that a crying baby is not a bad baby who needs to be spanked or disciplined. Prenatal care, home visits to low-income single mothers, and caregiver training in nurturing skills can significantly reduce child abuse. Studies show that more than a fourfold reduction in child abuse is achievable by home visitation before birth

in the classroom, and in the wider community.

The opportunity to become involved is not enough, however. A second condition of effective bonding is *having the skills needed* to succeed once involvement gets underway. Young people need to be taught the skills without which they will be unable to pursue opportunities effectively. Examples of skills that have been shown to protect children include good cognitive skills, such as problem-solving and reading abilities, and good social skills, including communication, assertiveness, and the ability to ask for support. The third condition of bonding is *a consistent system of recognition or reinforcement for skillful performance*. Young people often receive little or no recognition for doing the right thing. The focus is on what they have done wrong; much less frequently are their accomplishments acknowledged. The efforts they put forth, the challenges they face, and the contributions they make should be celebrated in personally and culturally accepted ways.

Thus, along with opportunities and access to skills, recognition or appreciation provides an incentive for continued contribution and is a necessary condition for enabling young people to form close attachments to their communities, schools, and families. Exhibit 2 shows how protective factors are

5. JUVENILE JUSTICE

and during the first few months of infancy.[5]

Prevention programs need to reach those who are at high risk by virtue of exposure to *multiple risk factors.* These multiple risks require multiple strategies that also are sensitive to the cultural diversity that characterizes many communities.

Commitment to risk-focused prevention programs arises only when there is buy-in by the community; that is, when the programs are felt to be "owned and operated" by the community. This sense of proprietorship evolves when all the various stakeholders in the community—the key leaders through the grassroots members—come together representing their diverse interests and develop a strategy for how to implement risk-focused prevention. The "Communities That Care" approach is one such strategy.

Implications for criminal justice

The inclusion of prevention as a central element of criminal justice policy and practice is emblematic of a new emphasis reflecting the realization that enforcement alone is not enough to reduce youth violence. This realization reflects the recognition that, in spite of geometrically increasing investments in enforcement, the courts, and corrections, violent crime, especially among young people, has continued to rise over the past decade.

For criminal justice, the orientation to prevention means establishing partnerships with other organizations, groups, and agencies in the community to identify and reduce risks for crime and violence and to strengthen protective factors that inhibit violence in the community. Community policing represents a clear example of this shift in criminal justice from an exclusive focus on the "back end"—after the crime has been committed. Integral to the intervention process is the involvement of the community and of social service and other agencies at the "front end"—working in tandem with law enforcement to identify problems and design strategies to solve them. In refining its role, criminal justice is taking on a much greater challenge than in the past, but doing so holds the promise of reducing crime in the long term.

Notes

1. Stuart, R.B., "Teaching Facts About Drugs: Pushing or Preventing?" *Journal of Educational Psychology* 37 (1974): 98–201; and Weaver, S. C. and F. S. Tennant, "Effectiveness of Drug Education Programs for Secondary School Students," *American Journal of Psychiatry* 130 (1973): 812–814.

2. See, for example, William DeJong's *Preventing Interpersonal Violence Among Youth: An Introduction to School, Community, and Mass Media Strategies*, Issues and Practices, Washington, D.C.: U.S. Department of Justice, National Institute of Justice, August 1994: 12–15.

3. From a speech delivered at the National Academy of Sciences in January 1994, by Kenneth I. Shine, M.D., President of the National Institute of Medicine.

4. See Hawkins, J. D., R. F. Catalano, and J. M. Miller, "Risk and Protective Factors for Alcohol and Other Drug Problems in Adolescence and Early Childhood: Implications for Substance Abuse Prevention," *Psychological Bulletin* 112 (1992): 64–105; Werner, E. E. and R. S. Smith, *Overcoming the Odds: High Risk Children From Birth to Adulthood,* New York: Cornell University Press, 1992; and Rutter, M., "Resilience in the Face of Adversity: Protective Factors and Resistance to Psychiatric Disorder," *British Journal of Psychiatry* 147 (1987): 598–611.

5. Olds, David L., C. R. Henderson, Jr., R. Chamberlin, and R. Tatelbaum, "Preventing Child Abuse and Neglect: A Randomized Trial of Nurse Home Visitation," *Pediatrics* 78 (1986): 65–78.

6. For information about the Communities That Care comprehensive community prevention planning approach, contact Developmental Research and Programs, 130 Nickerson Street, Suite 107, Seattle, WA 98109. Phone: (800) 736–2630; Fax: (206) 286–1462.

J. David Hawkins teaches social work at the University of Washington in Seattle and directs the University's Social Development Research Group.

Article 29

Street Gangs—
Future Paramilitary Groups?

By Robert J. Bunker, Ph.D., Adjunct Professor, National Security Studies Program, California State University, San Bernardino

The New York and Oklahoma City bombings have shown that the United States is no longer immune to politically motivated terrorist attacks. The latter proved that no part of the country was invulnerable; even worse, the perpetrators may be our own disenfranchised citizens.

Is it possible that street gangs' engaging in such activity looms on the horizon? Although it is unlikely that they would act on a political agenda, the emerging patterns are all too familiar. The expanding presence of street gangs in the United States can be linked both to military trends in the non-Western world and to future warfighting concerns—particularly in terms of the disruption of a society's social organization. One important implication coming from recognition of these trends is that the concept of terrorism itself is being reevaluated by scholars.

Street Gangs

At the August 1995 CGIA/ATF National Gang Violence Seminar held in Anaheim, California, Sergeant Jerry Flowers of the Oklahoma City, Oklahoma, Police Department spoke eloquently about law enforcement's life-and-death struggle with this growing criminal sector. The most reliable estimates are that some 4,881 gangs with 249,324 members now exist within the United States' major urban centers.[1]

Curious about the extent to which street gangs had set up franchises throughout the country for the purposes of narcotrafficking, I questioned Sergeant Wes McBride of the Los Angeles County, California, Sheriff's Department, a recognized authority on L.A.-based street gangs. He explained that the initial movement of L.A.-based street gangs, primarily Crips and Bloods, had little—if anything—to do with narcotics trafficking. On the contrary, he said, the initial moves were typically family relocations. One of the more common reasons for such relocations was to remove the youthful gang member from the influence of the local gang—parents were trying to re-establish a non-criminal lifestyle for the gang member.

Unfortunately, in many cases, the move did not achieve the hoped-for result, and the youth proceeded to establish his gang lifestyle in the new territory. On occasion, he would call some of his fellow gang members to come help him establish a gang in new turf, and some narcotic connections would be made, McBride said.[2]

An organized strategy by L.A.-based street gangs to expand their narcotics trade would have meant that some sort of command-and-control hierarchy existed with these gangs. Such a hierarchy would provide a target set that would facilitate combating the problem. Instead, street gangs had spread because of family relocations that failed to end the gang lifestyle.[3] McBride also noted, "We don't have drug gangs; we have gangs that have some members who deal drugs." Drug trafficking, it seems, has very little to do with street gangs. In fact, in Los Angeles, only about 25 percent of drug-trafficking instances can be tied to gang members.[4]

What is the potential for street gangs to engage in domestic acts of terrorism? "Certainly they have the potential," McBride said, "but probably not the need or desire to attract that kind of attention. We are not dealing with the sophistication of the [Colombian] cartels, [nor is there] the deep-rooted dependency on hierarchical leadership within gangs for domestic terrorism to become an issue." McBride did, however, make a distinction between "conventional" domestic terrorism—a force with a political agenda—and the terrorizing effect of random and pervasive violence. "I believe if we look at the disconnected violence issue involving the gangs," McBride said, "we are 'hip deep' right now in domestic terrorism created by the gangs. Their gang wars and disregard for innocent victims certainly ha[ve] an effect on . . . the well-being of our citizens, but it is not a planned action by the gangs—simply disorganized crime in action."[5]

Of course, it is much harder to deal with vast numbers of isolated nodes of criminal activity than with a few street gangs that systematically engage in terrorism for some defined political end.

Certain themes in McBride's assessment of L.A.'s street gangs stand out—with an organized pattern of chaos emerging as the dominant attribute of these themes. Accordingly, street gangs can be broadly characterized as

- spreading as a result of family relocations that fail to remove the youth from the gang lifestyle but instead introduce that lifestyle into new communities;
- possessing a nonhierarchical decision-making structure based on uncoordinated nodes (e.g. individual gangs) that take part in seemingly random patterns of activity; and
- engaging in criminal activity that is equivalent in effect to that of endemic low-grade terrorism.

These themes parallel those found in research on emerging forms of warfare and the new form of soldier developing in much of the non-Western world.

Emergent Warfighting Themes

Military scholars recognize that a new form of soldier, with no allegiance to the nation-state, is developing in much of the non-Western world. Major Ralph Peters, U.S. Army, who is responsible for evaluating emerging threats for the Office of the Deputy Chief of Staff for Intelligence, terms this threat "The New Warrior Class."[6] It is being taken seriously enough by the U.S. Army to be included in its perceptions of early 21st-century Army operations.[7]

This type of soldier, which has developed as an outcome of a breakdown in social organization in many failed nation-states, operates in subnational groups such as armed bands, private armies, crime networks and terrorist organizations. Debate in professional U.S. military and affiliated journals over the past two years has dealt with concerns that this

---

Reprinted from the *Police Chief* magazine, June 1996, pp. 54-58. © 1996 by The International Association of Chiefs of Police, Inc., 515 N. Washington St., Alexandria, VA 22314, U.S.A. Further reproduction without express written permission from IACP is strictly prohibited.

5. JUVENILE JUSTICE

new form of soldier may be developing within the United States.

Street gangs would be one logical source from which this new form of soldier could emerge in this country. These gangs have developed in failed inner cities, where poverty and crime run rampant and family social structures have been severely eroded.

Drawing parallels between a city such as Beirut and some U.S. inner-city cores, where many gang members grew up, is not overly difficult. The threat of death or physical harm is significant for a young male growing up in both surroundings, and both fail to provide educational opportunities that can allow for the transformation of this segment of the population into productive and responsible citizens. Today's pre-teenage inner-city children—termed the "super-predators" by Dr. John J. DiIulio, Jr., of Princeton University—bear a striking resemblance to the child soldiers found in numerous private armies throughout the non-Western world.

Further, social norms for many of our youths have become twisted. For example, says Anne Powell, project director of the California Family Impact Seminar on Teenage Pregnancy for the California State Library Foundation, in "street gang culture . . . men get 'points' for how many underage girls they have impregnated. Many of the men are jobless and achieve a sense of dominance through sex. Many of the girls have been abused as children and accept sex with older males as normal."[8] After two generations (about 30 to 34 years), children born into such family circumstances would likely consider them a normal pattern of inner-city life. Other skewed patterns of "normalcy," such as a basic disregard for human life or organized looting are not incomprehensible developments in children reared in such environmental conditions.

The nonhierarchical nature of street gangs is also an important factor. In the Army's Force XXI Operations, a new form of battle command based on a nonhierarchical—or "Internetted"—structure is envisioned.[9] Internetted structures refer to those entities that rely upon a structure resembling neural networks, with individual nodes connected to one another in "web-like" patterns. Such structures are viewed as applying only to complex, adaptive armies fielded in the future by technically advanced political entities. Such structural concepts can be found in the 1969 creation of the ARPNET, an early predecessor of the Internet. Because of the robust properties of this design, it was foreseen during the Cold War that such an Internetted U.S. communications structure would have a better chance of surviving a potential nuclear exchange than the more traditional existing structure.[10]

Street gangs appear to represent a type of Internetted structure based on self-sufficient individual nodes never considered by futuristic Army planners. In this case, it is based on a form of social mutation being spread throughout society by individual families attempting to remove their children from street gang influences and, to a lesser extent, by normal family migrations and local gang genesis. A street gang can be eradicated in any one city or town but, because the structure as a whole is based on Internetted gang nodes, fully eliminating this social cancer will be a monumental task.

Reevaluating Terrorism

The concept of what terrorism represents *vis-à-vis* future modes of warfare is currently being reevaluated by scholars. The traditional view holds that terrorism is a method by which "terror" or the "threat of terror" is used to obtain some political end. A common image is that of an airliner being hijacked by men in ski masks, whose political demands must be met if the plane and its passengers and crew are to be spared.

Today's terrorism, however, is a far more insidious form of warfare based on social rather than political considerations. It represents a process by which the social fabric of a nation or other form of political community is gradually compromised by repeated trauma to the social psyche. In a war waged between differing forms of social organization, terrorism represents the means by which one society attacks the core beliefs of another.

As early as 1983, Dr. Brian Jenkins of RAND wrote that "[t]errorists are primitive psychological warriors in an information war."[11] It is not surprising, then, that the disorganized criminal actions of street gangs are wreaking "social terrorism" in their areas of operation, as McBride suggests. These gangs are systematically eradicating the older social fabric in their territories and replacing it with their competing form of social organization. In essence, environmental modification is taking place.

The Implications

Of all the domestic concerns related to street gangs, probably the one that should be most closely watched is the interrelationship of these gangs to the U.S. military. Street gang members with military training would bring a whole new dimension to law enforcement's struggle with these criminal groups. With members having successfully transformed themselves from gangster to the new form of soldier, street gangs would take on the organization of paramilitary groups and actively combat all attempts to restore the rule of law.[12]

Such paramilitary groups would likely prove more than a match for current domestic law enforcement capabilities. With this in mind, the following survey of references to gang activity related to U.S. armed forces has been compiled.

• March 3, 1996, *Los Angeles Times:* On March 5 at Camp Pendleton, California, in response to a minor incident that had occurred two days earlier, Sergeant Jesse Quintanilla shot and killed Colonel Daniel Kidd and wounded Lieutenant Colonel Thomas A. Heffner with a .45-caliber pistol. After the shootings, Quintanilla calmly walked over to a group of Marines in a helicopter hanger and told them, "I just shot the XO and the CO. I did it for the brotherhood and the brown side. This is only the beginning. We have a hit list. The brothers have been wronged, and others are in the pen, and more will die unless they are released." Quintanilla, who has a tear-drop tattoo at the corner of his eye, had previously come to the attention of base authorities investigating Marines suspected of gang activity.

• July 24, 1995, *Newsweek:* Street gangs from Los Angeles (the Crips and Bloods) and Chicago (the Folk Gangsters) are active within all of the armed services. While gang activity has been reported at over 50 military bases, most criminal activity is said to be committed off-base. A report generated by a Department of Justice street gang symposium in November 1994 said, "[S]ome gangs have access to highly sophisticated personal weapons such as grenades, rocket launchers and military explosives. Some street gang members who are or have been in the military are teaching other gang members concerning the use of tactics. . . . With arms, weapons proficiency and tactics, some street gangs now have the ability to effectively engage in terrorist activities within the United States."

• January 21, 1995, *Deutsche Presse:* Gang members who are attempting to escape the gang lifestyle have been volunteering for military service in Texas and California. In the process, they are normally given specialized combat training, which some bring back to their old neighborhoods when they revert to their criminal ways.

• December 29, 1994, *Austin American-Statesman:* On August 25, 1994, in Arlington, Texas, a member of one of the city's most active street gangs was confirmed to be an off-duty member of one of the Army's special long-range reconnaissance units stationed at Fort Hood. On August 31 in San Diego, California, two soldiers were arrested for stealing a case of hand grenades from a Navy vessel. Eighteen of those grenades were delivered to a Los Angeles street gang and never recovered. On September 3, Arlington police arrested six soldiers from Fort Riley, Kansas, for attempting to enter the Six Flags Over Texas amusement park without paying admission. Five of these soldiers claimed to be in a Southern California gang, and some were armed with serrated, folding knives.

• October 25, 1994, *Omaha World Herald*: Child dependents of Air Force service personnel have brought the gang lifestyle with them to Capehart military housing, near the city of Bellevue, from San Diego and other large cities.

• July 30, 1994, *Houston Chronicle*: Two members of the Southeast Crips were arrested for the murder of a sixth-grader. The assault rifles they used in the crime were stolen by their street gang during Operation Desert Shield.

• November 19, 1993, *Washington Post*: Stolen military equipment belonging to the Department of Defense, such as machine guns and grenades, is being stockpiled by street gangs, white supremacists and other groups. The Los Angeles Police gang unit frequently recovers grenades, explosives and booby traps. In six Army and National Guard sites, a Government Accounting Office report concluded that "internal controls were deficient."

These incidents of military-related gang activity should be cause for concern,[13] suggesting as they do that a trend of increased gang involvement within the military may be developing. While the existence of such a trend cannot be confirmed, private conversations with numerous military officers indicate that many bases, both domestic and international, have gang or gang-like problems and that the armed services are actively addressing them.

Conclusions

It would be premature to conclude that street gang members are actively evolving into the new form of soldier developing in much of the non-Western world. In fact, research suggests a far more haphazard history.

At the same time, the gangster lifestyle as a nucleus from which this soldier could develop constitutes a very real threat. It represents an alternative form of social organization that has become alienated from more mainstream forms of society based on the rule of law.[14] It closely parallels Major Peters' assessment of "[t]he archetype of the new warrior class . . . a male who has no stake in peace, a loser with little education, no legal earning power, no abiding attractiveness to women, and no future."[15] Further, while street gang members join the military primarily in order to leave the gang lifestyle behind them and become law-abiding citizens, some of those who return to their former neighborhoods after leaving the service revert back to their old ways with the addition of military combat skills.[16] The power of their former lifestyle is apparently too strong a bond to break—despite boot camp and military resocialization.

We must ultimately recognize that where street gangs operate, a process of environmental modification based on "social terrorism" appears to be taking place.[17] This poses a fundamental problem because war in much of the non-Western world now represents a struggle between competing forms of social and political organization, rather than over traditionally defined issues of national sovereignty.

Street gangs will likely represent a fundamental threat to U.S. security in the future. To respond to this potential threat, law enforcement officials and scholars must begin to establish closer ties to their counterparts in military and national security studies. We must create a coordinated watch on street gang genesis to ensure that the new form of soldier is not allowed to emerge in our neighborhoods.

---

[1] G. David Curry, Richard A. Ball and Robert J. Fox, "Gang Crime and Law Enforcement Recordkeeping," *Research in Brief*, National Institute of Justice, August 1994, p. 1.

[2] Interview with Sergeant Wes McBride, L.A. County Sheriff's Department, conducted at the 1995 National Gang Violence Seminar held in Anaheim,

California on August 17, 1995.

[3] The migration of the L.A. Crips and Bloods has been reported in 45 western and midwestern cities. Preliminary research findings suggest family migration and local gang genesis may be the predominant factors. James C. Howell, Ph.D., *Gangs. Fact Sheet #12*, Office of Juvenile Justice and Delinquency Prevention, April 1994, p. 1.

[4] *Ibid*.

[5] McBride.

[6] Ralph Peters, "The New Warrior Class," *Parameters*, Summer 1994, pp. 16-26. For more insights, see Martin van Creveld, *The Transformation of War* (New York: The Free Press, 1991), and Robert Kaplan, "The Coming Anarchy," *Atlantic Monthly*, February 1994, pp. 44-76.

[7] TRADOC Pamphlet 525-5, *Force XXI Operations: A Concept for the Evolution of Full-Dimensional Operations for the Strategic Army of the Early Twenty-First Century*, 1 August 1994, pp. 2-4.

[8] Tony Perry, "Getting Tough on Teenage Pregnancies," *Los Angeles Times*, January 7, 1996, p. A21.

[9] TRADOC Pamphlet 525-5., pp. 2-8 to 2-9.

[10] See Robert J. Bunker, Ph.D., "Internetted Structures and C2 Nodes," *Military Intelligence*, April-June 1996.

[11] Brian Michael Jenkins, *New Modes of Conflict*, R-3009-DNA. (Santa Monica, CA: RAND, June 1983), p. 10.

[12] We must also start collecting data on preemptive attacks directed toward police substations such as those that took place in Los Angeles. See "Gang is Blamed in Police Office Bombing," *Los Angeles Times*, Saturday, July 1, 1995, p. 13.

[13] Gang involvement with police forces may also be taking place. See "Chicago's Street Gangs Infiltrate Police Ranks," *Los Angeles Times*, Sunday, October 8, 1995, p. A16.

[14] Other Western industrialized countries are also being affected by such societal conflict. In France, many housing projects, known as *banlieues*, have become "virtual no-go areas for the police." "France: Burning 'burbs," *The Economist*, January 27, 1996, p. 42.

[15] Peters, p. 17.

[16] Although very few, if any, gang members are currently going into the services specifically to learn tactics or steal weapons, it is important to note that members of paramilitary groups such as the Provisional Irish Republican Army entered the British armed forces specifically to gain combat skills. If this should begin to take place with street gang members, we will have an entirely new problem on our hands.

[17] One method of combating this process is through the concept of "defensible space"—a major component of Crime Prevention Through Environmental Design (CPTED). See Jacob R. Clark, "LEN Salutes Its 1995 Man of the Year, Architect and Urban Planner Oscar Newman," *Law Enforcement News*, December 31, 1995, p. 1.

Article 30

STATES REVAMPING LAWS ON JUVENILES AS FELONIES SOAR

YOUTHS TRIED AS ADULTS

But Some Critics Say Changes in Justice System Fail to Enhance Public Safety

FOX BUTTERFIELD

In the most drastic changes to the juvenile justice system since the founding of the first family court a century ago, almost all 50 states have overhauled their laws in the past two years, allowing more youths to be tried as adults and scrapping longtime protections like the confidentiality of juvenile court proceedings.

The main thrust of the new laws is to get more juveniles into the adult criminal justice system, where they will presumably serve longer sentences under more punitive conditions.

Proponents of the changes say that getting tough with teen-agers is the only way to stop the epidemic of juvenile crime. Over the past decade, for example, arrest rates for homicides committed by 14- to 17-year-olds have more than tripled. And with the number of teen-agers projected to increase by 20 percent over the next decade, many criminologists expect a new surge in crime.

"The thinking behind the juvenile court, that everything be done in the best interest of the child, is from a bygone era," said Patricia L. West, director of the Virginia Department of Juvenile Justice, which was created by the State Legislature in April.

While the original juvenile court, established in Chicago in 1899, was intended to deal with miscreants who might throw a rock through a shop-keeper's window, "now we have juveniles committing violent repeat crimes no one ever anticipated," Ms. West said.

So Virginia has adjusted its thinking, she said, making issues of public safety and victims' rights as important as protecting the interest of the child.

Among the changes in Virginia's new law, which parallels those adopted recently in many other states, are provisions requiring any child 14 or older who is charged with murder to be tried as an adult.

The law also gives prosecutors and judges greatly expanded authority to transfer other juveniles into adult courts for crimes that include armed robbery and burglary.

And, in a sharp departure from a century of practices intended to protect youths, juvenile court proceedings in felony cases will now be open to the public, juveniles will be finger-printed, and their records will no longer be expunged.

In New York, Gov. George E. Pataki is pushing to increase the minimum sentences for many juvenile offenders, to transfer all 16-year-olds in detention centers run by the State Division for Youth to adult prisons and to sharply increase sentences for youths convicted of a second felony.

Critics say the political leaders and others clamoring for these measures are endangering children and are unaware of the consequences.

"We are stepping down a very grim path toward eliminating childhood," said Lisa Greer, an official of

176 From *The New York Times*, May 12, 1996, p. 1, 24. © 1996 by The New York Times Company. Reprinted by permission.

30. States Revamping Laws on Juveniles

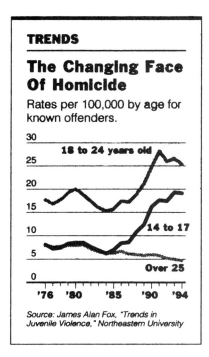

TRENDS

The Changing Face Of Homicide

Rates per 100,000 by age for known offenders.

Source: James Alan Fox, "Trends in Juvenile Violence," Northeastern University

the Los Angeles County Public Defender's Office who is a member of a state panel studying ways to overhaul the juvenile justice system in California. There are now several bills before the California Legislature that would at least double or triple the number of young people who could be tried as adults.

Howard Snyder, director of systems research for the National Center for Juvenile Justice in Pittsburgh, said, "The interesting thing is that these people yelling to put more kids into the adult system seem to be forgetting that they have been yelling that the adult prison system is a failure and is letting too many criminals out."

Barry Krinsberg, president of the National Council on Crime and Delinquency in San Francisco, said, "What we are really frightened about is guns, but instead of launching a war against guns we are launching a war against kids."

What is disturbing, he said, is that the public is trying to lower the age of adulthood rather than see what is happening as a failure of society.

Because the changes in juvenile laws are happening so fast, with some states altering their statutes almost every year, there are no national data on the total number of juveniles tried and incarcerated as adults, Mr. Snyder said.

But a new study of juvenile offenders tried in adult courts in Florida found that those sentenced to adult prisons reverted to a life of crime more quickly after they were released, and committed more crimes and more serious crimes, than those in juvenile institutions.

"Over all, the results suggest that transfer in Florida has had little deterrent value," wrote the authors, who include Donna Bishop and Charles Frazier, professors at the University of Florida. Nor, the authors concluded, has trying juveniles in adult courts "produced any incapacitative benefits that enhance public safety."

The study's findings are similar to those of a report that compared the records of 15- and 16-year-olds charged with robbery and burglary from Newark and Paterson, N.J., and Brooklyn and Queens. Under state law, the teen-agers in New Jersey were treated as juveniles while those in New York were treated as adults.

The survey found that offenders in both states were incarcerated for equal amounts of time, so that the juvenile court system was no more lenient than the adult courts, said Prof. Jeffrey Fagan, the author of the study and director of the Center for Violence Research and Prevention at the Columbia University School of Public Health.

More important, Professor Fagan said, he also found that the youths sentenced as juveniles in New Jersey "were significantly less likely to be re-arrested than those sentenced as adults" in New York.

"So it seemed that locking kids up as adults increases their propensity for offending, rather than lessening it," he said.

One reason being incarcerated in adult prisons may lead to worse outcomes, the professor suggested, is that youthful offenders suffer "contagion effects" from being housed with older, more hardened criminals. Another reason is that adult prisons tend to have fewer treatment services, like psychological counseling or job training programs.

Professor Fagan believes that incarcerating juveniles in adult prisons has another serious drawback: the dangers to the young people confined there.

On April 25, for example, a 17-year-old black youth, Damico Watkins, who was serving a 7-to-25-year sentence for acting as the lookout in a botched robbery of a pizza shop, was stabbed to death in an Ohio adult prison near Columbus by members of a white supremacist group.

His mother, Kimberly Watkins, has filed a $100 million wrongful death lawsuit against the prison, charging that the guards did not do enough to protect her son from the adult inmates.

A case that both proponents of the tough new laws and their critics agree may be a turning point in the debate is that of the 6-year-old-boy charged with attempted murder last month in Richmond, Calif., after being accused of dumping a neighbor's newborn baby out of its bassinet and beating it nearly to death. If the infant dies, the 6-year-old could be charged with murder.

"This case is a metaphor for the whole demand to eliminate childhood," said Mr. Krisberg of the National Council on Crime and Delinquency.

The incident is fraught with significance, he said, because under English common law children under the age of 7 could not be charged with the commission of a crime, and those from 7 to 14 were protected by a "presumption of infancy," a belief that they were too young to have a criminal intent.

American reformers in the 19th century tried a series of experiments to make the treatment of juveniles more humane, first by creating "houses of refuge" to separate youthful delinquents from adult prisoners, and later by establishing an independent juvenile court system.

The first juvenile court, created by the social worker Jane Addams,

5. JUVENILE JUSTICE

OVERVIEW

Changing Juvenile Laws

Fourty-four states have changed their juvenile laws in the past two years, or are debating changes currently in their legislatures.

KEY TO TYPES OF CHANGES IN LAWS

A TRANSFERRING JUVENILES TO THE ADULT COURT SYSTEM This covers three types of specific changes: 1, where the legislature has mandated that certain types of crimes automatically be transferred to adult court; 2, judicial waiver, where judges have the right to transfer youths; 3, prosecutorial discretion, where prosecutors can determine which youths to send to adult courts.

F FINGERPRINTING Allowing juveniles to be fingerprinted.

O OPENING JUVENILE COURT Opening court proceedings to the public or opening juvenile records to the public or selected law enforcement authorities.

P PARENTAL RESPONSIBILITY New laws forcing parents to take responsibility for the crimes of their children, sometimes paying fines or making restitution.

V VICTIMS' RIGHTS Extending victims' rights to juvenile courts. (Making sure victims get to sit in on juvenile court sessions or be notified of results, or in some cases to be paid restitution.

3 THREE STRIKES Equivalents of the "three strikes and you're out" laws, only in these cases it is three strikes and you are an adult.

STATE	CHANGES				STATE	CHANGES			
Alaska	A				Missouri	A	F	P V	
Arizona	A		P V		Montana*				
Arkansas	A		P		Nevada	A	O		
California	A	O	V		New Hampshire	A	O P		
Colorado	A		P		New Jersey	A			
Connecticut	A F	O			New York	A			
Delaware	A				New Mexico	A			
Florida	A	O	P	3	North Dakota	A	O P V		
Georgia		O			Ohio	A	O		
Hawaii		O			Oklahoma*				
Idaho	A F	O	P		Oregon	A F	P		
Illinois	A	O	P		Pennsylvania	F	O		
Indiana	A	O	P		Rhode Island		P		
Iowa	A F				South Carolina	A			
Kansas*					Tennessee	A			
Kentucky	A	O	P V		Texas	A F		3	
Louisiana	A	O	P		Utah	A			
Maine			V		Vermont	A	F P		
Maryland	A F				Virginia	A F	O	V	
Massachusetts	A				West Virginia	A	O		
Minnesota	A				Washington*				
Mississippi	A				Wisconsin	A			

*States making changes other than those listed.

Source: National Conference of State Legislatures

was designed to be a civil rather than a criminal court, and the accused were to be defined less by their offenses than by their youth. Children were thought to be still susceptible to rehabilitation, and the judges were to act informally, serving like doctors, to dispense the right treatment for the offender rather than punishment.

Now legislators are rushing to make sure juveniles receive the maximum punishment, turning the juvenile court system upside down.

"I'm not interested in legislating out childhood," said Gil Garcetti, the Los Angeles County District Attorney, who backs a bill now being considered by the California Legislature that would automatically transfer juveniles to adult court for serious crimes like murder.

"My concern is that juvenile crime has been rising unacceptably fast," Mr. Garcetti added, "and kids learn they can get away with it because there is no real punishment for the first few crimes."

Perhaps the most sweeping changes were instituted in Florida in 1994. Prosecutors now have the authority on their own to try juveniles as young as 14 as adults, and delinquents with three previous convictions are automatically tried as adults.

Moreover, judges have the authority to confine high-risk juveniles in temporary detention centers indefinitely until a place becomes available in a regular secure institution.

One result is that Florida is now sending more juveniles to adult courts than all the other states combined, some 7,000 cases last year, said Henry George White, executive director of the Florida Juvenile Justice Advisory Board.

But at the same time, Mr. White said, some of the temporary detention centers are now at a 200 percent of capacity, and the state is forced to let more young people out sooner, and with less treatment, than the law intended.

"At a cost of $93 a day" Mr. White said, "it would be cheaper just to put a kid in a hotel or send him to Harvard for a year."

Ultimately, critics of the new laws believe, these high costs may force a further revision, proving that there are cheaper and more effective alternatives to incarceration.

"The real driving force is money," said Mr. Snyder, of the National Center for Juvenile Justice. "We can no longer afford the luxury of incarceration."

The search for a proper punishment

Psychologists add fuel to the debate over whether young offenders should be tried as adults.

Randall Edwards

Randall Edwards is a freelance writer in Columbus, Ohio.

The newspaper headlines in a single week in September illustrate the reasons behind the public alarm over violent youths. A district attorney in Boston was slain in what was an apparent gang-ordered assassination. A 17-year-old Washington, D.C., boy was killed when a man he tried to rob at gunpoint wrested away the teen's handgun and shot him.

And even in a tranquil, rural community in Texas, 11 children between the ages of 8 and 14 clubbed a quarter horse to death, and some of them laughed and boasted when police arrested them at school.

Such reports have sparked a landslide of tougher juvenile crime laws. Many state legislatures have stiffened penalties for juvenile offenders and lowered the age at which adolescents can be tried as adults.

But many psychologists say that incarcerating children, in juvenile jails or adult prisons, fails to reduce juvenile crime. They warn that warehousing delinquent youth bleeds money from rehabilitation and treatment pro-

5. JUVENILE JUSTICE

grams that could more effectively prevent crime.

"Most violent acts [involving teen-agers] are acts of passion, and this notion that increasing the severity of the punishment will have an impact on crime is nonsense."

Arnold Goldstein, PhD
Syracuse University

"It's a valueless step taken solely for political showmanship," said psychologist Arnold Goldstein, PhD, director of the Center for Research on Aggression at Syracuse University. "Most violent acts [involving teen-agers] are acts of passion, and this notion that increasing the severity of the punishment will have an impact on crime is nonsense."

Criminals are younger

Statistics confirm the growth in juvenile crime, said John Reid, PhD, a psychologist at the Oregon Social Learning Center in Eugene. Ten years ago, defendants in homicide cases averaged between ages 20 and 25. Today, defendants are typically ages 15 to 20, he said.

State lawmakers have responded to public fears about this trend. Ohio, Colorado and Texas are softening the restrictions on trying juveniles as adults and sending them to adult prisons. Last year the Florida state legislature approved a juvenile crime bill that allows children to be shifted to the adult system at age 15. Georgia has dropped the age to 13. Some states have eliminated age restrictions entirely. And many are spending more on prison cells and less on early intervention, family counseling and treatment.

While Reid agrees that kids who kill should be locked up, he predicts that the thousands of juveniles being sent to adult prisons for, say, drug-trafficking or property crimes, may actually become more entangled in deviant behavior.

"You'll keep the violent kids off the street, but you'll also put many in jail who are not a threat," he said. Instead of rehabilitation, those juveniles will be exposed to deviant peer groups and become more entrenched in the criminal community, he said.

Treatment is more effective

An ongoing psychological study indicates that treatment programs may more effectively rehabilitate juveniles than traditional forms of incarceration.

Patricia Chamberlain, PhD, a psychologist and clinical director of Oregon's Social Learning Center, is in the final year of a five-year study funded by the National Institute of Mental Health. The project involves 80 children, ages 12 to 17, each of whom has 14 or more criminal convictions. The children have been placed in two different types of treatment situations.

Some are housed in traditional group homes, while others are placed with families in a program known as treatment foster care. The first group receives group therapy, while the foster care homes provide intensive supervision and individual treatment. The youth in the latter program are isolated from their peer group, earn privileges for good behavior and punishment when they violate the rules.

Compared to the subjects in group care, the children in treatment foster care run away less, are placed in detention less often and experience fewer mental problems, Chamberlian said.

"The problem with group placements is the power of the peer culture and the influence the kids have over each other," she said. "The children in foster care, in terms of their own self-reporting of psychiatric problems, seem to be happier and function better in families than they do in group situations."

Also, treatment foster care costs the state $76 per day for each child, compared to $118 a day to house children in the MacLaren School, Oregon's largest "training school," Chamberlain said.

An early start

Juvenile offenders in their late teens who have a progressive series of increasingly serious offenses probably cannot be rehabilitated in the limited time before they reach 21, the age when most juvenile prison systems must release inmates, said psychologist Solomon M. Fulero, PhD, JD, who heads the Center for Forensic Psychiatry in Hamilton, Ohio. But younger teens who commit serious crimes shouldn't be placed in prison with hardened 40-year-old criminals, he said.

"When you have a kid who is 13, you've got eight years to work with him. If more attention were paid to that side of the coin, instead of just to sentencing, we might have more success," he said.

But some psychologists find merit in treating young criminals as adults. Many delinquent juveniles are "far more calculating than the stereotype would suggest" and need to be held accountable, said John Gibbs, PhD, a developmental psychologist at Ohio State University who was recently named to a task force considering juvenile justice issues.

Although he is collaborating with Goldstein on a soon-to-be-published book, Gibbs does not share the belief that most juveniles commit crimes in spontaneous fits of passion. Through his work with delinquent youth, Gibbs has learned that many young of-

31. Search for a Proper Punishment

fenders are rational, pragmatic planners who revel in their ability to escape justice and carefully plan their crimes. And they know how to use laws to their advantage, he added.

In Ohio, for example, where juveniles cannot face adult justice until they are 15, children 14 or younger serve as couriers for drug traffickers.

"Knowing that they will be sent to the 'big house,' would be an added deterrent for a majority of defendants," he said.

But what if the youth repeat their crimes, regardless of the consequences? To suppress the number of multiple offenders, the system needs to deal more aggressively with first-time offenders to discourage them from further criminal activity, according to John Coie, PhD, a Duke University psychology professor who has studied juvenile aggression and antisocial behavior.

Most juvenile justice systems are either unwilling or unable to punish nonviolent offenders, he said. Children who commit theft or other less-serious crimes usually are placed on unsupervised probation, or are lost in overloaded court systems until the victim gives up and drops the case. The system instead should use a combination of punishment and treatment with fledgling criminals, Coie said. He recommends that first-time offenders of, for example, property crimes, should be forced to pay restitution and be placed in a community-works program.

Psychologists say they can't guess how the political shift toward incarceration will last, or how profound its long-term effects will be.

"I hope we can at least be smart enough to evaluate what we're doing," said Reid. "How are we going to know in five years if we were mean to a bunch of puppies or we really threw a bunch of bad-assed kids in jail?" Reid wonders. "It would be a shame if, after we got tough and slammed these kids in jail, we didn't have a clue what we had done."

Punishment and Corrections

In the American system of criminal justice, the term "corrections" has a special meaning. It designates programs and agencies that have legal authority over the custody or supervision of persons who have been convicted of a criminal act by the courts. The correctional process begins with the sentencing of the convicted offender. The predominant sentencing pattern in the United States encourages maximum judicial discretion and offers a range of alternatives from probation (supervised, conditional freedom within the community) through imprisonment, to the death penalty.

Selections in this unit focus on the current condition of the U.S. penal system and the effects that sentencing, probation, imprisonment, and parole have on the rehabilitation of criminals.

The report that opens this unit, "Correctional Populations in the United States" states that an estimated 5.1 million adults were under some form of correctional supervision in 1994. The fact that nearly three-quarters of these people were on probation or parole attests to the widespread use of these options. In "Probation's First 100 Years: Growth through Failure," Charles Lindner asserts that, through the years, probation's ineffectiveness has been linked to inadequate resources available to do the job. Adrian Nicole LeBlanc states in "A Woman behind Bars Is Not a Dangerous Man" that "the treatment of imprisoned women is based on a correctional model that is based on murky assumptions about violent men."

The article that follows, "The Color of Justice," points out that there are more nonwhite men on death row than their Caucasian counterparts, according to the numbers. Is the disparity due to racial discrimination or some other not-so-black-and-white issues? Governments are identifying alternative ways to sentence and rehabilitate offenders, according to Jon Jefferson in "Doing Soft Time." The stimulus for this approach is linked to rising crime rates and declining financial resources.

"Going to Meet the Man" offers practical advice from a former inmate to fellow inmates about parole officers and parole supervision. Mansfield Frazer asserts that the new-breed parole officer would rather keep parolees out of the joint than send them back. "Eddie Ellis at Large" is the story of a man who spent 23 years in New York State's toughest prisons for a crime he did not commit. Released several years ago, he has worked vigorously to effect change in his own community and in the justice system. And David Kaplan, in "Anger and Ambivalence," explores why citizens in this country have mixed feelings about putting people to death.

This unit closes with a Legal Defense Fund report, "Death Row, U.S.A.," indicating that there are 40 jurisdictions with capital punishment statutes and over 3,000 inmates on death row.

Looking Ahead: Challenge Questions

What issues and trends are most likely to be faced by corrections administrators at the close of this century?

What are some of the reasons for overcrowding in our nation's prisons?

Why have prisons become so violent and difficult to manage in recent years?

Discuss reasons for favoring and for opposing the death penalty.

UNIT 6

Correctional Populations in the United States, 1994

An estimated 5.1 million adults were under some form of correctional supervision in 1994. Nearly three-quarters of these people were on probation or parole. About 2.7% of the U.S. adult resident population were under correctional care or supervision in 1994, up from 1.1% in 1980.

Jails

Local jails are facilities that hold inmates beyond arraignment, usually for more than 72 hours but less than a year. Local jails are administered by city or county officials.

Local jails held an estimated 484,000 adults, or about 1 in every 398 adult U.S. residents, on June 30, 1994. Men made up 90% of adult jail inmates. White non-Hispanic inmates accounted for 39% of the total jail population; black non-hispanics, 44%; and Hispanics, 15%.

The total number of adults in jail increased by an estimated 28,200 inmates during the year ending June 30, 1994, or 6.2%. The overall increase of 301,400 adult inmates between 1980 and 1994 represents an average annual increase of 7.2%.

Probation

Nearly 3 million adults were on probation on December 31, 1994. Probationers made up 58% of all adults under correctional supervision in 1994.

Approximately 20% of the probationers were women, a larger proportion than for any other correctional population. About 66% of adults on probation were white, and 32%, black. Six in ten persons discharged from probation had successfully completed their sentences.

The number of adults on probation in the United States increased by 61,100 (2.1%) between yearend 1993 and 1994. From 1980 to 1994 the probation population grew by more than 1.8 million, an average of 7.2% annually.

Prisons

An estimated 992,000 men and women were in the custody of State and Federal prisons at yearend 1994. About 94% of all prisoners were men; 47% were white, and 51%, black.

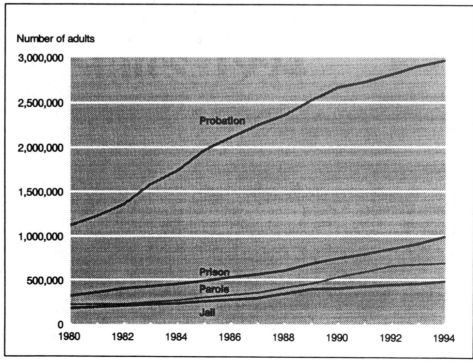

32. Correctional Populations

Two-thirds of sentenced prisoners entering prison in 1994 were new court commitments, and nearly a third were parole or other conditional release violators. Among persons released from prison in 1994, 77% were placed on probation, parole, or some other type of conditional release.

The number of prisoners rose by 9% during 1994, the equivalent of 82,200 inmates. This brought the total increase in prisoners between 1980 and 1994 to 672,014, which translates to an average growth rate of 8.4% each year.

Parole

An estimated 690,000 adults were on parole at yearend 1994, an increase of 2.1% from 1993. Nine of every ten parolees were men. An estimated 53% of persons on parole were white; 46%, black; and 1%, of other races.

About half of all entries to parole were based on a parole board decision. Nearly half of all exits from parole were categorized as successful completions. Most of the remainder were returned to incarceration, but only a tenth of parolees were returned to incarceration with a new sentence.

While the parole population increased by only 2% during the year, the average annual rate of increase from 1980 to 1994 was 8.5%, more than that of any other correctional population. The number of adults on parole tripled during the 14-year period (from 220,438).

Capital punishment

During 1994, 306 inmates were received under sentence of death by State and Federal prisons, and 112 had their death sentences removed by means other than execution. State and Federal prisons held a total of 2,890 prisoners under sentence of death on December 31, 1994.

An estimated 57% of those under sentence of death at yearend were white and 41% were black. Half of the inmates had been under sentence of death for at least 6 years.

Thirteen States executed 31 male prisoners during 1994. The total number of prisoners executed under civil authority in the United States from 1977 to 1994 was 257.

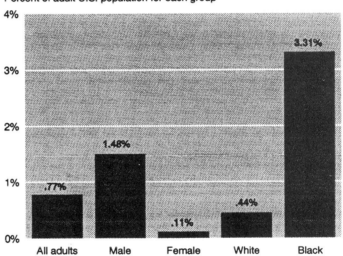

Incarceration rates

Adults in local jail or in State or Federal prison, 1994

Percent of adult U.S. population for each group

- All adults: .77%
- Male: 1.48%
- Female: .11%
- White: .44%
- Black: 3.31%

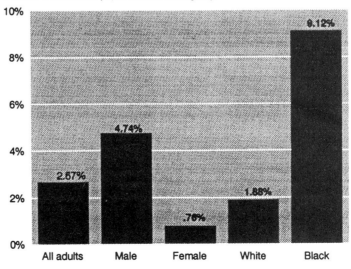

Adults in jail, on probation, in prison, or on parole, 1994

Percent of adult U.S. population for each group

- All adults: 2.67%
- Male: 4.74%
- Female: .76%
- White: 1.88%
- Black: 9.12%

6. PUNISHMENT AND CORRECTIONS

Military confinement

In 1994 the U.S. Department of Defense Correctional Council established an annual military confinement report. The council, comprised of representatives from each branch of military service adopted a standardized questionnaire and a common set of definitions. With the Correctional Council, the Bureau of Justice Statistics has produced a series of tables, which provide a unified profile of persons in the custody of U.S. military authorities.

Summary of U.S. military confinement, December 31, 1994

| | Number of prisoners | | | | |
	Branch of service holding prisoners	Branch of service to which prisoners belonged	Number of facilities	Design capacity	Percent of capacity occupied
All services	2,782	2,782	33	5,910	47%
Air Force	--	453	--	--	--
Army	1,779	1,311	12	3,358	53
Marine Corps	405	485	5	1,180	34
Navy	598	526	16	1,372	44
Coast Guard	...	7	...	...	...

—Data for Air Force confinement facilities were not reported.
...Not applicable. The Coast Guard does not operate confinement facilities.

On December 31, 1994, the Army, Marine Corps, and Navy held a total of 2,782 prisoners in 33 facilities, including 324 persons in pretrial detention and 2,458 in post trial confinement. The Coast Guard did not operate confinement facilities. Prisoner data from the Air Force were not reported; however, a total of 453 Air Force personnel were held by other branches of service. Slightly less than half of military prisoners reported at yearend 1994 (47%) belonged to the Army. The remainder were nearly equally divided among members of the Navy (19%), the Marine Corps (17%), and the Air Force (16%). Less than 1% belonged to the Coast Guard.

Approximately 98% of military detainees were men and 2% were women. Half were non-Hispanic whites; 39%, non-Hispanic blacks; 7%, Hispanics; and 4%, other races.

About 89% of prisoners held by the Army, Marine Corps, and Navy at yearend 1994 were convicted inmates; and 11% were unconvicted persons whose cases had not been tried.

A third of convicted military prisoners were confined for rape (17%), or sexual assault offenses (15%); and nearly a fifth (19%) were confined for military infractions, such as desertion, AWOL, insubordination, or failure to obey a lawful order.

Prisoners convicted of murder or nonnegligent manslaughter accounted for 11%, as did those convicted of larceny/theft. Drug law violators made up 9%, and assaulters, 8%. Each of the remaining categories of offenders accounted for 3% or less.

Approximately 90% of the 3,657 admissions to military confinement during 1994 were new commitments from a military court. The remainder were transfers from other military confinement, and parolees and escapees returned.

More than three-fifths of the 5,181 persons released from military confinement in 1994 were released through expiration of sentence or other form of unconditional release. About a fifth left on parole or other conditional release, and nearly a fifth were transferred, either within the same confinement branch or to another branch of service.

The Army, Marine Corps, and Navy operated a total of 33 confinement facilities, as of December 31, 1994. These included 11 local and 10 regional facilities, 1 long-term facility inside the continental United States, and 11 facilities outside the continental United States. The number of Air Force facilities was not reported.

The Navy maintained 16 facilities, and the Marine Corps, 5. The Army operated 12 facilities, including the U.S. Disciplinary Barracks, Fort Leavenworth, Kansas, which is the only U.S. military confinement facility holding prisoners with sentences of more than 5 years.

The design capacity of the 33 U.S. military confinement facilities was 5,910. At yearend 1994, these facilities were operating at 47% of their design capacity.

Article 33

DOING SOFT TIME

Jon Jefferson

Jon Jefferson is a free-lance writer in Knoxville, Tenn.

With 1.25 million people behind bars in the United States, even the law-abiding are prisoners of sorts. Locked into a system that spends more for jails and prisons than for job training, unemployment benefits and medical research combined, society has begun to look for an escape route.

While much of the public debate remains mired in simplistic labels—"soft on crime" or "law-and-order mentality"—more cash-starved governments are seeking new ways to curb their corrections budgets and still mete out the punishment, deterrence and security that the public demands. In New York City, where crime rates and jail crowding have forced the corrections system into the national forefront of alternatives to incarceration, the story of one young offender has an all-too-common beginning. Anthony G. grew up on the edge of Harlem, dropped out of school, and at age 18 faced one to three years in prison for beating and robbing two teen-agers. In the typical version of this story, Anthony would be behind bars.

Instead, he's at large and at "Liberty," literally: Two hundred feet below the statue's golden torch, Anthony works in the bookstore housed in the base of the nation's symbol of freedom. Amid a swarm of tourists—on peak summer days, as many as 16,000 will visit—he stocks shelves, runs the cash register, and answers questions about how the statue was built, how many stairs to the crown or how soon the next ferry leaves.

What has given Anthony's story another twist—and given him another chance—is the alternative program to which a judge sent him instead of prison. For six months, he reported to the program's Harlem office every weekday and met with a caseworker at least once a week; he also took classes, passed a high school equivalency test, learned basic computer skills and practiced interviewing for jobs. By the time he left the program, he had already landed his bookstore job.

For a now 21-year-old with a criminal record, it's a remarkable turnaround. For an overburdened prison system, it's a tiny but noteworthy measure of relief.

The nation's estimated inmate population of 1.25 million is roughly four times what it was in 1973, when a sharp 20-year climb in incarceration began. Most inmates—about 728,000—are in state prisons;

FACED WITH RISING CRIME AND FALLING REVENUES, GOVERNMENTS ARE LOOKING FOR NEW WAYS TO SENTENCE AND REHABILITATE OFFENDERS

the rest are in federal prisons and city and county jails.

The statistics, abstractly impersonal and ungraspably large, represent hundreds of overcrowded facilities, thousands of double-bunked inmates, and dozens of court orders to reduce prison crowding. They also represent the gradual ascent of a get-tough, lock-'em-up philosophy that, over the past two decades, has turned U.S. imprisonment rates into the world's highest.

In addition to those actually confined, another 3 million are on probation or parole, or are awaiting trials or appeals. When the relatively small numbers of incarcerated women, youths and elderly are factored out of the totals, roughly one of every dozen adult males in the United States is being held or watched by the criminal justice system.

"Over a lifetime, it turns out, something like a third of white men will be arrested at some point for a nontrivial crime, and something like 40 percent of black men," said Michael Tonry, a University of Minnesota law professor who also edits the bimonthly newsletter *Overcrowded Times*, which tracks the prison-population crisis and the efforts to solve it.

At an average annual price tag of $30,000 per inmate, prisons and jails now cost the nation $37.5 billion a year to operate. With the public clamoring for even tougher anti-crime measures and President Clinton backing so-called three-time-loser legislation for federal offenses, the pressures show no signs of letting up.

The best hope for relief, Tonry contended, lies in alternative sentences—or "intermediate punishments" as he prefers to call them—that mete out punishment without adding to the prison population. In a book entitled "Between Prison and Probation" (Oxford University Press, 1990), Tonry and Norval Morris, a University of Chicago law professor, urged far greater reliance on fines, community service, strictly supervised probation, electronic monitoring and day-reporting programs.

Their clear favorite is the means-based fine, or "day fine," named for the price of a day's freedom from prison. In one version of this system, a day's freedom equals a day's net income; in practice then, a convicted burglar might be fined a year's income instead of spending a year in jail.

Reprinted with permission from the *ABA Journal*, April 1994, pp. 62-66. © 1994 by the *ABA Journal*, a publication of the American Bar Association.

6. PUNISHMENT AND CORRECTIONS

Tonry and Morris downplayed concerns that criminals might commit additional crimes to raise cash for their fines: "No doubt some offenders will commit more crimes to pay their fines," they wrote. "If that be a serious risk, then there is merit to adding controls in the community for a period to reduce the risk. ..." They also rejected the argument that fines are unfair to the poor, citing a 1986 analysis of fines in the Staten Island area of New York City, which showed that students and unemployed offenders who had been fined did as well at paying them as others did.

Even if day fines were limited to nonviolent offenders, Tonry explained, they still could ease dramatically the burden on prisons. "In 1991, only 27 percent of the people sent to state or federal prison had been sentenced for a violent crime," he said. "So for the other 73 percent, there's a real possibility we could do something different [impose fines] that wouldn't cost $30,000 a year, wouldn't ruin their lives, and would actually generate revenues."

Day fines are widely used in Europe. In what was West Germany before unification, for example, adoption of fines 25 years ago gradually reduced the number of short prison sentences (six months or less) by three-fourths. In 1968, just before the move to fines began, 184,000 prison sentences were handed down; by 1989, the number had shrunk to just 48,000. During the same period, the number of criminal convictions in West Germany rose from 573,000 to 609,000.

But in the United States—which relies on the dollar for incentive and disincentive in most other arenas—fines are a form of punishment reserved almost exclusively for traffic offenses and misdemeanors. The reason, Tonry said, is "the idea that no punishment is serious unless it involves imprisonment." But if financial alternatives aren't yet helping relieve prison crowding, the same can't be said of technological ones.

Beep. "John Doe is not at home." Sounds like a message machine and it is, but not the usual sort: A version of this message has just flashed onto a computer screen at Vorec Corp., a New York company that makes electronic monitoring systems for corrections agencies. Nationwide, some 35,000 ankles are currently adorned with electronic "bracelets"; about 10 percent of them wear Vorec's version, which uses a fiber-optic circuit to increase tamper resistance. In New York, the state Department of Correctional Services has about 75 people on bracelets at a time; New York City has a similar number.

Built into the bracelet is a radio-frequency transmitter, explained David Manes, Vorec's president. The transmitter sends signals to a "smart" telephone receiver in the prisoner's home. "Typically, an individual is confined to his home for some periods of the day," Manes said. "At other times he's allowed—in fact, he's expected—to be at work, at counseling, at anger control, and so on."

A schedule of curfews and permitted travel periods is entered into the telephone unit and into the system's computers; if the bracelet moves beyond range of the phone unit during a curfew period, a computer immediately signals an operator, who notifies corrections officers. Vorec also makes a tracking antenna similar to those used to follow radio-collared wildlife that lets officers tell, simply by driving past a workplace or drug-treatment program, whether an inmate is there when required.

With a day of jail now costing $162, electronic monitoring has powerful financial advantages, said Carol Shapiro, New York City's assistant commissioner for alternatives to incarceration. The technology is cheap—

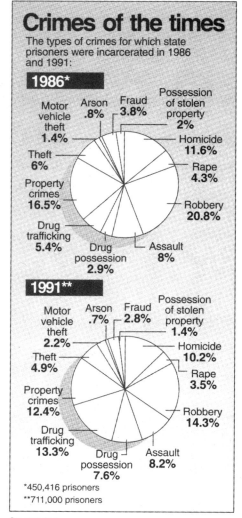

Global prisoners

Incarceration rates during 1990/1991 per 100,000 population:

U.S.	455
South Africa	311
Venezuela	177
Hungary	117
Canada	111
China	111
Australia	79
Portugal	77
Czechoslovakia	72
Denmark	71
Albania	55
Netherlands	46
Rep. of Ireland	44
Sweden	44
Japan	42
India	34

Note: Nations from the former Soviet Union were not included in study.
Source: The Sentencing Project "America behind bars: One year later"
ABA Journal research by Joseph Wharton

Source: FBI

Crimes of the times

The types of crimes for which state prisoners were incarcerated in 1986 and 1991:

1986*
- Motor vehicle theft 1.4%
- Arson .8%
- Fraud 3.8%
- Possession of stolen property 2%
- Homicide 11.6%
- Theft 6%
- Rape 4.3%
- Property crimes 16.5%
- Robbery 20.8%
- Drug trafficking 5.4%
- Drug possession 2.9%
- Assault 8%

1991**
- Motor vehicle theft 2.2%
- Arson .7%
- Fraud 2.8%
- Possession of stolen property 1.4%
- Homicide 10.2%
- Theft 4.9%
- Rape 3.5%
- Property crimes 12.4%
- Robbery 14.3%
- Drug trafficking 13.3%
- Drug possession 7.6%
- Assault 8.2%

*450,416 prisoners
**711,000 prisoners

Source: FBI

"the device itself costs us $2.47 per person per day," said Shapiro—but the program as a whole averages about $75 per day. This is still $87 a day less than jail for every person wearing a bracelet.

"By the end of this year," said Shapiro, "we expect to have 100 to 150 on [electronic monitoring]. By then we'll begin to see some significant cost savings."

Electronic monitoring has another advantage, Shapiro said, as "a real support for the prisoners—we're rooting them in their communities," where they can work, stay with their families, and receive social services such as job training and drug treatment. For Shapiro, who said she believes that in this country "we overuse our capacity for imprisoning people," the community ties allowed by incarceration alternatives seem at least as important as the cost savings. "We only get [offenders] for a blink of a moment. So we really try to work with other programs and services."

In fact, other programs and services outside the corrections department provide the vast majority of New York City's alternatives to incarceration. Last year some 5,000 offenders were sent, either before trial or as part of a sentence or plea bargain, to a community-based incarceration alternative program. Services offered range from drug treatment for addicts to job training for unemployed mothers who have been arrested.

The largest of these programs is the Center for Alternative Sentencing and Employment Services (CASES), which handles more than half the city's participants in alternative programs. With 180 staffers and an annual budget of $8.5 million, the center is practically a mini-corrections system, existing in a sort of parallel corrections universe where alternative sanctions are the rule, prison the exception.

At the milder end of the center's spectrum, its Community Service Sentencing Project took in about 1,800 parole violators and chronic misdemeanants last year. Instead of going back to jail—increasingly the fate of parole violators, as New York parole officers struggle with caseloads of 200 or more—these offenders each spent 70 unpaid hours cleaning playgrounds, painting senior-citizen centers, renovating apartments or planting gardens.

The center estimates the value of this work at about $500,000 a year. That's a couple of million dollars less than the program cost. But by keeping participants out of jail—at least, the 62 percent who fulfilled the program requirements—the community service program saves on jail costs.

The center's other program, the Court Employment Project (CEP), operates at a darker end of the spectrum: prison-bound felony offenders only. When Anthony G. was arrested, for example, it was the Court Employment Project that kept him out of prison, helped him earn a high-school equivalency certificate, and arranged a job interview at the Statue of Liberty.

Begun in 1967, the project now enrolls nearly 1,000 participants a year. Like Anthony, who completed the CEP program two years ago, most are first-time youthful offenders; also like Anthony, most—nearly two-thirds—have committed crimes involving violence or weapons.

"We're clearly the biggest alternative program in New York state," said Oren Root Jr., project director. "We also take much heavier offenders than most programs. Our 'big three' crimes are robberies, including armed robberies; drug sales; and possession of weapons."

The reasons for the project's parameters are simple: Prisons are full, and money talks. "Virtually all our money comes from the city and the state," said Root, "and their principal interest is in creating jail displacements."

At an average cost of about $9,400 per participant, the CEP program costs far less than a year in state prison ($32,000) or in the city's 20,000-bed corrections complex on Rikers Island ($59,000).

In addition—harder to calculate but maybe more valuable—there's the difference between a stint with the center and a stint behind bars. During participants' six months in the CEP program, each spends 20 to 30 hours a week in counseling, classes (at their own schools or at one of CASES' two centers), vocational training and other activities designed to land them on their feet in society.

Some, but Root conceded not enough, get jobs after graduation. Most common (but least rewarding) are fast-food jobs; more promising are the linkages the alternative sentencing center is building with more prestigious employers, including The Nature Company, Limited Express and the Statue of Liberty.

Although it's hard for the center to track the long-term fate of its graduates, Root is convinced that the two-thirds who finish the CEP program have a better shot at going straight than if they had gone to prison. "When you're in prison," he said, "it's a lot easier to learn to be a better criminal than it is to learn to be a law-abiding citizen."

The worst nightmare for an alternative sentencing program like CASES is that a participant commits a violent crime like murder or rape while released to the program's supervision. So far, center officials said, nothing like that has happened.

"We'd be foolish to be unconcerned about the risk of violence," Root said. "But we've carved out a mission of getting the most serious cases we can into the program."

But is the center possibly playing it too safe, working what law professor Tonry called the "Milquetoast" factor?

"If a program has virtually no significant failures," Tonry argued, "what that tells you is not that the program is magically perfect; what that tells you is that they're creaming off incredibly lightweight offend-

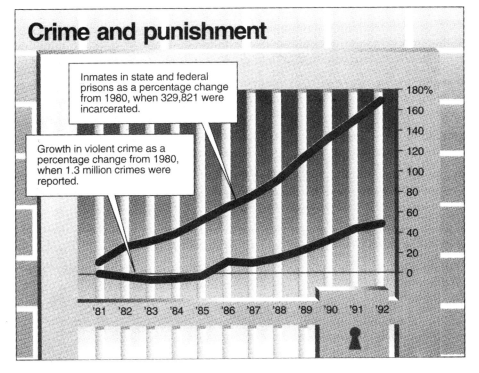

Source: FBI

6. PUNISHMENT AND CORRECTIONS

ers who should be fined and put on probation instead."

But Root challenged that description of Court Employment Project participants. "These aren't people who would be spending 10 or 20 years in prison," he conceded, "but they are felony offenders, and some are second-felony offenders." (Indeed, their offenses are serious enough to keep many CEP participants out of boot camps—ironic, since CEP participants have relative freedom while New York's boot-camp inmates are guarded 24 hours a day.)

The center's good record stems not from Milquetoast, Root said, but from case managers' intensive supervision of only 15 to 20 individuals at a time and their readiness to act swiftly if a participant shows signs of trouble.

"A third of the people fail the [CEP] program," Root pointed out. "In those instances, we tell the judges why, and tell them we're no longer supervising that person. We've worked out an elaborate system not only to get accurate information to judges, but to get it to them very quickly. We help make it possible for judges to take the risk they're taking in sending these people to us."

In Manhattan Supreme Court, Judge Michael Corriero is taking that risk again. A judge since 1980, Corriero spent four years as a prosecutor and another seven as a defense attorney. He also spent his childhood years on some rough Manhattan streets; a black-and-white photo on his desk shows a youthful Corriero sporting a dangling cigarette and a tough-guy attitude.

Last year about 200 defendants—mostly young men with attitudes as well as crimes—stood before Corriero. He sent a tenth of them to CASES. In his recent risk-taking decision, he sent Deshawn M., a 15-year-old who committed armed robbery and who faced one to three years in prison. "The reason I'm prepared to sentence you to youthful-offender treatment and alternative sentencing is that you're in school," Corriero told him, "and there are what may be called mitigating circumstances." (The main one: The gun was unloaded.)

Having leaned thus far in the direction of compassion with Deshawn, Corriero tilted abruptly back toward toughness: "You put a pistol in a man's back and stole his wallet," he said with an in-your-face intensity. "Don't think for one minute that just because I'm not putting you in jail, I won't put you in jail. Every week, I'm going to check up on you. If you foul up, I'm going to put you in jail for a minimum of two years and a maximum of six."

As if for emphasis, a half-hour later Corriero confronted Charlene E., a 15-year-old he had sent to CASES' Court Employment Project for beating and robbing a woman. "As far as I can tell, nothing has changed," he snapped. "I warned you. Remanded." Handcuffed and returned to jail, Charlene could face two to six years in prison.

Compassion and consequences—justice and just deserts: Like Corriero, the nation's entire criminal justice system teeters between these polarities daily. With the system running on overload—with more than one million persons already behind bars, tens of thousands more on the way this year, and public fears of crime growing—the balance point has become elusive.

Meanwhile, from courtrooms and classrooms and electronic monitoring centers, a message—sometimes hopeful, sometimes desperate—is emerging: There is an alternative.

Article 34

GOING TO MEET THE MAN

Mansfield B. Frazier

You always walk into the office with your fists balled up; you don't want to be there.

You've stepped off your time—had someone looking over your shoulder 24-7 for X number of years—and now you have to report to someone else, who is going to continue to look over your shoulder for X more years. The only other option was to turn down parole and remain in prison—which didn't seem like too much of an option at the time. Sure, there are some tough guys who tell the parole board that they'll "bring it to the door," but there aren't that many of those types left around anymore; you wanted out.

When you got busted and sentenced, that he will be dressed in a black suit with a black shirt and tie, with one of those goddam handcuff tie tacks, and a monocle in one eye. He'll stand, rhythmically slapping a riding crop against highly-polished black boots, with a loaded cigarette holder clenched between his teeth and speak with a guttural high-German accent. His cubicle reeks of the fear of the thousand men who have preceded you through these portals on the road back to the penitentiary. The room is lit with one bare overhead 200 watt bulb, and the only thing on his desk will be a cartoon of a poor guy slipping on a banana peel and getting butt-fucked before he hits the ground. The legend will read, "One required to violate you. They get promotions based on how many people they successfully negotiate through the parole period, not on how many violations they can make a month. True, you can draw a parole officer who can't be satisfied; personality clashes happen. But there are ways to handle this type of situation, as I learned while attending an orientation meeting at the federal parole office in Cleveland a few months back.

The conference room was spacious and well-lit. If it wasn't for us—a motley crew of twelve ex-cons sitting around the huge table—you would have thought that the board meeting of some large, successful corporation was about to

For the most part the new-breed parole officer would rather keep you out of the joint than send you back.

there were numerous people involved in the process. Even in the joint or at the parole board there were many people involved in determining your fate, but now you'll have just one person holding the cocked shotgun of revocation to your head: your P.O. This makes it an up-close and personal relationship.

And the horror stories you've heard while stepping off your bid don't help. Every convict has heard a prisoner, recently returned for a violation, tell how his P.O. was a power-crazed maniac who ate babies for breakfast and was out to get him straight off the dribble. Before the bullshit session welcoming the returnee back is over, everyone in the unit who has ever been on parole chimes in with their favorite P.O. tale. The consensus comes quickly: the people who regulate, or attempt to regulate, the lives of others are demented, nosey, twisted individuals. You wouldn't piss on them if they were on fire.

Before you meet this person who'll have the awesome power of allowing you to remain at liberty or sending you back whence you came, you might imagine slip and your ass is MINE!"

But what happens when reality doesn't jibe with your preconceived notions? What happens when the dude (or dudette) is pleasant, helpful, decent, brave and reverent? Not that they're going to personally go out and find you a twenty-five-dollar-an-hour job testing mattresses, spring for a pair of first-class tickets to Las Vegas with a pre-paid room at Caesar's, or arrange for you to be able to work the late-shift at a local strip joint—but a regular good scout nonetheless. It's got to be a trick, right? Not necessarily so.

Granted, there are probably still some troglodytes from the *Shawshank Redemption* era lurking around parole offices, a few who take perverse delight in telling some ex-con, "The only thing that's going to beat you back to prison will be the headlights on the fuckin' bus!" but those types are—thankfully—few and far between nowadays.

For the most part the new-breed parole officer would rather keep you out of the joint than send you back—if for no other reason than all the paperwork jump off. I was almost expecting some mini-skirted little thing (who couldn't type fifteen words a minute) to pop in and pass around leather-covered binders with profit-and-loss statements enclosed; I felt like lighting up a foot-long stogie, sitting back and blowing smoke rings.

The parole supervisor, John Peet, soon brought me back to *terra firma* by shooting straight from the hip. He started by acknowledging the fact that we no doubt weren't too thrilled by our required presence in the room, nor by the period of supervision we were about to embark on. He cited chapter and verse the laws which give parole officers the authority to govern our movements, living arrangements, and what chemicals we take into our bodies. He then outlined what would be expected from us. It was abundantly clear that the Northern Ohio District office intended to run a fairly tight ship. No, I couldn't jet down to South America for the weekend to visit my old friend Carlos, and yes, I would be required to remain gainfully employed— or at least attempt to.

"We don't have any deep, dark

From *Prison Life,* October 1996, pp. 17-18. © 1996 by Joint Venture Media of Texas, Inc. Reprinted by permission.

6. PUNISHMENT AND CORRECTIONS

secrets," said Peet. "Everything, except for specific information regarding a particular offender, is pretty open and straightforward. Our mission, first and foremost, is to insure that everyone under our supervision complies with the terms of that supervision as set down by the court."

A few people around the table looked mildly surprised. I imagine they thought the first priority was to assist them in readjusting to society. Not so. This is where the confusion begins. Their second concern is to protect the public. For instance, if an offender was incarcerated for rape, parole officials would look dimly on him working as a custodian at a girls' high school. While they normally don't go to employers and inform them of the offender's past, in this case they certainly would. Lastly, they concern themselves with the offender's reintegration into society.

"Parole—or supervised release under the new-law federal system—is far more intrusive today than it was twenty years ago," Peet admitted. "We have more tools at our command now: urine testing, home confinement and drug treatment facilities. While most people don't like this increased level of intrusion in their lives, it allows us to spot a potential problem and take action more quickly. In the past a parolee could pretty much do anything except catch a new case and we'd never know about it unless a family member informed us. Now we intervene early on, at the first sign of a problem."

The most prevalent problem is drug use. Roughly 60 percent of the violations in the Northern District of Ohio (which covers Cleveland, Akron, Youngstown and Toledo) are for dirty urine. Out of the 1,300 individuals on the caseload (77 percent men) 946 dirty urines were recorded in 1995: 369 cocaine; 252 marijuana (a one-third increase over the previous year); 149 opiates; and 110 for prescription drugs like Valium. Not that 946 people tested dirty, some were repeat offenders; a few gave as many as five or six dirties before being shipped back to the joint.

Parole officers hear every conceivable tale in regards to how urine can be dirty without using drugs: being in a room full of people who were smoking marijuana and catching a little passive smoke, having sex with a partner who used cocaine, touching a table some drugs had been on (osmosis I guess). Offenders tell these whoppers with straight faces, which I imagine is the hard part. Approximately twelve percent wind up back behind bars, but not before intervention efforts by the parole officer.

True, parole is more intrusive nowadays, but sending an offender back for the first dirty urine is rare. Outpatient drug rehab treatment, drug treatment at a locked facility, or home confinement is ordinarily tried first. Parole officers usually try to find something that works. Sometimes they can't.

"A guy gets out of prison after being locked up for a number of years," said Peet, "and the first thing he wants to do is let his hair down a bit. But he can't do it; we test from day one. And if he hooks back up with an old girlfriend who is still using, he hasn't got a chance. Within a few months he's going to be on his way back, guaranteed."

Peet readily admits that for some people old associations and habits die hard, but he also admonishes offenders to be well aware of the do's and don'ts of their new situation.

The next biggest problem area is firearms. Some men, before going to prison, had firearms around them all of their lives. But unless an offender can get an exemption from the rules (a one-in-a-million chance), they can never even get caught in the same residence with a firearm—unless they want to step off a buffalo for the feds. A felon with a firearm is a dead-bang case that carries a mandatory minimum of five years, yet some still get caught strapped. Even if the parolee is living with someone who has a permit for the weapon, they'd still better check with their parole officer and make them aware of the situation.

Travel restrictions are another area which makes parolees chafe. For the feds Vegas is off limits, but anyone who can go to Vegas and make it back without something dirty coming across his parole officer's desk probably doesn't need to go in the first place.

Changes in lifestyle, that's the message John Peet delivers. As society changes, so must the offender. A few years back domestic violence wasn't such a big issue; it is now. A dude who, prior to going to the joint, was used to punching his old lady's lights out whenever there was a disagreement had better understand that this type of behavior today is a sure ticket back to prison. If he can't get along with his spouse without throwing punches, then he had better make other living arrangements.

"Some guys have poor problem-solving skills. I know of a guy who got a damn good job as soon as he got out of prison, but he got into an ongoing argument with his wife and felt that he couldn't leave the house to go to work until the issue was settled. He missed three days of work. Naturally he got fired, and it took him over a year to get another job half as good," recounts Peet. And the issue probably still wasn't settled.

"I don't think anyone sets out to violate," says Peet, "but too often the offender doesn't do enough to correct a problem in his or her life."

There are cases where an offender has a real problem with his parole officer. All too often the individual will wait until the problem comes to a head before speaking up, and by then it's usually too late. Ignoring problems doesn't make them go away. "What happens is that the person will come to me when they are about to get violated," says Peet, "and in cases like that I get suspicious. Is the offender saying that there's a personality conflict just as an excuse? We don't routinely switch an offender to another parole officer, but if there's a real problem, the proper way to handle it is to have a talk with the supervisor early on, not when the papers are on their way to the judge."

The bottom line from John Peet is fairly simple and straightforward, albeit maybe not what a parolee wants to hear.

"Parole officers don't violate offenders," he says, "offenders violate themselves."

Article 35

MAN OF THE YEAR

EDDIE ELLIS AT LARGE

Former Black Panther Eddie Ellis spent 23 years in New York State's toughest prisons for a crime he did not commit. Released just three years ago, he hit the streets running and hasn't stopped since, taking the organizational skills he honed in prison back to his community, where he works ceaselessly to help those who suffer most from America's latest economic boom: the prison business. *Prison Life* salutes Eddie Ellis for his tireless efforts to make desperately needed changes in his own community and in the justice system at large.

Pam Widener

The Negro race, like all races, is going to be saved by its exceptional men.

W.E.B. Du Bois

With his usual red-faced exuberance and borderline Hell's Angel demeanor, this evening's moderator, activist-lawyer and William Kunstler protégé Ron Kuby never for a moment lets us forget why we have gathered. We are in the Puffin Room, a small gallery in downtown Manhattan hung with hauntingly beautiful art created by and for political prisoners the world over, a large number of whom are in the US. The panel is *The Politics of Incarceration*.

"Just imagine," Kuby says, "that there was some sort of disease that hit one white high school student in four. And what this disease did was it robbed these young white people of three, four, five, ten years, 20 years of their youth—their most productive years. Some of them it would cripple, and some of them it would kill. First it hit one in four young white high school students. And then one in three. And then finally people predicted this plague would hit one in two. You know what would happen in this country. There would be outrage. Hundreds of billions of dollars would be spent to cure this problem; no expense would be spared.

"That's the reality of what happens when white people are afflicted. As those of us here tonight know, when African-Americans and Latinos and when poor people generally are afflicted, the system is much different.

"I want to introduce to you a man, " he continues, "who has suffered tremendously, and in his suffering has given incredible things to a generation of young people this country is trying to destroy. A man who is truly one of society's unsung heroes."

Enter Eddie Ellis. He is a tall, lean, dignified man in his early 50s, bespectacled, with soft white hair and a white-speckled moustache. He looks his age, but has the bearing of a wise village elder. Nothing about him suggests he spent 23 years in prison. He seems calm, at ease, grounded in thought. Yet there is an energy hovering with studied patience behind his eyes and there is a constant purse to his lips, making them seem like a floodgate about to give from the intellectual pressure behind them.

"It is a tremendous honor and a pleasure to be asked to speak here," he says, "particularly in the company of such distinguished panelists. Indeed, I think that we've come a long, long way for just being asked."

His voice is distinctive. Once you hear it you'll recognize it in a heartbeat, even from several rooms away. It is the first of countless times I will hear Eddie refer to himself as "we," and I will come to understand that it's a reflection of his community-based world view.

"Unfortunately," he continues, "I have—since I got out of prison, which has been about three years—a set, prepared speech that I normally give. And over the three years I've gotten fairly good at delivering it." Laughter. "When I spoke to Ron Kuby about what I would talk on tonight, of course I had in mind my set speech. And he asked me to deviate from that speech. He said that the other presenters—the other illustrious presenters—would be using all of the material that I had in my set speech." Laughter. "Which they did." More laughter. "So I'm left here with this set speech that everybody else has already spoken about."

In the last three years, the set speech Eddie emerged from prison with has evolved into at least four versions, each of which can be customized on the spot to meet any occasion. His habit is to scribble a list of key words on whatever piece of paper is nearest while the other guests are speaking. When his turn comes, he speaks off the cuff, waving the piece of paper as though conducting his own symphony, consulting it only occasionally to make sure he hasn't left anything out, which is highly unlikely.

"The title of the speech," says Eddie slowly, pausing between each phrase and dragging his s's like snakes, "is From the Plantations to the Projects to the Prisons.

"And I think that somewhat describes

From *Prison Life*, October 1996, pp. 44-58. © 1996 by Joint Venture Media of Texas, Inc. Reprinted by permission.

6. PUNISHMENT AND CORRECTIONS

"From the plantations to the projects to the prisons.

I think that somewhat describes the journey that African Americans have taken in this country."

the journey that African-Americans have taken in this country. We went from a plantation... to a project... to a prison."

THE WAR COMES HOME

The same sense of outrage and urgency that dissidents took to the streets in the '60s to protest the war in Vietnam now drives countless seminars, conferences, lectures, marches and rallies throughout the nation and across the World Wide Web in response to the tragic failure of the War on Crime. In 1990, the debate was significantly stirred when The Sentencing Project, a non-profit research organization in Washington, D.C., released a report called *Young Black Men and the Criminal Justice System: A Growing National Problem.* The report revealed that almost one in four African-American males in the age group 20-29 was under some form of criminal justice supervision on any given day: in prison or jail, on probation or parole.

The Project's update in October 1995, *Young Black Men and the Criminal Justice System: Five Years Later*, revealed an even more outrageous situation: the numbers were up to one out of three young black men now under some form of criminal justice supervision, with predictions that the number would increase to one in two in the next several years. Already in some cities, like Baltimore, the number was more than one in two.

The report documented the cost of criminal justice control for these nearly one million young black males at about $6 billion a year; and went on to say that African-American women are the fastest growing prison population, rising 78 percent between 1989 and 1994. The number of black women incarcerated for drug offenses increased 828 percent from 1986 to 1991; African-Americans and Hispanics constitute almost 90 percent of offenders sentenced to state prison for drug possession.

"It would behoove us," the report admonished, "to learn from the mistakes of recent years and to begin implementing a strategy that will insure that the next generation of children will face a future filled with greater opportunity and promise."

In the months following the report, a new war has ensued. Special interest groups bent on building more prisons and prosecuting that "next generation of children"—already labeled "super-predators"—as adults to insure that the new human warehouses are well stocked, are up against community-based organizations working to stop them before the bottom of the pyramid erupts. It's a war being waged on our own soil, and if the prison expansion lobby isn't halted by the millennium, The Sentencing Project's year 2000 report may very well be called *Slave Times*, and none of us will be able to afford it.

"Very soon," Eddie says, "we will see prison colonies all over this country that feed the local economies. And very soon we're going to run out of inner-city people to put in these prisons. And I think at that point all of us will be in some serious, very serious trouble."

As staggering as The Sentencing Project's findings were, the disproportionate rate of Black male incarceration is nothing new. African-Americans have been over-represented in prisons since the beginning of the American penitentiary system in 1790. During the period of Reconstruction following the Civil War (1865-66), Southern states enacted the Black Codes as a system of social control. Blacks who were unemployed or without a permanent residence were declared vagrants; they could be arrested and fined and, if unable to pay, be bound for terms of labor. By 1878, just five years

35. Eddie Ellis at Large

"Attica was one of the most brutal, oppressive and racist prisons that I have ever been in. There was no rehabilitation, there was no education. There was nothing going on except brutality."

after emancipation, Blacks represented 33 percent of the American prison population and 95 percent of most prison populations in the South. Black prisoners were separated from white prisoners and subjected to more brutal and inhumane conditions than those suffered under slavery. During the 1880s, the death rate of Black prisoners was as high as 25 percent in some states—even while the disproportionate number of blacks in prison continued to grow.

"Prior to 1954," wrote noted '60s prisoner Eldridge Cleaver, "we lived in an atmosphere of Novocain. Negroes found it necessary, in order to maintain whatever sanity they could, to remain somewhat aloof and detached from 'the problem.' We accepted indignities and the mechanics of the apparatus of oppression without reacting by sitting-in or holding mass demonstrations."

In the prisons, Blacks were severely punished for protesting their condition. They had no political or legal influence, and no opportunity to complain or press charges against their white jailers. They lived with the constant threat and fear of lynching. Black prisoners were frequently taken from jails and hanged with the support and assistance of law enforcement officials.

In the late '50s, mirroring the attitudes and activities in the communities, black prisoners began to protest segregation and discrimination. Black Muslims initiated the prison protest movement, first by challenging discriminatory treatment of Muslims, and later expanding the struggle to include the constitutional rights of all prisoners.

The late '60s and early '70s saw the birth of radical urban political movements. The burgeoning Black and Latino prison population, many of whom were involved in radical movements such as the Black Panther Party and the Young Lords, began to apply their urban philosophies to the prison struggle. Black prisoners argued that they should be considered political prisoners; whether or not their crimes were political, their condition derived from political, economic and legal inequality.

Also in the '60s, the FBI began their infamous COINTELPRO operation, a systematic attack on organizations like the Panthers and other radical groups. Eddie Ellis was one of scores of leading Panthers targeted by COINTELPRO. The illegal operation decimated the Panthers with 768 arrests and almost five million dollars in bail bonds between 1967 and 1969. Thirty-eight Panthers were killed.

AMERICA AFTER ATTICA

Born and raised in Harlem, by 1966 Eddie was 25 years old and director of community relations for the New York City branch of the Black Panther Party. In 1969, as part of COINTELPRO, he was arrested and accused of killing a man he'd never seen before, had no connection to, and no motive for killing. There was no physical evidence linking him to the crime. He was sentenced to 25-years-to-life and wound up at Attica penitentiary in New York State.

"I was convicted," Eddie says, "on the testimony of two police officers who got on the stand and perjured themselves—said that they actually saw me shoot this individual."

To this day, Eddie maintains that evidence exists which can exonerate him, but the New York City Police Department and the FBI refuse to turn the records over on the basis that it would compromise national security. A more likely reason is that in the few incidents where records have been made available—most prominently in the case of Dhoruba Bin Wahad—they exposed illegal covert operations specifically designed to pervert the criminal justice system and use it to remove people with undesirable political views.

Dhoruba Bin Wahad, like Eddie, was a Black Panther convicted of murder and sentenced to 25-to-life. It took him three years of his prison time just to read through the 300,000 pages of documents turned over to him under the Freedom of Information Act, but eventually he discovered that the FBI had withheld evidence and "disappeared" witnesses, leaving Dhoruba in no position to mount a credible defense. In 1990, after serving 19 years, his conviction was reversed and he was released.

Several other political prisoners—some still incarcerated, some finally released after serving their entire sentences—continue to argue their cases. Eddie, though he spent every moment of his 25-year bid working toward his exoneration and release, has never been inclined to dwell on his own case. He's too busy moving forward.

"Attica was one of the most brutal, oppressive and racist prisons that I have ever been in," Eddie remembers. "There was no rehabilitation taking place, there was no education. There was nothing going on except brutality and racism. And it was this brutality and oppression which ultimately led the guys to rebel."

In September, 1971, the growing revolutionary consciousness erupted at Attica. At the first signs of revolt, the school where Eddie was working was sealed off and abandoned by the guards, who joined forces to repel the prisoners back through B-Block and C-Block to D-Block, where the standoff took place. Eddie was locked down in C-

"The day they took the prison back was the day I witnessed state-sponsored murder. That was a turning point, not just for me, but for criminal justice in America."

6. PUNISHMENT AND CORRECTIONS

Block, with a window overlooking the D-Block yard.

"The day they took the prison back," he recalls, "was the day I witnessed state-sponsored murder. That was a definitive turning point, not just for me, but for criminal justice in America. Attica was a watershed."

In what still stands as America's deadliest prison revolt, 32 prisoners and 11 state employees were killed.

"After Attica, there was a tremendous spotlight focused on the criminal justice system and on the prison system. The 19 demands made by the brothers at Attica ultimately became the groundwork for a minimal set of standards by which prisons would be run."

THE THINK TANK

In the wake of the Attica rebellion, a number of political prisoners from throughout the state were transferred to Green Haven prison near Poughkeepsie, New York. Most of these prisoners shared a background of political activism and consciousness raising, and they were concerned with trying to make sense of the prison experience: what they were doing there, what the purpose of prison was, and how they could best prepare themselves and other prisoners to return to their communities.

By the time Eddie arrived at Green Haven, he had already been in five of New York's 13 prisons. There are now close to 70 prisons in the state.

"Every prison I was in," he says, "I seemed to know everyone, they seemed to be very familiar to me. People who came from the neighborhood. And if I didn't know them personally, some friend of mine knew them. We discovered that we knew almost everyone in the prison system. Which seemed to suggest that the pool from which prisoners come is a very small pool."

Under the "guiding intellectual spirit" of Papa Rage, a/k/a Larry White, who had been transferred to Green Haven as a leader of the 1970 Auburn prison rebellion, and energized by the creative mindset of Senior Chaplain Ed Muller, a group of prisoners—mostly lifers—formed a "think tank" to begin investigating just

how small that pool was. They soon discovered that over 75 percent (the figure is closer to 80 percent now) of all the people in the New York State prison system come from just seven neighborhoods in New York City: Harlem, the Lower East Side, the South Bronx, Bedford Stuyvesant, Brownsville, East New York, and South Jamaica.

How is it, they asked, that in a state as large as New York, with 150 assembly districts, just 18 of them produce such a disproportionate number of people in the prison system?

"If you look at those seven communities," says Eddie, "you find some common characteristics. One of them, of course, is that they're populated by people who are of African-American and Latino descent. You find social conditions that by every possible measure—health care, housing, family structure, substance abuse, employment, education—rank at the very bottom in the state."

As Eddie explains it, people born and raised in inner-city areas where basic social institutions that should support and sustain their lives are dysfunctional develop a different way of seeing themselves and a skewed world view.

"We call it a 'crime-generative attitude.' And that attitude basically says that I'm living in a society where my community has been written off, relegated to the back of the bus...and so consequently I have to get mine; I have to do what I can do for myself; and I have to do it however I have to do it.

"By the time children get to be eight or nine years old, they've already formulated some very concrete ideas about themselves, about the world, about law enforcement, about what's acceptable and what's not acceptable. And in communities such as this, where unemployment is as high as it is, people automatically gravitate towards income generation that is marginal at best, and in the worst case scenario is criminal, so-called.

"One of the first things that happens in prison," he continues, "is you become very isolated. You begin to feel that the prison experience is a total experience in which you are totally powerless. And that feeling of powerlessness on the part

of prisoners, I think, feeds a feeling of powerfulness on the part of the administrators and the guards. And that power relationship is the relationship that dominates the entire time that people are in prison."

Over the next 10-15 years, the Think Tank's five core members—Larry White, Cardell Shaird, Charles Gale (all of whom are still locked up), Lawrence Hayes and Eddie Ellis—continued to analyze the umbilical relationship between the communities and prison. They began to publish papers, using what they described as a Nontraditional Approach to Criminal and Social Justice, emphasizing that the fundamental solution to crime, violence and drugs lies in the community and that the relationship between prisoners and the communities should be enhanced.

"It's an analysis based in fact," says Eddie. "It's a fact that close to 90 percent of all the people in the New York prison system are either Black or Latino. It's a fact that over three quarters of them come from seven neighborhoods in New York City. It's a fact that approximately 90-95 percent of everybody who is in the prison system will one day come out. And it's a fact that over 90 percent of the people who come out go back to the same communities they lived in prior to going in."

The Think Tank did a study of the New York State prison population between 1940 and 1990 and discovered that most of the prisoners in 1940 were Irish, Italian, German and Jewish, and up until the 1960s the rate of recidivism was relatively low. The reason, they found, was that the white prisoners got vocational training and were welcomed into union positions when they got out of prison. But as the minority prison population grew, the job market for released convicts shrank, and so the notion of rehabilitation was discredited.

The Nontraditional Approach says that education in prison can no longer be based in a white, middle class, Eurocentric foundation, but must be rooted in African-American/Latino value systems.

In the tolerance for reform that followed Attica, the prisoners at Green Haven began to develop programs they

"Ninety percent of all the people in the New York prison system are either Black or Latino. Three quarters of them come from seven neighborhoods in New York City."

35. Eddie Ellis at Large

could suggest to state prison authorities. Among the ideas that were ultimately co-opted from prisoner proposals were pre-release centers, regular phone calls, and special trailers for weekend family visits. Under an umbrella prison organization, Political Action Committee (PAC), they developed model programs, such as The Resurrection Study Group, that teach prisoners individual and civic responsibilities and prepare them to return to their communities committed to educating young people before they too get into trouble. The programs teach Afrocentric values, history, economics, politics, and belief systems designed to build self-esteem, enhance self-confidence, and encourage constructive social attitudes.

The Green Haven think tank was instrumental in implementing the first prison baccalaureate program in the state in 1973, and, by 1982, the first masters degree program.

"I spent most of my time in prison in some degree program," says Eddie. "And the other portion of the time I spent developing programs and teaching various kinds of educational classes." Eddie went into prison a college dropout and came out holding associates degrees in liberal arts and in paralegal studies, a B.S. in business administration, and a masters degree in theology.

"If I had more time," he says, "I probably would have gotten more."

He credits one man in particular, Marist College professor Lou Howard, with helping to develop his command of language.

"He had a drill," says Eddie. "I still remember it—A parts and B parts—you've got to know them backwards and forwards, you've got to be able to diagram sentences and pick out the verb and the preposition, and understand the relationship of adjective to adverb. It was almost paramilitary the way the guy drilled it into us. But most of us really needed that kind of approach to education, and certainly to the English language."

Professor Howard remembers not so much what he taught Eddie as what he learned from him.

"I think we assessed Eddie's progress," he told me recently from his office at Manhattan Borough Community College, where, at age 71, he continues his language drills, "by the extent to which he could help me to see that a particular author had written something that was relevant to some social problem." For an entire semester, the two studied world literature together in private, one-on-one classes. Eddie had enrolled in a course that wasn't actually being offered, and Howard had shown up to teach it anyway. Eddie remembers it as the most rigorous—20 books in 12 weeks—and the most enriching of his career.

"It was incredible," he says. "For a whole semester I was immersed in the classics. It really broadened my scope, gave me a whole other dimension—experiences I would not have gotten otherwise."

Prisoners, prison administrators, and even politicians know that lack of education is largely what lands people in prison in the first place. A 1994 study by the federal Bureau of Prisons found that the more education a person receives in prison, the less likely he is to return to prison. Yet an amendment to the 1994 crime bill banned federal grants to prisoners for post-secondary education, and in June, 1995, prisons throughout the nation faced the painful reality of commemorating their last college graduation ceremonies. The amendment was sponsored and pushed by a handful of politicians who claimed, falsely, that prisoners were receiving a significant amount of federal money that should rightfully go to more deserving students on the outside. In fact, prisoners received about 6 cents of every 10 program dollars, and no qualifying student on the outside would have been denied a grant, regardless of how many prisoner applicants there were.

At Green Haven, where higher education in New York prisons had been conceived 23 years earlier, the last graduation was an especially charged occasion.

"This ceremony," said graduate and prisoner Mario Andre in his valedictorian speech, "marks the end of a 23-year relationship between Marist College and this prison. Like many other efforts at engineering a more just and equitable society in this country, it, along with college programs for prisoners all over America, has fallen victim to a chilling wind that at the moment is blowing uncompromisingly hard to the political right."

Former prisoner Latif Islam reminded the graduates and their families that there was a time when young men entering the system were immediately taken under the wings of prisoner-scholars like Eddie Ellis and shown something in themselves they hadn't seen before.

"Maybe," said Latif, in a practiced speech-maker's voice with a hint of street in it, "we need to begin to see something in those brothers who are not here tonight enjoying this. Maybe we need to begin to see something in them that they don't see in themselves. Don't let this adversity knock us down. Don't let it stop us. Make this degree your teaching degree."

During slavery, when literate slaves risked losing their fingers—the penalty for breaking the illiteracy law—to pass their knowledge on to the others, a tradition developed in African-American scholarship: a Black scholar owes the rest of the Black community a commitment to service. W.E.B. Du Bois canonized the commitment at the beginning of this century in *The Talented Tenth*, and today, the grandchildren of the talented tenth, scholars like Cornel West and Henry Louis Gates, Jr., are vociferously keeping that commitment alive and in the mainstream. In *The Future of the Race*, published earlier this year, Gates and West explore the paradox of the largest black middle class ever coexisting today with one of the largest black underclasses. In the last quarter of a century, the size of the black middle class—primarily because of expanded opportunities afforded by gains in civil rights—has quadrupled, while the size of the black underclass has grown disproportionately as well. In 1995, 45 percent of all black children were born at, or beneath, the poverty line.

"If it is the best of times for the black middle class," write Gates and West, "it is the worst of times for an equally large segment of our community."

When Eddie Ellis entered prison in 1969, West and Gates were entering the "first-generation Ivy" Black student bodies at Harvard and Yale. While Eddie was helping to create Afrocentric programs in the New York prison system, Gates and West were helping to establish African-American Studies as an academic field at universities throughout the country. The underlying premises of *The Future of the Race* are that American society has failed to protect the basic, ostensibly inalienable rights of its people—equal access to education, adequate housing, affordable medical care, and, finally, equal economic opportunity, "equal access, indeed, to hope itself"—and that the leadership of the African-American community has a special responsibility to attend to these rights and to "design, promote,

197

6. PUNISHMENT AND CORRECTIONS

lobby, and agitate for bold and imaginative remedies to the conditions of inequality and injustice." The underlying premise of the Think Tank's Nontraditional Approach is that these failed social institutions (education, housing, medical care, economic opportunity)—and hope itself—are directly responsible for generating crime and imprisonment, and that prisons must be converted from "warehouses for the living dead" into universities that teach self-identity, sense of community, commitment to social change and empowerment. And that it is the special responsibility of those who have been imprisoned to attend to these rights and agitate for reform.

NEIGHBORHOOD DEFENDER

Eddie Ellis sits in his office at the Neighborhood Defender Service of Harlem on 125th Street. Below, beyond the floor-to-ceiling window of the second floor office, the pride and tragedy of this legendary boulevard bustles by as Eddie regales me with another breathless marathon sentence.

"So what I'm saying is that in these communities, there are these crime-generative factors that produce a certain kind of an attitude, and if you live in a community you acquire that attitude, and you begin to act it out. Now, if that's true—and we work on the assumption that it's true—then the prescription for law enforcement that deals specifically with criminal behavior, that is, the identification, apprehension, conviction, sentencing and incarceration of so-called criminals, that approach is doomed to fail, because the people who are involved with this criminal behavior are involved in this criminal behavior because of larger, systemic, socioeconomic reasons."

Looking down at the stream of activity in the street, I think about how extraordinary it must be for Eddie to be in this office every day—to be on this block—to be in this village of Harlem.

"All the time I was in prison," he had told me, "the 23 years I was in prison, I just thought about and worked towards one thing, and that was coming out."

Twenty-six years later he's the Coordinator of Community Education for the Neighborhood Defender Service of Harlem, an agency set up in 1990 by the Vera Institute for Justice to provide free, high-quality legal defense to residents of Harlem and East Harlem who are accused of crimes but cannot afford to hire private lawyers.

One of the many distinctions between NDS and other legal defenders is the degree to which it maintains a close connection with the community. Unlike most public defenders, they don't get appointed to cases, which means that if nobody calls them for help, they go out of business. Part of Eddie's job is making sure the community knows the service is available. Most people who get into trouble with the police don't know that they can call a lawyer. Most people, even if they know what their rights are, do not know how to exercise them in a moment of crisis. Eddie works to educate the community about how to respond if they or somebody they care about is arrested; how to avoid confrontation with police; how to avoid making the legal trouble worse than it is.

When designing NDS, Vera Institute Director Christopher Stone drew primarily on his experiences as a Yale Law School student in the early 1980s—not his time at the school, but the time he spent working in prison. In 1980, as a first year law student, he helped develop a program eventually known as PACT, or Project for a Calculated Transition, that brought Yale law students to Green Haven prison for discussion groups. In the classes, students kept prisoners—mostly lifers—up to date on current law, and prisoners lectured students about prison and crime in the streets.

From these early discussion groups at Green Haven, Stone gained valuable insights that helped him meet his goal of designing a truly helpful, client-oriented public defender.

Though he wasn't working closely with Eddie, Stone met him on several occasions over the two-and-a-half years he visited Green Haven. He remembers being particularly impressed with how smart and organized Eddie was at editing and publishing the Green Haven newspaper; and at how little he focused on his own case.

"A lot of the more sophisticated lifers," says Stone, "had figured out that it wasn't the first thing they should talk about. But it was rare that I'd meet someone who over time wouldn't find a way to bring up his case and ask for help. Eddie was always focused on the people, on organizing."

About a year after NDS was formed, a staff member came into Stone's office to ask him if he would add his signature to a petition to urge the release—or work-release—of a prisoner by the name of Eddie Ellis. Although Stone hadn't seen Eddie in almost ten years, he recognized the picture of him immediately.

"Does he have a job?" he asked, "because a job is probably more important than an extra signature on this petition." When he discovered that there was in fact no job waiting for Eddie, Stone created one for him.

"Most guys," he says, "when they get out, if they have a job at all, they're lucky to have a manual labor job. And those things are hard—tough hours, occasional work, low pay. It's really hard."

Having not only a job, but a job with an organization that understood where he was coming from, what his own needs were, and that meshed with his personal gifts and interests, has probably made all the difference in the world for Eddie.

As much as Stone was doing Eddie a favor, it felt more like he was repaying a debt.

"The men at Green Haven," Stone says, "really taught me a huge amount, and it influenced the work I've done in my life a lot. Being able to create that job for Eddie felt like we were giving him something he deserved. He did a lot for other people along the way, long before he ever got out of prison."

Anyone who's ever had any kind of involvement with the prison system knows that there is prison time and there is freeworld time, and the two are entirely different. In prison, no matter how much you try to maintain your connections to the outside world, it's ultimately impossible to hold onto the big picture. Even Eddie, who was known for how able he was to keep up with things while he was locked up, was stunned when he got out.

"He just couldn't believe it," says Stone. "He couldn't believe what happened to Harlem. He couldn't believe the way the kids were acting, he couldn't believe the music, he couldn't believe life in the streets."

One of the things that carried Eddie through 23 years in prison was a tireless fascination with the world—an ability to keep learning and to keep moving forward. He came out of prison convinced that community education should be based in an Afrocentric curriculum, and within a few months, he was able to incorporate it into a much broader political view of the world and how rich and diverse it is.

"It's a rare gift," says Stone, "and it's why he's so good at what he does. And it's why the connection between what he does for a job—education and outreach work for NDS—and what he does as an avocation with his political work in the community, is such a nice mix. He manages to use the connections in his

35. Eddie Ellis at Large

life—his time in, his time out, his politics, his profession, his skills—in a powerful way to advance the causes he's interested in."

Eddie's avocation is his work as co-founder and president of the Community Justice Center a few blocks east of NDS on 125th Street. One of the things the Think Tank resolved was that they needed to develop an organization in the street that could carry out the work—the research, publishing papers, policy advocacy and development—as well as continue to create innovative programs for prisoners and analyze existing programs to determine their efficiency and cost-effectiveness. Shortly after Eddie's release, he helped set up this outside arm. The uniqueness of CJC is that it is operated entirely by prisoners and ex-prisoners, and the Board of Directors, with one or two exceptions, is comprised of people in prison.

Just as the Nontraditional Approach provides an analysis of the prison population and determines what kinds of programs that specific population needs, the Community Justice Center strives to determine and define what changes people in inner-city communities want to see in the criminal justice system.

"One of the big problems," Eddie maintains, "is that someone else always gets to speak for us. The academicians speak for us, the professional penologists speak for us, the law enforcement people speak for us, the politicians speak for us, the media speak for us. We haven't really heard from the people in our communities." CJC holds forums and conferences all over the state in predominantly black and Latino and poor communities to get a sense of what the leadership, the community-based organizations, the clergy and the elected officials want to see the criminal justice system do, so that they'll be able to make specific recommendations to the Legislature and the governor.

Thanks largely to Eddie's unusual organizational capacity, the CJC has a dozen major programs in action or development, including Operation Cease Fire, their major youth program; a Food Services Program which works with disabled veterans; a Post-Release Program; a Drug Elimination Program, which works with the Housing and Urban Development Corporation to rid drugs from public housing developments; a Work Study Program which unites City University students with recently-released prisoners; a rally to commemorate the 25th anniversary of the insurrection at Attica; an educational and vocational skills program for adolescents on Rikers Island; a voter education and registration campaign called Operation Big Prison Vote, which will soon be in every county jail in the state; and their most ambitious undertaking, the Uptown Development Project, a multi-million dollar plan initiated and run by prisoners to rebuild four square blocks of land in northern Harlem into a model community with commercial businesses, public housing for special-needs populations and a state-of-the-art educational & entertainment complex.

Because of their expertise and education, the CJC is fast becoming one of the DOC's most valuable resources. Soon they will work exclusively on a consulting basis, hired by state offices such as HUD, Corrections, Parole and Probation, to solve problems that up to now have been unsolvable, largely because, according to Eddie, "the perspective has not been as good as it could be."

"Eddie is a real force for progress," says Stone. "He never stops working, moving the ball forward. And as a result, he brings people who are working with him forward. It's very rare. Not just for people who've been inside, it's very rare among humanity."

"There's a group of men who formerly were incarcerated in many prisons throughout the state of New York," Eddie says, "who made a commitment while we were in prison that once we got out of prison, we would try to do something to assist our brothers and sisters who were still in prison to come out; but even more importantly, begin to try to make some fundamental changes in the society out here so that many of our younger brothers and sisters will not ultimately have to go in."

THE REAL WAR ON CRIME

On a clear April morning, I'm driving toward Rikers Island to teach when Eddie's unmistakable tenor torrent comes sailing into my car over the WBAI airwaves.

There's something immensely appropriate about listening to WBAI New York on your way to jail. No other station devotes so much air time to prison issues, prison voices, and to the direct relationship between the street and the yard. No other station gets so many calls from concerned mothers needing advice on how to keep their sons from being arrested or killed.

Brother Shine, the station's resident recovering prisoner and producer of most of the prison shows, is broadcasting a speech Eddie delivered a few days earlier at Medgar Evers College in Brooklyn.

"Over the last few months," Eddie says, "I have been rapidly coming to the conclusion that we seem to be stuck in what Martin Luther King used to call the 'paralysis of analysis.' That is to say, we become paralyzed by analyzing and re-analyzing and discussing and re-discussing these issues over and over again. And while I agree that there is a need to share information and fellowship and to be able to feed off one another's positive energy, I think at some point we have to make some distinctions, we have to draw some lines, we have to come to terms with the fact that while we're analyzing this problem, it's getting worse and worse.

"What we have here, essentially," he continues, "is a serious assault and attack on poor people all over America, and people of color in particular: Latinos and people of African descent. And depending on where you line up in the spectrum, sometimes you can see this war and sometimes you can't. And the serious problem for most of us is that we don't even know that we're in a war. And because we don't know that we're in a war, we're losing the battle very rapidly."

Twenty-three years down, this man never lost the ability to see himself—to see us all—in a larger historical perspective.

"Some people take the position," he says, "and I think I stand with them, that from the point that Europe invaded Africa we've been at war. Sometimes it's a hot war, sometimes it's a cold war, sometimes it's more overt than others, but at least since then we've been at war. Our organization has an analysis, and we say that we've simply moved from the pyramids to the plantation to the projects to the prisons. That has been the sojourn of African people: from the pyramids to the plantation to the projects to the prisons."

In 23 years, he never lost the ability to expand his world view.

"We look at what's going on in New York

"More Americans were killed by gunfire at Attica than at any other event since the Civil War."

6. PUNISHMENT AND CORRECTIONS

Crabs in a Barrel

It's about as difficult for a young white female to get to Rikers Island as it is easy for a young black male. It takes three passes and one guard trailer just to get to the Control Building.

I exit the Control Building. Two turnstiles, one DOC bus, a metal detector and five iron gates later—I arrive in the classroom in the catacombs of one of Rikers 10 jails.

On any given day, there are about 20,000 people at Rikers. Thirteen are in my writing class. I know how slim their chances will be. When they are released, just getting home from Queens Plaza, where the DOC bus will leave them at 4:30 in the morning—after 10 hours in a small, overcrowded, stinking bullpen—will be an unlikely victory. Not buying a quart of beer from Brothers & Son Deli will be the first thing not likely to happen. Not picking up as many cracks as $4.00 can buy from the dealer who greets the bus every morning is also a low odd. The flow between Rikers

enraged. As the semester wears on and the drugs in Clarence's system wear off, he has become more frustrated with his situation, with the disunity in his community, with his own shame at being unconscious all these years, and with the unconsciousness of the men around him.

"Crabs in a barrel," he says now, "pulling each other down." He tells us that this awakening occurs every time he's in jail, but then when he leaves, his Master (drugs) takes over again. This time feels different: he finally understands the futility of complaining; he finally feels compelled to take responsibility for his own life. Unfortunately, he also feels compelled to preach it to the others, who are growing increasingly tired of it. Listening to him sermonize to the young, headstrong guys in the class is heartbreaking—mostly because they don't want to hear him.

This morning, Clarence's recitation of his epic *Master Plan*, about how the Black community has been divided to be at war with itself, sends some of the younger guys off on a violence tangent, wanting to shoot leaders and blow up buildings.

"If you feel so helpless because your leaders were killed," Clarence yells despairingly, "you need to learn what they knew so you can continue the struggle!"

and the street is constant and seamless.

Clarence, a student this term, has been one of two things for most of his life: high in the street or sobering in jail. The sober periods are filled with sudden clarity and hope, but mostly with remorse over a wasted and offensive life. He is weary, but still has the trickster's gleam in his eye. I imagine he'd frighten me in the street, and I'm not easily frightened.

As it turns out, Clarence is a wandering bard. Scores of poems, all in his head. Long, rhyming histories and morality tales. Sometimes I think he must have written the verse long ago, before the drugs took over, and that the lyrics resurface during his straight times. Or I imagine he creates the poems constantly, whether he's straight or high, but only cares enough to recite them when he is sobering in jail.

At the other end of the spectrum is Kevin, one of the younger students, a bright-eyed bundle of conflict crying out in subtle ways to be saved while demanding overtly to be killed. He's the sort of kid I imagined when I read Cornel West's description in *Race Matters* of "the nihilism that increasingly pervades black communities... a numbing detachment from others and a self-destructive disposition toward the world." Only there's something trying to shine through in Kevin. His eyes tell me that, his eyes and the fact that he shows up every day.

Kevin has a lot to say, but it's nearly impossible for him to speak. The language just isn't there for him. He makes all the motions—he even raises his hand politely when he wants to offer something—but what comes out is a muffled, halting, nearly aborted effort. Usually, he manages to get a key word out so that we can all finish his thoughts for him. Clarence, being a trickster, can sometimes get Kevin to elucidate—and he can always get him to smile—by pretending to be deaf in one ear.

An ongoing debate about victimhood and empowerment has dominated our class all semester. The men have a deeply ingrained belief in conspiracy theories and none has enough education to argue his way out of feeling oppressed and

"If you feel so helpless because your leaders were killed," Clarence yells despairingly, "you need to learn what they knew so you can continue the struggle!"

All Kevin knows is that he has no power and no voice, and that talking and marching don't seem to get anyone anywhere.

"Guns," he says. "Bombs. Blow up all—just—everything. Total—"

I wish Eddie Ellis were here. Kevin needs to meet a man who understands his rage, who has taken arms for it, served legendary time for it, and is now more powerfully able to avenge it—with his mind.

After class, moving past streams of brown and black men in green uniforms strutting in haphazard single-file from mess hall to yard, I catch up with Kevin.

"Listen," I say. "I've been meeting a lot of these men lately." He's listening. "Guys who were leaders in the Black Panther Party and who were targeted by the government and locked up and—"

"Those were, they—" he waves a hand to indicate total destruction. "*Set up.*"

"Totally shafted," I agree. "But I gotta tell you, these guys are doing some powerful things now. These are the men who are going to be making the changes you want to see. A lot of these men are coming out now after doing 20, 25 years. They're coming out committed to fighting. And they're the ones who can do it. Because they know *everything*. They just spent half their lives in prison, no one knows as much as they do—"

Kevin nods, respectful of that kind of time in.

"Yeah," he nods, "they know."

"Not only do they know the system," I say. "While they were locked up, they got educated. They got college degrees. Masters degrees. They got as many degrees as they could. There's nothing these guys don't know. They stand a better chance of making changes than anyone."

Kevin nods some more and looks sideways at me.

"You mean," he says, "you actually met some of these brothers?"—*PW*

35. Eddie Ellis at Large

City. The mayor has declared war on the so-called 'quality of life' type crime. I'm not really sure what that means or what that is, but I know that ultimate effect of it is that young Black and Latino men and women are now being arrested for things that they normally would not have been arrested for.

"We know for a fact that young truants—juveniles—are being picked up by the police, in some cases fingerprinted and photographed. We heard this morning about the kinds of abuses police brutality brings. We know that the police department has been picking up young men, school age, and putting them in line-ups without authorization from their parents.

"There's a war going on. This is not accidental, this is not coincidental, this doesn't just happen in a vacuum."

Hearing Eddie's voice on the airwaves makes me consider just how profound and far-reaching his accomplishments have been.

In addition to his normal workload, his calendar includes countless speaking engagements at high schools, colleges, churches and community centers, talk show appearances, lectures to parole boards, presentation of proposals to the Department of Corrections, and lobbying the State Legislature in Albany. He has become a primary source for local papers, radio and television. There simply isn't anything happening in the criminal justice system—and particularly in the New York prison system—that Eddie isn't aware of or involved in.

He serves as a member of the National Criminal Justice Commission, a diverse, nonpartisan group of about 40 citizens, scholars, criminal justice experts and community leaders from across the nation who originally came together two years ago to assess the state of crime policy in America. The result of their efforts, a report called *The Real War on Crime*, published earlier this year, provides the most definitive analysis of crime and punishment in the United States since the 1968 Kerner Commission report on civil disorder. It offers solutions for reducing violence and provides a set of recommendations that will fundamentally reform the criminal justice system and begin to cure its deep afflictions.

The Real War on Crime concludes that the criminal justice system is in crisis. Although the prison population has tripled and law enforcement expenditures have quadrupled since 1980, citizens in record numbers report that they feel unsafe in their homes and

on the streets while crime rates have remained virtually unchanged. In order to fund jails and prisons, state and local governments have been forced to divert money from education, health care, job programs and community development. Moreover, our practices and policies have helped set the nation back on the same "separate and unequal" racial divide the Kerner Commission observed more than a quarter of a century ago. The rate of incarceration for African-Americans is six times the rate for whites, "a fact that has much to do with discrimination," the report states, "as it does with rates of crime."

The very first, and most critical, recommendation the Commission makes is that "all states—absent some demonstrated urgent need—should impose a three-year moratorium on new prison construction."

The most effective campaign for this recommendation, at least in New York State, has been launched by the Community Justice Center. Their latest program, the Prison Moratorium Project, has united community-based organizations throughout the state to lobby for a halt to prison construction over the next five years, and to establish an "Alternative Budget" to re-allocate the $900 million dollars Governor Pataki currently proposes for building three new maximum-security prisons and creating an additional 4,300 cells.

Based on proposals for criminal justice change and changes in the juvenile justice law (trying 13-year-olds as adults and moving 16-year-olds into enhanced penalties), Pataki anticipates needing 10,000 new cells between now and the year 2000 to accommodate the new prisoners coming in.

"And we don't have to ask what those people are going to look like," Eddie tells the students at Medgar Evers. "And we don't have to ask where they're coming from. What we need to do is we need to begin to stop the process.

"We're asking everyone in this audience to join us in calling for a moratorium on prison construction for the next five years.

"We believe that the linchpin of social policy in America is built upon the construction and the maintenance and the development of this prison-industrial complex. And if we do not bring it to a halt—or in the worst-case scenario slow it down—we've got a serious problem on our hands. This is what we intend to do."

The applause ringing through my car speakers begins to subside, but Eddie is

not finished.

"Frederick Douglas," he begins again softly, "used to say that power concedes nothing without demand. And Marcus Garvey said that world history is never kind to weak people. And part of the reason that we're in this quandary, part of the reason that we're in this problem, part of the reason that we're even here today at Medgar Evers talking about this issue, has to do with our weakness, has to do with our disunity, has to do with the fact that although we're all warriors in a battle, we don't have a strategic plan.

"We say that if we can do this, we can begin to formulate the beginnings of another movement. A movement that may have as profound and deep ramifications as the human rights movement of the '60s and the anti-war movement of the '70s.

"We're in the beginnings right now, we think, of the development of a movement that will have major implications—socially, politically, economically, educationally, recreationally, religiously. A movement that must, at this time, begin its forward assault on those forces that are assaulting us.

"We say that we will begin this movement—and we're in the process of beginning this movement—from this day forward."

Twenty-five years ago, Eddie Ellis survived the watershed Attica revolt. In its aftermath, he and a handful of other prisoners initiated a wave of reforms in the prison system, critical reforms that sought to enable prisoners to make the positive changes in themselves that ultimately would impact on the communities they came from. Eddie and his peers identified the vital relationship between prisoners, their neighborhoods and the conditions that create criminal behavior.

In just the past few years, short-sighted politicians have wiped out post-Attica prison reforms and assured the perpetuation of the root causes of crime—lack of education, few job opportunities and poverty—and thus ensured the continued boom in the prison-industrial complex.

Eddie now stands at the center of another maelstrom. The war has spilled out onto the streets. Men like Eddie Ellis, who lived through Attica and decades of life in some of America's worst prisons, know how to deal with this kind of ignorance.

We need to listen to Eddie Ellis, I think yet again as the applause subsides. He knows. He's been there.

And now he's out of the cage.

Article 36

PROBATION'S FIRST 100 YEARS: GROWTH THROUGH FAILURE

Charles J. Lindner, Ph.D

Charles Lindner is a Professor of Law, Police Science and Criminal Justice Administration at the John Jay College of Criminal Justice, where he is coordinator of the Corrections Major. He has a J.D. from Brooklyn Law School and a M.S.W. from Fordham University. He has over 20 years of experience as a practitioner in the field of probation.

Professor Lindner is the author of numerous articles in professional journals, frequently addressing issues related to community-based corrections. He is a training consultant to many law enforcement agencies, including police, probation, and parole departments. Among other awards, Professor Lindner was the recipient of the American Probation and Parole Association's University of Cincinnati Award (1985) for "significant contributions to the probation and parole field."

The author is grateful to Professors Thomas Eich, John Kleinig and Maria Volpe for their constructive criticisms and insightful comments.

With the turn of the century, many of the early probation agencies will be commemorating their 100th anniversary. Over the years, probation has outgrown even the most optimistic expectations of a handful of pioneering reformers and is now the most frequently used sentencing alternative (Dawson, 1990:1). Moreover, while all correctional populations are increasing, during the years of 1982-1990 the number of sentenced offenders placed on probation surpassed any other correctional sentence (U.S. Department of Justice, 1992).

While the questions of probation's success in terms of offender rehabilitation, recidivism rates, and public safety continues to be problematic, its contribution to a perilously overcrowded criminal justice system is critical. Probation serves as a spillway for the overflowing of correctional institutions. Without the option of probation supervision, correctional institutions would be in chaos, local and state governments would be bankrupted by jail and prison costs, and inmates would of necessity be released after serving mere fractions of their sentences.

As probation becomes increasingly essential to the continued functioning of an already besieged justice system, probation agencies throughout the country are similarly facing new challenges never imagined by the early pioneers of this community-based corrections service. The probationer population has dramatically changed, so that caseloads are increasingly populated with "felony probationers" or by offenders who would have, with certainty, been incarcerated in the recent past (Petersilia, 1985; Stewart, 1986). Consistent with societal changes,

substantial numbers of probationers suffer from mental and physical illnesses, including AIDS, and regularly abuse alcohol, drugs, or both. Moreover, long-term increases in violent crimes and a proliferation of firearms on the streets of our cities, including more sophisticated and potent weapons, all contribute to the increased challenges faced by probation.

Ironically, despite the increased reliance of the justice system on probation services and the changed nature of the probationer population, many probation agencies are experiencing budgetary cutbacks. The author of this article contends that the diminution of resources at the time of increased demands upon probation agencies, is consistent with the low esteem in which probation is viewed within the criminal justice system. Moreover, in being compelled unrealistically to "do more with less," probation agencies can never really meet the dual test of increasing public safety through reduced probationer recidivism rates.

THE EARLY YEARS

The voluntary and unofficial contributions of John Augustus, "father of probation," and his small band of followers, to the creation of a probation system have been well chronicled. Based on the seminal work of Augustus, it is not surprising that the first probation law, limited to the criminal courts in the City of Boston, went into effect in the State of Massachusetts in 1878 (Chute & Bell, 1956). Vermont passed a probation law in 1898, followed by Rhode Island in 1899, and by 1910, thirty-seven states and the District of Columbia had enacted probation laws (Chute & Bell, 1956).

In retrospect, probation may have erred early on by justifying its very existence as a "cheap alternative" to other components of the criminal justice system. Augustus (1852: 100) for example made frequent reference to the savings accruable to the municipality through the use of probation as an alternative to incarceration. Unfortunately, through his own and other charitable contributions, he also set the pattern of relieving the State of the costs of probation services. At one point, for example, he bitterly denied accusations that he benefitted from his work, noting that neither the offender, nor the municipality, nor the State relieved him of the financial burdens of his volunteer efforts:

> While it saves the county or State hundreds, and I may say, thousands of dollars, it drains my pockets, instead of

From the *Journal of Probation and Parole,* Spring 1993, pp. 1-7. © 1993 by the New York State Probation Officers Association, Inc. Reprinted by permission.

36. Probation's First 100 Years

enriching me. To attempt to make money by bailing poor people would prove an impossibility (1852: 103).

The pattern of equivocating probation services in terms of financial considerations was further demonstrated with the very creation of a formal system of probation. In the Chicago Juvenile Court, for example, despite frequent judicial attributions of probation as the essential ingredient to an effective court system (Schultz, 1973), the original law establishing a juvenile court deliberately avoided the payement of salaries to probation officers, as it was feared that the cost of officer salaries might imperil the passage of such a bill (Bartelme, 1931; Schultz, 1973). To eschew the cost of professional probation officers, the early juvenile court depended upon services from civil servants, including police, court, and truant officers, all of whom were paid by their own Agency, social workers paid by private or religious organizations, and volunteers (Lindner & Savarese, 1984a). This practice was not unique to Illinois, but was also found in other jurisdictions (Linder & Savarese, 1984a), and helps to understand the proliferation of volunteers in early probation (Linder & Savarese, 1984b).

Similarly, over the years, probation was generally touted as a "cheap alternative" to incarceration. Illustrative is an early statement of the NYS Probation Commission (1906; 44-5) which cited the financial advantages, among others, of probation.

> The probation system has also another and important value to the community in its economy. The cost to the community of maintaining prisons and reformatory institutions is large. The actual saving in dollars and cents by reducing the number of persons committed to penal institutions, to be maintained therein at the expense of the public, is no inconsiderable item. The additional saving involved in the wages of men who would otherwise be unproductive is also large. Not infrequently a family has to be supported by charity while the bread winner is imprisoned.

A review of the early literature indicates that cost-savings was traditionally cited as an advantage of probation, both in official reports (NYS Probation Commission, 1907; NYS Probation Commission, 1922; and in academic publications (Morrisson, 1896), and continues to be cited today as a primary advantage of probation.

Accordingly, probation has been traditionally underfunded over the years, with chronically high caseloads from its inception to today (Mack, 1906; NYS Probation Commission, 1912; Flexner and Baldwin, 1914; NYS Probation Commission, 1915; NYS Probation Commission; 1917; Young, 1937; Rothman, 1980). Unlike institutional corrections, where even overcrowded facilities are eventually subject to the finite limitations of steel bars and concrete walls, there are no caps on the size of a probation caseload. And unlike institutional overcrowding,

often monitored by court appointed masters, probation caseloads, like watered down soup, always have room for one more. Moreover, unlike the police, probation is not considered primarily as a law enforcement organization in which there is a perception that funding is related to public safety. Finally, unlike public service organizations with a strong public constituency, as in the case of elementary schools, public support for probation services is minimal. Indeed, few lay persons can accurately articulate the difference between probation and parole, and those who are more knowledgeable of probation services, are likely to be critical of probation for being "soft on criminals."

TODAY'S PROBATION

Probation caseloads are far more difficult to manage than in the past years. Today's caseloads tend to be populated with greater numbers of violent offenders, felons, substance abusers, and physically and emotionally ill persons than every before. Moreover, many probation departments also report high numbers of recidivists on the supervision caseload, "who pose a higher risk for failure and, as such, can require more staff resources" (Irish, 1990: 90). Many of today's probationers would have been incarcerated in the recent past, and their placement on probation can be attributed only to the overcrowding of our correctional institutions. As noted by Stewart (1986), "probation departments have become spillways for overflowing prisons — an abuse of the whole probation system."

Traditionally, probation was intended to serve a misdemeanant population, generally first-time offenders who had committed non-violent acts and were believed capable of rehabilitation (Petersilia: 1985). Over the first half century of probation supervision, rarely would the number of convicted felons placed on probation exceed 10% of the total probation population. In New York State, for example, over a 14-year period ending on September 30, 1921, the number of convicted felons on probation amounted to approximately nine percent of the total population (N.Y.S. Probation Commission, 1923: 11, 20). Similarly, Rothman (1980: 108) found that "In a state like New York, a little over 90 percent of probationers in 1914 were misdemeanants and only 10 percent felons; in fact, the percentages did not vary much over the next decades."

With the insatiable demands of our correctional facilities for more space, probation nation-wide was rapidly transformed from a misdemeanant to a felony population, and by the 1980's, the term "felony probation" was popular in the literature. Petersilia (1985: 2) reported that "over one-third of the Nation's adult probation population consists of persons convicted in superior courts of felonies (as opposed to misdemeanors)." Similarly, New York State is illustrative of the dramatic increase of convicted felons under probation supervision:

> "In 1984, 47% of cases under supervision were for felony convictions. By the end of the first quarter of 1989, the felony population had increased to 54% (Seymour et al. 1989: 2).

203

6. PUNISHMENT AND CORRECTIONS

Predictably, the growth of "felony probation" has been especially pervasive in large urban areas. In New York City, for example, the felony population in 1989 represented 70% of the total caseload, as opposed to 54% statewide (Seymour et al., 1989: 2).

Although it might be argued that "felony probation" does not of necessity pose an increased risk to public safety in that many of the felons placed on probation did not commit crimes of violence, it is in reality only an argument as to the degree of increased risk. While many felons placed under probation supervision may not have been convicted of violent crimes, it is probable that many of those who *were* convicted of violent acts would not have been placed on probation in the recent past. Moreover, a recent study of recidivism among felony probationers during the years of 1986 through 1989 found that:

> Within 3 years of sentencing, while still on probation, 43% of these felons were rearrested for a felony. Half of the arrests were for a violent crime (murder, rape, robbery, or aggravated assault) or a drug offense (drug trafficking or drug possession) (Langan & Cunniff, 1992: 1).

Not only is supervision more difficult because of the growth of "felony probation," but studies reflect similar increases in special needs offenders. Substance abusers, for example, an especially difficult category to manage, are being placed on probation in unprecedented numbers. Smyley (1989: 34), When Commissioner of the New York City Department of Probation, reflected the concern of many urban probation departments when he estimated that between 9,000 and 13,000 crack abusers were under the supervision of his agency, with possibly as many as 40% of the probationer population "afflicted by one or more forms of chemical dependence." On the opposite coast, Nidord estimated that between 60% and 80% of the Los Angeles County probationers need drug testing and treatment programs for their addictions (Labaton, 1990).

The changed nature of the probationer population is a matter of concern to probation staff. In a nationwide study of probation/parole personnel, it was reported that "at least three-fourths of the respondents believe that the supervision needs of offenders are greater now than in the past. Thus, not only are the numbers larger, the offenders are also a more difficult group to manage." (Guynes, 1988; 8). A suburban probation agency, for example, reported that:

> More difficult offenders continued to enter the supervision program in 1990. The monitoring of undocumented aliens, mentally impaired chemical abusers, HIV positive offenders, and homeless individuals challenged supervising probation officers. The high level of recidivists or repeat offenders presented additional issues for the supervision program, as offenders with prior records pose a higher risk for failure on probation and often require increased staff

resources (Nassau County Probation Department, 1990: 19).

Recent evidence further reflects concerns as to probation officer victimization, especially as related to field activities (Ely, 1989; Holden, 1989; Parsonage, 1989; Serant, 1989; Labaton, 1990; Parsonage & Miller, 1990; Lindner, 1991; Martin, 1991; Pshide, 1991; Lindner & Koehler, 1992). Although some concern during field visits may have always existed, this is not reflected in the early literature (Hussey & Duffee, 1980; Smykla, 1984; Carter et al., 1984). Recent officer concern appears to be related not only to the new "felony probation," but their disquietude is further attributable to having to make visits to high-crime, drug ridden areas in which there is a proliferation of dangerous weapons (Linder & Koehler, 1992). As a result, many officers are reluctant to make field visits, which they view as unusually stressful and an undesirable component of their work (Ely, 1989; Parsonage, 1990; Lindner & Koehler, 1992). Probation officer victimization concerns may also be responsible, at least in part, to an increase in the number of officers carrying firearms (Brown, 1989 and 1990) and radical changes in the fieldwork policies of a number of large probation agencies (N.Y.C. Department of Probation, 1989).

A HABITUAL PAUCITY OF RESOURCES

During the 100 year existence of probation, inadequate resources have frequently been identified as an underlying factor contributing to the ineffectiveness of offender supervision. Inadequate resources are characterized by staff shortages, insufficient funding, and a lack of appropraite probationer services. The underfunding of probation, characteristic of so many of today's agencies, is especially doleful when one considers the chronic nature of the problem, little changed over the years. Moreover, since the truest test of governmental commitment to any of its public services is resource allocation, the historical underfunding of probation agencies is symptomatic of the low status awarded probation. In light of the chronic resource deprivation experienced by so many probation agencies, advocates argue that it is not that probation over the years has failed, but that it never had the opportunity to succeed. Because of chronic underfunding, inadequate resources, excessive caseloads, and policies more often shaped by politics than by reason, probation's true potential remains untested.

The historical underfunding of probation services, generally reflected in excessive caseloads and inadequate services, is well chronicled in the literature (Mack, 1906: 129; N.Y.S. Probation Commission, 1912: 87-93; Flexner & Baldwin, 1914: 116; N.Y.S. Probation Commission, 1915: 217; N.Y.S. Probation Commission: 114; Rothman, 1980). Moreover, over the years, a chronic underfunding of probation services remained the rule, rather than the exception. Lundberg's (1923: 4) contemporaneous plea for greater resources is illustrative of what is perhaps the total probation experience:

36. Probation's First 100 Years

the probation staff is deplorably inadequate, both in numbers and in equipment for the work...in very many courts the average number of cases handled by each probation officer runs up to one hundred or even two hundred.

Some fifteen years later, Young (1937: 14) would similarly warn that "most probation officers carry too heavy a load of cases to put into practice the ideals prescribed for them," while Tappan (1960: 552) later cautioned that "much that has been written...has little relevance to practice and little proof of its validity because the staff in most departments carries an overload of work."

Probation supervision, as an alternative to incarceration, is ailing, and some believe that it provides neither the necessary controls to insure public safety nor offender services essential to rehabilitation.

In his monumental review of the failed promise of probation, Rothman (1980: 92) recounted the chronic shortage of probation officers, inadequate salaries, and excessive caseloads, and concluded that probation failed quickly and uniformly. Interestingly, it was his contention that probation's failures were related to grandiose promises typical of the Progressive Movement, despite a "flimsy quality of reform theory" (1980: 92). Moreover, Rothman believed that the reformers failed to understand the economic and political realities of probation, in that while probation salaries were paid by local government, the primary beneficiary of diversion from prison was the State. This was because "the state government paid the costs of incarceration in state prisons, but the locality paid the costs of release on probation" (1980: 94). As a result, each case diverted from prison and placed on probation reduced state costs, but at the same time, increased municipal costs. As a result, while probtion was cheaper than incarceration, it was only the state, and not the municipality, which benefited from the diversion to probation supervision.

Finally, and perhaps most importantly, Rothman asserted that despite its many failings, probation survived because it facilitated the "specific interests of those who administered criminal justice: the prosecuting attorneys, the judges, the criminal lawyers" (1980: 98). Basically, it was the promise of a probation sentence that often convinced a defendant to accept a plea bargain, thereby expediating the process for all.

PROBATION: A PROBLEMATIC PROCESS

Whether probation will survive another hundred years is debatable. Probation supervision, as an alternative to incarceration, is ailing, and some believe that it provides neither the necessary controls to insure public safety nor offender services essential to rehabilitation. Byrne (1988: 1) argues that the crowding of probation "poses a more immediate threat to the criminal justice process and to community protection" than does prison crowding, while Lauen (1988: 33), after studying the effectiveness of a number of probation and parole programs, reported that "the evidence that probation and parole are effective correctional treatments is weak..." and we can conclude only that they might "have a marginal effect on some offenders for short periods of time." Morris and Tonry were especially forceful in rejecting traditional probation supervision, which they concluded "degenerated into ineffectiveness under the pressure of excessive caseloads and inadequate resources" (1990: 6). Similar criticisms of probation effectiveness were recently expressed by other highly respected sources (Silberman, 1978; Forer, 1980; Wilson, 1983; Conrad, 1985). Most painful is the recognition that many of the criticisms of today's probation, is consistent with those expressed in the past (NYS Probation Commission, 1906; NYS Probation Commission, 1912; NYS Probation Commission, 1922; NYS Crime Commission, 1927; Glueck, 1933; Young, 1937; US Attorney General, 1939; Tappan, 1960; President's Commission on Law Enforcement and the Administration of Justice, 1967).

Unfortunately, many of the major studies of probation effectiveness have been equally discouraging. In 1976 the Comptroller General of the United States (74) concluded that "state and county probation systems are not adequately protecting the public." One year later, the Comptroller General, based on a study of five Federal Probation districts, reported a number of serious problems in the supervision of offenders, and concluded that "higher risk offenders are still not getting the required amount of personal supervision" (1977: 9-10).

More recent studies question probation's ability to

6. PUNISHMENT AND CORRECTIONS

effectively supervise "felony probationers." Petersilia (1985: 3) found that the emergence of "felony probation" presented "a serious threat to public safety," noting that "as far official records indicate, during the 40-month period following their probationary sentence, 65 percent of the total sample were rearrested and 53 percent had official charges filed against them." Although other studies of the supervision of felony probation caseloads were more positive (Ficter, M., Hirschburgh, P. & McGaha, J. 1987; 9), a very recent study of 79,000 felons sentenced to probation in 1986 and tracked for a 3-year period commencing with the date of sentence, is strongly supportive of the Petersilia research (Langan & Cuniff, 1992). It was found that 43% of the felons, while still on probation, were rearrested for a new felony, almost half of which were for violent crimes or a drug offense (Langan & Cuniff, 1992).

Walker (1985: 176), a critic of probation services, was especially acerbic in stating that:

> Probation supervision, in fact, is essentially a myth. The supervision amounts to little more than bureaucratic paper shuffling. The offender reports to the probation officer once a month and has a brief conversation about work, drugs, alcohol, crime, whatever. The probation officers fills out the required reports and that is that.

While some would take exception to Walker's definition of probation supervision, few would deny that probation is in need of a major overhaul. Rosecrance (1986: 25) perhaps best summarizes the desperate situation faced by probation:

> Judicial support for probation services has eroded, public support has diminshed; legislative backing has wavered. Probation officers themselves question the efficacy and purposefulness of their actions, while probationers seriously doubt that any good will come from their contacts with probation officials.

FUTURE PROSPECTS FOR PROBATION

The problems facing probation, as outlined above, are serious enough to raise concern as to probation's future. As stated by Conrad (1985; 421), "in the present circumstances the survival of the idea of probation as a service is in jeopardy."

At the very least, it would appear that probation's survival is linked to adequate funding, serving both to insure quality control of the offender's behavior and to provide sufficient services to make rehabilitation viable. Ideally, this would allow for manageable work loads, adequate and competent staffing, and the provision of offender services which are both plentiful and meaningful. While it is recognized that caseload size per se, as is true of the other components of this wish list, are not a guarantee of success (Champion, 1990: 284; McShane & Krause, 1993: 106), excessive

caseloads, inadequate staffing, and a lack of offender services are a guarantee of failure.

Future determinations of "adequate funding" should no longer be based on the "cheap alternative" formula which has so long controlled the financing of probation agencies, but must be based on legitimate organizational needs. Obviously, this requires that budgetary decision-makers no longer view probation as an after-thought, whose status is at the very bottom of the correctional scale. Finally, it must be understood that probation costs are of necessity greater than ever, as probation now supervises a higher-risk and higher-needs population.

Unfortunately, recent indiciations, although admittedly limited, lead us to believe that many probation agencies will not only not receive increased funding, but will more likely, experience drastic budgetary reductions. Fiscal cutbacks will be justified on the basis of the financial difficulties experienced by local governments, although, as in the past probation agencies will proportionately suffer more than other criminal justice agencies. As noted by Allen (1985: 196), "in tax shortfall situations and inadequate public resource allocations, there is a tendency to underallocate resources to communuity corrections, particularly probation," Allen believes in addition that probation is considered to be of low-priority in the funding of municipal agencies:

> Finally, there is some evidence that elected officials are unwilling to make the necessary hard decisions on community corrections. The easiest escape from conflicting demands is to "fund-out" all resources to meet higher priority needs (police protection, fire, mandated school programs, cost-sharing welfare programs, and so on) . . .

Similarly, Petersilia (1988) found that the funding of probation agencies has not kept up with the increased number of offenders under probation supervision. She reported that 25 cents of every dollar spent on criminal justice goes to correction, with only three cents of that quarter spent on probation. Most important, she found that whereas most criminal justice agencies on a nationwide basis received increased funding over the past ten years, only probation received fiscal reductions.

Not only did Petersilia (1985: 2) conclude that budget cuts were experienced by probation on a nationwide basis, but she also reported that:

> With Proposition 13 and other fiscal constraints, California's probation agencies may have suffered the most severe cuts of all. Since 1975, the state's probation population has risen 15 percent, while the number of probation officers has fallen by 20 percent. In the same time period, the state has spent 30 percent more on criminal justice in general, but 10 percent less on probation."

36. Probation's First 100 Years

The Nassau County Probation Department experience further illustrates the funding problems noted by Allen and Petersilia, and experienced by many probation agencies. The civil servants of Nassau County, a comparatively wealthy suburb of New York City, are traditionally well compensated. Nevertheless, when faced with serious budgetary problems in the early 1990s, caused in part by a downturn in tax revenues, the County chose to substantially reduce the probation budget. It was publicly announced that the Agency faced severe staffing cutbacks, including the lay-offs of employees with years of service. These staffing reductions were planned despite increasing caseloads, a felony offender population of 34 percent of the total cases under supervision in 1991 (New York State Division of Probation & Correctional Alternatives, 1991), and the fact that "the increased numbers of high risk offenders has required more stringent standards and the use of intermediate sanctions as special conditions of probation" (Nassau County Probation Department, 1980: 7). Although public pressure caused fewer probation officers to be discharged than originally announced, the trend towards larger caseloads is apparent.:

1990 . . . . 75 cases per probation officer.
1991 . . . . 85 cases per probation officer.
1992 . . . . . . 103 cases per probation officer.

Unfortunately, because of the chronic underfunding of probation departments, even agencies that have not suffered cutbacks, fear the possibility of budget reductions. Rocco A. Pozzi, director of the Westchester County (N.Y.) Department of Probation, for example, stated to the media, that although his Agency had not experienced major cutbacks, "he feared that the final state budget could include huge cuts for probation officers" (1991: 6).

Chronic underfunding has so diluted the quality of offender supervision, both in terms of community protection and effective treatment and services, as to debase the promise of probation.

A proposed downsizing of the New York City Department of Probation, if carried out, would be even more extreme. Although not finalized, it is projected that probation officer staffing would be reduced by approximately 25 percent by 1995 (Office of the Mayor of the City of New York). Ironically, these cutbacks will be made by an Agency with a "felony probationer" population of about 70 percent (Seymour, Lockhart & Ely, 1989), and where it is estimated that the under supervision caseload includes between 9,000 and 13,000 crack abusers and "that as much as 40 percent of the probationer population may have been afflicted by one or more forms of chemical dependency" (Smyley, 1989: 34). Moreover, an Agency which has suffered from chronically high caseloads, including undifferentiated adult caseloads of approximately 200 (Lauen, 1988: 31), and where, even in a depressed economic climate, probation turnover rate was approximately 22 percent in the fiscal year ending June 30, 1991 (New York City Department of Probation, 1991). If these proposed staffing reductions come to fruition, then the New York City Department of Probation may become Jacob's classic example of a probation so watered down "that it is widely regarded as providing no punishment or control" (n.d.: 2).

At this time, the chronic underfunding of probation agencies is especially serious because of a nationwide economic downturn. In a 1991 survey of its Executive Committee, Board of Directors, and selected chief probation administrators, the American Probation and Parole Association reported that nearly half of the respondents (30 of 70) "stated that they (or their states or agencies) had experienced or anticipated cutbacks in providing services. Among the services mentioned most often as suffering cutbacks were: intensive supervision, sex offender or substance abuse treatment" (Reeves, 1991: 11).

While othe publicly funded agencies have also experienced budgetary reductions, probation is often among the departments proportionately suffering the most severe cutbacks (Allen, 1985; Petersilia, 1985). Moreover, in many instances, probation is already underfunded, struggling with high caseloads, low salaries, and insufficient programs. Most importantly, today's typical probationer caseload is likely to be populated by higher risk and special needs probationers. These types of offenders are more likely to present a multiplicity of serious problems, and as a result, usually require more intensive controls, experience the greatest likelihood of probation sentences which include intermediate sanctions, and need more extensive and expensive services.

Unfortunately, as we enter the 21st Century, the hope of adequate funding of probation agencies, is understandably pessimistic. Chronic underfunding has so diluted the quality of offender supervision, both in terms of community protection and effective treatment and services, as to debase the promise of probation. A continued diminution of an already diluted probation service may lead to its demise.

6. PUNISHMENT AND CORRECTIONS

REFERENCES

Allen, H.E. (1985). The organization and effectiveness of community corrections in L.E. Travis, 111 (ed). *Probation, Parole, and Community Corrections.* Prospect Heights, Illinois: Waveland: 185-199.

Augustus, J. (1972). *John Augustus: First Probation Officer.* (S. Glueck, Introd.) Montclair, N.J: Patterson Smith. (Original work published 1852 under the title, "A report of the labors of John Augustus."

Bartelme, M.M. (1931). *Twenty-five years ago and since.* The Yearbook. A record of the 25th Annual Conference of the National Probation Association, Minneapolis, MN, June 12 to 19, 1931. NY: The National Probation Association.

Brown, P.W. (1989). Probation and parole officers up in arms over the gun issue. Corrections Today, 51(2): 194-196.

Brown, P.W. (1990). Guns and probation officers: the unspoken reality. *Federal Probation, 54(2): 21-25.*

Byrne, J.M. (1988). *Probation.* U.S. Department of Justice, National Institute of Justice Crime File. Washington, DC: U.S. Government Printing Office.

Carter, R.N., Glasser, D., & Wilkins, L.T. (1984). *Probation, Parole, and Community Corrections.* (3rd ed.) NY: John Wiley & Sons.

Champion, D.J. (1990). *Probation and Parole in the United States.* Columbus, Ohio: Merrill.

Chute, C.L. & Bell, M. (1956). *Crime, Courts and Probation.* NY: MacMillan.

Comptroller General of the United States, General Accounting Office. (1976). *Report to the Congress: State and County Probation: Systems in Crisis.* Washington, DC: U.S. Government Printing Office.

Comptroller General of the United States, General Accounting Office. (1977). *Report to the Congress: Probation and parole activities need to be better managed.* Washington, DC: U.S. Government Printing Office.

Conrad, J.P. (1985). The penal dilemma and its emergeing solution. *Crime and Delinquency, 31: 411-422.*

Dawson, J.M. (1990). *Felons sentenced to probation in state courts, 1986.* U.S. Department of Justice, Bureau of Justice Statistics, Washington, DC: U.S. Government Printing Office.

Ely, R.E. (1989) *Report on the safety concerns of probation and alternatives to incarceration staff in New York State.* Albany, NY: New York State Division of Probation and Correctional Alternatives.

Fichter, M., Hirschburg, P. and McGaha, J. (1987). Felony probation: A comparative analysis of public risk in two states. *Perspectives.* 11(2): 6-11.

Flexner, B., & Baldwin, R.N. (1916). *Juvenile Courts and Probation.* NY: Century.

Forer, L.G. (1980). *Criminals and victims.* NY: Norton.

Glueck, S. (1933). *The signficance and promise of probation.* In S. Glueck (ed.) *Probation and criminal justice.* NY: MacMillan.

Guynes, R. (1988). *Difficult clients, large caseloads plague probation, parole agencies.* U.S. Department of Justice, National Institute of Justice, Research in Action. Washington, DC: U.S. Government Printing Office.

Holden, T. (1989). Point and counterpoint: Firearms-Debating the issues for probation and parole. *Perspectives.* 13(3): 6-8

Hussey, F., & Duffee, D.E. (1980). *Probation, parole and community field services.* NY: Harper and Row.

Irish, J.F. (1990) *Crime, criminal justice and probation in 1989.* Mineola, NY: Nassau County Probation Department.

Jacobs, J.B. (n.d.) Inside Prisons. *U.S. Department of Justice, National Institute of Justice Crime File.* Washington, DC: U.S. Government Printing Office.

Labaton, S. (1990). Glutted probation system puts communities in peril. *The New York Times,* AI, A16.

Langan, P.A., and Cunniff, M.A. (1992). *Recidivism of felons on probation, 1986-89.* U.S. Department of Justice: Bureau of Justice Statistics, Special Report. U.S. Government Printing Office.

Lauen, R.J. (1988). *Community managed corrections.* American Correctional Association.

Lindner, C., (1991). The refocused probation home visit: A subtle but revolutionary change. *The Journal of Contemporary Criminal Justice,* 7(2): 115-127.

Lindern, C., & Koehler, R.J. (1992). Probation officer victimization: An emerging concern. *Journal of Criminal Justice,* 20: 53-62.

Lindner, C., & Savarese, M.R. (1984a). The evolution of probation: early salaries, qualifications and hiring practices. *Federal Probation,* 48(1): 3-10.

Lindner, C., & Savarese, M.R. (1984b). The evolution of probation: The historical contribution of the volunteer. *Federal Probation,* 48(2): 3-11.

Lundberg, E.O. (1923). *The probation officer and the community: An address.* Albany, NY: The New York State Probation Commission: 1-8.

McShane, M.D., & Krause, W. (1993). *Community Corrections.* New York, Macmillan.

Mack, J.W. (1906). *The juvenile court: The judge and the probation officer.* Proceedings of the National Conference of Charities and Correction at the Thirty-Third Annual Session. Philadelphia, Pennsylvania: Press of Fred J. Heer.

Martin, D.R. (1991). Probation and parole officer safety: Examining an urgent issue. *Perspectives,* 15(1): 20-25.

Morris, N., & Tonry, M. (1990). *Between prison and probation.* NY: Oxford University Press.

Morrison, W.D., (1975). *Juvenile Offenders.* (J.F. Short, Jr., Introd.). Montclair, N.J.: Patterson Smith. (Original work printed in 1896.)

Nassau County Probation Department. (1991). *Annual Report: 1990.* Nassau County, NY.

New York City Department of Probation. (1989). *Executive policy and procedure 40-1-89: Field activity,* NY

New York City Department of Probation. (1991). *Staffing report as of 6/28/91.* NY.

New York State Crime Commission. (1927). *Report of the Crime Commission* (New York Legislative Document No. 94.) Albany, NY: J.B. Lyon Co., Printers.

N.Y.S. Probation Commission. (1906). *Report of the Temporary State Probation Commission of 1905-6.* Brandow Printing Co., Albany, NY.

N.Y.S. Probation Commission. (1907). *A Study of Probation in Yonkers, N.Y.,* Albany, NY: J.B. Lyon Company, State Printers.

N.Y.S. Probation Commission. (1912). *Fifth annual report.* Albany, NY: J.B. Lyon Company, State Printers.

N.Y.S. Probation Commission. (1915). *Eighth annual report.* Albany, NY: J.B. Lyon Company, State Printers.

N.Y.A. Probation Commission. (1917). *Tenth annual report.* Albany, NY: J.B. Lyon Company, State Printers.

N.Y.S. Probation Commission. (1923). *Sixteenth annual report.* Albany, NY: J.B. Lyon Company, State Printers.

N.Y.S. Division of Probation and Correctional Alternatives. (1991). *All-case report; Client data system.* Albany, NY.

Nidorf, B.J. (1988). Sanction-oriented community corrections: Sales job? Sellout? Or response to reality? *Perspectives,* 12(3): 6-8.

Office of the Mayor of the City of New York. *Mayor's management report for the City of New York..*

Parsonage, W.H. (1989). Worker safety in probation and parole. Washington, DC: U.S. Department of Justice, National Institute of Justice.

Parsonage, W.H., & Miller, J.A. (1990). A study of probation and parole worker safety in the Middle Atlantic region. Middle Atlantic States Correctional Association.

Petersilia, J. (1985). Probation and felony offenders. U.S. Department of Justice, National Institute of Justice Research in Brief. Washington, DC:

36. Probation's First 100 Years

U.S. Government Printing Office.

Petersilia, J. (1988). Probation reform in J. Scott (ed.), *Controversial Issues in Crime and Justice*. Newbury Park, CA: Sage.

Pozzi, R.A. (1991, March 3). Probation officers adapt to a changing caseload. *The New York Times, Westchester Weekly*, 1, 6.

Pshide, W. (1991). Probation officer field safety in the 90's. *Perspectives*, 15(1): 26-27.

Reeves, R. (1991). A report of the 1991 fiscal survey results: Down, but not out. *Perspectives*, 15(4): 11-12.

Rosecrance, J. (1986). Probation supervision: Mission impossible. *Federal Probation*, 50(1): 25-31.

Rothman, D.J. (1980). *Conscience and convenience: The asylum and its alternatives in progressive America*. Boston, Mass.: Little, Brown.

Schultz, J.L. (1973). The cycle of juvenile court history. *Crime and Delinquency*, 19(4): 457-476.

Seymour, J., Lockhart, P., & Ely, R. (1989). *Felonization of the probation caseload in New York State*. Albany, NY.: N.Y.S. Division of Probation and Correctional Alternatives.

Silberman, C.E. (1978). *Criminal violence, criminal justice*. New York, NY: Random House.

Smykla, J.O. (1984). *Probation and parole: Crime control in the community*, NY: Macmillan.

Smyley, K.T. (1989). *The new probation*. *Perspectives* 13(2): 34-36.

Stewart, J.K. (1986). Felony probation: An ever increasing risk. *Correction Today*, 48(8): 94-102.

Serant, C. (1989). Dangerous drug visits. *New York Daily News*, 49.

Tappan, P.W. (1960). *Crime, justice and correction*. NY: McGraw-Hill.

The President's Commission on Law Enforcement and Administration of Justice. (1967). *Task force report: Juvenile delinquency and youth crime*. Washington, DC: U.S. Government Printing Office.

U.S. Attorney General. (1939). *Survey of release procedures: Vol. 2: Probation*. Washington, DC: U.S. Government Printing Office.

U.S. Department of Justice. (1992). *National Update*. Office of Justice Programs, Bureau of Justice Statistics. Vol. 1(3), Washington, DC: U.S. Government Printing Office.

Walker, S. (1985). *Sense and Nonsense about Crime*. Monterey, CA: Brooks/Cole.

Young, P. (1937). *Social treatment in probation and delinquency*, NY: McGraw-Hill.

Article 37

A Woman Behind Bars Is Not a Dangerous Man

More women than ever are doing time in prison, and they're beginning to create a world all their own—one without weight lifting, gangs and violence.

Adrian Nicole LeBlanc

Adrian Nicole LeBlanc is a contributing writer for the Magazine. Her last article was "Gang Girl."

ON AN AIRLESS THURSDAY AT THE CENTRAL California Women's Facility, the largest women's prison in the nation, a 40-foot tractor-trailer parks beneath the awful sun. It carries 54 prisoners from Los Angeles County.

Although it's still morning, the women already look ransacked. They have been returned to their own clothes for the county-to-state transfer, which means they are wearing whatever they had on at the time of their arrest. Without easy access to drugs, the addicts among them have returned to eating, and with the added weight, their clothes no longer fit. Zippers open to protruding bellies with tattoos of the names of children and C-section scars.

Two officers—a man and a woman—step forward to begin the clothed body search, which they conduct in pairs. Like sorry starfish, the women spread their legs, hold up their arms.

The prisoners will serve their sentences at this five-year-old institution or at Valley State Prison, the nation's second-largest women's prison, which recently opened across the street. The compounds occupy the tiny farm town of Chowchilla, where almond and alfalfa groves surround the 50,000-volt electrified fence. To the crop dusters above, the flat gray-and-peach buildings must look like a giant corrections butterfly, shielding up to 8,000 women in the 1,340-acre spread of its cinderblock wings.

The predominant types of offenses women tend to commit—petty theft, check forgery, drug possession—are nonviolent and low-level, yet women's rates of incarceration have steadily gone up, surpassing men's for the past 14 years. The increases are largely due to changes in sentencing and drug laws, and all the trouble that rides the particular poverty track most of these women are on. Many receive state-prison terms for crimes that previously earned probation. Between 1986 and 1991, the number of women in state prisons for drug offenses increased 433 percent (compared with 283 percent for men). Nationally, at the beginning of this year, there were 69,028 women in state prisons—more than 9,600 in California alone. What this means is that the days of minivans with matrons escorting serious offenders to reformatory-style prisons are receding as more tractor-trailers pull into view.

In the world of corrections, an inmate is an inmate is an inmate. In the nation's imagination, too, all inmates are the same. Yet prison administrators, corrections officers and inmates consistently express an awareness of the differences between incarcerated women and men.

Nearly half of male inmates are serving time for violent offenses: among women, it's 1 in 3, and they are also significantly less violent once they're imprisoned. Women show a greater responsiveness to prison programs yet have less opportunity to participate in them than male inmates do. Men appear to weather years of solitary confinement, while the few women who receive it tend to break down in the hole in weeks. Male inmates work their bodies constantly, doing hundreds of squat thrusts and jumping jacks even when restricted to a maximum-security cage. Women, who fear the central yard, work out their anxiety with too much sleep, food and prescription pills.

Men's prisons divide the population by security level; women under minimum, medium and maximum security freely mix. Men tend to congregate by race, whether or not they prefer to in the free world. This is less true for women. Male gangs thrive in prison. Female gangs leave their colors on the street, some creating small families in prison—with designated mothers, fathers, siblings—for support.

Rarely do men become intimate with their keepers. Many women share their lives with officers shift after shift after shift. Men either honor orders or they defy them. Women ask why.

Only 29 percent of the guards at the Central California Women's Facility are women. This fact worsens the already-ancient problems of troubled women, many of whom are accustomed to coercive relationships, when they are placed in a highly sexualized, paramilitary setting in the custody mostly of men. An ongoing investigation of state prisons by the Human Rights Watch Women's Rights Project found that female inmates experienced some form of custodial sexual misconduct regardless of the prison or state; inappropriate sexual contact, verbal degradation, rape, sexual assault and unwarranted visual supervision were reported from California to New York.

Women require more medical care. Up to 6 percent of female inmates are pregnant; approximately 80 percent have two or more children under 18. When a father goes to prison, his children often become members of a single-mother household. When a mother heads to prison, her children lose their home.

Despite the differences, the treatment of imprisoned women is based on a correctional model that is based on muddy assumptions about violent men. Here are four prisoners whose complicated lives shed some light on the experiences of women in the rapidly expanding correctional system: Angela Bolden, 23, and Sandra Maple, 24, among the few younger women serving time for a violent crime; Pamela Kaufman, 35, whose low-level criminal history is entrenched in her lifelong abuse of drugs, and Shirley Carone, 27, who shares the turbulent history of Angela, Sandra, Pamela and so many women but who has a chance to change that and to stay out.

Angela and Sandra

ANGELA BOLDEN COULD HAVE LEFT THE Central California Women's Facility in April, but she didn't want to abandon her girlfriend, Sandra Maple, who is doing life. "I hate to see her stay and me leave," Angela said last summer in B-yard, outside the housing unit where they lived when I met them.

They are a striking couple by any standard, but they are especially striking in this dreary prison—their unscarred skin, animated eyes, voices that still emphasize and lift.

They are a striking couple by any standard, but they are especially striking in this dreary prison—their unscarred skin, animated eyes, voices that still emphasize and lift. When they aren't "programming" in jobs or classes, Angela and Sandra do whatever they can think of to do: aerobics, eat cookies, argue over who has the hairbrush and other "stupid things." Outdoors, they search for bugs. Indoors, they play Yahtzee. On weekends, unlike most of the other inmates, they venture to the main yard, where residents of the separate units—B, C and D—interact. Those inmates who socialize there—gossiping, flirting, fighting and contraband-scheming—are part of the scene known as "the mix." Their hearts are still tied to the street.

Angela and Sandra, in their early 20's, are younger than the general female prison population, whose average age is 31, but their biographies have in common the types of trouble found in the histories of older inmates—running away in their early teens, older boyfriends and early pregnancies, abusive men, mothers in violent relationships and with addictions to alcohol and drugs. The group homes that tried to help the girls when they began to run away or try to kill themselves instead refined the destructive habits they had picked up at home and on the street. Sandra drank and used drugs and had three children; Angela just stayed angry and fought and had one.

In 1992, after pleading guilty to second-degree murder, Sandra was sentenced to 15 years to life. She was 20 years old. She says she manipulated her estranged father, Danny Reloba, into killing the man she says raped her when she was 18. "If I wouldn't have held a vengeance, I wouldn't be in prison," Sandra often says. "Because I could have let that go and lived on in my life." Her father, convicted of the murder, is serving 29 years to life. They no longer correspond, and Sandra says her family has disowned her. She has not received a visit in at least a year.

6. PUNISHMENT AND CORRECTIONS

Angela is serving five years for second-degree robbery and threatening a witness. She demanded money from a woman at a bus stop in San Diego the night of her 19th birthday, a "stupid and impulsive" response to the realization that her Navy boyfriend, the father of the baby she was carrying, stood her up. A 15-year-old girlfriend who was with Angela—the witness she later threatened—turned her in. The court put her on probation and sent her to a residential drug treatment program that accepts pregnant women. According to her records, she threatened another resident with a fork and was discharged for being unable to adhere to the rules. "I'm like, 'Boring—I want to take my baby and go,'" Angela recalls. "And I just, I have this anger thing, so I can't control my anger. And they tell me constantly what to do, and I can't stand to be bossed around." Angela returned to court for the probation violation and was sent to prison to serve the rest of her five-year sentence. The baby was left in the custody of Angela's mother.

These days, when Angela gets angry, she feels that the whole world owes her. The debt is the kind of childhood she never had. "Everything I didn't get, I should get, double time, now," she says. Sandra tries to hold her anger in, and down, for fear it will do her in if it resurfaces, as it has before.

Disruptive inmates may be assigned to Administrative Segregation or the Security Housing Unit, known as Ad Seg and SHU. Angela has been a frequent resident of both; two of her three rocky years in the prison system have been spent in one or the other.

In these special units, shouting is the regular tenor, above the already unbearable decibel level of crackling intercoms, televisions blasting in the day rooms and the general curse-filled daily din. During her Ad Seg and SHU terms, Angela accumulated write-ups, called 115's. Plenty of them were for yelling, as much to express herself as to give her something to do.

"I was yelling out the door, disrespect to others, disrespect to staff, yelling yelling yelling," she says. "I was yelling at the police, (expletive), all that stuff, you know." She enjoyed her growing reputation as an entertainer, but when all the laughter became a chorus, the officers called it "inciting a riot," and she would get another 115. "I was on dog status," she says, which she claims included delayed meals (staff members call them "feedings") and withheld mail, toilet paper and sanitary pads. The Department of Correction denies the withholding of food or essentials.

Long-termers who are eligible for parole frequently have two or three 115's in their central file; to date, Angela's write-ups run more than 70 pages—for assaultive behavior, starting a fire, de-stroying state property (her prison-issued clothes), resisting staff members and at least one suicide attempt. She has thrown objects at the guard tower while exercising in the restricted exercise cage. She has been shot at by the guards twice, with rubber rounds out of a .37-caliber rifle, for refusing to stop fighting.

At 23, Angela believes the worst of her fighting days are over, a change of heart she attributes to coming of age in SHU. "Sometimes I feel it broke me," says Angela, whose high cheekbones add an elegance to her serious, intelligent face. "I'm used to getting in trouble all the time. Then I think, maybe I'm just better." "Better" to Angela means going about your business without commotion, "how to not get seen." But despite her troubles, she believes anger is better than the depression that seems to be a more common inmate state. At least with anger, whatever's underneath it, you express it. "With depression," she says, "you're just giving in to your weakness, and people can take advantage of you even more."

These days, if someone gives her trouble, she'll either ignore the person or mock her in the day room. If public humiliation doesn't do the trick, Angela says she may schedule a fight with her rival in the presence of a trustworthy referee, "somebody that's not going to let the other one pick up a chair, a razor." She says she is getting too old to risk having her face cut up.

Months after I meet Angela and Sandra in B-yard, Angela calls me collect. She's on closed B, a form of on-unit restricted movement. She says she is being punished for a suicide attempt—swallowing all the blood-pressure pills she had been saving after receiving a letter that her father died. She then tore her cell apart.

While the officer was placing handcuffs on Angela to take her to the infirmary, an inmate stood nearby and mocked her. 'That's my baby,' Sandra thought, and jumped the girl. Sandra got herself shipped to C-yard.

While the officer was placing handcuffs on Angela to take her to the infirmary, an inmate stood nearby and mocked her. Sandra, who was watch-

37. Woman behind Bars

ing, thought, "That's my baby," and jumped the girl. She got herself shipped to C-yard.

According to a cell mate of Sandra's, Sandra received a "beat-down" from another inmate in C-yard. Within weeks, she was transformed from a feisty girl to a scared one, no longer venturing from her cell for meals. Defiant as she was for Angela, Sandra has no fight left for herself.

Pamela

AFTER HER FATHER'S STRICT DISCIPLINE and the volatility of her first marriage, Pamela Kaufman feels that her violent life with Robbie Cisneros wasn't so bad. "And me and Robbie have a drug addiction together, so there's a lot of good with the bad," she says of her partner of 15 years.

"She always woke up mad," Robbie recalls over the telephone from Bent County Correctional Facility in Colorado, where he's serving six years for vehicular assault. The first time they were together, Robbie says, she hit him in the face with a closed hand. "Of course, I hit her back," he admits, acknowledging that he knocked her out. What stayed with him, however, was the depth of her combativeness. "She's just waking up, and she's swinging! That's the first thing that comes to her mind!"

At the heart of their heroin addiction was an unspoken deal. If Robbie couldn't "get the hustle up" for drugs or money, Pamela would. It's hard to see the fighter or the hustler in Pamela now. Her 35-year-old exhausted body looks punched in. When she was in state prison the first time, in 1988 for petty theft, Pamela was in the mix, but now, she's avoiding the fun, which means avoiding trouble. She is doing what she calls straight cell time now—reading historical romance novels, spending whole days in bed. Like an estimated 3 percent of California's female prisoners, Pamela is H.I.V.-positive.

"This is sad, but before I got busted I told Robbie, 'We need a prison break,'" she says. "You didn't have to worry about bills, you didn't have to worry about getting up, finding drugs, you didn't have to worry about kids getting dressed for school. Now I regret saying that."

Pamela believes she's in prison not because she stole 20 to 30 pairs of Levis a day for heroin, setting them in the stroller with her daughter and pushing them out of the store, but because of the impact her drug-using life style has had on her five children, ranging in age from 5 to 18. When they weren't with Pamela's father, who was raising them, they accompanied her when she went out to steal.

Sears was the easiest, according to her daughter Regina, 18, who is in the maximum-security Colorado Women's Correctional Facility, serving a three-year term for second-degree assault and attempted escape. (She had been placed in juvenile detention for stealing another girl's coat. After stealing the coat, Regina says, she pushed the girl through a window.) Regina and her 16-year-old brother, Jason, were lookouts for their mother. If they helped Pamela steal, they each received a cut. Before the cut was money, it was candy.

Shoplifting remains Jason's happiest memory of his mother. He tells me this from the Contra Costa County Juvenile Detention Center in California, where he's being held, for the second time, for stealing cars. "When I heard she was going to die, when I heard she had H.I.V., you know what I thought?" says Jason, a wired boy with a shaved head and skinny body that give the impression of a drumstick. "I thought, man, me and my mom had a hell of a lot of fun. She would steal pants and stuff, boost pants. And she would always give me a pair, off the top. And my mom just would be laughing. We pulled that one off, you know, I started crying when I thought of that."

Jessica, 13, inherited the role of lookout when her older siblings took to the streets. "Mom," Jessica would say, exhilarated, "they're on us. Dump!" It made Jessica giddy to save her mother. "It was a cat-and-mouse game for her, too, " Pamela says. "It was our way of life." In the same way Pamela made adjustments for the presence of violence in her world, her children's priorities about Pamela realigned. Pamela was their mom. Having her steal and shoot up was better than seeing her heroin-sick.

Regina, Pamela's most apparent heir, dreaded her mother's frequent arrests. She had to feed her little sisters and get them of to school. She also had to deal with Robbie, whose $100-a-day heroin habit had shriveled to twice a month because his veins were so overused. He would cry, then get drunk. "He slaved me," says Regina. "He wouldn't even let me to go school sometimes. He made me stay home and clean and cook." Robbie denies this. Pamela says, "He kind of wanted her to do all my things."

Above her lower bunk in her eight-woman cell in C-yard, Pamela has basted Regina's prison artwork. Unicorns leap at eye level next to the thin pillow where Pamela rests her head. She believes that her daughter, with all the gang-banging and glue-sniffing and chores at home, subconsciously came to need a prison break herself.

Jessica, Pamela's middle child, is a chubby girl with jet-black hair and crumpled lips. She is Pamela's ally and protector. "My mother loves me the best because I've been through everything, and

6. PUNISHMENT AND CORRECTIONS

I know how she feels and stuff like that," declares Jessica, the words falling out so quickly that she gulps whole phrases just to catch her breath. Jessica wants to make sure I understand that just because she's not in prison doesn't mean that she's no unhappy.

Jessica and I sit in my rental car beside her grandfather's stucco tract house near the window where Pamela and Regina must have climbed out when they were about Jessica's age. When Pamela was 15, her father, crouching between the trucks and cars that line his yard, caught her and a 25-year-old boyfriend necking. He struggled with the young man, who then drove away with Pamela. She didn't return until she called her father collect from Dallas almost two years later, beaten up and pregnant with Regina. When Regina began to run away at 12, she only stayed away in spurts. Jason left home at 15. Although he's part Mexican, he identifies himself as a white supremacist. "Jess," he tells his little sister when he calls or passes through, "you deserve a better life than this."

Jessica thinks running away is a bad idea. She wants to be home when her mom, Pamela, returns from prison. Jessica worries most about the AIDS, how it might make Pamela die no matter what.

Jessica thinks running away is a bad idea. She wants to be home when her mom returns from prison. On that special day, all happiness begins.

Though Jessica can't know it now, what will happen when Pamela is released is that she will marry a former love the first week. By the second week, she will be drinking, "kicking it" with the old friends she had planned to avoid. At a probation appointment, she'll test positive for heroin, then sign up for methadone treatments, and her husband will land in the county jail. Jason will escape from the juvenile detention center. Pamela will take Jessica's younger sisters back. Regina will get in trouble and land in segregation. Jessica's old hopes will fall down. Right now, she's worried most about the AIDS, how it might make Pamela die no matter what. That's the worst thing. And although Jessica tells her best friend everything—even admitting that her mother is in prison—Jessica cannot tell her best friend this.

As the sun sets, Jessica's two younger sisters, ages 5 and 8, chase each other around the car, the thistles, the scrawny trees, the flattened yard. Jessica asks me to put the car light on. Then she adds: "So like, if nobody could help us or anything with our life? They can't help us?" She turns her eyes on me, such sad eyes, their gravity shadowing her chunky cheeks with the nighttime dark. "Can you help a girl like me?"

Shirley

IN NOVEMBER OF 1994, WHEN SHE STEPPED into the receiving cage at Central California Women's Facility, her doleful eyes cast downward, Shirley Carone was a 24-year-old mother of three, twice divorced, depressed, drinking heavily, using drugs and about to finish the 11 months remaining on a suspended three-year sentence for a grand theft conviction for stealing clothes from a department store. When she was pulled over for speeding in the cab she drove to earn her living, the police ran a license check and discovered an outstanding warrant for probation appointments she missed. The police also discovered methamphetamine in a Marlboro box under her seat.

Shirley had recently discovered she was pregnant by her boyfriend, David Smith, 34. That David, already a father of two, would prove to be loyal through her 10-month incarceration—and not only take care of their son when he was born but also marry Shirley and visit her four times a week—makes Shirley's experience an aberration. It was her first state prison term. She had served one year in the county jail for stealing jeans and had also been arrested for soliciting cocaine.

When David visits Shirley, they may share one brief kiss at the beginning and end of their time together. Holding hands is allowed. When David leaves, Shirley is strip-searched.

When David visits Shirley at the prison, they may share one brief kiss at the beginning and the end of their time together. Holding hands is allowed. When David leaves, Shirley is strip-searched.

37. Woman behind Bars

To be searched, an inmate steps out of the prison-issue muumuu and stuffs the uniform in a hole on the search-cell door where a handle should be. Then she spreads her legs while a female officer slides a mirror on the end of a long instrument, like an oversize spatula, on the floor. The inmate squats over it and coughs. She also opens her mouth, runs her finger along her gums and under her breasts and through her pubic hair. She folds back her ears and wiggles her toes. Then she bends over, as if to touch her toes, and spreads her buttocks and coughs again. Shirley appreciates it when an officer doesn't stare. Some of the officers stare.

David tries not to think about what's happening to Shirley because he can't harness the intrusion of other explosive thoughts that the strip search brings to mind—strangers frisking the body that holds his baby when Shirley heads to work exchange, being able to watch Shirley dress and shower, having the right to read his mail. David's frustration is worsened by the shame he feels at being unemployed. He has always worked—two jobs, three—and now here he is, relocated to be near Shirley, about to go on welfare and, effectively, be the mother to their son.

If an infant born in custody is not collected by a family member within 48 hours, the baby becomes a dependent of the juvenile court. After David Sr. collected David Jr., he booked a tiny, long-term room at the B&Z Motel in nearby Madera. How did Shirley find a man so unlike her first two husbands, guys who, according to Shirley, beat her and stalked her? "Purely by accident," she says.

On his calendar at the B&Z Motel, David has drawn a circle around the date Shirley is scheduled for parole. Beside it he has placed a question mark, which speaks to the worry at the forefront of his anxious mind: Shirley, free.

Shirley met David at a Walmart store in Palmdale, Calif., at a strip mall on the Mojave Desert an hour and a half northeast of Los Angeles. His was the cab dispatched to pick her up, and he pulled up two hours late. She cussed him out, apologized and did not give him a tip. The next day, her housemate called a cab, and once more it was David, with his long hair and tentative smile, which Shirley later discovered was because he was embarrassed by his teeth. The housemate invited David in to share a line of methamphetamine. "And I just sat there the whole time staring at him," says Shirley. "I was attracted to him, but. . . ."

Shirley needed a cab the next day to visit her drug connection. She requested David. "He pulled up real fast," she says proudly. She asked if she could stay in the cab and drive awhile because she hates to be alone. They drove all night.

On his calendar at the B&Z, David has drawn a circle around the date Shirley is scheduled for parole. Beside it, he has placed a question mark, which speaks to the worry at the forefront of his anxious mind: Shirley, free. Might she lose her good-time days? Take the risk of going to the main yard, where she could end up in a fight? Will a bureaucratic error create some unforeseeable delay?

At 6 feet 2 inches, David overwhelms the small motel room, and it's an airless room already, swallowed by the baby's crib and a lumpy bed. David Jr. props up in his father's arm like an overstuffed grocery bag, his sprocket of hair grazing the ceiling, yellow-stained from smoke. It's spooky—his baby blank eyes, how someone so little makes so little sound. But the freight train screams as it blasts by the B&Z what seems like every hour. And there's the rattling of the air cooler and buzzing flies and car doors slamming, the children of other B&Z residents slapping empty beer cans on dry dirt.

On the wall is a perfectly positioned lineup of the visiting-room Polaroids of the Smiths, although, because Shirley and David married in prison, Shirley has to keep her maiden name for identification purposes. Only four more strip searches until his wife is released. David's keeping Count.

"You weren't kidding when you said it was small!" says Shirley on the sunny day of freedom when she steps into the dim motel room, bumping right into the bed.

"You think this is small," says David, "you should have seen the last space." He moved into this slightly larger room in preparation for her release, scouring it down and setting it up during his sleepless nights—the floor is bright, the tub has been scrubbed, he has changed the lined. The cooler's filled with Pepsi, Shirley's favorite drink.

David bends down awkwardly to hug Shirley, who sits smoking on the bed. He mock commands, "No contact with the inmate!"—it's a joke—and Shirley rolls her eyes. Her weariness is beginning to show the slightest edge of disappointment, on its way to what looks like an unrelated, titanic contempt or rage. David Jr. crams a stuffed animal in his gooey mouth and David Sr. moves to intercept it.

"He seems happy, let him play," says Shirley.

6. PUNISHMENT AND CORRECTIONS

"You're going to tear the whole end of it off," David says to his son.

"I can always sew it," Shirley says.

"Not if he swallows—."

"Give it to him," snaps Shirley, irritably, surveying the room with a sniffy air. "Well," she says, to no one, sighing. "I'm used to living in small, confined spaces." David Jr. lets out a howl.

THINGS ARE REALLY STARTING TO COME into place," Shirley reports over the phone one month later from the two-bedroom apartment where she and David now live. Unlike the 95 percent of parolees who return to the communities they came from, Shirley moved to Madera, one town over from Chowchilla, away from her drug-using friends and ex-husbands, where she and David had a wobbly but at least fresh start. David works at whatever he can find—stocking inventory at a warehouse, packing cardboard boxes, putting rubber rings on pipes—riding to jobs on a bicycle donated by the church ladies Shirley met through her prison Bible study group.

"We haven't peaked yet or anything," David says. "We're still getting furniture, that kind of thing, but we are making it." David worries that the work will dry up. Shirley worries about the time alone. She fills it up watching soap operas and her son. "And I don't even like soap operas," she says.

She thinks of the prison as a sort of distant parent who, in its unclear way, forced her to grow. "I used to want so many things for myself, I wanted so much, I wanted—I just wanted," Shirley says. "And now I don't care if I ever get the things in life that I want, as long as I have my family there."

Still, she wishes she had a friend her own age. It's hard to make friends David will approve of, and although the ladies from the church are sweet, they are rather old. When Shirley feels she's going crazy with isolation, "cooped up, as if I was in lockdown," she heads to Walmart. The two-mile trip can take up to four hours on the Dial-a-Ride, which schedules rides based on demand. She and the roly-poly David Jr. stroll up the chock-full aisles, down them, looking at all the brand-new things. "I think I know the inventory there now," Shirley says, with a whispery laugh. But the presence of the objects are a comfort, and the other women make her feel less alone.

Article 38

THE COLOR OF JUSTICE

When the question of equal treatment for people of all colors is discussed, it makes some capital punishment scholars see red.

JOHN H. TRUMBO

John H. Trumbo is a reporter and columnist for the daily Auburn Journal in Placer County, Calif. He covers primarily law enforcement and courts.

It appears that a defendant who has enough money to hire a high-priced lawyer has better odds of beating the death row rap.

The fact that there are more non-white men on death row than their Caucasian counterparts is a fact supported by the numbers. The real question is this: Is the disparity due to racial discrimination or some other not-so-black-and-white issues?

If black men who are accused of killing white victims are prime candidates for death row, then why isn't O.J. Simpson facing the ultimate punishment?

And why aren't there more women on death row? It's discrimination, but a closer look at the numbers will show it has nothing to do with color.

Racial discrimination on death row has become a familiar refrain among public defenders and non-profit organizations dedicated to protecting the rights of condemned men and women. But there may be bigger, less well-defined factors that determine who gets a cell on death row and who doesn't.

Organizations whose focus includes death row issues have sprung up from San Francisco to Washington, D.C., ever since civil rights became a national outcry three decades ago. Not surpris-

ingly, many southern states are home to the most active of these organizations.

"Everyone would concede there is racial discrimination," says Clive Stafford Smith of the Louisiana Crisis Assistance Center in New Orleans. "Debate is absurd. Who could pretend it doesn't have an impact?" he said.

A look at the statistics seems to support Smith's contention.

The Death Penalty Information Center in Washington, D.C., reports that 65 blacks have been executed for murders of whites since 1976, compared to one white person executed for the death of a black victim. However, a look at the race of victims for capital cases shows whites are way ahead of blacks—85 percent to 11 percent. Hispanic victims make up 2 percent and Asians represent 1 percent.

When you remove the racial aspect, the statistical portrait shifts dramatically. From 1976 to 1991, there were 157 executions in the United States. Ninety-four of them were Caucasians and 63 were African-Americans. That is 59.9 percent white and 40.1 percent black, which is almost a perfect match to the ratio of white and black people who occupy the nearly 2,500 death row cells in this country.

If we are to assume that Smith is correct and racial discrimination is significant, then who is to blame?

From *Death Row*, 1995, pp. 8-15. © 1995 by Glenn Hare Publications. A division of Dyna Corporation. Published annually by Hare Publications.

6. PUNISHMENT AND CORRECTIONS

Americans can blame the decision-makers, says Smith. Like many death penalty defense lawyers, Smith believes that racial bias occurs at every step in the criminal justice process—from the time the officer flicks on the red light for a traffic stop to that moment when the jury foreperson declares that the maximum penalty should be imposed.

Justice Comes With a Price

The first problem, says Smith, is for a death row candidate to get an adequate defense.

"Often, you have a bunch of town drunks representing people who don't have a lot of money," Smith said. In 10 years of wrangling with death penalty cases at the Louisiana Crisis Assistance Center, Smith says death penalty case defendants almost never have hired attorneys to represent them. He can recall only two cases out of 200 in the past decade where the hapless defendants have had hired attorneys.

"And those," he says wryly, "were $5,000 lawyers here in Louisiana who were no better than public defenders."

It appears, then, that a defendant who has enough money to hire a high-priced lawyer has better odds of beating the death row rap.

For example, Smith was not surprised when the Los Angeles District Attorney's Office chose not to pursue the death penalty with O.J. Simpson.

Even though he is black, Simpson is also rich—and that is a different kind of color issue. Some would call it green.

It's simple, Smith says. Prosecutors are less inclined to press for capital punishment when the defense is well-financed. "They (Simpson's prosecutors) aren't charging the death penalty because they won't get it. His defense is too well equipped," Smith said.

Prosecutor Bill Murray, who is black and number two in the San Joaquin County District Attorney's Office in Stockton, Calif., doesn't buy into the poverty factor in death row cases.

"That's not accurate in this county," Murray said. "We don't spare the expense for court-appointed or public defenders." He says even the middle-class defendants who can afford their own attorneys by mortgaging everything they own still end up on death row if they deserve it.

Murray believes Simpson escaped the death penalty phase for the simple reason that there is too much positive history with the defendant. "That case is not strong factually, and there are too many mitigating circumstances on the positive things he's done in his life. They would have been crazy to seek the death penalty on Simpson because the jury may not return that verdict," Murray said.

That argument flies in the face of a quote from U.S. Supreme Court Justice William O. Douglas, who in 1972, observed there were no examples of the wealthy on death row in America.

"One searches our chronicles in vain for the execution of any member of the affluent strata of this society," Justice Douglas wrote.

More recently, Associated Press Writer Bob Egelko reported that there appears to be a direct relationship between dollars and death row.

According to his September 1994 report, every one of the 384 men and four women awaiting execution as of July 1, 1994, was poor enough to quality for a lawyer at state expense.

Atlanta lawyer Stephen Bright concurs.

"The death penalty is for poor people," said Bright, who serves as the director of the Southern Center for Human Rights in Atlanta and has handled capital cases for 15 years.

"Unlike most of my clients, whose IQs are in the high 60s or low 70s, you're talking about people (rich defendants) who have their lives together, who have the ability to make money . . . You would think those would be the cold, calculated murderers most fit for the death penalty. But the death penalty is for poor people," Bright told the Associated Press.

The Gender Debate

Actually, statistics show that death row is for men who, for the most part, are poor, have never married and didn't complete high school. As of 1994, 98.5 percent of death row inmates in this country were men.

This in itself indicates discrimination, albeit in favor of women, says Smith. Since society still sees women as fairer and less violent than men, women who are accused of murders where there are special circumstances that could lead to the death penalty often obtain an escape route that is not available to men.

A typical, little-known case in nearly all-white, upper-middle class Placer County, Calif., illustrates the point.

Aaron S. Harper, 25, was found guilty of a first-degree, lying-in-wait murder of a white man in July 1994. Harper, who is black, faced the death penalty but ended up with life in prison without the possibility of parole.

Trial testimony showed that Harper agreed to do the February 1993 murder as a favor for a white woman, Trina Werly. She wanted revenge on her former boyfriend, whom she believed had molested their young daughter.

Werly was tried for murder and found guilty of a lesser charge of voluntary manslaughter. She was the mastermind of the crime—a capital of-

38. Color of Justice

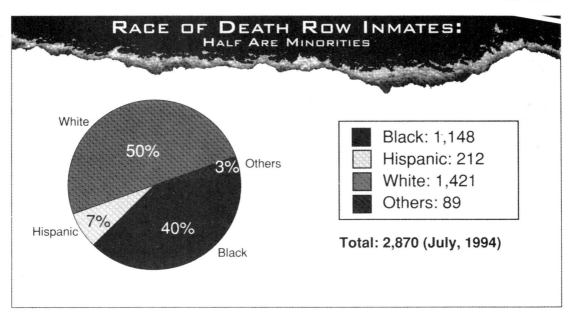

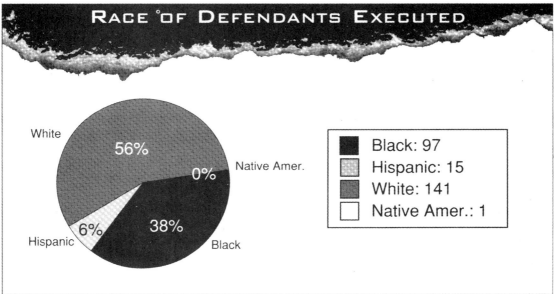

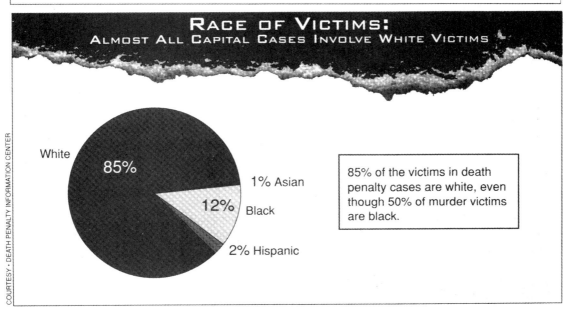

6. PUNISHMENT AND CORRECTIONS

fense that warrants the death penalty—but expects to serve only 12 years in prison. Harper, who was the only defendant who faced the death penalty, got life in prison.

"It's sexist, and women are the beneficiaries of discrimination, but I don't think we should start executing more women just to be fair," Smith said.

Racial Bias Seen at Every Level

Although Bright observes that in Georgia, 65 percent of all murder victims are black and most perpetrators are black, discrimination enters when there is a white victim. And, he says, there are at least three opportunities for racial discrimination that play a role in bringing about the death penalty: the race of the victim, the skin color of the prosecutor and racial makeup of the jury.

First, police investigators tend to invest "huge responses of resources and effort when white victims are involved," Bright said. He added that Georgia prosecutors go for the death penalty in 70 percent of interracial crime. "It becomes an issue of who you kill," Bright noted.

Take the example of Jerry Walker, who made the mistake of killing the son of a white brigadier general from Fort Benning, Ga., in 1991. It was a convenience store robbery, and the jury gave Walker death, partly, Bright believes, because the victim and his family had the politically-correct skin color and social status. However, Walker was re-sentenced to life in 1993.

Or, consider the murder case of black defendant John Michael Davis who went to death row in 1985 after the district attorney in Georgia's Muscogee County asked the stepfather of the young, white female victim if he wanted Davis to be imprisoned for life or get the electric chair.

Three years after the conviction, the grateful stepfather contributed $5,000 to the district attorney's judgeship campaign.

A second factor which can lead to discrimination on the way to death row, Bright notes, is the color of the prosecutor.

"In a lot of places in the country, a white person is the one who is making the decision to pursue the death penalty," he said.

That's not the case in Stockton, Calif., where the number two prosecutor Murray is African-American and has the responsibility to make final calls on death penalty cases. "As long as I've been here, race has not been an issue," said Murray, who came to California after being a prosecutor in New York.

Typically, any case which has death penalty potential goes through a two-tier process. There is a general discussion on the merits among staff,

then one person—in Stockton it is Murray—makes the decision on whether or not to seek capital punishment.

But Murray acknowledges that biases may exist in other parts of the country.

"The southern states have a different situation which they haven't quite shaken," he said.

Even though racial discrimination doesn't appear to be an issue in his San Joaquin County now, they do have three cases pending in federal courts in which the black defendants are appealing based on racial discrimination, Murray said. All three were handled prior to his arrival, he noted.

The third factor—the color of the jury—can also make a difference, said Bright.

William Henry Hance, a black man who was executed in Georgia in March 1994, was given the death penalty by a jury composed of one African-American and 11 Caucasians.

Ensuring there is a racially color-blind jury isn't that easy. Often in predominantly black Atlanta, said Bright, the black defendants are accused of killing white victims in predominately white neighborhoods. Consequently, the trials are in those mostly white counties, and the jury pools contain few non-whites.

In such situations, it becomes relatively easy for a prosecutor to excuse a black juror without cause. And even when good cause is required, Bright said, any attorney "with brains can come up with another reason that isn't race-related."

Bright likes to make an example of Ocmulgee County (Ga.) District Attorney Joe Briley, who has sought the death penalty in 30 cases. Twenty-four of those were black defendants, and in 20 cases, Briley used 169 jury strikes against black citizens and only 19 against white citizens.

In cases where victims were white, Briley exercised 94 percent of his jury strikes against black jurors, Bright said.

There are other examples from Bright's files, including a district attorney in Hinds County, Miss., whose public policy is to "get rid of as many" black jurors as possible. And there's documented evidence in Chambers County, Ala., that a prosecutor there ranked prospective jurors as "strong," "medium," "weak," and "black."

Murray acknowledges the problem with trying to obtain an unbiased jury.

"Selecting jurors is not a perfect process. You just can't control them," he said.

Even with all the opportunities for racial bias to occur, Murray has noticed a safety net that exists on death penalty issues because of human nature.

"People just aren't all that anxious to render death verdicts," he said. "If anything, in this state jurors are going the other way," Murray said.

Since 1977, only two California death row inmates have seen the inside of this gas chamber at San Quentin State Prison. There are 397 California inmates still awaiting execution—149 of whom are black.

38. Color of Justice

EXECUTIONS BY RACE — BY STATE
(1977-1994)

STATE	B	H	I	W	Count
AL	7	0	0	3	10
AR	2	0	0	7	9
AZ	0	0	0	3	3
CA	0	0	0	2	2
DE	2	0	1	1	4
FL	11	0	0	22	33
GA	12	0	0	6	18
ID	0	0	0	1	1
IL	0	0	0	2	2
IN	1	0	0	2	3
LA	9	0	0	12	21
MD	0	0	0	1	1
MO	5	0	0	6	11
MS	3	0	0	1	4
NC	0	0	0	6	6
NE	1	0	0	0	1
NV	0	0	0	5	5
OK	1	0	0	2	3
SC	0	0	0	4	4
TX	29	15	0	41	85
UT	2	0	0	2	4
VA	14	0	0	10	24
WA	0	0	0	2	2
WY	0	0	0	1	1
Count:	**99**	**15**	**1**	**142**	**257**

K. WILLIAM HAYES/CAPITAL PUNISHMENT STUDY

> "The system is nothing to write home about, especially when it deals with the question of who should live and who should die."
>
> —Stephen Bright
> Director, Southern Center
> for Human Rights

An Act of Racial Justice

The Racial Justice Act, which proponents tried to include in President Clinton's Crime Bill, would have been a small step toward bringing accountability for racial disparity, Bright said.

"It was a very watered-down remedy and would not have been that effective. It would have just forced the prosecutors to come up with other reasons to put non-whites on death row," he said, even though he was one of its early supporters.

Watered-down or not, Stockton prosecutor Murray is relieved that the Racial Justice Act was rejected.

"It would have been a nightmare for district attorneys," he said, noting that a quota or statistical basis for determining death row cases would be impossible because the Supreme Court has already decided pure statistics are not enough to prove racial bias.

The case that triggered the Supreme Court decision involved Warren McCleskey of Georgia, who was executed September 1991 for shooting a white police officer. His defense referred to a study, conducted by the National Association for the Advancement of Colored People (NAACP), which indicated that blacks who killed whites were more likely to receive the death penalty than whites who killed whites. A review of the NAACP study by an expert methodologist showed that black-on-white murders—including the McCleskey case—often involved other aggravating elements like armed robbery.

The 1987 Supreme Court decision followed the logic represented with Georgia's homicide statistics, which showed that 67 percent of black-on-white killings involved armed robbery, compared with 7 percent of black-on-black killings.

6. PUNISHMENT AND CORRECTIONS

Rep. Don Edwards, D-Calif., told the Wall Street Journal in July 1994 that the Racial Justice Act was an attempt to root out bias among decision-makers on death sentencing.

"Decision-makers in death sentencing—like those in other endeavors, such as voting, employment or jury selection—rarely, if ever, admit that they are racially biased," said Edwards, who at the time, was chairman of the House Civil and Constitutional Rights Committee.

According to the National Center for Policy Analysis in Dallas, the racial makeup of murderers indicates no great disparity nationally for the percentage of blacks on death row (42 percent) and the percentage charged with homicide (48 percent).

In July 1991, Bright testified before the House Subcommittee on Civil and Constitutional Rights. "We make significant public policy decisions based upon a finding that a smoker is 1.7 times more likely to die of heart disease than a nonsmoker," he said, "but we ignore the fact that in Georgia, a person accused of murdering a white person is 4.3 times more likely to be sentenced to death than a person accused of murdering a black (person)."

Bright noted that prosecutors' decisions on who will face the death penalty are highly subjective, and there are no statewide standards that govern when the death penalty is sought.

Mississippi, for example, can impose the death penalty for forcible rape of a person under 14 years old. And in Montana, a state prison inmate who has a prior homicide conviction, or been previously declared a persistent felony offender, can be executed for a deliberate attempted homicide, aggravated assault or aggravated kidnapping.

"The system is nothing to write home about, especially when it deals with the question of who should live and who should die," Bright said.

Article 39

Anger and Ambivalence

Most Americans support capital punishment, yet few inmates are actually executed. Why the country has mixed feelings about putting people to death.

DAVID A. KAPLAN

F IT'S SWIFT PUNISHMENT YOU want, you'll love the case of Giuseppe Zangara. Back on Feb. 15, 1933, in the middle of Miami, this slightly deranged malcontent pulled a gun on President-elect Franklin Roosevelt and fired repeatedly. He missed, but mortally wounded the mayor of Chicago. Thirty-three days later—after arrest, guilty plea and sentence—Zangara was electrocuted in Florida's "Old Sparky." In the good old days of capital punishment, there wasn't even enough time to sign a book deal.

The machinery of capital justice cranks a lot more slowly now. Death row is a growth industry. The rare inmate to die hangs on close to 10 years before meeting the executioner. In Florida, triple-killer Gary Alvord is celebrating his 22d year, still hoping, still appealing. Up the interstate, one quarter of Georgia's 109 death-row prisoners have been there since at least 1980. And in Montana, until May 10, Duncan McKenzie had avoided the lethal needle for 20 years. In fact, he fell just one vote short of gaining his eighth stay of execution. He may have been the cold-blooded murderer of a schoolteacher, but he had chutzpah. His last argument in court: two

decades on death row was itself "cruel and unusual" punishment, and therefore a violation of his constitutional rights. Never mind that McKenzie's lawyers had asked for the prior stays and had helped to create the judicial black hole he found himself in. A federal court didn't buy the claim and within days McKenzie became the first inmate executed in Montana since FDR's third term.

Give or take a few miscreants, there are currently 3,000 inmates on American death rows. That's more by far than at any time in world history. California alone has 407, followed by Texas with 398 and Florida with 342. Yet for each of the last 19 years—ever since the U.S. Supreme Court allowed states to resume capital punishment—no more than about 2 percent of the death-row total has ever been executed. In 1994, the number was 31; this year, the figure might reach 50. Spending a reported annual $90 million on capital cases, California has managed to gas just two inmates—and one of them waived all his appeals.

Capital punishment in America is a paper tiger. Despite tough political bluster and overwhelming poll numbers, the nation is ambivalent about the ultimate penalty. For

many years, legislators, governors, judges and victims'-rights activists have vowed to finally get on with it—to bar endless appeals, sanction mollycoddling defense lawyers, root out of office bleeding-heart governors. Congress passed reforms and cut funding for defense lawyers, the U.S. Supreme Court cracked down, and leaders like New York Gov. Mario Cuomo were voted out. The press, NEWSWEEK included, proclaimed in various aqueous illusions that the floodgates would soon open or that the logjam was about to be broken.

It's never happened. State prosecutors' offices remain understaffed and overwhelmed, courts have hopelessly long backlogs (assuming they can find lawyers for the defendants in the first place) and juries in most states enthusiastically continue to send killers to death row. For every inmate to die, though, there are five new ones to take his (or, in the rare case, her) cell. To clean up the backlog, states would have to execute a killer a day (Christmas and Easter included) through 2021. Even Texas—far and away the nation's death-penalty capital, with a third of all executions since 1976—manages to dispatch only about one in eight condemned inmates.

From *Newsweek*, August 7, 1995, pp. 24-26, 28. © by Newsweek, Inc. All rights reserved. Reprinted by permission.

6. PUNISHMENT AND CORRECTIONS

At the water cooler and in the streets of Union, S.C., people argue about what fate the Susan Smiths of the world deserve. And race and poverty have never gone away in the vexing national debate over the death penalty. But those moral and ideological questions have now been overshadowed by a simpler fact: people sentenced to death nonetheless live on in prison. What's the most frequent cause of death for death-row inmates? As of 1992, according to the U.S. Bureau of Justice Statistics, electrocution and lethal in-

---

Oscar Ortiz III
Age: 19
San Antonio, Texas, July 6.
One death sentence.

Every year, about 260 Americans are sentenced to die—though actual executions are usually delayed for years. Oscar Ortiz III and the men whose profiles follow are among those whose juries, unlike Susan Smith's, gave them the death penalty last month. Ortiz abducted businessman Joe Ince Jr., 38, from an ATM on Jan. 19, 1994. After forcing Ince to divulge his personal identification number, Ortiz drove him, in Ince's truck, to a second ATM. When the PIN worked, Ortiz rolled down the passenger window, presumably to keep blood from splattering the upholstery, and shot Ince in the head. Ortiz drove to three more ATMs, then dumped Ince on a highway. He died 12 hours later.

---

jection were mere runnerups. The No. 1 killer: "Natural Causes." What becomes of a penal policy that on its face is a sham?

Ask Alex Kozinski, one of the country's most outspoken and conservative federal judges who almost always upholds death sentences. "We have constructed a machine that is extremely expensive, chokes our legal institutions, visits repeated trauma on victims' families and ultimately produces nothing like the benefits we would expect from an effective system of capital punishment," he wrote in a recent, controversial op-ed article in The New York Times. "This is surely the worst of all worlds."

The systemic ambivalence about the death penalty is reflected in virtually all the 38 states that have death chambers open for business. During his election campaign last year, South Carolina's new attorney general, Charlie Condon, was so taken with a triple execution in Arkansas that he proposed doing away with his state's electric chair. His reform? An "electric sofa," to juice several inmates at a time. South Carolina's death-row population is 59; its last execution was in 1991. Ambivalence there may best be demonstrated by the Smith verdict itself last week. While polls showed

wide support for her execution, it took jurors less than three hours to reach a unanimous verdict to spare her.

NEW YORK, AFTER 20 YEARS OF abolitionist administrations in Albany, this spring became the newest state with capital punishment on the books. When it will post a job listing for executioners is another matter. It typically takes a decade before all courts sign off on a death statute. New York's is so full of procedural safeguards that some wonder if executions will ever resume. "That new law essentially says, 'KICK ME'," observes law professor Franklin Zimring, of the University of California, Berkeley. "They'll be lucky to have an execution in the 21st century." In a liberal state like New York, that may be the perfect political outcome for Republican Gov. George Pataki. He got the death penalty out of legislative purgatory, but he'll never actually have to deal with administering it.

That may also be the strategy of Bill Clinton. Already his re-election-campaign spots disingenuously boast of adding dozens of new crimes to the federal death statute. And the U.S. government is busily building its own death row in the Midwest, complete with a $300,000 death chamber, even though currently there are only six federal inmates convicted of capital crimes. Trouble is, federal executions, assuming they even get underway this decade, are unlikely to be more than a criminal-justice blip. The new laws contain such everyday offenses as killing a chicken inspector of the Agriculture Department.

Nobody in the capital-punishment system wants to accept blame for the current stalemate. Prosecutors blame judges, who blame courts, who blame the law, which gets passed down by Supreme Court justices, who don't speak, except to Nina Totenberg on occasion. But the primary whipping boys for execution gridlock have long been defense lawyers. It's true that a ferociously dedicated group of abolitionists, among them David Bruck, Smith's counsel, have fought the death penalty in every venue across the land. The fact is, judges are the ones who grant stays of execution, courts come up with incredibly complex rules and prosecutors don't push cases along. In one Indiana case, the state took two years to transcribe the trial record of a case. In most state A.G.s' offices in the death-belt states, appeals sit around because there aren't enough government lawyers to handle the load.

AT THE TOP OF THE SYSTEM, THE U.S. Supreme Court has labored hard to get out of the death-penalty business. But the justices every year get drawn into a few major cases and wind up having to revise doctrine. Worse, while there are no justices anymore like William Brennan

or Thurgood Marshall—who voted against all death sentences all the time—the high court often still splits 5-4 on capital cases, indicating that even the Supremes can't figure things out. That leads to further confusion for lower-court judges, who have enough trouble keeping up with legal changes from two years prior. Chief Judge Gerald Tjoflat of the 11th U.S. Circuit Court of Appeals in Atlanta says that some of his colleagues spend half their time wading through capital cases. "I've been in the judging business for 28 years," Tjoflat says, "and there's nothing harder."

Some judges take an especially long time to make up their minds. In 1986, an Arizona killer named Ruben Zaragoza exhausted his state remedies and appealed to the federal district court in Phoenix. Zaragoza's case hasn't been heard from since. Judge Earl H. Carroll, who has had the case for the last nine years, declined to comment. Two years ago, Arizona Attorney General Grant Woods got so annoyed with slow federal judges in his state that he took an extraordinary step.

Michael Clagett
Age: 34
Virginia Beach, Va., July 13.
Five death sentences.

Michael Clagett liked to hang out at the Witchduck Inn in Virginia Beach, where his girlfriend had once worked as a waitress. So when the couple needed cash for a trip to Oregon, they knew they would find gas money at the "Cheers"-like pub. They arrived shortly before midnight on June 30, 1994, and found four people inside, including the owner, whom Clagett later described as his "buddy." Clagett told everyone to lie on the floor while the girlfriend took $400 from the register. Then he shot them one by one in the head. Although his attorneys attempted various defenses—including blaming the girlfriend—Clagett was his own worst enemy. He gave police a weeping, videotaped confession in which he detailed each grisly shot he fired and told reporters that the police that he deserved to die. After deliberating for five hours, the jury agreed.

Woods asked the Ninth U.S. Circuit Court of Appeals, based in San Francisco, to order the judges to rule on 30 cases that had languished for a decade. The appeals court refused. "That was real smart of Arizona," says a deputy attorney general of one Southern state. "Trying to move a federal judge is like trying to make a pig dance. It doesn't work and it annoys the pig."

The Ninth Circuit itself has come under frequent attack from politicians. That court "is the most liberal of the circuits in the United States," complains California Attor-

39. Anger and Ambivalence

ney General Dan Lungren. "Some members appear to have a strong bias against the death penalty." Lungren has in mind the notorious case of Robert Alton Harris in 1992 that embarrassed the entire federal judicial system. Harris had been before both the California and the U.S. Supreme Courts six times in his 13 years on San Quentin's death row. On the eve of his scheduled April 21 appointment with the executioner, the Ninth Circuit kept issuing stays and the justices in Washington kept lifting them—into the predawn hours. Finally, an enraged Supreme Court—citing the Ninth Circuit's "civil disobedience"—ordered the circuit judges to abstain from any further interference. Harris was executed in the gas chamber forthwith. The case continues to haunt all participants in the California system.

Lungren correctly notes that the 24-member Ninth Circuit appeals court does in fact have several judges—from both ends of the political spectrum—who consistently vote against death sentences and thereby slow down the tumbrels. But so what? Of California's 407 death-row inmates, only eight have cases pending before the Ninth Circuit. And what of Lungren's own office? Of the state's 407 condemned prisoners, 120 are totally stalled before the state supreme court because there are no defense lawyers for them. (Constitutional law entitles them to representation.) "We haven't appointed counsel for anyone in 1993, 1994 and 1995," says Robert Reichman, a court administrator.

Douglas Kelly
Age: 37
Van Nuys, Calif.,
July 10.
One death sentence.

Five times over the years, Douglas Kelly had been convicted of sexually or violently assaulting women. But Sara Weir, a woman who befriended Kelly at the health club where he worked as a janitor, didn't know that. On or before Sept. 7, 1993, Kelly lured Weir, 19, to the apartment he shared with his girlfriend and her 10-year-old son. He raped and stabbed Weir 34 times with a pair of sewing scissors, then pushed Weir's body under the boy's bed. He put a plastic bag on Weir's head, a plastic Dodgers helmet on top of that, and stole her Ford Bronco. Though the defense admitted the murder, Kelly said that he did not rape Weir or steal from her—aggravating factors triggering the death penalty. But after four women testified that Kelly had raped them, the jury chose death.

"We're on 1992's cases." In short, that means at least three extra years of life and free meals for California's condemned. Capital punishment is about the only area of litigation where there aren't lawyers climbing over each other to earn a fee.

With his considerable political skills, why doesn't Lungren press the state supreme court to find lawyers, or urge the state bar to get members to take their ethics obligations seriously? Or, as one Ninth Circuit judge asked, why doesn't he simply call a press conference to explain why more than one quarter of California's condemned population is no closer to execution now than three years ago when the Ninth Circuit was being pummeled for its handling of the Harris case? "While this may be an area of legitimate concern," Lungren answered in a prepared statement, "we do not have any direct jurisdiction over it and, at a time when my own department is facing cuts of $10 million, it is questionable how much leverage we would have in achieving funding for court-appointed defense lawyers."

Ambivalence is not limited to judges and prosecutors. Earlier this year, the Florida clemency board voted to defer a decision on Danny Doyle—a mentally impaired murderer who was sentenced 13 years earlier—until the year 2020. He'll remain in death-row lockup, says Joe Bizarro, spokesman for the Florida attorney general. Jurors, too, seem to have mixed feelings. In 1987, Louisiana's electric chair got humming. It claimed four lives in one nine-day period and four more in a five-week period later in the year. In the following 21 months, juries throughout the state imposed only two death sentences. Homicide rates, among the highest in the nation, hadn't changed. Observers suggested that jurors lost their nerve, now that a death sentence was no longer an illusion.

There are really only two political positions to take on the death penalty. You can support it or oppose it. The great irony about American capital punishment, as Zimring says, is that "no one on either side can defend the current system, which is hypocritical and unprincipled." Unless the purpose of the penalty is to create a gruesome illusion, there are just two alternatives. Those who write the statutes can narrow the category of killers eligible for death down to a manageable few, as many advocates of capital punishment are beginning to suggest. Single out the terrorists, mass murderers and contract killers. Use limited resources and political capital to maneuver them into the death chambers. After all, they're the ones—not the liquor-store holdup guy who panicked—that most citizens want dead anyway.

The other choice, of course, is to summon up the political will to commence executions

---

Rogers Lacaze
Age: 18
New Orleans, July 21.
Three death sentences.

On March 4, 1995, at the Kim Anh Vietnamese restaurant in New Orleans, two employees and a police officer moonlighting as a security guard were killed during an armed robbery. At first, Rogers Lacaze claimed he wasn't even in the restaurant. Then he admitted he was there but denied having a gun. His lawyer argued that Lacaze would have been splattered with blood (he wasn't) if, as prosecutors contended, he had shot policeman Ronald Williams at close range. Lacaze even took the witness stand to say, "I didn't pull no trigger, I didn't kill those peoples. Please spare my life, please!" But two eyewitnesses fingered him. Even though Lacaze's father attempted to deflect the blame by testifying he had been absent for most of his son's life, the jury took fewer than four hours to give Lacaze three death sentences.

---

in record numbers—at the very least, more than the nationwide high-water mark of 199 in 1935. That means devoting millions of tax dollars for more prosecutors, and new U.S. Supreme Court policy to give those prosecutors more leeway. In turn, that would mean more tolerance of imperfect justice. "I tell folks that if they want appeals limited to two or three years, some time we'll execute the wrong person," says Georgia Attorney General Michael Bowers. "Of course we will. We're human. But it's a question of will."

Which brings us back to Judge Kozinski, who kindled much of the current debate with his scathing indictment of the modern capital-punishment charade. Kozinski was appointed by President Reagan. Though a judicial independent and freethinker, Kozinski is firmly rooted in the tradition of judging that tries to keep one's personal views out of the courtroom. At times, he's excoriated his colleagues on the Ninth Circuit for not getting on with the death penalty. How would Kozinski feel about a system that produced several hundred executions a year?

"I'd hope it wouldn't affect how I handled cases, but I just don't know," he says. "I just don't know."

With GINNY CARROLL in Houston, PETER KATEL in Miami, THOMAS HEATH in Denver, KAREN SPRINGEN in Chicago and ANTHONY DUIGNAN-CABRERA in New York

Article 40

Death Row, U.S.A.

TOTAL NUMBER OF DEATH ROW INMATES KNOWN TO LDF: 3,153 (As of July 31, 1996)

Race of Defendant:

White	1,509	(47.86%)
Black	1,291	(40.94%)
Latino/Latina	234	(7.42%)
Native American	49	(1.55%)
Asian	23	(.73%)
Unknown at this issue	47	(1.49%)
Gender: Male	3,104	(98.44%)
Female	49	(1.55%)

DISPOSITIONS SINCE JANUARY 1, 1973:

Executions:	335	
Suicides:	45	
Commuta-tions:	74	(including those by the Governor of Texas resulting from favorable court decisions)

Died of natural causes, or killed while under death sentence: 99

Convictions/Sentences reversed: 1,537

JURISDICTIONS WITH CAPITAL PUNISHMENT STATUTES: 40

(Underlined jurisdictions have statutes but no sentences imposed)

Alabama, Arizona, Arkansas, California, Colorado, Connecticut, Delaware, Florida, Georgia, Idaho, Illinois, Indiana, Kansas, Kentucky, Louisiana, Maryland, Mississippi, Missouri, Montana, Nebraska, Nevada, <u>New Hampshire</u>, New Jersey, New Mexico, <u>New York</u>, North Carolina, Ohio, Oklahoma, Oregon, Pennsylvania, South Carolina, South Dakota, Tennessee, Texas, Utah, Virginia, Washington, <u>Wyoming</u>, U.S. Government, U.S. Military.

JURISDICTIONS WITHOUT CAPITAL PUNISHMENT STATUTES: 13

Alaska, District of Columbia, Hawaii, Iowa, Maine, Massachusetts, Michigan, Minnesota, North Dakota, Rhode Island, Vermont, West Virginia, Wisconsin.

execution update

July 31, 1996

Total number of executions since the 1976 reinstatement of capital punishment (there were no executions in 1976): **335**

'77	'78	'79	'80	'81	'82	'83	'84	'85	'86	'87	'88	'89	'90	'91	'92	'93	'94	'95	'96
1	0	2	0	1	2	5	21	18	18	25	11	16	23	14	31	38	31	56	22

Reprinted with permission from the *NAACP Legal Defense and Educational Fund*, Summer 1996.

40. Death Row, U.S.A.

gender of defendants executed

total number 335
Female . . . .   1 (.30%)
  Male 334 (99.70%)

race of defendants executed

White 187 (55.82%)
Black 128 (38.21%)
Latino 17 (5.07%)
Native American . . . .   2 (.60%)
Asian . . . .   1 (.30%)

gender of victims

total number 451
Female 194 (43.02%)
  Male 257 (56.98%)

race of victims

White 370 (82.04%)
Black 57 (12.64%)
Latino 17 (3.77%)
Asian 7 (1.55%)

defendant-victim racial combinations

White Defendant and
  White Victim   259   (57.43%)
  Black Victim   5   (1.11%)
  Asian Victim   2   (.44%)
  Latino/a Victim   8   (1.77%)
Black Defendant and
  White Victim.   102   (22.62%)
  Black Victim   51   (11.31%)
  Asian Victim   2   (.44%)
  Latino Victim   1   (.22%)
Latino Defendant and
  White Victim   9   (2.00%)
  Latino Victim.   7   (1.55%)
  Asian Victim   1   (.22%)
Native American and
  White Victim.   2   (.44%)
Asian Defendant and
  Asian Victim   2   (.44%)

Crime Statistics

CRIME CLOCK
1995

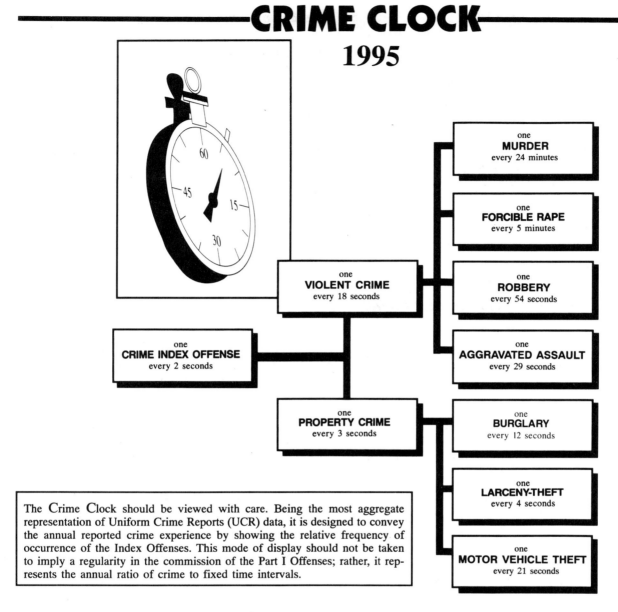

The Crime Clock should be viewed with care. Being the most aggregate representation of Uniform Crime Reports (UCR) data, it is designed to convey the annual reported crime experience by showing the relative frequency of occurrence of the Index Offenses. This mode of display should not be taken to imply a regularity in the commission of the Part I Offenses; rather, it represents the annual ratio of crime to fixed time intervals.

Crime in the United States, 1995

The Crime Index total, 13.9 million offenses in 1995, was the lowest serious crime count since 1987. The 1-percent decline in the total, 1995 versus 1994, was the fourth consecutive annual decline. Among the Nation's cities collectively, the Index decreased 2 percent, with the greatest decrease, 6 percent, reported in cities having a million or more inhabitants. Similar to the national experience, the suburban counties recorded a 1-percent decrease, but rural county law enforcement agencies registered a 4-percent rise.

Geographically, the largest volume of Crime Index offenses was reported in the most populous Southern States, which accounted for 38 percent of the total. Following were the Western States with 25 percent, the Midwestern States with 21 percent, and the Northeastern States with 16 percent. All regions except the west showed Crime Index decreases during 1995 as compared to 1994 figures.

As in previous years, Crime Index offenses occurred most frequently in August and least often in February.

Rate

Crime rates relate the incidence of crime to population. In 1995, there were an estimated 5,278 Crime Index offenses for each 100,000 in United States population, the lowest rate since 1985. The Crime Index rate was highest in the Nation's metropolitan areas and lowest in the rural counties. The national 1995 Crime Index rate fell 2 percent from the 1994 rate, 11 percent from the 1991 level, and 4 percent from the 1986 rate.

Regionally, the Crime Index rates ranged from 6,083 in the

Table 1.—Index of Crime, United States, 1986–1995

Population[1]	Crime Index total[2]	Modified Crime Index total[3]	Violent crime[4]	Property crime[4]	Murder and non-negligent man-slaughter	Forcible rape	Robbery	Aggravated assault	Burglary	Larceny–theft	Motor vehicle theft	Arson[3]
					Number of Offenses							
Population by year:												
1986–241,077,000	13,211,900		1,489,170	11,722,700	20,610	91,460	542,780	834,320	3,241,400	7,257,200	1,224,100	
1987–243,400,000	13,508,700		1,484,000	12,024,700	20,100	91,110	517,700	855,090	3,236,200	7,499,900	1,288,700	
1988–245,807,000	13,923,100		1,566,220	12,356,900	20,680	92,490	542,970	910,090	3,218,100	7,705,900	1,432,900	
1989–248,239,000	14,251,400		1,646,040	12,605,400	21,500	94,500	578,330	951,710	3,168,200	7,872,400	1,564,800	
1990–248,709,873	14,475,600		1,820,130	12,655,500	23,440	102,560	639,270	1,054,860	3,073,900	7,945,700	1,635,900	
1991–252,177,000	14,872,900		1,911,770	12,961,100	24,700	106,590	687,730	1,092,740	3,157,200	8,142,200	1,661,700	
1992–255,082,000	14,438,200		1,932,270	12,505,900	23,760	109,060	672,480	1,126,970	2,979,900	7,915,200	1,610,800	
1993–257,908,000	14,144,800		1,926,020	12,218,800	24,530	106,010	659,870	1,135,610	2,834,800	7,820,900	1,563,100	
1994–260,341,000[5]	13,989,500		1,857,670	12,131,900	23,330	102,220	618,950	1,113,180	2,712,800	7,879,800	1,539,300	
1995–262,755,000	13,867,100		1,798,790	12,068,400	21,600	97,460	580,550	1,099,180	2,595,000	8,000,600	1,472,700	
Percent change: number of offenses:												
1995/1994	−.9		−3.2	−.5	−7.4	−4.6	−6.2	−1.3	−4.3	+1.5	−4.3	
1995/1991	−6.8		−5.9	−6.9	−12.6	−8.6	−15.6	+.6	−17.8	−1.7	−11.4	
1995/1986	+5.0		+20.8	+2.9	+4.8	+6.6	+7.0	+31.7	−19.9	+10.2	+20.3	
					Rate per 100,000 Inhabitants							
Year:												
1986	5,480.4		617.7	4,862.6	8.6	37.9	225.1	346.1	1,344.6	3,010.3	507.8	
1987	5,550.0		609.7	4,940.3	8.3	37.4	212.7	351.3	1,329.6	3,081.3	529.4	
1988	5,664.2		637.2	5,027.1	8.4	37.6	220.9	370.2	1,309.2	3,134.9	582.9	
1989	5,741.0		663.1	5,077.9	8.7	38.1	233.0	383.4	1,276.3	3,171.3	630.4	
1990	5,820.3		731.8	5,088.5	9.4	41.2	257.0	424.1	1,235.9	3,194.8	657.8	
1991	5,897.8		758.1	5,139.7	9.8	42.3	272.7	433.3	1,252.0	3,228.8	659.0	
1992	5,660.2		757.5	4,902.7	9.3	42.8	263.6	441.8	1,168.2	3,103.0	631.5	
1993	5,484.4		746.8	4,737.6	9.5	41.1	255.9	440.3	1,099.2	3,032.4	606.1	
1994[5]	5,373.5		713.6	4,660.0	9.0	39.3	237.7	427.6	1,042.0	3,026.7	591.3	
1995	5,277.6		684.6	4,593.0	8.2	37.1	220.9	418.3	987.6	3,044.9	560.5	
Percent change: rate per 100,000 inhabitants:												
1995/1994	−1.8		−4.1	−1.4	−8.9	−5.6	−7.1	−2.2	−5.2	+.6	−5.2	
1995/1991	−10.5		−9.7	−10.6	−16.3	−12.3	−19.0	−3.5	−21.1	−5.7	−14.9	
1995/1986	−3.7		+10.8	−5.5	−4.7	−2.1	−1.9	+20.9	−26.6	+1.1	+10.4	

[1] Populations are Bureau of the Census provisional estimates as of July 1, except 1990 which [is] the decennial census count.

[2] Because of rounding, the offenses may not add to totals.

[3] Although arson data are included in the trend and clearance tables, sufficient data are not available to estimate totals for this offense.

[4] Violent crimes are offenses of murder, forcible rape, robbery, and aggravated assault. Property crimes are offenses of burglary, larceny-theft, and motor vehicle theft. Data are not included for the property crime of arson.

[5] The 1994 figures have been adjusted.

Complete data for 1995 were not available for the states of Illinois, Kansas, and Montana; therefore, it was necessary that their crime counts be estimated. See "Offense

All rates were calculated on the offenses before rounding.

West to 4,180 in the Northeast. Two-year percent changes (1995 versus 1994) showed rate declines in all regions.

Nature

The Crime Index is composed of violent and property crime categories, and in 1995, 13 percent of the Index offenses reported to law enforcement were violent crimes and 87 percent, property crimes. Larceny-theft was the offense with the highest volume, while murder accounted for the fewest offenses.

Property estimated in value at $15.6 billion was stolen in connection with all Crime Index offenses, with the greatest losses due to thefts of motor vehicles; jewelry and precious metals; and televisions, radios, stereos, etc. Law enforcement agencies nationwide recorded a 35-percent recovery rate for dollar losses in connection with stolen property. The highest recovery percentages were for stolen motor vehicles, consumable goods, clothing and furs, livestock, and firearms.

Law Enforcement Response

Law enforcement agencies nationwide recorded a 21-percent clearance rate for the collective Crime Index offenses in 1995 and made an estimated 2.9 million arrests for Index crimes. Crimes can be cleared by arrest or by exceptional means when some element beyond law enforcement control precludes the placing of formal charges against the offender. The arrest of one person may clear several crimes, or several persons may be arrested in connection with the clearance of one offense.

The Index clearance rate has remained relatively stable throughout the past 10-year period. As in 1995, the clearance rates in both 1991 and 1986 were 21 percent.

The number of persons arrested for Index crimes decreased 1 percent in 1995 when compared to 1994. Juvenile arrests for Index crimes decreased 2 percent, while those of adults showed virtually no change. By gender, arrests of males decreased 2 percent, but arrests of females increased 2 percent for the 2-year period.

CRIME INDEX OFFENSES REPORTED

Between 1994 and 1995, the number of persons arrested for the individual offenses composing the Index decreased for murder and motor vehicle theft, 6 percent; forcible rape, 5 percent; burglary, 4 percent; arson, 3 percent; and robbery, 2 percent. The number of larceny-theft arrests showed virtually no change, while those for aggravated assault increased 1 percent during the same 2-year period.

As in previous years, larceny-theft arrests accounted for the highest volume of Crime Index arrests at 1.5 million.

MURDER AND NONNEGLIGENT MANSLAUGHTER

DEFINITION

Murder and nonnegligent manslaughter, as defined in the Uniform Crime Reporting Program, is the willful (nonnegligent) killing of one human being by another.

TREND

Year	Number of offenses	Rate per 100,000 inhabitants
1994	23,326	9.0
1995	21,597	8.2
Percent change	−7.4	−8.9

Volume

The number of persons murdered in 1995 was estimated at 21,597, down 7 percent from the 1994 count and 13 percent below the 1991 total. The 1995 total was, however, 5 percent above the 1986 level.

The murder volumes decreased 9 percent in suburban counties and 8 percent in the Nation's cities in 1995 from the 1994 level. The greatest decrease—14 percent—was registered in cities with populations of 50,000 to 99,999. In the rural counties, murder increased 2 percent for the 2-year period.

When viewing the four regions of the Nation, the Southern States, the most populous region, accounted for 42 percent of the murders. The Western States reported 24 percent; the Midwestern States, 20 percent; and the Northeastern States, 15 percent. All the regions showed declines in the number of murders reported from 1994 to 1995. The greatest drop was in the Northeast, 13 percent. Decreases in the remaining regions were 8 percent in the Midwest, 7 percent in the South, and 3 percent in the West.

Monthly figures showed that the greatest number of murders occurred in the month of August in 1995, while the fewest occurred in February.

Rate

Down 9 percent from 1994, the national murder rate in 1995 was 8 per 100,000 inhabitants, the lowest rate since 1985. Five- and 10-year trends showed the 1995 rate was 16 percent lower than in 1991 and 5 percent below the 1986 rate.

Murder by Month, 1991–1995

[Percent distribution]

Months	1991	1992	1993	1994	1995
January	8.0	8.1	8.1	8.2	8.3
February	7.0	7.5	6.7	7.6	6.8
March	7.7	8.2	7.9	8.8	7.7
April	7.8	8.0	7.6	8.1	8.4
May	8.1	8.5	7.8	8.2	7.9
June	8.6	7.9	8.6	8.3	8.2
July	9.1	9.1	9.3	9.0	8.9
August	9.4	9.1	9.2	9.2	9.8
September	8.8	8.7	8.3	8.3	8.7
October	8.6	8.0	8.4	8.5	8.8
November	7.8	8.1	8.2	7.9	8.1
December	9.0	8.8	9.8	8.0	8.5

On a regional basis, the South averaged 10 murders for every 100,000 people; the West, 9 per 100,000; the Midwest, 7 per 100,000; and the Northeast, 6 per 100,000. Compared to 1994, murder rates in 1995 declined in all of the four geographic regions, with the Northeast experiencing the greatest change, a decrease of 13 percent, and the West, the smallest, a 4-percent drop.

The Nation's metropolitan areas reported a 1995 murder rate of 9 victims per 100,000 inhabitants. In the rural counties and in cities outside metropolitan areas, the rate was 5 per 100,000.

Nature

Supplemental data were provided by contributing agencies for 20,043 of the estimated 21,597 murders in 1995. Submitted monthly, the data consist of the age, sex, and race of both victims and offenders; the types of weapons used; the relationships of victims to the offenders; and the circumstances surrounding the murders.

Based on this information, 77 percent of the murder victims in 1995 were males; and 88 percent were persons 18 years of age or older. Forty-five percent were aged 20 through 34. Considering victims for whom race was known, 49 percent were black, 48 percent were white, and the remainder were persons of other races.

Supplemental data were also reported for 22,434 murder offenders in 1995. Of those for whom sex and age were reported, 91 percent of the offenders were males, and 85 percent were persons 18 years of age or older. Sixty-eight percent were aged 17 through 34. Of offenders for whom race was known, 53 percent were black, 45 percent were white, and the remainder were persons of other races.

Murder is most frequently intraracial among victims and

Murder Victims by Race and Sex, 1995

Race of Victims	Sex of Victims			
	Total	Male	Female	Unknown
Total White Victims	9,613	6,939	2,674	—
Total Black Victims	9,694	7,913	1,781	—
Total Other Race Victims	542	387	155	—
Total Unknown Race	194	117	44	33
Total Victims[1]	20,043	15,356	4,654	33

[1]Total murder victims for whom supplemental data were received.

offenders. In 1995, data based on incidents involving one victim and one offender showed that 94 percent of the black murder victims were slain by black offenders, and 84 percent of the white murder victims were killed by white offenders. Likewise, males were most often slain by males (89 percent in single victim/single offender situations). These same data showed, however, that 9 of every 10 female victims were murdered by males.

FORCIBLE RAPE

DEFINITION

Forcible rape, as defined in the Program, is the carnal knowledge of a female forcibly and against her will. Assaults or attempts to commit rape by force or threat of force are also included; however, statutory rape (without force) and other sex offenses are excluded.

TREND

Year	Number of offenses	Rate per 100,000 inhabitants
1994	102,616	39.3
1995	97,464	37.1
Percent change	−4.6	−5.6

Volume

The 97,464 forcible rapes reported to law enforcement agencies across the Nation during 1995 represented the lowest total since 1989. The 1995 count was 5 percent lower than in 1994, 9 percent below the 1991 level, but 7 percent higher than the 1986 volume.

Geographically, 39 percent of the forcible rape total in 1995 was accounted for by the most populous Southern States, 25 percent by the Midwestern States, 23 percent by the Western States, and 13 percent by the Northeastern States. Two-year trends showed that forcible rapes declined in all regions. The Northeast and Midwest each registered decreases of 6 percent; the South, 5 percent; and the West, 2 percent.

Monthly totals show the lowest rape volume occurred in December, while the most forcible rapes were reported during August.

Forcible Rape by Month, 1991–1995

[Percent distribution]

Months	1991	1992	1993	1994	1995
January	7.1	7.0	7.7	7.5	7.7
February	7.0	7.6	6.9	7.3	7.1
March	7.9	8.6	8.5	8.3	8.5
April	8.3	8.5	8.2	8.4	7.9
May	9.2	8.9	8.9	8.9	8.8
June	9.2	8.7	9.2	9.2	8.5
July	9.5	9.4	9.7	9.7	9.4
August	9.7	9.6	9.3	9.6	9.9
September	8.8	8.7	8.3	8.7	8.8
October	8.6	8.4	8.4	8.5	8.8
November	7.8	7.6	7.5	7.3	7.8
December	6.8	7.0	7.7	6.5	6.8

Rate

By Uniform Crime Reporting definition, the victims of forcible rape are always female, and in 1995, an estimated 72 of every 100,000 females in the country were reported rape victims. The 1995 female forcible rape rate was 6 percent lower than the 1994 rate and 13 percent lower than the 1991 rate.

The highest rate in 1995 was recorded in the Nation's metropolitan areas where it was 76 victims per 100,000 females. In cities outside metropolitan areas, the rate was 73 per 100,000 females, and in rural counties, it was 49 per 100,000 females. Although metropolitan areas record the highest rape rates, they have shown the only rate decline over the past 10 years (1986–1995), 10 percent. During this same time, the rate increased in cities outside metropolitan areas by 70 percent and in rural counties by 40 percent.

Geographically, in 1995, the highest female rape rate was in the Southern States, which recorded 80 victims per 100,000 females. The Midwestern States followed closely with a rate of 78; the Western States registered 75; and the Northeastern States, 49. For the 2-year period, 1994 and 1995, the changes in the forcible rape rates ranged from a decline of 7 percent in the Midwest to a 4-percent decrease in the West.

Over the last 10 years, regional increases in the female forcible rape rate were 13 percent in the Midwest and 1 percent in the South. Forcible rape rate decreases were reported in the Northeast and West, 11 and 13 percent, respectively, for the same timeframe.

Nature

Rapes by force constitute the greatest percentage of total forcible rapes, 87 percent of the 1995 incidents. The remainder were attempts or assaults to commit forcible rape. The number of rapes by force decreased 5 percent in 1995 from the 1994 volume, and attempts to rape decreased 6 percent.

As for all other Crime Index offenses, complaints of forcible rape made to law enforcement agencies are sometimes found to be false or baseless. In such cases, law enforcement agencies "unfound" the offenses and exclude them from crime counts. The "unfounded" rate, or percentage of complaints determined through investigation to be false, is higher for forcible rape than for any other Index crime. In 1995, 8 percent of forcible rape complaints were "unfounded," while the average for all Index crimes was 2 percent.

Law Enforcement Response

In 1995, over half of the forcible rapes reported to law enforcement nationwide and in cities were cleared by arrest or exceptional means. Rural and suburban county law enforcement clearance rates, each at 52 percent, were slightly higher than the cities' rate, 51 percent.

Geographically, forcible rape clearance rates in 1995 were 46 percent in the West, 49 percent in the Midwest, 50 percent in the Northeast, and 56 percent in the South.

Of the total clearances for forcible rape in the country as a whole, 15 percent involved only persons under 18 years of age. The percentage of juvenile involvement varied by community type, ranging from 13 percent in the Nation's cities to 22 percent in suburban counties.

Law enforcement agencies nationwide made an estimated 34,650 arrests for forcible rape in 1995. Of the forcible rape arrestees, about 4 of every 10 were under age 25. Over half of those arrested were white.

The number of arrests for forcible rape declined 5 percent nationwide from 1994 to 1995. Arrests fell 4 percent in the Nation's cities, 6 percent in the suburban counties, and 14 percent in the rural counties.

ROBBERY

DEFINITION

Robbery is the taking or attempting to take anything of value from the care, custody, or control of a person or persons by force or threat of force or violence and/or by putting the victim in fear.

TREND

Year	Number of offenses	Rate per 100,000 inhabitants
1994	618,949	237.7
1995	580,545	220.9
Percent change	−6.2	−7.1

Volume

The 1995 estimated robbery total, 580,545, was the lowest since 1989. Nationally, the 1995 robbery volume was down 6 percent from the 1994 total. In the Nation's cities, robberies decreased 7 percent. The largest decline—12 percent—was experienced in cities with a million or more inhabitants. During the same period, the robbery volume dropped 3 percent in the suburban counties but increased 1 percent in the rural counties.

Regionally, the Southern States, the most populous region, accounted for 34 percent of all reported robberies. The West-

ern States followed with 24 percent, the Northeastern States with 23 percent, and the Midwestern States with 19 percent. Two-year trends show the number of robberies in 1995 was down in all regions as compared to 1994. The declines ranged from 11 percent in the Northeast to 3 percent in the South.

Monthly volume figures for 1995 show robberies occurred most frequently in October and least often in February.

Rate

The national robbery rate in 1995 was 221 per 100,000 people, 7 percent lower than in 1994. In metropolitan areas, the 1995 rate was 268; in cities outside metropolitan areas, it was 72; and in the rural areas, it was 17. With 768 robberies per 100,000 inhabitants, the highest rate was recorded in cities with populations 1 million and over.

Robbery rates per 100,000 inhabitants declined in all regions from 1994 to 1995. The rates of 260 in the Northeast and 242 in the West were down 11 and 6 percent, respectively. The South's rate of 212 was 4 percent lower; and the Midwest's rate of 182 was down 9 percent.

Nature

Losses estimated at $507 million were attributed to robberies during 1995. The value of property stolen averaged $873 per robbery, up from $801 in 1994. Average dollar losses in 1995 ranged from $400 taken during robberies of convenience stores to $4,015 per bank robbery. The impact of this violent crime on its victims cannot be measured in terms of monetary loss alone. While the object of a robbery is to obtain money or property, the crime always involves force or threat of force, and many victims suffer serious personal injury.

Robberies on streets or highways accounted for more than half (54 percent) of the offenses in this category during 1995. Robberies of commercial and financial establishments accounted for 21 percent, and those occurring at residences, 11 percent. The remainder were miscellaneous types. All robbery types declined in 1995 as compared to 1994 totals. The decreases ranged from 10 percent for convenience store robberies to 4 percent for those of gas or service stations.

Robbery by Month, 1991–1995

[Percent distribution]

Months	1991	1992	1993	1994	1995
January	8.7	9.0	8.8	8.7	8.6
February	7.5	8.0	7.1	7.7	7.3
March	8.0	8.1	8.3	8.6	8.1
April	7.4	7.8	7.4	8.0	7.5
May	7.8	7.9	7.5	8.0	7.8
June	7.8	7.9	8.1	8.0	8.0
July	8.4	8.4	8.7	8.5	8.5
August	8.8	8.6	8.8	8.8	8.9
September	8.5	8.3	8.4	8.3	8.5
October	9.2	8.7	9.0	8.8	9.2
November	8.7	8.3	8.5	8.2	8.7
December	9.2	9.0	9.4	8.4	8.9

Robbery, Percent Distribution, 1995

[By region]

	United States Total	North- eastern States	Mid- western States	Southern States	Western States
Total[1]	100.0	100.0	100.0	100.0	100.0
Street/highway	54.3	64.1	61.6	50.7	48.8
Commercial house	12.3	9.0	10.4	12.4	15.5
Gas or service station	2.3	1.9	2.8	2.3	2.4
Convenience store	5.2	2.9	3.8	6.6	5.6
Residence	10.8	10.1	9.6	13.5	8.4
Bank	1.6	.9	1.3	1.3	2.6
Miscellaneous	13.4	11.0	10.6	13.3	16.6

[1] Because of rounding, percentages may not add to totals.

AGGRAVATED ASSAULT

DEFINITION

Aggravated assault is an unlawful attack by one person upon another for the purpose of inflicting severe or aggravated bodily injury. This type of assault is usually accompanied by the use of a weapon or by means likely to produce death or great bodily harm.

TREND

Year	Number of offenses	Rate per 100,000 inhabitants
1994	1,113,179	427.6
1995	1,099,179	418.3
Percent change	−1.3	−2.2

Volume

For the second consecutive year, aggravated assaults declined 1 percent to a total of 1,099,179 offenses in 1995. Aggravated assaults in 1995 accounted for 61 percent of the violent crimes.

Geographic distribution figures show that 40 percent of the aggravated assault volume was accounted for by the most populous Southern Region. Following were the Western Region with 25 percent, the Midwestern Region with 20 percent, and the Northeastern Region with 15 percent. Among the regions, only the Midwest registered an increase in the number of reported aggravated assaults.

The 1995 monthly figures show that the greatest number of aggravated assaults was recorded during July, while the lowest volume occurred during February.

Aggravated Assault by Month, 1991–1995

[Percent distribution]

Months	1991	1992	1993	1994	1995
January	6.9	7.3	7.5	7.2	7.6
February	6.6	7.3	6.5	7.0	7.1
March	7.7	8.0	8.1	8.3	8.1
April	8.1	8.7	8.3	8.5	8.3
May	9.1	9.2	8.9	8.8	8.8
June	9.3	8.9	9.1	8.9	8.8
July	9.7	9.4	9.6	9.5	9.4
August	9.9	9.1	9.2	9.4	9.3
September	9.0	8.6	8.3	8.9	8.9
October.	8.6	8.5	8.5	8.7	8.8
November	7.6	7.6	7.4	7.7	7.6
December	7.6	7.4	8.6	7.3	7.4

The Nation's cities collectively experienced a decrease of 3 percent in the aggravated assault volume from 1994 to 1995. Among city population groupings, both cities with populations over a million and cities with populations from 250,000 to 499,999 recorded 5-percent declines. The number of aggravated assaults decreased 1 percent in suburban counties but increased 6 percent in the rural counties during the same 2-year period.

Five- and 10-year trends for the country as a whole showed aggravated assaults 1 percent higher than in 1991 and 32 percent above the 1986 experience.

Rate

There were 418 reported victims of aggravated assault for every 100,000 people nationwide in 1995, the lowest rate since 1989. The rate was 2 percent lower than in 1994 and 3 percent below the 1991 rate. The 1995 rate was, however, 21 percent above the 1986 rate.

Higher than the national average, the rate in metropolitan areas was 459 per 100,000 in 1995. Cities outside metropolitan areas experienced a rate of 369, and rural counties, a rate of 187.

Regionally, the aggravated assault rate was 319 per 100,000 people in the Northeast, 359 in the Midwest, 474 in the South, and 481 in the West. Compared to 1994 rates, 1995 aggravated assault rates were down in all regions except the Midwest, which registered a 3-percent increase.

Nature

Thirty-three percent of the aggravated assaults in 1995 were committed with blunt objects or other dangerous weapons. Of the remaining weapon categories, personal weapons such as hands, fists, and feet were used in 26 percent of the assaults; firearms in 23 percent; and knives or cutting instruments in the remainder.

Three of the four categories of weapons decreased in use during 1995, with personal weapons (hands, fists, feet, etc.) showing the only increase, less than 1 percent. Those aggravated assaults involving firearms decreased 9 percent; assaults with knives or cutting instruments, 2 percent; and those with blunt objects or other dangerous weapons, 1 percent.

Aggravated Assault, Types of Weapons Used, 1995

[Percent distribution by region]

Region	Total all weapons[1]	Firearms	Knives or cutting instruments	Other weapons (clubs, blunt objects, etc.)	Personal weapons
Total	100.0	22.9	18.3	32.9	25.9
Northeastern States	100.0	14.3	21.1	35.3	29.3
Midwestern States	100.0	25.4	19.7	34.0	20.9
Southern States	100.0	25.4	18.8	34.3	21.5
Western States	100.0	22.1	14.4	29.2	34.3

BURGLARY

DEFINITION

The Uniform Crime Reporting Program defines burglary as the unlawful entry of a structure to commit a felony or theft. The use of force to gain entry is not required to classify an offense as burglary.

TREND		
Year	Number of offenses	Rate per 100,000 inhabitants
1994	2,712,156	1,042.0
1995	2,594,995	987.6
Percent change	−4.3	−5.2

Volume

The estimated 2.6 million burglaries in the United States during 1995 represented the lowest total in the past two decades. Distribution figures for the regions showed that the highest burglary volume in 1995 (40 percent) occurred in the most populous Southern States. The Western States followed with 25 percent, the Midwestern States with 20 percent, and the Northeastern States with 15 percent.

The greatest number of burglaries was recorded during August of 1995, while the lowest count was in February.

Burglary by Month, 1991–1995

[Percent distribution]

Months	1991	1992	1993	1994	1995
January	8.1	8.6	8.3	7.9	8.4
February	7.3	7.7	6.9	7.1	7.2
March	8.1	8.2	8.2	8.2	8.2
April	7.9	7.8	7.7	8.0	7.7
May	8.3	8.2	8.0	8.5	8.4
June	8.2	8.1	8.4	8.3	8.3
July	9.2	9.0	9.0	9.2	9.0
August	9.2	9.0	9.1	9.4	9.2
September	8.6	8.4	8.5	8.6	8.5
October	8.6	8.3	8.4	8.6	8.8
November	8.0	8.2	8.1	8.4	8.3
December	8.6	8.3	9.3	7.9	8.0

Overall, the burglary volume dropped 4 percent in 1995 from the 1994 total. Among the Nation's cities, decreases were registered in all groupings; the largest decrease was in cities with populations of 1 million and over which showed a 9-percent decline. The suburban counties also showed a decrease, 5 percent; however, an increase of 2 percent was reported for the rural counties.

All four regions of the United States reported decreases in burglary volumes during 1995 as compared to the 1994 figures. The Northeastern States experienced a 6-percent decline; the Southern States, a 5-percent decrease; the Midwestern States, a 4-percent decline; and the Western States, a 3-percent drop.

Longer term national trends show burglary down 18 percent from the 1991 level and down 20 percent from the 1986 volume.

Rate

Lower than in any other year of the past two decades, the burglary rate was 988 per 100,000 inhabitants nationwide in 1995. The rate was 5 percent lower than in 1994, down 21 percent from the 1991 level, and 27 percent below the 1986 rate. In 1995, for every 100,000 in population, the rate was 1,048 in the metropolitan areas, 924 in the cities outside metropolitan areas, and 634 in the rural counties.

Regionally, the burglary rate was 1,137 in the Southern States, 1,111 in the Western States, 841 in the Midwestern States, and 758 in the Northeastern States. A comparison of 1994 and 1995 rates showed decreases of 6 percent in both the Northeast and the South, 5 percent in the Midwest, and 4 percent in the West.

Nature

Two of every 3 burglaries in 1995 were residential in nature. Sixty-seven percent of all burglaries involved forcible entry, 25 percent were unlawful entries (without force), and the remainder were forcible entry attempts. Offenses for which time of occurrence was reported showed that 52 percent of burglaries happened during daytime hours and 48 percent at night. More residential burglaries (59 percent) occurred during the daytime, while 61 percent of nonresidential burglaries occurred during nighttime hours.

The value of property stolen in burglaries was estimated at $3.3 billion in 1995, and the average dollar loss per burglary was $1,259. The average loss for residential offenses was $1,211 and for nonresidential offenses, $1,257. Compared to 1994 losses, the 1995 average loss for both residential and nonresidential property decreased.

Both residential and nonresidential burglary volumes also showed declines from 1994 to 1995, 4 and 5 percent, respectively.

LARCENY-THEFT

DEFINITION
Larceny-theft is the unlawful taking, carrying, leading, or riding away of property from the possession or constructive possession of another. It includes crimes such as shoplifting, pocket-picking, purse-snatching, thefts from motor vehicles, thefts of motor vehicle parts and accessories, bicycle thefts, etc., in which no use of force, violence, or fraud occurs.

TREND		
Year	Number of offenses	Rate per 100,000 inhabitants
1994	7,879,812	3,026.7
1995	8,000,631	3,044.9
Percent change	+1.5	+.6

Volume

Larceny-theft, estimated at 8 million offenses during 1995, comprised 58 percent of the Crime Index total and 66 percent of the property crimes. Similar to the experience in previous years, larceny-thefts were recorded most often during August and least frequently in February.

Larceny–Theft by Month, 1991–1995

[Percent distribution]

Months	1991	1992	1993	1994	1995
January	7.8	8.2	7.7	7.4	7.9
February	7.5	7.8	6.8	7.1	7.1
March	8.2	8.3	8.0	8.1	8.2
April	8.1	8.1	8.0	8.1	7.8
May	8.4	8.2	8.2	8.5	8.5
June	8.5	8.5	8.7	8.6	8.7
July	9.2	9.1	9.2	9.2	9.1
August	9.3	9.1	9.3	9.5	9.3
September	8.3	8.4	8.3	8.5	8.5
October	8.7	8.6	8.6	8.9	8.8
November	7.9	7.9	8.0	8.3	8.1
December	8.2	8.0	9.1	7.9	8.0

Viewed geographically, the Southern States, the most populous region, recorded 38 percent of the larceny-theft total. The Western States recorded 25 percent; the Midwestern States, 22 percent; and the Northeastern States, 15 percent.

The 1995 volume of larceny-thefts nationwide was 2 percent higher than the 1994 total. By community type, increases of 1 percent were recorded both in cities collectively and suburban counties, and a 6-percent rise was experienced in the rural counties.

Larceny volumes increased in all four geographic regions. The increases were 3 percent in the West and 1 percent in the Midwest, Northeast, and South.

Long-term national trends indicate larceny was up 10 percent when compared to the 1986 total but was 2 percent below the 1991 level.

Rate

The 1995 larceny-theft rate was 3,045 per 100,000 U.S. inhabitants. Two-, 5-, and 10-year trends showed the rate was 1 percent higher than the rates in 1994 and 1986 but 6 percent below the 1991 rate. The 1995 rate was 3,278 per 100,000 inhabitants of metropolitan areas; 3,669 per 100,000 population in cities outside metropolitan areas; and 1,091 per 100,000 people in the rural counties.

By region, the 1995 larceny-theft rate per 100,000 people in the West was up 2 percent, and the Northeast's rate rose 1 percent. Showing virtually no change from 1994 were the rates in the Midwest and the South. The regional rates ranged from 2,296 per 100,000 people in the Northeast to 3,435 per 100,000 population in the West.

Nature

During 1995, the average value of property stolen due to larceny-theft was $535, up from $505 in 1994. When the average value was applied to the estimated number of larceny-thefts, the loss to victims nationally was nearly $4.3 billion for the year. This estimated dollar loss is considered conservative since many offenses in the larceny category, particularly if the value of the stolen goods is small, never come to law enforcement attention. Losses under $50 and those over $200 jointly ac-

counted for 77 percent of the thefts reported to law enforcement. The remainder involved losses ranging from $50 to $200.

Losses of goods and property reported stolen as a result of pocket-picking averaged $350; purse-snatching, $279; and shoplifting, $108. Thefts from buildings resulted in an average loss of $891; from motor vehicles, $531; and from coin-operated machines, $283. The average value loss due to thefts of motor vehicle accessories was $329 and for thefts of bicycles, $286.

Thefts of motor vehicle parts, accessories, and contents made up the largest portion of reported larcenies—36 percent. Also contributing to the high volume of thefts were shoplifting, accounting for 15 percent; thefts from buildings, 13 percent; and bicycle thefts, 6 percent. The remainder was distributed among pocket-picking, purse-snatching, thefts from coin-operated machines, and all other types of larceny-thefts.

Larceny Analysis by Region, 1995

[Percent distribution]

	United States Total	North-eastern States	Mid-western States	Southern States	Western States
Total[1]	100.0	100.0	100.0	100.0	100.0
Pocket-picking	.6	2.0	.3	.5	.4
Purse-snatching	.6	1.2	.6	.6	.5
Shoplifting	15.1	14.6	13.6	14.6	16.8
From motor vehicles (except accessories)	24.3	22.7	22.3	22.0	29.7
Motor vehicle accessories	12.1	11.1	13.1	12.9	10.7
Bicycles	6.3	7.9	6.7	5.3	6.6
From buildings	12.5	17.6	15.8	9.8	12.2
From coin-operated machines	.6	.7	.5	.7	.6
All others	27.9	22.2	27.1	33.7	22.5

[1] Because of rounding, percentages may not add to totals.

MOTOR VEHICLE THEFT

DEFINITION

Defined as the theft or attempted theft of a motor vehicle, this offense category includes the stealing of automobiles, trucks, buses, motorcycles, motorscooters, snowmobiles, etc.

TREND

Year	Number of offenses	Rate per 100,000 inhabitants
1994	1,539,687	591.3
1995	1,472,732	560.5
Percent change	−4.3	−5.2

Volume

The nearly 1.5 million thefts of motor vehicles occurring in the United States during 1995 represented the lowest total since 1989. The regional distribution of thefts in 1995 showed 33

235

percent of the volume was in the Southern States, 30 percent in the Western States, 19 percent in the Midwestern States, and 18 percent in the Northeastern States.

The 1995 monthly figures show that the greatest numbers of motor vehicle thefts were recorded during the months of August and October, while the lowest count was in February.

Motor Vehicle Theft by Month, 1991–1995

[Percent distribution]

Months	1991	1992	1993	1994	1995
January	8.3	8.8	8.5	8.2	8.6
February	7.5	7.9	7.3	7.4	7.5
March	8.2	8.2	8.2	8.5	8.2
April	7.8	7.8	7.8	8.0	7.8
May	8.1	8.1	7.9	8.2	8.2
June	8.2	8.2	8.4	8.3	8.2
July	8.7	8.8	8.9	8.9	8.6
August	8.9	8.9	8.9	9.1	8.9
September	8.3	8.2	8.4	8.4	8.4
October	8.7	8.6	8.6	8.8	8.9
November	8.5	8.3	8.3	8.4	8.5
December	8.8	8.2	8.8	7.8	8.2

Motor vehicle thefts declined 4 percent nationally from 1994 to 1995. The Nation's cities collectively experienced a 6-percent decline, but among city population groupings, the changes ranged from a 12-percent decline in cities with populations of 1 million or more to a 4-percent increase in those with populations under 10,000. During the same 2-year period, a 2-percent decrease in the volume of motor vehicle thefts occurred in the suburban counties, while rural counties registered an increase of 8 percent.

Geographically, decreases in motor vehicle thefts were recorded in the Northeast, 14 percent, and in the West, 3 percent. Both the South and Midwest regions showed decreases of 1 percent.

Rate

The 1995 national motor vehicle theft rate—560 per 100,000 people—was 5 percent lower than in 1994 and 15 percent below the 1991 rate. The 1995 rate was 10 percent above the 1986 rate.

For every 100,000 inhabitants living in metropolitan areas, there were 660 motor vehicle thefts reported in 1995. The rate

in cities outside metropolitan areas was 240 and in rural counties, 125. As in previous years, the highest rates were in the Nation's most heavily populated municipalities, indicating that this offense is primarily a large-city problem. For every 100,000 inhabitants in cities with populations over 250,000, the 1995 motor vehicle theft rate was 1,310. The Nation's smallest cities, those with fewer than 10,000 inhabitants, recorded a rate of 261 per 100,000.

Declining among all regions in comparison to 1994, motor vehicle theft rates ranged from 766 per 100,000 people in the Western States to 451 in the Midwestern States. The Southern States' rate was 530, and the Northeastern States' rate was 516. The Northeast reported the greatest rate decrease, 14 percent. The West reported a decrease of 4 percent; the South, a decrease of 3 percent; and the Midwest, a decrease of 2 percent.

An estimated average of 1 of every 139 registered motor vehicles was stolen nationwide during 1995. Regionally, this rate was greatest in the West where 1 of every 100 motor vehicles registered was stolen. The other three regions reported lesser rates—1 per 190 in the Midwest, 1 per 148 in the South, and 1 per 132 in the Northeast.

Nature

The estimated value of motor vehicles stolen nationwide in 1995 was nearly $7.6 billion. At the time of theft, the average value per vehicle was $5,129. The recovery percentage for the value of vehicles stolen was higher than for any other property type. Relating the value of vehicles stolen to the value of those recovered resulted in a 62-percent recovery rate for 1995.

Seventy-eight percent of all motor vehicles reported stolen during the year were automobiles, 16 percent were trucks or buses, and the remainder were other types.

Motor Vehicle Theft, 1995

[Percent distribution by region]

Region	Total[1]	Autos	Trucks and buses	Other vehicles
Total	100.0	78.4	16.3	5.4
Northeastern States	100.0	92.8	4.4	2.9
Midwestern States	100.0	75.1	18.2	6.7
Southern States	100.0	82.9	12.1	5.0
Western States	100.0	71.5	22.9	5.5

[1]Because of rounding, percentages may not add to totals.

Glossary

Abet: To encourage another to commit a crime.

Accessory: One who harbors, assists, or protects another person, although he or she knows that person has committed or will commit a crime.

Accomplice: One who knowingly and voluntarily aids another in committing a criminal offense.

Acquit: To free a person legally from an accusation of criminal guilt.

Adjudicatory hearing: The fact-finding process wherein the court determines whether or not there is sufficient evidence to sustain the allegations in a petition.

Admissible: Capable of being admitted; in a trial, such evidence as the judge allows to be introduced into the proceeding.

Affirmance: A pronouncement by a higher court that the case in question was rightly decided by the lower court from which the case was appealed.

Affirmation: Positive declaration or assertion that the witness will tell the truth; not made under oath.

Alias: Any name by which one is known other than his or her true name.

Alibi: A type of defense in a criminal prosecution that proves the accused could not have committed the crime with which he or she is charged, since evidence offered shows the accused was in another place at the time the crime was committed.

Allegation: An assertion of what a party to an action expects to prove.

American Bar Association (ABA): A professional association, comprising attorneys who have been admitted to the bar in any of the 50 states, and a registered lobby.

American Civil Liberties Union (ACLU): Founded in 1920 with the purpose of defending the individual's rights as guaranteed by the U.S. Constitution.

Amnesty: A class or group pardon.

Annulment: The act, by competent authority, of canceling, making void, or depriving of all force.

Appeal: A case carried to a higher court to ask that the decision of the lower court, in which the case originated, be altered or overruled completely.

Appellate court: A court that has jurisdiction to hear cases on appeal; not a trial court.

Arbitrator: The person chosen by parties in a controversy to settle their differences; private judges.

Arraignment: The appearance before the court of a person charged with a crime. He or she is advised of the charges, bail is set, and a plea of "guilty" or "not guilty" is entered.

Arrest: The legal detainment of a person to answer for criminal charges or civil demands.

Autopsy: A postmortem examination of a human body to determine the cause of death.

Bail: Property (usually money) deposited with a court in exchange for the release of a person in custody to ensure later appearance.

Bail bond: An obligation signed by the accused and his or her sureties, that ensures his or her presence in court.

Bailiff: An officer of the court who is responsible for keeping order in the court and protecting the security of jury deliberations and court property.

Bench warrant: An order by the court for the apprehension and arrest of a defendant or other person who has failed to appear when so ordered.

Bill of Rights: The first 10 amendments to the U.S. Constitution that state certain fundamental rights and privileges that are guaranteed to the people against infringement by the government.

Biocriminology: A relatively new branch of criminology that attempts to explain criminal behavior by referring to biological factors which predispose some individuals to commit criminal acts. *See also* Criminal biology.

Blue laws: Laws in some jurisdictions prohibiting sales or merchandise, athletic contests, and the sale of alcoholic beverages on Sundays.

Booking: A law-enforcement or correctional process officially recording an entry-into-detention after arrest and identifying the person, place, time, reason for the arrest, and the arresting authority.

Breathalizer: A commercial device to test the breath of a suspected drinker and determine that person's blood-alcohol content.

Brief: A summary of the law relating to a case, prepared by the attorneys for both parties and given to the judge.

Bug: To plant a sound sensor or to tap a communication line for the purpose of surreptitious listening or audio monitoring.

Burden of proof: Duty of establishing the existence of fact in a trial.

Calendar: A list of cases to be heard in a trial court, on a specific day, and containing the title of the case, the lawyers involved, and the index number.

Capital crime: Any crime that may be punishable by death or imprisonment for life.

Career criminal: A person having a past record of multiple arrests or convictions for crimes of varying degrees of seriousness. Such criminals are often described as chronic, habitual, repeat, serious, high-rate, or professional offenders.

Case: At the level of police or prosecutorial investigation, a set of circumstances under investigation involving one or more persons.

Case law: Judicial precedent generated as a byproduct of the decisions that courts have made to resolve unique disputes. Case law concerns concrete facts, as distinguished from statutes and constitutions, which are written in the abstract.

Change of venue: The removal of a trial from one jurisdiction to another in order to avoid local prejudice.

Charge: In criminal law, the accusation made against a person. It also refers to the judge's instruction to the jury on legal points.

Circumstantial evidence: Indirect evidence; evidence from which a fact can be reasonably inferred, although not directly proven.

Clemency: The doctrine under which executive or legislative action reduces the severity of or waives legal punishment of one or more individuals, or an individual exempted from prosecution for certain actions.

Code: A compilation, compendium, or revision of laws, arranged into chapters, having a table of contents and index, and promulgated by legislative authority. *See also* penal code.

Coercion: The use of force to compel performance of an action; The application of sanctions or the use of force by government to compel observance of law or public policy.

Common law: Judge-made law to assist courts through decision making with traditions, customs, and usage of previous court decisions.

Commutation: A reduction of a sentence originally prescribed by a court.

Complainant: The victim of a crime who brings the facts to the attention of the authorities.

Complaint: Any accusation that a person committed a crime that has originated or been received by a law enforcement agency or court.

Confession: A statement by a person who admits violation of the law.

Confiscation: Government seizure of private property without compensation to the owner.

Conspiracy: An agreement between two or more persons to plan for the purpose of committing a crime or any unlawful act or a lawful act by unlawful or criminal means.

Contempt of court: Intentionally obstructing a court in the administration of justice, acting in a way calculated to lessen its authority or dignity, or failing to obey its lawful order.

Continuance: Postponement or adjournment of a trial granted by the judge, either to a later date or indefinitely.

Contraband: Goods, the possession of which is illegal.

Conviction: A finding by the jury (or by the trial judge in cases tried without a jury) that the accused is guilty of a crime.

Corporal punishment: Physical punishment.

Corpus delicti **(Lat.):** The objective proof that a crime has been committed as distinguished from an accidental death, injury, or loss.

Corrections: Area of criminal justice dealing with convicted offenders in jails, prisons; on probation or parole.

Corroborating evidence: Supplementary evidence that tends to strengthen or confirm other evidence given previously.

Crime: An act injurious to the public, that is prohibited and punishable by law.

237

Crime Index: A set of numbers indicating the volume, fluctuation, and distribution of crimes reported to local law enforcement agencies for the United States as a whole.

Crime of passion: An unpremeditated murder or assault committed under circumstances of great anger, jealousy, or other emotional stress.

Criminal biology: The scientific study of the relation of hereditary physical traits to criminal character, that is, to innate tendencies to commit crime in general or crimes of any particular type. *See also* Biocriminology.

Criminal insanity: Lack of mental capacity to do or refrain from doing a criminal act; inability to distinguish right from wrong.

Criminal intent: The intent to commit and act, the results of which are a crime or violation of the law.

Criminalistics: Crime laboratory procedures.

Criminology: The scientific study of crime, criminals, corrections, and the operation of the system of criminal justice.

Cross examination: The questioning of a witness by the party who did not produce the witness.

Culpable: At fault or responsible, but not necessarily criminal.

Defamation: Intentional causing, or attempting to cause, damage to the reputation of another by communicating false or distorted information about his or her actions, motives, or character.

Defendant: The person who is being prosecuted.

Deliberation: The action of a jury to determine the guilt or innocence, or the sentence, of a defendant.

Demurrer: Plea for dismissal of a suit on the grounds that, even if true, the statements of the opposition are insufficient to sustain the claim.

Deposition: Sworn testimony obtained outside, rather than in, court.

Deterrence: A theory that swift and sure punishment will discourage others from similar illegal acts.

Dilatory: Law term that describes activity for the purpose of causing a delay or to gain time or postpone a decision.

Direct evidence: Testimony or other proof that expressly or straightforwardly proves the existence of fact.

Direct examination: The first questioning of witnesses by the party who calls them.

Directed verdict: An order or verdict pronounced by a judge during the trial of a criminal case in which the evidence presented by the prosecution clearly fails to show the guilt of the accused.

District attorney: A locally elected state official who represents the state in bringing indictments and prosecuting criminal cases.

Docket: The formal record of court proceedings.

Double jeopardy: To be prosecuted twice for the same offense.

Due process model: A philosophy of criminal justice based on the assumption that an individual is presumed innocent until proven guilty.

Due process of law: A clause in the Fifth and Fourteenth Amendments ensuring that laws are reasonable and that they are applied in a fair and equal manner.

Embracery: An attempt to influence a jury, or a member thereof, in their verdict by any improper means.

Entrapment: Inducing an individual to commit a crime he or she did not contemplate, for the sole purpose of instituting a criminal prosecution against the offender.

Evidence: All the means used to prove or disprove the fact at issue. *See also Corpus delicti.*

Ex post facto **(Lat.):** After the fact. An *ex post facto* law is a criminal law that makes an act unlawful although it was committed prior to the passage of that law. *See also* Grandfather clause.

Exception: A formal objection to the action of the court during a trial. The indication is that the excepting party will seek to reverse the court's actions at some future proceeding.

Exclusionary rule: Legal prohibitions against government prosecution using evidence illegally obtained.

Expert evidence: Testimony by one qualified to speak authoritatively on technical matters because of her or his special training of skill.

Extradition: The surrender by one state to another of an individual accused of a crime.

False arrest: Any unlawful physical restraint of another's freedom of movement; unlawful arrest.

Felony: A criminal offense punishable by death or imprisonment in a penitentiary.

Forensic: Relating to the court. Forensic medicine would refer to legal medicine that applies anatomy, pathology, toxicology, chemistry, and other fields of science in expert testimony in court cases or hearings.

Grandfather clause: A clause attempting to preserve the rights of firms in operation before enactment of a law by exempting these firms from certain provisions of that law. *See also Ex post facto.*

Grand jury: A group of 12 to 23 citizens of a county who examine evidence against the person suspected of a crime and hand down an indictment if there is sufficient evidence. *See also* Petit jury.

Habeas corpus **(Lat.):** A legal device to challenge the detention of a person taken into custody. An individual in custody may demand an evidentiary hearing before a judge to examine the legality of the detention.

Hearsay: Evidence that a witness has learned through others.

Homicide: The killing of a human being; may be murder, negligent or nonnegligent manslaughter, or excusable or justifiable homicide.

Hung jury: A jury which, after long deliberation, is so irreconcilably divided in opinion that it is unable to reach a verdict.

Impanel: The process of selecting the jury that is to try a case.

Imprisonment: A sentence imposed upon the conviction of a crime; the deprivation of liberty in a penal institution; incarceration.

In camera **(Lat.):** A case heard when the doors of the court are closed and only persons concerned in the case are admitted.

Indemnification: Compensation for loss or damage sustained because of improper or illegal action by a public authority.

Indictment: The document prepared by a prosecutor and approved by the grand jury that charges a certain person with a specific crime or crimes for which that person is later to be tried in court.

Injunction: An order by a court prohibiting a defendant from committing an act, or commanding an act be done.

Inquest: A legal inquiry to establish some question of fact; specifically, and inquiry by a coroner and jury into a person's death where accident, foul play, or violence is suspected as the cause.

Instanter: A subpoena issued for the appearance of a hostile witness or person who has failed to appear in answer to a previous subpoena and authorizing a law enforcement officer to bring that person to the court.

Interpol (International Criminal Police Commission): A clearing house for international exchanges of information consisting of a consortium of 126 countries.

Jeopardy: The danger of conviction and punishment that a defendant faces in a criminal trial.

Judge: An officer who presides over and administers the law in a court of justice.

Judicial notice: The rule that a court will accept certain things as common knowledge without proof.

Judicial process: The procedures taken by a court in deciding cases or resolving legal controversies.

Jurisdiction: The territory, subject matter, or persons over which lawful authority may be exercised by a court or other justice agency, as determined by statute or constitution.

Jury: A certain number of persons who are sworn to examine the evidence and determine the truth on the basis of that evidence.

Jury, hung: A trial jury which, after exhaustive deliberations, cannot agree on a unanimous verdict, necessitating an mistrial and a subsequent retrial.

Justice of the peace: A subordinate magistrate, usually without formal legal training, empowered to try petty civil and criminal cases and, in some states, to conduct preliminary hearings for persons accused of a crime, and to fix bail for appearance in court.

Juvenile delinquent: A boy or girl who has not reached the age of criminal liability (varies from state to state) and who commits and act which would be a misdemeanor or felony if he or she were an adult. Delinquents are tried in Juvenile Court and confined to separate facilities.

Law Enforcement Agency: A federal, state, or local criminal justice agency or identifiable subunit whose principal functions are the prevention, detection, and investigation of crime and the apprehension of alleged offenders.

Libel and slander: Printed and spoken defamation of character, respectively, or a person or an institution. In a slander action, it is usually necessary to prove specific damages caused by spoken words to recover, but in a case of libel, the damage is assumed to have occurred by publication.

Lie detector: An instrument that measures certain physiological reactions of the human body from which a trained operator may determine whether the subject is telling the truth or lies; polygraph; psychological stress evaluator.

Litigation: A judicial controversy; a contest in a court of justice for the purpose of enforcing a right; any controversy that must be decided upon evidence.

Mala in se **(Lat.):** Evil in itself. Acts that are make crimes because they are, by their nature evil and morally wrong.

Mala fides **(Lat.):** Bad faith, as opposed to *bona fides,* or good faith.

Mala priohibita **(Lat.):** Evil because they are prohibited. Acts that are not wrong in themselves but which, to protect the general welfare, are make crimes by statute.

Malfeasance: The act of a public officer in committing a crime relating to his official duties or powers. Accepting or demanding a bribe.

Malice: An evil intent to vex, annoy, or injure another; intentional evil.

Mandatory sentences: A statutory requirement that a certain penalty shall be set and carried out in all cases upon conviction for a specified offense or series of offenses.

Martial law: Refers to control of civilian populations by a military commander.

Mediation: Nonbinding third-party intervention in the collective bargaining process.

Mens rea **(Lat.):** Criminal intent.

Miranda rights: Set of rights that a person accused or suspected of having committed a specific offense has during interrogation and of which he or she must be informed prior to questioning, as stated by the Supreme Court in deciding *Miranda v. Arizona* in 1966 and related cases.

Misdemeanor: Any crime not a felony. Usually, a crime punishable by a fine or imprisonment in the county or other local jail.

Misprison: Failing to reveal a crime.

Mistrial: A trial discontinued before reaching a verdict because of some procedural defect or impediment.

Modus operandi: A characteristic pattern of behavior repeated in a series of offenses that coincides with the pattern evidenced by a particular person or group of persons.

Motion: An oral or written request made to a court at any time before, during, or after court proceedings, asking the court to make a specified finding, decision, or order.

Motive: The reason for committing a crime.

Municipal court: A minor court authorized by municipal charter or state law to enforce local ordinances and exercise the criminal and civil jurisdiction of the peace.

Narc: A widely used slang term for any local or federal law enforcement officer whose duties are focused on preventing or controlling traffic in the use of illegal drugs.

Negligent: Culpably careless; acting without the due care required by the circumstances.

Neolombrosians: Criminologists who emphasize psychopathological states as causes of crime.

No bill: A phrase used by a Grand jury when they fail to indict.

Nolle prosequi **(Lat.):** A prosecutor's decision not to initiate or continue prosecution.

Nolo contendre **(Lat., lit.):** A pleading, usually used by a defendant in a criminal case, that literally means "I will not contest."

Notary public: A public officer authorized to authenticate and certify documents such as seeds, contracts, and affidavits with his or her signature and seal.

Null: Of no legal or binding force.

Obiter dictum **(Lat.):** A belief or opinion included by a judge in his or her decision in a case.

Objection: The act of taking exception to some statement or procedure in a trial. Used to call the court's attention to some improper evidence or procedure.

Opinion evidence: A witness' belief or opinion about a fact in dispute, as distinguished from personal knowledge of the fact.

Ordinance: A law enacted by the city or municipal government.

Organized crime: An organized, continuing criminal conspiracy that engages in crime as business (e.g., loan sharking, illegal gambling, prostitution, extortion, etc.).

Original jurisdiction: The authority of a court to hear and determine a lawsuit when it is initiated.

Overt act: An open or physical act done to further a plan, conspiracy, or intent, as opposed to a thought or mere intention.

Paralegals: Employees, also know as legal assistants, of law firms, who assist attorneys in the delivery of legal services.

Pardon: There are two kinds of pardons of offenses: the absolute pardon, which fully restores to the individual all rights and privileges of a citizen, setting aside a conviction and penalty, and the conditional pardon, which requires a condition to be met before the pardon is officially granted.

Parole: A conditional, supervised release from prison prior to expiration of sentence.

Penal code: Criminal codes, the purpose of which is to define what acts shall be punished as crimes.

Penology: The study of punishment and corrections.

Peremptory challenge: In the selection of jurors, challenges made by either side to certain jurors without assigning any reason, and which the court must allow.

Perjury: The legal offense of deliberately testifying falsely under oath about a material fact.

Perpetrator: The chief actor in the commission of a crime, that is, the person who directly commits the criminal act.

Petit jury: The ordinary jury composed of 12 persons who hear criminal cases and determines guilt or innocence of the accused. *See also* Grand jury.

Plaintiff: A person who initiates a court action.

Plea-bargaining: A negotiation between the defense attorney and the prosecutor in which the defendant receives a reduced penalty in return for a plea of "guilty."

Police power: The authority to legislate for the protection of the health, morals, safety and welfare of the people.

Postmortem: After death. Commonly applied to an examination of a dead body. *See also* Autopsy.

Precedent: Decision by a court that may serve as an example or authority for similar cases in the future.

Preliminary hearing: The proceeding in front of a lower court to determine if there is sufficient evidence for submitting a felony case to the grand jury.

Premeditation: A design to commit a crime or commit some other act before it is done.

Presumption of fact: An inference as to the truth or falsity of any proposition or fact, make in the absence of actual certainty of its truth or falsity or until such certainty can be attained.

Presumption of innocence: The defendant is presumed to be innocent and the burden is on the state to prove his or her guilt beyond a reasonable doubt.

Presumption of law: A rule of law that courts and judges must draw a particular inference from a particular fact or evidence, unless the inference can be disproved.

Probable cause: A set of facts and circumstances that would induce a reasonably intelligent and prudent person to believe that a particular person had committed a specific crime; reasonable grounds to make or believe an accusation.

Probation: A penalty placing a convicted person under the supervision of a probation officer for a stated time, instead or being confined.

Prosecutor: One who initiates a criminal prosecution against an accused. One who acts as a trial attorney for the governments as the representative of the people.

Public defender: An attorney appointed by a court to represent individuals in criminal proceedings who do not have the resources to hire their own defense council.

Rap sheet: Popularized acronym for record of arrest and prosecution.

Reasonable doubt: That state of mind of jurors when they do not feel a moral certainty about the truth of the charge and when the evidence does no exclude every other reasonable hypothesis except that the defendant is guilty as charged.

Rebutting evidence: When the defense has produced new evidence that the prosecution has not dealt with, the court, at its discretion, may allow the prosecution to give evidence in reply to rebut or contradict it.

Recidivism: The repetition of criminal behavior.

Repeal: The abrogation of a law by the enacting body, either by express declaration or implication by the passage of a later act whose provisions contradict those of the earlier law.

Reprieve: The temporary postponement of the execution of a sentence.

Restitution: A court requirement that an alleged or convicted offender pay money or provide services to the victim of the crime or provide services to the community.

Restraining order: An order, issued by a court of competent jurisdiction, forbidding a named person, or a class of persons, from doing specified acts.

Retribution: A concept that implies that payment of a debt to society and thus the expiation of one's offense. It was codified in the biblical injunction, "an eye for an eye, a tooth for a tooth."

Sanction: A legal penalty assessed for the violation of law. The term also include social methods of obtaining compliance, such as peer pressure and public opinion.

Search warrant: A written order, issued by judicial authority in the name of the state, directing a law enforcement officer to search for personal property and, if found, to bring it before the court.

Selective enforcement: The deploying of police personnel in ways to cope most effectively with existing or anticipated problems.

Self-incrimination: In constitutional terms, the process of becoming involved in or charged with a crime by one's own testimony.

Sentence: The penalty imposed by a court on a person convicted of a crime; the court judgment specifying the penalty; and any disposition of a defendant resulting from a conviction, including the court decision to suspend execution of a sentence.

Small claims court: A special court that provides expeditious, informal, and inexpensive adjudication of small contractual claims. In most jurisdictions, attorneys are not permitted for cases, and claims are limited to a specific amount.

Stare decisis (Lat.): To abide by decided cases. The doctrine that once a court has laid down a principle of laws as applicable to certain facts, it will apply it to all future cases when the facts are substantially the same.

State's attorney: An officer, usually locally elected within a county, who represents the state in securing indictments and in prosecuting criminal cases.

State's evidence: Testimony by a participant in the commission of a crime that incriminates others involved, given under the promise of immunity.

Status offense: An act that is declared by statute to be an offense, but only when committed or engaged in by a juvenile, and that can be adjudicated only by a juvenile court.

Statute: A law enacted by, or with the authority of, a legislature.

Statute of limitations: A term applied to numerous statutes that set a limit on the length of time that may elapse between an event giving rise to a cause of action and the commencement of a suit to enforce that cause.

Stay: A halting of a judicial proceeding by a court order.

Sting operation: The typical sting involves using various undercover methods to control crime.

Subpoena: A court order requiring a witness to attend and testify as a witness in a court proceeding.

Subpoena duces tecum: A court order requiring a witness to bring all books, documents, and papers that might affect the outcome of the proceedings.

Summons: A written order issued by a judicial officer requiring a person accused of a criminal offense to appear in a designated court at a specified time to answer the charge(s).

Superior court: A court of record or general trial court, superior to a justice of the peace or magistrate's court. In some states, an in-termediate court between the general trial court and the highest appellate court.

Supreme court, state: Usually the highest court in the state judicial system.

Supreme Court, U.S.: Heads the judicial branch of the American government and is the nation's highest law court.

Suspect: An adult or juvenile considered by a criminal agency to be one who may have committed a specific criminal offense but who has not yet been arrested or charged.

Testimony: Evidence given by a competent witness, under oath, as distinguished from evidence from writings and other sources.

Tort: The breach of a duty to an individual that results in damage to him or her, for which one may be sued in civil court for damages. Crime, in contrast may be called the breach of duty to the public. Some actions may constitute both torts and crimes.

Uniform Crime Reports (U.C.R.): Annual statistical tabulation of "crimes known to the police" and "crimes cleared by arrest" published by the Federal Bureau of Investigation.

United States claims court: Established in 1982, it serves as the court of original and exclusive jurisdiction over claims brought against the federal government, except for tort claims, which are heard by district courts.

United States district courts: Trial courts with original jurisdiction over diversity-of-citizenship cases and cases arising under U.S. criminal, bankruptcy, admiralty, patent, copyright, and postal laws.

Venue: The locality in which a suit may be tried.

Verdict: The decision of a court.

Vice squad: A special detail of police agents, charged with raiding and closing houses of prostitution and gambling resorts.

Victim and Witness Protection Act of 1984: The federal VWP Act and state laws protect crime victims and witnesses against physical and verbal intimidation where such intimidation is designed to discourage reporting or crimes and participation in criminal trials.

Victimology: The study of the psychological and dynamic interrelationships between victims and offenders, with a view toward crime prevention.

Vigilante: An individual or member of a group who undertakes to enforce the law and/or maintain morals without legal authority.

Voir dire (Fr.): The examination or questioning of prospective jurors in order to determine his or her qualifications to serve as a juror.

Warrant: A court order directing a police officer to arrest a named person or search a specific premise.

White-collar crime: Nonviolent crime for financial gain committed by means of deception by persons who use their special occupational skills and opportunities.

Witness: Anyone called to testify by either side in a trial. More broadly, a witness is anyone who has observed an event.

Work release (furlough programs): Change in prisoners' status to minimum custody with permission to work outside prison.

World court: Formally known as the International Court of Justice, it deals with disputes involving international law.

SOURCES

The Dictionary of Criminal Justice, Fourth edition, © 1994 by George E. Rush. Published by Dushkin Publishing Group, Guilford, CT 06437.

Index

Adams, Randall Dale, 115–116
adjudication, 7
adjudicatory hearing, 8
adolescents, drug programs for, 35–37
advisory groups, citizen participation and, 97
African Americans. *See* blacks
Alfred, King of the Saxons, 143
alternative sentencing, 187–190
antifederalism, of William Rehnquist, 121–123, 124–130
Antiterrorism and Effective Death Penalty Act of 1996, 122
appellate review, 8
arbitration, community policing and, 102–103
arraignments, 7
Augustus, John, 202–203

bail: crimes committed during, 11; revocation of, 11
Baker Act, 58
beat meetings, 94
behavior restraints, 15
bench trials, 8
Black Gangster Disciple Nation (BGDN), 32, 33–34
blacks: prison and, 193–201; racial discrimination in capital punishment and, 217–222; as victims of crime, 43, 44; violent crime and, 29–30
Bloods, 31, 32–33, 173
Body Shop, 65
Boleyn, Susan V., 125–126
boot camp, 17
Botuin, Gilbert J., 36–37
Breakey, Gail, 69
Brennan, William J., 123
Bright, Stephen, 218, 220, 221, 222
Britain, 142–144, 145
Brown, Joseph, 115–116
Brown v. Allen, 122
Buel, Sarah, 61–64, 66
Burger, Warren E. 123, 124

capital punishment. *See* death penalty
case management, 106
Cayouette, Susan, 65
child abuse, Hawai'i Healthy Start program and, 67–75
child development, 22
children, risks during critical years of, 21–22. *See also* juvenile court; juvenile crime; juvenile justice system; juvenile offenders
Chinese triads, 25, 26–27
citations, juvenile civic, 103
citizen police academies, 98
civic citations, juvenile, 103
Clayton, Richard R., 35, 36
Clinton, Bill, 224
cocaine. *See* crack cocaine
COINTELPRO operation, of FBI, 195
Coleman v. Balkcom, 122
colleges, recruitment of police from, 104–105
community college programs, to prepare police officers, 104–105
Community Justice Center (CJC), 199

community policing, 89, 101–108, 110; multiculturalism and, 98–99; role of community in, 93–95
community, role of, in community policing, 93–95
"compurgators," 143
corrections, 8
"corsnaed," 142
Cosa Nostra, La. *See* Mafia
courts, public relations and, 13. *See also* Supreme Court
crack cocaine, 20, 32
crime laboratories: inadequate technical training in, 11; lack of quality control in, 11
crime prevention, community policing and, 93
Crimes Against the Elderly Unit (CATE), 58
criminal cases, excessive length of, 12
criminal justice process, 6–8
criminology, 101, 106
Crips, 31, 32–33, 173, 175
curfews, 18

DARE (Drug Abuse Resistance Education), 35–36, 37
day fine, 187
death penalty, 8; ambivalence of public feelings about, 223–225; racial discrimination in, 217–222; sex discrimination in, 218, 220
death row: gender and, 227; number of inmates on, 185, 223, 226; race and, 227
defense counsel, 7
detainer, 8
deterrence, 187
direct victimization, of crime, 78
discretion: in criminal justice system, 9; abuse of, by prosecutors, 114–120
dispositional decision making, 148
diversion programs, 8
Domestic Abuse Intervention Project, 62
domestic violence, 61–66
dropping charges, 7
drug convictions, percentage of inmates and, 20
drug dealers, replacement of, 20
drug markets, 19
drug offenders, 15, 18; imprisonment of, 20; alternative discipline for, 20
drug programs, for teenagers, 35–37
drug testing, 18, parole and, 192
due process, 9, 154
duty, for jurors, 138

early intervention, 21
elder abuse, 57–60
Elder Referral Card System (ERCS), 60
electronic monitoring, of offenders, 188–189, 190
Ellis, Eddie, 193–201
evidence: inadvertent contamination of, 11; suppression of, by prosecutor, 115–117
Ex Parte Yerger, 126
"exclusionary rule," 12, 132–133

Fagan, Jeffrey, 177
family assessment workers, 72

family, crime and, 28–30, 79
Family Development Research Project, 22
family environment, 21
Family Violence Prevention Fund, 65
family-preservation movement, 16
FBI (Federal Bureau of Investigation), 81, 195
federalism, William Rehnquist and, 121–123, 124–130
Felker v. Turpin, 121–122, 124–127
felony probation, 204, 205
Fifth Amendment, 133
fines, 8
firearms, parole and ownership of, 192
first impressions, effect of, on jurors, 117
"first responders," 57–58
Folk Gangsters, 174–175
Ford, Robert E., interview with, 101–107
formal charges, 7
foster homes, 8, 180
Fourth Amendment, exclusionary rule and, 132–133
Fry v. United States, 127
Future of the Race, The (West and Gates), 197

gangs. *See* street gangs
Gangster Disciples. *See* Black Gangster Disciple Nation
Gates, Daryl, 36
Gates, Henry Louis, Jr., 197
Gibbs, John, 180–181
Goldstein, Arnold, 180
grand juries, 7, 135
group homes, 23, 180
group therapy, 180
gun control, 17
guns, parole and ownership of, 192
Gwinn, Casey, 63

habeas corpus, Supreme Court and, 122–123, 124–130
harmless error doctrine, 119–120
Hawai'i Healthy Start, child abuse and, 67–75
Head Start, 22
Healthy Families America (HFA), child abuse and, 69
Healthy Start, Hawai'i, and child abuse, 67–75
Hispanics, 43, 44
Hoffa, James, 115
home visitation programs, Hawai'i Healthy Start and, 67, 68, 71, 72, 73–84
homicides, 14–15
Hoover, Larry, 34
Howe, William, 144–145
"hundredors," 143
hung juries, 139–140

illegitimacy, 22
illegitimate personal objectives, 115
immigrations, 107
inadmissible statements, use of, by prosecutors, 118
incarceration, 8
indictments, 7
indirect victimization, of crime, 78

Individual Family Support Plan, of Hawai'i Healthy Start, 67, 71
infant mortality, Hawai'i Healthy Start program and, 68
INS (Immigration and Naturalization Service), 107
insider trading, 76

Jackson, Eric, 115–116
jail, population of, 184
judges, inadequate numbers of, 12
juries, 134–140, 141–142, 144–145; flaws in, system, 12; hung, 139–140; instructions to, 133; peremptory challenges and, 133, 137–138; prosecutors and, 117–119
jury pay, 138
justiciars, 143
juvenile civic citations, 103
juvenile court, 8, 21, 148; "criminalized" or "punitive," 148; intake departments, 8; prosecuting attorneys, 8
juvenile crime: community guide for prevention intervention and, 171; prevention of, 167–172; protective factors in, 167, 170–171; rising rates of, 164–166; risk factors, 167–170
juvenile justice system, 8–9, 21; juvenile probation and, 159–163; sanctions, treatment, and rehabilitation in, 167
juvenile offenders: rehabilitation of, 17; trials as adults for, 176–178, 179–181
juvenile probation, 159–163

Katz, Jackson, 65
Kempe, Henry, 68
Kennedy, Anthony, 121, 124, 129, 136
King, Rodney, 89
Kleber, Herbert, 35, 36
Krinsberg, Barry, 177

lead poisoning, 23
leadership: multiculturalism and, 99–100; police cynicism and, 109–110
legal aid, lack of, 12
Levant, Glenn, 36
Life Skills Training, 36–37
Lindh v. Murphy, 127
Liz Claiborne Inc., 65

Mafia, 25–26, 31, 32
mandatory release, 8
manganese, elevated levels of, 23
McBride, Wes, 173
McCleskey v. Zant, 123, 221
mens rea, 76
mentors, police cynicism and, 110
meta-analysis, for pooling subjects of studies, 17
military confinement, number of people in, 186
Milquetoast factor, alternative sentencing and, 189–190
Miranda warning, 132
Monaghan, Henry P., 124–125
morale, low, of police, 101
Morris, Norval, 187–188
multiculturalism, police response to, 96–100
Murray, Bill, 218, 220, 221
Musto, David, 35

National Commission on Criminal Justice Standards and Goals, 88
National Committee to Prevent Child Abuse (NCPCA), 69

National Crime Victimization Study (NCVS), 40–47, 50, 51
National Workplace Resource Center, 65
Neighborhood Defender Service of Harlem, 198
New York Times Co. v. United States, 124
NIOSH (National Institute for Occupational Safety and Health), 83
nolle prosequi, 7
nolo contendere, 8
Nontraditional Approach to Criminal and Social Justice, 196–197, 198, 199
note taking, on juries, 139
Nursing Child Assessment Satellite Training (NCAST), 69, 71

O'Connor, Sandra Day, 125
O'Dell, Anne, 63
opening statement, importance of, in trials, 117–118
oral advocacy, 117
organizations, community policing and, 93, 95
organized crime, 25–27, 31, 32, 76
OSHA (Occupational Safety and Health Administration), 82, 83
overcharging, 12

PACT (Project for a Calculated Transition), 198
paramilitary groups, street gangs as future, 173–175
Parent-Child Development Center, 22
parole, 8, 189, 191–192; abolishment of, 12–13; number of people on, 185; prison overcrowding and, 13
parole officers, 8, 191–192
pat-downs, 17
peer counselors, police cynicism and, 110
Peet, John, 191–192
peremptory challenges, 133, 137–138
perjury, 116
Perry Preschool Project, 22
Petersika, Joan, 203, 206–207
Planned Parenthood of Southeastern Pennsylvania v. Casey, 121
poison, trial by ordeal and, 142
Polaroid Corp., 65
police, 24; black, 53; brutality, 89; community college programs to prepare, 104–105; criminology and, 106; cynicism and, 108–111; leadership and, 109–111; multiculturalism and, 96–100; training and, 97, 104–105; 110; writing skills of, 104–105
police academies, citizen, 98
police professionalism, 88–89
police substations, 97–98
poverty, crime and, 28–29, 78
power, abuse of, by prosecutor's office, 114–120
preliminary hearings, 7
President's Crime Commission, 82
pretrial detention, 7
pretrial-release decision, 7
prisons: limited space in, 12, 24; population of, 184–185; women in, 210–216
probation, 8; history of, 202–209; juvenile, 159–163; number of people on, 184
probation departments: organization of, 159–160; size of, 160–161
probation officers: caseloads of, 160; juvenile, 160, 161; number of juvenile, 160; salary of, 161

problem-oriented policing, 17
Project Fresh Start, 164
prosecutors, 7, 12; abuse of power by, 114–120; stress and, 119
public defenders, limited resources of, 12
punitive model, 148

race, crime and, 29–30, 178
racial discrimination, in capital punishment, 217–222
Racial Justice Act, 221, 222
Racketeer Influenced and Corrupt Organizations (RICO) Act, 26
recidivism, 17; probation and, 202–209
rehabilitation: goals of, 149; probation and, 202–209; reintegration approach to, 156; soft time and, 187–190
Rehnquist, William H., 121–130
Reid, John, 180, 181
reintegrative shaming, 154
relocation, of families to better neighborhoods, 23
restitution, 8, 154
restorative justice, 148, 150, 151–156; community service and, 154; restorative justice sanctioning, 156. See also sanctioning
"retributive justice" paradigm, 148–151, 153, 154, 156
Richardson, James, 115–116
right to counsel, 133
robbery, rates of, 14
Roe v. Wade, 121
Romans, law and order and, 142
Romer v. Evans, 121
Ronald McDonald Children's Charities (RMCC), 69
Root, Oren, 189, 190
Rothwax, Harold J., 131–133
Russian mob, 25, 26

safety, workplace, and white-collar crime, 81–83
sanctioning: goals and objectives of, 153–154; in juvenile court, 148–158; models of restorative, 156; reparative, 151
sanctions, 8
Scalia, Antonin, 125
Scandinavians, juries and, 142
"second wound," 94
Seminole Tribe of Florida v. Florida, 127
Seniors and Law Enforcement Together (SALT), 58
sentencing, 8; alternative, 187–190; hearing, 8; shorter effective, 19; soft time and, 187–190
sentencing hearings, 8
Sentencing Project, 194
serial jurors, 138
sex discrimination, capital punishment and, 218, 220
Shapiro, Carol, 188–189
Shaw, Clay, 115
SHOCAP (Serious Habitual Offender Comprehensive Action Program), 164–165, 166
Sia, Calvin, 68–69
Smith, Clive Stafford, 217, 218
Souter, David H., 127, 128
Stamper, Norm, 63, 64
State Farm Life Insurance Co., 65
Stevens, John Paul, 124
Stone, Christopher, 198

street crime, harm of, vs. white-collar crime, 76–85
street gangs: as future paramilitary groups, 173–175; shift of, toward organized crime, 31–34
stricken testimony, 118
substations, police, 97–98
Supreme Court, U.S., 14; death penalty and, 224–225; William Rehnquist as chief justice of, 121–130
surgery, unnecessary, as white-collar crime, 83–84

teenagers, drug programs for, 35–37
therapeutic interventions, 150
Things (tribunals), 142
"three strikes and you're out," 13, 17
Tocqueville, Alexis de, 135, 136
Tony, Michael, 187–188, 189–190
travel restrictions, parole and, 192
TRIAD, 58
triads, 25, 26–27
trial by combat, 143–144
trial by jury. See juries
trial by ordeal, 142–143

truancy, enforcement of, laws, 18
"tythings," 143

underclass, crime and, 77, 78
unfair selectivity, 115
Uniform Crime Reports (UCRs), 50, 51
United States v. Lopez, 121, 127

"victimless" prosecution, in domestic abuse cases, 63
victim-offender mediation, 154
victims: awareness education for, 154; community policing and, 94; domestic abuse, 64; insensitivity to, by justice system, 13; National Crime Victimization Survey on, 40–47; needs of, 152; restitution for, 151
violence, 15; characteristics of youthful offenders, 16; percentages of, 16; youthful, 15
violent crime, family and, 28–30
Vollmer, August, 88
Volunteers in Policing, 107

Wahad, Dhoruba Bin, 195

weapons, concealed: technology for detection of, 18; rewards for information on, 18
"weed and seed" program, for juvenile offenders, 166
welfare reform, 22
West, Cornel, 197, 200
white-collar crime, harm of, vs. street crime, 76–85
Wickersham Commission, 88
Wilson, William, 78
witness-protection program, 11
women: domestic violence and, 61–66; as police officers, 91–93; in prisons, 210–216
workplace safety, white-collar crime and, 81–83
writ of certiorari, 8
writing skills, of police, 104–105

Yale Child Welfare Project, 22
youth programs: drug use and, 35–37; multiculturalism and, 98

zone officers, 103

Credits/Acknowledgments

Cover design by Charles Vitelli

1. Crime and Justice in America
Facing overview—Illustration by Mike Eagle for Dushkin/McGraw·Hill Companies.

2. Victimology
Facing overview—United Nations photo by P. Sudhakaran.

3. The Police
Facing overview—© Daemmrich/Stock·Boston.

4. The Judicial System
Facing overview—AP Photo/Marcy Nighswander.

5. Juvenile Justice
Facing overview—United Nations photo by Paulo Fridman.

6. Punishment and Corrections
Facing overview—© John Eastcott/Yva Momatiuk/Photo Researchers.

PHOTOCOPY THIS PAGE!!!

ANNUAL EDITIONS ARTICLE REVIEW FORM

■ NAME: _____ DATE: _____

■ TITLE AND NUMBER OF ARTICLE: _____

■ BRIEFLY STATE THE MAIN IDEA OF THIS ARTICLE: _____

_____

■ LIST THREE IMPORTANT FACTS THAT THE AUTHOR USES TO SUPPORT THE MAIN IDEA:

_____

_____

_____

_____

■ WHAT INFORMATION OR IDEAS DISCUSSED IN THIS ARTICLE ARE ALSO DISCUSSED IN YOUR
TEXTBOOK OR OTHER READINGS THAT YOU HAVE DONE? LIST THE TEXTBOOK CHAPTERS AND
PAGE NUMBERS:

_____

_____

_____

_____

_____

■ LIST ANY EXAMPLES OF BIAS OR FAULTY REASONING THAT YOU FOUND IN THE ARTICLE:

_____

_____

_____

_____

_____

■ LIST ANY NEW TERMS/CONCEPTS THAT WERE DISCUSSED IN THE ARTICLE, AND WRITE A SHORT
DEFINITION:

_____

_____

_____

_____

*Your instructor may require you to use this ANNUAL EDITIONS Article Review Form in any
number of ways: for articles that are assigned, for extra credit, as a tool to assist in developing
assigned papers, or simply for your own reference. Even if it is not required, we encourage
you to photocopy and use this page; you will find that reflecting on the articles will greatly
enhance the information from your text.

We Want Your Advice

ANNUAL EDITIONS revisions depend on two major opinion sources: one is our Advisory Board, listed in the front of this volume, which works with us in scanning the thousands of articles published in the public press each year; the other is you—the person actually using the book. Please help us and the users of the next edition by completing the prepaid article rating form on this page and returning it to us. Thank you for your help!

ANNUAL EDITIONS: CRIMINAL JUSTICE 97/98
Article Rating Form

Here is an opportunity for you to have direct input into the next revision of this volume. We would like you to rate each of the 40 articles listed below, using the following scale:

1. **Excellent: should definitely be retained**
2. **Above average: should probably be retained**
3. **Below average: should probably be deleted**
4. **Poor: should definitely be deleted**

Your ratings will play a vital part in the next revision. So please mail this prepaid form to us just as soon as you complete it.
Thanks for your help!

Rating	Article	Rating	Article
	1. An Overview of the Criminal Justice System		20. Abuse of Power in the Prosecutor's Office
	2. The Real Problems in American Justice		21. The Rehnquist Reins
	3. What to Do about Crime		22. 'We're in the Fight of Our Lives'
	4. Who Is the Mob Today?		23. Unlocking the Jury Box
	5. Disintegration of the Family Is the Real Root Cause of Violent Crime		24. Do You Swear That You Will Well and Truly Try . . . ?
	6. The Evolution of Street Gangs: A Shift toward Organized Crime		25. Rethinking the Sanctioning Function in Juvenile Court: Retributive or Restorative Responses to Youth Crime
	7. Experts Are at Odds on How Best to Tackle Rise in Teen-Agers' Drug Use		26. Juvenile Probation: The Workhorse of the Juvenile Justice System
	8. Criminal Victimization 1994		27. Crime Time Bomb
	9. True Crime		28. Controlling Crime before It Happens: Risk-Focused Prevention
	10. Protecting Our Seniors		29. Street Gangs—Future Paramilitary Groups?
	11. Nobody's Victim		30. States Revamping Laws on Juveniles as Felonies Soar
	12. Helping to Prevent Child Abuse—and Future Criminal Consequences: Hawai'i Healthy Start		31. The Search for a Proper Punishment
	13. Is Street Crime More Harmful than White Collar Crime?		32. Correctional Populations in the United States, 1994
	14. Police and the Quest for Professionalism		33. Doing Soft Time
	15. Police Work from a Woman's Perspective		34. Going to Meet the Man
	16. The Community's Role in Community Policing		35. Eddie Ellis at Large
	17. Incorporating Diversity: Police Response to Multicultural Changes in Their Communities		36. Probation's First 100 Years: Growth through Failure
	18. LEN Interview: Police Chief Robert E. Ford of Port Orange, Fla.		37. A Woman behind Bars Is Not a Dangerous Man
	19. Police Cynicism: Causes and Cures		38. The Color of Justice
			39. Anger and Ambivalence
			40. Death Row, U.S.A.

(Continued on next page)

ABOUT YOU

Name _____ Date _____

Are you a teacher? ☐ Or a student? ☐

Your school name _____

Department _____

Address _____

City _____ State _____ Zip _____

School telephone # _____

YOUR COMMENTS ARE IMPORTANT TO US !

Please fill in the following information:

For which course did you use this book? _____

Did you use a text with this *ANNUAL EDITION*? ☐ yes ☐ no

What was the title of the text? _____

What are your general reactions to the *Annual Editions* concept?

Have you read any particular articles recently that you think should be included in the next edition?

Are there any articles you feel should be replaced in the next edition? Why?

Are there other areas of study that you feel would utilize an *ANNUAL EDITION?*

May we contact you for editorial input?

May we quote your comments?

No Postage
Necessary
if Mailed
in the
United States

ANNUAL EDITIONS: CRIMINAL JUSTICE 97/98

BUSINESS REPLY MAIL

First Class   Permit No. 84   Guilford, CT

Postage will be paid by addressee

Dushkin/McGraw·Hill
Sluice Dock
Guilford, Connecticut 06437